D1279195

WATERGATE INVESTIGATION INDEX

Senate Select Committee Hearings and Reports on Presidential Campaign Activities

THE WATERGATE INVESTIGATION INDEX

Senate Select Committee Hearings and Reports on Presidential Campaign Activities

Compiled by
Hedda Garza

SR *Scholarly Resources Inc.*
Wilmington, Delaware

UNIVERSITY OF TOLEDO LIBRARIES

© 1982 by Hedda Garza
All rights reserved
First published 1982
Printed and bound in the United States of America

Scholarly Resources Inc.
104 Greenhill Avenue
Wilmington, Delaware 19805

Library of Congress Cataloging in Publication Data

Garza, Hedda.
  The Watergate investigation index.

  1. United States. Congress. Senate. Select
Committee on Presidential Campaign Activities. Presiden-
tial campaign activities of 1972—Indexes. 2. Watergate
Affair, 1972– —Indexes. 3. Presidents—United States
—Election—1972—Indexes. 4. United States—Politics and
government—1969–1974—Indexes. I. Title. II. United
States. Congress. Senate. Select Committee on Presiden-
tial Campaign Activities. Presidential campaign
activities of 1972.
KF26.5.P7 1973 Suppl. 3   364.1'324'0973 82-7353
ISBN 0-8420-2175-2

KF
26.5
. P7
1973
Suppl. 3
Reference
Ref

PREFACE

Richard M. Nixon received a decisive mandate in the 1972 presidential election. With a popular vote exceeding 60 percent, he carried forty-nine states, losing only Massachusetts and the District of Columbia. The president shattered the old New Deal coalition by winning the Democratic South as well as the blue-collar vote in the industrial cities of the North. His campaign commitments—restraint in social programs, defense of traditional values, and a new balance in international relations—clearly had won the support of the American electorate. Without a doubt, the president had gained one of the most impressive victories in the history of presidential politics. For Nixon, the election of 1972 had to be a personal and emotional triumph. Yet, within two years, this man who saw his political career in terms of crises was to endure his greatest, one so serious and so encompassing that resignation became the only alternative to impeachment.

Watergate, now a synonym for moral corruption and illegal coverups, rapidly entangled the Nixon presidency and snared in its web the very men who ran the Government of the United States. The dimensions of this political scandal, one of the most serious in American history, and the constitutional crisis that followed strained the very structure and foundations of the nation.

The crisis began with a bizarre break-in at Democratic party national headquarters in Washington's elegant Watergate hotel-apartment-office complex on 17 June 1972. An alert watchman called the police. The arrest was unusual: two former White House aides with five accomplices were caught with sophisticated burglary tools. A pair of *Washington Post* reporters revealed that the accused had access to funds collected by the Nixon campaign organization, the Committee to Re-Elect the President (CRP). Hastily, in an almost panic state, the president and his closest associates secretly orchestrated a cover-up to obstruct justice under the pretext of national security. After the trial of the Watergate Seven in early 1973 but prior to sentencing, one of the convicted admitted to the presiding judge that highly placed White House advisors had known in advance of the break-in and that perjury had been committed during the trial. As one disclosure followed another, the burglary became only one piece in a much larger political puzzle. Finally, Republican congressional leaders joined Democrats in demanding the truth. It was hoped that all the facts would be brought out through public hearings conducted by a bipartisan seven-member Senate select committee. Thus, on 7 February 1973, by a unanimous vote of the Senate, its Select Committee on Presidential Campaign Activities, or the Watergate Committee, as it came to be called, started its work.

On 17 May 1973, the committee, chaired by Senator Sam J. Ervin, Jr., of North Carolina, opened the hearings to the public. Millions of television viewers watched the testimony unfold a record of political sabotage carried out by the senior staff of the White House. Several witnesses, most spectacularly John W. Dean, III, implicated themselves as well as key White House aides and the President of the United States. New words and phrases—hush money, "deep throat," "stonewall it," "CREEP"—dominated the news as the 1972 presidential campaign was dissected. Week after week throughout the summer and into September, the hearings continued. Daily coverage and nightly reruns on the public broadcasting network made the Watergate hearings the most watched program in the history of television. More than seven million words were recorded before the public hearings concluded.

The committee proceedings became an invaluable seminar in public enlightenment, and the public did not like what it heard. The American people served as jurors and registered their verdict in public opinion polls. Before the televised hearings began, 53 percent of the public thought Watergate was "just politics," and President Nixon received an approval rating of 54 percent. By September-October 1973, however, Watergate replaced crime and lawlessness on the list of the nation's most important problems; dissatisfaction and lack of trust in government ranked second only to the high cost of living. The president's approval rating dropped to 30 percent. Nearly a third of those polled thought that Nixon should be impeached and compelled to leave the presidency; half responded that they had little or no trust in the Nixon administration, which began to disintegrate rapidly and publicly.

The material in these voluminous hearings transcends the crime committed at the Watergate complex. A study of the hearings raises fundamental questions about the nation in the late 1960s and early 1970s. Was Watergate a one-time event, the product of unique political circumstances, or was it an extension of trends already under way in American politics and society? How should governmental power and authority be used? Was there, as Dean said, a Watergate climate—an "inevitable outgrowth of . . . excessive concern over leaks, and an insatiable appetite for political intelligence all coupled with a do-it-yourself White House staff regardless of the law"? What is presidential power, and what are the checks on its unlawful use? Should Congress hold Executive Branch officials accountable for the honest and ethical performance of their responsibilities and for attaining objectives defined in authorizing legislation? The principal use of the invaluable material compiled by the Watergate Committee should be not in detailing horrors and scandals but in responding to such questions. Perhaps, in retrospect, Senator Ervin and his colleagues demonstrated the crucial importance of a systematic legislative overview of the Executive Branch of government. For this lesson, we must be grateful to them.

Fred L. Israel

City College of New York
May 1982

GUIDE TO THE USE OF
THE WATERGATE INVESTIGATION INDEX

The hearings of the Senate Select Committee include public testimony, Executive Committee testimony, and numerous exhibits from both, as well as a Final Report of the Select Committee. This short guide to the Watergate Investigation Index will make it easier for the user to find the specific information he is seeking and will provide a long-awaited key to these historically important events.

Volume and Page Number: All of the numerical references are to volume and page number. The volume number is set in boldface (heavy) type in order to set it apart in a series of page references. The volumes are numbered consecutively. The Final Report is numbered separately from the volumes and is indicated by the abbreviation "FR."

Example: Jones, John **4**, 1675 **12**, 4927 FR 183

This would indicate that the subject can be found in Volume 4, page 1675; Volume 12, page 4927; and in the Final Report, page 183. The reader will notice some page references with the letter "E" appended to the page number citation; this indicates that the entry in question is an Exhibit. In some volumes the Exhibits are all at the end of the volume; in others they are placed at the end of the specific testimony referring to them. They include, as in a court of law's exhibits, tangible proof of the testimony: actual reproduced copies of checks, letters, photographs, affidavits, political leaflets.

Alphabetization: The entries are arranged in alphabetical order by the word-by-word system. Most readers are familiar with this method, where, for example, "West Virginia" is placed before "Western." When headings have the same first word, alphabetical order is determined by the second word. A comma stops this process.

Example: New, David L.
New, Henry S.
New Jersey
New York
Newark
Newton, Sir Isaac

Prepositions and conjunctions (of, by, in, to, and, etc.) are ignored in the alphabetization process.

Example: Committee of Human Rights
Committee for Preservation of Landmarks

However, if two entries are identical *except* for a preposition, their order is decided by the preposition.

Example: Committee *for* Human Rights
Committee *of* Human Rights

Subentries: The same basic rules of alphabetization hold for subentries. Prepositions, other than *at*, and conjunctions are ignored and are alphabetized word by word.

Example: Jones, John
           trip to Europe
           and visitors to Alabama

When dates occur in subentries, however, they are *not* alphabetized by the spelling of the month but are arranged by the actual chronological sequence.

Example: Smith, Robert, testimony of
           on meeting of May 9, 1971
           on meeting of May 12, 1972
           on meeting of April 2, 1973
           on meeting of June 12, 1973

Hyphenated compound words are treated as two separate words.

Cross References: These are indicated by the word *see* and refer the reader from one heading to a more frequently used alternative form.

Example: Bribes *see* Hush money

See Also References: These are listed at the end of a given entry and direct the user to related entries.

Special Cases: Because of the nature of these hearings, the names of people who actually testified are treated in a special way. For their direct testimony the heading reads:

    Alagia, Damian Paul, testimony of

However, when they are discussed by *other* people or are mentioned in exhibits, the entries look like this:

    Alagia, Damian Paul
        Haldeman on meeting with
        relationship with Sloan
        in Treasury report

Often the two different categories have very similar (or even identical) subentries, but their separation will provide Index users with a valuable tool for sifting out differences in the listed person's own version of an event and the versions of other witnesses.

General Notes: Subentries under particular names also may bear important clues to other entries that might throw further light on a particular topic. For example, the following might lead the user to entries under AMPI and/or Connally:

    Alagia, Damian Paul, testimony of
        on AMPI contacts with Connally

Important general topics often have been divided into more specific categories. For example, "Financial matters" is cross-referenced to "Hush money" and "Campaign contributions," since they have very special significance for these hearings and deserve separate categories of their own.

Care has been taken to index many names that only occur once or twice in the long hearings, since the Indexer realizes that any one of these single- or double-mention items might be the sole reason for a painstaking researcher's consulting the work.

Members of the Senate Select Committee
on Presidential Campaign Activities

Sam J. Ervin, Jr.   Howard H. Baker, Jr.
Herman E. Talmadge   Edward J. Gurney
Daniel K. Inouye   Lowell P. Weicker, Jr.
Joseph M. Montoya

Witnesses before the Committee

Damian Paul Alagia
Attorney in Louisville, KY;
employed by Dairymen, Inc. (DI)

Gerald Alch
Former counsel to James McCord

Carl F. Arnold
Business consultant in Arkansas and
Washington, D.C.; fund raiser for
Draft Mills campaign of 1972

Orin E. Atkins
Chairman of the board of Ashland
Oil Co., Inc.

Alfred C. Baldwin, III
Former security aide, Finance Committee to Re-elect the President

Anthony H. Barash
Former chief of convention security
activities for Senator McGovern's
staff at the 1972 Democratic National
Convention

Bernard L. Barker
Convicted participant in Watergate
burglary

Robert W. Barker
Counsel to Maurice Stans

Joseph Baroody
Employed by Wagner & Baroody,
a public relations consulting firm
retained by Associated Milk Producers, Inc. (AMPI)

John Bruce Barrett
Officer with the Metropolitan Police
Department, Washington, D.C.

Roger V. Barth
Former assistant to the commissioner
and deputy chief counsel, Internal
Revenue Service (IRS)

Robert E. Bartolme
Secretary, American Ship Building
Co.

Joe Bell
Pilot for Tandy Corp.; former pilot
for AMPI

Robert M. Benz
Employed by Donald Segretti during
the 1972 Democratic primary campaigns

Berl Bernhard
Former director of the Commission
on Civil Rights; general counsel,
Democratic Senatorial Campaign
Committee; manager of Senator
Muskie's presidential primary
campaign

Monroe Bethke
President, Citizens' National Bank,
Austin, TX

Paul E. Blanton
Pilot for Rockwell International;
former pilot for AMPI

Paul Brindze
Los Angeles McGovern campaign canvasser; delegate to Democratic nominating convention

Jack Warren Brown
Auditor for Key Biscayne Bank & Trust Co., FL; former assistant to bank president, Andrew C. Hall

Patrick J. Buchanan
Special consultant to President Nixon

John R. Buckley
Former investigator with the FBI and Office of Economic Opportunity

John E. Butterbrodt
President of Associated Milk Producers, Inc. (AMPI)

Alexander P. Butterfield
Administrator of the Federal Aviation Administration (FAA); former deputy assistant to the president in charge of administration

J. Frederick Buzhardt
Special counsel to the president

J. Phil Campbell
Undersecretary of U.S. Department of Agriculture (USDA)

Truman F. Campbell
Chairman of the Republican Central Committee of Fresno City, CA

Tim Lee Carter
Congressman; delegate to Republican National Nominating Convention

John J. Caulfield
Former aide to John Dean

Jack L. Chestnut
Minneapolis, MN attorney; chairman for the Humphrey senatorial and presidential campaigns

Lynda E. Clancy
Secretary at the National Republican Senatorial Committee

Matthew E. Clark, Jr.
Director of purchasing, American Ship Building Co.

Sidney Cohen
Chief of Dairy Branch of Commodity Operations Div., Agricultural Stabilization and Conservation Service of USDA

Joseph E. Cole
Cleveland, OH businessman; finance chairman for Humphrey presidential campaign, 1972

John B. Connally
Secretary of the treasury; former governor of Texas; chairman of Democrats for Nixon, 1972 campaign

Robert E. Cushman, Jr.
Commandant, U.S. Marine Corps; former deputy director of the Central Intelligence Agency (CIA)

John W. Dale
Staff member of the Senate Select Committee on Presidential Campaign Activities

Richard G. Danner
Employed by Summa Corp. of Las Vegas; former 1968 Nixon campaign worker

A. Darius Davis
Vice chairman of the board, Winn-Dixie Stores, Inc.

Chester C. Davis
Counsel for Summa Corp.

John W. Dean, III
Former counsel to the president

Russell DeYoung
Chairman of the board and chief executive officer of Goodyear Tire & Rubber Co., Akron, OH

David Dubin
Associate of Chester C. Davis

Barton D. Eaton
Secretary, Hertz Corp.

Sol M. Edidin
Former vice president and general counsel of the Hertz Corp.

Rufus Edmisten
Deputy chief counsel for the Senate Select Committee on Presidential Campaign Activities

John D. Ehrlichman
Former assistant to the president in charge of domestic affairs

John A. Elmore
Staff member of the Senate Select Committee on Presidential Campaign Activities

L. J. (Bud) Evans, Jr.
Deputy assistant director, Office of Policy, Planning & Action; former staff assistant to President Nixon for elderly affairs

Camilo Fabrega
Regional vice president, Braniff Airways, Panama

Ben E. Fellows
Attorney for National City Bank of Minneapolis, MN; auditor of campaign finances for Hubert Humphrey

Benjamin Fernandez
Former chairman of the board and president of the National Economic Development Association; chairman of National Hispanic Finance Committee for the Re-election of the President

Gordon L. Freedman, Jr.
Staff assistant for Senate Select Committee on Presidential Campaign Activities

Leonard Garment
Assistant to the president

Kenneth W. Gemmill
Attorney for C. G. Rebozo

Walter Glaeser
Employee of the Summa Corp.

John Goggans
Pilot for Tandy Corp.; former pilot for AMPI

Stanley P. Goldstein
Former Muskie Election Committee volunteer who handled payments to committee creditors

L. Patrick Gray
Former acting director of the FBI

William E. Griffin
Secretary and former general counsel to Robert Abplanalp, owner of Precision Valve Corp.

Alexander M. Haig, Jr.
Staff coordinator for President Nixon

H. R. Haldeman
Former assistant to the president in charge of operations

W. A. Hamilton
Telephone company executive

Gary E. Hanman
Senior vice president of Mid-America Dairymen, Inc.; chairman of Agricultural and Dairy Education Political Trust

Clifford M. Hardin
Vice chairman of the board of the Ralston Purina Co.

Sally J. Harmony
Former secretary to G. Gordon Liddy

Marion E. Harrison
Attorney with the former firm of Reeves & Harrison; retained by AMPI

Jane S. Hart
Secretary to Stuart H. Russell

Michael B. Heller
California coordinator of Jewish Youth for Humphrey; later a volunteer for Democrats for Nixon

Richard M. Helms
Ambassador to Iran; former CIA director

Gary Hickman
Lieutenant, Los Angeles Police Department

Lawrence M. Higby
Special assistant with the Office of Deputy Director, Office of Management & Budget (OMB); former chief deputy to H. R. Haldeman

E. Howard Hunt
CIA retiree; former consultant to Executive Office of the President

Jake Jacobsen
Counsel for Associated Milk Producers, Inc.

Joseph Johnson
Former AMPI official; chairman of the Mills for President Committee, 1972

Roger E. Johnson
Special assistant to the chief of protocol, U.S. Department of State; former special assistant to the president

Kirby Jones
Executive director of the National Executive Conference, Washington, D.C.; former consultant with Ted Van Dyk Associates; former employee, McGovern for President Committee

Herbert W. Kalmbach
Personal legal counsel to President Nixon; associate finance chairman and fund raiser for Finance Committee to Re-Elect the President

Alexander W. Keema
General Accounting Office staff member for Senate Select Committee on Presidential Campaign Activities

Bruce A. Kehrli
Special assistant to the president

Martin D. Kelly
Employed by Donald Segretti during 1972 Democratic primary campaigns

Richard G. Kleindienst
Former U.S. attorney general

Marc Lackritz
Assistant majority counsel of Senate Select Committee on Presidential Campaign Activities

Frederick C. LaRue
Former White House aide; assistant to John Mitchell on Committee to Re-Elect the President

Paul W. Leeper
Sergeant with the Metropolitan Police Department, Washington, D.C.

Matthew L. Lifflander
Attorney; former vice president and corporate counsel of Hertz American Express International; treasurer, NY State Muskie Finance Committee

Robert A. Lilly
Legislative director, AMPI; secretary of Committee for Thorough Agricultural Political Education (CTAPE)

Joe E. Long
Former law partner of Jake Jacobsen

Clark MacGregor
Director of Committee to Re-Elect the President following resignation of John Mitchell

Jeb Stuart Magruder
Former special assistant to the president; former deputy campaign director for Committee to Re-Elect the President

Frederick V. Malek
Deputy Director, Office of Management & Budget (OMB); former Deputy Director, Committee to Re-Elect the President; former special assistant to the president

Barnard M. Malloy
CIA employee on the psychiatric staff of the Office of Medical Services

Frank Mankiewicz
Political director of the McGovern presidential campaign

Eleanor Manuel
Supervisor of Telephone Operations within national headquarters of the Republican National Committee

Robert C. Mardian
Campaign coordinator and legal assistant to the director of the Committee to Re-Elect the President; former assistant attorney general in charge of internal security

William Marumoto
Presidential assistant for coordination of administration affairs for Spanish-speaking Americans

Frank D. Masters
Attorney employed by AMPI

James W. McCord, Jr.
Convicted participant in Watergate burglary; former office security assistant to director of security for Committee to Re-Elect the President

Stanley W. McKiernan
Counsel to Edward C. and F. Donald Nixon

Richard W. McLaren
U.S. district judge of the Northern District of IL; former assistant attorney general, Antitrust Division

Michael W. McMinoway
Employed by personnel associated with Committee to Re-Elect the President

Dr. George L. Mehren
Former assistant secretary, USDA; president of AgriBusiness, Inc.; consultant and director of Programming for AMPI; general manager of AMPI

John N. Mitchell
Former U.S. attorney general; former chairman of Committee to Re-Elect the President

Nicole Moncourt
Bookkeeper for C. G. Rebozo

Richard A. Moore
Special counsel to the president; former special assistant to Attorney General Mitchell

Ben F. Morgan, Jr.
President of Community National Bank, Austin, TX

Dwight Morris
Former secretary of the board, AMPI

John Morrison
Chairman of the board, Eldorado International, Inc.; deputy campaign manager for Hubert Humphrey in 1972

Stewart R. Mott
McGovern campaign backer

Harold S. Nelson
Former general manager of AMPI

Edward C. Nixon
Brother of President Nixon

F. Donald Nixon
Brother of President Nixon

Lee Nunn
Director of the Republican Senatorial Campaign Committee; former vice chairman of the Finance Committee to Re-Elect the President

Robert P. Odell
Executive director of the Republican National Finance Committee

Robert C. Odle, Jr.
Former director of administration of the Committee to Re-Elect the President

Don Paarlberg
Director of Agricultural Economics for the Department of Agriculture

Clarence D. Palmby
Vice president of the Continental Grain Co.; former assistant for international affairs and commodity programs, USDA

John Parker
Cashier with Citizens' National Bank, Austin, TX

David L. Parr
Former special counsel to the general manager of AMPI

Marian R. Pearlman
Former treasurer of McGovern for President, Inc.

Gerald R. Pepper
Executive director of the Iowa Institute of Cooperation (farmer co-op)

Henry E. Petersen
Assistant attorney general in charge of the Criminal Division

William D. Pleasant
Former cab driver and chauffeur for AMPI officials

Herbert L. Porter
Former White House communications aide; director of scheduling for the Committee to Re-Elect the President

John J. Priestes
Building contractor, Coral Gables, FL

Charles G. "Bebe" Rebozo
Friend and confidant of President Nixon

Robert A. Reisner
Former administrative assistant to Jeb Stuart Magruder; staff assistant to Clark MacGregor

Neal Robinson
Assistant treasurer of Braniff Airways

Mitchell Rogovin
Attorney; general counsel for the Institute for Policy Studies

Donald H. Segretti
Former employee of the Committee to Re-Elect the President, engaged in "dirty tricks"

Milton P. Semer
Counsel to President Johnson; former partner, Semer, White & Jacobsen; retained by AMPI

Gerald Shapiro
President of Carl Ally, Inc. (ad agency); former president of Hertz Corp.

Carl M. Shoffler
Officer with the Metropolitan Police Department, Washington, D.C.

Earl J. Silbert
Former principal assistant U.S. attorney for Washington, D.C.

William E. Simon
Secretary of the treasury

Hugh W. Sloan, Jr.
Former treasurer for the Committee to Re-Elect the President; former staff assistant to the president

George A. Spater
Former chairman and chief executive officer of American Airlines, Inc.

Maurice H. Stans
Former secretary of commerce; director of the Finance Committee to Re-Elect the President

Richard G. Stearns
Regional director of McGovern campaign

Marvin Stetler
President of First National Bank, Arlington, TX; former president of Citizens' National Bank, Austin, TX; hired by Jake Jacobsen

Gordon C. Strachan
Staff assistant to H. R. Haldeman

Jeremiah P. Sullivan
Police superintendent, Boston, MA

Frederick J. Taugher
Chief administrative officer of the California State Assembly; former Southern California coordinator with McGovern campaign

Thomas W. Townsend
Former special assistant to the general manager of AMPI

Anthony T. Ulasewicz
Former investigator for Nixon's personal lawyer; aide to John Caulfield

Ted Van Dyk
Head of Ted Van Dyk Associates, a consulting firm in Washington, D.C.; former assistant and campaign manager for Humphrey; former AMPI consultant

Thomas H. Wakefield
Vice chairman of the Key Biscayne Bank & Trust Co., FL; counsel to President Nixon and C. G. Rebozo

Don Wallace
Loan officer with Citizens' National Bank, Austin, TX

Johnnie M. Walters
Former commissioner of IRS; former assistant attorney general, Tax Division

Vernon A. Walters
Deputy director of the CIA

Robert F. Wearley
Employee, Summa Corp.

Alan S. Weitz
Assistant counsel to Senate Select Committee on Presidential Campaign Activities

Claude C. Wild, Jr.
Vice president for governmental relations of the Gulf Oil Corp.

Bruce B. Wilson
Deputy assistant attorney general, Antitrust Division

Rose Mary Woods
Personal secretary to President Nixon

John Zittle
Manager, Unit I Central District, Southwestern Bell Telephone Co., San Antonio, TX

"A.B.M. (anything but Muskie)" 10, 4026, 4289E
A.G. 3, 1244E
   on Nixon-Dean meeting agenda **4,** 1485-86
A.T. & T.
   and Ragan **21,** 9699-9700
Abbott, Steve 12, 5159E
Abel, Alice 2, 747, 909E, 910E **8,** 3207
   letter from Linde to Ervin on Supreme Court
     opinion on **8,** 3207, 3327-28E
   text of Supreme Court opinion in **8,** 3207, 3329-
     68E
Abel, I.W. 10, 4060E
Abelman, Diane
   See Mott, Stewart, statement of
Abernathy, Ralph 3, 1141E **10,** 3952
ABM missile issue
   bogus ads in support of **FR** 320-31E
   and Citizens Committee to Safeguard America **FR**
     155
   Hughes and **20,** 9596, 9597-98
   and Hughes contribution **24,** 11610
   memo from Danner to Rebozo on **20,** 9597-98 **21,**
     10045-48
   Woods denies knowledge of Rebozo involvement
     with **22,** 10230-31
Abortion issue
   in anti-Muskie leaflet **10,** 4058E
   and assault strategy on McGovern **10,** 4242E
   Buchanan on **10,** 3976
   and fissures in Democratic party **10,** 4201E,
     4203E
   and McGovern **10,** 4257-58E
   and Mott **25,** 12099
   and Muskie campaign **10,**4150E **11,**4670
   and Segretti's activities against Muskie **10,** 3992
Abourezk, James 14, 6150-51 **15,** 6843 **16,** 7008,
7025
   and Valentine, Sherman **16,** 7035-36
Abplanalp, Robert 5, 1911 **20,** 9454, 9550 **22,** 10213,
10214, 10240, 10279 **24,** 11471-72, 11549
   areas of waiver of attorney-client privilege to Grif-
     fin by **23,** 10755
   at lunch with Rebozo and Danner **24,** 11471-72
   at meetings with Nixon and Griffin **22,** 10412-13
   bowling alley to Nixon from **23,** 10781-83
   business dealings with Nixon **22,** 10510-11
   business dealings with Rebozo **21,** 10135-36
   22,10497, 10498-99
   checks from Precision Valve Corp. to **23,** 10821E,
     10822E
   and Cox investigation **23,** 11033
   and creation of trust for purchase of Rebozo's
     share of San Clemente partnership **23,** 10749-50
   Danner and **24,** 11434
   denies knowledge of Hughes contribution **FR**
     1012-13
   Griffin and **22,** 10440
   Griffin claims attorney-client privilege on ques-
     tions relating to **23,** 10756-60, 10774-79
   Griffin claims he had no knowledge of Hughes
     contribution **22,** 10466-68
   Griffin's reasons for not discussing Hughes contri-
     bution with **22,** 10472

and Griffin's refusal to act on Rebozo's behalf in
   return of Hughes money **FR** 1009-10
   hotel registration for **22,** 12581E
   and Hughes contribution **FR** 1016
   introduces Griffin to Rebozo **22,** 10411-12
   IRS sensitive case report on **23,** 10938
   loan to Nixon for San Clemente property pur-
     chase **23,** 10739
   meeting with Danner and Rebozo **20,** 9563-64
   meeting with Nixon and Rebozo **22,** 10448
   and Nixon's purchase of Key Biscayne property
     23, 10769
   and Nixon's sale of San Clemente property **23,**
     10740-41
   partnership agreement with Rebozo in B & C In-
     vestment Co. **23,** 10823-44E
   partnership document for San Clemente property
     23, 10804-18E
   promissory note to Rebozo **23,** 10746
   purchase of pool furniture **FR** 1041
   purchase of Rebozo's share in B & C Investment
     Co. **23,** 10744-46
   and Rebozo's loan for $225,000 **23,** 10760-65
   Rebozo's reasons for selling his share of San Cle-
     mente partnership to **23,** 10747
   relationship with Danner **20,** 9564
   relationship with Griffin **22,** 10412
   relationship with Rebozo **22,** 10452
   and Resorts International **23,** 10792-93
   and San Clemente property **23,** 11087
   trip with Rebozo and Danner **20,** 9547-48, 9556-
     57 **21,**10100-10101 **24,** 11407-11408, 11450
   trip with Rebozo and Griffin to Saranac Lake **22,**
     10423, 10464-66
   waiver of attorney-client privilege **23,** 10738
   Wakefield and **24,** 11330-31
Abramson, Mike 11, 4642 **FR** 202
Abzug, Bella
   Baldwin surveillance of **1,** 396
Acker, Marjorie P. 4, 1409 **21,** 10001 **22,** 10202,
10203, 10267, 10268, 10275, 10281
Acree, Vernon (Mike) 21, 9711 **22,** 10246, 10361 **23,**
11222, 11255 **FR** 113
   Caulfield and **FR** 113, 114, 134, 135, 138
   Caulfield on **22,** 10391-95
   and Caulfield's investigation of Cortese **22,** 10396
   and Caulfield's investigation of Hughes-O'Brien
     relationship **22,** 10409
   and Caulfield's relationship with IRS **22,** 10388
   and Caulfield's requests for tax information **22,**
     10361-79
   described by Caulfield in Sandwedge proposal **FR**
     139
   and information to Barth **23,** 11270
   and Operation Sandwedge **22,** 10342, 10343,
     10344, 10345, 10352-53, 10354 **FR** 248E
   and pretext interviews for Caulfield **22,** 10396-97
   and tax audit on Greene **22,** 10372, 10375
ACTION 13, 5536E **20,** 9437
   CRP use of **FR** 150
   memo from Rietz to Magruder on **FR** 285E
Action Committee on Arab Relations
   endorsement of McGovern campaign by **11,** 4629

and loan to ADEPT from SPACE **17**, 7738-39

meeting at Louisville airport with dairy cooperative representatives **16**,7083-84 **17**,7731-40 **FR** 655-57

meeting with Nelson **15**, 6685

Parr and **15**, 6818

Parr, Hanman, and Nelson fly to Louisville to meet with **15**, 6819-27

role in Dairymen, Inc. **FR** 585

Alagia, Damian Paul, testimony of 16, 7059-84

on AMPI contacts with Connally **16**, 7075

on contribution of March 24 **FR** 657-58

on dairy coops' contributions to Democrats in 1972 **16**, 7082-83

on decision making in SPACE on political contributions **16**, 7061, 7080-81

denies discussing contributions to Nixon campaign with representatives of other dairy coops **16**, 7068-69

denies knowledge of AMPI contributions to Nixon's re-election campaign **16**, 7079

denies knowledge of SPACE contribution campaigns through committees to Nixon's re-election campaign **16**, 7077-83

on formation of AMPI, TAPE, and ADEPT **16**, 7062

on formation of Central America Cooperative Federation **16**, 7069

on formation of SPACE **16**, 7060, 7061

on legal advisors to SPACE **16**, 7061-62

on loan from SPACE to ADEPT **16**, 7072-75

on meeting between Nixon and dairy coop representatives **16**, 7063-66

on meeting Chotiner **16**, 7064

on meeting with AMPI representatives **16**,7064, 7076-77

on meeting with Campbell, Clark, Marx, and Moser **16**, 7068

on meeting with Moser on SPACE contributions to Nixon's reelection **16**, 7069

on meeting with Nelson, Parr, Hanman, and Lilly at Louisville airport **16**, 7071-75

on Morgan's contacts with Connally **16**, 7079-80

on Morgan's meetings with Kalmbach **16**, 7081-82

on Moser's assessment of meeting between Nixon and dairy coop representatives **16**, 7067-68

on reasons for lack of SPACE contributions to CRP just prior to election **16**, 7081

on role with Dairymen, Inc. **16**, 7059-60

on SPACE fulfilling reporting requirements for political contributions **16**, 7060-61

on SPACE purchase of tickets for Republican fundraising dinner **16**, 7069-71, 7075-76

on SPACE refusal to participate in AMPI fund requests **16**, 7083-84

Alagia, Mrs. Damian Paul 16, 7071, 7075

Albert, Carl 14, 6185

AMPI contributions and **16**, 7301, 7338-39

and Committee for TAPE contributions **17**, 7572-73

meeting with Mehren, MacGregor, and Mills **16**, 7319-20

meeting with Mills **16**, 7118-20

Mehren and **16**, 7334

and milk price supports **16**,7401 **FR** 630, 634

Albuquerque, New Mexico

vandalism against Nixon headquarters in **12**, 5143-46E

Alch, Gerald 1, 198 **3**, 976 **9**, 3704

denies Executive clemency offers to McCord **FR** 63

and efforts to blame CIA for Watergate **9**, 3443-44

in Fensterwald's statement **7**, 3012E

Hunt dismisses **9**, 3835E, 3837E

in Hunt's notes **9**, 3838E

McCord and **1**, 131, 134, 150, 161, 242-43 **3**, 974, 975 **7**, 2736

McCord letter to CIA on **9**, 3443-44

and McCord's attorney-client privilege **1**, 221

meeting with Mitchell and O'Brien **4**, 1580-81

and offers of Executive clemency for McCord **1**, 188

and pressure on McCord to blame CIA for Watergate operation **1**, 193-95

Alch, Gerald, testimony of 1, 294-310, 312-56

on attempt to blame CIA for Watergate **1**, 299-301, 309, 313-16, 321-22, 328-29, 334-35

on Barker **1**, 347, 361

on conflicting testimony **1**, 333-41

on consultations with Bailey on McCord's defense **1**, 314-15

on Fensterwald **1**, 307-308, 322-23

letter from McCord on plan to prove wiretap on his telephone **1**, 339-40

on McCord's alternatives **1**, 349

on McCord's bail **1**, 305-307, 321

on McCord's belief that Watergate was legal **1**, 341-42, 353-54

on McCord's charges that he pressured him to plead guilty **1**, 309-10, 313, 316-19, 321, 329-30, 330-33, 336-37, 349-50, 352-53

on McCord's finances **1**, 333

on McCord's informing him that Mitchell was involved in Watergate **1**, 341-42

on McCord's letter to Sirica **1**, 303, 306-307

on McCord's motivation for Watergate break-in **1**, 336-37

on McCord's note to Caulfield **1**, 315-16

on McCord's plan for using his tapped telephone **1**, 320, 339

on McCord's proposed book **1**, 320-321

on McCord's reaction to Magruder's testimony at Watergate trial **1**, 343-44

on relationship with Bailey **1**, 347-48

on relationship with CRP **1**, 348

on relationship with McCord **1**, 294-310, 325-33, 343-44

on selection by McCord **1**, 341

on source of McCord's fee **1**, 312

suggests polygraph test for himself and McCord **1**, 335, 336

on visit to Bittman's office **1**, 323-325, 326-27, 347, 349-50

Alcohol, Tobacco, and Firearms Bureau **4**, 1637
and domestic intelligence reports to White House
3, 1071, 1072
Alderman, Joe **25**, 12267, 12292, 12321
Alexander, Donald **23**, 11022 **24**, 11656
and Barth's call to Rebozo **23**, 11232
discussion at IRS briefing of Treasury on placing
date on issuance of currency **23**, 10939-40
Garment and **23**, 11063
Garment discusses audit of Nixon with **23**, 11059-
60
Gemmill and **23**, 11209
informs Barth of letter of complaint from O'Brien
23, 11225
and IRS interview of Rebozo **23**, 11233
and IRS investigation of Rebozo **23**, 11251
and IRS sensitive case reports to Treasury Department **23**, 10928
memo to Simon on Hughes contribution and
Rebozo **23**, 10932-33, 10934, 10936
memo to Simon on IRS sensitive case report on
Rebozo **23**, 10935-36
reports from Walters to **24**, 11652
telephone call to Simon on IRS sensitive case re-
port on Rebozo **23**, 10933
work liaison with Simon **23**, 10926
Alexander, John **24**, 11622-23
Alexander, Dr. W.H. **14**, 6296
Alinsky, Sol **11**, 4463
Allan, Robert **2**, 781
Allen, David **1**, 34-35
Allen, Dick **3**, 1119E
Allen, James **18**, 8189-90
guilty plea of **FR** 486-87
See also Northrop Corp.
Allen, Robert H., testimony of
on Mexican checks **FR** 516-17
See also Mexican checks
Allen, Robert S. **3**, 1147E, 1191E
Allen v. *United States* **4**, 1788-89E
Allin, Mort **3**, 1115E **10**, 3905, 3913, 4180E
memo to Haldeman on Checkers speech film **22**,
10388
Allison, Jimmy **10**, 4122E
Allison, Richard L.
See Lehigh Valley Cooperative Farmers, Inc.
Almaguer, Frank **1**, 35
Alonso, Jose **23**, 10966
Alsop, Don **16**, 6961
Alsop, Joseph **11**, 4586 **16**, 6962-63
Alter, Seymour **20**, 9449, 9610
Amarata Hess Co. **25**, 12201
Amato, Thomas **9**, 3751
Ambassadorships
contributions by appointees to **FR** 492-96
and de Roulet **FR** 501-503
non-career **FR** 494
and Symington **FR** 497-501
and Whitney **FR** 504-505
Ambrose, Miles **22**, 10247, 10344 **FR** 113
on Griffin's records **22**, 10414-15

on Griffin's telephone records **23**, 10794
objections to Armstrong's characterization of
Griffin's testimony **22**, 10468
objections to line of questioning of Griffin
22,10444-45, 10470-71, 10472 **23**, 10755-60,
10765-68, 10774-79, 10786
on prevention of leaks **23**, 10793-94
on relevance of Precision Valve documents **22**,
10424
on return of Griffin's records **22**, 10473-74
on return of Griffin's telephone records **22**, 10473-
74
on scheduling of further testimony by Griffin **22**,
10474, 10475
on Senate vote on transcript of Griffin testimony
23, 10734
statement on leaks from Select Committee on
Griffin testimony **23**, 10733-34
and submission of Griffin exhibits **23**, 10734-38
See also Griffin, William E., testimony of
Ambrose, Mrs. Myles **FR** 157
Ambrose operation **4**, 1639
Amendment to End the War Committee **25**, 12182-83
American Airlines, Inc.
CAB calendar listing status of regulatory proceedings **13**, 5513, 5842-49E
check to Chemical Bank **13**, 5504, 5838E
disclosure of illegal campaign contribution by **FR**
449
"good government" fund **13**, 5508, 5519-20
letter from Barrick to Miller on return of illegal
campaign contribution of **13**, 5504, 5840E
letter from Miller to Parkinson on return of illegal contribution to CRP of **13**, 5504, 5839E
proposed merger with Western Airlines **13**, 5508-
10, 5512-14 **FR** 449-51
solicitation of contribution from **FR** 447-48
supplement to memo on regulatory matters affect-
ing **13**, 5513, 5850-51E
See also Spater, George A., testimony of
American Bar Association Center for Professional
Discipline
and computer printout information from Select
Committee **FR** 1093
American Bar Association Criminal Justice Project
Standard **6**, 2432-34, 2593
American Broadcasting Co. **5**, 1998-99
American Civil Liberties Union **11**, 4543
and FBI raw data used in Segretti matter **5**, 2034
American Express card **4**, 1593
in alias for Ulasewicz **FR** 110, 231E
Dean's use of **4**, 1514, 1515
American Independent Party **FR** 358E
and vote-siphoning scheme of CRP **FR** 203-205
Walters' efforts to re-register **11**, 4643-44
American Law Institute
Model Penal Code **FR** 103-104
American Nazi Party **11**, 4644
and re-registration scheme in California **FR** 204-
205
American Nurses Association, Inc.
Code of Ethics sent to Ervin **9**, 3559, 3855-59E

American Polygraph Association **1,** 335

American Ship Building Co. **13,** 5431, 5770E, 5792-93E

    campaign contribution by **FR** 451-59

    dealings with Government agencies **FR** 452

    financial records of **13,** 5431, 5778-82E

    memo to file on employee bonuses **13,** 5431, 5784E

    scheme to conceal corporate contribution **FR** 447

    statement of Clark to FBI agents on finances of **13,** 5431, 5771-76E

    subpoenas from grand jury to **FR** 456-58

    See also Bartolme, Robert, testimony of; Clark, Matthew E., testimony of

Amnesty issue

    McGovern record on **10,** 4066-67E

    and Muskie campaign **11,** 4670

AMPAC **13,** 5475, 5476

AMPI

    See Associated Milk Producers, Inc. (AMPI)

"AMPI Outline Proposal" **15,** 6836, 6912-18E

Anderle, Ed **25,** 12280

Anderson, Jack **1,** 297 **5,** 1978 **9,** 3475 **15,** 6525 **22,** 10654, 10659 **23,** 11136E **24,** 11416-17

    and AMPI reimbursement scheme **15,** 6530-31

    article on Ashland Petroleum agreement with Iran **13,** 5453-54

    bogus press releases to **11,** 4381

    on campaign against Stearns **11,** 4582-83

    on Davis brothers contributions to Nixon campaign **26,** 10577-79, 10590E

    on Dean's firing **5,** 1971, 1980

    on ex-Nazi in CRP **11,** 4586

    on financing of Cuban Watergate burglars **21,** 10106

    on Hughes **21,** 9992

    on Hughes contribution **21,** 9999-10000, 10067, 10407, 10651-52

    on ITT-Dita Beard memo **5,** 1873-74, 1949 **23,** 11264 **FR** 127

    and leaks from Select Committee **22,** 10198, 10199, 10218

    link Nixon with Nazis **12,** 4970

    on Maheu relationship with O'Brien **21,** 9719

    McCord memorandum on **1,** 407

    memo from Colson to Dean on **4,** 1687E

    on plot to kill Castro **21,** 9723-24

    prints documents from National Security Council meeting **3,** 921

    and Responsiveness Program **18,** 8179

    source of information on CRP **2,** 502

    Ulasewicz and **FR** 110

    using Hughes memo to Maheu **20,** 9608-10

    Washington Post columns of **12,** 4970, 5026-30E **17,** 7615, 7624E

    and White House concern over leaks **3,** 1101-1102E

Anderson, Leon **22,** 10670, 10671

Anderson, Noble **16,** 7314, 7315

Anderson, Richmond **24,** 11571, 11598

Anderson, Stanton D. **13,** 5322 **18,** 8201, 8227, 8230, 8234 **19,** 8902E **23,** 11260 **FR** 416

    affidavit of **19,** 8897-98E

    letter to Hamilton with list of Departmental contacts for "Responsiveness Program" **19,** 8751-53E

    memo to Malek on Responsiveness Program **18,** 8232, 8366E

    memo to Warren on Cohen **18,** 8227, 8365E **FR** 416-17

    and Responsiveness Program **FR** 379

    and Symington's ambassadorial appointment **FR** 498

Andrade, Carolyn

    letter from Ely on appearance of Fernandez before Select Committee **13,** 5398, 5747E

Andreas, Dwayne O. **2,** 730, 749, 750, 781 **7,** 2735 **25,** 11774, 11783, 11810 **FR** 561, 562

    affidavit of **25,** 11922E, 11924-25E **FR** 888-90

    check to Humphrey Volunteer Committee **25,** 11953-55E

    and Dahlberg checks **2,** 699-701, 722 **FR** 37

    Fellows on **25,** 11778-79

    and Humphrey contribution through sale of stocks **FR** 888-91

    and second Duncan loan **25,** 11802-11804

    subpoena by Patman Committee **3,** 1191E

    See also Dahlberg checks

Andrews, Dave **12,** 5170E

Andrews, Vincent **22,** 10230, 10488

Andrews Air Force Base

    demonstration at **1,** 397, 398

Anfinson, Tom **22,** 10669-70

Annenberg, Walter **FR** 940

Another Mother for Peace **11,** 4543

Answer Desk **10,** 4210-11E

Anti-Defamation League **12,** 5029E

Anti-Semitism

    Nixon accused of **12,** 5026-30E

    See also Heller, Michael, testimony of

Antitrust laws

    and AMPI "base-excess plan" marketing arrangements **FR** 646

Antitrust suit against AMPI **14,** 6251-52, 6325 **15,** 6464-65, 6673-77 **16,** 6940, 7177-80

    alluded to in meeting between Nixon and Government agricultural leaders **17,** 7768-69

    and AMPI contributions **FR** 722-29

    and AMPI contributions to Democrats **15,** 6468

    and AMPI payments to Russell **16,** 7310

    Butterbrodt on **17,** 7640

    campaign contributions and **FR** 699-729

    and commitments to Republican campaigns **16,** 7285-86

    and destruction of AMPI files in Little Rock **15,** 6895

    discussed at meeting with Kalmbach and AMPI representatives **15,** 6447-49

    discussed at meetings with Connally **15,** 6460, 6461-62

    Ehrlichman on **16,** 7397-98

    Harrison on **17,** 7680-88

    Jacobsen on **15,** 6469-72

    Kalmbach denies discussions with milk people on **17,** 7613-14

    Kalmbach on contacts with Mehren on **17,** 7615-17

contacts with White House after March 12 milk price-support decision **FR** 633-37

contacts with White House officials after 1969 contribution **FR** 595-96

contribution to Democratic Convention program **15,** 6467-68

contribution to Kalmbach in 1969 **FR** 587-611

contributions for Mills from employees of **15,** 6868-70

contributions to congressional campaigns **16,** 7737-38

contributions to Democratic party candidates in 1970 and 1971 **FR** 611

contributions to Democratic presidential candidates **16,** 7005-7006 **17,** 7662

contributions to Humphrey campaign through bogus billings by Valentine, Sherman **15,**6458-59 **FR** 872-81

contributions to Johnson **14,** 6088

contributions to Mills campaign **15,**6603-13 **16,** 7083, 7313-16 **FR** 904-23

contributions to Muskie campaign **15,** 6615-16 **16,** 7012-23

contributions to Nixon campaign through committees **15,** 6885-93

contributions to Republicans, in Hillings letter to Nixon **15,** 6701-6702E

contributions to Wallace campaign **15,** 6613-15

correspondence with Valentine, Sherman **25,** 11840-46E

and Dairy Marketing Advisory Committee **14,** 6296

decision making on political contributions **15,** 6880-81

destruction of documents by **16,** 6959

and disposition of IRS investigation of MPI **FR** 721-22

and disposition of 1969 contribution **FR** 595

efforts to have Nixon attend annual meeting **15,** 6405

efforts to have Nixon attend first convention **17,** 7633-34

employees working for Mills in 1971 **16,** 7108-7109, 7110-11

employment of Townsend by **16,** 7087-88

file on Mills campaign **25,** 12077-87E

financial contributions to congressmen **15,** 6882

and first milk price-support decision **16,** 7134

formation of **15,** 6632 **16,**6946, 7062 **FR** 583-84, 904-905

and formation of TAPE and CTAPE **14,** 5911-12 **FR** 584-85

and Gallup poll on presidential candidates in 1972 **16,** 7004-7009

Harrison's legal role at **17,** 7679-80

and Hillings letter to Nixon **FR** 619-21

and Humphrey campaign **16,** 7114-15

and Humphrey's presidential campaign of 1968 **15,** 6616-17

and import quotas issue **15,** 6405, 6798-99

increased retainer for Van Dyk from **16,** 7022-23

invoice and check to Jones for expenses **17,** 8071-72E

invoice from Jacobsen and Long for legal fees and expenses **15,** 6383, 6435, 6480E, 6499E

IRS audit of **15,** 6461, 6464

and IRS investigation of MPI **FR** 715-18

and Jacobsen contribution to Mills campaign **15,** 6434

Jacobsen offers Connally contribution for Democrats for Nixon from **15,** 6428-29

Jacobsen on contributions to Republicans of **15,** 6415-19

Jacobsen on Kalmbach and **15,** 6437-46

Jacobsen on transactions between Jacobsen and Long and **15,** 6435-37

and Jacobsen's contacts with Connally on milk price supports **15,** 6407-15

and Jacobsen's offered contribution to Connally **15,** 6421-25

and Johnson King Air **14,** 6181-82

and Johnson's book **15,** 6696-97, 6906

Jones' retainer ended at **16,** 7329-31

last-minute pre-election campaign contribution **FR** 732-43

lawyers representing **16,** 6961-64

letter from Harrison to Russell on *United States* v. *AMPI* **16,** 7262, 7351E

letter from Isham to Betke on his resignation from **17,** 8163E

letter from Isham to Mehren resigning from **17,** 8159-62E

letter from Jacobsen and Long on billing for services **14,** 5940, 6012E **15,** 4938, 6007E

letter from Jones to Ervin on his involvement with **17,** 8058-60E

letter from Kennelly to Dorsen on Jones' billing to **17,** 8061-64E

letter from Lilly to Jacobsen on IRS audit of **17,** 8155-56E

letter from Russell to Weitz on money delivered to employees of **15,** 6779, 6910E

letter from Valentine to Parr on payment to Valentine, Sherman from **15,** 6840, 6923E

letter of agreement and related correspondence with Valentine, Sherman on compilation of master file of farmers **14,** 6148, 6193-6215E

letter of recommendation of Chestnut from Connell to Parr **25,** 11839E

letter to Van Dyk with checks for Muskie campaign **16,** 7013, 7055-56E

letters from Mehren to Weitz **16,** 7187, 7220-23E

Lilly's role with **14,** 5908

and loan taken by Lilly for contribution to Republicans **14,** 5921-24

lobbying efforts on milk price supports **14,**5871, 5975, 5984-86, 5986-88 **15,**6804-6805, 6814 **FR** 630

Masters' billings to **16,** 6943-52, 6957-58

Masters denies knowledge of political contributions by **16,** 6941-42

Masters denies solicitation for contributions by **16,** 6965-68

Masters on duties for **16,** 6938-39

Masters on lawyers representing **16,** 6939-40

meeting between McGovern and representatives of **16,** 7009-10

meeting with representatives of Nixon administration **16,** 7069

meetings with ADEPT and SPACE **15,** 6417

on Ashland Petroleum's contributions to Democrats **13,** 5457

on Ashland Petroleum's operations **13,** 5440

on decision to contribute $100,000 to CRP **13,** 5441-42, 5451-52

denies contribution to CRP produced benefits to Ashland Petroleum **13,** 5446-48, 5453-56

on guilty pleas to misdemeanor charges by Ashland Petroleum, Gabon, and himself **13,** 5446

on letter from Finance Committee **13,** 5448

on letter from Parkinson of Finance Committee to Re-Elect the President on source of contribution **13,** 5445-46

on letter from Vinson to Stans on source of contribution and requesting refund **13,** 5445-46

on letter to Berdes on benefits of contribution to CRP **13,** 5447

on motivation for contribution to Finance Committee **FR** 460-62

on reasons for making illegal corporate campaign contribution to CRP **13,** 5442, 5448, 5453-56

on reforms needed for campaign financing **13,** 5449

on refund from Finance Commitee **13,** 5446

on relations with Stans **13,** 5459

on reporting illegal contribution to Special Prosecutor's Office **13,** 5446

on role of Yancy and himself in Ashland Petroleum **13,** 5451-52

on sources of campaign contribution to CRP **13,** 5442-44, 5452

on Stans' request for list of Ashland Petroleum contributors **13,** 5444-45

on telephone call from Stans soliciting campaign contribution **13,** 5440-41, 5450-51, 5457-58

See also Ashland Oil Co., Inc.

Atkins, Mrs. Orin E. 13, 5448

letter from Parkinson on $100,000 contribution to Finance Committee by **13,** 5448, 5796E

letter from Vinson to Stans on contribution of **13,** 5448, 5797E

Atlantic Investors of Miami, Ltd., contribution FR 999

Atomic Energy Act 4, 1459

Atomic tests in Nevada 22, 10521 **23,** 10895-96

Danner's letter to Rebozo on **20,** 9587-88, 9591-98

Davis on Maheu and **24,** 11578-79

Rebozo and **21,** 10041-44

"Attack" commercials 6, 2474-75, 2489 **10,** 4216-18E

"Attack strategy" of Nixon campaign FR 108, 158-60

Colson and **5,** 1930

Magruder on **10,** 4179-84E

and McGovern **10,** 4252-53E, 4254E, 4259-63

memo from Khachigian to Mitchell on **10,** 4209-20E

Odle on **1,** 26

Attorney-client privilege

Alch on **1,** 294

Ambrose-Griffin claims of **23,** 10756-60, 10765-68, 10774-79

Barth takes on discussions with Gemmill **23,** 11247

and Buckley **11,** 4454, 4459

Buzhardt and **23,** 10916

Buzhardt claims for conversations with Garment **22,** 10540-44

and Buzhardt sources for memo on Dean-Nixon conversations **23,** 10896-10900

Danner-Davis discussions and **24,** 11562-63

Davis invokes on discussion of Winte-Hunt meeting **24,** 11598-99, 11605-11609

and Davis testimony **24,** 11568, 11569, 11570, 11571, 11587-88

Dean and White House use of **4,** 1496-97

and Dean's testimony **3,** 914, 995, 1041, 1042 **4,** 1422

debriefing of Liddy **4,**1643-44, 1648, 1673 **5,** 1905, 1918-20, 1922-24 **6,** 2286-89, 2309-10, 2317-18, 2320-21, 2278, 2304, 2337, 2395-98 **7,** 2822

and Ehrlichman's memo to Dean on written retainer arrangement for Kalmbach **7,** 2812-15

and Fellow's testimony **25,** 11765

and Griffin exhibits **23,** 10736

and Griffin's testimony on San Clemente property transaction **23,** 10742, 10755, 10756-60, 10765-68, 10774-79 **25,**11765

Hunt and **9,** 3698-99, 3699-3703

and Lifflander relationship with Hertz Corp. **25,** 12266-67

Mardian and **6,** 2347, 2376-77, 2401-2402, 2414-15

and Mardian testimony on Liddy **6,** 2345-46

and Nixon's assignment of Dean to Watergate **7,** 2854

and Rebozo-Kalmbach discussions **21,** 10185-87 **23,** 10856-57

Rebozo's partial waiver for Gemmill's testimony **23,** 11173, 11174, 11182, 11184, 11186, 11189-91, 11194-95, 11206-11207, 11210, 11211, 11218

and Segretti-Dean relationship **10,** 3984-85, 4035-42, 4047

Select Committee recommendations on study by state and local bar associations on **FR** 1074

Wakefield claims for testimony on Nixon and/or Rebozo **24,** 11279, 11280, 11284, 11286-88, 11290-94, 11297, 11298, 11300-11302, 11303-11305, 11306, 11307 **FR** 943-94

and Wakefield testimony **FR** 969

Attorneys' fees scheme FR 910

and AMPI contributions **14,** 5953-54, 5956-57 **15,** 6398-6406, 6528-35, 6691-92, 6772-74, 9780-82

in AMPI payback scheme **14,** 5973-74

and AMPI's relationship with Wagner & Baroody **15,** 6651-55

as conduit for concealing TAPE contribution **FR** 596-611

Jacobsen on **15,** 6435-37

Mehren on **16,** 7306-12

for payment of Muskie debt to Hertz

see also Lifflander, Matthew L., testimony of

in scheme for Hertz Corp. contribution to Muskie campaign **25,** 12230-35, 12238, 12241-49, 12250-51 **FR** 475-81

See also Masters, Frank D., testimony of; Van Dyk, Ted, testimony of

Auchincloss, Eve **1**, 32, 35
Audience
  Baker admonishes **7**, 2830, 2905-2906
  behavior during Ehrlichman's testimony **7**, 2863, 2904-2906
  Ervin admonishes **7**, 2795 **8**, 3151
  photographers during Hunt's testimony **9**, 3667, 3731
  requests for silence from **7**, 2657
Aurelia, Emily FR 563
Aurelio, Richard FR 559, 560
Austin, Texas, Republican Party
  fire at **12**, 5176-80E
"Authority to Investigate" document of Select Committee 23, 10996, 11038-41E
Avis Corp. 25, 12250
B & C Investment Co. 21, 10135-36
  and Abplanalp-Rebozo partnership agreement **23**, 10823-44E
  check from Precision Valve Corp. **23**, 10845-46E
  IRS audit of **23**, 10754-55, 11205
  loans from Precision Valve Corp. **23**, 10752-53
  Nixon-Rebozo business relationship and **22**, 10492-93
  Rebozo sells share of interest in **23**, 10744-46
  and San Clemente property transaction **23**, 10742-43, 10751
  statements on total funds given by Rebozo to **23**, 10819E, 10820E
Bab, Dr. Emerson 14, 6296
Babcock, Tim 2, 710, 717 **6**, 2296, 2320, 2334, 2335
  money to LaRue **6**, 2342
Bache & Walston 21, 10081
Bachelor, Ray 18, 8443, 8444
Backers of Humphrey
  banking authorization card for **25**, 11892E
  checks and deposit tickets of **25**, 11889-91E
  deposits of **25**, 11897-11906E, 11945-48E
  and Jackson & Co. contributions **FR** 883-84, 887
Bacon, Donald 4, 1685E
Badden, Walter J. 21, 9720-21
Baez, Joan 3, 1141E
Bagdones, Susan 21, 10015 **23**, 10966
Bagmen
  in proposal for Sandwedge Plan **FR** 17
Bahamas Exploration, Ltd. 13, 5469-70
  as source of funds for Gulf Oil Co. contribution to CRP **13**, 5462-63, 5464 **FR** 923-24
Bahr, Leil E. 22, 12537E
Bail money
  Dean asks Walters about CIA raising **9**, 3816-17E, 3818E
  for McCord **1**, 260
  See also Hush money
Bailey, F. Lee 3, 1001 **4**, 1574-75, 1580 **5**, 2129-30
  consultations between Alch and **1**, 314-15
  reason for turning down McCord case **1**, 347
Bailey, John 9, 3737, 3742
Bain, Byford 15, 6503 **16**, 7316
Baker, Arnold, interview of
  on OEO grant to J. A. Reyes & Associates **FR** 385

Baker, Howard H., Jr. 1, 35, 36, 55, 59
  on acceptance of affidavits in lieu of direct testimony **12**, 5007-17
  admonishes audience **7**, 2830, 2905-2906
  agenda for Nixon's meeting with **3**, 998, 1245-46E
  announces FBI is investigating hoax call **6**, 2372
  announces intention of finding out more about McCord's letters to CIA **9**, 3447
  asks for Democratic National Committee records on cash contributions **2**, 767
  on attitudes toward presidency and Watergate **5**, 2153, 2155-56
  on attorney-client privilege and Segretti-Dean relationship **10**, 4023
  on bipartisan nature of Select Committee **FR** 1105
  on Brown's sworn statement **4**, 1557
  on campus politics **11**, 4514
  on Carter's position on Vietnam War **12**, 4993-94
  on categorizing of evidence **4**, 1465-66, 1537
  comments on Ervin **4**, 1508
  on conflicts in regard to tapes and recollection of tapes **8**, 3090
  conversation with Johnson on selection of minority counsel **3**, 986
  on Dash's line of questioning of Hunt **9**, 3670, 3671
  on Dash's questioning Ehrlichman about receipt of campaign funds **7**, 2859
  on Dean's request for privilege against testifying **3**, 912
  on denial of request by special prosecutor of Watergate case **2**, 458
  on difference between Committee hearing and trial **1**, 333-34
  discussion with Haldeman on Presidency and White House staff system related to Watergate **8**, 3183-88
  on efforts to intimidate Select Committee members or witnesses **4**, 1504
  Ehrlichman wants Johnson to visit on selection of minority counsel **3**, 984
  Ehrlichman's reaction to **3**, 983-84
  on Ervin's questions to Moore **5**, 2019
  on Ervin's request for copy of Stans' statement to prosecuting attorney **7**, 2797-98
  on executive privilege and White House tapes **9**, 3604
  on exhibits put into record **10**, 3955-56
  on FBI **9**, 3543
  on FBI reports on Ellsberg investigation **7**, 2665
  on future questioning of Ulasewicz on confidential assignments for Caulfield **6**, 2265, 2266, 2267
  on grant of use immunity for Strachan **6**, 2436
  on Haldeman hearing tapes **7**, 2894, 2895, 2896
  on Helms' testimony before Senate Foreign Relations Committee and Committee on Appropriations **8**, 3262-63
  on Hunt's attorney-client privilege **9**, 3699, 3700-3701
  on Hunt's double-agent theory **9**, 3754
  on immunity from prosecution for Baldwin **1**, 390-91
  on impact of Watergate **FR** 1105
  on institutional arrangements at White House related to Watergate **5**, 2170-71

on Joe Woods **22**, 10243
Kleindienst seeks meeting with **3**, 992
on lack of complaints to police about hecklers at political events **12**, 4963, 4964
on leaks from Select Committee **10**, 3903-3904
on legality and ethics of political intelligence gathering **11**, 4513-14
letter from Barker **7**, 2974E
letter from Colby on Select Committee CIA report **FR** 1158-59, 1160
letter to Nixon requesting documents on domestic intelligence **3**, 1060
on letters from McCord to CIA **9**, 3440-41
on McCord's characterization of Schlesinger **9**, 3444
on McCord's request to testify again **1**, 312
McKiernan letter on treatment of Nixon brothers to **23**, 10975-77, 10984-87E
meeting with Kleindienst **4**, 1493
meeting with Nixon **3**, 988-89, 991-92, 1243E **4**, 1483
meeting with Timmons **4**, 1483-84
on method of questioning Moncourt **22**, 10491, 10492
motion for litigation against Nixon on refusal of subpoena for tapes **7**, 2660-61
on Muskie **11**, 4686
Nixon and **3**, 1002
on Nixon appearing before Select Committee **5**, 1838-39
Nixon questions on **7**, 2748, 2749
on Nixon-Dean meeting agenda **4**, 1486-88
on Nixon's ability to provide important testimony **5**, 2022
on Nixon's refusal to obey subpoenas for White House tapes **7**, 2659-60
on Nixon's refusal to testify or give material to Select Committee **5**, 1837-38
on nominal secret classification of Helms' testimony to Committee on Armed Services **8**, 3243
opening statement of **1**, 4-6
overrules Weicker's objection to Haldeman testifying on basis of Nixon tapes **8**, 3066, 3067
on Porter's testimony **2**, 680
on Presidency and Watergate **8**, 3160-62
on Presidential campaigns **11**, 4686
on Presidential powers and Ellsberg break-in **6**, 2595-96
on private vs. public financing of Presidential campaigns **13**, 5475-76
proposed Kleindienst meetings with **4**, 1396
proposed meeting with Nixon **3**, 988
on public financing of campaigns **11**, 4689-93
on questioning of Mardian **6**, 2427, 2433
on questioning of Woods and Sirica's silence order **22**, 10255-56
on *Quicksilver Times* being put into record as exhibit **10**, 3956
on Rayburn **10**, 3947
on reasons for not issuing subpoena for Woods **22**, 10195
recommendations
  on campaign and electoral reforms **FR** 1108-12
  on establishment of Office of Public Prosecutor within Department of Justice **FR** 1105-

1106
  on establishment within Congress of Joint Intelligence Oversight Committee for monitoring governmental intelligence activities **FR** 1106-1107
  on increased national party committee role in federal elections **FR** 1114
  on Presidency **FR** 1112-14
  on reformation of congressional investigatory hearing procedures **FR** 1107-1108
request counsels annotate their notes with page references to previous testimony **8**, 3044, 3045
request for inclusion of summary of investigation of CIA activity in Watergate incident by **FR** 1115
on request for Nixon tapes and papers **5**, 2137
requests consent for executive session to hear Ehrlichman testimony on missing paragraph from Young memo **7**, 2704
requests further information from McCord **1**, 188-89, 191-92
on respect for Helms **8**, 3279
on role of Select Committee **5**, 1837
on rotation of questioning **2**, 810
ruling on Wearley exhibits **20**, 9465
rulings on Moncourt's testimony **22**, 10487
on security of "Dean Papers" **2**, 602
on Select Committee calling Democrats **11**, 4587, 4588
on Select Committee's methods of obtaining immunity for witnesses **4**, 1348
on Senate Resolution 60 and inquiries into political spying in past campaigns **11**, 4466, 4471
on Stans' request for deferment of testimony **2**, 687
and Stennis Compromise **FR** 1081
submits letter by Brown **4**, 1597-98
on subpoena for Caulfield **1**, 132-133
on subpoena for Chestnut **17**, 7699
on subpoena for Mitchell **4**, 1602
on subpoena for Nixon tapes and presidential papers **6**, 2480-81
summarizes Mitchell's testimony **5**, 2020-21
in taped telephone conversation between Kleindienst and Ehrlichman **4**, 1500-1501 **7**, 2944E
on tests of Dean's testimony **4**, 1482
thanks LaRue for testimony **6**, 2344
on use of rules of evidence by Select Committee **4**, 1524
on violence at Republican National Convention **12**, 4991-93
wants Kleindienst as contact with White House **3**, 989
on Weicker's comments on line of questioning of Marumoto **13**, 5310
on Wilson's meeting with Foreign Relations Committee **4**, 1557
on Wilson's request for time for statement on Inouye **8**, 3228, 3229
on Woods' objections to Select Committee obtaining her unlisted number **22**, 10198
on Zweig opinion **7**, 2805-2806, 2807

Barbanti, Robert A. **12**, 5113E
Barker, Bernard L. **21**, 9971
    background **FR** 28
    convicted in Fielding break-in **FR** 15-16
    letter to Ervin on Stans **13**, 5714-15E
    and locksmith for Greenspun break-in **20**, 9381
    and Mexican checks **FR** 519
    role in Watergate break-in **FR** 1
    See also Dahlberg checks
Barker, Desmond J. **18**, 8443 **19**, 9137E, 9217-18E, 9220E
    memo from Wright to **13**, 5323, 5622-23E
    memos to public information offices on aging program information **19**, 9205-06E
Barker, Margaret **1**, 375, 389 **22**, 10453, 10513 **23**, 11178 **24**, 11290 **FR** 1015
Barker, Noland **15**, 6859
Barker, Norman **14**, 5973, 6162
Barker, Robert W.
    letter to Ervin on Dunnells' affidavit **13**, 5348, 5733-35E
    letter to Ervin on Ervin's characterization of Stans' testimony **13**, 5348, 5714-15E
    letter to Ervin on Stans' statement **13**, 5348, 5706-07E
Barnes, Michael **11**, 4773E
Barnhardt, Bill **25**, 12277
Baron, M. **25**, 12277, 12283
Baroody, Joseph **14**, 6278 **16**, 7176, 7395-96
    affidavit of **17**, 7817-20E
    and AMPI **FR** 694-98
Barr, Charlie **26**, 10339
    Caulfield denies knowing **22**, 10355-56
Barrera, Roy **14**, 6173
Barrett, John Bruce **18**, 8237
    and Watergate break-in **1**, 103, 104, 105, 107, 113, 114, 118, 119, 123
Barrick, Paul E. **22**, 12532E, 12533E, 12572E **FR** 564
    letter from Parkinson on return of Goodyear Tire & Rubber Co. contribution to FCRP **13**, 5526, 5857E
    letter to Mellott on return of Gulf Oil campaign contribution **13**, 5466, 5806E
    letter to Miller on return of American Airlines' campaign contribution **13**, 5504, 5840E
    letter to Myers on return of Goodyear Tire & Rubber Co. contribution to FCRP **13**, 5526, 5856E
    letter to Vinson on return of Ashland Petroleum contribution **13**, 5448, 5798-99E
Barrigan, Polly Baca **19**, 8771E
Barron, Barbara **10**, 4026, 4296-97E **FR** 173
    signature on Segretti's false letter on McCarthy campaign stationery **10**, 4002-4003
Barry, A. Frank
    letter to Robinson on tax matters re political contributions **11**, 4806-4808E
Barry, Bob **25**, 11755
Bart, Ross **15**, 6503

Barth, Charles
    Caulfield and **22**, 10244-46
Barth, Roger Vincent **22**, 10249, 10361
    affidavit on memo of beginning portion of testimony before Executive Session of Senate Select Committee **23**, 11275E
    on alerting Ehrlichman to sensitive case reports **23**, 11267-68
    assignment changes at IRS **24**, 11625-26
    on audit of Graham **FR** 137
    briefings on IRS sensitive case reports to Walker **24**, 11631
    and Caulfield **22**, 10395 **FR** 113, 114, 138, 142
    Caulfield denies discussing IRS sensitive case reports with **22**, 10363-64
    communication with White House **23**, 10941
    contacts with Gemmill **23**, 11208
    discusses IRS interviews with Rebozo and F. Donald Nixon with Ehrlichman **21**, 9684
    and Ehrlichman's interest in audit of O'Brien **FR** 1025-30
    employment history **23**, 11276E
    information from IRS to White House and **21**, 9710-11
    informs Ehrlichman of impending IRS investigation of Rebozo **21**, 9679-85
    informs Rebozo of forthcoming IRS interview **24**, 11651-52
    informs Walters that F. Donald Nixon will be informed of forthcoming IRS interview **24**, 11651-52
    and investigation of Hersh **22**, 10378
    material to Haldeman from **23**, 11111-12
    meeting with Ehrlichman on IRS interview of Rebozo **FR** 1003
    and Operation Sandwedge **22**, 10342, 10343, 10345
    and reports on sensitive cases from IRS to Treasury Department **23**, 10926, 10927
    sensitive case reports given to Ehrlichman by **FR** 134, 1002-1003
    and tax audit of Greene **22**, 10376-77
    telephone conversation with Ehrlichman, Walters, and Shultz on O'Brien tax audit **24**, 11638, 11640-41, 11644-46
    Walters on appointment as IRS Commissioner **24**, 11624-27
    Walters on handling of sensitive case reports by **24**, 11628
Barth, Roger Vincent, testimony of **23**, 11221-74
    on access of White House staff to IRS information **23**, 11260-61
    advises Ehrlichman on O'Brien's tax return **23**, 11222, 11224
    on anonymous informants and IRS audits **23**, 11272-73
    on Caulfield's inquiries on status of tax-exempt organizations **23**, 11262-67
    on Caulfield's requests for tax information **23**, 11261-72
    claims he only talked with Ehrlichman about O'Brien's tax returns **23**, 11240
    on contacts with Colson **23**, 11250

Barth, Roger Vincent, testimony of *(Continued)*
on contacts with DeMarco **23,** 11249-50
on date of call to Rebozo on IRS interview **23,** 11234
on dates of meetings with Ehrlichman on IRS sensitive case report on Hughes **23,** 11238-39
denies familiarity with Operation Sandwedge **23,** 11273
denies knowledge of IRS interview of Danner **23,** 11255
denies knowledge of meetings between Dean and Walters on enemies list **23,** 11244
on Dent's complaint about IRS harassment of Republicans **23,** 11242-43
on destruction of copies of tax returns **23,** 11228-29, 11239
on discussions with Gemmill **23,** 11247
on Ehrlichman's concern over unresponsiveness of IRS **23,** 11229, 11242
on Ehrlichman's report on discussion with Nixon on forthcoming IRS interview with F. Donald Nixon **23,** 11232
on Ehrlichman's requests on sensitive case reports **23,** 11230
on files taken from IRS when leaving **23,** 11273
on handling of sensitive case reports **23,** 11227
on instances of harassment at IRS against him **23,** 11242
on IRS and minority business enterprises **23,** 11260
on IRS investigation of Rebozo **23,** 11251-54
on IRS investigation of Winn-Dixie **23,** 11268-69
on IRS report to Caulfield on Goldberg **23,** 11261-62
on IRS sensitive case report on Graham **23,** 11270-72
on IRS sensitive case report on "Hughes Project" **23,** 11221-32, 11235-44
on IRS sensitive case report on Wayne **23,** 11269-70
on IRS sensitive case reports discussed with Ehrlichman **23,** 11267-69
on ITT case and Beard matter **23,** 11264-65
on learning about Hughes contribution **23,** 11255
on letter of complaint from O'Brien **23,** 11225
on meeting with Ehrlichman on forthcoming IRS interviews with Rebozo and F. Donald Nixon **23,** 11231-33, 11244-46
on meeting with Shultz and Walters on O'Brien tax report **23,** 11223-24, 11241
memo on beginning portion of **23,** 11276-78E
on memo to Haldeman on harassment at IRS **23,** 11248-49
on *Newsday* investigation of Rebozo **23,** 11266
on notification of Rebozo of IRS investigation **FR** 1067
on precedents for Ehrlichman's access to tax information **23,** 11227-28
on preparation of sensitive case reports by IRS **23,** 11255-56
on problems with Walters and Thrower at IRS **23,** 11248-49
on purpose of sensitive case reports **23,** 11256-57
on Rebozo telling Meier not to talk to IRS **23,** 11231

on recordkeeping procedure for requests from White House for IRS information **23,** 11250-51
on relationship with Caulfield **23,** 11259
on requests for IRS material through Morics **23,** 11273
on source of allegations in sensitive case report on Hughes Tool Co. **23,** 11258-59
on source of IRS sensitive case report on Hughes **23,** 11256
on telephone call from Ehrlichman on tax report on O'Brien **23,** 11224, 11243-44
on telephone call to Rebozo on forthcoming IRS interview **23,** 11232, 11233-34, 11245-48
on White House method of obtaining tax information and/or tax returns **23,** 11259-60, 11261

Bartlett, John 23, 11179-80, 11182
contacts with Gemmill **23,** 11209-10, 11211-14, 11219-20
Gemmill denies asking him to call Buzhardt **23,** 11212-14
and serial numbers on Hughes money **23,** 11203-11204, 11219
telephone call to Gemmill on Rebozo's contribution from Hughes **23,** 11180
and Woods' letter on Hughes contribution **22,** 10202, 12534E **26,** 10283E
See also IRS, interview of Rebozo

Bartlett Construction Co. FR 1036

Bartolme, Robert E.
check to Dedicated Americans for Effective Government **13,** 5431, 5783E
statement to FBI on salary, finances and political contributions **13,** 5785-91E
See also American Ship Building Co.

Bartolme, Robert E., testimony of 13, 5419-38
on American Ship Building Co. bogus bonus plan **13,** 5420-38 **FR** 454-55
on amounts of bonuses **13,** 5432-35
on bookkeeping methods for records of bonuses and campaign contributions **13,** 5424-25
on dealings with Steinbrenner **13,** 5427-30, 5434
duties and salary at American Ship Building Co. **13,** 5419
on false certificates to employees **13,** 5425-26
on false memo on bonuses for file **13,** 5425
on false statements to FBI **13,** 5426-27, 5428-29
on Kalmbach's role in American Ship Building Co. contributions **13,** 5431, 5436-37
meeting with Steinbrenner and Lepkowski on need for contribution **13,** 5421
obtains counsel **13,** 5430-31
on origins of decision on campaign contributions **13,** 5435-36
on prevention of future illegal corporate contributions **13,** 5437-38
on Slater as courier from American Ship Building Co. to CRP **13,** 5422-23
on Steinbrenner destroying records on transactions involving bonuses **13,** 5424
on Steinbrenner's motivations for illegal campaign contributions **13,** 5435
on Steinbrenner's personal contribution to CRP **13,** 5423-24
on testimony before grand jury **13,** 5431

Bennett, Robert *(Continued)*
  inquiries as to terms of arrangement between
    Hughes Tool Co. and O'Brien **24,** 11593-94
  and ITT-Dita Beard memo **FR** 129
  knowledge of roles of Hunt and Colson at White
    House **20,** 9366-68
  letter from Petrie enclosing payment of bills from
    Hertz Corp. to Muskie campaign **25,** 12331-32E
  memo from Colson to Goodearle on Hughes and
    23, 11079, 11123E
  and Mullen and Company **FR** 1121-26, 1151-52
  and provision of committee names for milk pro-
    ducers' contributions **FR** 689
  report from Hunt on meeting with Winte **20,**
    9380, 9390-91
  requests trash-inspection operation at Suskind
    home **20,** 9404
Bennett, Wilbur
  and 3M contribution to Mills campaign **FR** 926-
    27
Bennett, William Edward 18, 8226
  memo from MacGregor to Kingsley on **18,** 8226,
    8363E
Benz, Robert M. 10, 3996 **11,** 4397, 4640, 4666 **FR**
  166-67, 168, 169, 174-75, 176, 177, 178
  collaboration with Segretti in Florida **10,** 3983
  collaboration with Segretti in Milwaukee **10,** 3984
  and Jackson-Humphrey letter **FR** 169-70
  Kelly denies knowledge about **11,** 4395-96
  payments received by **10,** 3983
  persons recruited by **FR** 174
  and Segretti **10,** 4015-16
  Segretti contacts after *Washington Post* story **FR**
    182
  Segretti on contact with **10,** 3993
Benz, Robert M., testimony of 11, 4403-32
  activities against Muskie campaign **11,** 4408-13
  on activities of Frolich as infiltrator in Jackson
    campaign **11,** 4407
  on activities of Griffin as infiltrator in Muskie
    campaign **11,** 4406-4407
  attitude toward Jackson-Humphrey letter **11,**
    4419, 4421
  attitude toward participation in dirty tricks cam-
    paigns **11,** 4425-26, 4429-30
  on bogus Muskie literature against Wallace **11,**
    4410
  claims information on dirty tricks against Repub-
    licans was given to FBI **11,** 4424-25
  on contacts with CRP or Republican Party **11,**
    4415-16
  on conversation with Segretti about Democratic
    National Convention **11,** 4414
  on destruction of documents on dirty tricks **11,**
    4414-15
  on dirty tricks against Republicans **11,** 4429-31
  on dirty tricks in Milwaukee **11,** 4413
  on dirty tricks in Pittsburgh **11,** 4413
  on dirty tricks played on him in 1970 **11,** 4422-25
  on "Duke" **11,** 4426
  on employment by Segretti **11,** 4403-4405, 4415
  on FBI contacting **11,** 4415
  on halting dirty tricks in future campaigns **11,**
    4419, 4433

  on hiring of Frolich **11,** 4431
  on hiring of Griffin **11,** 4430-31
  immunity for **11,** 4403
  on Jackson-Humphrey letter **11,** 4411, 4421-22
  on legality of dirty tricks **11,** 4427-28
  on letter requesting pickets at Nixon rallies **11,**
    4407
  on motivation for dirty tricks **11,** 4416-17, 4417-
    19, 4420, 4432
  persons recruited by **11,** 4405-4407
  political background **11,** 4403
  on prior use of dirty tricks in other campaigns **11,**
    4419
  on reasons for Cramer losing 1970 election **11,**
    4431-32
  on stinkbombs at Muskie picnic **11,** 4412-13, 4414
  on stinkbombs in Muskie headquarters **11,** 4411-
    12, 4427-28
  on telling FBI about alleged dirty tricks of Demo-
    crats **11,** 4428-29
  working relationship with Segretti **11,** 4409
Berde, Sidney 16, 6939, 6961, 6962, 6963
Berdes, George R.
  letter from Atkins on illegal corporate contribu-
    tion to FCRP **13,** 5447, 5448, 5802E
Berens, Fred 13, 5373
Berentson, Buehl 16, 7419, 7421, 7424 **17,** 7559 **FR**
  741-42
  Clancy on duties of **16,** 7404
  letter and check from Lilly for National Republi-
    can Senatorial campaign **16,** 7300, 7363E
  and TAPE contributions through committees **16,**
    7406, 7407, 7410
Berger, Elmer
  letter from Stearns to **10,** 4102E
Berger case 6, 2592
Bernard, Frank S. 11, 4461, 4891E
Bernard, Mary 25, 11790
Bernhard, Berl 11, 4623, 4817E **25,** 12104, 12128 **FR**
  158, 205, 206
  letter from Jones with record of contributions to
    Muskie campaign **11,** 4792-94E
  memo from Billings on "funny phones" **11,** 4888E
  memo from Kline on Muskie fundraising schedule
    11, 4795-99E
  memos on financial matters relating to Muskie
    campaign **11,** 4767-85E
Bernhard, Berl, testimony of 11, 4644-96
  on background to Muskie's candidacy in Demo-
    cratic primaries **11,** 4645-46
  on belief that Democratic opponents were respon-
    sible for dirty tricks **11,** 4669-70
  on bogus demonstrations against Muskie **11,** 4668-
    70
  on Canuck letter **11,** 4685
  on chart of dirty tricks related to polls on candi-
    dates **11,** 4679-80
  on "Citizens for Liberal Alternative" pamphlet
    11, 4671-72
  on confidentiality of campaign contributions **11,**
    4649-50
  on dirty tricks at fundraising dinner for Muskie
    11, 4666
  on electronic surveillance of Muskie campaign **11,**

4665-66

on extent of bogus literature distribution **11,** 4670-71

on fair campaign practices vs. dirty tricks **11,** 4655-56

on financial problems and practices of Muskie campaign **11,** 4646-52, 4680, 4687-88

on Florida primaries **11,** 4662-65

on fundraising for Muskie campaign **11,** 4646-47

on impact of dirty tricks **11,** 4653-68, 4672-73, 4683-84

on Kennedy's candidacy **11,** 4659-60

on link between Buchanan memos and Segretti operations **11,** 4680-81

on Lofton's activities **11,** 4681-82

on money spent by Muskie campaign compared with costs of Liddy operation **11,** 4673-74

on Mott's role **11,** 4678-79, 4681

on Muskie's reaction to attacks on his wife **11,** 4653

on New Hampshire primaries **11,** 4660-62

opening statement of **11,** 4645-68

on pickets vs. bogus demonstrations **11,** 4683

on political background **11,** 4645

on political infiltrators in Muskie campaign **11,** 4657-60

on political problems of Muskie campaign **11,** 4652

on Presidential election campaign reform **11,** 4651-52, 4674-80, 4686-87

on public financing of election campaigns **11,** 4689-93

on purpose of dirty tricks against Muskie **11,** 4654-55

on selection of Vice Presidents **11,** 4688-89

on theft of documents from Muskie campaign **11,** 4657-60, 4672-73

on United Democrats for Kennedy **11,** 4671

on Watergate and erosion of public confidence **11,** 4694-95

Bernstein, Carl

and Segretti matter **FR** 184

Bernstein, Leonard 7, 2762-63 **8,** 3155

on enemies list **4,** 1698

Berrigan, Daniel 12, 5151E **FR** 62

Berry, Dr. Calvin 14, 6298, 6299

Besemer, Melvin 16, 7301, 7339 **17,** 7627, 7670, 7671

letter from Mehren on campaign proposal **14,** 6119, 6186E

and TAPE contributions to Humphrey campaign **16,** 7313 **17,** 7659

Bethke, Monroe

affidavit with attachments of **17,** 7832-38E

letter from Isham on resignation from AMPI **17,** 8163E

Bevens, Tom 1, 205

Beyer, Nat 18, 8250

Bezdek, Sarah 14, 5910, 5911 **FR** 672

Bible quotations

Ervin and **7,** 2697-98, 2904 **8,** 3272 **9,** 3541 **FR** 1102

Bierbower, James J.

See Magruder, Jeb Stuart, testimony of

Bierne, Joe 25, 12145

Big Sky project 4, 1528-29, 1702E

Bigda, Richard J. 12, 5170E

affidavit of **12,** 5009, 5165-67E

"Bigot list" of CIA FR 1138

Bill of Rights

refusal to sign copy of **FR** 1175

and Watergate **FR** 1189-95

Billings, Leon 11, 4666

memo dealing with unusual occurrences on telephones of Subcommittee on Air and Water Pollution Office from **11,** 4695, 4886-87E

memo to Bernhard on "funny phones" **11,** 4888E

Billy Graham Day 8, 3152, 3322-23E **FR** 201

Binda, Jeffrey 18, 8443, 8444-45, 8459, 8460

Binh, Madame Nguyen Thi 12, 5199E

BIPAC 13, 5475, 5476

Bird, Robert J. 21, 10121-22

Bishop, George Norman, Jr.

affidavit of **12,** 5009, 5076-77E

Bittenbender, Gary 1, 54, 194

and CIA blamed for Watergate **1,** 215, 313

Hunt on **9,** 3836E, 3838E, 3839E

McCord letters on perjury by **9,** 3443, 3445

Bittman, William O. 1, 135, 150, 161, 188, 196, 301-302 **3,** 949 **4,** 1673

assured by Colson of Executive clemency for Hunt **FR** 67

and attempt to blame CIA for Watergate **1,** 194, 207-208, 219

Barker and **1,** 361-62

Colson and **3,** 1053 **6,** 2608 **7,** 2847

contacts with Ulasewicz **6,** 2225-27, 2228E

demands money from Parkinson **6,** 2368

disbursement of money from LaRue to **23,** 11160

discussions with Hunt on CIA relationship to Plumbers activities **9,** 3755-56

discussions with Mardian **FR** 51

and Executive clemency offers **1,** 316-317, 329, 330-331, 349-350, 351-352 **3,** 973, 974 **4,** 1484

and Executive clemency offers to McCord **FR** 63

funds to **9,** 3696

Hunt asks Colson to see him **3,** 1234E

and Hunt's affidavit on Colson **9,** 3793, 3794

Hunt's fees to **9,** 3703, 3755

and Hunt's status after death of Mrs. Hunt **3,** 971, 972

and hush money **FR** 55

involvement in coverup, Dean on **3,** 1054

LaRue's disbursements to **23,** 11156, 11162

lawyers' meeting at offices of **1,** 315, 323-325, 326-327, 347, 350-351

letter to Colson on Hunt's motion **4,** 1587

Mardian on fee charged by **6,** 2394

and McCord's tapped telephone **1,** 228

and meeting between Hunt and O'Brien **FR** 57

meeting with Barker and McCord **1,** 133-134

meeting with Colson **9,** 3697-98

messages from Hunt on hush money **3,** 969

and money from "Mr. Rivers" **9,** 3692, 3695

Boll, Joe **14**, 6311
Bolz, Charles **9**, 3522
Boman, Wally **11**, 4461, 4890E
Bombings
    of Capitol **4**, 1637
    of CIA headquarters in Chicago
        See Plamdon case
    of CRP headquarters **12**, 5012-13
    Ehrlichman on **6**, 2512-13
    Mardian on **6**, 2422-24
    of Nixon headquarters **8**, 3080
    of North Vietnam **7**, 2870
    See also Violence
Bond, Doyle **FR** 715
Bond, Julian **16**, 6983
Bonecroy, Robert
    letter from Mehren on campaign proposal to **14**,
        6119, 6186E
Bonnet, Walter J. **2**, 687
Bonus plans **13**, 5405-18, 5420-38
    and campaign contribution by American Ship
        Building Co **FR** 452-58
Borash, Anthony **11**, 4504, 4532, 4617, 4717E
Boston, Mass.
    demonstration in **12**, 5102-06E, 5110-15E
Boston Globe **12**, 5009, 5102-06E
Boston Herald Traveler and Record American **12**,
    5113-15E
Boston Police Department
    photograph of injured officer during demonstra-
        tion **12**, 4999, 5031E
    photograph of repelling crowd of demonstrators
        on surge toward armory **12**, 4999, 5032E
    See also Sullivan, Jeremiah P., testimony of
Boudin, Leonard **1**, 198, 246 **FR** 123
    Hunt article on **9**, 3673, 3735
    Hunt's allegations about terHorst story on **9**,
        3759, 3895-96E
    in memo from Young to Ehrlichman **FR** 13-14
Bouman, Jack **9**, 3751
Bouterse, Borrelli & Albaisa
    and improvements on Nixon's Key Biscayne prop-
        erty **FR** 1034-35
Bowen, Gene **22**, 10707, 10708
Bowles, Charley **9**, 3620
Boyarsky, Bill **11**, 4585-86
Braden, Tom **11**, 4604
Bradford
    See LaRue, Fred C. (code name for)
Bradley, Tom **25**, 12151
Brady, Richard
    declines to name attorneys used in pay-back
        scheme of Muskie campaign and Hertz Corp.
        25, 12232-33
    See also Edidin, Sol M., testimony of
Brady v. *United States* **9**, 3631
Brand, Herbert **FR** 513
Braniff Airways, Inc.
    contribution by **FR** 462-63
    guilty plea by **FR** 463
    press release on 1972 contributions to Finance
        Committee to Re-Elect the President **13**, 5483-
        84

See also Fabrega, Camilo, testimony of; Robinson,
    Neal, testimony of
Braniff International
    account analysis of debits and credits of **13**, 5491,
        5830-31E
    miscellaneous financial records of **13**, 5491, 5813-
        29E, 5832-33E, 5834-36E
    record of payment to CAMFAB **13**, 5491, 5810-
        11E
Branner, John W.
    relationship to McGovern campaign **25**, 12175
Bratiass, Nancy **1**, 35 **19**, 8663E
Brawley, William **13**, 5464, 5468 **FR** 473
Bray, John **25**, 12166
    letter to Dorsen on immunity for Strachan **16**,
        7455, 7472E
    See also Strachan, Gordon C., testimony of
Break-ins
    attempted at McGovern Washington headquarters
        FR 27-28
    in Gemstone plan **FR** 21
    planned for Bremer's apartment **FR** 130
    See also Watergate break-in
Breed, Abbott, and Morgan, New York City **5**, 1998
Bremer, Arthur **9**, 3735, 3807
    Colson's plan to investigate **FR** 129-30
    Segretti denies knowing **10**, 4044
Brennan, Charles **6**, 2421, 2435
Brennan, Jack **FR** 782E
Brennan, Peter **19**, 8815E
Brenneman, Hugh W. **18**, 8461
    letter to Brody on radio programs **18**, 8461, 8533-
        35E
Brereton, Charles **3**, 1135E
Bress, David
    asks for ruling from chair on questions about
        Mardian's role at Internal Security Division **6**,
        2425
    on line of questioning of Mardian **6**, 2433
    on Mardian's use of attorney-client privilege **6**,
        2345, 2346, 2383
    on memo of Mardian-Stans telephone call **6**, 2367
    See also Mardian, Robert C.
Breuil, James F. **22**, 12568-69E
Brewer, Michael **3**, 1134E **4**, 1581-82 **16**, 7206, 7378
    23, 11090-91 **FR** 594, 595
    source of contribution to **17**, 7580-81
Brezhnev, Leonid I.
    visit to U.S., Select Committee postpones hearings
        during **2**, 875 **20**, 9549
    and Watergate coverup **4**, 1485
Brierly, Lee A. **20**, 9415
Briggs, George **12**, 5114-15E
Brill, Theodore **2**, 659 **11**, 4641, 4644 **FR** 198-99
Brindze, Paul, testimony of **12**, 4975-85
    on attitude toward dissemination of anti-Nixon lit-
        erature **12**, 4983
    on duties for McGovern campaign **12**, 4976, 4981
    on Los Angeles Board of Rabbis' endorsement of
        McGovern **12**, 4980-81
    on "Nixon Is Treyf" leaflet **12**, 4976-79

Buchanan, George FR 483

Buchanan, Henry 2, 627

Buchanan, Patrick J. 1, 82 2, 545, 623 3, 988, 1075
10, 4111E, 4112E, 4126E, 4130E 25, 12112
 Assault book on strategy for undermining
  McGovern election bid 10, 3975, 4240-46E
 and Citizens for a Liberal Alternative FR 157-58
 and dirty tricks operation FR 160
 letter to editor drafted by 10, 4133-44E
 letter to Kilpatrick on Nixon's press conferences
  10, 4145E
 memo to Mitchell, "Attack Organization and
  Strategy" 10, 3975, 4209-20E
 memo to Mitchell and Haldeman on fourth-party
  candidacies FR 203
 memo to Mitchell on advance people FR 201
 memo to Mitchell on use of citizens committees
  in 1972 campaign FR 156-57
 memos on political strategy for 1972 campaign
  FR 158-60
 as observer spokesman 3, 1243-44E
 and Plumbers operation FR 120
 and preparations for press conferences 5, 1973
 in Rogovin affidavit 10, 4370-74E
 and Shumway's alleged slander of Stearns 11,
  4567, 4592, 4593
 and stock ownership in Fishers Island Corp. 24,
  11284, 11285
 and write-in campaign for Kennedy in New
  Hampshire FR 203

Buchanan, Patrick J., testimony of 10, 3899-3977
 on activities of Democratic party 10, 3899-3977
 on ads against McGovern 10, 3928-30
 on analysis of possible Kennedy candidacy 10,
  3928
 on appointment of Supreme Court judges 10, 3927
 on Assault Strategy memo 10, 3913-14
 on attack material on McGovern 10, 3961-63
 on attitudes toward Democratic opponents to
  Nixon 10, 3921-22
 on break-ins at candidates' headquarters 10, 3970
 on brochure on Muskie's position on Blacks 10,
  3965-67
 and Brookings Institution FR 124
 on campaign ethics 10, 3957-60
 on campaign practices in 1972 compared to other
  Presidential campaigns 10, 3956-57
 on Canuck letter 10, 3967-68
 on Caulfield's activities 10, 3974
 and "Citizens for a Liberal Alternative" 11, 4611,
  4638-39
 complains of inadequate time to examine his
  memos 10, 3907, 3908, 3909-10
 confidential memo to DeBolt, Finch, Harlow,
  Moore, Nifziger, Price, Timmons and Walker
  on topics for discussion at meeting of June 24,
  1971 10, 3975, 4173E
 on covert activities by Republican party at Democratic National Convention 10, 3932-33
 on crossing over of Republicans in 1968 Wisconsin campaign 10, 3959-60
 on Democratic party primaries 10, 3921-22
 on Democrats for Nixon 10, 3929-30

 on demonstrations during campaign 10, 3931-32
 denies role in political sabotage 10, 3901
 on Ellsberg investigation 9, 3806 10, 3912-14
 and enemies list 4, 1689E
 on ethics of political actions during campaign 10,
  3968-77
 on Fielding break-in and coverup 10, 3964-65
 on ghosted letters 10, 3938
 on incumbent administration using Justice Department CIA, FBI, and State Department for
  political purposes 10, 3963-65
 on information from Muskie campaign 10, 3920-
  21
 on institutionalized power of Left FR 124
 on investigations of private lives of candidates 10,
  3975
 on IRS personnel 10, 3919-20
 on lack of impact of Segretti's dirty tricks 10,
  3901-3902
 on leaks to press damaging to opposition candidates 10, 3960
 on learning about Fielding break-in 10, 3913
 on letter-writing campaigns 10, 3976
 on McGovern as best opposing candidate for Nixon 10, 3925-26
 on McGovern's "encouragement" of Ellsberg 10,
  3914
 on Mitchell's comment that he would do anything
  to reelect Nixon 10, 3922-23
 on "Muskie Watch" 10, 3915-16, 3922, 3936
 on Nixon's election victory 10, 3902-3903
 on Nixon's instructions on Eagleton 10, 3940
 on O'Brien's campaign manual 10, 3944-46
 opening statement 10, 3900-3903
 on paid infiltrators 10, 3970-71
 on pamphlet issued by Citizens for a Liberal Alternative 10, 3933-34
 plan for activities at the Democratic National
  Convention 10, 4221-24E
 on Plumbers unit 10, 3912-13
 on political action memos on Muskie's primary
  campaign 10, 3921-22
 on political association with Nixon 10, 3904
 on political attacks 10, 3935-36
 on political espionage and political tricks 10,
  3924-25
 on political monitoring activity as usual election
  practice 10, 3946-47
 on political rhetoric 10, 3922
 on political sabotage and dirty tricks and pranks
  10, 3942, 3958-59
 on political strategy memos becoming part of
  Presidential papers 10, 3905-3906, 3907
 on political strategy memos obtained by Select
  Committee from CRP 10, 3907-10
 on Presidency 10, 3939
 protests lack of notification of scheduling of his
  testimony 10, 3900
 protests leaks to media prior to his appearance
  before Select Committee 10, 3900-3901
 on reasons for Nixon's victory 10, 3901
 on reasons for Republicans concentrating political
  resources on Muskie 10, 3902
 on recipients of memos from 10, 3940

on role in Gardner's campaign for governor of
North Carolina **11**, 4437
on role in Underwood's campaign for governor of
West Virginia **11**, 4437
on size of spying operation **11**, 4451-52
on termination of infiltration of Muskie campaign
11, 4444-45
on violation of Hatch Act **11**, 4450-51, 4454-55
Buckley, Mrs. John R. 14, 5962
**Budget Committee of Finance Committee to Re-Elect
the President**
MacGregor on role in **12**, 4911-12
membership of **2**, 704, 764
Stans on organization of **2**, 704-705
and Stans memos on expenditures **2**, 746-47
and use of money designated **2**, 741
See also Finance Committee to Re-Elect the President
Buffham, Benson 9, 3401E
Bulgo, Joseph E. 3, 1117E
Bulkley, Eula 14, 5935, 5936, 6002E, 6003E **15**,
6398-6404, 6432-33, 6484-87E, 6495-96E
Bull, Stephen 3, 1017, 1170E **5**, 2075, 2078, 2080 **7**,
2896 **22**, 10239, 10726
investigates Dean's awareness of White House
taping system **FR** 95
Bumper stickers
bogus **FR** 172
Bumpers, Dale 16, 7025
Bundy, McGeorge 9, 3881E, 3882E, 3883E **10**, 3952
Bungato, Nick FR 200
memo from Odle to **FR** 353E
Burch, Dean
and White House use of FCC **FR** 149
Burck, R. H., Jr. 12, 5030E **FR** 462
Burden, Earl 12, 5162E
Burdick, Jess FR 168
activities campaign of **11**, 4639-40
Burglaries
break-ins in Huston Plan **FR** 3-4
Colson's plan to burglarize Brookings Institution
3, 919-20
report on Jenkins **11**, 4561, 4727-42E
See also Break-ins
Burkard (Chestnut's law partner) 25, 11755
and loan to Humphrey campaign **25**, 11741-42
Burke, Bruce 20, 9486
Burke, David 16, 7006
Burke, Edmund 11, 4568
Burning Tree Country Club, Washington, D.C. 2,
820, 823 **9**, 3560, 3561-62, 3577, 3612 **10**, 3904
Burns, Diana FR 153
Burns, Martin 5, 1866 **16**, 6961
and suit against AMPI **FR** 703-704
Burr, Aaron 5, 1866
Burstein, Lawrence S.
See Danner, Richard, testimony of; Davis, Chester
C., testimony of
Burtost, Donald 22, 10513
Bush, George 7, 2803

Business Executives Move for Vietnam Peace 3,
1138E, 1141E
Businessmen's Alliance Against the War 25, 12143,
12157
Busing issue 10, 4199E
and dirty tricks against McGovern **10**, 4261E **12**,
5017
and dirty tricks against Muskie **10**, 3982, 4000 **11**,
4379, 4394-95, 4410, 4662-63, 4671
in memo from Failor to Magruder **12**, 5265E
Morgan's brief on **24**, 11458
in Segretti activities against Muskie **10**, 3995-96
Butcher, Bill 25, 12166
bogus Muskie poster on **10**, 3996, 4267E
Butterbrodt, John E. 14, 5875 **15**, 6873 **16**, 7233,
7248 **17**, 7621 **FR** 583
and AMPI contributions to congressional campaigns **16**, 7302
and antitrust suit against AMPI **16**, 7310
discussions with Mehren on AMPI commitments
16, 7247-48
discussions with Morris on antitrust suit against
AMPI **16**, 7444-45, 7447-50
letter from Mehren on campaign proposal **14**,
6119, 6186E
Morris on remarks on AMPI contributions and
antitrust suit **16**, 7445-46
Parr denies AMPI commitment to **16**, 7317
and Russell payback scheme **FR** 601-602
speech on milk import quotas given by **15**, 6545,
6703E
Townsend's relationship with **16**, 7101
Butterbrodt, John E., testimony of 17, 7625-73
on AMPI contributions approved by **17**, 7646
on AMPI contributions to Democratic Senatorial
and House committees **17**, 7670-71
on AMPI rally for Mills in Ames, Iowa **17**, 7663-
66
on AMPI's efforts to have Nixon attend convention in 1970 **17**, 7633-34
on antitrust suit against AMPI **17**, 7640
on attending Nixon's meeting on world development at White House **17**, 7635-36
on contacts with senators or congressmen on milk
price supports **17**, 7662
contradicts Morris testimony **17**, 7650-51
denies knowing Hillings or Colson **17**, 7637
denies knowledge of AMPI contributions to Nixon campaign in 1971 **17**, 7637, 7639-40
denies knowledge of contacts between AMPI representatives and Colson or Kalmbach in 1970
17, 7633
denies knowledge of Lilly's delivery of funds for
Humphrey campaign **17**, 7669
denies meeting with Kalmbach and agreeing to
AMPI contributions **17**, 7650
denies solicitation of AMPI by Humphrey campaign **17**, 7671
denies telephone conversation with Mehren on
contributions to Republicans **17**, 7645-46
on financial arrangements with AMPI **17**, 7658
on financial authority at AMPI **17**, 7671-72
on Johnson's activities in Mills campaign **17**,
7667-69

Butterbrodt, John E., testimony of *(Continued)*
on Kalmbach's suggestion that AMPI contributions go through state committees 17, 7643-44
on learning about increase in price supports 17, 7638-39
on letter on TAPE contribution for purchase of Democratic and Republican National Convention booklets in 1972 17, 7651-52
on meeting between Mehren and Kalmbach 17, 7641-43
on meeting with Morris 17, 7648-51
on meetings between Nixon, Nelson, and Parr in 1970 17, 7634-35
on Mehren-Connally meeting 17, 7645
on Mehren-Nunn meeting 17, 7645-47
on Mehren's report that Kalmbach refused funds from AMPI for Nixon campaign 17, 7644-45
on milk price-support issue 17, 7635-39
on Nelson and Isham explaining high fees to Russell 17, 7628-29
on Nixon's meeting with dairy industry leaders FR 646
on notification about meeting with Nixon 17, 7635
on professional affiliations other than AMPI 17, 7657-58
on proposals for contributions to Democratic Presidential candidates 17, 7659
on reasons for not withholding payments to Russell 17, 7632-33
refutes Wright report on conversation with Morris 17, 7672-73
on relationship with Humphrey 17, 7671
on relationship with Parr 17, 7660
on role as president of AMPI board 17, 7626
on role with TAPE and Committee for TAPE 17, 7626-27
on Russell's billings to AMPI 17, 7628-33
on Russell's explanation of high fees 17, 7629-30
on Russell's loan from AMPI 17, 7631-32
on Semer's delivery of $100,000 to Kalmbach 17, 7627-28
on TAPE contribution to Mills 17, 7659-62
on TAPE contributions to Humphrey campaign 17, 7658-59, 7660
on TAPE contributions to Republican and Democratic congressional campaign committees 17, 7653-57
on voided Committee for TAPE checks 17, 7647-48
Butterfield, Alexander Porter 3, 931, 980 5, 2179 6, 2503 8, 3053, 3058, 3101-3102, 3175, 3193 12, 4939 13, 5531 23, 10901
contacted by FBI on Hunt's probable involvement in Watergate FR 33
and FBI check on Hunt's employment by White House 9, 3526
and FBI investigation 8,3157-58 9,3534
Haldeman says he had access to tapes prior to testimony of 8, 3050
interviewed as result of satellite chart on Haldeman FR 29
memo for Caulfield 3, 919, 1107E, 1108E
memo from Brown 3, 919, 1103E

memo to Haldeman on Fitzgerald 8, 3146-48
and money returned to CRP 6, 2462
and revelation of Nixon taping system FR 29-30, 49, 1114
role at White House 1, 85
and transfer of money from CRP to White House 6, 2461, 2473, 2494, 2497
work relationship with Haldeman 8, 3154
Butterfield, Alexander Porter, testimony of 5, 2073-90
on authority for installation of listening devices 5, 2077
on availability of Nixon tapes 5, 2079
on checking and maintenance of Nixon tapes 5, 2078
claims Ehrlichman and Dean had no knowledge of Nixon's listening devices 5, 2078
claims no one has asked for Nixon tapes 5, 2089-90
on Dean's suspicions of being tape recorded 5, 2081
on duties at White House 5, 2074
on listening devices at Nixon's Oval Office and Executive Office Building Office 5, 2074-90
on Nixon's innocence of any offense 5, 2090
opening statement on lack of counsel 5, 2073-74
on operation of recording devices 5, 2079-80, 2086-87
on persons knowing about Nixon's tape recorders 5, 2077-78
on reason for installation of listening devices 5, 2077, 2087-88
on recording devices away from White House 5, 2085-86
on reluctance to reveal existence of White House listening devices 5, 2088
on tapped telephones 5, 2082-83
on tests of Nixon's tape recording system 5, 2080-81
on use of tapings by other administrations 5, 2084
Butz, Earl 4, 1536
appearance at Lehigh Valley Cooperative Farmers annual dinner FR 481-82
meeting with Mehren, Campbell, and Lyng 16, 7279
See also Nader v. *Butz*
Buzhardt, J. Frederick 3, 985, 1060 6, 2409 7, 2670 10, 3906 23, 10788, 10877-10924, 11064
affadavit and detailed notes by Thompson of telephone conversation with 4, 1794-1800E
attitude toward full disclosure to Watergate Committee 22, 10631-32
and booklet on Nixon brothers 22, 10652
and Dean's request for access to his files 4, 1532
discussion with Garment on Nixon booklet 23, 11071
discussion with Gemmill on his testimony 23, 11215-16
discussion with Higby prior to Executive session interview 23, 11080-81
discussion with McKiernan on *Vesco* case 22, 10621
discussions with Garment on investigation of Hughes Tool Co. 23, 11054, 11059

Calley case **3,** 1027 **4,** 1357

Calloway, Howard **14,** 5966

Caltigirone, Samuel R.
affidavit of **12,** 5009, 5173E

Cambodia
and Ehrlichman's reasons for wiretapping Kraft **21,** 9688
memo from Haldeman to Magruder on advertisements about administration policy on **10,** 3975, 4128E
memo from Magruder to Nixon on reaction to response to bombing of **FR** 317-19E

CAMFAB
and conduit for Braniff Airways contribution to Finance Committee of CRP **13,** 5484-85, 5487, 5489-93 **FR** 462-63
record of payment by Braniff International to **13,** 5491, 5810-11E

Camp David
listening devices at **5,** 2077
See also Dean Report

CAMPA **14,** 5909 **15,** 6755

Campaign contributions
of ADEPT, *see* Hanman, Gary Edwin, testimony of
of American Ship Building Co., *see* Bartolme, Robert, testimony of; Clark, Matthew, testimony of
Anderson column on Davis brothers **26,** 10590E
anonymous **2,** 706
Stans on **2,** 729-31, 750-56, 780-81
Arenas' **13,** 5324-25
of Ashland Oil, *see* Atkins, Orin E., testimony of
Atkins' letter from Vinson to Stans on **13,** 5448, 5797E
Atkins' letter from Parkinson on **13,** 5448, 5796E
of Bartolme **13,** 5431, 5785-91E
and Black groups **18,** 8257, 8259
bogus, to McCloskey **FR** 197-98
of Braniff Airways, *see* Fabrega, Camilo, testimony of; Robinson, Neal, testimony of
Buckley asked to identify memos on **11,** 4461
Casanova affidavit on **13,** 5375, 5737-39E
cash, and Federal Election Campaign Act of 1971 **FR** 445-46
check from Republican Campaign Committee to Republican Committee **17,** 8170E
check from Republican Campaign Committee to Republican Senatorial Campaign Committee **17,** 8170E, 8171E, 8173E
check from Republican National Associates Committee to National Republican Congressional Committee **17,** 8172E
check from Republican National Associates Committee to National Republican Senatorial Committee **17,** 8172E
check from Republican National Finance Committee to Congressional Boosters Club **17,** 8169E
check from Republican National Finance Committee to Republican Congressional Campaign Committee **17,** 8169E
check from Republican National Finance Committee to Republican Senatorial Campaign **17,** 8169E

committed as of April 7 **2,** 749-50
corporate, *see* Corporate contributions
by dairy coops, *see* ADEPT; AMPI; SPACE; TAPE
Danner denies discussing using for Nixon's expenses **24,** 11453-54
Danner's solicitation of **24,** 11440-42, 11443-44
of Davis, A. D., *see* Davis, A. Darius, testimony of
of Davis brothers **23,** 11018
for Democratic National Convention **3,** 1154E
and enemies list **4,** 1409, 1691E, 1733E
F. Donald Nixon on involvement in **22,** 10710-12
from Belcher campaign funds **14,** 5958, 6041E
from foreign nationals **2,** 713 **23,** 10855-56 **25,** 12156-58
from Kovens **FR** 147
from Lagdameo **2,** 713
from Spanish-speaking Americans to Nixon campaign **13,** 5277, 5315
funds given to Nixon brothers from **23,** 10896, 10924
given to LaRue by Rebozo **23,** 11152-71
of Goodyear Tire & Rubber Co., *see* DeYoung, Russell, testimony of
of Gulf Oil Corp., *see* Wild, Claude C., Jr., testimony of
by Hispanic American recipients of government contracts **13,** 5298-99
to Hispanic Finance Committee **13,** 5371, 5736E
by Hughes, *see* Danner, Richard G., testimony of; Hughes contribution
to Humphrey campaign, *see* Chestnut, Jack L., statement of
to Humphrey campaign from dairy industry, *see* Dairy industry, contributions to Humphrey campaign
and ITT-Dita Beard memo **FR** 127-29
Kalmbach destroys files of **5,** 2092, 2094
Kalmbach on disbursal to Edward Nixon **23,** 10858, 10859
Kalmbach's methods of soliciting **5,** 2126, 2139
Kline's thank-you letter to Muskie contributors **11,** 4809E
letter from Chotiner to Parr on use of political committees for **15,** 6888, 6930E
letter from Firestone to Parkinson on **13,** 5526, 5854E
letter from Garment to Dash with list of pre-April 7 **26,** 10284E
letter from Hanman to Harrison on ADEPT's **17,** 8150E
letter from Harrison to Isham on use of political committees for **15,** 6645, 6730-41E
letter from Harrison to Nelson on **14,** 6264, 6287-92E **15,** 6644, 6723-29E
letter from Heininger to Parkinson on **17,** 7653, 7674-77E
letter from Isham to Harrison on **15,** 6647, 6742E
letter from Jones to Bernhard on **11,** 4792-94E
letter from Parkinson to Firestone on **13,** 5526, 5852-53E
letter from Parkinson to Wild on **13,** 5466, 5803E
letter from Parr to Isham on mailing of **15,** 6890, 6931E

Campaign contributions *(Continued)*
letter from Russell to Muskie Election Committee on **16,** 7015, 7057E

letter on appreciated properties and gift-tax committees for Muskie **11,** 4695, 4806-08E

letter returning, from corporations **11,** 4695, 4809E

limitation on, Select Committee recommendations for **FR** 570-71

to Lindsay campaign **FR** 558-63

made in 1968 and used in 1972 for Caulfield-Ulasewicz activities **22,** 10570-71

to McGovern, investigation of **21,** 9727-28

memo from Kline to Bernhard on schedule for Muskie's fundraising **11,** 4795-99E

memo from Nelson to Muskie staffers on **11,** 4804E

to McCloskey campaign **3,** 1137-38E

Mott's **25,** 12116-23, 12136E

Mott's philosophy of **25,** 12107-12108

Mott's recommendations on **25,** 12120

to Muskie campaign **4,** 1700E, 1734-53E, 1495 **11,** 4691, 4890-91E **14,** 5951, 6029-40E **16,** 7013, 7016, 7055-56E, 7058E **25,** 12106, 12107

to National Hispanic Finance Committee **13,** 5292-93

to National Republican Senatorial Campaign **16,** 7300, 7354-56E

new law and **2,** 710-11

Palmby on relationship to milk price-support decision **16,** 7148-51

personal notes of Lilly on **14,** 5972, 6045-49E

and placement on Presidential Board **FR** 415

pre-April 7 **FR** 564

pre-April 7 list of **26,** 10285-10338E

press release admitting Gulf Oil's **13,** 5466, 5808-09E

Rebozo's correspondence on **22,** 11529-74E

to Republican members of Select Committee from White House **4,** 1501-1502

retained by Rebozo after 1968 campaign **21,** 9945-52

Rubin's, to McGovern campaign **25,** 12138-43

and Seafarers' Political Action Donation Committee **FR** 512-13

Select Committee recommendations on **FR** 443-44, 573-76

solicited from recipients of federal moneys **FR** 409

Steinbrenner's **13,** 5423-24

stocks as **2,** 736

tax credit for
Select Committee recommendations for **FR** 572

tax problems and **11,** 4806-4808E

through multiple committees
legal reasons for **FR** 884-85

Ulasewicz develops lists of potential **6,** 2273-74

unauthorized collections in Maryland **12,** 5095-96E

used for defense funds **4,** 1570 **8,** 3092-93, 3197-98

by Wakefield **24,** 11281, 11346-51E

to Weicker **8,** 3203-4

Woods denies knowledge of Rebozo's activities in **22,** 10231-34

See also Campaign financing; Dahlberg checks; Fernandez, Benjamin, testimony of; Mexican checks; Milk Fund report; Mills campaign finances report; Parr, David L., testimony of; Rebozo, Charles Gregory, testimony of; Rubin, Miles L., statement of; Strachan, Gordon C., testimony of

Campaign financing
Bernhard's recommendations for **11,** 4651-52, 4677, 4687-93

and corporate contributions, *see* Corporate contributions

and corporate good government committees **FR** 550-53

and corporate-oriented solicitations **FR** 544

and discretionary fund at Commerce Department **2,** 873-74

Ervin on **11,** 4696

general guidelines for Muskie campaign **11,** 4800-4803E, 4805E

impact of dirty tricks on Muskie's **11,** 4667

industry-by-industry program for **FR** 548-50

and labor unions, *see* Labor unions

letter from Stans to Mrs. Swanke on distribution of **16,** 7429, 7436E

and Lindsay campaign **FR** 558-63

MacGregor's recommendations on **12,** 4912, 4927-28

and Mexican checks and Allen matter **FR** 514-22

and misuse of money **FR** 108

Montoya statement on **FR** 1167-69

for Muskie **11,** 4646-52, 4680

and National Hispanic Finance Committee **FR** 522-26

and Nixon appointments to ambassadorships **FR** 492-96

role of Kalmbach in raising **FR** 505-10

Select Committee investigation of **FR** 445-46

Select Committee recommendations for legislation on **FR** 563-77
amendment of Internal Revenue Code to provide credit for campaign contribution **FR** 572

establishment of Federal Elections Commission **FR** 564-67

prohibition of Government officials on Executive Office of President payroll or whose appointment required Senate confirmation from soliciting or receiving campaign contributions **FR** 575

statute prohibiting campaign contributions from foreign nationals **FR** 573-75

statute prohibiting cash contributions and expenditures in excess of $100 **FR** 567-68

statute requiring candidates for President or Vice President to centralize campaigns **FR** 568-69

statutory limitation on campaign expenditures of Presidential candidates **FR** 569-70

statutory limitation on political contributions **FR** 570-71, 575-76

timing of **FR** 563-64

violations of major provisions of campaign financing law constituting felony **FR** 576-77

See also Campaign contributions; Humphrey cam-

discusses Sandwedge proposal with Caulfield and Dean **FR** 116

discussion with Rose Mary Woods on private security agency plan **FR** 113-14

and efforts to hire Joe Woods **22,** 10243, 10244-45

and FBI **FR** 143-45

funds from Kalmbach to **22,** 10570-71

and grants to foundations **FR** 142-43

Higby on role of **23,** 11094-95

hired by Ehrlichman **FR** 107

information from FBI on DeAntonio to **FR** 144-45

informs Ulasewicz that Segretti works for CRP **FR** 165

and investigation of Fund for Investigative Journalism **FR** 143

and investigation of Potomac Associates **FR** 143

involvement with McCord after Watergate break-in **3,** 974-76 **4,** 1545, 1580 **23,** 10865-67

and IRS audits on DeAntonio, Talbot, and New Yorker Films **FR** 136-37

and ITT case **23,** 11265

Kalmbach's payments to **2,** 10184-85 **23,** 10865-67, 10870E, 10875E

and Kraft wiretap **FR** 111-12

letter to Kalmbach with travel expenses **22,** 12472E **23,** 10864E

on Maheu relationship with Frank **21,** 9716-17

and McCord **1,** 126, 150-51, 182-83, 198 **4,** 1649-50, 1673

and McCord's letter on effort to place blame for Watergate on CIA **1,** 196-197

McCord's note on plan to blame CIA to **1,** 241, 315-316

and McCord's plan for case being thrown out **1,** 227-28, 243-244

meets with McCord **FR** 64-66

memo from Dean on *Newsday* article on Rebozo **21,** 10126

memo on IRS audits **23,** 11270

memo to Dean on antitrust action against *Los Angeles Times* **FR** 145

memo to Dean on ballot security for 1972 **26,** 10339E

memo to Dean on Hughes retainer to O'Brien **23,** 11079, 11131E

memo to Dean on IRS sensitive case report on Graham **23,** 11271, 11272

memo to Dean on *Newsday* article on Rebozo **23,** 11101, 11143-44E **FR** 135-36

memo to Dean on Sandwedge plan applicability to 1972 campaign **FR** 115

memo to Dean on "Sixty Minutes" show on Hughes-Maheu **23,** 11079, 11132E

memo to Dean re Kennedy people and Toyota franchise **23,** 11098, 11138E

monitoring of wiretap of F. Donald Nixon **FR** 112-13

and political enemies project **FR** 131

press statement on Hunt and Segretti **3,** 965, 1209E

Ragan's payments to **FR** 112

report on demonstrations **10,** 4109-10E

requests to Barth for IRS information **23,** 11259, 11261-72 **FR** 138-39

and Sandwedge Plan **2,** 786 **6,** 2536-37, **8,** 3032 **FR** 17-18, 113-17

source of payments to **23,** 10860 **FR** 942-43, 1060

special account set up by Kalmbach for payments to **22,** 12473

subpoena by Patman Committee **3,** 961, 1191E

subpoena for **1,** 132-133

summary of Ulasewicz' activities **3,** 926

and surveillance of Kennedy **3,** 923 **4,** 1532 **8,** 3158-59

telephone call to Dean after Watergate arrests **3,** 932 **4,** 1356

tells Dean about Colson's plan to burglarize Brookings Institution **3,** 919-20

tells Dean about Plumbers' unit **3,** 921

tells Dean about wiretap on newsman's telephone **3,** 919

and Ulasewicz **4,** 1590 **6,** 2244

and Ulasewicz surveillance of Kennedy **FR** 117-18

and Ulasewicz's calls to McCord **1,** 285-292 **6,** 2271

Ulasewicz's investigative assignments for **6,** 2268-69, 2271-76 **7,** 2274

Ulasewicz's reasons for not telling him about money to Watergate defendants **6,** 2260

and wiretapping of Kraft **23,** 10912

Woods on **22,** 10241-47, 102277-78

works for Mitchell **3,** 925-26

Caulfield, John J., testimony of 1, 248-184 **21,** 9687-9737 **22,** 10341-10410

on Acree's role **22,** 10391-95

on Anderson's columns on CIA plot to kill Castro **21,** 9723-24

on anonymous letters to IRS **22,** 10368

on Badden **21,** 9720-21

on Barth's relationship with Walters at IRS **22,** 10358-59

on belief he was serving Nixon **1,** 274-75

on "black bag capability" in Operation Sandwedge **21,** 9731-33

on Brookings Institution matter **22,** 10356-61

on Buckley **22,** 10355

on "capability at IRS" in memos **22,** 10387-88

on Castro assassination attempt **21,** 9719

on CIA **1,** 280-83

on contacting Ragan about wiretapping of Kraft **21,** 9688-90

and CRP **1,** 251-52

on CRP hiring of McCord **1,** 270-71

on De Galindey and Trujillo assassinations **21,** 9717

on dealings with Department of Justice **22,** 10399-10400

on Dean's rejection of Sandwedge Plan **22,** 10353-54

denies discussing tax information with Haldeman **22,** 10379

denies gathering information from Hughes Tool Co. employees **21,** 9721

denies investigation of Fund for Investigative Journalism **22,** 10377-78

denies knowledge of electronic or physical surveillance of *Newsday* reporters **22,** 10374

denies knowledge of file at White House on F. Donald Nixon **21,** 9704

Celbard case **1**, 340
Cellini, Eddie 20, 9568
CEMI 22, 10608
Census Bureau
deletion of material on Hispanic Americans from Census Report for 1972 **13**, 5324
report on Spanish-speaking Americans CRP efforts to delay **FR** 404-405
Center for Community Change 25, 12113
Center for Corporate Responsibility
denial of tax-exempt status of **FR** 143
Center for Political Reform 25, 12113
Central America Cooperative Federation (CACF) 14, 5898, 6247 **16**, 6985
formation of **16**, 7062, 7069
Central Arkansas Milk Producers Association
See CAMPA
Century Plaza Hotel, Los Angeles
demonstration against Nixon at **8**, 3081, 3205 **11**, 4538-55, 4719-24E
See also Hickman, Gary, testimony of
Cernan, Eugene 20, 9448 **21**, 10053 **24**, 11548
Cerny, Howard 22, 10711-12
Cerrell, Joe 11, 4490
CGSP
See Corporate group solicitation program
Chairamonte, Robert 12, 5161E
Chambers, Arden 2, 469, 535, 571, 689
subpoena by Patman Committee **3**, 1191E
Chambers, Whittaker 5, 2047-48
Chandler, Norman 5, 1999
Chapin, Dwight 1, 84, 252 **2**, 850 **3**, 941, 954 **10**, 4132E **16**, 7164 **22**, 10268 **FR** 205
alias used by **FR** 162
at meeting on Segretti matter **5**, 2022-23
at Segretti's meeting with Dean and Fielding **10**, 4050
on boat ride on Potomac **2**, 623
code names used by **10**, 3988-89
contacts with Segretti **10**, 4030-31
in Dean's taped conversation with Segretti **10**, 4041
discussion with Moore on Segretti matter **5**, 2006
Ehrlichman on role in Segretti matter **7**, 2846-47
and employment of Segretti **10**, 3980, 4029-30
and FBI contact with Segretti **FR** 178
and FBI files held by Dean **4**, 1362
and hiring of Segretti **FR** 160-63
in hypothetical question and answer session to prepare Ziegler for press conference **3**, 965, 1200-1208E
interviewed by Moore on Segretti matter **5**, 1954, 1955
and Jackson-Humphrey letter **FR** 170
knowledge of Nixon office tape recorders **5**, 2075
letter to Hardin on milk producers' meeting with Nixon **17**, 8135E
letter to Segretti entitled "Politics" **10**, 4271-72E
MacGregor asks about Segretti's role **12**, 4905
meeting with Segretti on duties in campaign **FR** 162
meeting with Sloan **2**, 545, 579, 593-94, 611-12, 623, 628, 629

and meetings on Segretti matter **5**, 1955 **6**, 2485-86
memo regarding signs to be used at rallies **11**, 4695, 4858E
memo to Dean on hiring of Segretti **FR** 186
memos to Segretti **11**, 4607-4608, 4656-57
Moore on hiring of Segretti by **10**, 4043
news summary on Muskie appearance at Whittier College **10**, 3992
Nixon's decision on Segretti matter and **FR** 183
and Nixon's trips abroad **3**, 1301-1302E
number of contacts with Segretti **10**, 4025
offers "thugs" to get rid of antiwar demonstrator **3**, 917, 918
press statement on Segretti **FR** 184
relationship with Segretti **3**, 963, 965-66, 1212-13E, 1295-1307E **4**, 1374 **5**, 2132 **6**, 2502 **7**, 2736, 2877 **9**, 3621 **10**, 3923-24, 3980, 3982, 4007, 4029 **FR** 163-65
reporting relationship with Segretti **10**, 4028
resignation from White House staff **3**, 966, 969
role on White House staff **1**, 78, 85, 89
and Segretti **FR** 169, 172, 174
and Segretti coverup **FR** 179-82
and Segretti's activities **10**, 3086-94, 3996, 4001, 4004, 4013, 4016
Segretti's duties outlined by **10**, 3981
in Segretti's grand jury testimony **10**, 4049
and Segretti's letter on fake Muskie letterhead about Humphrey and Jackson **10**, 3997
and Sloan **5**, 1884
Sloan expresses concerns to **FR** 41
sworn deposition draft of **3**, 1210E, 1214-21E
telephone log from Morris (Segretti) **10**, 4026, 4314E
transfer from White House staff **1**, 80
Chapman, William 11, 4884E
operatives of **11**, 4637E, 4638 **FR** 199-200
Chappaquiddick incident 4, 1532-33 **10**, 4176E **22**, 10241 **23**, 11097, 11099
Buchanan on **10**, 3936, 4171E
Colson investigation of **8**, 3077
material in Hunt's file on **3**, 938
Ulasewicz investigation for Caulfield of **7**, 2774-75 **8**, 3159 **21**, 9725 **FR** 110
Charles, Fred
See Colson, Charles
Charlotte, North Carolina
memo from Walker to Haldeman on demonstrations in **8**, 3190, 3191, 3194, 3322-23E
Charlotte Observer **4**, 1533
on White House campaign to discredit Ervin **8**, 3201-3202
Charney, Joseph 12, 4979, 4984-85
Chase, Warren 11, 4658 **12**, 5114E
Chavez, Cesar 12, 4951, 4959, 4960 **13**, 5291, 5303 **19**, 8772E **25**, 12166
Chavez, Richard 12, 4951
Chavira, Nat 19, 8771E
Checkers speech 22, 10383-84, 10388-89
Chemical Bank
check from American Airlines **13**, 5504, 5837E, 5838E

Chennault, Anna 2, 721 3, 981 23, 11155-56

Chenow, Kathleen 1, 80 4, 1438 9, 3722, 3752, 3789
  briefing before FBI interview FR 46-47
  FBI interview with 3, 941 9, 3455-56
  role on White House staff 1, 79

Chern, Vicki 1, 32, 34 2, 489, 491, 503 6, 2401
  entry from diary of 2, 490, 889E

Cherry, Don 1, 107, 108

Chestnut, Jack L. 14, 5970-71, 6155 15, 6600, 6601
  16, 6961, 7112 17, 7671 25, 11719-46
  advice to Valentine on retention of AMPI corpo-
    rate check FR 874-75
  and AMPI payment for Humphrey Presidential
    campaign through Valentine, Sherman FR 877-
    80
  and AMPI relationship with Valentine, Sherman
    15, 6843, 6856-58
  on arrangements to pick up Loeb contribution 25,
    11726-27
  asks Morrison to take money to West Virginia to
    cover bounced checks from Humphrey cam-
    paign 25, 11755-56
  on banks used by Humphrey campaign 25, 11729
  on becoming campaign manager for Humphrey
    Presidential campaign of 1972 25, 11719-20
  on Broome's role in Humphrey campaign 25,
    11735-36
  business associations 25, 11719
  calendar page with notes on Valentine, Sherman
    25, 11845E
  check of Valentine, Sherman 25, 11886E
  on contributors of $100,000 or more to Hum-
    phrey campaign 25, 11744-45
  delivery of funds by Lilly to 17, 7669
  denies campaign contributions by corporations he
    served in official capacities for 25, 11721
  denies knowledge of contributors to Humphrey
    campaign requesting anonymity 25, 11723
  denies knowledge of earlier Loeb contributions 25,
    11728
  denies knowledge of use of safe-deposit boxes by
    Humphrey campaign 25, 11729, 11730
  denies receiving contributions of $1000 or more
    25, 11723
  denies surplus from 1968 for Humphrey campaign
    25, 11730
  on deputies in Humphrey campaign 25, 11721-22
  destruction of Humphrey campaign records by FR
    884, 891
  on direct mail fundraising by Humphrey cam-
    paign 25, 11744
  on disclosure of contributors by Humphrey cam-
    paign 25, 11745-46
  on discussion with Thatcher of Loeb contribution
    25, 11727
  on disposal of Humphrey campaign records 25,
    11731-40
  on Duncan loan 25, 11728-29
  Fifth Amendment taken by FR 880, 890, 898
  on financial condition of Humphrey campaign 25,
    11729-30
  on GAO audit of Humphrey campaign finances
    25, 11732, 11742-43
  on Goldbloom contribution 25, 11741

on handling of money taken to California 25,
  11742-43
on Humphrey campaign setting up committees for
  contributions 25, 11729
on Humphrey's 1968 campaign 25, 11730-31
invokes Fifth Amendment 17, 7700-7703
letter of recommendation from Connell to Parr on
  25, 11839E
on loan to Humphrey campaign arranged by
  Thatcher 25, 11741-43
on Loeb contribution 25, 11723-28 FR 894-95,
  896, 898
on material turned over to GAO 25, 11737, 11740
Mehren denies knowing 16, 7346-47
and money left in Morrison's desk 25, 11757-58
Morrison and 25, 11748
on official functions for corporations 25, 11721
on pre-April 7 records 25, 11733-34
and proceeds from Duncan loan 25, 11758-59
on publicity over Loeb contribution 25, 11727-28
refusal to testify under oath FR 871
on reimbursement for expenses in Humphrey
  campaign 25, 11720-21
and relationship between AMPI and Valentine,
  Sherman 15, 6581, 6582-83, 6587, 6589
on relationship with Cole 25, 11788
on responsibilities in Humphrey campaign 25,
  11720
on solicitation of campaign contributions for
  Humphrey 25, 11722
subpoena from Select Committee for 17, 7704-05E
on trust account funds used by Humphrey Presidential campaign FR 886-87
on use of committees for contributions to Humphrey campaign 25, 11743-44
on use of computer organization by Humphrey
  campaign 25, 11736-37
use of part of proceeds of Duncan loan 25, 11772
and Valentine, Sherman 25, 11861-78E
Van Dyk on Valentine, Sherman and 16, 7039

Chew, David 1, 35

Chicago, Illinois
  anti-Nixon demonstrations in 12, 5082-83E

Chicago Seven FR 62

Chicago Tribune
  interview with Ehrlichman on Gray nomination 7,
    2812

Chile
  See ITT matter

Chilean embassy, Washington, D.C.
  burglary at 9, 3825-26E
  McCord's calls to 3, 975-76 9, 3442, 3836E

China
  Bruce nominated as first representative to 5, 1973
  McGovern on 10, 4076E
  Nixon's trip to 1, 9 7, 2870

Chinni, Andy 14, 6148

Chisholm, Shirley 25, 12032 FR 164
  Baldwin's surveillance of 1, 396
  bogus letter to supporters of 10, 4296E
  "Dear Chisholm Supporter" letter signed by Bar-
    ron 10, 4026, 4296-97E
  on enemies list 4, 1557

Mott campaign contribution to **25,** 12116

Segretti activities against **10,** 3995, 4004 **FR** 172

Chotin, Art 25, 12144

Chotiner, Murray M. 1, 17-18 **10,** 3970 **11,** 4625 **14,** 5975, 6296-98, 6314, 6315, 6372E **14,** 6314 **15,** 6625, 6639-40, 6658-59, 6688, 6700, 6795 **16,** 6958 **17,** 7596, 7738, 7752 **20,** 9478

Alagia and **16,** 7064

and AMPI contributions **14,** 6273

and antitrust suit against AMPI **FR** 723-24

association with Harrison's law firm **14,** 6248-49

at milk producers' meeting with Kalmbach in 1970 **17,** 7590-91, 7593-94

Butterbrodt and **17,** 7637

Caulfield on duties of **21,** 9733

and contributions from Mid-America **14,** 6280-81

conversation with Mitchell on antitrust suit against AMPI **17,** 7683-84, 7686-87

and dairy industry contributions **15,** 6443 **16,** 7168, 7169, 7391-92 **17,** 7545

discussed in Mehren-Harrison meeting **16,** 7255

discussion with Ehrlichman on milk price supports **FR** 635

Ehrlichman denies contacts with White House during period between milk price-support decisions **16,** 7384-85

Ehrlichman denies discussions on milk industry contributions with **16,** 7387

financial arrangements with AMPI **14,** 6249-50

Haldeman and **16,** 7180

on Harrison informing him of delay in milk producers' contributions **FR** 691

hiring of Freidin and Goldberg to travel as newspaper reporters with Democratic candidates **FR** 199-200

informs Kalmbach of reaffirmation of AMPI $2 million pledge **17,** 7601, 7602

involvement in milk price-support issue **14,** 6312-13

letter to Parr on use of political committees for contributions **15,** 6888, 6930E

in list from Harrison to Hardin **15,** 6553-54

meeting with Kalmbach and Nelson on March 24 **17,** 7809-11, 7812-13 **FR** 659-68

meeting with Nelson **15,** 6570-75

meetings with Colson on March 23 **FR** 643

meetings with Kalmbach **17,** 7600-7603, 7689-92

Mehren denies knowing **16,** 7237

memo from Colson on Harrison and dairy contributions to unopposed candidates **FR** 792E

memo from Colson with complaint about Harrison and Hillings **FR** 793E

and milk industry contributions **16,** 7172

and milk price support-decision reversal **FR** 633-35

and milk price-support issue **15,** 6637-38

Nelson on meetings with **15,** 6632-33

and Nixon's appearance at 1971 AMPI convention **15,** 6892

Nunn's contacts with **17,** 7539

receipt of milk producers' contributions by **FR** 691

and Reeves and Harrison **15,** 6806 **16,** 7168 **FR** 633

relationship with Colson **17,** 7601-7602

role in milk price-support decision reversal **16,** 7237-38 **FR** 673

and solicitation of funds by Colson **17,** 7552

and SPACE contributions to Nixon's re-election **16,** 7078

subpoenaed by Patman Committee **3,** 1091E

and TAPE committees **14,** 6315-16

telephone call to Nelson on Nixon's reversal of milk price-support decision **FR** 649

Christian Science Monitor

interview with McGovern **10,** 4081-82E

Chupka, Bernard 12, 5162E

Church, Frank 23, 11221, 11237, 11257-58

Churchill, Winston 12, 4935

CIA

assistance to Hunt in Fielding break-in **FR** 16-17

at Key Biscayne **6,** 2280

and bail money **9,** 3816-18E

and Caulfield's investigation of O'Brien-Hughes relationship **22,** 10409-10

comments on Baker's revised staff report "CIA investigation" **FR** 1161-65

comments on Committee report on action required for further CIA investigation **FR** 1164-65

communication channel with Saigon station **9,** 3669

connections with Watergate burglars **9,** 3427-28

contacts Ulasewicz for investigative job **6,** 2220

coverage of American students traveling or living abroad **3,** 1321-22E

Dean and **3,** 1067

Dean requests bail and salary money for Watergate defendants from **3,** 1037 **4,** 1449 **8,** 3240-42 **9,** 3409

Dean requests financial assistance for Watergate defendants from Walters **FR** 51

Dean's attempts to involve in Watergate investigation **3,** 945-48 **4,** 1368-69

Dean's efforts to recover photos of Fielding break-in from **FR** 75-76

and Dean's messages to McCord **1,** 318, 326, 346

destruction of tapes **FR** 1154

and document from McCord on "Relevancy of Intercepted Communications" **3,** 976, 1236-37E

and domestic intelligence gathering for White House **3,** 1072 **8,** 3251

Ehrlichman and **1,** 82

Ehrlichman on meeting after Watergate break-in with **6,** 2555-56

Ehrlichman's call to Cushman requesting aid for Hunt from **8,** 3290-91

and Ellsberg case **6,** 2553, 2606-2607

employment of Mrs. Hunt at **8,** 3262

and enemies lists **4,** 1531

former employees involved in Watergate break-in **8,** 3247-48, 3249

and Executive clemency for McCord **1,** 228-29, 231 **3,** 1079-80, 1089 **4,** 1378-79 **9,** 3795

and FBI investigation of Watergate **3,** 1080 **7,** 2712-13, 2782-86, 2799, 2833-34 **9,** 3648

film delivered by Hunt to **8,** 3264-65

Gray's theory on involvement in Watergate **3,** 943 **9,** 3150-67, 3509-12

CIA *(Continued)*

handwritten note from McCord on CIA taking blame for Watergate **3**, 974, 1235E

Helms assures Gray of noninvolvement in Watergate **8**, 3237-38, 3247-48, 3249

Helms' attitude toward **8**, 3252

and hiring of Ulasewicz **7**, 2775

Hunt and **3**, 1160E

Hunt letters given to Senate Appropriations Committee **9**, 3443, 3834-42E

Hunt's career with **9**, 3662, 3725-26, 3754-56

and Hunt's employment at White House **1**, 386-87 **8**, 3257 **9**, 3727-30

and Hunt's role in Ellsberg break-in **8**, 3234

and hush money **3**, 950

and Huston Plan **5**, 1822-24

information to FBI on Martinez **9**, 3426-27

and intelligence gathering at CRP **3**, 926

involvement in domestic affairs **5**, 1822 **9**, 3756

involvement in Watergate **3**, 943 **9**, 3509-12

and IRS audits **3**, 1072 **4**, 1410, 1529-30

and Kalmbach's contact with Ulasewicz **6**, 2239

legal fees and salaries of exposed agents of **9**, 3661

legality of IEC and **4**, 1457

letter from Colby to Baker on Select Committee report on **FR** 1158-59

letters from McCord to **9**, 3440-47

as liaison between White House and Interagency Evaluation Committee **3**, 916

and Liddy plan **6**, 2326

Liddy tells Mardian about involvement of **6**, 2359

loan of equipment to Hunt **8**, 3259

and Maheu **21**, 9719

Mardian on involvement in Watergate break-in **6**, 2383-84

Martinez on retainer at time of Watergate break-in from **8**, 3237-48, 3249

and material for Hunt's interview of DeMotte **FR** 119

material on Hunt **3**, 977-79 **9**, 3677-78

McCord as security officer with **1**, 125, 155-56

McCord's letters on efforts to implicate in Watergate **9**, 3442-47

McCord's "Relevancy of Intercepted Communications" paper to **3**, 1236-37E

memo from Butterfield to **3**, 919, 1107E, 1108E

memo to Haldeman on leaks **3**, 919, 1101-1102E

memos to Dean **3**, 919, 1108E, 1146-48E **4**, 1688E

and Mexican checks **2**, 774

Mitchell on **4**, 1605-1606

Mullen and Company relationship with **9**, 3726 **FR** 1121-26, 1151-52

and newspaper story on Baldwin **1**, 226-227

Nixon's concern over Watergate investigation and **7**, 2694-95

in Nixon's May 22, 1973, speech on Watergate **FR** 1118-19

Odle on **1**, 27-28

offer of clemency to McCord **7**, 2771

and Operation Sandwedge **3**, 924-25, 1149E **4**, 1444-45

people assisting Hunt at **9**, 3752

plan to blame Watergate on **1**, 129-30, 192-99, 206-08, 213-16, 241, 264-67, 280-83, 299-301, 309, 329, 334-35, 350-51 **2**, 805, 867 **3**, 974,

1235E **4**, 1415, 1416 **5**, 884 **9**, 3834E, 3837-40E, 3842E

plans private investigative security consulting corporation **3**, 924

and plot to kill Castro **21**, 9723-24

and political intelligence gathering **3**, 922, 931

prediction on leaks **3**, 1114E

pressure on McCord **1**, 155, 161-62

and processing of photos from Fielding break-in **9**, 3729

and psychiatric profiles **6**, 2601-2602, 2605 **7**, 2674

and psychological profile of Ellsberg **6**, 2546 **8**, 3235-26 **9**, 3674-75, 3724 **25**, 12421-26E

reaction to Watergate break-in at **8**, 3237

reasons for appearing to be involved in Watergate break-in **8**, 3266-67

reports on antiwar demonstrators and radical groups to Dean's office **3**, 916

routing slip and memo on Hunt's request for agency support **8**, 3266, 3277-79E, 3280-82E

as source of coverup money **5**, 1899-1900

use by White House **3**, 1071

Walters on Dean's attempt to blame for Watergate **9**, 3408-3409, 3410

Walters on importance of **9**, 3435

Walters on legislation to prevent political involvement of **9**, 3426

and Watergate **FR** 1099

and Watergate break-in **1**, 360, 379-81 **4**, 1621

and Watergate coverup and domestic intelligence **FR** 102

and Watergate investigation **9**, 3616-17, *see also* CIA Watergate investigation

Watergate memos given to FBI **9**, 3423-25, 3428

White House control of **1**, 195-196

White House efforts to restrict FBI Watergate investigation through use of **FR** 37-40

as White House liaison to IEC **3**, 1055

and wiretaps **6**, 2535

CIA tapes

CIA comments on Committee report on **FR** 1162

CIA Watergate investigation FR 1115-57

action required to complete

    on CIA tapes **FR** 1154

    on Martinez relationship to CIA **FR** 1150-51

    miscellaneous needs **FR** 1154-57

    on Mullen and Company **FR** 1151-52

    on psychological profile of Ellsberg **FR** 1153-54

    on Technical Services Division of CIA support of Hunt **FR** 1152-53

background **FR** 1118-20

and Bennett's relationship with Mullen and Company **FR** 1121-26

and Bennett's report to CIA on plan for Watergate break-in **FR** 1124-26

CIA preliminary comments on **FR** 1161-65

and destruction of tapes on CIA discussions of Watergate **FR** 1131-34

and Martinez's relationship with CIA **FR** 1145-49

organization of **FR** 1115-17

and Pennington matter **FR** 1127-30

on financial arrangements with Humphrey campaign **25,** 11804

on financial condition of Humphrey campaign **25,** 11813-14, 11815

on fundraising role in Humphrey campaign **25,** 11788-89

on Humphrey campaign office **25,** 11789-90

on loans made to Humphrey campaign **25,** 11792, 11793E, 11794-95, 11807-08

on Loeb contribution **25,** 11804-11806

on other fundraisers in Humphrey campaign **25,** 11789

on professional associations **25,** 11787

on records kept during fundraising for Humphrey campaign **25,** 11790-92

on relationship with Chestnut **25,** 11788

on repayment of his loans to Humphrey campaign **25,** 11807-08, 11812

on reporting methods of Humphrey campaign **25,** 11813-15

on Rickless contribution **25,** 11811-12

on role in Humphrey's 1968 campaign **25,** 11788

on staff aid in Humphrey campaign **25,** 11790

on top contributors in Humphrey campaign **25,** 11810-11

Cole, Kenneth R., Jr. 2, 545 **3,** 1115E **13,** 5282 **23,** 11094

memo from Armendariz on Raza Unida programs **13,** 5323, 5697-98E

memo from Evans on Social Security increase **19,** 9222E

memo from Malek on Social Security increase **19,** 9223E

memo from Malek on White House staff support for Nixon re-election **18,** 8208, 8325-41E

and OMBE grants **13,** 5542E

and Responsiveness Program **18,** 8187-88

Cole, Robert C.

memo to Mitchell on support for Nixon's Vietnam speech **FR** 301-304E

Coleman, Barbara 11, 4774E, 4817E

Coleman, Jeff 12, 5161E

College press credentials

forgery of **1,** 222, 230

College Republican National Committee 10, 4122-23E

Colleges

recommendation to relax restrictions on FBI coverage of **3,** 1321-22E

Collie, Marvin 14, 6077 **15,** 6464, 6470, 6471 **FR** 715-16

contacts with Phinney **FR** 717-18

and IRS audit of Milk Producers, Inc. **15,** 6672-73

Collier, Calvin 20, 9430, 9541

Collins, George 6, 2466 **23,** 11090

affidavit of **12,** 5009, 5102-06E

Collins, John 14, 6084

Collins, Judy 12, 5133E, 5134E

Colom, Audrey 12, 5187E

Colson, Charles 2, 506, 792 **3,** 954 **4,** 1469 **6,** 2519 **7,** 2879 **10,** 4182E **14,** 5879-80, 6296, 6297, 6298 **15,** 6690, 6796 **16,** 7211 **17,** 7596, 7766 **19,** 8813E

alleged telephone conversation between Magruder and **2,** 517-18

and AMPI contributions 14, 6262-67 **15,** 6560, 6797 **16,** 7462-63 **17,** 7597-98, 7747

AMPI representatives and **14,** 5975 **17,** 7633

and AMPI's efforts to have Nixon attend first convention **15,** 6539-40, 6549, 6792

and AMPI's relationship with Wagner & Baroody **15,** 6651-55 **FR** 694-98

appearance before grand jury **3,** 954

assigned to "outside projects" in Haldeman memo **FR** 776E

assigned to "outside projects" in Magruder memo **FR** 777-78E

at meeting with Dean and Ehrlichman **FR** 34-35

at meeting with Parr, Gleason, and Kalmbach **15,** 6784-86

at post-Watergate meeting **7,** 2822

and "attack" operation **1,** 26 **4,** 1533-34 **6,** 2474-75, 2489

Baroody and **FR** 695-96

and Beard memo **5,** 1950

and Black advance projects **8,** 3025

and bogus contributions to McCloskey **FR** 198

briefs Nixon on $2 million pledge by dairy industry **16,** 7376-77

and Brill's infiltration of peace vigil **FR** 198-99

and CRP **1,** 39

call from Hunt demanding money **3,** 969-70

Camp David report on **3,** 1206E

and Caulfield's investigation of Meany **22,** 10403

and citizens committees **FR** 156-57

and Committee for a Responsible Congress **FR** 155-56

and Committee for the Congress of 1970 **FR** 156

concern about attending Mrs. Hunt's funeral **3,** 971-72

and conflict in Ehrlichman-Dean testimony **7,** 2718-19

contacts with Barth **23,** 11250

contacts with Mitchell after Watergate **5,** 1931-32

conversation With Hunt on Ellsberg **9,** 3812

in Cushman's memo instead of Ehrlichman **8,** 3296-99, 3308-3309

and dairy industry contributions **15,** 6469 **16,** 7375, 7377, 7392

Dean memo to Mardian on **6,** 2381

Dean suspects Watergate involvement of **3,** 932, 955, 1040

on Dean testifying that Ehrlichman told him to deep-six Hunt's briefcase **7,** 2830

on Dean's indictable list **5,** 1989

and Democrats for Nixon **5,** 1931-32

and Department of Labor and Office of Economic Opportunity grants **18,** 8445

and Diem cable incident **5,** 1920 **9,** 3672-73, 3733 **FR** 125-27

and direct mailings **FR** 153

discussed by Hunt and Shapiro **9,** 3706

discusses FBI interview with Dean **3,** 939

discussion on forthcoming testimony of **8,** 3219-21

discussion with Caulfield on proposed firebomb at Brookings Institution **22,** 10360-61

discussion with Nixon on Executive clemency for Hunt **5,** 2003

discussions on dairy import quotas **15,** 6545

Colson, Charles *(Continued)*

discussions with Kalmbach on dairy contributions **17,** 7600

and DNC civil suits **FR** 74

duties in campaign **5,** 1930-31

and efforts to embarrass Weicker **4,** 1502-1503

and efforts to obtain milk price-support increases **15,** 6570

efforts to place in IRS **7,** 2684

and Ehrlichman **16,** 7382

Ehrlichman calls after learning about Watergate **6,** 2580

Ehrlichman refutes testimony that he requested money for Krogh from **16,** 7394-95

Ehrlichman suspects involvement in Watergate affair **3,** 932

and Ehrlichman telling Dean that Liddy should leave country **FR** 34

and Ellsberg matter **FR** 14-15

and employment of Hunt by White House **9,** 3662

and enemies list **4,** 1411, 1459, 1498, 1499, 1529, 1689E **6,** 2487 **FR** 8

Evans' reporting relationship with **18,** 8438

excused from grand jury testimony **9,** 3619, 3636-37

and Executive clemency offers to Hunt **3,** 973-74, 1079, 1080 **4,** 1451, 1484 **5,** 1862 **7,** 2847-48 **FR** 66

and Executive clemency offers to McCord **4,** 1379

FBI interview with **3,** 939-40, 1160E

and Fielding break-in **9,** 3717, 3723-24

first meeting with Liddy **20,** 9383, 9391-92

and funds from Baroody for Fielding break-in **FR** 696

and Gemstone **9,** 3765

given responsibility for special-interest groups **FR** 612

gives Dean copy of transcript of telephone conversation with Hunt on hush money **FR** 56

gives information to Ehrlichman on O'Brien's meeting with racketeers **21,** 9682-83

and Government brochures published in 1972 **18,** 8475-77

and Greenspun matter **20,** 9365-66

Harrison and **14,** 6270, 6274-75

and Harrison replacing Semer as AMPI lawyer for White House matters **FR** 613

and Hillings letter to Nixon **14,** 6261 **15,** 6544

and Hunt **2,** 851 **3,** 921 **4,** 1632, 1673 **7,** 2732

Hunt affidavit on **9,** 3793-94

and Hunt interview of DeMotte **9,** 3677-78 **FR** 118-19

Hunt leaves his number at White House with Cushman **8,** 3306-3307

Hunt on participation in clandestine operations **9,** 3734-35

and Hunt on responsibilities to Watergate defendants **9,** 3776

Hunt's activities for **3,** 938 **9,** 3807

and Hunt's affidavit denying his prior knowledge of Watergate break-in **9,** 3680-81, 3887E

and Hunt's assignment to collect derogatory information on Ellsberg **9,** 3666-67

and Hunt's employment at White House **3,** 940 **6,** 2532 **9,** 3514, 3666

and Hunt's interview with Beard **9,** 3753

and Hunt's interview with Conein **9,** 3667, 3668-69

Hunt's letter to **9,** 3757-58

in Hunt's notes **9,** 3839E

and hush money **5,** 2149

information from Secret Service on Democratic candidates to **FR** 148

instructions to Ulasewicz **FR** 110

and investigation of O'Brien's relationship with Mafia figures **21,** 9723

involvement in coverup **2,** 835 **3,** 1054

involvement in Liddy plan **9,** 3679-84

involvement in Watergate **1,** 143 **3,** 1050-51, 1091 **8,** 3116

and ITT-Dita Beard matter **FR** 128-29

Kalmbach on relations between dairy people and **17,** 7595

knowledge about Gemstone plan **9,** 3715-22, 3776-77

knowledge of Plumbers' operations **9,** 3724

and Labor for America Committee **FR** 157

and Lambert **20,** 9367

and Las Vegas matter **20,** 9347, 9391

letter from Hunt to **7,** 2770-71 **9,** 3696-97, 3698, 3807, 3892E, 3897E, 3898E **FR** 66

letters from Harrison to **15,** 6634-35, 6711-12E **FR** 635

and Liddy **7,** 2801 **9,** 3748-49

and Liddy plan **5,** 1929-30 **20,** 9386

and list of Muskie's campaign contributors **4,** 1495

and Magruder **2,** 512 **3,** 954 **5,** 1933-34 **6,** 2302

and Marumoto **13,** 5276, 5314 **18,** 8248, 8250

and Marumoto memo on report on Brown Mafia **13,** 5323, 5536-41E

and meeting between Nixon, Parr, and Nelson **15,** 6794

meeting with Bittman **9,** 3697-98

meeting with Dean after Watergate **4,** 1672

meeting with Harrison **14,** 6257-58

meeting with Kalmbach and dairy industry representatives **15,** 6536, 6539-41 **17,** 7590-91, 7593-94, 7598

meeting with Liddy **9,** 3683-84

meetings with AMPI leaders and Harrison in 1970 **FR** 613-14

meetings with Chotiner **FR** 643, 649

meetings with Ehrlichman **6,** 2608-12 **7,** 2800-2801

meetings with Hunt on Gemstone plan **9,** 3766-67

meetings with Moore on ITT matter **5,** 1949

meetings with Parr and Nelson **14,** 6259-60 **15,** 6657-58, 6770-71, 6787-89, 6798, 6806, 6813-14, 6876-78

Mehren claims Parr denied commitment to **16,** 7232-33

memo from Hunt on neutralization of Ellsberg **9,** 3675, 3886E

memo from Hunt on Plumbers' unit **3,** 937-38

memo from Krogh and Young on Hunt's memo on neutralization of Ellsberg **9,** 3730, 3893E

memo from Marumoto on activity report for Spanish-speaking Americans **13,** 5323, 5556-60E, 5561-65E, 5566-70E, 5571-75E, 5576-78E, 5579-82E, 5583-87E, 5599-5606E, 5607-10E,

Congressmen
on enemies list **4**, 1713E
Connally, Bob 23, 11263-64
Connally, John B. 3, 989 **5**, 1929, 1932, 2110 **10**,
4260E, 4262E **11**, 4616 **12**, 5187E **14**, 5984, 6312
16, 6968, 7298, 7446 **17**, 7689, 7738
affidavits of **14**, 6102-03E, 6104E
Alagia on AMPI contacts with **16**, 7075
Alagia on Morgan's contacts with **16**, 7079-80
and alleged AMPI payment **FR** 684-85
AMPI and **15**, 6405
and AMPI lobbyists **14**, 5975-82
and AMPI retainer for Collie **FR** 716
and antitrust suit against AMPI **15**, 6466
and appointment of Walters as commissioner of
IRS **24**, 11624
at Nixon-Mitchell meeting **4**, 1676-77
attends Nixon's meeting with dairy industry representatives **16**, 7388
Butterbrodt denies knowledge of contacts between
dairy coop representatives and **17**, 7638
and campaign contributions from AMPI **14**, 6106
contact with Lilly at Page Airways **14**, 6308-12
15, 6617-24 **FR** 638-40
contacts with Jacobsen **15**, 6567-68 **FR** 637-38
and contribution from ADEPT and SPACE to
Democrats for Nixon **FR** 729-31
conversation with Mills on milk price-support increases **FR** 907
conversations with Walters after leaving as secretary of treasury **24**, 11653
dairy industry leaders' contacts with **FR** 637-40
and Dairymen, Inc., contributions **15**, 6456
deliveries of money from AMPI to Jacobsen for
FR 673
discussion with Walters on Barth problem **24**,
11625
discussions with Ehrlichman on dairy industry **16**,
7385-86
and Ehrlichman **16**, 7382
and formation of TAPE **FR** 584
handwritten notes by Walters for briefing with **24**,
11632, 11665E
as head of Democrats for Nixon **11**, 4625-26
and IRS audit of Milk Producers, Inc. **15**, 6672-
73
and Jacobsen **14**, 5989 **15**, 6557-59, 6560-63, 6567
16, 7180, 7239
Jacobsen denies delivering money to **15**, 6426-27
Jacobsen on contacts with **15**, 6407-15
Jacobsen on money offered to **15**, 6421-25, 6427-
29
Jacobsen on relationship with **15**, 6461
Jacobsen transmits AMPI money to **FR** 682-87
Kalmbach and **17**, 7620
letter from Hanman on dairy industry needs for
federal assistance **14**, 6080, 6099-6101E
letter from Hanman to Jacobsen on followup letter to discussions with **14**, 5890, 5905E
letter from Westwater on federal programs relating to dairy industry **14**, 6080, 6095-98E
Lilly and contribution to **15**, 6647-49
meeting with Haldeman on dairy industry contribution **16**, 7163-64

meeting with Hanman **14**, 5889-90
meeting with Jacobsen **15**, 6806-07 **17**, 7747-48
meeting with Jacobsen, Mehren, and Nelson **15**,
6360-66, 6508
meeting with Jacobsen, Nelson, Mehren and
Kalmbach **15**, 6451-52
meeting with Jacobsen and dairy coops representatives **15**, 6472-75
meeting with Mehren **16**, 7263-71 **17**, 7645 **FR**
718-21
meeting with Mehren and Nelson **15**, 6668-69,
6675-78
meeting with Morgan, Parr, Westwater, Baldi,
and Hanman in 1972 **15**, 6901-6904
meeting with Nixon before meeting with dairy
leaders **17**, 7765 **FR** 648
meetings with dairy leaders **14**, 5890-97 **FR** 713-
14, 715
meetings with Lilly **15**, 6459-60, 6807-13
meetings with Parr in 1972 **15**, 6901-6904
Mehren discusses antitrust suit against AMPI
with **15**, 6470-71
Mehren reports to Lilly on meetings with **14**,
6107-18
and milk price-support issue **15**, 6638 **16**, 7401
FR 630
and Mitchell **15**, 6467
money delivered by Lilly to **14**, 5961-64
Nelson on relationship with **15**, 6508-6509
and Nixon's decision on milk-price supports **FR**
622
and Phinney **FR** 717-18
Parr on AMPI funds for **15**, 6897
records of phone calls and appointments **14**, 6056,
6080, 6092-94E **16**, 1972 **23**, 1971
refuses contribution from AMPI **15**, 5424-25
relationship and contacts with Lilly **14**, 6138-44
relationship with Jacobsen **15**, 6381-82
role in milk price-support decision reversal **FR**
651-56
telephone call to Dole **16**, 7268, 7269
telephone call to Mitchell **16**, 7267-69
telephone conversation with Nixon on meeting
with dairy leaders **FR** 829E
telephone conversation with Nixon on milk price
supports on March 23 **FR** 643
Van Dyk denies knowledge of AMPI contact with
16, 6987
visit to Jamaica **FR** 503
and Walters' briefings to Shultz on Hughes-Meier
investigation **24**, 11630-31, 11632, 11634
and Walters leaving IRS **24**, 11656
and White Paper justification for Nixon's reversal
of milk price-support decision **FR** 678
Connally, John B., testimony of
on Democrats for Nixon's policies on contributions **14**, 6070-71
denies attending "Kickoff 1972" Republican dinner **14**, 6065-66
denies discussing IRS audit with Mehren, Nelson,
and Jacobsen **14**, 6079
denies discussing milk price supports with Johnson **14**, 6088
denies discussing political contributions with
AMPI or TAPE representatives **14**, 6051, 6053-

54, 6060, 6067-69, 6071-72, 6077-78, 6079-80, 6083, 6084, 6086-87, 6088, 6102-6103E, 6104E

denies knowledge of Mehren-Johnson meeting in 1972 **14**, 6090

denies maintaining savings deposit box in Citizens' National Bank, Austin **14**, 6071

denies meeting with Jacobsen and Nelson after meeting with Nixon and dairy farmers **14**, 6065

denies meeting with Lilly **14**, 6066-68

denies meeting with Nelson, Jacobsen, and Mehren in 1972 **14**, 6059, 6068-69

denies speaking with AMPI people at Page Airways **14**, 6067-68

on discussion of milk price supports with Mills **14**, 6087-88

on discussion with Jacobsen and Nelson on formation of TAPE **14**, 6051-53

on discussion with Jacobsen on political contributions in 1971 **14**, 6069-73

on discussions with Jacobsen on milk price-support decision **14**, 6054-58, 6058-60

on IRS audit of MPI **14**, 6076-78

on meeting and telephone log **14**, 6056, 6059-60, 6080

on meeting with dairymen on August 2, 1972 **14**, 6080-83

on meeting with Jacobsen, Nelson, and Mehren in 1972 **14**, 6073-77

on meeting with Nixon and dairy farmers **14**, 6060-64

on Nixon-Humphrey election campaign **14**, 6053-54

on reasons for wanting to discuss with press **14**, 6090-91

on reception for Nixon in September 1972 **14**, 6083-84

on relationship with Nelson **14**, 6052-53

on role in ITT matter **14**, 6089-90

on SPACE AND ADEPT contributions to Democrats for Nixon **14**, 6084-86

on telephone call to Mitchell on antitrust suit against dairy coops **14**, 6075-76

on telephone conversation with Mitchell on milk price supports **14**, 6078-80

Connally, Merle 15, 6508

Connell, Gerald FR 700

Connell, William 16, 7028

and AMPI relationship with Valentine, Sherman **15**, 6581-82, 6843, 6844, 6856 **FR** 872-73, 874

letter to Parr on meeting in Louisville **15**, 6835-36, 6911E

letter to Parr recommending Chestnut for services to AMPI **25**, 11839E

memo from Valentine on pending projects **25**, 11822E

and milk price-support issue **16**, 7326

and recommendations to Valentine, Sherman **16**, 7029, 7038

relationship with Townsend **16**, 7114-15

Valentine, Sherman and **16**, 7039

Conspiracy law

and Responsiveness Program **FR** 438-39

Constitution

and appointment of Public Attorney **FR** 98-100

and establishment of office of independent Public Attorney **FR** 1173-74

and Presidential power **FR** 1102

and Watergate **FR** 1177-96, 1223-24

Constitutional amendment

for direct popular election of President **12**, 4928

Conyers, John 10, 3969-70

on enemies list **4**, 1695E

Cook, Richard 4, 1479

and House Banking and Currency investigation **4**, 1509

Cook, Dr. U. 14, 6296, 6303

Coombs, Merle 20, 9584

Cooney, Eldora 12, 4949, 5052E

Cooper, Elmer 12, 4979, 4984

Cooper, Richard

See Cole, Joseph E., statement of

Cooper, W. J.

memo to Managers and Controllers on rentals to political campaign organizations **25**, 12326E, 12329E

Cooper and Lybrand Report 23, 11106 **24,** 11322 **FR** 1032-33

expenditures by Rebozo concealed in **FR** 1033-34

Lenzner requests worksheets from Gemmill **23**, 11220

Copeland, Miles FR 1119

Coplon case 1, 198

Copperman, Diane 1, 34

Corporate conduit program

See Corporate group solicitation program (CGSP)

Corporate contributions FR 548-50

and American Airlines, Inc. **FR** 447-51

by American Ship Building Co. **FR** 451-59

of Ashland Co, Inc. **FR** 459-62

and Braniff Airways, Inc. **FR** 462-63

of Carnation Co. **FR** 464

and Common Cause suit **FR** 447

and Diamond International Corp. **FR** 464-65

extent of in 1972 Presidential campaign **FR** 446

fines for *See* Fines for corporate contributions

and good government committees **FR** 550-53

of Goodyear Tire & Rubber Co. **FR** 465-68

of Gulf Oil Corp. **FR** 469-73

of Hertz Corp. **FR** 473-81

illegality of **FR** 446-47

and Kalmbach **FR** 506

of Lehigh Valley Cooperative Farmers, Inc. **FR** 481-84

letters returning from Muskie campaign **11**, 4695, 4809E

of Minnesota Mining & Manufacturing Co. **FR** 484-86

of Northrop Corp. **FR** 486-89

and Phillips Petroleum Co. **FR** 489-92

Select Committee questionnaires on **FR** 487N, 527-29

unpaid bills to corporations as **25**, 12330E

by Vesco *See* Vesco case

Wakefield correspondence on **24**, 11352-69E

Corporate contributions *(Continued)*
  Woods denies knowledge of Rebozo solicitations
    of **22,** 10232-34
  See also Corporate group solicitation program
    (CGSP) *and under individual names of corpora-
    tions*
"Corporate Executives Committee for Peace" 4, 1410
  on enemies list **4,** 1730-32E
Corporate group solicitation program (CGSP) FR
544-48
  direct-mail campaign compared with **FR** 547-48
Correa, Marilyn R. FR 216E
Corrupt Practices Act of 1925 2, 590 **5,** 1875 **14,**
5917 **FR** 551, 904
  and AMPI contributions through committees **17,**
    7594
  Colson memo to Dean with question on **FR** 787-
    91E
  and contributions from foreign nationals **2,** 713
  Dahlberg check and **1, 2,** 748-50
  Dean-Petersen consultations on **9,** 3613
  and Ehrlichman's interest in O'Brien's taxes **23,**
    11222, 11229
  Jacobsen on AMPI contributions and **15,** 6388-89
  Nelson on **15,** 6517
  Parr on **15,** 6788-89
  and political contributions of SPACE **16,** 7060
  Silbert tells Segretti he did not violate **FR** 179
  See also Fines for corporate contributions
Cortese, Antonio 23, 11265-66
  Caulfield investigation of **22,** 10395-96
Costa, Robert J.
  letters from Walters re deposits to Jackson and
    Company by Backers for Humphrey **25,** 11897-
    11906E
  memo to Sanders and Hamilton **25,** 11852-60E
  memo to Sanders on Humphrey campaign bank
    accounts **25,** 11960-68E
  memo to Sanders on meeting with Joe Walters on
    Humphrey campaign finances **25,** 11969-72E
Costa, Robert J., questioning by
  Chestnut **25,** 11732, 11740-41, 11743, 11744
  Fellows **25,** 11765-73, 11783
  Mott **25,** 12121-22
  Pearlman **25,** 12197-99
  Rubin **25,** 12151-53
Council of Economic Advisors (CEA)
  review of Department of Agriculture March 12
    milk price-support decision **FR** 631-32
**"Counter Espionage Agent for the Republicans--The
True Story of the Watergate Case"**
1, 297, 320-21
Courtelis, Alec 22, 12547E **FR** 999
Cousin (police officer) 9, 3491
Covens, Cal 22, 10518, 10519
Cox, Archibald 3, 1096E **4,** 1503 **8,** 3233
  disclosure from IRS on Hughes contribution **23,**
    11211-12
  discussions between Buzhardt and Richardson on
    investigations by **23,** 10915-17
  dismissal of **FR** 1081
  efforts to proscribe radio and TV coverage of
    Dean and Magruder testimony **FR** 32

Haig's discussions with Richardson on investiga-
    tion by **23,** 11013-15, 11020, 11031
  investigation of Abplanalp **23,** 11033
  investigation of Hughes contribution **23,** 10888-89,
    11219-20
  investigation of Hughes-Rebozo matter **FR** 1020-
    24
  investigation of Rebozo **22,** 10206
  and letter from Young on Segretti **10,** 4008-4009
  letter on agreement with LaRue **6,** 2333
  letter to Vinson from **6,** 2328, 2634E
  meeting with Moore **5,** 1979
  press release on American Airlines disclosure of
    illegal campaign contributions **13,** 5498
  public response to firing of **FR** 32
  and receipt of IRS information on Hughes contri-
    bution **FR** 1020, 1022
Cox, Charles C. 22, 12542E
Cox, Dan, interview of
  on OEO grant to J. A. Reyes & Associates **FR**
    385
Cox, Tricia Nixon 4, 1385 **8,** 3080 **12,** 5011, 5181E
  22, 12052 **23,** 10773 **24,** 11332-33
Coyle, James J. FR 983, 987
  and Dunes Hotel matter **FR** 989-91
  report from Jones on Dunes Hotel acquisition
    proposal **26,** 12902-12E
Craig, Stephen FR 938, 959
Cramer, Congressman 3, 983 **11,** 4424
  Benz alleges dirty tricks by Democrats against **11,**
    4429, 4431-32
Cramer, Joan 10, 4280E
Cramer, Julian 25, 12201
Cramer, Mary Ann 10, 4033, 4280E
Cranston, Alan 9, 3571 **FR** 429
Cravath, Mr. and Mrs. 24, 11311
Crawford, Jack 18, 8258, 8260-61 **FR** 376-77, 409
  letter to Mardian accompanying proposal for
    Black Voter Program **19,** 8743-47E
  memo from Mardian to Malek on Black Voter
    Program **19,** 8742-47E
Crime
  McGovern record on **10,** 4068-69E
Cromer, Jack 20, 9489-90 **23,** 10924
Cronkite, Walter 10, 3962
  bogus telephone call to **11,** 4629
Crosby, James 20, 9449, 9568 **23,** 11105 **FR** 242E
  campaign contribution of **21,** 10183
  Danner and **20,** 9519-21, 9524
  Griffin and **22,** 10472
  Griffin on dealings with **23,** 10791-93
Crosmun, Homer 24, 11633, 11634
Cross, Burt S.
  See Minnesota Mining & Manufacturing Co.
Crouch, Nancy 1, 34
Crude oil quotas
  Atkins denies as motivation for Ashland Pe-
    troleum campaign contribution to CRP **13,**
    5453, 5454-55, 5456
Cruikshank 18, 8448, 8456

Cuban defense fund **8,** 3046
Cuban Revolutionary Council **1,** 375 **9,** 3726
Cuban voters
and false advertising on Muskie **11,** 4394, 4396, 4663, 4670 **FR** 173
and intelligence gathering in Miami against Democrats **3,** 1152E
in memo on Spanish-speaking voters **19,** 8624E
and National Hispanic Finance Committee in Florida **13,** 5365-66
Cuban Watergate burglars
attitude toward Hunt **9,** 3788
Dash on McCord's references to **1,** 191
Dean learns about arrest of **3,** 932
and Fielding break-in **9,** 3774-75
guilty pleas of **9,** 3787
Hunt on silence of **9,** 3803-3804
and LaRue's money to Bittman **6,** 2313
lesser amounts of money given to **6,** 2242
Liddy to Dean on involvement of **3,** 933
McCord on **1,** 158
offers of Executive clemency from Hunt to **1,** 208-210, 212-13
Rebozo denies knowing **21,** 10105-10106
recruitment of **1,** 197
and Watergate **9,** 3820E, 3831E
Cuban-Americans **9,** 3751 **11,** 4382-83
Cubans for Nixon Committee **22,** 10605
Cudd, Connie **1,** 32, 35
Culver, John **14,** 6150 **15,** 6844
letter from Valentine on Iowa Voter Information Survey **25,** 11828E
Cunningham v. *Nagle* **6,** 2633
Curtis, Kenneth M. **12,** 5086E, 5093-94E **FR** 465
Cushenan **13,** 5429
Cushman, Ian **FR** 453
Cushman, Robert E., Jr. **9,** 3678
and CIA aid to Hunt **FR** 1135-36, 1152-53
Ehrlichman contacts on help for Hunt **8,** 3281, 3285
and Hunt **9,** 3728
in Hunt's notebook **9,** 3751-52
informs Helms of authorization to give Hunt tape recorder and camera **8,** 3233
knowledge of Hunt's reasons for needing equipment **8,** 3283
memo to Helms on Hunt **8,** 3265-66
and retrieval of CIA material on Hunt from Justice Department **3,** 977-78
routing slip to Helms on materials given to Hunt **8,** 3282-83
supplies Hunt with materials **FR** 119
tape of discussion with Hunt **FR** 1132-34
and technical assistance to Hunt **8,** 3263-64 **FR** 16-17
transcript of taped meeting with Hunt **8,** 3292, 3383-89E **9,** 3728-29
Cushman, Robert E., Jr., testimony of **8,** 3289-3311
on additional requests from Hunt **8,** 3293-94
on authorization for Hunt's request for CIA aid **8,** 3305-3306
on call from Ehrlichman requesting aid from CIA for Hunt **8,** 3290-91

on camera given Hunt and camera used for photographs in Fielding's office **8,** 3308
on career **8,** 3289-90
on CIA aid for internal activities **8,** 3302
on CIA psychiatric profiles **8,** 3310-11
on delivery of equipment to Hunt **8,** 3303-3304
denies other demands for assistance from White House **8,** 3308
on Hunt's poor judgment **8,** 3307-3308
on Hunt's reasons for wanting equipment from CIA **8,** 3292-94, 3301-3302
memo on request for guidance on extent of assistance to Hunt **8,** 3311, 3392-93E
memo to Ehrlichman on contact with Hunt **8,** 3295, 3390E, 3391E
on Pentagon Papers matter **8,** 3304-3305
on preparation of memos on contacts with Hunt **8,** 3295-3300, 3308-10
on relationship with Hunt **8,** 3303, 3306
on relationship with Nixon **8,** 3305-3306
on taped conversation with Hunt **8,** 3291-90, 3297-98, 3300-3301, 3306-3307
Cutler, Eliot **11,** 4658-59, 4817-46E
Cutler, Lloyd N.
See Spater, George A., testimony of
D'Agostino, Carl **25,** 12166
Daguerre, Manuel Ogarrio
See Ogarrio, Manuel
Dahlberg, Kenneth H. **1,** 356 **2,** 574-76, 587-88, 617, 620, 630-31, 781
Hunt on **9,** 3730
subpoenaed by Patman Committee **3,** 1192E
Dahlberg checks **2,** 631, 896E **3,** 942-43, 944 **4,** 1415
Mitchell on **4,** 1659-60
and Patman hearings **FR** 73
Stans on **2,** 699-701, 725, 728, 717, 748-50
Stans-LaRue meeting on **2,** 738
and Watergate coverup **FR** 37
and White House efforts to use CIA to restrict FBI Watergate investigation **FR** 37-40
Dailey, Peter **1,** 32, 35 **5,** 1878
Dairy import quotas **15,** 6798-99
AMPI and **15,** 6405
and AMPI contributions in 1970 **15,** 6543
campaign contributions and **16,** 7162, 7164
Campbell on **17,** 7754-55, 7771
comparison of actual and recommended **FR** 621
and dairy industry contributions **FR** 580
Masters denies involvement with **16,** 6967-68
in memo from Colson to Ehrlichman on **FR** 816-17E
in memo from Colson to Chotiner **FR** 792E, 793E
in memo from Gleason to Colson **FR** 772-75E
Nelson on **15,** 6544-46
Nixon action on **FR** 619-21
in Rice memo **FR** 800-803
Townsend on **14,** 6296-99
Dairy industry
antitrust suit against **14,** 6075-76
campaign contributions through secret committees **FR** 689-94
contribution activity prior to Nixon's reversal of milk price-support decision **FR** 640-42
contributions after milk price-support decision **FR** 682-99

and Hughes contribution **20,** 9408-10 **22,** 12428-29E

and Hughes-Maheu conflict **21,** 9987-88

informs Davis that Hughes contribution is for congressional campaigns in 1970 **24,** 11582-84

informs Maheu of Rebozo's feeling on O'Brien's involvement with Hughes **21,** 10056

instructed by Hughes through Maheu to meet with Mitchell on Dunes acquisition **FR** 983-84

interdepartmental correspondence to Hirsch on expenses account **24,** 11392, 11502E

introduces Nixon to Rebozo **FR** 934

IRS interviews of **24,** 11654 **FR** 1017-18

and IRS investigation of Rebozo **21,** 10068

lends money to Rebozo **21,** 10087-88

letter from Woods to Bartlett re campaign contribution delivered to Rebozo by **26,** 10283E

letter to Nigro with expense vouchers **22,** 12475-80E

letter to Rebozo on AEC underground testing **20,** 9588, 9674E

letter transmitting documents of **24,** 11391, 11492-93E

letters to Rebozo **20,** 9588, 9675E **21,** 10059

list of items not to be produced on grounds of privilege **24,** 11392, 11501E

meeting with Morgan, Rebozo, and Mitchell **21,** 9976-77

meeting with Nixon and Rebozo at Camp David **23,** 10894-95, 11005-11006, 11019-20 **FR** 1011-12, 1066-67

meeting with Rebozo and Morgan **21,** 9939-44 **FR** 936-37

meeting with Rebozo in San Clemente **21,** 9975-76

meeting with Rebozo in Washington **21,** 10094

meetings with Mitchell **22,** 10231 **FR** 984-89

memo to Levy with notes covering expenses **22,** 12484-89E

memo to Rebozo on ABM issue **21,** 10045-48

objections to line of questioning of **20,** 9592-93

payments from Hughes Tool Co. **FR** 984

professional background **FR** 934

and Rebozo **21,** 9939 **23,** 11186-87

Rebozo decides to accept Hughes contribution from **21,** 9961-62

Rebozo denies discussing TWA suit with **21,** 10054

in Rebozo records **21,** 10022, 10023

and Rebozo testimony **21,** 9939-44 **FR** 954-56

and Rebozo's decision to return Hughes contribution **21,** 10090-10100

Rebozo's efforts to return Hughes contribution to **22,** 10446-48, 10465 **24,** 11585-56

Rebozo's handling of money delivered by **21,** 9966-72

relationship with Mitchell **21,** 10044-45

and return of Hughes contribution **21,** 10060-65 **23,** 11198, 11204, 11205-11206

Smathers and **21,** 10106

and Smith's report to Garment on Hughes matter **23,** 11058

submission of documents by Davis for **24,** 11391-11401

telephone calls from Nixon to **21,** 10066-68

telephone conversations with Rebozo in 1968 on "house project" **FR** 939-40

telephone records **21,** 9976

tells Gemmill Davis will contact him **23,** 11176, 11190

trip to Washington with Rebozo and Maheu **21,** 10055-56

Wakefield and **24,** 11330

Wearley denies flying to Texas for visit with President Johnson **20,** 9458

Wearley denies knowledge of contributions taken to Rebozo by **20,** 9488-90

Danner, Richard G., testimony of 20, 9495-9554, 9555-89, 9591-9612 **24,** 11387-11478, 11539-66

on advising Rebozo to discuss Hughes contribution with attorney **24,** 11545

affidavit for IRS, contradictions with testimony **20,** 9510

and analysis of delivery dates of Hughes contribution **FR** 962-68

on Anderson column on Hughes memo to Maheu **20,** 9608-10

on appearance of Hughes money **24,** 11540

on arrangements for returning money to Hughes **20,** 9552-54, 9557-60

at Waldorf Hotel, New York City, for election returns **24,** 11424-25

on attending party in Washington in October 1973 **20,** 9551-52

on business dealings with Morgan **20,** 9497-98

on campaign contributions by Hughes in 1968 **20,** 9501-9502

on changeover in Hughes organization in 1970 **20,** 9540-41

on check cashed with Rebozo **20,** 9604-9605

conflict with other testimony on Hughes contribution **24,** 11418-19 **FR** 1053-67

conflicting statements on Bell deliveries of Hughes contributions **FR** 961

conflicts in testimony during Maheu-Hughes litigation **24,** 11451

on conflicts in testimony with Rebozo on initiation of discussion on Hughes contribution **24,** 11445-46

on conflicts on date of visit with Nixon on Walker Cay **24,** 11450-52

contact with Hughes **24,** 11415

on contact with Rebozo on Air West matters **20,** 9585-86

on contacts between Gay, Davis, and Rebozo **24,** 11557

on contacts with Greenspun **24,** 11550

on contacts with Kalmbach **24,** 11564

on contacts with Mitchell after Dunes Hotel acquisition matter **20,** 9606

on contacts with Rebozo in 1968 **24,** 11412-32

on contacts with Rebozo on return of Hughes contribution **FR** 1010, 1011-12

on contacts with Smathers **24,** 11551

contradictions between other testimony and **24,** 11439

contradicts prior testimony on meeting with McLaren **20,** 9576-77

on contributions to Rebozo **20,** 9562-63

Danner, Richard G., testimony of *(Continued)*

on conversation with Maheu on Hughes contribution **24,** 11541-44

on conversation with Nixon and Rebozo at San Clemente **20,** 9538-40

on conversation with Rebozo at time of delivery of Hughes contribution **24,** 11542-44

on conversation with Rebozo on *Newsday* investigation **24,** 11546-47

on conversation with Woods at San Clemente **20,** 9539

on correspondence with Rebozo **24,** 11455-60, 11462

on date of Smathers mentioning forthcoming sale of his house to Nixon **24,** 11452-53

on dealings with Crosby and Davis **20,** 9519-21

on deliveries of Hughes contribution to Rebozo **20,** 9531-39, 9543, 9555-56, 9563 **24,** 11464-68, 11539-40

denies cash contributions in 1968 **24,** 11445

denies contacts with Rebozo since last session of Senate Committee **24,** 11551-52

denies discussing business problems of Hughes Tool Co. with Mitchell **20,** 9507

denies discussing direct payment of contributions to Nixon **20,** 9500-9501

denies discussing Hughes contribution with Nixon in 1973 **20,** 9549-50

denies discussing Hughes Tool Co. business problems with Rebozo **20,** 9500, 9524

denies discussing use of contribution with Rebozo **20,** 9560

denies discussion on Hughes contribution being considered as gift **24,** 11470

denies discussion with Greenspun on Meier relationship with F. Donald Nixon **20,** 9607-9608

denies discussion with Smathers, Rebozo, or Nixon on raising campaign contributions to pay Nixon's expenses **24,** 11453-54

denies going to SEC on Dunes Hotel acquisition matter **20,** 9584-85

denies knowledge of Davis contribution **24,** 1142

denies knowledge of "house project" in 1968 discussions with Rebozo **FR** 939-40

denies knowledge of Hughes contribution to Nixon campaign through Laxalt **20,** 9504

denies knowledge of letter sent to Metzner on Dunes Hotel acquisition **20,** 9586-87

denies knowledge of Morgan discussion with Kalmbach on Hughes contribution **24,** 11550

denies knowledge of payments from Florida for Nixon to Rebozo **24,** 11545

denies knowledge of Rebozo consulting lawyers on Hughes contribution **24,** 11476

denies knowledge of Rebozo consulting with Nixon, Kalmbach, and Griffin on return of Hughes contribution **24,** 11469

denies knowledge of Rebozo financing improvements on Nixon's Key Biscayne home **24,** 11544-45

denies link between campaign contributions and Dunes Hotel acquisition efforts **20,** 9581-82

denies meeting with Meier or F. Donald Nixon in 1968 **20,** 9510-11

denies offering Rebozo envelope with money **20,** 9516

denies Rebozo specified cash form of contribution **20,** 9534

denies recent conversations with Mitchell or McClaren on Dunes Hotel acquisition effort **20,** 9584

denies soliciting campaign contributions from Resorts International, Davis, or Crosby **20,** 9520

denies telling Rebozo that Hughes' contributions were tied to meeting with Nixon **20,** 9515

denies telling Rebozo that Morgan had personal contribution to make **20,** 9500

denies transfer of funds during trip with Abplanalp and Rebozo **20,** 9557

denies visiting Nixon's home in Key Biscayne **24,** 11544

on diaries for 1968 **24,** 14401-32

on diaries for 1969-72 **24,** 11433

on diaries for 1973 **24,** 11432-38

differentiates between contribution from Hughes and Hughes Tool Co. **20,** 9500

on discussing accepting employment with Hughes Tool Co. with Rebozo in 1969 **20,** 9511-12

on discussion with Nixon on role in 1968 campaign **24,** 11409-11

on discussion with Rebozo on nerve gas issue **24,** 11464

on discussion with Stans **20,** 9506

on discussions of Greenspun break-in **20,** 9609 **24,** 11561-62

on discussions of Hughes contribution with Danner **24,** 11555-56

on discussions with F. Donald Nixon **20,** 9604

on discussions with Golden on Hughes contribution **24,** 11459-60, 11552-55

on discussions with Mitchell on TWA litigation **20,** 9605

on discussions with Nixon in 1968 **20,** 9502, 9503

on discussions with Rebozo and Nixon on contributions **20,** 9540

on discussions with Rebozo on contributions to Nixon campaign in 1969 **20,** 9512-17

on discussions with Rebozo on IRS interviews **24,** 11558-60

on discussions with Rebozo on Nixon's financial dealings **20,** 9525

on discussions with Rebozo on Watergate break-in **24,** 11548-49

on discussions with Smathers on Hughes contributions **20,** 9544-45

on discussions with Winte on rumored Rebozo denial of receipt of Hughes contribution **24,** 11554-55

on Federal Reserve Board checking Hughes money **24,** 11558

on first meeting with Maheu **20,** 9498

on flights on Hughes' planes **20,** 9523

on Florida real estate developers **24,** 11428-29

on gaps in travel records **20,** 9522-23

on Hughes attempted acquisition of Dunes Hotel **20,** 9576-85

on Hughes contributions **20,** 9511-15, 9540 **FR** 934-35, 1053

Hughes organization instructs him to end political concerns **20,** 9540-41

on improvements at Nixon's home in Key Biscayne **24,** 11544

on informing Hughes Tool Co. officers of contributions by Hughes **20**, 9541-42
on informing Rebozo of IRS deposition **20**, 9543-44
on investigation of delivery of Hughes contribution **24**, 11568-70
and job offer from Hughes organization **24**, 11430-31
on Key Biscayne meeting with Nixon and Rebozo **24**, 11410, 11411
on letter from McGrath **24**, 11460-62
on letter to Rebozo on atomic energy tests in Nevada **20**, 9587-88, 9591-98
on loan to Rebozo **24**, 11456-57
on location of correspondence with Rebozo **24**, 11458-59
on Maheu authorization of Hughes' contribution **20**, 9531-32, 9533, 9564
on meeting in Davis' office on Watergate **24**, 11437-38
on meeting with Abplanalp and Rebozo **20**, 9547-48, 9563-64 **24**, 11471-72
on meeting with Davis and Crosby **20**, 9524
on meeting with Maheu in Las Vegas in 1968 **24**, 11446-48, 11449
on meeting with Mitchell and Rebozo **24**, 11444-45 **FR** 937-38
on meeting with Morgan and Rebozo **20**, 9498-99, 9505-9506 **24**, 11444
on meeting with Nixon and Rebozo in 1968 **20**, 9503-9505 **24**, 11421-22, 11439-42
on meeting with Rebozo and Garcia **24**, 11445
on meeting with Rebozo and Nixon at Camp David **20**, 9548-50 **24**, 11472-76
on meeting with Rebozo on dumping of nerve gas into Atlantic **20**, 9596
on meetings with Rebozo on contributions in 1969 **20**, 9515-17, 9526-27
on Meier and F. Donald Nixon **20**, 9598-9604
on memo on ABM to Rebozo **20**, 9597-98
on Mitchell and Dunes Hotel acquisition **FR** 991
on Nixon's interest in Hughes' 1969 Congressional campaign contributions **20**, 9526-28
on Nixon's purchase of Smathers' house **24**, 11425-26
on physical appearance of Hughes money **24**, 11466
on presence of Maheu during delivery of Hughes contribution to Rebozo **24**, 11476-78
on reasons for requesting guest list from Rebozo for dinner for Prince Philip of England **24**, 11457
on Rebozo and Hughes contributions in 1968 **20**, 9495-97, 9498-99
on Rebozo and TWA litigation **20**, 9569-72
on Rebozo's first request for return of Hughes contribution **24**, 11469-71
on Rebozo's reasons for believing Hughes should contribute in 1969 **20**, 9528-30
on Rebozo's reasons for returning contributions **20**, 9569
on Rebozo's refusal of campaign contributions **20**, 9513, 9515, 9517, 9527
on Rebozo's remodeling of home in Key Biscayne **24**, 11545

on Rebozo's return of Hughes contribution **20**, 9546-47
on Rebozo's visit to Las Vegas of 1973 **20**, 9523-26, 9561-62
on recording of telephone calls in diary **24**, 11429
on records of appointments **24**, 11436-37
on relationship between Hughes contribution and Dunes acquisition **24**, 11564
on relationship with Abplanalp **20**, 9564
on relationship with Rebozo **20**, 9496
on report to board of directors on Hughes contribution **24**, 11557
on return of Hughes contribution **24**, 11462-63
on role in acquisition of Dunes Hotel **20**, 9572-75
on role in TWA litigations **20**, 9565-68
on rumor that Rebozo would deny Hughes contribution **20**, 9545
on solicitation of contributors **24**, 11440-42, 11443-44
on source of second Hughes' contribution **20**, 9542-43
on stag dinner for Prince Philip of England in 1969 **24**, 11457
on storage of money used for Hughes contribution **FR** 961-62
summary of **FR** 949-51
on telephone call from Kessler of *Washington Post* **24**, 11436
on telephone conversations with Rebozo in 1969 **20**, 9521-22
on telephone records **20**, 9582-83
on testimony before Judge Pregerson in Las Vegas trial **24**, 11449
on testimony before Securities and Exchange Commission **20**, 9587
on timing of discussions with Rebozo on Hughes contribution **24**, 11546
on travel records **20**, 9517-18, 9556
on trip to Key Biscayne to deliver money **20**, 9536-37
on trip to Miami with Maheu **20**, 9535-36
on trip to San Clemente to deliver contribution to Rebozo **20**, 9538-40
on trip to Texas in 1968 to solicit campaign funds **24**, 11512-13
on trip to Washington in 1973 on Air West acquisition **20**, 9551
on trip with Abplanalp and Rebozo **20**, 9556-57
on trip with Nixon, Rebozo, and Abplanalp **24**, 11407-11408
trips with Rebozo on Hughes Tool Co. plane **24**, 11547-48
on use of Hughes contribution to 1970 senatorial campaigns **20**, 9530-31
on visit with Rebozo in May 1973 **20**, 9546-48
on Winte's contacts with Hunt **24**, 11560-61
on word "project" in diary **24**, 11429-30
on Xeroxes of checks paid to campaign committees by Hughes **20**, 9501

Danner, Robert 24, 11555-56
Darman, Dick 19, 9098E
Dash, Samuel 1, 1, 6, 9, 40, 109 **3**, 1246E **11**, 4892-95E
on Alch's opening statement **1**, 293-294

Dash, Samuel *(Continued)*
application for use immunity for Strachan **6,** 2436-37
arrangement with Frates on Rebozo testimony **21,** 10070
on Baker's request that counsel annotate notes with page references to previous testimony **8,** 3044
on Bellino and Armstrong **21,** 10125
and booklet on Nixon brothers **22,** 10631-32
on Buzhardt representing Nixon and Haig **23,** 10997-98
on committee investigators **21,** 10086
on conflicts between testimony of Haldeman and others **8,** 3222
correspondence with Gartner on provision to Committee of specific information and documents **25,** 11816-22E
on damage done by Segretti **10,** 4046-47
on Edmisten, Lackritz, and Dubin returning with envelopes subpoenaed from Davis **20,** 9415
on enemies list **4,** 1400
on false advertising in election campaigns **11,** 4634
on Frates' objections to line of questioning of Rebozo **21,** 9945, 9951, 9957, 9959, 10127
on Garment's request that Moore testify after Mitchell **5,** 1992
Greer's agreements with **22,** 10514-15, 10532-37
on Haig's testimony **23,** 11036
on Hunt **9,** 3661, 3665-69, 3703-3707, 3804-3808
on Hunt's attorney-client privilege **9,** 3701-3702
and identification of exhibits by Dean **4,** 1408-1412
on impact of investigation **21,** 10085-86
on investigation of Rebozo by Committee staff **21,** 10123, 10124
on leaks from Select Committee **10,** 3903 **22,** 10263
on length of interviewing sessions with Hunt **20,** 9376, 9377
letter from Davitt of Justice Department on absence of records on criminal acts of Democrats **8,** 3132, 3321E
letter from Garment with pre-April 7 list of contributors **26,** 10284E
letter from Hershman on allegations about Wallace **19,** 8857-58E
on letter from Krogh to Ehrlichman reported in *New York Times* **6,** 2661-63
letter from Miller on grant to Farmer **19,** 8839-41E
letter from Silbert accompanying affidavit **25,** 12401-12404E
letter from Taugher on McGovern campaign **25,** 12419-20E
letter to Dash on absence of information in Justice Department or FBI files on criminal acts of Democrats **8,** 3132, 3321E
letter to Walters on confidentiality of affidavits **25,** 11926-28E
on line of questioning of Marumoto **13,** 5310-11
on line of questioning of Rebozo **21,** 10076, 10078, 10080, 10085, 10093
on MacGregor's voluntary appearance and cooperativeness with Select Committee **12,** 4897-98

on McCord's reference to "Cuban-Americans" **1,** 191
Memorandum of Law, Admissibility of Hearsay Statements of Co-conspirator submitted by **4,** 1783-90E
on Nixon's logs of meetings with Dean **2,** 531-32
on objections to further questioning of Woods **22,** 10193-97
on reasons for subpoena for Haig **23,** 11025-26
on Rebozo documents **21,** 9938, 10021, 10023-24, 10024-25, 10026, 10027, 10028, 10029, 10030-31, 10032, 10033, 10034, 10035, 10037, 10089, 10140-41, 10142
on release of enemies list **4,** 1400
on relevance of calling Stearns to testify **11,** 4594-95
on relevancy of line of questioning of Woods **22,** 10224-25, 10227
on rules of evidence **4,** 1523-24
on sequencing of witnesses **1,** 263-264
on staff of committee **21,** 10088-89
on subpoena for Caulfield **1,** 132-133
on subpoena for Haldeman's tapes **2,** 833 **8,** 3053-54, 3061
thanks Weicker for spending time in executive hearings **21,** 10139
on Vinson's request for copy of LaRue's transcript **23,** 11171-72
Wilson's advice to McKiernan on turning over booklet on Nixon brothers to **22,** 1065
on Woods' objections to Select Committee obtaining her unlisted number **22,** 10198, 10199
on wording of Strachan's testimony on Haldeman's instructions on files **8,** 3061, 3062

Dash, Samuel, questioning by 5, 2079-81
Bartolme **13,** 5419-31, 5437, 5438
Brindze **12,** 4975-81
Buchanan **10,** 3899-3934, 3976, 3977
Campbell **12,** 4953-55, 4962, 4963
Caulfield **1,** 264-267
Clark **13,** 5403-16
Dean **3,** 1021-31 **4,** 1349, 1350, 1386, 1387, 1408-11, 1564-80
Ehrlichman **6,** 2522-54 **7,** 2815-60
Haldeman **8,** 3017-61, 3207-3222
Harmony **2,** 458-64, 487-88
Heller **12,** 4964-70
Hunt **20,** 9359-60, 9396, 9379, 9382, 9385-87, 9390, 9391-92, 9396, 9397, 9398-99, 9400, 9401, 9402, 9404, 9405
Jacobsen **15,** 6392-93, 6413, 6460-61
Kalmbach **5,** 2091-2112
Kehrli **1,** 75-76, 77-80
LaRue **6,** 2277-2301 **23,** 11151, 1158-89, 11163-64, 11165-66, 11168-69
Leeper **1,** 95-109
MacGregor **12,** 4897-4912
Malek **18,** 8265-66, 8276-77, 8278
Mankiewicz **11,** 4601-20, 4634
Marumoto **13,** 5273-96, 5319-25 **18,** 8277
McCord **1,** 125-135, 137, 141, 232-37
McMinoway **11,** 4477-4500
Mitchell **4,** 1602-36 **5,** 1896-1928
Moore **5,** 1992, 2066

Odle **1,** 12-14, 52-59
Petersen **9,** 3611-32
Priestes **13,** 5326-39, 5355, 5356
Rebozo **21,** 9968, 9985-86, 9987, 9988, 9992,
    9993, 9997-98, 10001, 10004, 10005, 10006,
    10014, 10016, 10062-63, 10064, 10073, 10115-16
Segretti **10,** 3979, 3985-4005, 4046-49, 4052
Shoffler **1,** 117-118, 123,124
Sloan **2,** 630-31
Strachan **6,** 2445-66
Ulasewicz **1,** 284-88
Walters **9,** 3403-19, 3426, 3427
David, Ed 22, 10703
David H. Murdock Development Co. 12, 5046E
Davidoff, Sidney
  on enemies list **4,** 1695E
Davidson, Bob
  discussion with Goldstein at HUD **FR** 434
  memo to Malek on Responsiveness Program **18,**
    8232, 8366E
Davidson, Irving 24, 11416
Davies, John 3, 919 **21,** 9692-93
  and telephone installer's card to Caulfield for
    Kraft wiretap **FR** 112
Davis, A. Darius 22, 10232, 10518, 10519 **23,** 11268
  24, 11330
  Anderson column on contribution of **22,** 10577-79
    26, 10590E
  campaign contribution of **22,** 10238-39, 12429-30E
    23, 11160, 11161 **FR** 1000-1001
  Danner denies knowledge about contribution of
    24, 11442
  Danner's business relationship with **20,** 9497-98
  LaRue denies knowledge of campaign contribu-
    tion of **23,** 11157, 11158, 11159
  letter from Stans to **22,** 12576E
  Rebozo on contribution from **21,** 10116-18
Davis, A. Darius, testimony of 22, 10561-89
  on acknowledgements for contributions **22,** 10576
  on anonymity of contribution **22,** 10565-66
  on belief that Rebozo transmitted contribution to
    campaign **22,** 10572-73
  on business of Winn-Dixie Stores, Inc. **22,** 10562
  Cole's objections to line of questioning of **22,**
    10570-71
  on contribution to Rebozo for Nixon's 1972 cam-
    paign **22,** 10562-63, 10564-67
  on decision to make contribution to Nixon cam-
    paign **22,** 10568-69
  denies contributions to Florida Nixon for Presi-
    dent Committee **22,** 10579-80
  denies discussions with Rebozo on handling and
    recording of campaign funds **22,** 10579
  denies efforts to acquire Las Vegas property or
    doing business with Government as supplier **22,**
    10583
  denies financial dealings or discussion of cam-
    paign contributions with Danner **22,** 10582-83
  denies Government investigated Winn-Dixie Co.
    or himself or his brothers **22,** 10584
  denies having business or financial transactions
    with Rebozo **22,** 10569-70, 10584-87
  denies knowledge of list of contributors **22,** 10581

denies solicitation of campaign contributions **22,**
  10587-88
desire to avoid discussion of amount of campaign
  contribution **22,** 10562-63
on division of contribution among committees **22,**
  10581
on first meeting with Danner **22,** 10581-82
on letter from Republican National Committee
  after campaign contribution to Rebozo **22,**
  10572, 10576
meeting with Rebozo to make contribution **22,**
  10564-67
on previous contributions to Nixon's campaigns
  22, 10576-77
reasons for cash form of contribution **22,** 10575-
  76, 10580
reasons for contributing to Rebozo **22,** 10570,
  10587-88
reasons for contribution to Nixon campaign **22,**
  10565
relationship with Rebozo **22,** 10569
on son's campaign contribution **22,** 10573
source of contributions **22,** 10566, 10580, 10588
telephone call from Rebozo informing him of
  investigation by Select Committee **22,** 10567-68
Davis, Angela
  defense fund for **6,** 2567, 2570
Davis, Chester C. 20, 9457, 9542, 9560-61, 9562,
  9568, 9606-9607 **22,** 10232 **23,** 10786, 10800E,
  10905, 11190, 11200
  accepts envelopes after Xeroxing of money **20,**
    9417
  advises Moncourt of IRS investigation of Rebozo
    22, 10519-20
  on Armstrong's conduct **24,** 11406
  on conflicts in Danner's testimony before Senate
    Committee staff and in Maheu-Hughes litigation
    24, 11451-52
  Danner and **20,** 9524
  and Danner's arrangements for returning money
    to Hughes **20,** 9552, 9553, 9558-60
  discussion with Gemmill **23,** 11206
  discussions with Danner on Winte-Hunt contact
    24, 11562-63
  Gemmill and **23,** 11201-11202
  letter from Ervin denying request for open hear-
    ing for Winte **24,** 11615-16, 11619E
  letter from Lackritz requesting Henley documents
    24, 11536-37E
  letter from Lenzner on arrangements for question-
    ing Hughes **22,** 12451E
  letter of reply from Ervin to **24,** 11389, 11488-91E
  letter to Ervin on legality of some of Staff's activi-
    ties **24,** 11389, 11479-87E
  money delivered by Gemmill to Glaeser for **20,**
    9410-15
  on Muse calling Pregerson's court on his testimo-
    ny **24,** 11567
  objection to repeating Danner's prior testimony
    24, 11413
  objections to characterization of Danner's testimo-
    ny **24,** 11446
  objections to Glaeser's testimony in executive ses-
    sion **20,** 9414-15

See also Davis, A. Darius

Davis-Bacon Act 13, 5534E

Davison, Robert 13, 5289, 5290, 5291 **18,** 8201, 8230 **19,** 8901E **FR** 410-12

  and Malek's progress reports on Responsiveness Program to Haldeman **18,** 8234, 8235

  memo from Evans on Federation of Experienced Americans **18,** 8449-50

  memo from Evans on "Public Awareness" proposal **18,** 8449, 8487E

  memo from Marumoto on Development Associates **13,** 5318-20, 5323, 5635-36E

  memos from Marumoto on grants **FR** 387

  report on EEOC-University of Texas matter **FR** 410

  and Responsiveness Program **18,** 8245-46, 8251, 8252-53 **FR** 379

  telephone report to Hamilton on Responsiveness Program **19,** 8752E

Davitt, John H. FR 210

Dawson, Anne 22, 10383-84 **FR** 249E

Day, Floyd C. 19, 8902E

Day, John S. 11, 4812-13E

Dayton, Ohio

  actions against Nixon campaign in **12,** 5163-64E

Dean, John W., III 1, 25, 82, 88 **2,** 753, 754 **5,** 1855, 1950

  abilities of **6,** 2450-51

  absent from meetings on Segretti matter **5,** 1955

  advice to Segretti **10,** 4046, 4051

  alleged involvement in Watergate **1,** 242-43

  and anonymous letter from McCord to Caulfield **FR** 64

  and antitrust suit against AMPI **16,** 7178

  asked to brief cabinet on Watergate **8,** 3167-68

  asks CIA to retrieve Hunt files from FBI **9,** 3529

  asks Gray to delay interview of Chenow **9,** 3455-56

  asks Kalmbach to raise money for Watergate defendants **5,** 2105, 2110-12, 2149, 2151-52 **7,** 2885 **FR** 51-52

  asks Petersen to excuse several White House staff members from grand jury testimony **9,** 3619-20

  asks Schlesinger for CIA to get Hunt's material back from FBI **9,** 3438-39

  asks Walters to help raise bail money **6,** 2561-62

  assigned to Watergate case **6,** 2519 **7,** 2739-40, 2850 **9,** 3675-76

  assurances to Magruder **2,** 804-805, 850

  at FBI interviews **FR** 46

  at Liddy's first presentation of intelligence-gathering plan **2,** 787-88, 811, 838-39, 844-45, 855, 862-63 **5,** 1816

  at Liddy's second presentation of intelligence-gathering plan **2,** 789-91 **4,** 1611

  at meeting on June 19 **FR** 33-34

  at meeting with Kalmbach, Mitchell, and LaRue on hush money **5,** 2110-11, 2176

  at meeting with Kalmbach and Mitchell on raising hush money **4,** 1632

  at meeting with LaRue, Mardian, Magruder, and Mitchell **6,** 2286

  at meeting with Nunn, Kalmbach, and Evans on milk producers' contributions **17,** 7649-50

  at meetings to plan Magruder's grand jury testimony **6,** 2292

  at meetings with Kalmbach and LaRue **5,** 2113, 2134-35 **6,** 2290-91

  and attorney-client privilege in relationship with Segretti **10,** 4022-23, 4035-42

  and authorization for Brookings Institution firebombing **6,** 2536

  authorization of money to Hunt **23,** 11110-11

  bank statement on account of **4,** 1712E

  Bittman and **1,** 325

  blamed in Buzhardt memo **5,** 1817-18

  on boat ride on Potomac **2,** 623

  Brown's letter on Patman Committee testimony of **5,** 1815

  and Buckley's infiltration in Muskie campaign **21,** 9729-30

  Butterfield claims lack of knowledge on Nixon's listening devices **5,** 2078

  in Buzhardt memos **5,** 1817-18, 2065-69

  Buzhardt on persons with access to files of **23,** 10921-22

  Buzhardt's letter to Inouye and questions for **4,** 1754-82E

  Camp David trip of **7,** 2803 **FR** 89, *see also* Dean Report

  career **5,** 1841

  Caulfield and **1,** 251, 268, 269

  Caulfield informs about plan for private security agency **FR** 113

  Caulfield recommends he watch CBS-TV show "60 Minutes" on Hughes controversy **21,** 9724

  and Caulfield's investigation of DeAntonio **22,** 10379-90

  and Caulfield's investigation of film of Nixon's Checkers speech **22,** 10383-84

  and Caulfield's investigation of *Newsday* **22,** 10368-77

  and Caulfield's investigation of Udall and Overview Corp. **FR** 138-39

  and Caulfield's investigation of Virgin Islands Corp. **22,** 10400-10402

  and Caulfield's meeting with McCord on Executive clemency **FR** 65

  and Caulfield's offer of clemency to McCord **1,** 254-60, 264-67, 272-73, 277-78, 282-83, 318 **7,** 2771

  and Caulfield's proposal for "Operation Sandwedge" **21,** 9728-29

  and Caulfield's recommendations on *Millhouse* **FR** 136

  and Caulfield's requests to IRS for tax information **22,** 10361-79

  on cause of Watergate break-in **6,** 2395, 2419-20

  Chapin and **10,** 4041

  Colson gives copy of Hunt's letter to **FR** 66

  and Colson's plan on Brookings Institution **22,** 10359-60

  communications with Nixon in Buzhardt memo sent to Thompson, Buzhardt on sources for **23,** 10897-10900

  comparison of Moore's testimony with testimony of **5,** 1958-59, 1985-88

  concept of intelligence gathering held by **2,** 811

Dean, John W., III *(Continued)*

conflicts between Kalmbach testimony and **5,** 2176

conflicts between Mardian testimony and **6,** 2387-88

conflicts between Moore's testimony and **5,** 1959

contacts with Mitchell after Watergate **5,** 1883, 1885

contacts with Rebozo **21,** 10065-66

contacts with Walters **8,** 3288-89 **9,** 3439-40

and contents of Hunt's safe **FR** 35-37

in conversation between Kalmbach and Ehrlichman **6,** 2574, 2575

conversations with Moore on Watergate **FR** 89

conversations with Sloan **2,** 589-91

and coordination of intelligence-gathering activities **6,** 2471

and Cortese investigation **22,** 10395

in Cushman's memo instead of Ehrlichman **8,** 3296, 3308-3309

dealings with Walters **4,** 1682E

delivers Hunt files to Gray **7,** 2678

and deniability for Mitchell **1,** 218-219

denies involvement in Watergate planning meetings to Magruder **2,** 806, 842-43, 864-65

and Diem cables **5,** 1920

differences between testimony and Nixon tape on March 21 meeting **8,** 3118

discharged from first law job **5,** 1971

discloses coverup to Nixon **FR** 88-89

discusses Colson's plan on Brookings Institution with Ehrlichman **FR** 125

discusses possibility of public disclosure with Haldeman **FR** 89

discusses Sandwedge proposal with Mitchell **FR** 115-16

discusses theories of Watergate break-in with Gray **9,** 3525, 3528

discusses White House involvement in Watergate with Nixon on March 21 **8,** 3074-75

discussion with Gray on Dahlberg checks **FR** 37

discussion with Magruder on deniability for Mitchell **2,** 872-73

discussion with Nixon on Select Committee hearings **FR** 79-80

discussion with Petersen on Magruder's grand jury testimony **9,** 3617-18

in discussions between Nixon and Ehrlichman on Executive clemency **FR** 73

discussions with Ehrlichman on Executive clemency **7,** 2849

discussions with Haldeman on his own vulnerability **8,** 3077-78

discussions with Mitchell on McCord's revelations **5,** 1913-14

discussions with Nunn on milk producers' contributions **17,** 7548

discussions with U.S. attorneys reported to Kleindienst **9,** 3578-79

documents given to Gray by **9,** 3624-25

and draft of White House Executive privilege statement **5,** 1974-75

efforts to get CIA to stop FBI investigation of Mexican money **9,** 3648

efforts to retrieve Hunt photos of Fielding break-in from CIA **FR** 75-76

Ehrlichman and Nixon discuss his status at White House **7,** 2807-2808

Ehrlichman and planned firebombing of Brookings Institution **6,** 2535-36

Ehrlichman denies he told him to get rid of Hunt's briefcase **7,** 2824-28

Ehrlichman instructs to follow up on June 23 meeting with Walters **7,** 2835

Ehrlichman on falsehoods of **6,** 2513-14

Ehrlichman on involvement in Watergate of **7,** 2744

Ehrlichman refutes his testimony that Nixon gave Executive clemency assurances to Hunt **6,** 2610-11

Ehrlichman says he did conduct investigation of Watergate **6,** 2720-24

Ehrlichman tells Gray to deal with on all Watergate matters **9,** 3450, 3508-3509

Ehrlichman tells Nixon of his involvement in Watergate **7,** 2714

Ehrlichman testimony in conflict with **7,** 2718-20

on Ehrlichman-Kleindienst relationship **9,** 3565-66

and enemies list from Colson **6,** 2487

enemies list given to Walters by **24,** 11691-11716E

on Executive clemency for McCord **1,** 290 **9,** 3795

expresses fears to Nixon on unravelling of coverup **FR** 83-89

extent of reports to Mitchell **5,** 1904

"Eyes Only" memo from Ehrlichman on Kalmbach's written retainer arrangement **7,** 2813, 3005-3006E

and FBI check on DeAntonio **22,** 10380

on FBI checking Select Committee members **5,** 1975-76, 1995

and FBI Watergate investigation **9,** 3606

FBI 302s given to **9,** 3469-70, 3477-82, 3514-15, 3576-77, 3583

and follow-up with Walters **8,** 3064

gives material from Hunt's safe to Gray **FR** 36

goes to Camp David **7,** 2901

goes to U.S. attorneys **7,** 2903

Gray hearings and **5,** 1971

Gray on efforts to slow down investigation **9,** 3540-41

Gray on suspicions about **9,** 3530-32, 3548-50

Gray on Watergate investigation by **9,** 3529

Gray says he probably lies **9,** 3490

Gray tells him that Helms says there is no CIA involvement in Watergate **9,** 3509

and Gray testimony on Hunt's files **9,** 3467-71

on Gray's confirmation hearings **9,** 3488

and Gray's information on Dahlberg and Mexican checks **9,** 3451, 3452, 3453-55, 3456, 3457

Haldeman denies he reported on Liddy plan meetings **8,** 2098-99

Haldeman on denial that he conducted Watergate investigation **8,** 3099-3100, 3145-46

Haldeman's attitude toward **7,** 2885

Haldeman's notes on conversations with **7,** 2873-74

and Haldeman's order of 24-hour surveillance of Kennedy **FR** 118

and handling of Watergate situation **8,** 3163

hints about White House horror stories to Moore **5,** 1972

hiring of **8**, 3130
hiring of Caulfield and **4**, 1605
Hunt on Liddy plan and **9**, 3679
Hunt on responsibility for Watergate **9**, 3778
and Hunt's belief on authorization for activities **9**, 3764
and Hunt's files to Gray **9**, 3513-14
in Hunt's notes **9**, 3839E
and hush money **5**, 2156, 2161 **6**, 2295-96, 2313, 2320, 2324
immunity for **9**, 3643, 3654-55
and immunity powers of Select Committee **FR** 28
implicates Haldeman in coverup **8**, 3095-96
indictable list **4**, 1461 **5**, 1988-90 **7**, 2854-57 **8**, 3058
infers Nixon knew about coverup **5**, 1838
information from Petersen on grand jury hearings **FR** 80
information to Caulfield on Kennedy Foundation financing *Newsday* article on Rebozo **22**, 10374-75
information to Mitchell from **5**, 1905
information to Moore from **5**, 2029
information to Nixon from **7**, 2811 **9**, 3586
and information to White House from IRS **21**, 9710
informed by Strachan that files were destroyed **6**, 2472
informs Moore about his meeting with Nixon on coverup **5**, 1945
informs Moore of meetings on Liddy plan **5**, 1969-72
informs Nixon of Colson call to Magruder on Gemstone plan **FR** 24
instructed by Ehrlichman to gather information on Watergate **7**, 2759-61
instructed by Kleindienst to contact DeLoach for information on foreign travels of Kopechne **FR** 118, 144
instructs Young's secretary not to mention special unit's activities to FBI **6**, 2558
interviews Strachan and Chapin on Segretti matter **6**, 2451
introduces Liddy to Mitchell **4**, 1608-1609, 1637-38
and investigation of McGovern's fundraising **21**, 9727-28
and investigation of O'Brien's relationship with Hughes Tool Co. **21**, 9714-23
and investigation of Potomac Associates **21**, 9727
investigation of Watergate by **6**, 2502-2503
involvement in Watergate coverup **4**, 1671-72 **5**, 2007
involvement in Watergate plans **1**, 129, 159, 160, 165, 173, 199-202
and IRS **4**, 1684E **24**, 11634
and IRS audit of *Newsday* reporter **FR** 9
job offer to Segretti **10**, 4024
and Justice Department knowledge of Fielding break-in **7**, 2681-82
and Kalmbach **5**, 2092
Kalmbach asks Ehrlichman about his authority on raising money for Watergate defendants **5**, 2106-2107
Kalmbach denies he said he was speaking on behalf of Haldeman and Ehrlichman **5**, 2115-16
Kalmbach feels used by **5**, 2175, 2176

and Kalmbach's grand jury testimony discussed with Ehrlichman **5**, 2162-63
Kalmbach's reasons for accepting assignment to raise money for Watergate defendants **5**, 2100
and Kalmbach's talk with Magruder in 1973 **5**, 2148-49
Kalmbach's testimony compared with testimony of **5**, 2112-14, 2115-17
Kalmbach's trust in **5**, 2129, 2130-31, 2145-46, 2150, 2153, 2171
Kalmbach's use of funds and **16**, 7158
and Kennedy surveillance **6**, 2492 **21**, 9725
Kleindienst has no recollection of July 31, 1972, meeting with Ehrlichman and **9**, 3566-67
Kleindienst on telling him about meeting Liddy at Burning Tree Country Club **9**, 2562
and La Costa meetings **5**, 1940-42 **7**, 2890-92
LaRue on involvement in coverup of **6**, 2324, 2340-41
LaRue tells him he is going to U.S. Attorneys **6**, 2298-99
and LaRue's payments to Bittman **6**, 2312
learns of Watergate **3**, 1265-66E
letter to Ervin on investigation of Watergate matter **3**, 1252-57E
letter to Ervin on willingness to cooperate with Select Committee **3**, 1252-57E
letter to O'Brien on request to Nixon for appointment of Special Prosecutor **3**, 1163E
as liaison between CRP and White House **4**, 1624
as liaison between Kalmbach and Nixon **5**, 2093-94
as liaison to Haldeman **6**, 2451
and liberal foundations **FR** 142
Liddy and **2**, 471 **4**, 1670
and Liddy-Magruder problem **6**, 2466
and Liddy plan **1**, 221 **5**, 1843, 1857-58 **20**, 9385
and Liddy's employment by CRP **2**, 786, 810
list from Strachan on shredded documents **6**, 2459
MacGregor on being used by **12**, 4930
MacGregor on meeting with Stans and **12**, 4908
MacGregor on statement on Watergate prepared by **12**, 4908
and Magruder **4**, 1640
Magruder says he co-authored Liddy plan **7**, 2766
and Magruder's perjury **4**, 1628-29 **5**, 1896, 1897, 1914-15 **7**, 2845 **8**, 3144-45 **12**, 4906
Mardian contradicts testimony of **6**, 2368-69, 2370-71
on Mardian's suggestion that CIA be used **6**, 2368
and McPhee's talks with Richey **5**, 1908-10
meeting with Chapin and Strachan before FBI interviews **6**, 2464
meeting with Colson and Ehrlichman **6**, 2608-12
meeting with Ehrlichman and Gray **9**, 3483-84
meeting with Ehrlichman and Haldeman **7**, 2741-45
meeting with Ehrlichman and Haldeman on Segretti matter **FR** 182-83
meeting with Ehrlichman and Haldeman to discuss demands for hush money **FR** 56
meeting with Gray **9**, 3450-51, *see also* Gray-Dean meetings
meeting with Haldeman, Ehrlichman, and Mitchell **5**, 1888

and photographs of Fielding break-in **6**, 2552
and political intelligence **6**, 2493
political relationship with Haldeman **6**, 2460-61
on possibility of Cubans bearing responsibility for
 Watergate **9**, 3412
and preparation of Magruder for perjury **2**, 864,
 869-70 **4**, 1417
presence at FBI interviews **8**, 3142
and problems in Magruder-Liddy relationship **2**,
 793, 826, 863
public statement on not being made "scapegoat"
 in Watergate affair **FR** 95
questioned by Ehrlichman **7**, 2727
reaction to Anderson column on his firing from
 first legal job **5**, 1980
reaction to idea that everyone should go before
 grand jury **8**, 3071-73
reaction to Liddy plan **4**, 1611
reasons for McCord's silence on **1**, 247-248
Rebozo denies discussing O'Brien-Hughes-Maheu
 relationships with **21**, 10129
receives copy of transcript of Hunt-Colson telephone conversation **FR** 56
recommends against investigation of DeAntonio
 22, 10388
refuses to meet Gray at Department of Justice **9**,
 3476
and rejection of Sandwedge Plan **22**, 10353-54
relationship with Colson **3**, 1256-57E
relationship with CRP **1**, 18
relationship with Gray **9**, 3476
relationship with Haldeman **6**, 2449-50
relationship with Haldeman and Ehrlichman after
 decision to go to federal prosecutors **FR** 91
relationship with Kleindienst **9**, 3613
relationship with Liddy **3**, 1255-56E
relationship with Moore **5**, 1979-80, 2002
replaced by Ehrlichman as contact with Kleindienst **7**, 2750
and replacement of $350,000 **6**, 2472-73
replacement of money taken by **4**, 1801-1807E
reports to Ehrlichman on Watergate **6**, 2541
reports to Mitchell on Hunt's Executive clemency
 negotiations **4**, 1674
reports to Nixon **6**, 2525-26
request to CIA for money for Watergate defendants **9**, 3505 **FR** 51
requests for transportation for **4**, 1808E, 1809E
requests money from Kalmbach **2**, 711-12
requests money from Stans **2**, 717
resignation of **5** 1984 **7** 2678 **9** 3597-98 **FR** 92-93
and revelation of Huston Plan **FR** 3
role as liaison on intelligence programs **8**, 3030
role at meetings after Watergate **2**, 800
role in raising and distribution of money for Watergate defendants **5**, 2102, 2104, 2110-11, 2113-
 14, 2139-42, 2145
role on White House staff **1**, 78, 80-82 **2**, 764
and Sandwedge Plan **1**, 252 **2**, 862 **22**, 10355 **FR**
 114-15
scapegoat statement of **8**, 3079
and Segretti coverup **FR** 178, 179-80, 181, 182,
 186-87
and Segretti matter **3**, 1302E, 1303E **5**, 2031-32 **9**,
 3620

Segretti on relationship with **10**, 3984-85
and Segretti's attorney **FR** 183
as source of assurances to Watergate defendants **2**,
 810
Stans and **2**, 722
Stans claims he assured Kalmbach of legality of
 money-raising assignment **5**, 2133-34
statement and documents from Brown concerning
 allegations made by **5**, 2181-2208E
Strachan states belief in truthfulness of **6**, 2477
and Strachan's returning money to LaRue **6**, 2443
submits documents on La Costa meeting **FR** 78-
 80
subpoena to obtain logs of meetings with Nixon **2**,
 231-32
subpoena by Patman Committee **3**, 1192E
suggested as White House coordinator with Select
 Committee **5**, 1940-41
suspects taping of conversation with Nixon **5** 2081
 FR 29-30
talking paper for Nixon on meeting with Kleindienst **FR** 79
in taped conversation between Ehrlichman and
 Kalmbach **5**, 2177-78
taped conversation with Segretti **10**, 4040-42 **FR**
 182
in taped telephone conversation between Ehrlichman and Colson **7**, 2829-30
in taped telephone conversation between Ehrlichman and Gray **9**, 3537-38
and taped telephone conversation between Hunt
 and Colson **7**, 2853
taped telephone conversations with Ehrlichman **7**,
 2786-90, 2811-12, 2950-51E
and tax audit of Greene **22**, 10375-76
telephone call to Cushman on his name in memo
 on Hunt **8**, 3297
telephone call to Kalmbach **5**, 2097, 2112
telephone call to Petersen on Magruder testimony
 9, 3651 **FR** 46
telephone call to Schlesinger **9**, 3417-18
telephone call to Treese asking Sloan to take Fifth
 Amendment at Barker trial **2**, 585-86
telephone calls to Gray **9**, 3452, 3499, 3534, 3535
telephone calls to Walters **8**, 3270-71 **9**, 3408
telephone conversations with Haldeman while at
 Camp David **7**, 2901-2902
telephone conversations with Mitchell after Watergate **5**, 1879-80
telephone conversations with Moore from Camp
 David **5**, 1987-88
tells Ehrlichman about Cuban defense fund in
 Florida **6**, 2567-68
tells Ehrlichman about Hunt's blackmail threats
 7, 2853
tells Ehrlichman and Haldeman about meetings
 on Liddy plan **7**, 2753-54
tells Ehrlichman Petersen has pictures from Ellsberg break-in **6**, 2553
tells Gray he is reporting to Nixon directly **9**,
 3450-51
tells Gray not to interview Ogarrio and Dahlberg
 9, 3510, 3511-12
tells Gray of problem of FBI Watergate investigation uncovering CIA operations **9**, 3510

Dean, John W., III *(Continued)*

tells Haldeman about Liddy plan meetings **8,** 3034-36

tells Haldeman his attorneys are meeting federal prosecutors **8,** 3078

tells Kalmbach LaRue will distribute hush money **5,** 2098-99

tells LaRue that O'Brien says Bittman wants $75,-000 **6,** 2297-98

tells Magruder he won't be indicted **2,** 823-24

tells Mitchell about Colson's connection to White House horrors **5,** 1932-33

tells Mitchell about defendants' demands for money **5,** 1862

tells Moore about coverup **5,** 1955, 1968, 2043

tells Moore about discussion with Nixon on coverup **5,** 1981

tells Moore about Ehrlichman's involvement in Ellsberg case **5,** 1960-61, 1989

tells Moore about Fielding break-in **5,** 1960-61

tells Moore about Hunt's demands for money **5,** 1959-60, 1981-82, 2053-54, 2063-64

tells Moore about Magruder's perjury **5,** 1970-71

tells Moore about meetings presenting Liddy plan **5,** 1970-71, 1972

tells Moore about some Hunt-Liddy activities **5,** 1944

tells Moore about telling Nixon **5,** 1996-97

tells Moore he can't write report at Camp David **5,** 1971-72

tells Nixon about Liddy plan meetings **8,** 3074-75

tells Nixon Strachan had prior knowledge of Watergate break-in **FR 26**

testimony before U.S. attorney discussed at Kleindienst-Nixon meeting **9,** 3585-88

testimony on Kalmbach's meeting with Magruder **5,** 2148-49

testimony to prosecutors on Haldeman and Ehrlichman **9,** 3632-36

and transfer of funds from CRP to White House **7,** 2879-80 **8,** 3047

and transfer of funds from White House to CRP **8,** 3195-98

unaware of Nixon rescinding approval of Huston Plan **FR 4**

verification to Mitchell of White House horror stories **4,** 1647

visits to Magruder **2,** 506

Walters' memos on meetings with **9,** 3410, 3411, 3413, 3419, 3815, 3816-17E, 3818E, 3819-20E, 3827E

Walters' opinion of dealings with **9,** 3423

Walters' reports to Helms on meetings with **8,** 3240-42

wants to claim immunity to grand jury **7,** 2754

Watergate investigation by **7,** 2698, 2891-92 **8,** 3094-95, 3113

and White House fund of $350,000 **FR 56**

on White House involvement in coverup **5,** 1890

working relationship with Ehrlichman **6,** 2525-26

working relationship with Haldeman **6,** 2525 **8,** 3020-21

working relationship with Strachan **6,** 2450

Dean, John W., III, testimony of 3, 914-1020, 1021-94 **4,** 1348-1600

on ability to recall details of conversations with Nixon **4,** 1433-34

on access to his files in White House **3,** 1073 **4,** 1531-32

on access to Nixon **4,** 1488-90

and agendas for Nixon's meetings **3,** 988, 1243-44E, 1245-46E **4,** 1485-88

agrees to furnish financial statement to Select Committee **4,** 1378

on Alch's meeting with O'Brien and Mitchell **4,** 1580-81

on asking Gray about documents from Hunt's safe **4,** 1365-66

on attempt to get statement from Liddy **4,** 1452

on attempted retrieval of CIA material on Hunt from Department of Justice **3,** 977-79

on attempts to discredit Ervin **4,** 1533-34

on attempts to get Liddy to disavow his prior knowledge about Watergate **3,** 1005

on attempts to involve CIA in Watergate investigation **3,** 945-58 **4,** 1368-69

on attempts to recruit Tapman for undercover work at Democratic Convention **4,** 1448

on attitude of White House staff toward legality **3,** 915

on attitude toward Liddy's plan **3,** 930-31, 1087-88 **4,** 1413, 1414

on attitude toward meetings with Nixon **4,** 1406-1407

bank statement from National Savings & Trust Company **4,** 1392-93

becomes White House staff member **4,** 1413

on belief that April 15 meeting with Nixon was taped **4,** 1576-77

believes he is being made White House scapegoat for Watergate **3,** 956, 1018-20, 1050, 1077 **4,** 1424-25, 1449, 1490, 1587

believes he is involved in obstruction of justice **4,** 1402

on briefings of Ziegler after Watergate break-in **3,** 1074-75

on Brown's letter **4,** 1598

on burning Kalmbach's notes on distribution of hush money **4,** 1590

call to Sloan on taking Fifth Amendment **3,** 1039

Camp David report with attached handwritten notes **3,** 1006, 1263-93E, *see also* Dean Report

on campaign duties **4,** 1591

on career background **4,** 1413

on Caulfield's dealings with McCord **3,** 974-76

on Caulfield obtaining confidential information from IRS **FR 134**

on circumstances at time he replaced money **4,** 1587-88

claims lack of knowledge of approval by Mitchell of Liddy's plan **3,** 1088

claims privilege against testifying by self-incrimination clause of Fifth Amendment **3,** 912-13

closing statement **4,** 1599

on Colson's FBI interview **3,** 939-40

on Colson's prior knowledge of Watergate **3,** 1050-51

and Colson's taped conversation with Hunt **4,** 1419

on conflict between his testimony and Magruder's **4**, 1442-43

on conflict between Magruder and Liddy **4**, 1443

on conflict in his testimony on Fielding **4**, 1564

on conflicting testimony **4**, 1556

on contacts with Internal Security Division of Justice Deparment **3**, 1057-58

on contents of Hunt's files turned over to Gray **4**, 1362-66

on continuing intelligence activities since Watergate arrests **3**, 1090

on conversation with Mardian on wiretap logs related to newsmen and White House staffers **3**, 1068

on conversation with Moore after McCord's letter to Sirica is read in open court **3**, 1003-04

on conversations with Nixon on coverup **4**, 1521-23

on conversations with Walters **4**, 1449

corroborated by Nixon tapes **FR** 49

on countersuits **4**, 1470-71

on creation of IEC **4**, 1456

on credibility of Nixon vs. his own credibility **3**, 1044, 1094

on CRP fear of demonstrations **4**, 1458-59

on dealings with arrested persons **4**, 1418-19

on "Dean Report" **4**, 1427-28

decision to talk to federal prosecutors **4**, 1385-86, 1394-95

on demands for hush money **4**, 1402-1403,1449,1518

on denial of complicity in Watergate **3**, 1022-24

on desire for immunity as reason for testifying **3**, 1043-44

on difference between investigation and participation in coverup **4**, 1366-67

on discharge from law firm **3**, 1045-46, 1085-86 **4**, 1354-56

on discrepancies between White House memos sent to Select Committee **4**, 1496-97

on discrepancies on location of meeting with Kalmbach **4**, 1511-14

discusses hush money with Moore **3**, 997

discusses immunity with Nixon **4**, 1558

on discussions at White House on separation of powers and Executive privilege for Nixon **4**, 1508-11

on discussions with Nixon on Executive privilege **4**, 1422

on discussions with Walters of CIA **3**, 1037

on documents from Huston **3**, 1062-63

draft letter to Ervin **3**, 997, 1252-57E

draft statement for Nixon re grand jury's investigation into Watergate and leave-of-absence requests from Haldeman, Ehrlichman,and Dean **3**, 1018, 1317-18E

on duties in connection with demonstrations at Justice Department **4**, 1445-46

and early discussions on hush money **FR** 51

on efforts to discredit his testimony **3**, 1085-86

on efforts to obtain immunity **4**, 1436-37

on efforts to use CIA **4**, 1461

on Ehrlichman wanting Hunt to leave country **4**, 1417

on Ehrlichman's instructions to destroy material from Hunt's file **3**, 938

on enemies list **3**, 1073-74 **4**, 1498-99

on establishment of intelligence-gathering capability at CRP **3**, 926-29

evaluation of Petersen **4**, 1554

on events immediately after Watergate break-in **3**, 1048-49

on Executive clemency offers **3**, 972-74 **4**, 1378-79, 1521, 1522

on Executive clemency offers to Magruder **4**, 1443-44 **FR** 70

on Executive privilege waived by White House **4**, 1492-93

on exhibits demonstrating Nixon's knowledge of coverup **4**, 1470-73

exhibits submitted by **4**, 1386-89

expects to become scapegoat for Watergate **4**, 1579

F. Donald Nixon's attitude toward **22**, 10639

on FBI files from Gray **4**, 1358-62

on Fielding's knowledge of coverup **4**, 1438-39

firefighting role at White House **3**, 1027 **4**, 1356

on Fitzgerald's firing by Air Force **4**, 1559-61

on follow-up of decisions of La Costa meetings **3**, 986-91

on Gemstone plan **FR** 21, 22-23

goes to Camp David **4**, 1552

on grand jury hearings **4**, 1384

on Gray saying he lied about Hunt's office in White House **3**, 939-40

guilty plea of **25**, 12403-12304E

on Haldeman and Ehrlichman wanting Mitchell to take blame for Watergate **3**, 1011-13

on Haldeman and Ehrlichman's probable knowledge of Watergate break-in **3**, 1088-89

on Haldeman as his liaison to Nixon **4**, 1353-54

on Haldeman-Ehrlichman relationship **3**, 1052

on Haldeman's information to Nixon **4**, 1470

on handling of FBI interviews at White House **3**, 940-41

on handling of hush money **4**, 1437-39

on handling of press **4**, 1437

on hiring of Liddy by CRP **3**, 927-28 **FR** 18

on House Banking and Currency investigation **4**, 1509

on Hunt and Liddy working together **3**, 1087

on Hunt urged to leave country **4**, 1417

on Hunt's decision to plead guilty **3**, 1053

on Hunt's motion on materials from his safe **4**, 1587-88

and Hunt's safe **4**, 1416

on Hunt's status after death of his wife **3**, 971-72

on hush money **4**, 1390-93, 1416, 1418 **FR** 60-61

on identification of exhibits **4**, 1408-12

on illegality of domestic security methods **3**, 1073

on illegality of his actions in coverup **3**, 1093-94

immunity for and litigation on television and radio coverage of Senate Select Committee hearings **FR** 1079-80

on impact of McCord's letter to Sirica **3**, 1002-1003

on implementation of political enemies project **4**, 1528-31

on indictable list **3**, 1013, 1053-54, 1312E **7**, 2754-57

on information from Internal Security Division to CRP **3**, 1056-57

Dean, John W., III, testimony of *(Continued)*

informed of impending newspaper stories on his prior knowledge about Watergate **3,** 1004 **4,** 1385-86

informs Haldeman that he is talking to special prosecutors **3,** 1010-11

informs Nixon that he is testifying before special prosecutors **3,** 1015-17

on Interagency Evaluation Committee **3,** 1064-65

involvement in Watergate break-in, McCord on **1,** 127, 130, 139, 142-149

involvement with hush money **4,** 1589-90

on IRS and Nixon's friends **4,** 1558-59

and IRS audit on Ryland **22,** 10248, 10249

and IRS audits **4,** 1480-81

on Kalmbach and hush money **3,** 949-51 **4,** 1569-71

on Kalmbach's use of code names **4,** 1570-71

on La Costa meetings with Haldeman, Ehrlichman, and Moore **3,** 982-86 **4,** 1500, 1533-35

lawyers request that he not testify **3,** 1095-98E

on lawyers retained by **4,** 1377

on leaks **3,** 1068-71

on learning about Watergate break-in **3,** 931-38 **4,** 1356

on legality of IEC **4,** 1457

on length of time taken for honeymoon **4,** 1590-95

letter from Garment to **3,** 914, 1099E

on letters to Nixon requesting indefinite leave of absence **3,** 1017, 1018, 1314-15E, 1316E

on Liddy plan **3,** 929-31 **4,** 1417

on Liddy plan related to Watergate break-in **4,** 1351

on Liddy telling him Magruder pushed him into Watergate break-in **FR** 30-31

on Liddy's call to Krogh **3,** 976-77

on Liddy's employment by CRP **4,** 1351-52

on likelihood of Haldeman telling Nixon about Liddy plan **3,** 1024-25

on Magruder perjury **FR** 44-45

on Magruder's diary revealing meetings with Liddy in Mitchell's office **3,** 952-53

on Magruder's employment problems after Watergate **3,** 990-91

and Magruder's testimony before grand jury **3,** 1038

on Magruder's testimony on his involvement in Watergate break-in **4,** 1379-80

on meeting on domestic intelligence between Nixon, Huston, and others **4,** 1452

on meeting with Haldeman on campaign spending **3,** 968, 1226-30E

on meeting with Kalmbach on hush money **4,** 1511-14

on meeting with Kleindienst after Watergate arrests **4,** 1419-20

on meeting with Kleindienst on scope of Watergate investigation **3,** 936-37

on meeting with Krogh about Krogh's relationship with Liddy **3,** 1007-08

on meeting with Liddy after his presentation of intelligence plan **4,** 1353

on meeting with Liddy after Watergate arrests **3,** 993

on meeting with Liddy and Krogh **4,** 1442-43

on meeting with Liddy and Mitchell, agenda prepared by Liddy for **3,** 928, 1150E

on meeting with Mitchell, Mardian, and Magruder after Watergate arrests **3,** 935

on meeting with Nixon, Ehrlichman, and Haldeman **3,** 1000 **4,** 1383-84

on meeting with Nixon, Ehrlichman, Haldeman, and Mitchell **3,** 1000-1002

meeting with Nixon and Haldeman on **4,** 1371-73

on meeting with Nixon on coverup **3,** 1046-47

on meeting with Nixon on hush money **FR** 58

on meeting with Petersen on investigation of White House **3,** 1032-34

on meeting with prosecutors on coverup **3,** 1008-09

on meeting with Segretti **4,** 1373-74

on meeting with Strachan after Watergate arrests **3,** 933-34

on meetings to plan coverup **3,** 1089-92

on meetings with Gray on Watergate investigation **3,** 942-44

on meetings with Haldeman, Ehrlichman, and Mitchell during his talks with prosecutors **3,** 1011-12

on meetings with Mitchell and Magruder after Watergate **3,** 1005-07

on meetings with Mitchell on White House intelligence-gathering against demonstrators **3,** 1059

on meetings with Nixon where Watergate coverup was discussed **4,** 1400-1408

on mental state when taking money out **4,** 1588-89

on message to Liddy to get Hunt out of country **3,** 1037-38

on message to Nixon before going to federal prosecutors **3,** 1015, 1313E

on Mitchell and Magruder remaining at CRP after Watergate arrests **3,** 951-53

on Mitchell as scapegoat **3,** 1092-93

on Mitchell suggesting that Bailey see McCord **4,** 1575

on money from Howard **3,** 1025-26

on money from Strachan and Howard **4,** 1374-77

on money from 1968 primaries **4,** 1581-82

on money received in past year **4,** 1377-78

on money taken for personal use **4,** 1572-73, 1590-95, 1596-97

on money to Wallace's opponent in Alabama gubernatorial race **4,** 1536-37

motivation for replacing money **4,** 1586-90

on nature of his testimony **4,** 1466

on newspaper stories containing his allegations against Nixon **4,** 1440-41

on newspaper story that Segretti saw FBI files **4,** 1360-61

on *Newsweek* article on his prospective testimony **4,** 1441

on Nixon and Patman Committee **4,** 1575

on Nixon and Watergate break-in **4,** 1407

on Nixon and Executive clemency offers to Hunt **3,** 974 **4,** 1467 **5,** 2003

on Nixon receiving news summaries **3,** 1082

on Nixon tapes **FR** 83-89

on Nixon telling him to report directly **4,** 1400-1401

on Nixon wanting him to talk with Ervin and Baker **4,** 1494

Dean, John W., III, testimony of *(Continued)*
on removal of contents of Hunt's safe **3,** 934-35, 937-38
on replacement of money taken from safe **4,** 1573, 1584-87, 1596-97
on request by Haldeman to write report on Watergate **4,** 1384-85
on request for information on FBI activities for other presidents **3,** 1071
on requests by White House people on IRS audits **FR** 137
on resignation **3,** 1020, 1041 **4,** 1318, 1428-29, 1495
response to interrogation prepared by White House **4,** 1412-29, 1431-51, 1451-52
as restraining influence at White House on political intelligence **4,** 1445
on retaining attorneys **4,** 1393-96
on role in briefings of President after Watergate **3,** 1075-81
on role in Intelligence Evaluation Committee **4,** 1447-48
on role in intelligence operations at White House **4,** 1447-48
on role in political intelligence **4,** 1526-31
on role in Watergate coverup **3,** 1035, 1050 **4,** 1357-58
on role of Dent **4,** 1563
on role of Government agencies in domestic intelligence **3,** 10, 71-73
on San Clemente meetings on coverup **4,** 1510-11
on Secret Service report on McGovern **3,** 1071-72
on Segretti matter **3,** 962-66
on so-called Dean investigation of Watergate **3,** 955-56
on source of exhibits **4,** 1387
on Stans role in coverup **4,** 1572
statement of charges against White House and CRP **3,** 1004, 1261E
on statutes on immunity for witnesses before Senate committees **4,** 1349-50
submits exhibits from "Opponents List and Political Enemies Project" file **4,** 1349-50
suggests Sloan take Fifth Amendment **4,** 1418
on suit by DNC **4,** 1575-76
on surveillance of Kennedy **3,** 922-23
on talk with federal prosecutors **4,** 1552-56
on talks with Moore **4,** 1421-22
on taped conversation with Magruder with attached Camp David envelope **3,** 1004, 1258-60E
on taped conversation with Maroulis **4,** 1450
on taped interview with Segretti **3,** 965-66
on telephone call from Nixon after McCord letter is read by Sirica **FR** 89
on telephone conversations with Nixon **3,** 997-98 **4,** 1550-52
on telling Kalmbach about Haldeman's destruction of files **4,** 1369-70
on telling Nixon about coverup **4,** 1541-46
tells Caulfield to make offers to McCord **3,** 1089
tells Ehrlichman about meetings in Mitchell's office on Liddy's intelligence-gathering plans **3,** 934
tells Haldeman and Ehrlichman that they are indictable for obstruction of justice **3,** 1047 **4,** 1422

tells Haldeman he will expose coverup **3,** 1006 **4,** 1399
tells Mitchell and Haldeman White House should not raise hush money **3,** 970-71
tells Mitchell he might "disappear" before grand jury hearing **3,** 1310E
tells Nixon that Haldeman, Ehrlichman, and Dean are indictable **4,** 1547-48
tells Nixon judge will be influenced in civil suit **4,** 1565
tells prosecutors about Fielding break-in **3,** 1042-43
on testimony before grand jury **4,** 1518, 1519-20
on testing credibility with written statement **4,** 1464
on timing of private meetings with Nixon **4,** 1439-40
told by Nixon to deal directly with him **3,** 1078-79
told to "deep six" and shred Hunt's material **3,** 1049
on transmitting materials from Hunt's safe to FBI **3,** 948-49
on trip to Camp David after McCord's letter to Sirica is read in open court **3,** 1002-06
on trip to Manila **3,** 931-32
on use of credit cards **4,** 1514-15, 1516, 1592-94
on use of FBI by White House **3,** 1071-73
on use of IRS against enemies **4,** 1535
on Wallace's opponent receiving money **4,** 1581-82
and Walters **4,** 1415-16
and Watergate break-in **FR** 27-28
on White House allegations that he was participant in break-in and coverup **4,** 1412-29
on White House attitude toward Select Committee **4,** 1493-94, 1501-1502 **FR** 76-80
on White House concept of political enemies **4,** 1459
on White House concern about leaks **3,** 919-22, 1022
on White House efforts to block Patman Committee hearings **3,** 959-62
on White House fear of demonstrations and dissent **FR** 6-7
on White House handling of demands for hush money **3,** 967-71
on White House interest in political intelligence **3,** 922-24, 1021-22 **4,** 1452-59
on White House plan for perpetuation of coverup throughout Senate Watergate investigation **3,** 979-82
on White House reaction to DNC civil suits **FR** 74-75
on White House staff appearances before grand jury **3,** 953-54
on White House statement on Nixon's meetings with Dean **4,** 1422
on White House statement that he was assigned to write written report at La Costa **3,** 966-67 **4,** 1378, 1421-22
on White House violations of Fourth Amendment **4,** 1455
on wiretapping of White House staffers' conversations with newsmen **3,** 920-21

on Ziegler and coverup **3,** 1034-35
on Ziegler's briefings **3,** 1081, 1082-83
Dean, Mrs. John 3, 982, 986, 1310E **4,** 1385, 1441, 1551, 1556, 1592, 1594
Dean memos
on call from Dent re Magruder **3,** 991, 1251E
on counteractions on Democratic party civil suit against CRP **3,** 957, 1173-80E
on "Dealing with Our Political Enemies" **4,** 1526-27 **FR** 7-8, 130-32
on Maroulis conversation with Dean concerning Liddy **3,** 1005, 1262E
on meeting with LaRue on April 13, 1973, re La Rue's appearance before grand jury **3,** 1012, 1311E
on meeting with Mitchell **3,** 1011, 1308-10E
on Segretti matter for Nixon **3,** 1294E-1307E
to Caulfield on antitrust action against *Los Angeles Times* **23,** 11102, 11145E
to Caulfield on obtaining tax information on Goldberg **22,** 10366
to Caulfield to arrange viewing of "Sixty Minutes" show on Hughes-Maheu **23,** 11079, 11133E
to Colson on *Nader* v. *Butz* **FR** 867E
to Colson on O'Brien leasing Government building **23,** 11085, 11137E
to DeMarco, Evans, and Kalmbach on charter for committees working for Nixon's renomination **17,** 7596, 7623E, 8130-34E
to Ehrlichman on *Nader* v. *Butz* **16,** 7182-83, 7397 **FR** 710-11, 863-66E
to Haldeman and Ehlrichman on *Nader* V. *Butz* **16,** 7470, 7510-12E
to Haldeman and Erlichman re O'Brien letter concerning special prosecutor **3,** 943, 1161-68E
to Haldeman entitled "Talking Points for Meeting with Attorney General" **3,** 989, 1247-48E
to Haldeman on Hughes retainer of O'Brien **23,** 11079, 11127-29E, 11130E
to Haldeman on lack of cooperation by IRS on political enemies **FR** 132-33
to Haldeman on *Nader* V. *Butz* **16,** 7470, 7505-09E
to Haldeman re O'Brien's reported involvement in "international consulting firm" **23,** 11076, 11117-18E
to Haldeman re Watergate and Segretti with attachments **3,** 967, 1210-25E
to Higby on additional names for enemies list **4,** 1697-98E
to Higby with attachments **3,** 931, 1151-56E
to Kalmbach on bill from Gleason's lawyer on Common Cause lawsuit **3,** 968, 1231-32E
to Krogh on Brookings Institution **22,** 10356-57 **FR** 142-43
to Mitchell on domestic intelligence **3,** 1063-64
to Mitchell on Huston Plan **FR** 5-6
to Mitchell on IEC **4,** 1457
to Mitchell on Operation Sandwedge **3,** 926, 1149E
to Nixon re congressional hearings regarding Watergate **3,** 980, 1239E
to Strachan on antitrust exemption for Milk Producers Cooperative **16,** 7465, 7499E

to Strachan on possible antitrust exemption for AMPI **FR** 706
to White House staff on dealing with political enemies **4,** 1689-90E
from Colson **3,** 935, 954, 1157-59E, 1169-72E **4,** 1577
from Caulfield **3,** 919, 1108E
from Caulfield on antitrust action against *Los Angeles Times* **FR** 145
from Caulfield on ballot security for 1972 **26,** 10339E
from Caulfield on Hughes retainer for O'Brien **23,** 11079, 11124-26E
from Caulfield on IRS sensitive case report on Graham **23,** 11271, 11272
from Caulfield on McCloskey campaign **3,** 1146-48E
from Caulfield on *Newsday* article **21,** 10126 **23,** 11101, 11143-44E **FR** 135-36
from Caulfield on "opposition activity" **4,** 1688E
from Colson about McGovern staff members **10,** 3975, 4247E
from Colson on Corrupt Practices Act **FR** 787-91E
from Colson on Gibbons' tax return **4,** 1686E **FR** 136
from Colson on information concerning Anderson **4,** 1687E
from Colson on names given top priority on enemies list **4,** 1692-96E
from Colson on note from Hunt **9,** 3807, 3897E
from Colson on Smathers' request **FR** 147
from Colson re Kennedy people and Toyota franchise **23,** 11098, 11138-39E
from Colson with attached report on Hughes-Maheu conflict **23,** 11079, 11134-35E
from Ehrlichman on written retainer arrangement with Kalmbach **7,** 2812-15
from Haldeman on appointment of minority counsel to "Ervin Committee" **3,** 982, 1240-42E
from Haldeman on communist money used for demonstrations against Nixon **8,** 3171-74, 3177-79, 3188-90
from Haldeman on Hughes retainer of O'Brien **8,** 3136, 3137, 3369-71E **23,** 11079, 11130E
from Haldeman with *Newsweek* page "The Periscope" **23,** 11076, 11115-16E
from Haldman on selection of minority counsel by Select Committee **8,** 3203-3204
from Higby on campaign disruptions **3,** 1241E **8,** 3178-79, 3205
from Huston on O'Brien **23,** 11077, 11119-22E
from Jones on "Options for Jeb Magruder" **3,** 990, 1249-50E **4,** 1577-78
from Magruder on federal resources available for campaign **19,** 8597E
from Magruder on federal resources used by Eisenhower, Johnson, and Humphrey for campaign purposes **19,** 8597E **FR** 363-64
from Nixon re college students and demonstrations **3,** 918, 1100E
from Parkinson re 1972 political filings **3,** 961, 1183-89E
from Strachan with additions to enemies list **4,** 1700E, 1701-1702E, 1703-1704E

Dean memos *(Continued)*
from Wilson on proposed antitrust action against
Los Angeles Times **23,** 11102, 11146-48E

Dean Report 3, 955-56, 1002-1006, 1263-93E **4,** 1366-68
draft of Ziegler statement on **3,** 1211-13E
Ehrlichman on **7,** 2720-24
Haldeman on **7,** 2881-83
Mitchell's reaction to Nixon's announcement of **5,** 1900-1901
Nixon assigns Dean to **7,** 2746
Nixon on **4,** 1510
and Watergate coverup **FR** 47
White House questions on **4,** 1421-22, 1427-28

Dean-Nixon meetings *See* Nixon-Dean meetings

DeAntonio, Emile
Caulfield on investigation of **22,** 10379-90 **FR** 144-45

Deboer, Franklin 20, 9610

DeBolt, Ed
confidential memo from Buchanan on topics for discussion at meeting of June 24, 1971 **10,** 3975, 4173E

DeCain, Vincent F. FR 464

Dedicated Americans for Effective Government 13, 5431, 5783E

Dedicated Friends of America 9, 3487

DeDiego
Barker on **1,** 375-76
and Fielding break-in **9,** 3676

DeFalco, Tony 1, 35 **FR** 303E

Defense fund
Dean asks Walters for money from CIA for **8,** 3241 **9,** 3409, 3500
Haldeman on **7,** 2885-86 **8,** 3146-50, 3195-98
Hunt on silence in exchange for **9,** 3803-3804
on March 21 tape **8,** 3077
Parkinson and **9,** 3784
See also Hush money

DeGalindey assassination 21, 9717

DeGooyer, John G.
See Clancy, Lynda E., testimony of; Odell, Robert P., testimony of

Del Campo, Caridad 23, 10967

Del Real, Hilda 23, 10966

Del Real, Juan 23, 10966

Delaney v. *United States* **3,** 1195E

Delano, William A. 14, 5862, 5864 **FR** 688
and ADEPT **FR** 586

Delimitation agreement between CIA and FBI 8, 3239

Dellinger, David 12, 5151E

Dellums, Ronald
on enemies list **4,** 1696E

DeLoach, Cartha 21, 9939 **FR** 118, 144

DeLoach, Deke 3, 922, 981, 1240E **5,** 1824 **8,** 3030 **14,** 6119
and Haldeman memo to Dean on Kendall firing **8,** 3204-3205
meeting with Mitchell on Huston plan **4,** 1603
Nixon believes he is lying about wiretapping in 1968 **3,** 993

DeMarco, Frank 5, 2174 **16,** 7284 **17,** 7610 **23,** 10738
at meeting between Kalmbach, Mehren, Nelson, and Jacobsen **15,** 6443
at meeting with Mehren, Nelson, Jacobsen, and Kalmbach **16,** 7255-61
Barth's contacts with **23,** 11249-50
memo from Dean on charter for committees working for Nixon's renomination **17,** 7596, 7623E, 8130-34E
and Nixon's sale of San Clemente property **23,** 10740
and payment of B & C Investment Corp. taxes **23,** 10754
and refinancing of San Clemente property **23,** 10750
Wakefield reports expenditures on behalf of Nixon to **24,** 11341-42

"Democratic and Republican Contenders"
memo from Magruder to Mitchell **10,** 3975, 4174-84E

Democratic Campaign Manual 10, 3944-46

Democratic National Committee 1, 27
and actions against Nixon during campaign **8,** 3123-24
dirty tricks at **11,** 4377
discussed by Dean, Liddy, Magruder, and Mitchell as target for intelligence-gathering **2,** 789-90, 791, 795, 826
drawing of floor plan of headquarters of **1,** 102E
electronic surveillance plan for **1,** 184, 188
and Gemstone plan **9,** 3747-48
headquarters in Watergate Office Building
See Watergate break-in
Hunt on photos taken in headquarters of **3,** 925, 1133E **4,** 1642-43 **9,** 3735, 3741, 3796
Hunt's assignment to Barker for **9,** 3688
Hunt's investigation of financing of **3,** 1151-56E **9,** 3708, 3709-10, 3711, 3712
information taken from **1,** 206
lawsuit against CRP, *see* Civil suits
Liddy informs Magruder of first successful break-in at **2,** 796-97
wiretapping of headquarters of **1,** 128

Democratic National Convention (1968)
violence at **2,** 862 **12,** 4990, 4992

Democratic National Convention (1972) 10, 4059E, 4060E
airplane hired by Segretti and Kelly to fly over **FR** 174, 176
Barash on security at **12,** 5267-72E
Buchanan on Republican Party activities at **10,** 3932-33
kickbacks from business exposition at **2,** 790, 840-41 **3,** 1153-55E
letter from Strauss to Mehren with proposal for **14,** 6119, 6187-88E
Liddy plan to disrupt **2,** 524 **3,** 929
Mankiewicz on McMinoway's testimony on security job at **11,** 4616-17
Mankiewicz on possibly staged demonstrations at **11,** 4629-30
McGovern denies meeting McMinoway at **11,** 4743E
McMinoway activities at **11,** 4496-5000 **FR** 195-96

and Older Americans Division **19**, 9098E
and Troy **18**, 8482-83
use in Nixon re-election campaign **FR** 423-24
Department of Health, Education, and Welfare (HEW) film
memo from Malek to Novelli on **18**, 8479, 8582E
memo from Todd to Callahan on **18**, 8479, 8578E, 8581E
memo from Todd to Malek on **18**, 8479, 8583E
memo from Todd to Novelli on **18**, 8479, 8580E
Department of Housing and Urban Development (HUD)
Civil Service Commission investigation of **18**, 8228
information to Stans on Priestes **FR** 525
and Model Cities grant in Los Angeles **18**, 8220
Priestes' dealings with **13**, 5713E
and Responsiveness Program **18**, 8237-38, 8245-46, 8251 **FR** 433-34
and Sedan Chair II **6**, 2441
and suspension of Priestes **13**, 5347
Department of Justice 14, 5971
AMPI lawyers and **16**, 6958-59
Antitrust Division documents **26**, 12858-59E
antitrust suit against Hughes Tool Co. **26**, 12792-12818E
and antiwar demonstrations **3**, 917
and appointment of special prosecutor for Watergate case **9**, 3646
and attempts to discredit Ervin **4**, 1533 **8**, 3201, 3202
Caulfield denies getting information on Maheu-Hughes problem from **21**, 9722, 9724
complaints to Barth about tax investigation against Republican State Committee office **23**, 11242-43
conflict on date of knowledge about Ellsberg break-in **7**, 2681
on corporate group solicitation program **FR** 545
Dean's duties at **4**, 1445-46
and Democrats checking on members of Democrats for Nixon **11**, 4626
efforts to convince Alch to have McCord plead guilty **1**, 337-338
establishment of Office of Public Prosecutor within **FR** 1105-1106
guidelines on corporate acquisitions or mergers **26**, 12861-75E
and Intertel **21**, 9735-36
Kleindienst on work relationships at **9**, 3566
letter from Russell to Heininger on complaint of **16**, 7262, 7349-50E
letter to Dash on absence of information on criminal acts involving Democrats **8**, 3132-33, 3321E
and limitations on FBI Watergate investigation **9**, 3502
in Malek's Responsiveness Program **FR** 369
Mardian as assistant attorney general at **6**, 2346
Moore works at **5**, 2000-2001
Patman Committee and **5**, 1898-99
report on "Las Vegas Resort Hotel Situation" **26**, 12888-92E
report on tourism in Nevada **26**, 12881-86E
reports to CRP **1**, 178-181

Select Committee request for evidence on links between violence or disruption and Democrats **8**, 3124
Tax Division
See Walters, Johnnie M., testimony of
Watergate investigation **9**, 3600, 3612, 3620-21, 3637-39, 3640-43
Department of Justice, Antitrust Division
and acquisition of Dunes Hotel by Hughes Tool Co. **22**, 12429E **FR** 996-98
and "anticrime" factor in Dunes decision **FR** 992-94
and investigation of Hughes' hotel activities **FR** 981-83, 989-91
and Mitchell-Danner meeting **FR** 984-89
See also Antitrust suits
Department of Justice, Internal Security Division 1, 246-247
Dean on reasons for contacts with **4**, 1057-58
information to CRP **3**, 1056-57
information to McCord **1**, 217-18, 221-24, 229-32, 234, 237 **2**, 824
and Interagency Domestic Intelligence Unit **3**, 1066
investigations by **6**, 2398-99
Mankiewicz denies McGovern campaign received information from **11**, 4631
Mardian on role as head of **6**, 2420-29, 2434-35
and Pentagon Papers case **6**, 2408-10
reports to CRP **5**, 1842-43
request by Inouye for records on memos to McCord **1**, 348-349
White House use of **FR** 146-47
Department of Labor
contract to Federation of Experienced Americans **FR** 424-25, 428
Dock and Wharf Builders investigation **FR** 411
documents relating to Responsiveness Program in **19**, 8797-8812E
and financing of radio advertising by Federation of Experienced Americans **18**, 8446
grant to Federation of Experienced Americans **18**, 8439, 8440-42, 8447, 8451-57
grants
Responsiveness Program and **18**, 8234-36
and housing rehabilitation **19**, 9229-30E
memo to Malek on responsiveness of **19**, 9338-40E
migrant worker program grant controversy **FR** 433
Reports to Older Americans **19**, 9175-80E
resistance to Responsiveness Program **FR** 431-33
and Responsiveness Program **18**, 8238-39, 8239-40, 8250-51
Responsiveness Program documents **19**, 8797-8812E
Derge, David 19, 8595E
Des Moines Tribune **17**, 7721
Desautels
and White House investigation of Hughes Tool Co. relationship with O'Brien **21**, 9714-15

Detrich, Noah **22**, 10275

Devant, Harry **11**, 4378

Development Associates **13**, 5290-93, 5303, 5312, 5318-20 **18**, 8251, 8252
  letter from Small Business Administration to **13**, 5685E
  loss of grants by **FR** 387-90
  memo from Marumoto to Davison on **13**, 5635-36E

DeVilliers, Darrell C.
  affidavit of **25**, 11951-52E

Devine, Jim **3**, 1064, 1336E

Devine, Sam **18**, 8190-91

DeVos, Lloyd **11**, 4768-77E

DeYoung, Russell
  See Goodyear Tire & Rubber Co.

DeYoung, Russell, testimony of **13**, 5521-30
  on decision to volunteer information to Special Prosecutor **13**, 5529
  on judgment against Goodyear **13**, 5529-30
  on motivation for contribution to Finance Committee **13**, 5527
  on motivations for going to Special Prosecutor **FR** 467-68
  opening statement **13**, 5521-23
  on Parkinson's request for list of contributors **13**, 5525-26
  on return of contribution **13**, 5526
  on source of cash contribution to Finance Committee **13**, 5523-24, 5527-28

DI
  See Dairymen, Inc.

Diamond International Corp.
  campaign contributions by **FR** 464-65

Dibble, Robert **13**, 5412 **FR** 453

Dickerson
  on transcript of discussion with Gray and Von Tobel on Dunes Hotel acquisition **26**, 12790-91E

Diebold, Inc., Canton, Ohio **22**, 10529 **23**, 10948, 10949, 10951, 10954, 10958, 10959
  statements to Key Biscayne Bank & Trust Co. **23**, 10972-74

Diego, Felipe **1**, 235

Diem administration
  coup against **9**, 3808-11
  and Hunt's interview with Conein **9**, 3668-69

Diem cable incident **FR** 125-27, 128
  and Colson **5**, 1932-33 **9**, 3735
  as effort to prevent candidacy of Kennedy **9**, 3780
  Gray reads **9**, 3468, 3484, 3526-27
  Hunt on **9**, 3672-73, 3732-33
  Hunt's motivations for fabrication of **9**, 3741
  in Hunt's safe **FR** 35
  Mankiewicz on **11**, 4601
  Mardian debriefing report to Mitchell on **5**, 1920
  and Pentagon Papers **9**, 3808-3811

Diem papers **4**, 1644

"Dignity Instead of Desperation" **19**, 9187-99E

Dilbeck
  and Duncan loan to Humphrey campaign **25**, 11796, 11797, 11802-04, 11813, 11814

Direct-mail solicitations by CRP **FR** 153-54
  compared with corporate group solicitation program **FR** 547-48
  disguised sources and changes in **FR** 153-154

Dirty tricks
  Bernhard on legislation against **11**, 4674-78
  Buchanan on **10**, 3963-64
  Canuck letter **FR** 207
  Chapin memo on signs to be used at Muskie and Humphrey rallies **11**, 4858E
  and chart of standing of Democratic party primary candidates **11**, 4635-36, 4637E, 4638-44
  Colson and **1**, 89
  Dean's awareness of **4**, 1373-74
  by Democrats against Republicans **11**, 4566-67 **12**, 4925-26
  Ehrlichman on Nixon's desire for improvement in **6**, 2527
  and film strip viewing equipment bought by Porter **2**, 668-69
  fraudulent mailing of Harris poll critical of Kennedy and attributed to Muskie **11**, 4847-51E
  and "funny phones" in office of Senate Subcommittee on Air and Water Pollution **11**, 4665-66
  Gray denies engaging in **9**, 3553
  Haldeman on **7**, 2876-77
  impact on American people **11**, 4694-95
  impact on Democratic party campaigns **11**, 4603-4604 **FR** 205-207
  impact on Muskie campaign **11**, 4666-68, 4683-89
  Kelly on legality of **11**, 4389-91
  Kelly on purpose of **11**, 4393-98
  Kelly's attitude toward role in **11**, 4388-89
  and Lincoln **3**, 1295E
  MacGregor's recommendations for prevention of **12**, 4929
  Magruder asks Porter to lie about money for **2**, 635-36, 643-46
  Magruder tells Mardian about **6**, 2351, 2412
  Mankiewicz on **11**, 4601-4604
  by McGovern campaign, Pearlman denies knowledge of **25**, 12194-95
  by McGovern supporters **11**, 4522-27
  memo from Failor to Magruder on **12**, 5016, 5017
  Mitchell claims lack of knowledge of **4**, 1670
  Mitchell learns about **4**, 1645
  and Muskie campaign **2**, 658 **11**, 4656-57
  in New Hampshire primaries **11**, 4660-62
  and Nixon campaign **11**, 4680 **12**, 4973-4
  O'Brien on **7**, 2735-36
  in other campaigns **11**, 4385-86
  played on Benz in 1970 campaign **11**, 4422-25
  Porter asked by Magruder to give cash to Liddy for **2**, 633-34
  Porter on his involvement in **2**, 646-52
  and rally in support of mining of Haiphong **1**, 68
  reports made to Porter on **2**, 678-79
  Rubin on **25**, 12160
  and Sedan Chair I **FR** 190-92
  Sedan Chair II **FR** 192-96
  Sloan on **2**, 615
  Stearns denies knowledge of Democrats' involvement in **11**, 4590
  Strachan on **6**, 2474-76

Donley, Owen **25,** 12178, 12179-80
Donnelly, Joan **1,** 34
Dore, Ann **1,** 34
Dorn, Evelyn **22,** 10604, 10611, 10728
Dorsen, David M. **4,** 1791E
  on jurisdiction of committee in questioning Van
    Dyk **16,** 7014
  letter from Bray on immunity for Strachan **16,**
    7455, 7472E
  letter from Fortas enclosing transcript of Loeb's
    appearance before Judge Cannella **25,** 11976-
    85E
  letter from Jobe to **7,** 2963-65E
  letter from Kennelly on Jones' billing to AMPI
    17, 8061-64E
  letter from Malek on Responsiveness Program **19,**
    8748E
  letter from Malek with list of contacts for "Re-
    sponsiveness Program" **19,** 8749-50E
  letter from McLaren on *U.S.* V. *AMPI* **17,** 8151-
    54E
  letter from Whitney to **7,** 2959E
  letters from Barker to **7,** 2956E
Dorsen, David M., questioning by
  Campbell **17,** 7786-87, 7788-90
  Clancy **16,** 7403-12
  DeYoung **13,** 5521-27
  Fabrega **13,** 5483-87
  Fernandez **13,** 5359-82, 5399-5402
  Haldeman **16,** 7184-85
  Helms **8,** 3232-42, 3281-87
  Kleindienst **9,** 3560-75, 3608-3610
  Masters **16,** 6945-46, 6960, 6967-68, 6971-72
  Nelson **15,** 6613-16
  Palmby **16,** 7129-35, 7137-46, 7147-50
  Parr **15,** 6851, 6852, 6883-85
  Porter **2,** 631-37, 677-78
  Robinson **13,** 5488-91
  Van Dyk **16,** 7042
  Wild **13,** 5460-66, 5479-81
Dougherty, Richard **11,** 4620 **12,** 5020-21E
Douglas, Cathy **25,** 12166
Douglas, William O. **6,** 2590
Dow, Carolyn **12,** 5085E, 5088E
Downey, John W. **8,** 3277, 3401E
Draft
  McGovern record on **10,** 4066-67E
Draft Mills for President Committee **16,** 7104
  GAO registration form and statement of **25,**
    12072-74E
  letter from Gulf Oil requesting return of Wild
    contribution **25,** 12028, 12029E, 12030
Drew, Elizabeth **10,** 4167E
Drug Abuse Law Enforcement program
  See Dale program
Drug abuse task force
  See Operation Intercept
Du Chessi, William **10,** 4060E
Dubin, David, testimony of **20,** 9418
  on agreement with Edmisten's testimony on
    Xeroxing money from Davis' exhibits **20,** 9416-
    17

Dubrowin, Raphael **FR** 464-65
  guilty plea of **FR** 465
Duffy, Joe **16,** 7015
Duffy, John
  and security at Republican National Convention
    3, 1127E
Dugan, Pat **23,** 11093
"Duke" **FR** 174, 175
Dulles, Allen W. **9,** 3726
Duncan, Carol **20,** 9611, 9612
Duncan, Martha **2,** 650, 668-69
  and documents from Muskie's offices **2,** 669-71
Duncan, Sally **4,** 1495
Duncan, Wallace L.
  See Nunn, Lee, testimony of
Duncan, Walter
  See Duncan loan to Humphrey campaign
Duncan loan to Humphrey campaign **25,** 11728-29
  Cole on **25,** 11795-11804, 11813-14
  default on loan to Humphrey campaign **25,** 11810
  Fellows on **25,** 11771-73
  Morrison on **25,** 11751-53, 11754-59
  used to cover bad checks in West Virginia **25,**
    11771-72, 11773
Dunes Hotel acquisition and Hughes Tool Co. **20,**
    9572-75 **21,** 10055 **22,** 10231, 12429E **23,** 10895,
    11030 **24,** 11564, 11609-10 **26,** 12775-12943E
  Antitrust Division decisions on **FR** 989-91
  collapse of negotiations on **FR** 996-98
  Danner and **21,** 10044-45
  Danner on **20,** 9576-85, 9586-87
  Maheu testimony on **FR** 983-84
  materials pertaining to **26,** 12775-12943E
  and Mitchell **FR** 989-98
  Mitchell-Danner meetings on **FR** 984-89
  and prior Antitrust Division review of Hughes'
    hotel activities **FR** 981-83
  report to Garment on **23,** 11053-56
  Select Committee Final Report on **FR** 980-98
Dunn, Lesley G. **11,** 4859E
Dunn, Winfield **10,** 4207E
Dunnells, G. Richard **13,** 5345, 5348, 5733E
  affidavit of **13,** 5348, 5734-35E
  note to Stans on Priestes **13,** 5348, 5713E
Durand, Daniel M.
  affidavit of **12,** 5009, 5107-09E
Durante, Jimmy **21,** 10051, 10056
Durante, Lou **FR** 559
Durham, Don
  See Segretti, Donald
Dwight, Donald **12,** 5110E, 5115E
Dwinell, Lane **3,** 1139E
Dyson, Charles **8,** 3155
  on enemies list **4,** 1604E, 1698E
Dziekanowski, Tadeusz **11,** 4809E
Dzu, Nho **9,** 3882E
Eagleton, Thomas F. **4,** 1687EF **10,** 3936, 4254E **11,**
    4461, 4520
  invitation to Muskie **11,** 4890E
  McGovern's choice of **10,** 4251E
  Nixon's instructions on **10,** 3940

Eastland, James O.
discussions with Mehren on antitrust suit against AMPI **16**, 7335-36
letter of transmittal from Ervin of Final Report of Select Committee on Presidential Campaign Activities **FR** 5
TAPE contribution to **16**, 7334

Easton, Jack 12, 4950
affidavit on "Nixon is Treyf" leaflet **12**, 5048-50E

Eaton, Ann Schaeffer 25, 12248, 12249, 12275, 12308

Eaton, Barton Denis 25, 12243, 12245, 12246, 12249, 12251, 12275, 12296, 12349E **FR** 475
cancelled checks to Muskie Election Committee **25**, 12371-72E
invoices to Hertz Corp. **25**, 12338-41E

Eaton, Barton Denis, testimony of 25, 12299-12324
on billings to Hertz **25**, 12316-20
on career **25**, 12300
on contribution to Muskie campaign solicited by Edidin **25**, 12303, 12304, 12306-11
on delivery of contribution to Edidin **25**, 12307
denies knowledge of others in Hertz Corp. with knowledge of arrangement with Edidin for campaign contribution **25**, 12324
on duties with Hertz Corp. **25**, 12300-12303
on Edidin's role at Hertz Corp. **25**, 12322
on Hertz Corp. demanding money back for services not rendered **25**, 12322-23
on Hertz policy relative to campaign contributions **25**, 12303
immunity order by Sirica on **25**, 12299
on invoice to Edidin for contribution check **25**, 12309-10
on IRS investigation **25**, 12311-12
on meeting Edidin **25**, 12300
on other attorneys providing legal services for Hertz Corp. **25**, 12320-22
on purpose of billings to Hertz for services not rendered **25**, 12323-24
on purpose of special billing to Edidin **25**, 12314-15
on relationship with Edidin **25**, 12304-12305
on sources of work in Hertz Corp. **25**, 12321
on special projects for Hertz Corp. **25**, 12305-12306
telephone call to Edidin after IRS contact **25**, 12312
telephone call to Ticktin on IRS investigation **25**, 12312-13
on thank-you letter from Muskie committee **25**, 12311

Ebner, Stanley 21, 10189-90 **23**, 11030 **FR** 1064
and Kalmbach's advice to Rebozo on Hughes contribution **FR** 1006, 1007

Eccles, William 14, 5875

Echeverria Alvarez, Luis 13, 5276 **15**, 6549 **16**, 7376
activities planned for visit of **13**, 5605-5606E

Economic Opportunity Act 11, 4463

Edidin, Sol M.
Eaton on relationship with **25**, 12300
and Eaton's contribution to Muskie campaign **25**, 12303-12304, 12306-11
invoice from Lifflander to **25**, 12393E

Lifflander on relationship with **25**, 12262
and Lifflander's invoice for extra work on research project on Hertz franchising **25**, 12266, 12267-68, 12277-81
lunch with Lifflander **25**, 12271
and national campaign requests for rentals **25**, 12326E
Ohrenstein on immunity granted to **25**, 11257-58
relationship with Eaton **25**, 12304-12305

Edidin, Sol M., testimony of 25, 12221-51
on arrangement with Muskie campaign for free Hertz cars **25**, 12236-37
on attorney's fees used to pay bills for Muskie campaign car rentals **25**, 12230-35, 12238, 12241-49, 12250-51
on billing of Hertz vehicles used by Muskie campaign **25**, 12226-27, 12229
contact with Lifflander on bills owed to Hertz by Muskie campaign **25**, 12262-66, 12271-72
on delivery of checks to Muskie campaign **25**, 12233
denies informing Petrie of method of paying Hertz bills of Muskie campaign **25**, 12241
denies knowledge of billing by Hertz Corp. to other presidential candidates **25**, 12250
denies personal contribution to presidential candidates **25**, 12252E
on discussions with Petrie on car rental arrangement with Muskie campaign **25**, 12229-30, 12235, 12240
and Eaton's invoices **25**, 12306
employment history **25**, 12221-22
on events leading to arrangement for Hertz to provide vehicles to Muskie presidential campaign **25**, 12224-26
on Falk's refusal to write off bills to Muskie campaign from Hertz Corp. **25**, 12227-28
on Hertz accounting procedures and Muskie campaign free cars **25**, 12236-37
on Hertz billing system **25**, 12228
and Hertz charge privileges to political parties **25**, 12327E, 12328E
on late arriving bills for Muskie campaign use of Hertz cars **25**, 12235-36
on names of attorneys involved in Hertz Corp.-Muskie campaign bill payment scheme **25**, 12243, 12244-51
on officers reporting to at Hertz Corp. **25**, 12222-23
on persons aware of Hertz arrangement with Muskie campaign **25**, 12238-40
on payment of Hertz bills from Muskie campaign **25**, 12234
on reporting relationships at Hertz Corp. **25**, 12222-23
on responsibility for selection of outside law firms for Hertz **25**, 12223
role at Hertz Corp. **25**, 12322
Smalley's instructions on provision of vehicles to Muskie campaign **25**, 12226
statement of **25**, 12224, 12252-55E
on telephone call from English on Hertz rentals **25**, 12240-41
See also Hertz Corp.

Edmisten, Rufus 14, 6089-91
  on Xeroxing money from Davis' envelopes **20,** 9415-16
Edmisten, Rufus, questioning by 3, 1060 **4,** 1525 **6,** 2478
  Buckley **11,** 4436-48
  Gray **9,** 3473-88, 3551-54
  Spater **13,** 5498-5505, 5519
  Stans **2,** 694-703, 772-74
Edmondson, Senator 16, 7322, 7338
Educational Research Council of America 18, 8481-82
Edwardo
  See Hunt, E. Howard
Edwards, Kip 11, 4406, 4409 **FR** 174-75
EEOC
  See Equal Employment Opportunity Commission (EEOC)
Egan, Arthur C., Jr. 11, 4812-13E
  affidavit of **12,** 5009, 5127-34E
Ehrlichman, Jeanne 5, 2106
Ehrlichman, John D. 1, 25, 58, 80 **2,** 506, 721 **3,** 941 **5,** 1855 **14,** 6418 **17,** 7738, 7756 **22,** 10239, 10730
  access to Nixon **4,** 1489
  after Watergate arrests **5,** 1853
  and AMPI contribution **FR** 593
  and antiwar demonstrations **3,** 915, 917
  and appointment for Leanse **3,** 1103-1108E
  approval of payment of campaign funds to Edward Nixon **23,** 10859-60
  arranges meeting between Chotiner, Nelson, and Kalmbach **17,** 7810, 7812-13 **FR** 659-60
  asks Barth about O'Brien's taxes **23,** 11222, 11224, 11237-40, 11243-44
  asks Caulfield to investigate breaking of My Lai story **22,** 10378
  asks Cushman to supply material to Hunt **FR** 119
  asks Dean to check into Watergate break-in **3,** 1047-48
  asks Dean to retrieve CIA material on Hunt from Department of Justice **3,** 977-79
  asks Dean to retrieve Hunt photos of Fielding break-in from CIA **FR** 75
  asks Moore to investigate Segretti matter **5,** 1954-55
  asks Ulasewicz to locate F. Donald Nixon **22,** 10348
  assigned by Nixon to investigate Watergate break-in **5,** 1915
  and assignment of Buchanan to Ellsberg case **10,** 3911
  assures Colson of Executive clemency for Hunt **FR** 67
  at La Costa meetings with Dean, Haldeman, and Moore **3,** 982-86 **5,** 1940-42, 2049
  at meeting on Segretti matter **5,** 2022-23
  at meeting when Dean tells Nixon about coverup **3,** 1047
  at meeting with Malek, Mitchell, Shultz, and Nixon **18,** 8205-8206
  at Mitchell-Nixon meetings **4,** 1677
  at San Clemente meetings **4,** 1510-11
  and attempts to involve CIA in Watergate investigation **4,** 1368

attitude toward immunity **4,** 1427
attitude toward IRS "unresponsiveness" Barth on **23,** 11229, 11242
attitude toward Meier and Hatsis **22,** 10610-11
and authorization for Fielding break-in **3,** 1007
and authorization for Hunt's request for CIA aid **8,** 3304
and authorization for Ulasewicz payments **8,** 3103
Barth on precedents for allowing him to see tax information **23,** 11227-28
and Barth reports on IRS sensitive case reports **24,** 11628
and Barth's changed assignment at IRS **24,** 11627
and Barth's problems at IRS **23,** 11242
on belief in legality of defense fund for Watergate defendants **FR** 62
and briefing of Ziegler after Watergate **3,** 1074
Butterfield claims lack of knowledge on Nixon's listening devices **5,** 2078, 2085
calls off burglary at Brookings Institution **3,** 920
and cancellation of Gray's meeting with Helms and Walters **9,** 3531
and Caulfield **3,** 924
Caulfield does not inform of Kraft wiretap implementation **21,** 9695
Caulfield on authority for wiretapping of **21,** 9689
and Caulfield's investigation of Meany **22,** 10402
Caulfield's relationship with **1,** 82, 267-268, 270
Caulfield's telephone call after second Watergate break-in **1,** 279
and Chenow testimony to FBI **3,** 941
and CIA assistance to Hunt **FR** 1134
claims information on Fielding burglary was given to Department of Justice **9,** 3603
and Colson's repayment of expenses of Fielding break-in **FR** 698-99
and Colson's taped conversation with Hunt **4,** 1419
contact with Chotiner **FR** 633
contacts Colson on informing dairy leaders of Nixon's reversal of milk price-support decision **FR** 648-49
contacts with CIA **8,** 3281
contacts with Mitchell after Watergate **5,** 1883
conversation with Barth on IRS sensitive case report on Hughes **23,** 11222, 11225-26, 11228-30, 11235-36, 11237-38, 11243-44, 11258, 11277-78E
convicted in Fielding break-in **FR** 15-16
convictions for perjury **FR** 16
and coverup plan for Select Committee hearings **3,** 979-82
Cushman calls on Hunt's additional requests **8,** 3294
and Cushman's loan of equipment to Hunt **8,** 3255
in Cushman's memos on CIA contacts with Hunt **8,** 3295-3300, 3308-3309
and Dahlberg checks coverup **FR** 37
and Davies **21,** 9693
Dean as liaison between Mitchell and **5,** 1900
Dean informs of efforts to block Patman Committee hearings **3,** 960
Dean on role in Watergate break-in **3,** 1048-49

Dean report on **3**, 1267E

Dean reports conversation with Gray to **3**, 943, 944

Dean reports on FBI interview files to **4**, 1360

and Dean talking with federal prosecutors **4**, 1552

and Dean's decision to expose coverup **4**, 1398, 1399-1400

on Dean's "indictable" list **5**, 1989

and Dean's information for President **4**, 1381

and Dean's involvement in coverup **2**, 803-804

and Dean's meeting with Kalmbach on Segretti matter **5**, 2130

Dean's meetings after Watergate with **4**, 1420

and Dean's memorandum to Nixon on Senate hearings **3**, 979-80

and Dean's offer of Executive clemency to Magruder **4**, 1443-44

and Dean's reference to Walters in telephone call **8**, 3240

and Dean's report on Watergate **3**, 967

and Dean's tape of conversation with Segretti **3**, 966

Dean's testimony to prosecutors on **9**, 3632-36

delegation of political tasks to **6**, 2518-19

and demonstrations **4**, 1448

demonstrations during testimony of **7**, 2904-2905

and designation of Rebozo as Nixon's agent **24**, 11302-11305

directs Caulfield to send Ulasewicz to Chappaquiddick **FR** 110

discussion with Dean on Hunt's safe **FR** 35-36

discussion with Kalmbach on breaking off contact with "milk people" **FR** 726

discussions with Barth on IRS interviews of Rebozo and F. Donald Nixon **23**, 11244-46

discussions with Mitchell on Ellsberg matter **5**, 1905

discussions with Mitchell on White House horror stories **4**, 1625

discussions with Rebozo on Hughes **21**, 10129-30

dispute with Malek **12**, 4944

and efforts to involve CIA in Watergate investigation **3**, 946, 947 **5**, 1884

and efforts to obtain milk price-support increases **15**, 6570

and Ellsberg case **5**, 1960-61, 2061-62 **8**, 3032 **9**, 3806

and employment of Caulfield **1**, 251-252

and employment of Hunt at White House **9**, 3662

and Executive clemency offers to Hunt **3**, 973-74, 1079 **5**, 2003

and Executive clemency offers to McCord **1**, 257 **4**, 1379

and Executive privilege **5**, 1821

expresses concern for Krogh **3**, 1008

F. Donald Nixon denies notification of IRS audit by **22**, 10704

and F. Donald Nixon's financial activities **21**, 9701-9704

and F. Donald Nixon's relationship with Meier **22**, 10707-10708

and F. Donald Nixon's trip to Dominican Republic with Meier and Hatsis **22**, 10729-30

and FBI investigation **3**, 942, 943 **9**, 3532

and funding for Ulasewicz **3**, 926

and grand jury hearings **4**, 1384

Gray claims lack of knowledge of meeting with Haldeman and Walters **9**, 3499

Gray denies he made any inquiries on FBI Watergate investigation **9**, 3494

Gray on suspicions about **9**, 3530-31

and Gray's confirmation hearings **9**, 3488

in Gray's testimony on Hunt's files **9**, 3467-68, 3469, 3470-71

Haldeman on testimony on La Costa meetings **8**, 3055-56

handwritten notes re investigation into Watergate affair by **7**, 2730, 2915-43E

and help from CIA **3**, 1037

hiring of Caulfield by **21**, 9687 **FR** 107

Hunt threatens to testify about his role in Watergate **3**, 999 **4**, 1382, 1567

and Hunt's decision to plead guilty **3**, 1053

and Hunt's employment at White House **9**, 3779

and Hunt's files given to Gray **9**, 3513-14

and Hunt's requests from CIA for equipment **8**, 3234, 3283, 3284-85

and Hunt's safe **4**, 1416, 1588

and Hunt's threats **4**, 1426

and hush money **3**, 950, 951, 969-70, 971 **4**, 1370, 1402, 1416, 1648-49 **5**, 2149, 2161 **FR** 51-52

and information from Barth at IRS **21**, 9710-11

informed by Dean that material from Hunt's safe was going to FBI **3**, 948

informs F. Donald Nixon of forthcoming IRS interview **24**, 11651-52

informs Mitchell about Magruder's allegations on his involvement in Watergate **5**, 1915-16

informs Rebozo of IRS investigation **21**, 10090 **22**, 12441E

instructions to Dean on material from Hunt's file **3**, 938, 1008

instructions to Kalmbach for meeting with Nelson and Chotiner **17**, 7812-13

instructs Caulfield to desist from wiretapping Kraft **21**, 9694-95

and Intelligence Advisory Committee **1**, 201

interview of Ulasewicz **6**, 2220, 2239, 2264-65

investigation of Watergate by **8**, 3095

involvement in Watergate coverup **3**, 993, 1003, 1027, 1054, 1088-89 **5**, 2007

and IRS audit of O'Brien **FR** 1025-30

and IRS sensitive case reports **23**, 11267-68

justification for Fielding break-in **8**, 3304

and Kalmbach **5**, 2092

Kalmbach feels used by **5**, 2175

Kalmbach on awareness of AMPI contribution and objectives **17**, 7811

Kalmbach on Dean's claim that he was speaking on behalf of **5**, 2115-16

Kalmbach on knowledge of disbursement to Caulfield **21**, 10185

and Kalmbach's break with milk people **17**, 7618-19, 7622

Kalmbach's confidence in **5**, 2121

and Kalmbach's contacts with Semer **17**, 7583

and Kalmbach's decision to stop raising and delivering money for Watergate defendants **5**, 2110

Ehrlichman, John D. *(Continued)*
tells Nixon and Dean that everyone should go to grand jury **8**, 3071-73
tells Walters it is all right to talk with Dean **9**, 3408, 3409
and theory on Mitchell "taking the rap" **3**, 1011-13
Thompson on audience treatment of **7**, 2863
and threatening telephone call to Parr **16**, 7448
Ulasewicz and **1**, 289
urges MacGregor to make statement answering *Washington Post* article on Haldeman **12**, 4903
visit to Hallamore Homes project **22**, 10684-89, 10706
Wakefield and **24**, 11300-11305
Walters' affidavit on discussions with **9**, 3419, 3828-29E
in Walters memo **9**, 3816E
wants Dean to see FBI reports on Watergate investigation **3**, 944
wants Hunt told to leave country after Watergate arrests **3**, 934, 1037-38, 1091 **4**, 1417
and Watergate coverup **2**, 873
Watergate investigation by **9**, 3577-78, 3602
White House information withheld from **6**, 2503
and White House staff transfers to CRP **1**, 83
and White House Watergate investigation **FR** 90
and wiretap logs of conversations between White House staffers and newsmen **3**, 919, 920
and wiretapping of F. Donald Nixon **21**, 9700-9707
and wiretapping of Kraft **21**, 9687-99 **23**, 10912 **FR** 112
Young tells Malloy he requested CIA psychological profile of Ellsberg **25**, 12422E
and Young's request for CIA psychiatric profile of Ellsberg **8**, 3235
Ehrlichman, John D., testimony of 6, 2509-87, 2599-2632 **7**, 2663-2727, 2729-93, 2796-2865 **16**, 7373-7402 **18**, 8187-98 **21**, 9677-85
on access to records at White House **7**, 2859-60
on AMPI's contributions to legislators **16**, 7400
on antitrust suit against AMPI **16**, 7397-98
on apparent administration support for Gray nomination **7**, 2811-12
on assignment to investigate Watergate **7**, 2759-70
on attitude toward Fielding break-in becoming known to public **6**, 2541-53
on attitude toward Hoover's competency **7**, 2691-92
on attitude toward release of White House tapes **7**, 2687-90
on authorization for Brookings Institution fire-bombing **6**, 2536
on authorization for Fielding break-in **7**, 2771-72
on Barth informing him of IRS investigation of Rebozo **21**, 9679-85
on briefing on legal aspects of Watergate **7**, 2750-51
on briefings of Ziegler **7**, 2761-62
on career **6**, 2522-24
on Caulfield's offer of clemency to McCord **7**, 2771
on Chapin's role in Segretti matter **7**, 2846-47

on CIA and Watergate **6**, 2563-64
cites precedent for Stans not testifying before grand jury **7**, 2797-98
claims he did not tell Nixon about hush money **7**, 2726
claims national security privilege on wiretapping of F. Donald Nixon **FR** 113
closing statement **7**, 2864-65
on Colson's information on O'Brien **21**, 9682-83
on conflicts in testimony **7**, 2772-73
on congressional activity on milk price-support issue **16**, 7399-7400
on contacts with representatives of dairy industry during period between milk price-support decisions **16**, 7384-86
on contrasting procedures under Kennedy and Nixon administrations for White House access to tax records **7**, 2798, 2800
on contributions to Mills from dairy industry **16**, 7401-7402
on creation of CRP **6**, 2538-39
on criticisms of OMBE **18**, 8194-95
on dairy industry contributions and requests for quid pro quo **16**, 7374-75, 7377, 7399
on Dean having raw data from FBI **7**, 2722-23
on Dean memo on *Nader* v. *Butz* **16**, 7397
on Dean-Mitchell-Haldeman meeting **7**, 2745
on Dean-Nixon meetings **7**, 2715-16, 2853-54, 2855-57
on Dean's assignment to write Watergate report **7**, 2746
on Dean's claim that he told Nixon everything **7**, 2746-47
on Dean's investigation of Watergate **7**, 2720-24, 2753
on Dean's involvement in Watergate **7**, 2743-44
on Dean's indictable list **7**, 2714, 2716, 2855-56
on Dean's report about photographs of Fielding break-in **6**, 2553
on Dean's report on Watergate **6**, 2541
on Dean's testimony **6**, 2561-62 **7**, 2824-28
on Dean-Walters meeting **7**, 2835
on defense funds for Ellsberg and Davis **6**, 2567, 2570
on delay of Gray's resignation **7**, 2678-79
on demonstrations against Nixon **FR** 209
on demonstrations and political climate during Nixon administration **6**, 2512-13
denies approving Liddy's assignment to CRP **FR** 18
denies awareness of contacts between Kalmbach and dairy people in 1972 **16**, 7398-99
denies Chotiner contact with White House in period between milk price-support decisions **16**, 7384-85
denies Colson's testimony that he requested money for Krogh **16**, 7394-95
denies discussing Fielding break-in with Mitchell **7**, 2781-82
denies discussing grantsmanship plan with Nixon **18**, 8195-96
denies discussing milk industry issues with Mitchell **16**, 7399
denies discussions with Kalmbach on contributions **16**, 7390

denies early knowledge of CRP involvement in Watergate **6**, 2583-84

denies instructing Dean to tell Hunt to leave country **7**, 2718-20

denies knowledge about Nixon's first meeting with dairy industry representatives **16**, 7376-77

denies knowledge of Baroody or Webster's role in Colson's use of milk fund **17**, 7896

denies knowledge of Colson contact with dairy industry representatives **16**, 7375

denies knowledge of contact between dairy industry representatives and White House staff members **16**, 7391-93

denies knowledge of dairy industry pledges in 1971 and 1972 **16**, 7394

denies knowledge of Dita Beard matter **7**, 2832-33

denies knowledge of Huston plan **7**, 2817-20

denies knowledge of initiation of Responsiveness Program **18**, 8192-93

denies knowledge of Liddy budget money **7**, 2717-18

denies knowledge of White House taping **6**, 2585

denies prior knowledge of Watergate break-in **6**, 2579-80

denies secrecy of Plumbers **7**, 2691

denies seeing Dean's indictable list **7**, 2857

denies seeing documents sent by Fielding on Fishers Island **21**, 9678

denies telling Dean to "deep-six" briefcase with Hunt's documents **6**, 2613

on discussion of his testimony with Haldeman **7**, 2860

on discussion with Nixon on Watergate break-in· **6**, 2554-55

on discussions of campaign contributions with Haldeman **16**, 7375-76

on discussions with Byrne on directorship of FBI **6**, 2617-22

on discussions with Connally on dairy industry **16**, 7385-86

on discussions with Kalmbach on dairy contributions through Semer in 1969 **16**, 7373-74, 7375, 7377, 7378

on Dita Beard matter **6**, 2622-23

on duties as White House counsel to Nixon from 1969-70 **6**, 2514-15

on duties at White House after Watergate break-in **7**, 2717-18

on enemies list **7**, 2683-86

on events leading up to Nixon's announcement of new developments in Watergate **7**, 2757-58

on Executive clemency offers **6**, 2607-12 **7**, 2847-50

on factual basis for Nixon's statement of April 17 **7**, 2857-58

on FBI investigation of Ellsberg case **7**, 2667-82

on FBI leaks **7**, 2675

on FBI Watergate investigation and CIA **7**, 2799

on Fielding break-in **6**, 2536, 2551-52, 2599-2607 **7**, 2681 **FR** 13-16, 122

on forthcoming criminal trial **16**, 7396

on Gifford's role during campaign **18**, 8195

on Gray confirmation hearings **7**, 2679

on Gray destroying documents from Hunt's safe **6**, 2615-16 **7**, 2675-76

on Gray nomination by administration **7**, 2788-89

on Gray resignation over refusal to suppress FBI investigation of Watergate **7**, 2711-13

on Haldeman and Nixon wanting improved domestic intelligence program **6**, 2527

on Helms-Walters meeting **7**, 2833-35

on Hillings' letter to Nixon **16**, 7377-81

on hiring of Hunt **6**, 2532

on hiring of Ulasewicz **7**, 2775-76

on his loyalty to Nixon **7**, 2864

on his own and Nixon's belief that there was no White House involvement in Watergate **7**, 2769-70

on Hoover's attitude toward Ellsberg case **6**, 2606

on Hoover's letter to Krogh **6**, 2627-28

on Hunt's demands for money **6**, 2550-51 **7**, 2770-71, 2852

on Hunt's safe **6**, 2612-16

on Huston Plan **6**, 2527-29

on information on Watergate given to Nixon **7**, 2810-11

on innocence of wrongdoing **6**, 2624

on inquiry into Watergate **7**, 2713-14, 2727, 2857

on instructions to Hunt to leave country **7**, 2718-20

on interview notes kept during inquiry into Watergate **7**, 2729-31

on interview with Colson **7**, 2800-2801

on interview with Kalmbach **7**, 2768-69

on interview with Magruder **7**, 2765-66

on interview with O'Brien **7**, 2731-36, 2751-52

on interview with Strachan **7**, 2767-68, 2864

on interviews during his inquiry into Watergate **7**, 2727, 2763-70

on investigations of candidates **7**, 2776-80

on investigations of Watergate **6**, 2555-56 **7**, 2698-99

on IRS audit of Rebozo **21**, 9684-85

on IRS investigation against Hughes Tool Co. involving O'Brien **21**, 9683-84

on issues of importance at White House after Watergate break-in **6**, 2519-20

on justification for Fielding break-in **6**, 2575-79, 2629-30, 2632-33 **7**, 2692-93

on justification for intelligence gathering by White House **6**, 2537-38

on Kalmbach raising money for Watergate defendants **6**, 2568-69, 2570-75 **7**, 2840-45

on Kalmbach's use of milk fund **16**, 7378

on knowledge about Magruder's involvement in Watergate **7**, 2845-46

on knowledge of AMPI contributions to congressional elections of 1970 **16**, 7378

on La Costa meetings **7**, 2849-51 **FR** 77

on LaRue's role in raising money for Watergate defendants **7**, 2853

on leaks at FBI **6**, 2562

on learning about Liddy plan meetings from Dean **7**, 2753-54

on learning facts about Watergate break-in **6**, 2539-41, 2580-87

on learning of Hunt's involvement in Watergate **6**, 2540-41

on legality of actions **6**, 2569-70

Ehrlichman, John D., testimony of *(Continued)*
on legality of Fielding break-in **7,** 2815-21
on legality of Ulasewicz's activities before Watergate **7,** 2773-80
on Malek's political capabilities to execute Responsiveness Program **18,** 8197
on Marumoto's role in campaign **18,** 8197-98
on meeting to discuss Huston Plan **6,** 2527-28
on meeting with Dean, Clawson, Colson, and Kehrli **7,** 2822
on meeting with Haldeman, Helms, Walters **7,** 2823-2824
on meeting with Haldeman and Dean **7,** 2741-45
on meeting with Haldeman and Malek on Responsiveness Program **18,** 8188-89
on meeting with Rebozo on *Newsday* series **21,** 9681-82
on meeting with Shultz and Hardin **16,** 7383-84
on meetings and telephone calls after Watergate break-in **6,** 2581-87
on meetings with CIA after Watergate break-in **6,** 2555-56
on meetings with Colson **6,** 2608-12
on meetings with Dean **6,** 2521, 2522 **7,** 2740, 2754-57, 2759-61, 2821-22, 2835-36
on meetings with Helms and Walters **6,** 2558, 2559 **7,** 2694-95, 2782-86, 2823-24
on meetings with Nixon **6,** 2556, 2584-87, 2609 **7,** 2770-71, 2807-2809, 2822-23, 2848-49
on memo for Walters on meetings with Haldeman, Helms **7,** 2786, 2948-49E
on memo from Young on Pentagon Papers Affair **6,** 2554, 2646-51E
on memo to Dean re written retainer arrangement with Kalmbach **7,** 2812-15
on method of preparing his testimony **7,** 2860
on milk price-support decisions **16,** 7381-90
on milk price-support decisions in other administrations **16,** 7400-7401
on Mills' activity on milk price-support issue **16,** 7399
on Mitchell's attitude toward Ellsberg matter **6,** 2543
on Mitchell's reactions to "White House Horrors" **7,** 2780-82
on Mitchell's resignation **7,** 2724-25
on Mitchell's testimony on White House horrors **7,** 2831-33
on money for Watergate defendants **6,** 2566-75
on Nixon appointing Dean as chief investigator of Watergate **7,** 2739-40
on Nixon calling Gray at urging of MacGregor **12,** 4916, 4918
on Nixon tapes supporting his contentions **6,** 2616-17
on Nixon's attitude toward Ellsberg matter **6,** 2543-44
on Nixon's attitude toward programs such as Responsiveness Program **18,** 8196
on Nixon's attitudes toward grants and regulatory bodies **18,** 8190-92
on Nixon's concern over CIA and FBI Watergate investigation **7,** 2824
on Nixon's discussion with him on leave of absence **7,** 2809

on Nixon's efforts to obtain information on Watergate break-in **7,** 2802-2803
on Nixon's instructions after Watergate break-in **6,** 2557-66 **7,** 2798-99
and Nixon's invitation to attend dairy industry convention in 1970 **16,** 7376
on Nixon's knowledge of dairy industry contributions **16,** 7386
on Nixon's knowledge of Special Investigations Unit **6,** 2564-65
on Nixon's meeting with Kleindienst and Petersen **7,** 2857
on Nixon's meeting with representatives of dairy industry **16,** 7382, 7387-90
on Nixon's methods of investigating Watergate break-in **7,** 2695-97
on Nixon's position on immunity for White House staff **7,** 2831
on Nixon's press statements on Watergate **7,** 2762-63
on Nixon's reaction to Gray's destruction of Hunt files **7,** 2677-78
on Nixon's reasons for appointing Dean as chief investigator **7,** 2740-41
on Nixon's request that Stans not be compelled to go before grand jury **7,** 2790, 2792
on Nixon's statement of May 22 on Watergate investigation **6,** 2555-56 **7,** 2858
on Nixon's statement on Fielding break-in **6,** 2553
on note from Young and Krogh on Pentagon Papers Project--Status Report **6,** 2554, 2643-45E
on notes of meeting with Kalmbach **7,** 2773, 2947E
on notifying Rebozo of IRS investigation **FR** 1067
on opening Hunt's safe **7,** 2824
on origin of suggestion of Byrne for FBI directorship **7,** 2811-12
on paragraph missing from memo from Krogh to Young to Ehrlichman **7,** 2702-10
on planned firebombing of Brookings Institution **6,** 2535-36
on political pressures on administration on milk price-support issue **16,** 7401
on possibility of conflict between his testimony and Haldeman's **7,** 2861-63
on possible content of Hunt's blackmail **7,** 2853
on presidency **6,** 2515-16
on press comments on his notes of interviews **7,** 2802
on prior testimony **6,** 2510-11
on psychiatric profile as reason for Ellsberg break-in **7,** 2673-74
on public defense fund in Florida for Watergate defendants **6,** 2567-68
questions he wishes to set the record straight on **6,** 2511-12
on reaction to Fielding break-in **6,** 2623-24
on reaction to Watergate break-in **6,** 2582
on reasons for creation of Plumbers **FR** 120
on reasons for keeping information away from Nixon **7,** 2716-17, 2804-2805
on receipt of campaign funds since January 1969 **7,** 2858-59
on recording conversaton with Kalmbach **6,** 2572-75

refuses to discuss private conversations with Nixon **16,** 7393

on relations of White House staff to President **6,** 2516-17

on relationship with Haldeman **6,** 2521-24

on reporting to Nixon about Dean's findings **7,** 2724, 2737, 2757-58

on Republican fundraising dinner in 1971 **16,** 7390-91

on request to Petersen not to ask Stans to testify before grand jury **7,** 2699-2701

on resignation **7,** 2809

on Responsiveness Program
  and Cabinet **18,** 8193-94
  denies familiarity with memos on **18,** 8187-88
  denies formal knowledge of **18,** 8198
  Nixon and **18,** 8189-92

on results of Watergate inquiry **7,** 2750-57

on role as assistant to President **6,** 2517-18, 2520-22 **7,** 2683-86, 2870

on role in preparations for 1972 Republican fundraising effort **16,** 7377

on role in selection of Presidential appointees **7,** 2682-83

on role in setting up special White House unit on leaks **6,** 2529-33

on role in Watergate-related issues **6,** 2521, 2522

on SALT leak **6,** 2533

on Sandwedge plan **6,** 2536-37 **FR** 17-18

says Magruder admitted approval of Liddy plan along with Mitchell and LaRue **7,** 2766

says Magruder named Dean as preparer with Liddy of break-in plan **7,** 2766

says Nixon told him Dean was involved in cover-up **7,** 2747

says Strachan never mentioned Haldeman's instructions to destroy documents **7,** 2745

on Sloan's efforts to inform him **7,** 2699

on sources of information on Watergate **7,** 2762-63

on statement by MacGregor that Ehrlichman lied to him **7,** 2803-2804

statement of **6,** 2510-22

on Strachan's advice to young Americans to stay out of government service **7,** 2864-66

on Strachan's memo to Haldeman on use of milk fund money **16,** 7395

on Strachan's working relationship to Haldeman **6,** 2526-27

on symbols used in interview notes **7,** 2736-37

on taped conversation with Gray **7,** 2786-90 **9,** 3469, 3512, 3536-39

on taped meeting with Mitchell **7,** 2736-37

on taped telephone conversation between Hunt and Colson **7,** 2852-53

on taped telephone conversation with Clawson **7,** 2826-2827, 3009E

on taped telephone conversation with Gray **7,** 2786, 2837, 2838-39, 2950E

on taped telephone conversation with MacGregor **7,** 2814, 2815, 3007-3008E

on taped telephone conversations with Dean **7,** 2786, 2838, 2950-51E, 2952-53E

on taped telephone conversations with Kalmbach **7,** 2737-39, 2842-44

on taped telephone conversations with Kleindienst **7,** 2714-15, 2747-50, 2944-46E

on termination of Special Investigations Unit **6,** 2556

on timing of knowledge about Watergate break-in **6,** 2554

on timing of learning about Liddy plan meetings **7,** 2804-05

on Ulasewicz's role at White House **6,** 2515

on use of IRS **7,** 2684-86

on use of Plumbers instead of FBI **6,** 2625-29

on use of psychiatric profiles **7,** 2673-74, 2690-91

on use of recording device **7,** 2738

on Walters-Gray meeting **FR** 37-38

on White House reaction to Watergate **6,** 2513-14

on White House requests for tax information **7,** 2684-86

on willingness to assist Select Committee in identification of his records **7,** 2860

on working relationship with Colson **6,** 2526

on working relationship with Dean **6,** 2525-26

on working relationship with Haldeman **6,** 2524-25

"8-A Program" 18, 8273, 8423-26

Eisenhower, David 22, 10633
  Barth and **24,** 11625
  Rebozo on purchase of house for **21,** 10132-33

Eisenhower, Dwight 9, 3432 **11,** 4478, 4584
  advice to Haldeman **7,** 2868
  use of Federal resources for campaign purposes **19,** 8597E-99E **FR** 363-64

Eisenhower, Julie Nixon 12, 5046E **21,** 10132-33 **FR** 1034

Eitreim, Irven M. 18, 8444-45, 8458
  on OEO grant to Federation of Experienced Americans **FR** 425-27

El Diario
  memo from Marumoto to Lynn on editorial in **13,** 5323, 5535E

El Pueblo con McGovern 12, 4950-51, 4959, 4960 **25,** 12183
  campaign contributions **FR** 511-12
  connection with Watergate **2,** 786

Elder, James Leo
  memo to "file" on Cole loans to Humphrey campaign **25,** 11793E

Elder, James Leo, questioning by
  Chestnut **25,** 11721, 11739-40, 11744
  Cole **25,** 11807-11808, 11814-15
  Hanman **14,** 5894-95
  Morrison **25,** 11759-60

Eldorado International, Inc.
  business dealings with Humphrey campaign **25,** 11753
  Morrison's position at **25,** 11747-48

Eldredge, Harold W. 10, 3975, 4264E **11,** 4811E

Election campaign law
  Baker on **11,** 4686
  Dahlberg check and **2,** 748-50
  and transfer of money from CRP to White House **6,** 2461
  See also Federal Election Campaign Act of 1971; Senate Select Committee Final Report

letter to Andrade on appearance of Fernandez before Select Committee **13,** 5398, 5747E

See also Fernandez, Benjamin, testimony of

Embassies

McCord's plan on **1,** 281-83 **3,** 975-76

"EMK--Political Memorandum"

from Buchanan to Nixon **10,** 3975, 4167-72E

Enemies list 3, 958-59, 1073-74 **4,** 1400, 1408-11

academics on **4,** 1725E

action on **4,** 1528-31

additions to **4,** 1408-12, 1556-57, 1713-24E, 1725-29E

Barth denies knowledge of Dean-Walters meeting on **23,** 11244

business people on **4,** 1721-23E

celebrities on **4,** 1720E

and concept of presidential power **FR** 7-12

Corporate Executives Committee for Peace Trip to Washington list on **4,** 1730-32E

and Dash's questions to Rebozo on use of IRS **21,** 10127

Dean memo to White House on dealing with **4,** 1689-90E

Dean on concept of **4,** 1459, 1498-99, 1526-31

and Democratic contributors in 1968 campaigns **4,** 1733E

discussion in Dean-Nixon meeting **8,** 3210-11

Ehrlichman denies knowledge of **7,** 2683-84

Fitzgerald case and **4,** 1559-61

Gibbons on **4,** 1686E

given to Walters by Dean **24,** 11691-11716E

and grant awarding by Nixon administration **13,** 5311

Haldeman on **8,** 3154-58, 3213-14

and IRS **4,** 1461-62 **6,** 2486-87 **FR** 51, 132-33

labor leaders on **4,** 1719E

and Lofton's activities **11,** 4682

Mankiewicz on **11,** 4602

McGovern campaign staff on **4,** 1707-11E

media and newspaper men and women on **4,** 1716-18E

memo from Colson to Dean on names given top priority on **4,** 1692-96E

memo from Dean to Higby on additional names for **4,** 1697-98E

memo from Strachan to Dean on Miller and **4,** 1703-1704E

memo from Strachan to Dean with additions to **4,** 1700E

Muskie contributors on **4,** 1734-53E

and Nixon **4,** 1479-80

organizations on **4,** 1715E

participants in National Labor for Peace Organization on **4,** 1705-1706E

Picker on **11,** 4649

politicians on **4,** 1713-14E

recipients of **4,** 1409

release of **4,** 1400

removal of Gues from **4,** 1691E

"Salute to Victor Reuther" sponsors on **4,** 1728-29E

Semer on **16,** 7212-13

Strauss and **4,** 1699E

and taped discussion between Nixon, Dean, and Haldeman **FR** 9-12

top **20,** 4, 1529

and Wallace **4,** 1536

and White House use of IRS **FR** 108

English, Jack 11, 4767E, 4772E, 4773E, 4775E **25,** 12109

telephone call to Edidin on Hertz rentals **25,** 12240-41

Engman, Lew 19, 8817E

Enthoven 10, 4151E

Environment issue

Muskie on **10,** 4151E

Epstein, Fred 11, 4548-49 **FR** 209

Equal Employment Opportunity Commission (EEOC) 18, 8243, 8389-92E

memo from Florence to Armendariz on termination of Pena from **13,** 5669E

Pena firing from **13,** 5293-94, 5304

and Responsiveness Program **18,** 8243

and University of Texas suit **18,** 8240-41 **FR** 410

Equal Employment Opportunity in the Federal Government; Executive Order 11478 19, 8706-8707E

Erikson, Ralph 4, 1559

Ervin, Sam J., Jr. 1, 6, 8, 9, 22, 23, 26, 28, 34, 35-36, 41, 56, 69, 75

absence for vote on nomination of Richardson for Attorney General **1,** 293

acceptance of affidavits in lieu of testimony **12,** 5008-5009

on access to Dean's files **4,** 1532

analysis of characterization of Stans' testimony by **13,** 5348, 5716-32E

announces Shultz call as hoax **6,** 2360-61

appearance on "Face the Nation" discussed at Dean-Nixon meeting **3,** 997

attempts to discredit **4,** 1533 **8,** 3201-3202

on attorney-client privilege **6,** 2382-83

on attorney-client privilege and Dean-Segretti relationship **10,** 4035-42

on audience demonstrations during Ehrlichman testimony **7,** 2904-2905

on Baker's request that counsels annotate their notes with page references to previous testimony **8,** 3045

on Baldwin's immunity from prosecution **1,** 391

on Bellino's whispering **22,** 10520

on Billy Graham Day ceremonies in North Carolina **8,** 3153

on Buzhardt's claim of attorney-client privilege covering discussions with Garment **22,** 10541, 10543, 10544

on Buzhardt's questions **4,** 1347-48, 1351

on campaign financing **11,** 4696

on Colson appearing as witness **8,** 3220, 3221

commends Atkins for voluntary disclosure to Special Prosecutor **13,** 5449

on Committee staff **7,** 2906

confidence of American people after Watergate **11,** 4694-95

on contributions to Young Republicans after Watergate **13,** 5478

on Davis' objections to Glaeser testimony in executive session **20,** 9414-15

Ervin, Sam J., Jr. *(Continued)*

on Dean and media requests for interviews **4,** 1600

on Dean's Fifth Amendment claim against testifying **3,** 912

denies he ever used political spying **11,** 4474

Dent and **4,** 1793E

on direct election of President **12,** 4934, 4935

on documents on Stans' million-dollar fund **7,** 2795-96

on documents wanted from White House **4,** 1389

draft letter from Dean to **3,** 997, 1252-57E

on Ehrlichman's justification for Ellsberg break-in **6,** 2577-79

on enemies list exhibit **4,** 1556-57

on excised version of Huston Plan **7,** 2820

on Executive privilege **10,** 3906-3907

on Executive privilege for Haig testimony **23,** 10996, 10998

on exhibits wanted from Dean **4,** 1388, 1389

on fact-finding mission of Select Committee **7,** 2773

on FBI reports on Ellsberg case **7,** 2664, 2665

on Frates' objections to line of questioning of Rebozo **21,** 9941-42, 9944, 9945, 9957, 9958-59

on grantsmanship **18,** 8276

on Greer's agreements with Dash **22,** 10532-33

on Greer's objections to line of questioning of Moncourt **22,** 10514, 10515

on Haldeman hearing White House tapes **7,** 2894, 2895, 2896

on Haldeman's interpretation of Nixon tapes **8,** 3066-67

on Haldeman's subpoena **8,** 3061, 3226-27

on hearsay evidence **1,** 132 **9,** 3813

as holder of information on Caulfield's friend helping with Kraft wiretapping **21,** 9691

on Hoover **7,** 2692

and Hunt's attorney-client privilege **9,** 3698, 3699

on Hunt's double-agent theory **9,** 3753-54

on illegal entry **6,** 2630-32

on immorality of dirty tricks **11,** 4397, 4398

on impact of dirty tricks **11,** 4402

on indictability of CRP officers if Stans had testified before grand jury **7,** 2793

on Inouye **8,** 3231

on issuing subpoena duces tecum requiring Nixon to turn over tapes and papers **6,** 2486

on Jonas **4,** 1563-64

Jonas' statement on honesty and integrity of **4,** 1536

on jurisdiction of Select Committee to investigate Fitzgerald case **4,** 1561

Kleindienst seeks meeting with **3,** 992

on laws on transfers of funds from foreign subsidiaries to American companies **13,** 5481

on leaks from congressional committees **21,** 9958

on leaks from Select Committee **10,** 3904

on legal telephone tapping **1,** 175

on legislation to prevent solicitation of corporate contributions **13,** 5474

letter canceling subpoenaed records of Griffin **26,** 10480E

letter from Barker on characterization of Stans' testimony by **13,** 5348, 5714-15E

letter from Barker on Dunnells' affidavit **13,** 5348, 5733E

letter from Barker on Stans **13,** 5348, 5706-07E, 5714-15E

letter from Brown on Dean's remarks **4,** 1791-92E **5,** 2181E

on letter from Buzhardt on Nixon tapes **5,** 2090

letter from Davis on legality of some of staff's activities **24,** 11389, 11479-87E

letter from Humphrey denying knowledge of Valentine, Sherman matter **FR** 871

letter from Jones on his involvement with AMPI **17,** 8058-60E

letter from Linde on Supreme Court opinion in *Abel* v. *United States* **8,** 3207, 3327-28E

letter from McGovern re his campaign financing **25,** 12219-20E **FR** 556-581

letter from McGovern re press accounts of corporate donations to political campaigns **25,** 12214-18E

letter from McKiernan on treatment of Nixon brothers **23,** 10975-77, 10984-87E

letter from Nixon on purposelessness of meeting with **6,** 2478

on letter from Nixon on subpoenas for tapes and records **7,** 2657-58, 2907E

on letter from Shaffer, McKeever and Fitzpatrick, law offices **3,** 913, 1095-98E

on letter from Sneed on Department of Justice investigation of telephone hoax **6,** 2383

letter from Stoner on statement of Sloan to **13,** 5379, 5740E

letter of transmittal to Eastland of Final Report of Select Committee on Presidential Campaign Activities **FR** 5

on letter requesting that Stans not testify **2,** 685, 697-98E

letter to Davis on request for open hearing for Winte **24,** 11615-18, 11619E

letter to Griffin re subpoenaing of telephone records **26,** 10479E

letter to Nixon requesting documents on domestic intelligence **3,** 1060

letter to Nixon requesting tapes and meeting **5,** 2178-79

letter of reply to Davis **24,** 11389, 11488-91E

letter to St. Clair on Rebozo-Nixon financial relationship **FR** 1051, 1069-70

letters from Barker **7,** 2796, 2954-73E, 2973-77E

letters from Jobe **7,** 2960-62E

letters to Humphrey requesting meeting with Committee member **FR** 899, 900

letters to Mills requesting interview **FR** 928, 929

on Liddy declining to testify **2,** 488

on Lincoln voluntarily appearing before House Judiciary Committee **4,** 1557

on line of questioning of Mardian **6,** 2425-27

mailgram from McKiernan on Nixon brothers' inability to comply with new subpoena **23,** 10988E

on McCarthyism **2,** 855

on McCord and Fensterwald requesting to testify **1,** 311

on mention of Vesco case **7,** 2808

on Miller's comments about questions relating to interviews of Moore by U.S. attorneys **5,** 2059-60

on Mitchell's role as Attorney General while engaged in political activity **5,** 1856-57

on Montoya's request for subpoena for Buzhardt **4,** 1430

on Nixon as best witness on his own knowledge about Watergate **5,** 2009

on Nixon's letter prohibiting Secret Service personnel from testifying before Select Committee **5,** 2136-37

on Nixon's letter refusing tapes **6,** 2479-80

on Nixon's refusal to testify or give access to presidential papers **5,** 1867

on objections to line of questioning of Moncourt **22,** 10530-31

on Omnibus Crime Act and testimony on content of wiretaps **1,** 400

on *Face the Nation* **3,** 1252E

on *New York Times* acquiring "Dean Papers" **2,** 601-602

opening statement by **1,** 1-14

on possibility of conflict between Ehrlichman's and Haldeman's testimony **7,** 2862-63

on possible impact of Stans' grand jury testimony **9,** 3581-82

on power and objectives of Select Committee hearings **5,** 2047-48

preface to Select Committee Final Report **FR** 7

on presidential duties **9,** 3603

on presidential powers **6,** 2587

on presidential powers and Ellsberg matter **6,** 2593-94, 2597

on prior dealings with Haldeman **4,** 1562

quotes from literature in reference to Watergate **FR** 1102-1103

on Rebozo documents **21,** 9938

on records of campaign contributions **FR** 891-92

on regulatory power of Government **13,** 5520-21

on repressive legislation **2,** 854, 855

on request of Special Prosecutor of Watergate case to postpone or terminate hearings **2,** 457-58

requests copy of Stans' statement to prosecuting attorney **7,** 2797-98

requests silence from audience **6,** 2616, 2630 **7,** 2657, 2795 **8,** 3151

on role of humor **10,** 3942

on role of White House staff **7,** 2697-98

on Rule 25 **2,** 625

on Rule 30 and Buzhardt's request for copy of transcript **22,** 10539

on rules against question on 1964 judgment against Haldeman **8,** 3170-71

on rules of evidence **1,** 129 **4,** 1524-25

ruling on attorney-client privilege between Kalmbach and Rebozo **FR** 1005

ruling on questions pertaining to 1968 campaign contributions **22,** 10579-80

on Saturday sessions **8,** 3177

on schedule for hearings **4,** 1507

on search warrants on McCord **9,** 3486-87

on Select Committee in relation to federal prosecutor **5,** 2060

on Select Committee methods of obtaining immunity for witnesses **4,** 1348

on Select Committee rules on admissibility of testimony **4,** 1520

selected to head Watergate hearings **3,** 980

on Senate resolution on Vesco case **11,** 4522

on staff conduct during questioning **21,** 9948

on Stans excused from grand jury testimony **7,** 2790-92, 2797-98

on Stans' request for deferment of testimony **2,** 684-86, 687

and Stennis Compromise **FR** 1081

submits exhibit from Linde **8,** 3207

on subpoena for Buzhardt **4,** 1569

and subpoena for financial records of Edward C. Nixon **22,** 10616

on subpoena requiring Haldeman to turn over notes or tapes to Select Committee **8,** 3954

on sympathy for Magruder **2,** 874-75

on telephone call from Shultz on Nixon's willingness to turn tapes over to Select Committee **6,** 2354-55

thanks staff **4,** 1507

on tragedy of Watergate **6,** 2343-44

on unavailability of Stans' deposition before grand jury **7,** 2792-93

on use of Helms' testimony to Committee on Armed Services **8,** 3244

on use of political spies **11,** 4420

on value of CIA **9,** 3440

on Vesco matter **7,** 2801-2802

on Watergate scandal as unprecedented **11,** 4419

on White House employees engaged in political activities **18,** 8275-76

on Wilson's complaint about incomplete documents **8,** 3217-18

on Wilson's request for time for statement on Inouye **8,** 3228, 3229

on witnesses to be called **8,** 3135

Ervin, Sam J., Jr., questioning by

Alch **1,** 325-33, 353-56

Atkins **13,** 5448, 5449

Barker **1,** 363-64

Benz **11,** 4419-21, 4428, 4432

Bernhard **11,** 4692-96

Buchanan **10,** 3938-42

Buckley **11,** 4471-74

Butterfield **5,** 2073, 2089

Campbell **12,** 4961

Carter **12,** 4990, 4991

Caulfield **1,** 282-283

Cushman **8,** 3299, 3300, 3308

Dean **4,** 1388, 1389, 1411, 1429, 1430, 1452-65, 1531, 1532, 1536, 1537, 1569, 1596, 1599, 1600

DeYoung **13,** 5528, 5529

Ehrlichman **6,** 2570-79, 2632 **7,** 2664-66, 2689-2701, 2790-93, 2797-99, 2814, 2815, 2862, 2863

Gray **9,** 3512-16, 3537-42

Haig **23,** 11004, 11008-11009

Haldeman **7,** 2866, 2894-96, 2906 **8,** 3081-86, 3114-18, 3132, 3133, 3138-42, 3162-65, 3177-80, 3195-98

Harmony **2,** 481-83, 486-87

Heller **12,** 4974

Helms **8,** 3267-73, 3279, 3280

Hickman **11,** 4563

on political activities of Government employees **18,** 8482-84

on Project FIND **18,** 8477-78

on projects worked on with Malek **18,** 8439

on radio advertising by Federation of Experienced Americans **18,** 8445-46, 8461-62

on Responsiveness Program **18,** 8438-39

on Richardson-Flemming film **18,** 8478-80, 8482

Evans, Thomas W. 14, 6254, 6258-59, 6264, 6265 **15,** 6406, 6539-40, 6542, 6598 **16,** 7161 **17,** 7590, 7591, 7594, 7595 **FR** 451, 513

and AMPI committees **14,** 6300

at meeting between Kalmbach and dairy industry representatives **15,** 6535-38

at meeting with Hillings, Harrison, Nelson, and Parr **15,** 6788

at meeting with Nunn, Kalmbach, and Dean on milk producers' contributions **17,** 7649-50

and letterwriting campaigns to senators **FR** 291E

meeting with Kalmbach and Dean **17,** 7605-7606

meetings with Kalmbach **15,** 6658

meetings with Parr **15,** 6787-89, 6790

memo from Dean on draft charter for committees working for Nixon's renomination **17,** 7596, 7623E, 8130-34E

memo to Mitchell on "Citizens Campaign for 1972" **FR** 325-35E

Evans and Novak 4, 1665 **7,** 2733 **8,** 3172 **FR** 78

bogus press releases to **11,** 4381

column on Muskie **10,** 4146E, 4147E **11,** 4695, 4814E **FR** 351E

"Lyndon B. Johnson: The Exercise of Power" **10,** 3937-38

and material from Buckley **11,** 4452

in memo from Haldeman to Dean **8,** 3188, 3189

stolen Muskie campaign documents sent to **11,** 4446, 4657-58

on '72 Sponsors Club **10,** 4196E

Evat, Gary 14, 5924 **15,** 6525

Ex parte Millikin **6,** 2631

Executive clemency 1, 231

and Barker **1,** 211-12, 359, 362-63, 379

and Bittman **1,** 302, 330-331, 351-352

Caulfield on source of offers of **1,** 268-269, 277-78, 280

Caulfield's contacts with McCord on **1,** 254-260, 264-67

for Cuban Americans **1,** 212-213

Dean and Mitchell offer to Magruder **2,** 804-805, 819, 836-37

Dean on sources of offers of **3,** 973-74

Dean talks to Haldeman about **7,** 2902

Dean's discussions with Nixon on **4,** 1400-1408

discussion at March 21 meeting **7,** 2898 **8,** 3075, 3076

Ehrlichman on **7,** 2771, 2847-50

and Ellsberg **6,** 2607-12

Haldeman on **8,** 3054-55

for Hunt **3,** 1053 **4,** 1403, 1485 **5,** 1910-11, 2003 **8,** 3076, 3116 **FR** 66-70

for Hunt and Colson **3,** 1042

Hunt denies promise of **9,** 3739, 3795

in hypothetical question-answer session to prepare Ziegler for press conference **3,** 965, 1200-1208E

Magruder asks Mitchell and Haldeman for assurances of **2,** 807-808

Magruder says Dean offered **4,** 1443-44

for McCord **1,** 131-41, 149-53, 155, 161-62, 163-64, 167-68, 182, 188, 231-32, 271-73, 290 **2,** 313, 316-19, 326-27, 328, 330-33, 337, 346, 350-52 **3,** 975 **4,** 1673-74 **7,** 2736 **FR** 63-66

for Mitchell **5,** 1911-12

Mitchell on **4,** 1634 **5,** 1821-22

Moore denies Dean told him about discussion with Nixon on **5,** 2004-2006

Nixon's attitude toward **FR** 68-69

Nixon's offer to Hunt of **1,** 208-10 **3,** 1017, 1020, 1077, 1079-80

offered to Magruder **FR** 70-71

offers of, as part of Watergate coverup **FR** 63-73

source of offers of **2,** 850

Executive pardon

for Tijerina **13,** 5315, 5316

Executive privilege

Baker urges Nixon to waive **3,** 988

and Buchanan's political strategy memos **10,** 3906-3907

and Butterfield **5,** 2082

Buzhardt claims **23,** 10911, 10912, 10913, 10914, 10918-19

and Buzhardt's letter on Haldeman's testimony **7,** 2893-96

and Caulfield **1,** 284

and Dean **1,** 81 **3,** 912-14, 994 **4,** 1405 **5,** 1971-72 **7,** 2739-40, 2741

Dean draft statement on **5,** 1974-75

discussed in Dean-Nixon meetings **3,** 996, 997

Ehrlichman advises Sloan to take **2,** 546, 579-80, 622

and Ehrlichman's testimony **16,** 7393

Ervin on **1,** 2 **10,** 3906-3907

and Haig's discussions with Richardson on Cox investigation **23,** 11031-32

and Haig's testimony **23,** 10849-50, 10995-96, 11036

Hauser objects to questions on wiretapping on grounds of **23,** 11096, 11097

and Kehrli **1,** 82

Kleindienst on **9,** 3589-90, 3609

Magruder on **2,** 852

Mitchell on **3,** 1001 **5,** 1863-64, 1866, 1888

Moore on **5,** 1942, 1943

Nixon asks Dean about **3,** 994

Nixon on **3,** 992, 993 **4,** 1405, 1463-64 **5,** 1838-39, 1974 **23,** 10853

Nixon waives for Dean **3,** 1099E

Nixon waives for Haldeman **8,** 3320E

Nixon-Mitchell discussions on **4,** 1663-64

and Nixon's attitude toward White House staffers testifying before Select Committee **5,** 1958

as part of coverup **3,** 1092

and questions on wiretapping of F. Donald Nixon **23,** 10942

Select Committee resolution on **23,** 10995, 11037E

Weicker on **23,** 11026

White House holds Dean responsible for **4,** 1422

and White House meetings **4,** 1548-49

Executive privilege *(Continued)*
    White House waives **4,** 1492-93
    See also White House tapes
Executive Protective Service **5,** 2074
Ex-FBI Agents Society
    resume from **1,** 393
Fabrega, Camilo **FR** 462-63
    See also CAMFAB
Fabrega, Camilo, testimony of **13,** 4584-88
    on cash sales of tickets **13,** 5485-86
    on contacts with South **13,** 5484-85, 5486-88
    on delivering money to South **13,** 5486
    on operations to raise money for Braniff **13,** 5484-88
    personal loan taken for South **13,** 5486-87
    on reasons for dealing in cash for South **13,** 5487-88
"Face the Nation" **3,** 997 **4,** 1562
    Ervin on **5,** 1974
Failer, Edward D.
    "attack" operation of **1,** 26
    memo from Howard on unsigned booklet on McGovern platform **FR** 205
    memo to Magruder on McGovern-Shriver confrontation **12,** 5016, 5017, 5265-66E **FR** 355E
    subpoenaed by Patman Committee **3,** 1192E
    and Young Voters for the President **FR** 200-201
Fair Campaign Practices Committee **11,** 4674
Fair Campaign Reform Act of 1971 **11,** 4675
Falk, Richard J. **25,** 12239
    approval of attorney's bills submitted to Edidin **25,** 12245
    refuses to write off bills to Muskie campaign from Hertz Corp. **25,** 12227-28, 12230
Fall River, Massachusetts
    vandalism at Nixon Campaign Headquarters at **12,** 5107-5109E
Fannie Mae inquiry **18,** 8237-39 **FR** 411-12
Fannin, Paul **12,** 5046E **16,** 7380, 7403
Farmer, James **18,** 8270-73, 8419E
    affidavit of **19,** 8843-47E
    documents on grant to **19,** 8837-47E
    HEW grant to **FR** 405-406
    letter to Dash on allegations about HEW grant **19,** 8842E
    memo from Jones to Malek on meeting with **19,** 8838E
Farmer, Jerry **14,** 5882
Farmers
    agreement between AMPI and Valentine, Sherman on compiling master file of **14,** 6148, 6164, 6193-6125E, 6216E
Farrington, Carl C.
    memo to USDA Administrator of Commodity Operations on dairy price support **17,** 8117-26E
Fasser, Paul J.
    memo from Lovell on distribution of funds for older workers program **19,** 9231E
"Fat Jack"
    See Buckley, John R. (alias of)

Fauntroy, Walter **12,** 4912
FBI **1,** 51
    Baldwin and **1,** 226, 408
    Bartolme on false statements to **13,** 5426-27, 5428-29
    and Beard memo **5,** 1950
    and Benz's information on dirty tricks against Republicans in 1970 **11,** 4424-25
    break-ins at offices of **2,** 861-62
    Buchanan on use in political campaigns **10,** 3964
    Buckley's employment at **11,** 4436
    Buzhardt on surreptitious entries by **23,** 10922-23
    bypassed for Kraft wiretapping **21,** 9687-88
    and Caulfield's investigation of O'Brien-Hughes relationship **22,** 10409-10
    and CIA involvement **5,** 1884
    CIA turns material on Watergate burglars over to **8,** 3278-79, 3280
    contact with Rebozo **23,** 10940
    and CRP documents **1,** 26-27
    Dean on past use of **5,** 1976
    Dean suggests investigation of campaigns of Select Committee members by **5,** 1975-76, 1995
    Dean's contacts with **3,** 1067 **5,** 1971
    denies Benz told them about dirty tricks against Republicans **11,** 4428-29
    and Dunes Hotel acquisition matter **23,** 11057-58 **FR** 991-92
    Ehrlichman discusses directorship with Byrne **6,** 2617-22
    Ehrlichman on justification for using Plumbers instead of **6,** 2625-29
    and Ellsberg matter **5,** 2016 **6,** 2544 **7,** 2661-82
    and Erlichman's papers **1,** 90, 91
    false information from CIA on Pennington to **FR** 1127
    Gray gives files to Dean **9,** 3564, 3576-77, 3583
    Gray on role of **9,** 3478, 3479, 3544-45
    Haldeman on political structure of **8,** 3226
    and Haldeman's records **1,** 91
    Hunt on Liddy's relations with **9,** 3709-10
    infiltration of Institute for Policy Studies **11,** 4434-35
    information from CIA on Martinez **9,** 3426-37
    information on Ellsberg to Plumbers from **9,** 3786
    information to Caulfield on DeAntonio from **FR** 144-45
    informed by Stans of Sloan's resignation **2,** 770
    in-house CIA investigation memos given to **9,** 3423-25
    and Internal Security Division **1,** 223
    interview of Chenow **3,** 941
    interview of Colson **3,** 939-40, 1160E
    interview of McMinoway **11,** 4478
    interview of Segretti **3,** 963 **FR** 178
    interview of Strachan **6,** 2464, 2502
    inventory of Jacobsen's safe-deposit box **15,** 6426-27, 6488-94E
    investigation of American Ship Building Co. contribution **FR** 454-55
    investigation of DeAntonio **22,** 10379-85
    investigation of Hatsis and Meier **22,** 10611
    investigation of plane crash that killed Mrs. Hunt **9,** 3507
    investigation of potential presidential appointees **7,**

2682-83

investigation of Schorr **3**, 1071 **FR** 144

Kleindienst recommends Byrne as Director of **9**, 3570-72

leaks **6**, 2557-58, 2562, 2613, 2626, 2655E, 2674-75 **9**, 3450, 3456, 3476-77

and Liddy plan **6**, 2326

and Liddy's firing from CRP **12**, 4910

Magruder tells false story on Liddy money to **2**, 803, 852, 853

Mardian and **6**, 2378-79, 2421, 2422-23

Mardian denies requesting wiretap of Division 5 of **6**, 2429

material from Hunt's safe given to **3**, 948-49

and materials from Magruder to Strachan **6**, 2449

McCord as special agent for **1**, 125

memo from Odle on payments to McCord **1**, 52

memo from Walters to Gray on information on Watergate incident provided by **9**, 3551, 3850-52E

and Mexican checks **3**, 942-43 **5**, 1860

misuse of **12**, 5010

Mitchell denies knowledge about Watergate to **5**, 1926-27

motivation for creation of Plumbers unit and **7**, 2780

Petersen on **9**, 3645, 3649-50

Porter lies about amount of Liddy money to **2**, 636

questions Stans **2**, 772

raw data to Dean from **7**, 2722-23

recruitment of Barker in Cuba **1**, 378

relations with White House **FR** 143-45

and reports from Internal Security Division **1**, 230

reports on antiwar demonstrators and radical groups to Dean's office **3**, 916 **4**, 1445-46

reports to CRP **1**, 178

Schorr investigation **6**, 2489 **8**, 3156-57

and Segretti **3**, 1302E-1303E **5**, 2033-34 **10**, 4005

Stans' statement on Liddy's role to **2**, 705-706

statement by Bartlome on his salary, finances, and political contributions to **13**, 5431, 5785-91

statements by employees of American Ship Building Co. to **13**, 5407-10, 5412-13, 5414-15, 5431, 5771-76E

statements from Chestnut and Thatcher on Loeb contribution **25**, 11727

subpoenas for files from CRP **1**, 37

and telephone tap on Halperin **11**, 4665

used for political purposes **3**, 993, 1071-73

and wiretap on Oliver's telephone **9**, 3595-96

and wiretaps against Nixon and Agnew in 1968 **3**, 1242E

FBI FD-302s

contents of **9**, 3616

Mardian denies he read **6**, 2370-71

Mitchell and **4**, 1678-79

in Moore's possession during meeting with Strachan and Chapin **6**, 2485-86

Petersen-Gray discussions on giving to Dean **9**, 3614-16

Segretti denies seeing **10**, 4008

shown to Segretti **10**, 4008, 4009-10

FBI Watergate investigation

beginning of **FR** 33

Dean and **8**, 3112-13 **9**, 3606

Dean on cooperation of White House staff with **3**, 1253E

Dean on interviews at White House **3**, 940-41

discussed in Dean-Gray meeting **9**, 3451

efforts to suppress **9**, 3413-14, *see also* Helms-Walters meeting

Ervin on Dean's presence during interviews **8**, 3142

and failure to interview Reisner **FR** 47

Gray offers files to senators **9**, 3553

Gray on **9**, 3500-3503, 3525-26, 3534-35, 3539, 3542, 3543, 3548, 3554-58

Gray on McCord's allegations about **9**, 3485-87

and Gray resignation over Ehrlichman's request for suppression of **7**, 2711-13

Haldeman and Dean's efforts to stop **9**, 3648

Haldeman on **8**, 3095, 3224-26

and interviews at CRP after Watergate arrests **2**, 521-22

and interviews with Mitchell **5**, 1926-27

and interviews with Sloan **2**, 544, 564-65, 566, 583 **FR** 41

and investigation of nonoperating bug of DNC in September 1972 **1**, 107, 111, 114 **5**, 1828-29, 2016 **7**, 2762-63, 2782-86, 2798-99 **9**, 3548, 3595-96, 3651-52

and Justice Department **9**, 3612

Kleindienst on **9**, 3582, 3591-92

MacGregor on **12**, 4933-34

and Magruder and Porter perjury **FR** 45

McCord's article on **9**, 3521-22, 3848-49E

and Mexican checks **9**, 3522-23 **FR** 37

Mitchell on **5**, 1926-27

reports given to Dean on **3**, 944-45, 1038-39

and Segretti matter **9**, 3620

in Walters memos to Gray **9**, 3815E, 3819E

and White House and CRP interviews **9**, 3512-13 **FR** 46-47

White House use of CIA to restrict **FR** 37-40

See also Helms-Walters meeting; Kissinger tapes

FEA

See Federation of Experienced Americans (FEA)

Fecteau **8**, 3277

Federal Bureau of Investigation

See FBI

Federal Communications Commission (FCC)

and Nixon administration **FR** 268E, 281-84E

White House misuse and attempted misuse of **FR** 149-50

Federal contracts and grants

See Grants; Grantsmanship

Federal Criminal Code

Select Committee recommendations for revision of **FR** 100-101

Federal Election Campaign Act of 1971 2, 6916 **16**, 7420

and corporate group solicitation program **FR** 545

filings of political committees registered under **3**, 1183-89E

and formation of CTAPE **FR** 585

Federal Election Campaign Act of 1971 *(Continued)*
impact of April 7 cutoff on campaign **FR** 564
impact on campaign contributions **FR** 445-46
limitations of **FR** 573
and privacy rights **FR** 892-93
and separate corporate funds for political purposes **FR** 550-52
Federal Elections Commission
Select Committee recommendation for establishment of **FR** 564-67
Federal employees
appointments and discharges tied to political support **FR** 400-403
Federal Housing Administration (FHA) 13, 5327-39, 5340-45, 5346-47, 5349
and Priestes contribution **FR** 522-26
See also Fernandez, Benjamin, testimony of
Federal "Political" Personnel Manual, 1972 19, 8903-9050E
Federal Reserve Bank
evidence on Hughes contribution money **FR** 972-80
report on Hughes contribution **FR** 1024
Federal resources
Magruder memos on use for campaign purposes by Eisenhower, Johnson, and Humphrey **19,** 8597E, 8598-99E
memo from Magruder to Horton on Martin's plan for use of **19,** 8604-8605E
memo from Magruder to Mitchell on use of **19,** 8595-96E
memo from Magruder to Strachan on use of White House computer for 1972 campaign **19,** 8600-8603
memos from Millspaugh to Flemming on use of **19,** 8606-12E
See also Grants; Grantmanship
Federation of Experienced Americans (FEA)
CRP documents on **19,** 9234-38E
distribution of campaign literature by **18,** 8450
Eitreim memo on grant application by **18,** 8458
Evans' opinion of **18,** 8448-49
GAO investigation of **18,** 8449, 8450-57
GAO report on, *see* General Accounting Office (GAO)
Government contracts and grants to **FR** 424-28
and grants **18,** 8439-42, 8451-62
memo from Todd to Malek on funding for **19,** 9239-41E
and OEO grant **18,** 8443-45, 8481
radio advertising by **18,** 8445-46, 8461-62
Federation of Homemakers
See Nader v. *Butz*
Federini
See Sturgis, Frank
Feld, Bernard T. 4, 1695E
Feldman, Meyer 10, 3937, 3938 **11,** 4622 **25,** 12122
Felds, Kevin 23, 11267
Fellows, Ben E. 25, 11762
Fellows, Ben E., testimony of 25, 11765-85
on Andreas contribution **25,** 11778-79
association with Thatcher **25,** 11766-67

on balance on hand when Humphrey campaign came into existence **25,** 11778
on cash deposits by Humphrey campaign **25,** 11784
on compensation received for audit of Humphrey campaign records **25,** 11773
on coordination of assignment for Humphrey campaign with O'Connor law firm **25,** 11775
on delay in deposit of Loeb cash contribution **25,** 11780
denies knowledge of Hughes contribution to Humphrey campaign **25,** 11785
denies knowledge of reimbursement of Andreas loan to Humphrey campaign **25,** 11779
on GAO criticisms of Humphrey campaign financial reporting **25,** 11782-83
on Humphrey campaign compliance with Federal Election Act **25,** 11783-84
on large cash disbursements by Humphrey campaign **25,** 11772-73
on large deposits of cash to Humphrey campaign accounts **25,** 11767
on leave of absence from National City Bank of Minneapolis **25,** 11773-74
on loan to Humphrey campaign **25,** 11771-73
location of checks returned for insufficient funds **25,** 11780-81
on methods used in examining Humphrey campaign financial records **25,** 11781
on money not included in opening balances shown in reports of GAO
on Humphrey campaign finances **25,** 11775-76
on persons responsible for Humphrey campaign recordkeeping **25,** 11771
on pre-April 7 records of Humphrey campaign finances **25,** 11768-71, 11776-78, 11783
on preparing amendments based on review of Humphrey records **25,** 11766-67
professional association with National City Bank of Minneapolis **25,** 11765-66
on record-keeping system used by Humphrey campaign **25,** 11767, 11779
on repayment of $57,000 loan by Humphrey campaign **25,** 11783-84
on request to review records of Humphrey campaign **25,** 11766
on Thatcher's request for review of records of Humphrey campaign **25,** 11774-75
Fellows, Boyd 3, 1045-46
Felt, Mark 3, 920, 921, 943, 1056, 1069, 1070 **9,** 3454, 3455, 3456-57, 3460, 3465, 3478, 3479, 3485, 3492-93, 3501, 3521, 3534-35
memo from Dalbey on dissemination of information to White House **9,** 3479-82, 3843-45E
Fensterwald, Bernard, Jr. 1, 125, 131, 191, 305-309, 319, 322-323, 328, 335-336, 346
polygraph test for **1,** 355
requests to testify **1,** 311
sworn statement of **7,** 2906, 3012-15E
Fernandez, Alex FR 381
Fernandez, Benjamin 13, 5277, 5305, 5306 **FR** 381, 391
and campaign contributions **13,** 5306-5307, 5314

letter from Ely to Andrade on appearance before Select Committee of **13**, 5398, 5747E

letter from Villalobos to Peterson and Kleppe on charges made against **13**, 5394, 5743-46E

letter to Ely with Villalobos monthly report on National Economic Development Association **13**, 5748-67E

meeting with Priestes and Stans **13**, 5335-37

Priestes on contacts with **13**, 5328-45, 5348-51, 5353-55, 5356

in Stans' statement on Priestes testimony **13**, 5346-47

See also National Hispanic Finance Committee

Fernandez, Benjamin, testimony of 13, 5360-5402

on accomplishments of National Hispanic Finance Committee **13**, 5360-61

on amount of Priestes contribution **13**, 5366, 5368-69, 5370-71, 5377, 5381-82

on arrangements for Priestes to see Stans **13**, 5376-77

attitude toward Stans **13**, 5383

on career background **13**, 5360

on cash contributions **13**, 5385-86

on contacts with Priestes **13**, 5372, 5374-76, 5384-88

on dealings with Sloan **13**, 5376-77

denies discussions with Marumoto or Rodriguez on grants **13**, 5399-5401

denies knowledge about memo from Marumoto to Lynn on NEDA editorial **13**, 5400-5401

denies violation of Hatch Act **13**, 5401-5402

on first contact with Priestes **13**, 5366-69

on formation of National Hispanic Finance Committee **13**, 5362-63

on functioning of National Hispanic Finance Committee **13**, 5364-66

on goal of National Hispanic Finance Committee **13**, 5362-63

on his record of volunteerism **13**, 5372-73

on instructions from Stans to return Priestes check **13**, 5380-81

on meeting with Priestes in Washington, D.C. **13**, 5373-76

on meeting with Stans and Priestes **13**, 5377-79

on motivation for working with National Hispanic Finance Committee **13**, 5363, 5365

on NEDA and Research, Inc. **13**, 5388-93, 5394-99

opening statement **13**, 5360-62

and Priestes contribution **FR** 522-26

on Priestes' lack of credibility **13**, 5381

on Priestes' reasons for approaching National Hispanic Association **13**, 5369-70, 5387-88

on reasons for Priestes' desire to contribute to Nixon campaign **13**, 5370-71

on relations with Stans **13**, 5373

on resignation as NEDA president **13**, 5391-93

on Sloan's statement on amount of Priestes contribution **13**, 5380

on Sloan's statement on meeting with Priestes and Stans **13**, 5380

and statement by Sloan on contact with Stans **13**, 5741-42E

states he believed Priestes problem was with *Miami Herald* **13**, 5369

on Villalobos letter in answer to Gonzalez **13**, 5395-99

Fernandez, Louis Andre 22, 12560-61E, 12546-65E

FHA

See Federal Housing Administration (FHA)

Ficker, Robin 10, 3975, 4266E **11**, 4642, 4671 **FR** 202-203

Fielding, Dr. (Ellsberg's psychiatrist)

See Fielding break-in

Fielding, Elizabeth B. 9, 3861E

Fielding, Fred 2, 720, 927, 928, 934, 935, 956 **3**, 1263E **4**, 1562, 1582 **7**, 2879 **8**, 3374E **23**, 11260

at FBI interviews **FR** 46

and Caulfield's proposal on IRS audits of persons associated with *Millhouse* **FR** 136-37

and Chenow briefing **FR** 46-47

Dean protests Nixon's announcement of "Dean report" to **4**, 1368

and Dean's firefighting role in White House **4**, 1356

delivers material on Dean's firing by law firm to Ehrlichman **7**, 2753

deposition in DNC suit on Ehrlichman telling Dean to "deep-six" Hunt's briefcase **7**, 2825-26

helps Dean sort through Hunt's file material **3**, 937-38

and Hunt's safe **4**, 1362, 1363 **7**, 2824

and hush money **3**, 969 **4**, 1438

informed by Caulfield of anonymous letter from McCord **FR** 64

informs Dean of Watergate arrests **3**, 932

investigates Air West merger with Hughes Tool Co. for Garment **23**, 11054, 11055

knowledge about coverup **4**, 1564

meeting with Dean and Segretti on October 10 **10**, 4042-43

meeting with Segretti after Watergate break-in **10**, 4024

meeting with Segretti and Dean after Watergate break-in **10**, 4034-35, 4036, 4050-51

memo of December 5, 1972, re TSD photographs on **9**, 3623, 3861-74E

and preparation of White House staff for grand jury testimony **3**, 953

reaction to Ehrlichman's instructions to destroy material from Hunt's file **3**, 938

Rebozo denies discussing libel suit against *Newsday* with **21**, 10128

and removal of contents from Hunt's safe **3**, 935, 948, 949

and replacement of $350,000 to CRP **6**, 2462, 2472-73

role at White House **1**, 93

and Segretti coverup **FR** 181, 182

sent by Ehrlichman to discuss libel suit against *Newsday* proposed by Rebozo **21**, 9677-79

tells Dean about McCord's letter to Caulfield **3**, 974

and Watergate coverup **4**, 1438-39

Fielding break-in 4, 1421, 1426, 1482, 1653 **6**, 2426 **7**, 2771-72 **10**, 3964-65 **16**, 7176 **22**, 10388

Barker and **9**, 3744

Fielding break-in *(Continued)*
Barker on **1,** 357-358, 388
Barker's motives for participation in **1,** 358, 365-367, 371, 385
Buchanan learns about **10,** 3913
camera used in **8,** 3308
and CIA aid to Hunt **FR** 16-17, 1136-41, 1152-53
Colby denies CIA knowledge of **FR** 1159
Colson and **9,** 3717, 3734
and Colson's reports from Hunt **9,** 3723-24
convictions in **FR** 15-16
coverup of **5,** 1901-1902, 1903-1905
Cushman on Hunt's equipment and **8,** 3303
Cushman on learning about **8,** 3295
Dean tells prosecutors about **3,** 1042-43
Dean's efforts to retrieve files with photos of Liddy at **9,** 3529-30 **FR** 75-76
discussed on March 21 tape **8,** 3076-77
discussions between Buzhardt and Krogh on **23,** 10917-18
Ehrlichman and **9,** 3724 **FR** 13-16
Ehrlichman on justification for **6,** 2536, 2541-53, 2575-79, 2599-2607, 2629-30, 2632-33 **7,** 2687, 2692-93, 2815-21
Ehrlichman on motivations for **7,** 2667-82
Ehrlichman's reaction to **6,** 2623-24
Ehrlichman's reasons for not telling Nixon about **7,** 2804
and equipment taken by Hunt from CIA **8,** 3276-77
funding of **FR** 694-99
Gray denies knowledge of **9,** 3463
Gurney on irrelevancy to Watergate hearing of **FR** 1171-72
Haldeman denies knowledge of **8,** 3032
Haldeman learns about **8,** 3139
Haldeman on attitude toward methods such as **8,** 3194
Helms on learning of **8,** 3234
Hoover's competency and **7,** 2691-92
Hunt not indicted for **9,** 3731, 3732
Hunt on **9,** 3663, 3675-76, 3711, 3741, 3796, 3797, 3807
Hunt on belief of Cuban participants in legality of **9,** 3787
Hunt on national security reasons for **9,** 3781-83
Hunt on White House staff after **5,** 2016-17
and Hunt's involvement in planned Greenspun break-in **20,** 9377, 9381-82
Hunt's role in **8,** 3234
Kleindienst denies knowledge of **9,** 3603
Kleindienst on **9,** 3587, 3592
Kleindienst on Nixon's reaction to **9,** 3607-3608
Krogh learns about picture of Liddy at **3,** 1007-08
Liddy tells Mardian about **6,** 2359, 2361-62
MacGregor on secrecy of Ehrlichman on **12,** 4930
in Mardian debriefing report to Mitchell **5,** 1918-19
milk money used for **15,** 6650 **FR** 682
Mitchell acknowledges awareness of **5,** 1858
Mitchell gets verification from Dean on **4,** 1647
Mitchell learns about **4,** 1622

Mitchell on **5,** 1890-92
Moore learns about **5,** 1960-62
Moore on Nixon's knowledge of **5,** 2069-70
motivation for **8,** 3304
as national security issue **9,** 3740-41
Nixon statement of May 22 on **6,** 2552-53
Nixon's knowledge of **4,** 1491 **5,** 2067-69 **6,** 2501
Petersen denies knowledge of **6,** 2606-2607 **9,** 3623
Petersen learns about **9,** 3630
photograph of Liddy at **3,** 979 **6,** 2607
and Plumbers **FR** 12, 13, 121-22
and preparation of White House staff for FBI interviews **3,** 941
and prosecution of defendants under existing law **FR** 101
secrecy of **7,** 2691
and Segretti **3,** 965
timing of FBI investigation of **7,** 2679-80
use of participants for Watergate break-in **9,** 3680
Wilson on legal justification for **6,** 2589-93
Fierce, Barbara 1, 34
Fifth Amendment
Buckley's reasons for taking **11,** 4451
Chestnut's use of **17,** 7700-7703 **FR** 880, 890, 898
Colson's use of **FR** 23
Dean suggests Sloan take **4,** 1418
Dean-Mitchell discussion on use of **4,** 1679-80
Dean's use of **3,** 912-13, 1044-45 **4,** 1518-19, 1520
and immunity **4,** 1437
Joseph Johnson's use of **FR** 904, 920, 925
Joseph Johnson's use of constitutional privilege instead of **17,** 7697
Liddy's use of **3,** 1262E
Magruder's use of **7,** 2845, 2846
McCord's use of **1,** 177-178
Sloan advised to take **2,** 582-83, 585-86, 612, 614, 778
Sloan's use of **2,** 709 **6,** 2300
Stans and **2,** 683-84, 685
Vanet plans to advise Townsend to take **16,** 7085
Fig Garden Village Shopping Center, Fresno, California
Nixon rally disrupted at **12,** 4948-51, 4953, 4955-63
Finance Committee to Re-Elect the President 1, 12, 13-14, 15E, 20
alleged passthrough of contribution from CTAPE to congressional committees to **FR** 736-43
bookkeeping arrangements with White House **17,** 7599-7600
Budget Committee of, *see* Budget Committee of Finance Committee to Re-Elect the President
Campaign Spending Act and **2,** 553-55, 559-61
check to Baldwin from **1,** 455E
checks from Republican Campaign Committee **16,** 7422, 7434E
and corporate contributions
  See Corporate contributions
and corporate group solicitation program **FR** 544-50
and dummy citizens committee **FR** 157
financial statements **22,** 12518-28E

and grants to Spanish-speaking Americans **13,** 5276-77

Kalmbach and **1,** 20

Kalmbach denies discussion of Watergate at daily staff meetings of **5,** 2139

legality of operations of **2,** 689-92

letter from Barrick to Myers on return of Goodyear Tire & Rubber Co.'s contribution to **13,** 5526, 5856E

letter from Firestone to Parkinson on contributions to **13,** 5526, 5854E

letter from Mellott to Parkinson on origin of contribution to **13,** 5466, 5804-05E

letter from Myers to Parkinson on return of Goodyear Tire & Rubber Co.'s contribution to **13,** 5526, 5855E

letter from Parkinson to Atkins on contribution to **13,** 5448, 5796E

letter from Parkinson to Barrick on return of Goodyear Tire & Rubber Co.'s contribution to **13,** 5526, 5857E

letter from Parkinson to Firestone on contributions to **13,** 5526, 5852-53E

letter from Parkinson to Wild on $100,000 contribution to **13,** 5466, 5803E

letter to Atkins on source of contribution **13,** 5445-46

and letters to corporate executives on disclosure of source of contribution **FR** 447

list of employees of **1,** 28, 437-447

location of cash kept by **2,** 535

mentioned in news stories on Watergate **2,** 740

and payment for Tell It To Hanoi Committee advertisement **FR** 316E

payments to Baldwin from **1,** 394

pick-up arrangements for contributions to **2,** 617-18

post-April 7 ADEPT and SPACE contributions to **FR** 731-32

and return of illegal contribution from Gulf Oil **13,** 5466, 5806E

Robinson denies knowledge of Braniff CAMFAB transaction connection to **13,** 5490

Sloan's role as treasurer of **2,** 532-99, 602-31

Stans employed by **2,** 696

Stans on contributions to **2,** 709-11

transfer of funds from Republican Senatorial and Congressional Campaign Committees to **17,** 7562-69, 7570-72, 7574

travel expenses paid to Baldwin **1,** 456E

unsigned letter to Atkins on illegal corporate contribution to **13,** 5448, 5800-01E

Wakefield's checks to **24,** 11281, 11346E

White House control of **FR** 20

See also Campaign financing; Nunn, Lee, testimony of

Financial matters

affidavit of Muskie campaign bookkeeper on **11,** 4695, 4786-89E

Bellino's affidavit on investigation of Rebozo's financial activities **26,** 12944-66E

between CRP and White House **1,** 83-84

between McMinoway and Rainer **11,** 4556, 4718E

Braniff International financial records **13,** 5491, 5813-29E

campaign contributions through donative sales of stock **25,** 12118-19, 12121-22

campaign funds paid to Edward Nixon **23,** 10858, 10859-60

checks and accounts for Ulasewicz **FR** 215-16E

checks missing from Rebozo's personal account **22,** 10506-10509

Chestnut's arrangements for reimbursement in Humphrey campaign **25,** 11720-21

cost of Letters to the Editor program **FR** 298E

CRP payments to Liddy and Hunt **1,** 62

CRP payments to McCord **1,** 52

Danner's expense accounts **26,** 12834-35E

Dean on money for Liddy's operations **4,** 1442-43

Dean's bank statement from National Savings and Trust Co., Washington, D.C. **4,** 1712E

Edward Nixon denies financial dealings with Rebozo **22,** 10591-92

and electronic equipment bought by McCord **1,** 184-185

F. Donald Nixon's financial affairs **22,** 10671-73, 10677-98, 11073

F. Donald Nixon's loan from United California Bank **22,** 10712-14

and Finance Committee for Re-Election of the President *See* Sloan, Hugh W., Jr., testimony of

financial statements of Finance Committee **22,** 12518-28E

financing of Gemstone plan **FR** 25-26

financing of Mills rally in Ames, Iowa **17,** 7715-16

Harmony on **2,** 471

Higby on Kalmbach's payments out of 1968 fund **23,** 11090-94

Hughes loan to F. Donald Nixon **20,** 9373-74

liability ledger from First National Bank of Miami to Richard and Patricia Nixon **26,** 12771-72E

loan to Humphrey campaign **25,** 11741-43

McCord on money received after arrest **1,** 130

McGovern campaign debt settlements and transfer of funds to senatorial committees **FR** 553-58

McGovern campaign financing of El Pueblo Con McGovern **12,** 4950-51, 4960

Meier and Hatsis paying F. Donald Nixon's travel expenses **22,** 10645-48

memos from Muskie campaign on **11,** 4767-85E

Moncourt on Rebozo's finances **22,** 10490-94, 10495-97, 10498-99, 10515-18

Moncourt's denial of unusual increases in compensation **22,** 10530-31

Mott money to Tuck **25,** 12113-14

and Muskie campaign **11,** 4646-52, 4786-89E, 4790-91E

Nixon's purchase and sale of Key Biscayne property **23,** 10768-75

Odle payment for rally in support of mining of Haiphong **1,** 68-69, 74

payments to F. Donald Nixon from surplus 1968 campaign funds **23,** 10860-61

personal finances of Edward Nixon **22,** 10597-99

police costs for Nixon's visit to Century City **11,** 4725-26E

proposed "Sandwedge" budget **1,** 252

Financial matters (Continued)
Rebozo on his personal finances **21**, 10070-89
Rebozo's loan to Nixon for purchase of Key Biscayne properties **22**, 12436-38E
Rebozo's loan from Hudson Valley Bank **22**, 10497-98
Rebozo's payment of Moncourt's legal fees **22**, 10531-32
Rebozo's payments for improvements and furnishings at Nixon's Key Biscayne properties **22**, 12430-36E, 12445-47E
records of American Ship Building Co. **13**, 5431, 5778-82E
Reisner on petty cash dispensed by Porter **2**, 498-99, 500
San Clemente property transaction
See Griffin, William, testimony of
source of funds for proposed Greenspun break-in **20**, 9384-85
various staff memos relating to **11**, 4695, 4766-85E
See also Campaign contributions; Clancy, Lynda E., testimony of; Hush money; Money; Odell, Robert P., testimony of; Wakefield, Thomas H., testimony of; White House payroll
Finch, Christopher **3**, 1135E
Finch, Robert **5**, 1999-2000 **9**, 3474, 3475 **13**, 5275, 5304 **20**, 9484 FR 939
confidential memo from Buchanan on topics for discussion at meeting of June 24, 1971 **10**, 3975, 4173E
Kalmbach loan to **5**, 2158
Malek memo on Farmer grant to **19**, 8837E FR 406
role at White House **1**, 91, 92
Fines for corporate contributions FR 927
American Shipbuilding Co. FR 459
Ashland Petroleum FR 462
Braniff Airways FR 463
Carnation Co. FR 464
Diamond International Corp. FR 465
Goodyear Tire & Rubber Co. FR 468
Gulf Oil Corp. FR 473, 925
Lehigh Valley Cooperative Farmers, Inc. FR 484
Northrop Corp. FR 489
Phillips Petroleum Co. FR 492
3M Corp FR 486, 894
Fiorini, Frank
See Sturgis, Frank
Firebombings
at anti-Nixon demonstration in Boston **12**, 4998
and political spying **11**, 4469
See also Brookings Institution
Firestone, Arden E. **13**, 5522, 5525, 5527, 5529 FR 465
Parkinson correspondence on contribution to FCRP **13**, 5526, 5852-53E, 5854E
Firestone, Leonard **22**, 10604, 10605, 10617
employs Edward Nixon at Richard Nixon Foundation **23**, 10857
and solicitation of Northrop Corp. FR 487
and suggested employment of Ehrlichman and Haldeman by Richard Nixon Foundation **23**, 11104-11105

First Amendment
Campbell on **12**, 4961
and CRP attitude toward demonstrators **4**, 1459
and demonstrations against Nixon **11**, 4552
and Stearns on demonstrations **11**, 4579
First National Bank of Washington, D.C. **13**, 5431, 5768E
First National City Bank of New York **13**, 5448, 5795E
Fischer, Kay **22**, 12552E, 12553E
Fischer, William F., Jr. **3**, 1141E
Fishbein, Michael J. **12**, 5113E
Fisher, Max **2**, 719, 721 **4**, 1677
Fishers Island Development **22**, 10529-30
Fishers Island stocks **20**, 9525 **21**, 9678, 10082, 10084, 10131 **22**, 10227
F. Donald Nixon on **22**, 10706
Moncourt on Rebozo's business dealings on **22**, 10529-30
and Wakefield **24**, 11282-84
Woods on **22**, 10224, 10225-26
Fitzgerald, A. Ernest
Dean on Air Force firing of **4**, 1559-61
memo to Haldeman from Butterfield on **8**, 3146-48
Fitzsimmons **23**, 11268
Five o'clock club in 1964 campaign **2**, 647 **11**, 4622-23
Fixman, Ben and Marilyn **25**, 11956-59E
Flake, Ronald R.
See Masters, Frank D., testimony of
Flanigan, Dent **4**, 1689E
Flanigan, Peter **3**, 1333E **4**, 1562 **13**, 5503 **17**, 7583, 7588 **23**, 11269
and American Airlines contribution to CRP **13**, 5509
and information from IRS to White House **21**, 9711
letter to Select Committee on discussions on ambassadorships with Kalmbach FR 499-500
role at White House **1**, 91, 92
and Symington's ambassadorial appointment FR 498-99
and Whitney FR 504-505
Flemming, Dr. Arthur S. **18**, 8212, 8284, 8448, 8456, 8478, 8479, 8482, 8483 **19**, 9053E, 9093-94E, 9096E, 9124E
appointment as Nixon's Special Consultant on Aging **19**, 9093-95E
memo from Evans to Malek on advance scheduling of **18**, 8483, 8584E
memo from Todd on second OA brochure **18**, 8485, 8593E
Flemming, Harry S. **1**, 10, 16, 17, 22, 34 **2**, 537 **3**, 1229E, 1331E **4**, 1606 **5**, 1845 **6**, 2281, 2305 **16**, 7170
meeting with LaRue, Magruder, and Mitchell in Key Biscayne **23**, 11150
memo from Millspaugh on patronage FR 364-65
memo from Millspaugh on resources of incumbency **18**, 8223, 8358-62E
memo from Sedam on Tennessee primary **10**, 4207-08E

memo to Malek on Fannie Mae inquiry **FR** 411-12

memo to Malek on Stack **18**, 8237, 8387E

memos from Millspaugh on meetings on federal resources for campaign **19**, 8606-12E

and Responsiveness Program **18**, 8237

role in campaign **18**, 8289

subpoenaed by Patman Committee **3**, 1192E

Fletcher, Robert 20, 9366

Florence, David E. 13, 5293-94

memo to Armendariz on Pena **13**, 5323, 5669E **FR** 402-403

Florida

Armendariz report on Spanish-speaking campaign in **19**, 8795-96E

See also Florida Democratic party primaries

Florida Criminal Code

McMinoway's activities as violation of **11**, 4521, 4676

Florida Democratic party primaries

Benz activities in **10**, 3982-83 **11**, 4403-32

Bernhard on **11**, 4662-65

Buchanan memo on **10**, 4192-95E

false advertising by Segretti during **FR** 173-74

false and misleading literature distributed by Segretti during **FR** 169-71

impact of dirty tricks on **11**, 4401-4402

Kelly activities during

See Kelly, Martin Douglas, testimony of

Kelly-Segretti discussion on **11**, 4379

memo from Buchanan to Magruder about **10**, 3975, 4192-95E

picketing organized by Segretti during **FR** 174-75

Segretti activities in **10**, 3982-83, 4020-21 **FR** 166-67

Florida Democrats for Nixon

and Danner **FR** 937

and Garcia **24**, 11415

Florida Department of Military Affairs

afteraction report on Republican National Convention **12**, 5014-15

Florida Finance Committee to Re-Elect the President

check from Wakefield to **24**, 11281, 11346E

Florida Nixon for President Committee 21, 10184 **22**, 10605 **23**, 10869E

check to Kalmbach from **23**, 10862E

Davis denies contributions to **22**, 10579-80

and payment for earrings for Mrs. Nixon **FR** 1047-48

payments to Caulfield with check from **23**, 10861

Rebozo and **21**, 10074, 10076-77, 10078 **24**, 11545 **FR** 1046-47

and Rebozo's money left over from 1968 campaign **21**, 9947-48

and Thomas H. Wakefield Special Account **24**, 11298

Florida Republicans for Nixon 22, 10241

Fluor Corp., Los Angeles, California 20, 9467-68

Foley, Tom 14, 5984

Fonda, Jane 9, 3712 **12**, 5201E

Fontaine, Frankie 12, 5115E

Fontainebleau Hotel, Miami, Florida 2, 790, 795, 826 **3**, 929, 1084

See also Democratic National Convention

"Food and Housing for the Elderly" 19, 9157-64E

Ford, Henry 12, 5026E

Ford, Tim 20, 9466

Ford Foundation 10, 4152E, 4241E

Buchanan on **10**, 3915-17, 3951-55

and Institute for Policy Studies **10**, 3952, 3955-56

and IRS **22**, 10357-58

Fore, Breck 1, 35

Foreign Agents Registration Act 6, 2424-25

Foreign Intelligence Advisory Board

Helms requested to assist in domestic operations of **8**, 3251-52

Foreign nationals

Select Committee recommendations for prohibition of solicitation or receipt of campaign contributions from **FR** 573-75

Foreign policy

of Kennedy **10**, 4170E

McGovern record on **10**, 4072-82E, 4251E, 4259-60E

Foreign relations

Haig on impact of Watergate hearings on **23**, 11014-15

Forest, Wisdom 14, 5909

Forman, Nanci Lee 23, 10966

Fort Wayne story 8, 3188, 3189

in memo to Dean from Haldeman on campaign disruptions **8**, 3179-80

Fortas, Abe 24, 11418, 11419

letter to Dorsen with transcript of Loeb's appearance before Cannella **25**, 11973-85E

"Fortune 500" FR 545

Forzberg, Miss (Mrs. Mitchell's secretary) 6, 2280

Foundations

Buchanan memo on **10**, 4114-19E

Buchanan on **10**, 3048-54, 3915-20, 3940-44

Fourth Amendment

and Ellsberg case **6**, 2632

and enemies list **4**, 1459

intelligence operations in violation of **4**, 1455

suspension of **8**, 3207

Foust, Jon 1, 34 **FR** 430

Fox, Francis 20, 9429, 9430, 9432, 9433-34

Frank, John

Caulfield on **21**, 9716-17

Frankfurter, Felix 4, 1524 **11**, 4593

Franklin, Barbara 18, 8201

Frates, William S. 22, 10560, 10622, 10653, 10893, 11185, 11211

on Armstrong's questions **21**, 10005, 10006

on Bellino and Armstrong **21**, 10123, 10124

on Bellino's disruptions **21**, 9948

contacts with Buzhardt **23**, 10901-10902

on Danner affidavit on delivery of money to Rebozo **21**, 9964

on Danner's records **21**, 9976

on documents brought by Rebozo **21**, 9937, 9938

Griffin discusses interview by staff of Select Committee with **23**, 10788, 10789-90, 10790-91

statement to Ted Van Dyk Associates for **16,**
7003, 7046E

Van Dyk on **16,** 7024

Garcia **24,** 11414-15, 11420, 11422, 11423, 11445

Garcia, Phillip **13,** 5629E

Garcia, Sylvia **13,** 5629E

Gardner, James F. **11,** 4437 **16,** 6938

Gardner, John **2,** 568 **3,** 1176E, 1180E **5,** 1907

Garland, Frank **12,** 5093E

Garment, Leonard **1,** 91 **3,** 917, 1019, 1055 **4,** 1503,
1567 **9,** 3585, 3589 **10,** 3906 **19,** 9096E **21,** 10062,
10064 **22,** 10232, 10240, 10622 **23,** 10788

approves Thompson's memo of Buzhardt's phone
conversation with him **5,** 2066

Buzhardt claims attorney-client privilege covers
discussions with **22,** 10540-44

Dean on Nixon's participation in coverup and **3,**
1077-81

discussions with Buzhardt on newspaper stories
about Hughes contribution **22,** 10540, 10544-45,
10548, 10552-53

discussions with Simon on Hughes matter **23,**
10934-35

discussions with Simon on Rebozo matter **23,**
10930-32, 10933, 10934-35, 10936

Gemmill and **23,** 11193

and hoax Shultz call **6,** 2360-61

informs Buzhardt of telephone call from reporter
on story about Rebozo's use of Hughes contribution **22,** 10544-45

and IRS investigation of Rebozo **22,** 12441E **23,**
10879, 10892

letter to Dash with pre-April 7 list of contributors
26, 10284E

letter to Dean **3,** 914, 1099E

letter to Select Committee **3,** 914

meeting with Haig, Chapman, and Buzhardt on
IRS investigation of Rebozo **23,** 10999, 11000-
11001, 11022-23

Moore's talks with **5,** 1992

Moore's testimony requested after Mitchell's by **5,**
1990

and Rebozo's proposed suit against Select Committee investigators **23,** 10893

recommends Gemmill as attorney for Rebozo **23,**
10999-11000, 11001, 11017 **FR** 1014

and requests by Select Committee for White
House records **2,** 532

telephone conversation with Gemmill **23,** 11175,
11199

Garment, Leonard, testimony of **23,** 11053-72

on conversations with Griffin **23,** 11069-70

denies knowledge of Camp David meeting of Nixon, Danner, and Rebozo **23,** 11069

denies knowledge of Greenspun break-in **23,**
11071

denies knowledge of meeting between McKiernan
and Nixon brothers **23,** 11071

on discussion with Buzhardt on Nixon booklet **23,**
11071

on F. Donald Nixon **23,** 11070-71

on Fielding's checking on Air West-Hughes Tool
matter **23,** 11054, 11055

on first knowledge of Hughes contribution **23,**
11068

on first knowledge of Kalmbach-Rebozo meeting
23, 11068

on Hughes contribution through Rebozo **23,**
11059-71

on inquiry to Smith of Attorney General's office
on Hughes Tool matter **23,** 11053-59

on meeting with Haig, Rose, and Buzhardt **23,**
11060-61, 11064-65

on Mitchell's memos to Hoover in Smith report
on Hughes Tool Co. **23,** 11057-58

on Nixon tapes **23,** 11071-72

on notes on report from Smith on Hughes Tool
Co. **23,** 11058-59

on positions held with Nixon since 1969 **23,**
11053

on recommendation of Gemmill as lawyer for
Rebozo **23,** 11066-67

on references to meetings between Mitchell and
Hughes representatives in Smith report **23,**
11056-57

Garner, Bobby **FR** 166, 168

Garrabrant, Ann **11,** 4886-88E

Garrish, Ted **1,** 34

Gartner, David **16,** 7321

correspondence with Dash on provision to Committee of specific information and documents
25, 11816-22E

Gaunt, Paulina **23,** 10967

Gay, Bill **20,** 9354, 9365, 9542, 9561, 9562 **24,** 11437,
11557, 11575-76

discussion with Winte on his conversation with
Hunt and Liddy **24,** 11600

meeting with Danner **24,** 11434-35

meeting with Winte **24,** 11604-11605, 11608

and Winte **24,** 11562

Gay, Frank **20,** 9483

Gay Liberation Front **11,** 4383

and bogus contributions to McCloskey **FR** 198

Gay liberation issue **11,** 4656

and Muskie campaign **11,** 4670

Gayler, Admiral **6,** 2409, 2527

Gaynor, Paul F. **9,** 3443, 3445, 3447, 3835E, 3838E,
3839E, 3840E

letters from McCord addressed to **9,** 3441-42

Gays for McGovern **11,** 4630

Geibel, Frank **23,** 11222, 12238, 11239 **FR** 1026

Gelb, Leslie **22,** 10359 **FR** 124

Gemmill, Kenneth W. **20,** 9457 **21,** 9994, 9995 **22,**
10275-76, 10655 **23,** 10754, 10800E **24,** 11291,
11435, 11585, 11654

and Buzhardt's preparation of letter for Woods to
IRS **23,** 10878-88

and Danner's arrangements for return of Hughes
contribution **20,** 9552-53, 9557-60

and Davis' investigation of Hughes contribution
24, 11609

discussions with Barth **23,** 11247

Garment and **23,** 11063

Garment on Rose's recommendation of **23,** 11066-
67

Griffin returns Hughes contribution to **22,** 10456-
58

and Hughes' campaign contribution **20,** 9408-10

Gemmill, Kenneth W. *(Continued)*
and IRS audit of B & C Investment Co. **23,**
10754-55
IRS interview with **FR** 1019-20
and letter from Woods to IRS **21,** 10107-10108
meeting with Rebozo in Philadelphia **22,** 10452
money delivered to Glaeser by **20,** 9410-15
Rebozo informs Griffin of agreement with **22,**
10449
and Rebozo's attempts to return Hughes contribution **22,** 10464-65
recommended by Garment as attorney for Rebozo
23, 10999-11000, 11001 **FR** 1014
reports to Haig that Hughes money was returned
23, 11019
requested by Armstrong to check with Nixon on
discussing Nixon's financial relationship with
Rebozo **23,** 11220
retained by Rebozo **21,** 10064, 10102
and return of Hughes contribution **21,** 10060-61,
10092, 10093, 10114 **23,** 11007, 11177-80,
11196-97, 11205-11206 **24,** 11471 **FR** 1014-16
telephone conversation with Davis **24,** 11586-87
Walters on relationship with **24,** 11621
and Woods' letter on Hughes contribution **22,**
10202
Gemmill, Kenneth W., testimony of 20, 9417, 9421
21, 10073 **22,** 10220, 10240, 12441E
on Bartlett's determinations on Hughes money **23,**
11219
claims no knowledge of asking Bartlett to contact
Buzhardt on Cox investigation of Rebozo **23,**
11212-14
on contact with Bartlett **23,** 11209-10, 11211-14
on contact with Rebozo and IRS on Hughes contribution **23,** 11174-81, 11185-88
on contacts with Barth **23,** 11208
on contributions received by Rebozo other than
Hughes contribution **23,** 11195-96
conversation with Davis on return of $100,000
Rebozo had received from Danner **20,** 9407-
9408
on conversations with Haig on Hughes contribution **FR** 1024
on Danner telling him Davis will contact him **23,**
11176, 11190
on Danner's affidavit on delivery of Hughes contribution **23,** 11200-11201
denies contact with Alexander on Hughes contribution **23,** 11209
denies discussing Hughes contribution with
Woods **23,** 11210-11
denies discussing O'Brien or Nixon brothers with
Rebozo **23,** 11208
denies foreknowledge of Rebozo's first contact
with him **23,** 11183
denies knowledge of Camp David meeting of
Rebozo, Danner, and Nixon **23,** 11198-99
denies knowledge of Rebozo converting campaign
contributions for own use **23,** 11207
denies knowledge of Rebozo's reasons for chang-
ing wrappers and destroying original envelopes
of Hughes contribution **23,** 11200
on discussion with Buzhardt on testifying on conversations with Nixon **23,** 11215-16

on discussion with Davis **23,** 11026
on discussion with IRS on Rebozo's statement
that he had not disclosed Hughes contribution
to anyone **23,** 11189
on discussions with Haig on IRS investigation of
Rebozo **23,** 11191-93, 11195
on discussions with Nixon on IRS investigation of
Rebozo **23,** 11193-94
on effects of Cox investigation on IRS clearance
of Rebozo **23,** 11211-14
on efforts to ascertain if Hughes money had remained in place **23,** 11203-11204
on efforts to talk with someone at IRS on return
of Hughes contribution **23,** 11178-79
on examining IRS report on Rebozo **23,** 11219
on first meeting with Rebozo **23,** 11185-86
on individuals within White House contacting
IRS on Rebozo case **23,** 11197-98
informs Garment he has contacted Rebozo **23,**
11175, 11199
on instructing Rebozo to list serial numbers of
Hughes money **23,** 11176, 11202-11203
on learning that Haig called Richardson on Cox
investigation **23,** 11214-15, 11216-17
on Lenzner's request for Cooper and Lybrand
worksheets **23,** 11220
on Maheu's role in Rebozo-Hughes matter **23,**
11200
on meeting between Griffin and IRS **23,** 11205
on meeting with Bartlett and Webb from IRS **23,**
11179-80
on meeting with IRS agents **23,** 11182
on meetings with Danner **23,** 11204
on other counsel Rebozo consulted with on
Hughes contribution **23,** 11184-85
on payment for legal work from Rebozo and Nixon **23,** 11218-19
on reasons for refusing to hold Hughes money for
Rebozo **23,** 11205
on Rebozo's agreement to partial waiver of attorney-client privilege on his testimony **23,** 11173,
11174, 11182, 11186, 11189-91, 11194-95,
11210, 11211, 11217, 11218
on Rebozo's reasons for keeping Hughes contribution **23,** 11186-88
on Rebozo's reasons for not depositing Hughes
contribution in CRP account in Key Biscayne
Bank **23,** 11195-96
on Rebozo's statement on Wakefield's knowledge
about Hughes contribution **23,** 11188
on relations with Nixon **23,** 11217-18
on relationship between Rebozo and Griffin **23,**
11204-11205
on relationship with Chester Davis **23,** 11201-
11202
on source of information on Cox investigation of
Hughes contribution **23,** 11219-20
on tax laws related to Rebozo's holding of
Hughes contribution **23,** 11175-76
on telephone call from Davis on return of Hughes
contribution **23,** 11177-78, 11199
on telephone call from Rose on Haig testimony
23, 11215-16
on Webb saying none of Hughes money was con-
verted **23,** 11180

Gemstone files
conflicting testimony on discussion of destruction
of **6,** 2356-57
decision to destroy **2,** 800
Magruder instructs Odle and Reisner to remove
FR 32-33
Reisner on Odle taking home **2,** 525-26
removal from Magruder's desk **2,** 511-12
Strachan denies Magruder showed him **6,** 2451-52
Gemstone plan 1, 49-50, 53, 71 **2,** 504 **20,** 9382-83
after June **2,** 513
budget for **9,** 3748
differentiated from general intelligence-gathering
plan by Hunt **9,** 3746-49
financing of **FR** 25-26
first presentation at meeting of Mitchell, Dean,
Magruder, and Liddy **FR** 21
Harmony on **1,** 488
Hunt on Colson's knowledge about **9,** 3715-22,
3758
Hunt's participation in drawing up **9,** 3734
impact on Democratic primaries **11,** 4636, 4637E,
4348
LaRue denies Rebozo's presence during discussions of **23,** 11171
Liddy and **20,** 9370
MacGregor and **2,** 530
MacGregor denies knowledge of **12,** 4907
Magruder and bill for **2,** 483-84
Magruder on contents of **2,** 848
Magruder shows to Mitchell **2,** 797
Magruder shows to Strachan **2,** 797-98, 827
in Magruder's file for Mitchell **2,** 503-504
material in Hunt's missing notebooks on **9,** 3751
McCord on **1,** 206
and McGovern headquarters break-in **FR** 27-28
Mitchell denies knowledge of **4,** 1618-20, 1622,
1641-42, 1669
Mitchell denies telling Magruder to destroy **5,**
1877
Mitchell on **5,** 1852
Mitchell tells Magruder to destroy **6,** 2286
Mitchell's reaction to **2,** 871
names in Hunt's notebooks as contacts on **9,**
3751-52
Operation Sandwedge as precursor to **FR** 117
Reisner asks Magruder about **2,** 504-505
Reisner on **2,** 513-15
and Ruby I **FR** 189
second meeting on **FR** 22-23
Select Committee's investigative work and **FR** 20
Strachan on **6,** 2442
third meeting on **FR** 24-25
and Watergate break-in **9,** 3663, 3792 **FR** 28-30
See also Liddy plan
Gemstone stationery 1, 450E, 464, 877E **FR** 29
cost of **2,** 479
Magruder shreds bill for **2,** 464
Reisner on **2,** 493-94
used for typing telephone logs **2,** 461-62, 467
Geneen, Harold 14, 6089-90
General Accounting Office (GAO) 3, 962 **5,** 1875
audit of Humphrey campaign finances **25,** 11732,
11737, 11742-43

and Democrat's civil suit **5,** 1887
and Draft Mills for President finances **FR** 903
and dummy committees **FR** 157
Fellows requested to review records of Humphrey
campaign in preparation for audit by **25,** 11766
and financing of United Farm Workers demonstration against Nixon **12,** 4950-51
interview with Sloan **2,** 599
investigation of Federation of Experienced Americans **18,** 8449, 8450-57
and Loeb contribution to Humphrey campaign **25,**
11727 **FR** 897
and McGovern campaign **25,** 12146
and Mexican checks **2,** 699, 701
Mitchell and **5,** 1906
Mott reports to **25,** 12110, 12118
on Nixon-Dean meetings **7,** 2892, 2896-98 **8,**
3076-77, 3115-18, 3142-46, 3211-12
registration form and statement of Mills for President Committee **25,** 12072-74E
report on Federation of Experienced Americans
18, 8457-58, 8459-61 **FR** 424-25, 428
report on Humphrey campaign finances **25,**
11782-83
report on McGovern campaign finances **25,** 12197
report on Older Americans brochures **19,** 9135-
9204E
report on TAPE contributions **14,** 6130, 6131
Select Committee recommendation on disclosures
of income by President and Vice President to
FR 1073-74
Sloan's reports to **2,** 605, 606
and SPACE contributions **16,** 7081
**General Agreement on Tariff and Trade (GATT
agreement) 14,** 5891
General Services Administration
Civil Service Commission investigation of **18,** 8228
and Civil Service violations **FR** 416-17
final decision of Civil Service Commission on violation of Hatch Act **19,** 8872-81E
and Responsiveness Program **18,** 8244-45 **FR** 412-
13
solicitation of political contributions by employees
of **FR** 413-14
Geneva, Switzerland
trip by F. Donald Nixon, Meier, and Hatsis to **22,**
10714-15
George, Charles 16, 7109 **FR** 915
George, Mrs. Charles 15, 6871-72
George Washington University Law School 9, 3474
Georgia CRP 12, 5009, 5080-81E
Gerard, Sumner FR 494
Gerity, Jim 22, 12529E
"Germaine" 9, 3882E, 3886E
Gesell, Judge FR 1082
Getty, J. Paul 21, 9974, 9975 **22,** 10232, 10519 **24,**
11441 **26,** 12428E **FR** 1059-60
campaign contribution **21,** 10181-82
Haldeman's memo to Ehrlichman on Rebozo's
planned contact with **22,** 12469E
Rebozo solicitation of contribution from **FR** 940-
41, 999

Giacana, Sam **21**, 9683

Gibbons, Harold J. **4**, 1480, 1498
Colson memo to Dean on IRS audit of **FR** 136
memo from Colson to Dean on **4**, 1686E

Gibbs, Phillip **FR** 1175

Gibson, Beatrice **10**, 4258E

Gibson, Fred
See Parr, David L., testimony of

Gifford, William L. **1**, 40, 449E **13**, 5282, 5542E **18**, 8276 **19**, 8606E, 8607E
Ehrlichman on role of **18**, 8195
letter to Hamilton with list of Departmental contacts at OMB for "Responsiveness Program" **19**, 8749-50E
in Malek's plan for Responsiveness Program **FR** 369-70
memo on milk price supports **FR** 815E
note with attachments from Horton on White House papers **18**, 8209, 8348-57E
and Responsiveness Program **18**, 8180-81, 8215, 8218, 8230-31, 8235

Gift tax law
evasion of **2**, 760, 766-67
and Muskie campaign contributions **11**, 4695, 4806-08E

Gill, Michael
Caulfield denies knowledge of surveillance of **21**, 9707-9708

Ginsberg, Allen **12**, 5201E

"Give Peace a Chance" **12**, 5092E

Gladieux, Virgil **22**, 10279, 10773-74, 10857

Glaeser, Walter, testimony of **20**, 9417-25 **22**, 10458 **23**, 11177, 11178, 11202 **FR** 1016
and return of Hughes contribution **20**, 9410-15, 9417-25 **23**, 11180

Glanzer, Seymour **1**, 111, 295, 389-90 **2**, 552, 565-66, 808 **9**, 3566 **25**, 12321, 12401E
Kleindienst on **9**, 3567
Porter's perjury on Liddy money and **2**, 642

Gleason, Jack A. **4**, 1582 **8**, 3376E **14**, 6255, 6256 **15**, 6535, 6784, 6795 **16**, 7157 **17**, 7578, 7583 **21**, 10182 **22**, 10488
and AMPI's concern over antitrust problems **FR** 705
at meeting with Parr, Colson, and Kalmbach **15**, 6784-86
FBI interviews **9**, 3526
informs Semer he is blacklisted at White House **16**, 7210
in Jacobsen's *Nader* v. *Butz* deposition **15**, 6441
letter to Semer on Department of Agriculture advisory board positions **16**, 7208, 7225E
letter to Semer on fundraising dinner for Nixon **15**, 6521-23
letter to Semer on TAPE contributions through committees **16**, 7208
meeting with AMPI officials **FR** 595-96
meeting with Parr **15**, 6766-69
meetings with dairy representatives **15**, 6521
meetings with Semer **15**, 6386 **16**, 1789-91
memo from Colson with article from *Washington Post* on dairy contributions to unopposed candidates **FR** 790-91E

memo from Dean to Kalmbach on bill to **3**, 968, 1231-32E
memo to Colson on milk producers **FR** 772-75E
memo to Wilson on corporate Good Government committees **FR** 551-52
Rebozo asks about contributions from foreign nationals **23**, 10855-56
Woods denies discussions on contributors' list with **22**, 10209-11

Glenn, Kay **20**, 9431, 9435, 9436

Glennon, Donald F. **12**, 5012-13, 5136E
affidavit of **12**, 5009, 5135-42E

Godoyn, Earl
See Gonzalez, Virgilio (alias of)

Goemans, John W. **3**, 1117E

Goering, Hermann **12**, 4966, 4972

Goggans, John **14**, 5981, 6311
affidavit with attachments of **17**, 7900-12E

Gold, Elliot **19**, 8872-81E

Gold Star Mothers, Inc. **FR** 784E

Goldberg, Lawrence **1**, 35
information from IRS to Caulfield on **22**, 10365-68 **FR** 138

Goldberg, Lawrence and Rosalee **23**, 11261-62

Goldberg, Lucianne C. **FR** 199-200

Goldbloom, Stanley **25**, 11740-41

Golden, James **20**, 9449 **21**, 9734 **22**, 10209, 10486-87, 10727 **24**, 11416-17 **FR** 242-43E
Caulfield and **21**, 9716
and Caulfield's investigation of O'Brien-Hughes-Maheu relationship **22**, 10204-10205
in correspondence between Danner and Rebozo **24**, 11459
discussion with Danner on Hughes contribution **24**, 11459-60, 11552-55
discussion with Davis **20**, 9569 **24**, 11610-11
discussions with Woods on Hughes organization **22**, 10212
flights on Hughes' plane **20**, 9487-88
Griffin on relationship with **23**, 10785-86
role on Nixon's staff **22**, 10211
visit to Rebozo **24**, 11553
Woods and **22**, 10274-75

Goldman, David **11**, 4809E

Goldman, Henry **9**, 3661

Goldsmith, Bertram J. **22**, 12544E

Goldstein, Jonathan J. **12**, 5113E

Goldstein, Richard A. **18**, 8245-46
affidavit of **18**, 8245, 8399-8404E **FR** 412, 433-34

Goldstein, Stanley P. **25**, 12268
affidavit of Hertz Corp. relations with Muskie campaign **25**, 12373-75E
Edidin referred by Lifflander to **25**, 12263, 12271-72, 12289
letter to Ediden on Johnson bill **25**, 12376E
Lifflander sends Hertz bills to Muskie campaign to **25**, 12272
memo from Lifflander on settling Hertz account **25**, 12282-83

Goldwater, Barry **9**, 3805, 3812 **10**, 4241E, 4245E **12**, 4927, 5076E
dirty tricks against **2**, 647

Johnson's campaign against **10**, 3937-38
Nixon wants him to blast antiwar activists and
    McGovernites **3**, 1100E
tax-exempt foundation supporting **10**, 3919
Gonzalez, Betty Jean 1, 35
Gonzalez, Corky 19, 8774E
Gonzalez, Henry B.
on Fernandez and NEDA **13**, 5392, 5394-99
Gonzalez, Kathy 3, 1135E
Gonzalez, Manuel 19, 8789-90E
Gonzalez, Virgilio 1, 108, 234
arrest of **1**, 106
and Executive clemency **1**, 212-13
and lawyers' meeting **1**, 326
meeting with Segretti in Miami **10**, 4011-12
money for **6**, 2235, 2252
role in Watergate break-in **1**, 367 **FR** 1
See also Cuban Watergate burglars; Watergate de-
    fendants
Good, Josephine 14, 6119
Good Government committees FR 550-53
Gould, Inc., Better Government Association **FR**
    552-53
Tennessee Eastman Co. Volunteers for Better
    Government **FR** 553
Good-bye Mr. Christian (Dougherty) **11**, 4620
Goodearle, Roy
memo from Colson on Hughes **23**, 11079, 11123E
Goodhart, Harry 20, 9487
Goodrich, Rich 25, 11771
Goodyear Tire & Rubber Co.
campaign contribution by **FR** 464-68
letter from Barrick to Myers on return of contri-
    bution to FCRP of **13**, 5526, 5856E
letter from Myers to Parkinson on return of con-
    tribution to FCRP of **13**, 5526, 5855E
letter from Parkinson to Barrick on return of con-
    tribution to FCRP of **13**, 5526, 5857E
See also DeYoung, Russell, testimony of
Gordon, Jack 3, 1152E
Gordon, Joanne FR 131
memo to White House staff with additional ene-
    mies list names **4**, 1691E, 1705-1706E, 1725-
    29E, 1734-53E
Gorton, George 1, 32, 35 **11**, 4641
and Brill's infiltration of peace vigil **FR** 198-99
Goss, Oscar E. (Gene) 15, 6831, 6832, 6863-64, 6865
    16, 7321, 7324 **FR** 908, 909, 921
on AMPI employees working for Mills campaign
    FR 914-15
money delivered by Townsend to **16**, 7088-90,
    7097-98, 7103-04
Gould, Inc.
loan and contribution by Better Government As-
    sociation of **FR** 552-53
Government contracts
and Black voters and Responsiveness Program **18**,
    8256-80
and Brookings Institution **22**, 10356-57
and Caulfield's investigation of Overview Corp.
    22, 10394-95
and documents related to Wallace matter **19**,
    8848-58E

Fernandez on **13**, 5400
and Hallamore Homes **22**, 10678
and industry-by-industry solicitation of campaign
    contributions **FR** 549-50
for Spanish-speaking firms, Marumoto on **13**,
    5284-85
See also Grants; Grantsmanship; Responsiveness
    Program
Government Operations Committee 13, 5311
Graham, Billy 8, 3151, 3152, 3153, 3322E **11**, 4598
    22, 10397 **23**, 11112 **25**, 12120 **FR** 137
Caulfield on requests to IRS for tax information
    on **22**, 10361-62
IRS sensitive case report on **23**, 11267-68, 11269,
    11270-72
See also Billy Graham Day
Graham, Katherine FR 151
Grand Bahama
Rebozo on trips to **21**, 10054
Grant, Harold 11, 4891E
Grants
and appointment of Guerra as Deputy Director of
    OMBE **13**, 5535E
in Armendariz "Plan to Capture the Spanish
    Speaking Vote" **FR** 374
and campaign contributions **13**, 5316-23
Ehrlichman on Nixon's attitude toward **18**, 8190-
    91
and Federation of Experienced Americans **18**,
    8439-42, 8451-57, 8481-82
Fernandez denies discussions with Marumoto or
    Rodriguez on **13**, 5399-5401
to foundations **FR** 141-42
for Hispanic Americans, *see* Marumoto, William
    H., testimony of
Horton's "Discussion Draft" on **FR** 365-67
to La Raza Unida **13**, 5678E, 5697-98E **18**, 8252-
    53 **19**, 8774E
letter from Small Business Administration to
    Development Associates **13**, 5685E
to Lower Rio Grande Valley Department Council
    vs. consortium of OEO **18**, 8234-36
Malek denies discussing with Nixon **18**, 8207
Malek on **18**, 8214, 8215-20
in Malek's plan for Responsiveness Program **FR**
    367-73
Malek's role in **18**, 8280-81
memo from Dent on southern Black leaders and
    FR 365
memo from Marumoto to Davison on Develop-
    ment Associates **13**, 5635-36E
for National Conference of Southwest Council of
    La Raza **19**, 8797-98E
OEO document on FEA **18**, 8458, 8530-32E
OEO memo from Marumoto to Colson on **13**,
    5543-46
OMBE memo from Armendariz to Bayer on **13**,
    5653-57E
OMBE memo from Malek on **13**, 5323, 5542E
and political enemies **4**, 1526, 1528-29
and Responsiveness Program for Blacks **18**, 8256-
    80 **FR** 376
and Responsiveness Program for Spanish-speaking
    groups **FR** 382-94

Walters and **8,** 3270

Walters' memos on meetings with **9,** 3407, 3416, 3417, 3815E, 3821-22E, 3823E

Walters' reports to Helms on meeting with **8,** 3239-40

Walters told by Haldeman to discuss FBI investigation of Watergate with **8,** 3238-39

and Watergate coverup **2,** 822

and White House efforts to restrict FBI Watergate investigation **FR** 37-40

See also Gray confirmation hearings

Gray, Louis Patrick, testimony of 9, 3449-72, 3473-3558

on appointment as Acting Director of FBI **9,** 3450

asks MacGregor to inform Nixon on White House staff use of CIA and FBI **9,** 3462

on attitude toward Watergate break-in in Washington, D.C. **9,** 3527-28

on authority for keeping Hunt on payroll after Watergate burglary **9,** 3514

on belief that Dean, Ehrlichman, Mitchell, and Magruder were not involved in Watergate break-in **9,** 3550

on call to MacGregor **9,** 3530-31, 3542

on cancellation of meeting with Helms and Walters **9,** 3531

on career **9,** 3473-75

on CIA involvement in Watergate **9,** 3150-67

claims lack of knowledge of Walters' meeting with Haldeman and Ehrlichman **9,** 3499

on conclusions about Nixon being victimized **9,** 3535-36

on confirmation hearings **9,** 3488, *see also* Gray confirmation hearings

on conflict between Walters and Helms on CIA involvement in Watergate **9,** 3510-11, 3518-19, 3521

on conflicting testimony re meetings with Walters **9,** 3452-67, 3496-98, 3517-25

on connection between his call to MacGregor and Nixon's call to him **9,** 3536

on contact with CIA on Watergate matter **9,** 3509-12

on contacts with Weicker on destruction of Hunt's files **9,** 3471

on contemporaneous writings after conversations with Walters and telephone conversation with Nixon **9,** 3552

on Dean asking Walters for defense money **9,** 3500

Dean asks to delay interview with Chenow **9,** 3455-56

on Dean-Ehrlichman conversation on his confirmation hearings **9,** 3488

on Dean's calls to cancel interviews with Ogarrio and Dahlberg **9,** 3534, 3535

on Dean's investigation of Watergate **9,** 3529

denies he had Hunt's files **9,** 3470-71

denies knowledge of Dean's request for defense money from Walters **9,** 3505

denies knowledge of other papers in Hunt's file **9,** 3507-3508

denies Nixon requested Watergate information **9,** 3493

denies suspicions about Hunt's files **9,** 3531

denies taping conversations in his office **9,** 3542

on destruction of Hunt's files **9,** 3468, 3484-85, 3504-3506, 3513, 3533, 3605-3606, 3609, 3734

on Diem cablegram **9,** 3468, 3484, 3504-3505, 3513-14

on double-agent theory of Watergate break-in **9,** 3528

duties as assistant attorney general in 1971 **9,** 3487

on efforts of Dean to slow down investigation **9,** 3540-41

on Ehrlichman's telling him Dean is in charge of White House Watergate Investigation **9,** 3539-40

on examination of Hunt's papers **9,** 3504-3505

on FBI file materials given to Dean **9,** 3469-70, 3477-82, 3514-15, 3564, 3576-77

on FBI interview with Erhlichman **9,** 3532

on FBI interviews at CRP and White House **9,** 3512-13

on FBI teletypes **9,** 3477

on FBI theories of CIA involvement **9,** 3518

on following orders for illegal acts **9,** 3506

on getting Hunt's files from Ehrlichman and Dean **9,** 3513-14

Haldeman orders Walters to tell him to stop further investigation in Mexico **8,** 3281-82 **9,** 3405, 3425-26

on handling of classified material **9,** 3532-33

on harm to Nixon **9,** 3541

on Hunt's files **9,** 3467-71, 3494-95, 3503-3506

identifies memos from Walters for exhibits **9,** 3551

on impact of Watergate on lives of people **9,** 3550-51

on instructions from Ehrlichman and Dean on Hunt's papers **9,** 3530

on investigation of Dean and Ehrlichman **9,** 3527

on Kleindienst's attitude toward FBI investigation of Watergate **9,** 3529

on lack of suspicions about Dean **9,** 3548-50

on legality of destruction of Hunt's files **9,** 3508, 3554

on letter to Nixon in 1968 **9,** 3495-96

on McCord's allegations about inadequacy of FBI Watergate investigation **9,** 3485-87

on McCord's article in *Armed Forces Journal International* **9,** 3521-22

meeting with Ehrlichman and Dean **9,** 3483-84

meetings with Dean **9,** 3450-51, 3476-77

on meetings with Kleindienst during confirmation hearings **9,** 3553

meetings with Walters **9,** 3452-53, 3458-67, 3499-3500, 3530

on memo from Dalbey to Felt on dissemination of information to White House **9,** 3479-82

on memo from Walters on Hunt **9,** 3551-3853E

on memo from Walters on information provided by FBI on Watergate incident **9,** 3551, 3850-52E

on memo from Walters on Mr. "Cleo's" contacts with Hunt **9,** 3551, 3854E

on money found on Mrs. Hunt's body **9,** 3515

on nature and future role of FBI **9,** 3544-45

Gray, Louis Patrick, testimony of *(Continued)*
on Nixon campaign funds found on Watergate burglars **9**, 3515-16
on Nixon's confidence or lack of confidence in him **9**, 3545-46
on Nixon's statement of April 30, 1973 **9**, 3489-90
on nomination as FBI Director **9**, 3487-88
on nomination being withdrawn **9**, 3545-46, 3553
on nomination for deputy attorney general **9**, 3475
opening statement **9**, 3449-71
on orders from superiors **9**, 3508
on Petersen's comment that they were expendable **9**, 3547
on Petersen's determination of scope of Watergate investigation **9**, 3551-52
on photographs of Liddy in front of Fielding's office **9**, 3466-67, 3529-30
on plane crash that killed Mrs. Hunt **9**, 3507
on political activity in fall of 1972 **9**, 3547-48
on realization of involvement in Watergate problems **9**, 3525
on reasons for accepting files from Hunt's safe **9**, 3484
on reasons for giving FBI data to Dean **9**, 3482
on reasons for lack of suspiciousness over Hunt's papers **9**, 3526-37
on reasons for not reporting suspicions to Kleindienst **9**, 3536-37
on reasons for seeking advice of counsel **9**, 3547
on reasons for telling President he was being "mortally wounded" **9**, 3531
on reasons why FBI investigation stopped at Liddy and Hunt **9**, 3503
on reasons why he should be believed despite previous lies **9**, 3498-99
on receiving memo from Walters on CIA assistance to Hunt **9**, 3462-63
on recommendation for special prosecutor for Watergate case **9**, 3552-53
on relationship between FBI and White House **9**, 3557-58
on relationship of Watergate investigation to his attitude toward Government **9**, 3546-47
on relationship with Dean **9**, 3476
on relationship with Ehrlichman **9**, 3476
on relationship with Haldeman **9**, 3476
on relationship with Nixon **9**, 3474-75
on relationship with Walters **9**, 3517
on relationship with Weicker **9**, 3489
on rights of having counsel present during FBI interviews **9**, 3512-13
says Ehrlichman made no inquiries on FBI Watergate investigation **9**, 3484
on significance of Mexican checks in FBI Watergate investigation **9**, 3522-23
on summary of FBI Watergate investigation for Dean **9**, 3478
suspects his telephone conversation with Nixon was taped **9**, 3506-07
on suspicions about Dean **9**, 3531-32
on taped telephone conversation with Ehrlichman **9**, 3467, 3512, 3536-39
telephone call from Ehrlichman informing him that Dean will handle Watergate investigation **9**, 3508-3509

telephone call to MacGregor **9**, 3541
telephone calls from Dean **9**, 3452, 3497
telephone calls to Dean **9**, 3453-54, 3455-56, 3457
on telephone conversation with Nixon **9**, 3462, 3489-90, 3497-98, 3506-07, 3523-25, 3527, 3531, 3536, 3541
tells Dean about Dahlberg and Mexican checks **9**, 3451
tells Ehrlichman Hunt files were destroyed **9**, 3470
on visit from Helms **9**, 3466
on Watergate **FR** 1225-26
on worrying over Nixon's response to his warnings **9**, 3541
Gray, Mrs. Louis Patrick 6, 2311, 2314, 2332 **9**, 3476
Gray, Richard 26, 12775E **FR** 982
Jones report to Rashid on conference with **26**, 12923-24E
memo to Hughes on Justice Department antitrust suit and Dunes Hotel acquisition **26**, 12788E
in report on Dunes Hotel acquisition proposal **26**, 12903-10E
statements made before Nevada Gaming Commission in report from Jones to Rashid **26**, 12913-14E
Gray, Robert
on campaign contributions and ambassadorships **FR** 494-95
Gray confirmation hearings 3, 993, 994-95, 1092, 1252E **4**, 1403, 1422 **7**, 2811-12, 2899 **9**, 3598-99
Byrne and **6**, 2617
Dean and **4**, 1494, 1549, 1550 **5**, 1863, 1943, 1971, 1972, 1979-80 **7**, 2746
and Dean lying **5**, 2055
Dean-Nixon discussions on **4**, 1405, 1406
Krogh and **4**, 1491
Nixon's call to Gray on **9**, 3490
raised at Nixon's press conference **4**, 1404
and Segretti matter **5**, 2033-34, 2035, 2039
Grayham, Willy 23, 11255
Great Plains Wheat, Inc. 10, 4088-89E
Greaves, Roger 2, 658, 679 **FR** 184
sabotage activities **11**, 4638-39
and Sedan Chair I **FR** 190-92
Green, James Earl FR 1175
Green, Thomas C.
See Butterbrodt, John E., testimony of
Green Light Program 19, 9226-27E
Green Thumb Program 19, 9226-27E, 9229E
Greenbaum, Leon C. 25, 12222, 12301
See also Clark, Matthew E., Jr., testimony of
Greenberg, Carl 3, 1148E
Greene, Leon FR 139
Greene, Robert W. 21, 10127 **22**, 10387 **23**, 11266
Caulfield on IRS audit of **22**, 10368-77
IRS audit of **22**, 10390 **FR** 135-36
Greene, Saundra
message to Liddy **3**, 977, 1238E
Greenspun, Herman 7, 2801 **9**, 3686 **22**, 10661
contacts with Danner **24**, 11550
and Hughes contribution **23**, 11032

and Hughes memos **20**, 9608-10 **21**, 9724-25, 10130
on Hughes' plane **20**, 9477-78
inquiries about Hughes contribution **21**, 10130
and Maheu **20**, 9346, 9349, 9354-55, 9361-62, 9372-73, 9376, 9380
meetings with Kalmbach **20**, 9607
rumor on possession of information on Muskie by **20**, 9346, 9349-50, 9352, 9356-57, 9365-66, 9368, 9370-71
Wearley on planned break-in at office of **20**, 9483
See also Greenspun break-in; Las Vegas matter
Greenspun break-in 1, 202, 230 **2**, 790, 791 **23**, 11105-11106
Buzhardt denies discussion of material in Nixon tapes on **23**, 10908-10909
Danner on discussions of **24**, 11561-62
Davis and **24**, 11598-11601
Garment denies knowledge of **23**, 11071
Hunt and conversation between Davis and Bennett on **24**, 11601-11603
and Hunt-Winte meeting **24**, 11596-11601, 11604
Nixon tapes on **23**, 11033
Greenwood, Toni B. 12, 5011
affidavit of **12**, 5009, 5185-87E
Greer, Alan G.
on agreements with Dash **22**, 10532, 10533-37
on agreements with Dash on line of questioning of Moncourt **22**, 10514-15
at Armstrong interview of Wakefield **24**, 11287-88
and attorney-client privilege on Wakefield testimony **24**, 11293
and Committee's requests for documents **22**, 10533-37
on Ervin's absence **22**, 10500-10501
on his firm representing Rebozo's employees **22**, 10532
objections to line of questioning of Moncourt **22**, 10491, 10501, 10520, 10528, 10530-31, 10532
objects to Committee's investigations **22**, 10532
on Rebozo documents **21**, 10020-21, 10023, 10024, 10025-26, 10027, 10028, 10029, 10030, 10031, 10032, 10033, 10034, 10035, 10036, 10038-39
on Rebozo phone records **21**, 10021-22
on records of Rebozo safety deposit boxes **21**, 10011-12
requests Select Committee Staff question Moncourt one at a time **22**, 10487
Senate Select Committee subpoena for **22**, 12618-20E
See also Moncourt, Nicole, testimony of
Greer, Willie 12, 4987
Gregory, Charles
See Rebozo, Charles Gregory (alias of)
Gregory, Thomas 1, 164 **9**, 3685-86, 3761 **11**, 4657, 4658, 4672 **FR** 1123
and efforts to bug McGovern headquarters **FR** 27-28
Hunt and **20**, 9366, 9367
infiltration into Muskie campaign **11**, 4636, 4638
and Ruby II **FR** 196-97

Greigg, Stanley 1, 107
Grenold, Ben 3, 1152E
Gribbon, Daniel
See DeYoung, Russell, testimony of
Griffin, Patricia 8, 3375E **9**, 3574 **11**, 4405, 4408 **FR** 169
activities as infiltrator in Muskie Florida campaign **11**, 4406-4407
Benz on hiring of **11**, 4430-31
Griffin, Peg FR 167
Griffin, Robert P. 16, 7338
Griffin, William, Sr.
letter from Ervin re subpoenaing of telephone records **26**, 10479E
letter from Ervin to A. T. & T. canceling subpoena on telephone records of **26**, 10480E
Griffin, William E. 20, 9413 **21**, 9994, 9995, 10062, 10064 **22**, 10276, 10729 **23**, 10961, 11069-70 **24**, 11549 **FR** 174
airplane registration numbers **23**, 10795E
business and financial dealings with Rebozo **22**, 10497, 10498-99
Buzhardt denies knowing **23**, 10923-24
check to Nixon **23**, 10796E
check to West Republican County Committee **23**, 10798E
checks to Florida hotels written by **26**, 10481-82E
checks to Precision Valve Corp. **23**, 10795E, 10797E
discussion with Rebozo about Hughes money **21**, 10102
on learning about Hughes contribution from Rebozo **FR** 1063
McKiernan denies knowing **22**, 10653
in *New York Times* article on Hughes contribution **23**, 10800E
note for file on Rebozo's loan from Hudson Valley National Bank **23**, 10847E
purchase of Key Biscayne property from Nixon **24**, 11332-33
Rebozo discusses with Woods **22**, 10213-14, 10216
Rebozo's discussions on Hughes contributions with **24**, 11469
relationship with Rebozo **23**, 11204-11205
and return of Hughes contribution **21**, 10092-93, 10115-16 **FR** 1009-10
round-trip ticket from New York to Miami **23**, 10799E
scheduling of further testimony of **22**, 10474-75
subpoena for **26**, 10476-78E
Griffin, William E., testimony of 22, 10411-75 **23**, 10738-94
on Abplanalp's lack of knowledge of Hughes contribution **22**, 10466-68
on advising Rebozo to return Hughes contribution **22**, 10439-40
Ambrose's objections to line of questioning of **22**, 10470-71, 10472
on areas of waiver of attorney-client privilege from Rebozo and Abplanalp **23**, 10755, 10756-57
Armstrong's requests for waiver of attorney-client privilege from **23**, 10774-79, 10780
billings to Rebozo for representing in loan transaction **23**, 10765

Griffin, William E., testimony of *(Continued)*

on calculation of selling price for Rebozo's share of San Clemente partnership **23,** 10748-49

on checks from Precision Valve Corp. to Abplanalp **23,** 10746

on collateral for Abplanalp's loan to Nixon **23,** 10739

on communication with Rebozo unrelated to Hughes contribution **22,** 10415-16

on Cox investigation of Rebozo **22,** 10462

on dealings with Davis and Crosby of Resorts International **23,** 10791-93

on dealings with Moncourt on transfer of Rebozo's account to B & C account **23,** 10753-54

denies being source of leaks **23,** 10790

denies business or financial transactions with Kalmbach or DeMarco **23,** 10779

denies business or financial transactions with Nixon's family or relatives **23,** 10780

denies discussing return of Hughes contribution with anyone at White House **22,** 10461

denies discussing testimony with Rebozo **22,** 10462-63

denies efforts to identify $100,000 as original contribution **22,** 10445-46

denies knowledge of Nixon, Rebozo, or Mitchell maintaining cash currency in excess of $1000 **23,** 10793

denies knowledge of Rebozo meetings with Nixon and Abplanalp **22,** 10448

on discussions with Abplanalp **22,** 10350-51

on discussions with Rebozo on return of Hughes contribution **22,** 10446-48, 10461-62

on documents reflecting representation of Rebozo in B & C Investment Co. matter **23,** 10752

on documents related to San Clemente property transaction **23,** 10741-42

effects of leaks on his career **23,** 10791

on financial dealings between Rebozo, Woods, Nixon, and Abplanalp **23,** 10783-84

on financial transactions or business with Nixon **23,** 10768-75

on financial transactions with Rebozo **23,** 10768

on first learning of Nixon's interest in selling part of San Clemente property **23,** 10739-40

on first meeting with Rebozo **22,** 10411-12

on first meeting with Rebozo on Hughes contribution **22,** 10427-38

informs Rebozo of IRS audit of B & C Investment Co. **23,** 10755

on Kalmbach's testimony on Rebozo using Hughes contribution **23,** 10788-89

on legal research conducted on Rebozo's problem with Hughes contribution **22,** 10469

on loan from Rebozo to Nixon **23,** 10747

on loans from Precision Valve Corp. to B & C Investment Co. **23,** 10752

on meeting with Gemmill and IRS auditors for B & C Investment Co. **23,** 10754-55

on Nixon's interest in purchasing San Clemente property **23,** 10738-39

on Nixon's sale of San Clemente property **23,** 10739-40

on payment of taxes of B & C Investment Co. **23,** 10753, 10754

persons discussing meeting with Select Committee staff with **23,** 10786-91

protests Committee subpoena of mother's and father's telephone records **22,** 10416-17

on reasons for advising Rebozo to return Hughes contribution **22,** 10469

on reasons for not discussing Hughes contribution with Abplanalp **22,** 10472

on reasons for Rebozo selling share of San Clemente property to Abplanalp **23,** 10747

on Rebozo paying business or personal expenses for Nixon **23,** 10781-83, 10784-85

on Rebozo telling him $100,000 was identical money received from Danner **22,** 10436-37

on Rebozo's call to discuss problem **22,** 10413-14

on Rebozo's efforts to return money to Griffin **22,** 10464-65

on Rebozo's interest in selling his interest in San Clemente property **23,** 10744-46

Rebozo's loan of $225,000 from Precision Valve Corp. and/or Hudson Valley Bank **23,** 10756-57, 10760-65

on Rebozo's meeting with Gemmill in Philadelphia **22,** 10452

on Rebozo's need for cash **23,** 10746, 10747, 10755

on Rebozo's purchase of house in Maryland **23,** 10780-81

on receiving envelope from Rebozo **22,** 10453-56

on records brought for submission to Select Committee **22,** 10414-17

on refinancing of San Clemente property **23,** 10750-51

on relationship with Abplanalp **22,** 10412

on relationship with Golden **23,** 10785-86

on relationship with Nixon **22,** 10412-13

on representation of Rebozo in B & C Investment Co. transaction **22,** 10435-36

on research on statutes relating to Rebozo's holding of Hughes contribution **22,** 10433-34

on returning Hughes contribution to Gemmill **22,** 10456-58

on second meeting with Rebozo on Hughes contribution **22,** 10439-46

on source of Rebozo's payment to B & C Investment Co. **23,** 10743-44

on telephone calls on day of return of Hughes contribution **22,** 10458-59

on telephone calls to Rebozo **22,** 10425-29

on telephone calls to White House **23,** 10794

on telephone calls to White House on day of returning Hughes contribution **22,** 10459-61

on telephone records **23,** 10794

on trip to Saranac Lake with Rebozo and Abplanalp **22,** 10422-24, 10464-66

on trips to Florida from January 1 to June 30, 1973 **22,** 10417-24, 10425

on Wakefield's role in return of Hughes contribution **22,** 10451

on willingness to testify on return of Hughes contribution **22,** 10473

Griffin, Mrs. William E. **22,** 10421
Griffith, James **FR** 385
Griffith, W.R. (Preach) **14,** 5912, 5913, 5959 **16,**
7300 **17,** 7627, 7660
and AMPI reimbursement scheme **15,** 6531-32
letter from Mehren on campaign proposal **14,**
6119, 6186E
Griffiths, Arthur **FR** 894-95, 896-97
checks to Humphrey committees accumulated by
25, 11986-89E
and Hertz arrangement with Muskie campaign **25,**
12238
Grimes, John **16,** 6961
Grinalds, John
memo to Malek on military voters **19,** 9332-37E
FR 430-31
Griswold, Dean **8,** 3375E **9,** 3574
Grossman, Richard **15,** 6466-67 **16,** 7444 **17,** 7633,
7668
Groves **24,** 11431-32
Guatemala
Hunt and 1954 overthrow of regime in **9,** 3726
Guenther, George C. **FR** 432-33
memo on OSHA programs **19,** 8801-8803E
Guerra, Cip **13,** 5279-80, 5400, 5535E **FR** 391
Guest, Raymond **4,** 1691E **21,** 9974, 9975 **FR** 999
Guggenheim, Charles **3,** 1138E
Gulf Oil Corp., campaign contributions by **FR** 469-73
and Good Government Fund **FR** 925
letter from Barrick to Mellott on return of **13,**
5466, 5806E
letter from Mellott to Parkinson on origin of **13,**
5466, 5804-05E
letter on Wild contribution to Mills for President
Committee **25,** 12028, 12029E, 12030
press release admitting **13,** 5466, 5808-09E
See also Wild, Claude C., Jr., testimony of
Gulf Resources and Chemical Corporation **FR** 514
subpoenaed by Patman Committee **3,** 1192E
See also Allen, Robert H.
Gulledge, Eugene **13,** 5337
Gun control **10,** 4057E
Gurney, Edward J. **1,** 117 **5,** 2083, 2084, 2089, 2090
absence for vote on nomination of Richardson for
attorney general **1,** 293
on Buchanan's complaint about lack of time to
study his memos **10,** 3908
on Dash's interview with Alch **1,** 263-264
on decision on Colson's appearance as witness **8,**
3219-21
on dirty tricks as part of politics **11,** 4391
Ehrlichman's reaction to as member of Select
Committee **3,** 983
on Ervin's "harassment" of Stans **2,** 767
on his reaction to Watergate break-in **9,** 3527,
3528
on importance of Moore's testimony **5,** 1997-98
on legality of destroying records of contributions
5, 2131-32
letter and documents from Statler-Hilton Hotel,
Washington, D.C., on Kalmbach's registration
5, 2210-14
letter from the Mayflower Hotel **5,** 2009E

on McCall's testimony **1,** 132
on Moore's character **5,** 2001
on news of subpoena to obtain Nixon's logs **2,**
531-32
Nixon's attitude toward **3,** 992
on Nixon's involvement or noninvolvement as
central theme of Select Committee hearings **8,**
3181
opening statement **1,** 7-8
questions Dash's line of questioning of Hunt **9,**
3670, 3671
on reasons for appointment of special prosecutor
for Watergate case **9,** 3646
on reasons for calling Stearns to testify **11,** 4591
on Select Committee in relation to federal
prosecutor **5,** 2060
on Watergate hearings **8,** 3181 **9,** 3647
Gurney, Edward J., questioning by
Alch **1,** 342-347
Buchanan **10,** 3951-57
Buckley **11,** 4454-56
Caulfield **1,** 277-278
Cushman **8,** 3306-2208
Dean **4,** 1351-1407, 1511-23
Dole **1,** 23-26
Ehrlichman **6,** 2606-16 **7,** 2718-27, 2737-58, 2807-
10
Gray **9,** 3499-3503, 3527-30
Haldeman **7,** 2895, 2896 **8,** 3096-3100, 3124,
3125, 3142-46, 3165-69
Harmony **2,** 470-73
Helms **8,** 3254-56
Hunt **9,** 3736-39, 3763-68, 3792, 3793
Kalmbach **5,** 2131-35, 2148-42
Kehrli **1,** 84-88
Kelly **11,** 4391-93, 4400, 4401
Kleindienst **9,** 3590-93
LaRue **6,** 2311-15
Leeper **1,** 112
Magruder **2,** 838-44
Mardian **6,** 2394-98
McCord **1,** 135-137, 165-71, 210-17
McMinoway **11,** 4522-29
Mitchell **4,** 1667-81
Moore **5,** 1997-2009, 2060
Odle **1,** 62-69
Petersen **9,** 3646-50
Porter **2,** 657-64, 678-80
Reisner **2,** 518-22
Segretti **10,** 4019-21
Sloan **2,** 587-99
Stans **2,** 719-26
Stearns **11,** 4592, 4593
Strachan **6,** 2491-95
Ulasewicz **6,** 2249-61
Walters **9,** 3435-39
Gurney, Edward J., statement of **FR** 1171-74
on criticisms of Watergate hearings **FR** 1171-72
on opposition to committee's recommendation for
public attorney **FR** 1172-74
on reform of campaign laws **FR** 1172
Guthman, Ed **8,** 3155 **21,** 10127 **22,** 10373
on enemies list **4,** 1694E, 1698E

Gutierrez, Jose Angel **13,** 5679-80E, 5697-98E **19,** 8774E **FR** 398

Gutstein, Dr. T. **FR** 485

Gwirtzman, Milton
  letter to Muskie Accountability Project **25,** 12106-12107, 12131-32E

Habedank, Allan **12,** 5126E

Hackler, Dan **25,** 11722

Haddad, Frank E., Jr
  See McMinoway, Michael W.

Hagan, LaDonna **25,** 11776

Hagerty, Jim **11,** 4623

Haig, Alexander M., Jr. **1,** 75 **3,** 1072 **4,** 1662 **11,** 4884E **22,** 10268, 10275-76, 10551, 10554 **23,** 11054, 11183, 11198
  "Authority to Investigate" document of Select Committee on **23,** 10996, 11038-41E
  Barth denies discussing IRS Hughes report with **23,** 11246
  Buzhardt's preliminary statement on Executive privilege and testimony of **23,** 10996-97
  contacts with Edward Nixon **22,** 10655
  conversation with Buzhardt after appearance before Select Committee staff **23,** 10889, 10890-91
  discussion with Rebozo **22,** 10212-13
  discussions with Gemmill on Rebozo and Hughes contribution problem **23,** 11190, 11191-93, 11195
  discussions with Rebozo on Hughes money **21,** 10108-10109
  discussions with Simon on Rebozo matter **23,** 10930-32, 10933, 10936
  first subpoena served on **23,** 11049-50E
  informs Nixon of IRS investigation **23,** 11064, 11065-66
  and IRS investigation of Rebozo **22,** 12441E
  letter from Nixon invoking Executive privilege and directing him not to testify **23,** 10849-50
  meeting with Rose, Garment, and Buzhardt on IRS investigation of Rebozo **23,** 10999, 11000-11001, 11022-23, 11060-61, 11064-65
  and Nixon brothers **22,** 10622
  questions asked and answers refused from interview of **23,** 10996, 11042-48E
  refuses to answer all questions **23,** 10850-53
  reports on antiwar groups **3,** 917
  second subpoena served on **23,** 10996, 11051-52E
  Senate Select Committee resolution and other documents on testimony of **23,** 10995-96
  telephone call from Rose to Gemmill on testimony of **23,** 11215-16
  telephone call to Richardson on Cox investigation of Rebozo **23,** 10888-89, 10891, 11214-15, 11216-17 **FR** 1022-25
  telephone calls from Schultz on IRS sensitive cases **23,** 10928-29
  tells Higby that Dean authorized money for Hunt **23,** 11110-11
  Woods denies discussing Rebozo's return of Hughes contribution with **22,** 10239-40

Haig, Alexander M., Jr., testimony of **23,** 10849-53, 10998-11036
  on assignment to White House **23,** 11002
  on attitude toward person responsible for Hughes contribution **23,** 11015-17
  on attitude toward Rebozo-Hughes matter **23,** 11018-19
  on awareness that Hughes money was campaign contribution **23,** 11009-10
  on belief Nixon had no knowledge of Hughes contribution **23,** 11027
  on Camp David meeting between Nixon, Rebozo, and Danner **FR** 1012
  on conversation with Rebozo on recommendation of Gemmill **23,** 11017
  on conversations with Nixon on Hughes-Rebozo matter **23,** 11027-30
  on conversations with Rebozo on Hughes contribution **23,** 11023-24
  on conversations with Simon on IRS investigation of Rebozo **23,** 11002-11003, 11004-11005, 11020-21
  on Cox investigation of Hughes-Rebozo matter **FR** 1022-23, 1024-25
  denies being at Camp David at time of Nixon, Danner, Rebozo meeting **23,** 11019-20
  denies discussing Greenspun matter with Richardson **23,** 11032
  denies discussing Hughes-Rebozo matter with Haldeman, Ehrlichman, or Higby **23,** 11021-22
  denies knowledge of Defense Department procurement of airplanes **23,** 11035-36
  denies knowledge of Greenspun break-in **23,** 11033
  denies knowledge of investigations or electronic surveillance of Select Committee or staff **23,** 11034
  denies knowledge of other campaign contributions not turned over to CRP **23,** 11030
  denies knowledge of Rebozo-Kalmbach meeting **23,** 11031
  denies listening to Nixon tapes on conversations on Hughes-Rebozo matter **23,** 11023
  denies White House employee was assigned to monitor Hughes-Rebozo matter **23,** 11004
  on discussion with Nixon on testifying before Select Committee **23,** 11025
  on discussion with Rebozo on Hughes contribution **23,** 11034
  on discussion with Ziegler on Camp David meeting of Nixon, Danner, and Rebozo **23,** 11005-11006
  on discussions with Nixon on Hughes contribution **23,** 11011-12, 11019
  on discussions with Rebozo on IRS investigation **23,** 11003-11004
  on discussions with Richardson on Cox investigation **23,** 11013-15, 11020, 11032-33
  on duties as Chief of Staff **23,** 10998
  on duties with regard to Hughes contribution through Rebozo **23,** 10998-11000
  on first knowledge of IRS investigation of F. Donald Nixon **23,** 11034
  on Gemmill's statement about serial numbers on Hughes money **23,** 11009

on Hughes contribution and CRP **23,** 11010
on impact of Watergate hearings on foreign relations **23,** 11014-15
informed by Simon of IRS investigation of Rebozo **23,** 10999, 11000, 11002
informs Nixon of report from Simon on IRS investigation of Hughes contribution **23,** 10999, 11001
on leaks **23,** 11026
on meeting between Nixon, McKiernan, and Nixon brothers **23,** 11024-25
on meeting with White House staff and Nixon **FR** 1013-14
on Nixon telling him Rebozo did not use Hughes money **23,** 11024
on Nixon's request for lawyer for Rebozo **23,** 10999, 11000
on Rebozo's fundraising role **23,** 11017-18 **FR** 941
on Rebozo's return of Hughes contribution **23,** 11006-11009
on Rebozo's suits against *Washington Post* and Select Committee **23,** 11030
on recommending Gemmill to Rebozo **23,** 11011, 11023
on relationship with Rebozo **23,** 11016-17
on statement to press **23,** 11036
Haiphong harbor, mining of
and CRP campaign in support of **FR** 152
Haladay, Henry 11, 4773E
Halberstam, David 9, 3882E
Haldeman, Harry Robins 1, 13, 25, 31, 35, 54, 58, 75, 80 **2,** 506, 572, 623, 721 **4,** 1675, 1676 **5,** 1855 **6,** 2519 **21,** 10188 **22,** 10239
and access to Nixon **4,** 1489, 1542
and access to Nixon tapes **5,** 2089-90
after Watergate arrests **5,** 1853
and agencies responsive and unresponsive to White House **4,** 1481
agrees Dean should further inform Nixon on Watergate situation **3,** 998
aides of **6,** 2466-67
and AMPI contribution **16,** 7333, 7460
and antitrust suit against AMPI **FR** 705
and antiwar demonstrations **3,** 917, 918, 926-27, 1263E
approval of Segretti hiring **FR** 161
approval of Segretti's activities by **3,** 964
asks Dean for written report on Watergate **3,** 967 **4,** 1384-85, 1552
asks Dean to draw up agenda for meeting with Nixon on La Costa decisions **3,** 987-88
asks Dean to meet with Mitchell and Magruder **FR** 71, 89-90
asks Dean to prepare agenda for Nixon's meeting with Baker **3,** 988
asks Dean to prepare briefing paper for Nixon's meeting with Kleindienst **3,** 989
asks Dean to talk to Mitchell **3,** 1042
asks to meet with Mitchell and Magruder **4,** 1449
assessment of members of Select Committee **3,** 983-84
at La Costa meetings with Dean, Ehrlichman, and Moore **3,** 982-86 **5,** 1940-42, 2049
at meeting on Segretti matter **5,** 2022-23

at meeting when Dean tells Nixon about coverup **3,** 1047
at meeting with Malek, Mitchell, Ehrlichman, Shultz, and Nixon **18,** 8205-8206
at Nixon-Dean meetings **3,** 957-59 **4,** 1371-73, 1382-83, 1475, 1476, 1538, 1540 **5,** 1838
at Nixon-MacGregor meeting **12,** 4942
at Nixon-Mitchell meetings **4,** 1676, 1677
at San Clemente meetings **4,** 1510-11
and attacks on O'Brien **4,** 1471
and attempts to discredit Ervin **4,** 1533
authority of **5,** 2092
and awareness of Semer-Kalmbach meeting and agreement **17,** 7806
on belief of legality of defense fund for Watergate defendants **FR** 62
and briefing of Ziegler after Watergate **3,** 1074
briefing paper for meeting with head of IRS **4,** 1682-85E
Buchanan's memos and **10,** 3910
Buchanan's reporting relationship to **10,** 3905
and bugging, burglarizing, and mailcover plan against antiwar leaders and supporters **3,** 916
and Buzhardt memo on Dean-Nixon conversations **23,** 10900
California suit against in **5,** 2128
calls Magruder after Watergate arrests **2,** 799, 815-16, 820, 821, 828-29, 858-59
and campaign contributions **16,** 7374-75
cash disbursement made by Sloan to Kalmbach for **2,** 607-608
Caulfield and **1,** 251, 270 **22,** 10389 **FR** 109
Caulfield denies discussions on tax information with **22,** 10379
and Caulfield's investigation of Meany **22,** 10402
and "Chapman's Friend Reports" **FR** 199-200
and CIA involvement in Watergate investigation **3,** 946 **4,** 1416
and clearance of CRP personnel **1,** 72
Colson takes blame for **4,** 1491
and Colson's conversation with Hunt **4,** 1419
and Colson's repayment of expenses of Fielding break-in **FR** 698-99
and committees for milk producers' contributions **FR** 689-90
confidential memo to Colson, Buchanan, Cole, and Magruder on support for administration's Vietnam position **10,** 3975, 4120-26E
conflict between his testimony and Ehrlichman's **7,** 2861-63
control of surplus money from 1968 campaign **3,** 968
and countermoves against Democrats **3,** 1242E
and coverup plan for Select Committee hearings **3,** 979-82
and creation of Interagency Domestic Intelligence unit **3,** 1064
and Dahlberg checks coverup **FR** 37
Dean as liaison between Mitchell and **5,** 1900
Dean informs about newspaper stories that Magruder and Dean had prior knowledge about Watergate **3,** 1004
Dean informs of efforts to block Patman Committee hearings **3,** 960
and "Dean Report" **3,** 1075 **4,** 1422

Haldeman, Harry Robins *(Continued)*

Dean reports conversation with Gray to **3,** 943, 944

Dean reports on FBI interview files to **4,** 1360

Dean transmits facts to **6,** 2451

and Dean's decision to expose coverup **4,** 1398-99 **5,** 1987

and Dean's idea of independent panel to investigate Watergate **3,** 1005

on Dean's indictable list **5,** 1989

and Dean's investigation of O'Brien-Hughes relationship **23,** 10907-10908

and Dean's involvement in coverup **2,** 803-804

as Dean's liaison to Nixon **4,** 1358

and Dean's offer of Executive clemency to Magruder **4,** 1443-44

and Dean's preparation of agenda for meeting with Nixon **4,** 1486

and Dean's reaction to Nixon's announcement of "Dean report" **4,** 1367-68

and Dean's talking with federal prosecutors **4,** 1552

and Dean's tape of conversation with Segretti **3,** 966

Dean's testimony to prosecutors on **9,** 3632-36

demonstrations and dissent as reasons for Huston Plan **FR** 6

denies that he instructed Walters to talk with Gray **9,** 3448

and destruction of documents **3,** 1035, 1091 **4,** 1369-70, 1372, 1415

discussions with Mitchell on Ellsberg matter **5,** 1905

discussions with Mitchell on Watergate **4,** 1661

discussions with Mitchell on White House horror stories **4,** 1625

and DNC civil suits **FR** 74

duplicates of Mitchell's documents sent to **2,** 504

and Edward Nixon's employment by Richard Nixon Foundation **23,** 10857, 11104

efforts to get CIA to stop FBI investigation of Mexican money **9,** 3648

efforts to involve CIA **5,** 1884

efforts to restrict FBI Watergate investigation **FR** 37-40

Ehrlichman discusses Watergate with **6,** 2581-82

and employment help for Magruder after Watergate **3,** 990-91

and employment of Hunt at White House **9,** 3662

and employment of Sloan at CRP **2,** 533

and enemies list **3,** 958-59 **4,** 1408-1409, 1498, 1529

and Gemstone file **4,** 1619-20

gifts to personnel for moving expenses **23,** 11091-92

and grand jury hearings **4,** 1384

and grantsmanship **18,** 8218

Gray claims lack of knowledge of meeting with Ehrlichman and Walters **9,** 3499

Haig and **23,** 11002

and Halperin's tapped telephone **11,** 4665

Higby as deputy to **23,** 11074

Higby denies knowledge of funds received after leaving White House by **23,** 11108-11109

Higby discusses Nixon's mention of Rebozo's offer of legal fee money with **23,** 11082-84

and Hillings letter to Nixon **16,** 7378-79

and hush money **3,** 950, 951, 969-70, 971 **4,** 1391, 1392, 1648-49 **5,** 2149 **FR** 51-52

and Huston memo on IRS moving against leftist organizations **FR** 139

and Huston Plan **6,** 2528 **FR** 5

information from Connally on milk producers' contribution **FR** 653

and installation of Nixon's listening devices **5,** 2077

instructions to Kalmbach on handling of 1968 surplus funds **17,** 7579-80

instructions to Liddy to transfer intelligence from Muskie to McGovern **FR** 27

instructions to Ulasewicz **FR** 110

instructs Dean to write report on Watergate **3,** 1003 **FR** 89

instructs Strachan to clean files after Watergate break-in **3,** 934 **6,** 2471-72

instructs Strachan to destroy documents **7,** 2744-45

instructs Walters to go to Gray **8,** 3281-82

and Intelligence Advisory Committee **1,** 201

interest in political intelligence **6,** 2450

involvement in Watergate break-in **3,** 1088-89

and IRS audits **4,** 1480

and IRS responsiveness to White House **4,** 1410-11

Kalmbach feels used by **5,** 2175

Kalmbach informs of Semer's delivery of AMPI contribution **17,** 7582

Kalmbach on awareness of AMPI contribution and objectives **17,** 7811-12

Kalmbach on Dean's claim that he was speaking on behalf of **5,** 2115-16

and Kalmbach's efforts to obtain ambassadorship in Europe for Symington **FR** 498

on Kalmbach's handling of 1968 surplus funds **FR** 591

and Kalmbach's payment to Segretti **5,** 2132

and Kalmbach's payments out of 1968 fund **23,** 11090

and Kalmbach's role in 1972 campaign **17,** 7589-90

and Kalmbach's testimony before grand jury **5,** 2161, 2167-68

and Kingsley's reports on Responsiveness Program **18,** 8284-86

and Kissinger tapes **6,** 2406, 2408, 2533

knowledge of Colson's dirty tricks **6,** 2475

knowledge of Hughes contribution **FR** 1057

knowledge of Liddy plan **6,** 2490

knowledge of Magruder's perjury **2,** 832

knowledge of Nixon's tape recorders **5,** 2075, 2085

and leaks **3,** 921, 922 **6,** 2504-2505

learns about Liddy plan meetings from Dean **7,** 2753-54

learns Dean is talking to Government prosecutors **3,** 10-11 **FR** 91

leave of absence request of **3,** 1018, 1317-18E

as liaison between Dean and Nixon **4,** 1353-54

as liaison with CRP **2,** 675, 785

Liddy and **6,** 2475-76

and Liddy plan **3,** 1265E **4,** 1553
and Liddy's employment at CRP **2,** 871
and loan to Hitt **2,** 558
MacGregor answers *Washington Post* article on **12,** 4902-4904
and Magruder perjury **FR** 44
Magruder tells truth about Watergate to **2,** 806, 821, 850, 851, 860
Magruder threatens **4,** 1577-78
and Magruder's employment at CRP **2,** 784 **4,** 1606
Magruder's messages through Strachan to **2,** 819
and Magruder's plan to run for office **4,** 1380
Magruder's post-Watergate meeting with **2,** 831-32
and Magruder's statement to O'Brien on Nixon's involvement in Watergate **3,** 990-91
and Magruder's testimony before grand jury **3,** 952 **4,** 1624 **9,** 3651
Malek on work relationship with **18,** 8200
Malek takes blame for Schorr investigation for **4,** 1490
and Malek's plan for Responsiveness Program **FR** 367-78
Malek's progress reports on Responsiveness Program to **18,** 8234-39
Mankiewicz on allegations against Democrats of **11,** 4602-4603
material from Strachan to **6,** 2466
and McMinoway's reports **11,** 4479
and media reports on Watergate **5,** 2018
meeting with CIA people **2,** 867
meeting with Dean and Ehrlichman on Segretti matter **FR** 182-83
meeting with Dean on use of "milk money" **FR** 673
meeting with Magruder **4,** 1634 **FR** 71
meeting with Mitchell, MacGregor, and Nixon **12,** 4943
meeting with Mitchell after Key Biscayne **6,** 2476-77
meeting with Mitchell and Magruder after Watergate arrests **2,** 841-42
meeting with Mitchell and Moore **5,** 2062-63
meeting with Mitchell on antitrust suit against AMPI **FR** 706-707
meeting with Nixon, Dean, Ehrlichman, and Mitchell **3,** 1000-1002
meeting with Sloan **2,** 597-98, 608-10, 611, 612-14, 626-27, 628, 629
meeting with Stans on campaign spending **2,** 715-16
meeting with Strachan after Watergate break-in **6,** 2458
meeting with Strachan before his grand jury testimony **6,** 2464-65
and meetings to plan coverup **3,** 1089-92
meetings with Dean after Watergate **4,** 1420
meetings with Ehrlichman, Dean, and Nixon **3,** 1000 **4,** 1306-1307
meetings with Ehrlichman, Mitchell, and Nixon brothers **22,** 10640-42
meetings with MacGregor **12,** 4940
meetings with Mitchell after Watergate **5,** 1881, 1885

meetings with Mitchell on White House horror activities **5,** 1903-1904
methods of working **6,** 2456
Mitchell and **4,** 1613
Mitchell discusses Watergate with **5,** 1859-60
and money given to Kalmbach **2,** 724
and money transferred from CRP to White House **6,** 2495, 2497-99, 2500 **6,** 2295, 2461-64
Nixon's attitude toward testifying before Select Committee **5,** 1957-58
and Nixon's instructions on Watergate investigation and national security **7,** 2697
and Nixon's involvement in Watergate coverup **3,** 1078 **4,** 1468-69, 73-74
and Nixon's references to Executive clemency for Hunt **3,** 995-96
and Nixon's request for Dean's resignation **3,** 1018-20
and Nixon's request that Dean prepare counter-suit against Democrats **3,** 956-57
notes from meeting with Dean on campaign spending **3,** 968, 1226-30E
in notes from Petersen to Nixon on Watergate investigation **9,** 3634, 3875-76E
notified of Watergate break-in **FR** 33
obligation to inform Nixon of White House horror stories **5,** 1827
O'Brien asks for appointment with **7,** 2731
orders surveillance of Kennedy **FR** 117-18
orders to Walters **9,** 3433-34
and organization of CRP **FR** 18-19
and Patman Committee hearings **4,** 1566
and Pentagon Papers case **6,** 2410
and political intelligence **3,** 923
political relationship with Strachan **6,** 2439-40
and Porter's efforts to get Government job after Watergate trial **2,** 653
prior dealings with Ervin **4,** 1562
private polls by **6,** 2461, 2497-99
progress report on Responsiveness Program from Kingsley to **FR** 436-37
progress report on Responsiveness Program from Malek **FR** 410-12
questioned by MacGregor about Watergate **2,** 530
reaction to continued investigation by Select Committee **23,** 11081-82
reaction to Dean's indictable list **3,** 1054 **4,** 1547-48
reasons for destroying documents **3,** 1088
reasons for keeping truth from Nixon **2,** 860-61
on reasons for Watergate break-in **FR** 31
relationship with CRP **1,** 18
relationship with Dean **6,** 2449-50
relationship with Ehrlichman **1,** 84-85 **3,** 1052 **6,** 2522, 2523-24, 2447, 2521-22
relationship with Gray **9,** 3476
relationship with Higby **6,** 2447 **23,** 11083
relationship with MacGregor **12,** 4944-45
relationship with Mitchell **2,** 818 **4,** 1607-1608
relationship with Nixon **3,** 1051
relationship with Strachan **3,** 1024 **6,** 2440, 2441
relationships with staff **6,** 2503-2504
and reports from Interagency Evaluation Committee **3,** 916
and reports from Kalmbach on AMPI contribution **17,** 7591-92 **FR** 615

Haldeman, Harry Robins *(Continued)*
request for investigation of Public Affairs Analysts **21,** 9713
requests that Walters see Gray **9,** 3425-36
requests written report from Dean on Watergate **4,** 1378
resignation of **3,** 1020, 1318E **4,** 1495 **5,** 1894-95, 1984, 1997 **6,** 2624-25 **7,** 2809, 2904 **9,** 3597-98 **FR** 92-93
responsibility for cash disbursements **2,** 652
and Responsiveness Program **18,** 8211-12
role at meetings with Nixon **7,** 2744
role in campaign **6,** 2447-48
role in selecting White House staff **1,** 84-85
role on White House staff **1,** 76, 78, 79, 82, 84-85, 86-87, 88-89, 91, 92 **2,** 766 **5,** 2074
and Sandwedge proposal **FR** 116
and scapegoating of Mitchell **3,** 1092-93 **4,** 1665
and scheduling of Nixon's meeting with dairy leaders **FR** 644
and Schorr investigation **FR** 144
and security **3,** 1125E
and Segretti matter **3,** 1081, 1213E, 1221E **5,** 1955, 2037 **FR** 180, 186
and Select Committee **4,** 1499
and selection of members of CRP **1,** 13, 14
and Semer-Dent meeting **17,** 7584
and sensitive case reports from IRS **23,** 11112
Sloan and **2,** 578-79
Smathers on **FR** 280E
Stans' attitude toward after Watergate arrests **2,** 732
states Nixon rescinded approval of Huston Plan **FR** 4
Stearns on activities of **11,** 4598
Strachan destroys documents for **4,** 1357 **6,** 2459-60, 2490-91
Strachan on intelligence gathering discussed at meetings attended by **6,** 2492-94
Strachan on preparation of political memos for **6,** 2494
Strachan on role at White House of **6,** 2501
Strachan on testimony of **6,** 2504-2505
Strachan on work habits of **6,** 2448
Strachan takes blame for approving Segretti **6,** 2488-89
Strachan's destruction of political matters memo to **6,** 2442
Strachan's liaison role between CRP and **2,** 785, 830-31, 839, 846-47
and Strachan's return of money to CRP **6,** 2464
Strachan's role as staff assistant to **6,** 2446-47
Strachan's talking papers to **6,** 2448-49, 2470-71
subpoenas served on **8,** 3060, 3316-17E, 3318-19E
summary of meeting called by **23,** 11100, 11140-42E
sworn statement planned by Dean for **3,** 1210E
talking paper for meeting with Mitchell **6,** 2454
talking paper on milk producers **FR** 764E
in taped conversation between Ehrlichman and Kalmbach **5,** 2177-78, 2216-17E
Taugher on testimony about dirty tricks of Democrats **11,** 4537-55

telephone conversation between Kehrli and **1,** 90-91
telephone monitoring system **6,** 2453-54
tells Dean to return from Camp David for meeting with Mitchell and Magruder **3,** 1005
tells Higby Nixon says Rebozo has funds available for legal defense **23,** 11074-75, 11082-84
tells Magruder Nixon wants him to stay on at CRP **2,** 872
tells Strachan to clean out files **6,** 2458-59
tells Strachan to contact Liddy on political intelligence assignment **6,** 2455-56
tells Strachan to destroy materials in files **3,** 1048
tells Strachan to return $350,000 to CRP **6,** 2462
and test of Dean's testimony **4,** 1482
and theory on Mitchell "taking rap" **3,** 1011-13
and transfer of CRP money to White House **5,** 2096
transmittal of Responsiveness Program to Ehrlichman and Shultz **FR** 378
travels with Nixon **6,** 2521-22
and use of milk money **17,** 7605
and use of White House fund for Watergate defendants **FR** 56-57
Walters' affidavit on discussions with **9,** 3419, 3828-29E
Walters' reasons for not asking for more information on Mexican matter **9,** 3436-37
wants Dean to see FBI reports on Watergate investigation **3,** 944
Washington Post story on payments from secret cash fund **FR** 186
and Watergate coverup **2,** 808, 822, 834-35, 858-59, 873 **3,** 943, 1026-27, 1028, 1054 **5,** 2007
and White House staff transfers to CRP **1,** 83
and wiretap information from DNC **4,** 1543
work methods **6,** 2466-68
working relationship with Ehrlichman **6,** 2524-25
working relationship with Nixon **6,** 2467-68
working relationship with Strachan **6,** 2526-27
and write-in campaign for Kennedy in New Hampshire **FR** 202
Haldeman, Harry Robins, testimony of 7, 2866-2904 **8,** 3017-3227 **16,** 7155-85 **18,** 8175-85
on access to Nixon tapes **8,** 3050-54, 3057-58, 3101-3102, 3164-65, 3207-3208
on accomplishments of Nixon administration **7,** 2867-68
on accuracy of Butterfield's testimony **8,** 3058
on accuracy of his log **8,** 3035-36
on actions against Nixon campaign **8,** 3079-81
on advice from Eisenhower and Johnson **7,** 2868
on Alabama money **8,** 3093-94, 3104
on AMPI intention to contribute $2 million **FR** 614
on antitrust investigation of milk producers and milk fund **16,** 7177-80
on arrangements for Nixon's meeting with dairy industry **16,** 7164-65
asks Walters to speak to Gray **8,** 3286-87
assigned to handle leaks **8,** 3032
on association with Nixon **7,** 2873

Haldeman, Harry Robins, testimony of *(Continued)*
includes Jackson in apology on smear letter **8,** 3148

on information to Nixon **8,** 3126

informs Dash that he also had telephone tapes **8,** 3209-10

on initiatives taken to clear up Watergate matter **8,** 3108-3109

on instructions from Nixon on testimony on White House tapes **8,** 3132, 3320E

on Intelligence Evaluation Committee **7,** 2874-75

on interest in polls **7,** 2878

on interviews with Senate Committee staff and other official committees **7,** 2867

on investigations of Watergate **8,** 2093-95, 3112-13

on IRS checks **8,** 3175

on judgment in 1964 for illegal and unethical campaign activities **8,** 3169-71

on Justice Department report that Democratic party was not involved with violence **8,** 3132-33

on justification for use of campaign contributions for defense fund **8,** 3197-98

on Kalmbach and milk fund **16,** 7165-66, 7180, 7182-83

on Kalmbach's one-million-dollar fund from 1968 **7,** 2875-76

on Kleindienst nomination **8,** 3219

on knowledge about CRP connection with Watergate break-in **8,** 3139-40

on knowledge of Ellsberg break-in **8,** 3077

on La Costa meetings **7,** 2889-92 **8,** 3055-56, 3109 **FR** 77-78

on leaks **7,** 2874-75

on learning of Ellsberg break-in **8,** 3139

on learning of Watergate break-in **8,** 3039

on letter to Mitchell from Sloan on money requested for Walker **8,** 3190, 3324E

on listening to tape of March 21 meeting **7,** 2893

on Magruder's testimony on his involvement in Watergate **8,** 3056-57

on matters heard on tapes **8,** 3105-06

on meaning of "containment" **8,** 3200-3202

on media stories **8,** 3126

on meeting with Connally on dairy industry contributions **16,** 7163-64

on meeting with Dean after Watergate break-in **8,** 3039-40

on meeting with Dean and Ehrlichman **7,** 2741-45

on meeting with Dean and Nixon on September 15 **FR** 48-49

on meeting with Dean on milk fund **16,** 7169-70, 7171-73

on meeting with Ehrlichman and Nixon **7,** 2899

on meeting with Helms and Walters **8,** 3040-42, 3062-64

on meeting with Mitchell **7,** 2881 **8,** 3180-81

on meeting with Mitchell, Ehrlichman, Dean, and Nixon **7,** 2899-2900

on meetings after Watergate arrests **8,** 3039-40

on meetings between Nixon and dairy industry representatives **16,** 7159-60, 7164-65, 7168-69

on meetings with Nixon **7,** 2888-89 **8,** 3040-41

on memo from Dean to Ehrlichman on *Nader* v. *Butz* **16,** 7182-83

on method of listening to tapes **8,** 3109-12

on milk industry contributions in 1972 **16,** 7170-71, 7183

on milk price-support decision **16,** 7167-68, 7183-84

on milk producers' contribution and *quid pro quo* **FR** 690

on Mitchell's opposition to Huston Plan **8,** 3030

on Mitchell's resignation **8,** 3165-67

and Mitchell's testimony on meetings on Liddy plan **7,** 2752

on money left over from 1968 campaign **8,** 3118-19

on money transferred from CRP to White House **8,** 3092-93, 3115-16, 3119-20

on motivations for dairy industry campaign contributions **16,** 1766-68, 7184-85

on Nixon administration **7,** 2868-71 **8,** 3227

on Nixon tapes **8,** 3090-91, 3181-82

on Nixon telling Dean to brief cabinet **8,** 3167-68

on Nixon-Dean meetings **8,** 3100, 3138-42

on Nixon's awareness of milk industry pledge **FR** 616

on Nixon's behavior at March 21 meeting **7,** 2898

on Nixon's duties **7,** 2869-71

on Nixon's handling of Watergate situation **8,** 3162-63

on Nixon's reaction to media stories on White House involvement in Watergate **8,** 3125-26

on Nixon's reactions to Dean's implication of him **8,** 3095-96

on Nixon's remark to Dean about raising $1 million **8,** 3117

on Nixon's use of campaign funds **16,** 7158

on note on concern with results in memo to Magruder **8,** 3192-95

notes on Nixon tapes **7,** 2895, 2896 **8,** 3052, 3107

on O'Brien as target of White House **8,** 3214-15

on opinion of Strachan **8,** 3038

on Patman Committee **8,** 3201

on personal staff **8,** 3018-19

on persons aware of White House recording system **8,** 3181

on pledge of $2 million by dairy people **16,** 7159

on Plumbers **8,** 3030-32

on political career **8,** 3017-18

on political composition of FBI **8,** 3226

on political enemies project **FR** 132

on political matters memos **8,** 3036-38

on polling instructions **8,** 3121

on preparation of Magruder for perjury **8,** 3043

on preparation of testimony based and not based on tapes **8,** 3114-15

on preservation of White House memos **8,** 3177-78

on Presidency and White House staff system related to Watergate **8,** 3183-88

on prevention of Watergate-type events **8,** 3199

on purpose of enemies list **8,** 3155-56

on purpose of Nixon tapes **8,** 3182

on quality of Nixon tapes **7,** 2895

on reasons for not asking Mitchell about involvement in Watergate **8,** 3169

on reasons for not listening to some tapes **8,** 3208

on reasons for not using campaign funds for Watergate defendants **8,** 3148-49 on reasons for resignation **8**, 3058-59

on reasons for testifying on matters heard on tapes **8**, 3102, 3212-13

on Rebozo's fundraising efforts **FR** 1060

on relationship with Ehrlichman **8**, 3020

on relationship with Magruder **7**, 2886-88

on relationships with his staff **8**, 3154

on reporting to Nixon **8**, 3216

on request for FBI report on Schorr **8**, 3156-57

on resignation **7**, 2809, 2904 **8**, 3096

on Responsiveness Program **18**, 8175-85

    attitude toward seriousness and legality of **18**, 8185

    denies discussing grants with Malek **18**, 8183

    denies discussing with Nixon **18**, 8179-80

    denies discussion with Malek on rechannelling grants for political impact **18**, 8181

    denies final approval of **18**, 8178-79

    denies giving order to end **18**, 8184

    denies knowledge of Kingsley Report on **18**, 8184

    initiation of **18**, 8175-79

on role **7**, 2871

on role in 1972 election campaign **7**, 2877-78

on Sandwedge plan **8**, 3032-33

on security of September 15 tape **8**, 312, 322-23

on selection of White House staff **8**, 3128-32

self-evaluation as taskmaster **8**, 3021

on solicitation of funds from dairy industry in 1969 **16**, 7155-56

on Strachan cleaning out files **8**, 3037-38

on Strachan's advice to young people on Government service **8**, 3176

on Strachan's role and Higby's role **8**, 2019-20

on surplus 1968 campaign contributions **16**, 7157-58

on suspicions about Watergate **8**, 3088

on taped conversation with Magruder **7**, 2888

on taped March 21 meeting **8**, 3064

on taping system at White House **8**, 3222-24

on telephone conversations with Dean at Camp David **7**, 2901-2902

tells Select Committee he reviewed tapes of two meetings **7**, 2888-89

on transfer of funds from CRP to White House **7**, 2878-80 **8**, 3047-50

on transfer of funds from White House back to CRP **8**, 3195-98

on use of campaign donations for defense fund **8**, 3092-93

on use of milk money **16**, 7172-76

on Vietnam support advertisement **8**, 3120-21

on visits to White House after resignation **8**, 3059

on Walker's activities **8**, 3190-92

and Watergate coverup **7**, 2883-84 **8**, 3199-3200

on White House recording system **8**, 3181

on White House requests for audits into individuals' tax returns **8**, 3135-38

on White House staff moved to CRP **8**, 3023

on willingness to review tapes and papers **8**, 3060

on wording of Strachan's testimony on instructions about files **8**, 3061-62

on working relationship with Butterfield **8**, 3154

on working relationship with Dean **8**, 3020-31

on working relationship with Higby **8**, 3153-54

on working relationship with Mitchell **8**, 3026

Haldeman memos

on solicitation of campaign contributions **16**, 7462

to Buchanan, Keogh, Klein, and Nofziger on use of Lasky **10**, 3975, 4129E

to Colson, Dent, Klein, and Magruder on assigning Colson to "outside projects" **FR** 776E

to Colson on note from Dole **16**, 7456, 7474E

to Colson on outside fund handling **16**, 7456, 7474E

to Dean on Ervin Committee **FR** 78-79

to Dean on Hughes retainer of O'Brien **8**, 3221, 3369-71E **23**, 11079, 11130E

to Dean on putting out story on communist money used for demonstrations against Nixon in 1972 **8**, 3171-74, 3177-79, 3188-90, 3206-3207

to Dean on Select Committee selection of minority counsel **8**, 3203-3204

to Dean with *Newsweek* page "The Periscope" **23**, 11076, 1115-16E

to Dean re appointment of minority counsel to "Ervin Committee" **3**, 982, 1240-42E

to Ehrlichman on Getty contribution **FR** 1060

to Ehrlichman on Nixon's request for Rebozo to contact Getty **22**, 12443E

to Ehrlichman on Rebozo contact with Getty **22**, 12469E **FR** 940-41

to Huston **4**, 1455-56, 1604

to Huston on domestic intelligence review **3**, 1062, 1324E

to Huston on Nixon's approval of Huston Plan **FR** 4

to Magruder about press coverage for administration **10**, 3975, 4112E

to Magruder on advertisements against opponents of Cambodia policy **10**, 3975, 4128E

to Magruder on anti-Nixon media with Nixon's requests attached **FR** 267-72E

to Magruder on Harris poll on students' attitudes **10**, 4126E

to Magruder on "hatchetman operations" **FR** 310E

to Magruder on letters, telegrams, and telephone calls to senators opposing Nixon's positions **FR** 150-51

to Magruder on telegrams to Humphrey **FR** 286E

to Magruder requesting summaries of "hatchetman operations--letter to the editors, counterattack, etc." for Nixon **FR** 153

to Malek on leaks **3**, 922, 1113E, 1114-16E

to Walters on meeting with Helms and Ehrlichman **7**, 2786, 2948-49E

from Barth on harassment at IRS **23**, 11248-49

from Buchanan about strategy on McGovern **10**, 3975, 4235E, 4248-49E

from Buchanan and Khachigian on Democratic contenders **10**, 4226-34E

from Buchanan and Khachigian on Muskie campaign **11**, 4668

from Buchanan on basic attack strategy **10**, 3975, 4236E

from Buchanan on "McGovern Assault Book" **10**, 3975, 4252-53E

from Buchanan on political suggestions for attacks on McGovern **10**, 3975, 4254-55E

Hallamore Homes
Ehrlichman and Rebozo visit project **22,** 10685-89
F. Donald Nixon and **22,** 10643, 10644, 10652, 10677-98
Hallet, Douglas 2, 658
Halperin, Morton 8, 3155 **11,** 4665, 4676 **FR** 132
on enemies list **4,** 1695E, 1698E
Washington Post article on wiretap of **11,** 4695, 4884-85E
Hamilton, Alexander 5, 1868
Hamilton, Edward Joseph
See Sturgis, Frank (alias of)
Hamilton, James 7, 2737
on correct description of Responsiveness Program **18,** 8176
cover letter to Morris on questionnaire for Select Committee **16,** 7447, 7454E
letter from Anderson on Responsiveness Program **19,** 8751E
letter from Gifford on his work as Special Assistant to the President **19,** 8749-50E
letter from Gifford with list of departmental contacts for "Responsiveness Program" **19,** 8749-50E
letter from Hamilton with list of departmental contacts for "Responsiveness Program" **19,** 8751-53E
letters from Dent on southern Black leaders **19,** 8615-16E
lists items in Responsiveness Program **18,** 8181
requests list of cash contributions from Arnold **25,** 12031
telephone report from Davison on Responsiveness Program **19,** 8752E
on Vanet's request for recording executive session and reading transcript of previous session **16,** 7085-87
Hamilton, James, questioning by 18, 8224
Arnold **25,** 12024-27
Atkins **13,** 5439-48
Barker **1,** 357-359
Cushman **8,** 3289-97, 3309-11
Ehrlichman **18,** 8187-93
Evans **18,** 8437-86
Haig **23,** 11035-36
Haldeman **18,** 8175-85
Hickman **11,** 4556-61
Malek **18,** 8199-8205, 8207-11, 8212-13, 8214-19, 8220-21, 8223, 8225-41, 8242-51, 8252-63, 8266-69, 8270-74, 8281-88, 8289-90
Mardian **6,** 2345-77, 2429-33
Nelson **15,** 6575-82, 6588-97, 6601-6604
Parr **15,** 6833-48, 6852, 6860-65, 6872-75
Taugher **11,** 4536-42
Townsend **16,** 7104-7109, 7113, 7121
Van Dyk **16,** 7028-33, 7035-36, 7038-41, 7042
Hamilton, Russell, Jr.
letter to Sanchez on change in status of his business **13,** 5323, 5685E
Hamilton, W.A.
affidavit with attachments of **17,** 7913-15E

Hammond, Robert A., III 8, 3376E **26,** 12817-18E
Hammond, Sukie 11, 4773E
Hampton, Gordon
and Segretti case **FR** 183
Hampton, Lionel 2, 658 **12,** 5115E
Hampton (chairman, Civil Services Commission) 18, 8289, 8290
Hand, Learned 4, 1786-87E
Hanlon, John 23, 11232 **24,** 11638
and IRS investigation of Rebozo **23,** 11251
and O'Brien's tax case **24,** 11639
Hanman, Gary Edwin 14, 6080, 6082, 6083, 6143, 6296 **15,** 6556, 6684, 6905 **17,** 7750
and ADEPT **FR** 586
after meeting with Nixon **FR** 646
at meeting at Louisville airport on March 23 **16,** 7071-75 **FR** 655-57
at meeting with Connally **15,** 6472-75
and campaign contributions **FR** 688
on Campbell call to Parr **FR** 650
and formation of TAPE **15,** 6507
letter from Harrison on names and addresses of Republican committees **14,** 5883, 5901-02E
letter from Parr **14,** 6280-81
letter from Parr on contributions to political committees **14,** 6315, 6373-77E
letter on reasons for reversal of milk price-support decision **FR** 671
letter to ADEPT Committee on quarterly report **14,** 5888, 5903-04E
letter to Baumann on TAPE, ADEPT, and SPACE role in milk price-support decision **17,** 8139-40E
letter to Beezley on milk price supports **17,** 8127E
letter to Connally **14,** 6080, 6099-6101E
letter to Connally on dairy industry needs for Federal assistance **14,** 6080, 6099-6101E
letter to Harrison on ADEPT political contributions **17,** 8150E
letter to Jacobson on discussions with Connally **14,** 5890, 5905E
letter to Parr on AMPI committees **14,** 6315-16
letter to Parr on cover letter to Chotiner **14,** 6315, 6372E
meeting with Hardin and others after March 12 decision on milk price supports **FR** 629
and Mid-America contributions to Nixon campaign **15,** 6627, 6628, 6629, 6630, 6635
and Nixon fundraising dinner **FR** 642
Parr and **15,** 6818
role in Mid-Am **FR** 586
Hanman, Gary Edwin, testimony of 14, 5859-99 **17,** 7731-48
on ADEPT and SPACE contributions to CRP **14,** 5896-97
on ADEPT commitment of campaign contribution **17,** 7741-42
on ADEPT committee members meeting with Nelson and Parr after Republican fundraising dinner **17,** 7742-43
on ADEPT decision to contribute to Nixon's re-election effort **14,** 5868-69
on ADEPT'S contributions to Democrats **14,** 5888-89

See also Milk price supports

Hardin, Mrs. Clifford M. 16, 7141, 7142

Hare Krishna movement 11, 4383

Harkins, Mrs. John
affidavit of **12,** 5009, 5078-79E

Harkins, Paul 9, 3734, 3808

"Harlem for Muskie Committee" 11, 4660-61, 4675

Harlow, Bryce 4, 1675, 1676, 1677 **6,** 2519 **15,** 6523
confidential memo from Buchanan on topics for discussion at meeting **10,** 3975, 4173E
and Nixon fundraising dinner **15,** 6522

Harman, Dick 3, 1128E

Harmony, Sally J. 1, 13, 36 **2,** 501 **11,** 4638
and Hunt's memos to Liddy **20,** 9372
memos on Watergate for Liddy **1,** 39
on Patman Committee subpoena list **3,** 961, 1192E
picks up money envelope from Sloan for Liddy **2,** 613
tapes logs of DNC telephone conversations **FR** 29

Harmony, Sally J., testimony of 2, 458-88
on allegations that she committed perjury **2,** 477
on allegations that she received "award" for testimony **2,** 469-70
on attitude toward intelligence information **2,** 472
on attitude toward wiretapped telephone calls **2,** 487-88
on code names for sources of intelligence **2,** 462, 466, 467, 470, 472
on contacts between Liddy and Magruder **2,** 474-75
on content of wiretaps **2,** 465-67, 468-69, 472
on destruction of material in Liddy's files **2,** 464, 475, 485-86
on duties for Liddy **2,** 478
on employment by CRP **2,** 458-59
on employment by Liddy **2,** 470
employment on Inaugural Committee after Watergate break-in **2,** 473-74
on Gemstone bill destroyed by Magruder **2,** 464, 484-85
on Gemstone reports **2,** 483
on Gemstone stationery **2,** 461-62, 467, 479
on knowledge of Liddy's intelligence activities **2,** 475-76
on Liddy and Barker **2,** 463
on Liddy and Mitchell **2,** 478
on Liddy's reason for his discharge from CRP **2,** 487-88
on Liddy's telephone calls to White House **2,** 471-72
on Magruder reassuring Mitchell on her testimony **2,** 464, 467-68
on Magruder's discussion on her testimony **2,** 471
on material taken home from Liddy's desk **4,** 485-86
on memo on wiretaps from McCord **2,** 466-67
on November Group **2,** 476
on photographs from Democratic National Committee **2,** 479-80
on political spying at McGovern headquarters **2,** 482-83
prepares pass for McGovern headquarters **2,** 463

on reasons for four appearances before grand jury **2,** 477-78
on reasons for giving Gemstone bill to Magruder **2,** 483-84
on removal of contents of Liddy's desk **2,** 479, 480
on simulated McGovern stationery **2,** 463, 472-73
on transcription of tapes from wiretaps **2,** 459-62, 465-67
on visitors to Liddy **2,** 470-71, 474-75

Harper, Bruce 23, 11182

Harper, Dr. Edward 6, 2519

Harper's magazine **FR** 1119

Harrington, Mike 25, 12115

Harris, Angela 1, 32, 35

Harris, Fred 14, 5884 **25,** 12098

Harris, Sam 11, 4461, 4890E **FR** 409

Harris, Sidney 16, 6939,6940, 6959, 6961

Harris polls 8, 3121
on Cambodia **10,** 4128E
of Democratic party primaries **11,** 4635-36, 4637E, 4638-44
fraudulent, on Kennedy candidacy **11,** 4660, 4695, 4847-49E
on Nixon vs. Muskie **11,** 4646, 4656, 4695, 4764-65E
on Nixon vs. Muskie vs. Wallace **11,** 4695, 4764-65E
on students' attitudes **10,** 4126E

Harrison, Marion Edwyn 14, 5867, 5881, 5883, 5898, 5975, 6134, 6314 **15,** 6405, 6465, 6523, 6551, 6621, 6625, 6658-59 **16,** 6959, 7247, 7384 **17,** 7552, 7596, 7601, 7748 **22,** 10500
and Alagia's purchase of tickets for Republican fundraising dinner **16,** 7070-71
and AMPI **15,** 6522
and AMPI committees **14,** 6300, 6301, 6302
and AMPI contributions **15,** 6768-69, 6775-76, 6893
and AMPI efforts to obtain milk price-support increases **15,** 6552
and AMPI's relationship with Wagner & Baroody **15,** 6651-55
and arrangements for meetings between dairy industry representatives and Nixon **15,** 6798, 6814
at meeting between Kalmbach and dairy industry representatives **15,** 6535-38
at meeting between Nixon and dairy coop representatives **16,** 7063-64
at meeting with Hillings, Nelson, Evans, and Parr **15,** 6788
at meeting with Kalmbach **15,** 6658 **17,** 7593
attitude toward Republican fundraising dinner **15,** 6828
Butterbrodt and **17,** 7637
contacts with Nunn **17,** 7553
and dairy industry contributions **15,** 6642, 6644, 6646 **FR** 690-91
and dairy industry contributions to 1971 Republican fundraising dinner **17,** 7537
discussion with Nelson on antitrust suit against AMPI **15,** 6687-88
discussions with Nelson on AMPI contributions to Republicans in 1972 **15,** 6660

Harrison, Marion Edwyn *(Continued)*

efforts to get Nixon to attend AMPI convention in 1970 **15,** 6549

exhibits **14,** 6252, 6253, 6264, 6282-92E

firm fired by AMPI **FR** 724

involvement in price-support decision **14,** 6312

legal role with AMPI **17,** 7680

letter from Hanman on ADEPT political contributions **17,** 8150E

letter from Isham **15,** 6647

letter from Isham on contributions **15,** 6647, 6742-49E

letter to Colson **15,** 6634-35

letter to Colson on dairy industry parity **15,** 6634, 6711-12E

letter to Hanman on names and addresses of Republican committees **14,** 5883, 5901-02E

letter to Hardin **15,** 6553-54

letter to Hardin on arranging meeting with Nixon **15,** 6553, 6705-08E

letter to Isham on use of political committees for contributions **15,** 6645, 6730-41E

letter to Nelson on campaign contributions **14,** 6264, 6287-92E

letter to Nelson on TAPE activities **14,** 6252, 6282-84E

letter to Mehren on antitrust suit against AMPI **15,** 6465-66 **FR** 770E

letter to Mehren on Chotiner discussion with Mitchell on antitrust suit against AMPI **FR** 724

on letter to Nelson **15,** 6775-76, 6887

letter to Nelson on contributions to opposed candidates only **15,** 6538-39

letter to Nelson on political committees to use in contributions **15,** 6644, 6723-29E **FR** 672

letter to Russell on *United States* v. *AMPI* **16,** 7262, 7351E **FR** 771E

letter to Whitaker on dairy industry parity **15,** 6634, 6714-15E

letter to Whitaker on milk price-support increases **FR** 634

and meeting between Nixon, Parr, and Nelson **15,** 6794

and meeting between Parr and Colson **15,** 6771

and meetings between Colson and dairy industry representatives **15,** 6538

and meetings with Connally **14,** 6109-10

meetings with Mehren **16,** 7236-37, 7253-55

and Mehren-Nunn meeting **17,** 7557

memo from Colson to Chotiner on **FR** 793E

memo from Townsend to Nelson and Parr on Townsend's meeting **14,** 6297, 6331E

memo to Special Counsel to the President on milk import quotas **14,** 6296, 6328-30E

and milk price-supports issue **15,** 6634 **17,** 7758

on Mitchell's role in antitrust suit against AMPI **FR** 724

on moneys received by Chotiner **14,** 6249-50

Nelson denies discussions of TAPE contributions with **15,** 6534-35

and Nixon's appearance at AMPI 1971 convention **15,** 6892

note listing names of political committees from **15,** 6641, 6718-22E

Nunn and **17,** 7540, 7541, 7544

preparations for meeting between Nixon and dairy industry leaders **FR** 643-44

relationship with Colson **17,** 7602

replaces Semer as AMPI lawyer for White House matters **FR** 613

retained by AMPI **15,** 6511

retained by Mid-Am and DI **FR** 732

sends list of committee names to Nelson **FR** 689

and SPACE **16,** 7061-62

and TAPE committees **14,** 6315

and Townsend's papers on import quotas **14,** 6297-98

Van Dyk denies knowledge of meetings between dairy people and **16,** 6988

and White House contacts on milk price-supports issue **15,** 6805-6806

Harrison, Marion Edwyn, testimony of 14, 5983-84, 6246-81 **17,** 7679-92

on ADEPT campaign commitment **17,** 7741

on advice given to AMPI and TAPE on political contributions **14,** 6254-57

on alleged meetings with dairymen and Connally **14,** 6270

on AMPI campaign contributions and antitrust suit **17,** 7684-85

on AMPI cash contributions to Nixon's re-election campaign **14,** 6250-51

on AMPI committees **14,** 6274-75

on AMPI committees organized for Colson **14,** 6262-67

on AMPI contacts with Kalmbach **17,** 7688-89

on AMPI purchase of $1000 dinner tickets **14,** 6267-69

on AMPI retaining Harrison, Lucey, Sagle & Solter **14,** 6247-48

on anti-trust suit against AMPI **14,** 6251-52 **17,** 7680-88 **FR** 723, 724

on cash political contributions by TAPE **14,** 6251-53

on Chotiner and Hillings association with his law firm **14,** 6248

on Chotiner's conversation with Mitchell on antitrust suit against AMPI **17,** 7683-84

on Chotiner's financial arrangements **14,** 6249

on Colson's recommendations on AMPI political contributions **14,** 6255-56

on contacting Kleindienst on antitrust suit against AMPI **17,** 7682-83

on dairy industry and import quotas **14,** 6260-61

on delivery of AMPI contribution to Webster **14,** 6273-74

denies discussing AMPI contributions with White House staff members **14,** 6266

denies knowledge of dairymen meeting with Connally **14,** 6278-79

denies meeting with Jacobsen **14,** 6272

on fee arrangement with AMPI **14,** 6248-49, 6250

and import quota issue **14,** 6296-99

on letter from Hillings to Nixon **14,** 6253-54, 6260-62

on letter to Nelson on commitment to Republicans **14,** 6251-52, 6264-65, 6269-71

on letter to Russell on antitrust suit against AMPI **17,** 7687-88

and Lilly **14,** 6271-72

on McLaren confirmation **17,** 7687

on meeting between Nixon and dairy leaders **17,** 7689

on meeting with dairymen and Nixon **14,** 6265, 6279

on meeting with Dent **14,** 6265

on meeting with Mehren **14,** 6276-77 **16,** 7253-55

on meetings between Chotiner and Kalmbach **17,** 7689-92

on meetings with Colson **14,** 6257-58, 6264

on Mehren's attitude toward Nixon administration **17,** 7689

on name of firm **14,** 6246

on Nunn's listing committees for AMPI contributions **14,** 6259

on Parr's promise of $2 million for Republicans **14,** 6259-61

on recommendations to Mehren on AMPI contributions **14,** 6277-78

on relations with Colson **17,** 7691

on relationship with Jacobsen **14,** 6266

requests Montoya's continued presence at hearing **14,** 6262

requests open hearing **14,** 6245-46

on retainer arrangement with AMPI **17,** 7679

on special project in Hillings letter to Nixon **14,** 6262-64

on subpoenaed documents **14,** 6246-47

on TAPE's contributions **14,** 6266-67, 6275-76, 6280-81

Harrison, Lucey, Sagle & Solter

See Harrison, Marion Edwyn, testimony of

Harry Winston, Inc.

insurance appraisal for Mrs. Richard M. Nixon for diamond earrings **26,** 12765-66E

Hart, Gary 3, 1173E, 1178E **10,** 3922 **11,** 4497, 4502, 4504, 4585, 4621, 4717E **25,** 12095, 12101, 12109, 12123, 12124, 12126, 12167, 12174

bogus call to Meany **11,** 4628-29

memo to Mankiewicz, Gralnick, and Dougherty from **11,** 4620-21

Hart, Jane S. 14, 5965, 6043E, 6167 **FR** 600

affidavit with attachments of **17,** 7920-35E

Hart, Jim 25, 11831-36E

Hart, Milledge A., III

contributions to Mills campaign committees **25,** 12068-69E

Hartford, Milton 20, 9415

Hartke, Vance FR 280E

and Duncan loan to Humphrey campaign **25,** 11795, 11804

Harvey, Annette 5, 2094 **17,** 7808

Hass, Lew 11, 4548, 4549, 4550, 4582

Hass, Warren K. FR 912

Hastings, Doris L. 3, 1160E **FR** 888

affidavit on contribution to Humphrey campaign **25,** 11921E **FR** 888-90

Hatch, Frank, Jr. 12, 5115E

Hatch Act

Buckley denies violation of **11,** 4450-51, 4454-55, 4458, 4465

and Cabinet Committee for Opportunity for Spanish-Speaking People **18,** 8282 **FR** 394, 396

Fernandez denies violation of **13,** 5401-5402

and Government employees attending "advance school" for surrogate candidates **FR** 430

investigation by Special Subcommittee on Human Resources on violation of **19,** 8872-81E, 9242-48E **FR** 429

Malek on Government employees participating in campaign activities and **18,** 8282-84

Marumoto denies violations of **13,** 5313-14

Marumoto on grant recipients and **13,** 5289-90

and Pena **FR** 402

and Responsiveness Program **18,** 8255, 8256 **FR** 438

Select Committee recommendations on amending **FR** 444

and solicitation of campaign contributions by GSA employees **FR** 413-14

Hatsis, Anthony 20, 9455, 9601 **21,** 9701, 9703 **22,** 10279, 10609, 10625, 10633

Ehrlichman and **22,** 10611

F. Donald Nixon and **22,** 10645-48, 10730-31

trip with Meier and F. Donald Nixon to Geneva, Switzerland **22,** 10714-15

trip with Meier and F. Donald Nixon to the Dominican Republic **22,** 10709, 10729-30

Hauser, Richard 25, 12145

objection to questions to Higby **23,** 11087-88, 11096, 11097

requests copy of transcript of Higby testimony and relevant portions of Kalmbach's testimony **23,** 11112

See also Higby, Lawrence M., testimony of

Hawkins, Valerie 12, 5134E

Hay-Adams Hotel, Washington, D.C. 1, 253 **4,** 1514

Priestes-Fernandez meeting at **13,** 5332-34

Hayes, Helen 8, 3157

Hayes, James

letter to Metzner on Dunes acquisition matter **FR** 995-96

letter to Metzner on Hughes Tool Co. transactions **26,** 12937-38E

Haynes, Bob

and FBI check on DeAntonio **22,** 10380

Haynes, Richard FR 515

Hays, C. Lansing 21, 10181, 10182

Hazlett, Nick 12, 5093E

Health care

and older Americans **19,** 9017E

Healy, Patrick

letter from Palmby on dairy price-support level **16,** 7134, 7152E

letter to Harding on announcement of milk price supports **16,** 7134, 7153-54E

and SPACE **16,** 7064, 7065

Hearing, George 11, 4406, 4408, 4409 **FR** 174, 175, 177

Benz on prison sentence of **11,** 4425

guilty plea by **11,** 4422

indictment of **11,** 4421

and Jackson-Humphrey letter **FR** 169-70

and Jackson-Humphrey sexual misconduct letter **11,** 4406, 4410, 4411

prison sentence of **FR** 170

Hearing, George *(Continued)*
and stinkbombs at Muskie picnic **11,** 4412-13
and stinkbombs in Muskie headquarters **11,** 4412, 4427-28

Hearsay evidence 1, 132, 138-39, 163
Dash on **4,** 1523-24, 1783-90E
and Dean and Mitchell's involvement in Watergate **1,** 243
Dean on Nixon's involvement in Watergate and **3,** 1080-81
and Haldeman's testimony based on Nixon tapes **8,** 3065
and Segretti matter **5,** 2038
Talmadge on **1,** 160
Thompson-Ervin discussion on **9,** 3812-13
and Watergate trial **1,** 336 **3,** 1261E

Heckler, Margaret M. 12, 5115E

Hefner, Hugh 25, 12148
contribution to McGovern campaign **25,** 12170

Heimlich 20, 9403-9404

Heininger, Erwin C. 15, 6467, 6674 **16,** 6961, 7250, 7287, 7444 **17,** 7663 **FR** 704
letter from Russell on Department of Justice complaint **16,** 7262, 7349-50E
letter to Parkinson on contribution to CRP **17,** 7653, 7674-77E

Heininger, Erwin C.
See also Mehren, George L., testimony of

Held, Mr. and Mrs. Marvin 22, 12543E

Heller, Michael Barry
affidavit of **12,** 5009, 5059-60E

Heller, Michael Barry, testimony of 12, 4964-75
on Anderson columns linking Nixon with Nazis **12,** 4970
attitude toward politics **12,** 4974-75
on dirty tricks **12,** 4973, 4974
on involvement in Nixon campaign **12,** 4964-65
on Jews for McGovern-Shriver **12,** 4968
on "Nixon Is Treyf" leaflet **12,** 4965-69, 4971-72, 4973
on political background **12,** 4970-71

Hellinki Techiniki Corp.
F. Donald Nixon's employment with **22,** 10674-75

Helms (guard at Watergate complex) 1, 103, 196, 300 **3,** 1080

Helms, Richard M. 4, 1416, 1667 **9,** 3754-55
and CIA involvement in Watergate **9,** 3534
Cushman reports meeting with Hunt to **8,** 3293
Ehrlichman's meeting with after Watergate break-in **7,** 2695-96
Haldeman on **8,** 3130
in Hunt's notes **9,** 3839E, 3841E
and Huston Plan **6,** 2527
letter from McCord to **9,** 3445
McCord on resignation of **3,** 1235E **9,** 3444
meeting with Ehrlichman and Haldeman **2,** 867 **7,** 2782-86
meeting with Kleindienst **9,** 3608-09
memo for Walters on meetings with Ehrlichman and Haldeman **7,** 2786, 2948-49E
orders destruction of CIA tapes relating to Watergate **FR** 1131-34
and Pentagon Papers matter **8,** 3304-3305

resignation of **1,** 195
tells Gray CIA was not involved in Watergate **9,** 3428-29, 3451, 3509, 3518
tells Gray not to interview Wagner and Casell **9,** 3519-20
in Walters memo **9,** 3818E
Walters reports on meetings with Dean to **9,** 3410
and Watergate cover-up **1,** 213-16
and White House efforts to restrict FBI Watergate investigation **FR** 37-40
White House memo on domestic intelligence to **8,** 3311, 3394-3401

Helms, Richard M., testimony of 8, 3232-89
on amateurishness of Watergate break-in **8,** 3260
attitude toward CIA **8,** 3252
on career as ambassador to Iran **8,** 3232
on career as director of CIA **8,** 3232
on classified testimony before Senate Foreign Relations Committee **8,** 3262-63
on conflict of testimony on discussion of Watergate break-in at meeting with Walters, Haldeman, and Ehrlichman **8,** 3244-47, 3249, 3271-72
on contacts between CIA and White House **8,** 3281
on contacts between Ehrlichman and CIA **8,** 3281
on conversation with Gray on lack of CIA involvement in Watergate **8,** 3237-38
denies discussing FBI uncovering CIA operations with Gray **8,** 3242
denies knowledge of Hunt's illegal activities **8,** 3266
denies knowledge of Plumbers unit **8,** 3282
denies Liddy had any relationship to CIA **8,** 3261-62
discusses forthcoming Gray meeting with Walters **8,** 3239
on efforts to bring CIA into domestic investigation areas **8,** 3251-52
on equipment lent to Hunt **8,** 3254-55
on FBI-CIA relationship **8,** 3258
on first knowledge of Fielding break-in **8,** 3234
on first knowledge of Watergate break-in **8,** 3236-37
on former CIA employees involved in Watergate break-in **8,** 3247-48, 3249, 3262-63
on Haldeman's access to tapes **8,** 3254
on Haldeman's request that Walters talk to Gray **8,** 3252-53, 3281-82
on Hunt's assignments at CIA **8,** 3254
on Hunt's hiring at White House **8,** 3257
on Hunt's record at CIA **8,** 3260-61
on Hunt's request for CIA secretary in Paris to be assigned to him at White House **8,** 3233-34
on Hunt's requests for material from CIA **8,** 3233, 3234, 3263-64, 3268
on Hunt's retirement from CIA **8,** 3261
on Hunt's use of equipment gotten from CIA **8,** 3276-79
informs Gray that CIA had no involvement in Watergate break-in **8,** 3242
on investigation of leaks **8,** 3253
on lack of knowledge of connection between CIA and Watergate burglars **8,** 3278-79
on Liddy given alias and materials by CIA **8,** 3264

Hertz Corporation *(Continued)*
campaign contribution of **FR** 473-81
demands money back from Eaton **25,** 12322-23
Eaton bills to **25,** 12316-20
invoices from lawyers contributing to Muskie
campaign **25,** 12336-36E
letters accompanying payments to lawyers contributing to Muskie campaign **25,** 12347-51E
Lifflander's work relationship with **25,** 12262
memo from Cooper on national campaign requests
for rentals **25,** 12326E
memo from Cooper to Rybicki on charge privileges to political parties **25,** 12327E
memo from Massad on authorized signers **25,**
12325E
money owed by Muskie campaign to **25,** 12262-
66, 12271-72, 12273-74
organizational setup **25,** 12223
See also Eaton, Barton Denis, testimony of; Edidin, Sol M., testimony of
Hess, Leon 25, 12201
Hesser, Jack 14, 5974
HEW
See Department of Health, Education, and Welfare (HEW)
Hewitt, Robert
check to Catalina Pools, Inc. **24,** 11316, 11375E
Hickman, Gary, testimony of 11, 4556-63
on demonstration against Nixon at Century Plaza
Hotel, Los Angeles **11,** 4556-60, 4562
on Haldeman's testimony that Hollywood Nixon
headquarters was bombed **11,** 4560-61
on police man-hours expended at anti-Nixon
demonstration in Los Angeles **11,** 4561-62
position in Los Angeles Police Department **11,**
4556
Hidalgo, Ed 13, 5629E
Higby, Lawrence Mead 2, 852 **3,** 930, 931, 952, 986
4, 1409, 1578 **6,** 2442, 2458, 2466, 2467
advised by Haldeman that Rebozo has $400,000
available for legal expenses of Haldeman and
Ehrlichman **22,** 12428E, 12439E
and deliveries of monies by Kalmbach in 1970 **5,**
2142, 2143, 2144
and enemies list additions **4,** 1409-10, 1529, 1699E
on Firestone and Richard Nixon Foundation **23,**
11104-11105
Gray tells about his resignation **9,** 3493
and Haldeman's polling instructions **8,** 3121
and Haldeman's request to investigate Schorr **3,**
1071 **8,** 3156-57
information to Haldeman on contributions to
Weicker's campaign **8,** 3203
informs Kalmbach of Edward Nixon's employment at Richard Nixon Foundation **23,** 10857
Kalmbach and **16,** 7158
and Kalmbach's efforts to obtain ambassadorship
in Europe for Symington **FR** 498, 500
and knowledge of Nixon's taping devices **5,** 2077,
2084
and leaks at White House **3,** 921
and Magruder **7,** 2887
and Magruder's employment problems after Watergate **3,** 990

memo from Colson on fundraising **16,** 7456,
7476E
memo from Dean on additional names for enemies list **4,** 1697-98E
memo from Dean with attachments **3,** 931, 1151-
56E
memo from Jones on "Options for Jeb Magruder"
3, 990, 1249-50E **4,** 1577-78
memo from Strachan on White House polls **FR**
323E
memo to Dean on campaign disruptions **3,** 1241E
8, 3178-79, 3205
memo to Klein on White House polls **FR** 155,
322E
memo to Magruder on discrediting Huntley **10,**
3975, 4127E
memo to Magruder on Tell It To Hanoi advertisements **FR** 324E
and messages from Haldeman to Magruder **2,** 851
and milk fund **16,** 7175
and Nixon's friends with tax problems **4,** 1530
and political enemies project **FR** 131
reassures Barth on harassment at IRS **23,** 11249
recording apparatus used by **6,** 2482
relationship with Haldeman **6,** 2447 **8,** 3154
requests for intelligence reports on antiwar
demonstrations **3,** 917
requests money from Kalmbach for transfer from
CRP to White House **5,** 2095, 2096
role at White House **8,** 3019-20
Strachan calls after Watergate break-in **6,** 2457
and surveillance of Kennedy **3,** 923
Higby, Lawrence Mead, testimony of 23, 11073-
11113
on "account zero" **23,** 11093-94
on campaign contributions to Rebozo **23,** 11103
on Caulfield's role at White House **23,** 11094-95
claims no knowledge of F. Donald Nixon's tax
problems **23,** 11087
on Colson's interest in O'Brien **23,** 11077-78
contacts with Rebozo **23,** 11075
denies involvement in paying expenses at Nixon's
homes **23,** 11099-11100
denies knowledge of Haldeman or Ehrlichman receiving funds after they left White House **23,**
11108-11109
denies knowledge of Hughes contribution **23,**
11074
denies knowledge of IRS investigation of Rebozo
23, 11107
denies knowledge of Kalmbach's involvement in
Greenspun matter **23,** 11105-11106
denies knowledge of payments to Nixon brothers
23, 11089
denies knowledge of Rebozo's assets **23,** 11106-
11107
denies knowledge of Resorts International matter
23, 11105
on discussion with Buzhardt prior to Executive
session interview **23,** 11080-81
on Edward Nixon employed by Richard Nixon
Foundation **23,** 11089, 11094, 11103-11104
on employment history **23,** 11073-74
on employment on transition committee **23,**
11085-86

on F. Donald Nixon's financial problems **23,**
11088-89
on funds furnished by Kalmbach from 1968 trust
fund **23,** 11090-94
on Haldeman informing him of Rebozo's fund for
administration-connected costs **FR** 943
on Haldeman stating that Rebozo had funds
available for legal defense **23,** 11074-75
on hush money **23,** 11109-11111
identification of documents by **23,** 11076-80,
11084-85, 11098-99, 11101-11102
on informing Haldeman of forthcoming testimony
before Select Committee **23,** 11081-84
on Kalmbach's role as trustee of 1968 funds **23,**
11085-86
on material to Haldeman from Barth **23,** 11111-12
on *Newsday* investigation **23,** 11098-99, 11101-
11102
on Nixon tapes **23,** 11107
on Nixon's San Clemente purchase **23,** 11086-87
on payment of moving expenses for personnel out
of 1968 funds **23,** 11090, 11091-92
on reasons why grand jury called him back again
23, 11111
relationship with Haldeman **23,** 11083
on special fund for White House expenses **23,**
11092-93
on Ulasewicz's employment at White House **23,**
11097
Higgins, Robert L.
letter to Sanders re total receipts of Mills for
President Committee **25,** 12075E
Hildegard, James 20, 9428, 9444, 9487
Hilliard, Anita 20, 9583
Hillings, Patrick J. 14, 5866, 5898, 5970, 6258 **15,**
6405-6406, 6536 **16,** 7064, 7168, 7384, 7387 **17,**
7596, 7601 **20,** 9454
and AMPI efforts to obtain milk price-support increases **15,** 6552
association with Harrison's law firm **14,** 6248
at meeting with Harrison, Nelson, Evans, and
Parr **15,** 6788
at milk producers' meeting with Kalmbach **17,**
7590-91, 7593-94
Campbell denies knowing **17,** 7779-80
letter to Nixon **14,** 6253-54, 6260-64 **15,** 6541-42,
6544, 6701-6702E, 6789-90, 6798, 6814, 6884
16, 7161-63 **17,** 7546, 7594-95 **FR** 643, 757-58E
Ehrlichman on **16,** 7377-81
memo from Roger Johnson to Haldeman on
FR 755E
letter to Nixon on AMPI funding special project
FR 695
letter to Nixon on dairy import quotas and AMPI
$2 million pledge **FR** 619-21
letter to Nixon on implementation of Tariff Commission recommendation **14,** 6253, 6285-86E **15,**
6541, 6701-02E
memo from Colson to Chotiner on **FR** 793E
relationship with Nixon **15,** 6625-26
Himens, Stan 3, 1118E
Hinerfeld, Norman 11, 4461

Hirsch, Chick 24, 11392, 11502E
Hislop, Robert I., Jr.
affidavit of **12,** 5009, 5153-62E
Hispanic Finance Committee 13, 5371, 5736E
contributions to, *see also* Priestes, John J., tes-
timony of
Hiss, Alger 9, 3878E
Hiss case **3,** 906, 993, 994, 1075, 1076 **4,** 1405 **5,**
2047-48
Hitler, Adolf 11, 4426, 4663 **12,** 5027E
Hitt, Bob
cash disbursement from Sloan to **2,** 541, 558-59,
573
Ho Chi Minh 10, 4077E
Hoback, Judy 2, 549, 596, 689, 1255E **FR** 43
Hodgkin, John P. 25, 12120
memo to Sanders re Mott contribution **25,**
12136E
and Mott's campaign finances **25,** 12116-23
Hodgson, James 13, 5312 **FR** 431
Hoecker, Wayne
See Hanman, Gary Edwin, testimony of
Hoffa, James 23, 11268 **FR** 278E, 279E
Hofgren, Daniel 7, 2733 **13,** 5499
Hogan, Tom 3, 1004, 1009 **4,** 1377, 1395, 1573 **7,**
2734
Dean contacts **4,** 1385-86
Hogan and Hartson 9, 3703
Holiday Inn, Montego Bay, Jamaica
Segretti offered job at **FR** 183
Holland, Josiah Gilbert FR 1103
Holland, Todd 6, 2550
Holliday, Raymond 20, 9541
Hollowell, Wynn 15, 6780 **17,** 7630
Hollywood, California
bombing of Nixon headquarters in **8,** 3080
Hollywood Bowl 5, 2001
Holmes, E. P. FR 781E
Holmes, Johnny 15, 6871-72 **16,** 7109
Holt, Kathryn A. 12, 5127-28E, 5133-34E, 5135-36E
Holtsmith, C. R. 23, 11268
Hooper, Jack FR 962
flights on Hughes' plane **20,** 9488
Hoover, J. Edgar 8, 3226 **9,** 3605, 3645 **20,** 9347
Barker's assignment at demonstration after death
of **1,** 358, 365-66, 392
and Cash kidnapping case **24,** 11510E, 11511E
in correspondence between Krogh and Ehrlichman **7,** 2661-63
and creation of Interagency Domestic Intelligence
unit **3,** 1064, 1335E, 1337E
demonstration at funeral of **2,** 500, 512, 515 **9,**
3711-12
dissemination of information on criminal cases to
White House by **9,** 3844-45E
and Dunes Hotel acquisition **23,** 11055
Ehrlichman on **7,** 2691-92
and electronic surveillance **3,** 1320E
and Ellsberg case **5,** 2016 **6,** 2531, 2606 **7,** 2663-
82
FBI in later years of **9,** 3736

Huerta, Dolores 12, 4951 25, 12166 FR 511-12
Hugh, Harry
 See Pearlman, Marion, testimony of
Hughes, Harold 11, 4689 25, 12098
 and Valentine, Sherman 16, 7030-35
Hughes, Howard 7, 2801 15, 6844 16, 7014, 7041 20,
 9439 24, 11415
 and ABM issue 21, 9697-98 21, 10045, 10047-48
 aircraft log books 22, 12490E, 12512-14E
 and atomic bomb testing in Nevada 23, 10895-96
 and campaign contributions
  see Hughes contribution
 Caulfield investigation of relationship with O'Bri-
  en 22, 10404-10
 check to Maheu 24, 11526E
 conflict with Maheu 21, 9987-88 23, 11079,
  11134-35E
 contribution to Humphrey campaign 21, 9953,
  9955 24, 11614-15 25, 11764
 correspondence with Maheu on Dunes Hotel acquisition 26, 12775-89E
 Dean investigation of relationship between O'Bri-
  en and 23, 10907-10908
 and Greenspun break-in 1, 202 20, 9361-62
 and Irving biography 20, 9367
 job offer to Danner 24, 11430-31
 letter from Lenzner to Davis on arrangements for
  questioning 22, 12451E
 memo from Colson to Goodearle on Bennett and
  23, 11079, 11123E
 memo from Gray on Dunes Hotel acquisition
  proposal of 26, 12788E
 memo from Haldeman to Dean on retainer of O'-
  Brien by 8, 3214-15, 3217, 3221, 3369-71E
 memo to Maheu 20, 9608-10 21, 9724-25
 Moncourt denies knowledge of Rebozo dealings
  with 22, 10521-22
 and nerve gas dumping issue 20, 9535-36, 9596
 and O'Brien 21, 10056-59 24, 11638-42
 planned public relations activity to develop public
  image of 24, 11590-91
 Rebozo flights on his planes 21, 10050-51, 10053
 retainer for O'Brien 23, 11079, 11124-31E
 rumored contribution to Humphrey campaign 25,
  11784-85
 rumored loan to F. Donald Nixon 20, 9373-74
 subpoena for FR 933
 and Suskind book 20, 9404
 Wearly on use of aircraft by 20, 9434-35
 on Woods' contributors' list 22, 10266
 Woods on list of contributions of 22, 10238
 Woods on return of contribution of 22, 10276
 See also Hughes contribution; Hughes Tool Co.;
  Hughes-Rebozo investigation; Wearley, Robert
  Franklin, testimony of
Hughes, Phillip S.
 and Patman Committee 3, 1181E
Hughes contribution 1, 202 20, 9355-56, 9407-25
 analysis of possible sources of FR 956-62
 and atomic testing in Nevada 24, 11579
 Buzhardt denies assignment of White House per-
  son to monitor 23, 10902-10903
 Buzhardt denies discussion with Rebozo on 23,
  10877

Buzhardt on preparation of Woods letter to IRS
 on 23, 10878-88
conflicting evidence on initiator of FR 1053
conflicting testimony on delivery of FR 1055
conflicting testimony on storage of FR 968-72,
 1053-55, 1057-58
contradictory testimony of principals involved in
 FR 948-49
Cox investigation of Rebozo and 23, 10888-89
Danner and Rebozo testimony on initiation of dis-
 cussion of 24, 11445-46
Danner denies discussion at Camp David meeting
 with Nixon and Rebozo 24, 11473, 11474-75
Danner denies discussion with Maheu in 1968 on
 24, 11448
Danner discusses with family 24, 11555-56
Danner informs Davis money is for congressional
 campaigns in 1970 24, 11582-84
Danner on delivery of 24, 11464-68
Danner on return of 24, 11462-63
Danner on rumored denial planned by Rebozo on
 receipt of 24, 11553-55
Danner on storage before delivery of FR 961-62
Danner testimony on FR 949-51
Danner-Golden discussion of 24, 11459-60, 11552-
 55
Davis denies discussion of considering as gift 24,
 11588-89
Davis denies knowledge of exchange of original
 bills for other bills 24, 11589
Davis on knowledge of 24, 11567-70
Davis on motivation for 24, 11609-10
Davis-Hughes discussion on 24, 11569-73
decision to contribute to Nixon campaign through
 Rebozo FR 935
delivery dates in Key Biscayne FR 963-68
discussion by Danner, Nixon, and Rebozo in 1968
 on possibility of 24, 11439-42
discussion with Davis on campaign contribution
 through Rebozo 24, 11569-73
and Dunes Hotel acquisition
 See Dunes Hotel acquisition
Edward C. Nixon on 22, 10612-13
F. Donald Nixon's first knowledge of 22, 10710
Federal Reserve Board evidence on 24, 11558 FR
 948, 972-80
Garment on 23, 11059-71
Gemmill on return of 23, 11177-80
Gemmill's involvement with Rebozo and 23,
 11174-80
and Greenspun 23, 11032
Griffin and 23, 10791
Griffin denies discussing with anyone other than
 Rebozo or Gemmill 23, 10786, 10788, 10789-90
Griffin denies discussing with Golden 23, 10784-
 85
and Griffin's claims of attorney-client privileges
 on questions regarding Rebozo's finances 23,
 10767-68
Haig on return of 23, 11006-11009, *see also* Haig,
 Alexander, testimony of
Higby denies knowledge about 23, 11074
IRS discovery of FR 1017-18
and IRS investigation of Rebozo 21, 9680 23,
 10891-92, 11246 FR 1016-30

Hughes contribution *(Continued)*
IRS learns about **23,** 11233
IRS report to Gemmill on **23,** 11180
Kalmbach denies discussing with Nixon **21,** 10183
Kalmbach memo on discussions with Rebozo on **21,** 10187-91
LaRue denies discussing with Rebozo **23,** 11169-70
LaRue denies knowledge of **23,** 11163
and legislative recommendations **FR** 1071-74
Lenzner's question to Haig on discussion on **23,** 10852
in letter from Select Committee to White House requesting information and documents from Nixon **22,** 12428-29E
letter from Woods to IRS on **22,** 12584E
list of individuals interviewed by Select Committee on **FR** 1075-78
McKiernan's first knowledge about **22,** 10651-52
New York Times article on **23,** 10800E
Nixon-Haig discussions on **23,** 11027-30
and Nixon-Rebozo-Danner meeting at Camp David
    conflicts in testimony on **FR** 1066-67
persons with knowledge of receipt of
    conflicts in testimony on **FR** 1056-57
possible delivery dates
    conflicts in testimony on **FR** 962-68
purpose of
    conflicts in testimony on **FR** 1055
Rebozo's efforts to return **24,** 11585-86
Rebozo's reasons for keeping **23,** 11186-88, 11195-96
Rebozo's return of **22,** 12439-40E
and Rebozo's 1969 responsibilities for Nixon and the White House **FR** 940-44
and Rebozo's 1972 campaign fundraising role **FR** 998-1001
return of **20,** 9407-25 **FR** 1001-16
    conflicts in testimony on **FR** 1060-66
Select Committee report on return of **FR** 1001-16
Simon on attempts to trace dates of insurance of **23,** 10939-40
Simon on IRS sensitive case report on Rebozo and **23,** 10930-33
summary analysis of conflicting evidence on **FR** 1053-67
summary of facts on **FR** 944-48, 1068-71
total amount of **FR** 980-81
use of
    charts on **FR** 1052-53
    conflicts in testimony on **FR** 1064-66
    and Coopers & Lybrand report **FR** 1032-33
    expenditures by Rebozo concealed from accountants **FR** 1033-32
    and Florida Nixon for President account **FR** 1046-47
    and improvements on Nixon's Key Biscayne properties **FR** 1034-46
    investigation of **FR** 1030-31
    and loan note signed by Rebozo and used for purchase of Nixon's Key Biscayne property **FR** 1049-50
    and Nixon brothers **FR** 1052
    Nixon denial of Rebozo payments of expenses for **FR** 1051, 1069-70

and purchase of earrings for Mrs. Nixon from Winston **FR** 1047-48
and Rebozo's financial situation **FR** 1044-46
summary of facts on **FR** 1031-32
summary of total payments by Rebozo on behalf of Nixon **FR** 1049
Wakefield on **24,** 11295
Wakefield pleads attorney-client privilege on **24,** 11290-91
See also Hughes-Rebozo investigation

Hughes Tool Co.
acquisition of Dunes Hotel by **22,** 12429E **23,** 10895 **26,** 12775-12943E
Air West acquisition by **22,** 10730
antitrust suit against **26,** 12792-12818E
and Badden **21,** 9721
and Bennett **20,** 9349
business trips by Danner in 1969 for **20,** 9517-19
Caulfield on investigations of relationship between O'Brien and **21,** 9714-23
Danner denies contributions by **20,** 9500, 9501
Danner denies discussing business problems with Rebozo **20,** 9539
Danner denies request for information on Meier to **20,** 9603-9604
Danner discusses job offer with Rebozo **21,** 9953
Danner informs of contributions through Rebozo **20,** 9541-42
Danner on differentiation from Hughes **20,** 9507
Danner's discussions with Rebozo on issues relating to **21,** 10041-44
Davis denies discussions with Danner on **22,** 10582
directors inform Wearley that aircraft must not be flown for Maheu **20,** 9430
and F. Donald Nixon **20,** 9599-9604 **22,** 10626
Garment's inquiry to Smith on Air West and Dunes Hotel negotiations by **23,** 11053-59
and Greenspun break-in **20,** 9365, 9380-81, 9390, 9396, 9397
Hunt denies relationship with **20,** 9348
Hunt on plan to leave Las Vegas after Greenspun break-in with aircraft from **20,** 9351, 9358, 9363
Hunt on possibilities of employment for himself or others with **20,** 9403-9404
information from IRS to White House on **21,** 9711
and Intertel **20,** 9348
IRS investigation of **FR** 1017-18
IRS investigation of O'Brien and **21,** 9683-84
IRS investigation of Rebozo and **21,** 9680
and Maheu **20,** 9433
and Maheu-Greenspun relationship **20,** 9349, 9376
Meier and **22,** 10707
Moncourt denies correspondence file on **22,** 10519
and Mullen and Company **FR** 1122-23
and O'Brien **21,** 9956 **23,** 10943
O'Brien retainer with **20,** 9528-29, 9530 **21,** 9734-36 **22,** 10249 **24,** 11589-94
Simon on sensitive case report from IRS on **23,** 10927-28
suit and countersuit against Maheu **20,** 9541
and TWA litigation **20,** 9565-68
Walters on
    See Walters, Johnnie M., testimony of

Wood denies knowledge of file maintained by **22**, 10268-69

Woods denies knowledge of business transactions of **22**, 10231

See also Las Vegas matter; Wearley, Robert Franklin, testimony of

Hughes-Rebozo investigation

alternatives possible in conclusions on **FR** 1070-71

and attempted Hughes contribution at Palm Springs in 1968 **FR** 938-40

and background of Hughes' contribution commitment **FR** 933-38

and delivery and retention of Hughes contribution **FR** 944-80

and Dunes report **FR** 980-98

and Maheu testimony on Hughes contributions **FR** 933

organization of report on **FR** 931-33

and subpoena for Hughes' appearance **FR** 933

See also Hughes contribution; Rebozo, Charles Gregory "Bebe"

Hullin, Todd 3, 966 **FR** 182

Human Events **10**, 4126E

Hummell, Robert FR 700

Humphrey, Hubert 2, 700, 730 **3**, 1155E **8**, 3235 **10**, 4060E **10**, 4212E **16**, 7111, 7320 **20**, 9457

AMPI contributions to **14**, 6151, 6160-62, 6185, 6326-27 **15**, 6531, 6547-48, 6876 **16**, 7301

and AMPI contributions to Congressional candidates **16**, 7338-39

and AMPI contributions to Democratic Congressional and Senatorial committees **17**, 7670

article in *Washington Star* about **11**, 4439, 4697E

asks Chestnut to explain financial condition of campaign to Loeb **25**, 11723, 11725-26

attack pamphlet on **10**, 4299-4300E

attack strategy for **10**, 4188E

bill on milk price supports introduced by **25**, 11880E

"blind" trust of **FR** 888-90

bogus advertisement for free barbecue in Milwaukee for **11**, 4413

bogus "Democrats against Bossism" leaflet against **10**, 4001-4002

bogus press releases on Muskie stationery on **10**, 3942, 4026, 4280E **11**, 4380-81, 4392, 4395

bogus press releases on stationery of **FR** 172

Buchanan memo "Resurrection of Hubert Humphrey" on **10**, 3937, 3975, 4154-63E

Buchanan on **10**, 3926

Butterbrodt and **17**, 7671

campaign against Nixon **14**, 6053-54

and Chestnut disposing of campaign records **25**, 11734

contributions of dairy trusts to **FR** 883

contributions to 1968 presidential campaign **15**, 6616-17

declines interview by Select Committee **FR** 884

demonstrations against in 1968 **10**, 3942

dirty tricks against **2**, 679

discussions with Morrison **25**, 11763

disruption of fundraising dinner by McGovern supporters **11**, 4525-26

given Muskie schedules by McMinoway **11**, 4484

handling of hecklers and demonstrators by **11**, 4493

Hughes' contributions to **20**, 9512, 9513 **24**, 11614-15

impact of dirty tricks on **11**, 4682-83

intelligence gathering by supporters of **11**, 4502

invitation to bogus rally for **10**, 4026, 4285E

letter from Mott in 1968 **25**, 12096-97

letter on Muskie stationery about sexual improprieties of **10**, 3982-83, 3997, 4032-34

letter to Ervin declining to meet with Committee member **FR** 901

letter to Ervin denying knowledge of Valentine, Sherman matter **FR** 871

letters from Ervin requesting meeting with **FR** 899, 900

Lilly on contributions to 1968 campaign of **14**, 5932

and Loeb contribution **25**, 11723-26, 11741

MacGregor's news release charging McGovern with political espionage against **12**, 4903-4905

Magruder on **10**, 4175E, 4177E

Maheu contributions to **24**, 11575 **FR** 959

Maheu's employment for son of **20**, 9529

Masters' contribution to **16**, 6966-67

McMinoway activities in California campaign of **11**, 4492-94, 4506-4508

McMinoway on infiltration of Philadelphia campaign headquarters of **11**, 4486-91

meeting with AMPI officials and Chestnut **14**, 6155, 6158

memo from Strachan to Magruder on "Humphrey Watch" **10**, 3975, 4164-66E

milk industry support for **14**, 5916

and milk price-support issue **16**, 7317, 7318, 7399

Muskie schedule given to supporters of **11**, 4523-24

older voters in Gallup polls and **19**, 9079E

pamphlets against **10**, 4026, 4299-4300E **11**, 4492-93

political intelligence-gathering by Muskie campaigners against **11**, 4515, *see also* Humphrey Campaign

poster against **10**, 4026, 4295E

in primaries **10**, 4168E, 4228E, 4229E, 4230-31E

and relationship between AMPI and Valentine, Sherman **15**, 6575-98

relationship with Mehren **16**, 7322-23

and review of Committee for TAPE contributions **17**, 7572-73

rumored trip to Las Vegas **25**, 12160-63

Segretti activities against **10**, 4001-4002

Segretti letter on **10**, 4046-47, 4050

Segretti pamphlet against **FR** 172

and Segretti's activities in Florida primary **10**, 4020-21

in sensitive case report on Hughes Barth on **23**, 11221, 11237, 11257-58

speech in Senate on milk price supports **25**, 11879E

support from dairy industry **15**, 6385

TAPE contributions to **16**, 7323-24

telegram campaign to **FR** 286E

trip to New York during campaign **25**, 11723-25

Humphrey, Hubert *(Continued)*
 use of Federal resources by **19,** 8597E, 8598-99E
 FR 363-64
 and Valentine, Sherman relationship with AMPI
 15, 6834-35, 6845-46, 6846-50
 See also Humphrey campaign
Humphrey, Mrs. Hubert 11, 4493
Humphrey campaign 2, 848 **FR** 869-901
 AMPI contributions to **14,** 5970-71 **15,** 6458-59,
 7121 **17,** 7669
  Chestnut invokes Fifth Amendment on questions on **17,** 7700-7703
 and AMPI payments to Russell **16,** 7340
 and AMPI relationship with Valentine, Sherman
 15, 6858, 6860 **16,** 7345-46
 anti-McGovern literature of **11,** 4585-86
 bank deposit tickets **25,** 11881-82E
 and contribution from 3M **FR** 484, 893-94
 contributions from milk coops to **15,** 6880-81
 and corporate contributions by AMPI through
 Valentine, Sherman **FR** 870-81
 Dean discusses with Nixon **3,** 995, 996, 999, 1017,
 1020 **4,** 1381-82, 1402-1403, 1538-40, 1544 **8,**
 3125
 document from Democrats for a Peace Candidate
 on **11,** 4608-4609
 Dogole checks showing loans to **25,** 11883-85E
 and financial support from dairy industry **FR** 869-
 70
 Hughes contribution to **20,** 9528 **21,** 9953, 9955
 22, 10613
 and Humphrey's support for legislation favorable
 to milk producers **FR** 881-83
 impact of dirty tricks on **11,** 4613-14 **FR** 173
 impact on Muskie campaign **11,** 4653
 and Loeb contribution **FR** 894-98
 McMinoway infiltration of **FR** 194-95
 McMinoway on types of supporters for **11,** 4532
 Mid-Am contributions to **17,** 7745-46
 and MPI **16,** 7193
 and National Jewish Youth for Humphrey **12,**
 4964
 and Parr **15,** 6600-6601
 in Philadelphia **11,** 4712E
 political intelligence in **2,** 499-500
 pre-April 7 large individual contributions to **FR**
 883-93
 Sedan Chair and **2,** 523
 Segretti infiltration of **FR** 168
 and Select Committee mandate **FR** 869
 TAPE contributions to **17,** 7658-59, 7660
 and Townsend's relationship with Connell **16,**
 7114-15
 and Valentine, Sherman **16,** 7112, 7113 **25,** 11822-
 78E
 and Van Dyk **16,** 7039
 See also Backers of Humphrey; Chestnut, Jack L.,
 statement of; Cole, Joseph E., statement of; Fellows, Ben E., testimony of; Morrison, John,
 statement of
Humphrey for Senator Committee
 and Humphrey's presidential campaign **FR** 886

Humphrey Volunteer Committee 14, 5865-66
 Fixman checks to **25,** 11956-59E
"Humphrey Watch"
 memo from Strachan to Magruder on establishment of **10,** 3975, 4164-66E
Hundley, William G.
 See Mitchell, John N., testimony of
Hunt, Dorothy (Mrs. E. Howard Hunt) 1, 195, 196,
 197-98, 364, 375, 384 **5,** 2129, 2140, 2141, 2142,
 2146 **6,** 2267, 2290 **7,** 2801 **9,** 3704, 3890E
 amount paid to **6,** 2245 **9,** 3798, 3799E, 3800-
 3802
 asks for money for personal expenses **6,** 2235
 and attempt to blame CIA **1,** 207
 contacts with Ulasewicz **6,** 2225, 2227, 2228-30E,
 2231, 2234-36, 2236, 2237-38, 2246, 2250-56
 death of **3,** 971-72, 1234E **6,** 2608 **9,** 3663, 3738,
 3812, 3892E **FR** 66, 68
 gives money to McCord **1,** 130, 210, 241
 Gray on plane crash that killed her **9,** 3507
 Helms on relationship with CIA of **8,** 3262
 Hunt on amounts received and distributed by **9,**
 3750
 and hush money **3,** 970, 1001 **5,** 2104 **9,** 3691-92
 FR 53, 55
 increased demands by **6,** 2244, 2261
 McCord and **1,** 131, 150
 memo on money **7,** 2734
 and messages about Executive clemency **1,** 209-
 210
 money on person at time of death **6,** 2262-63 **9,**
 3515
 money to Barker from **1,** 359
 Ulasewicz denies discussion of pardons or light
 sentences with **6,** 2246, 2247
 Ulasewicz on her increasing demands for money
 6, 2241-42
 Ulasewicz on her probable contact with someone
 else **6,** 2242-43
 Ulasewicz on verification of money transmitted by
 6, 2238
 and Ulasewicz's delivery of money to Liddy **6,**
 2232
 visit to O'Brien **6,** 2367-68
Hunt, E. Howard 1, 39, 130, 133, 141, 155, 214 **2,**
 786 **3,** 931 **5,** 1858 **9,** 3612 **11,** 4666 **12,** 4922
 activities at Chappaquiddick **3,** 938
 arrest of **5,** 2013
 assigned to special unit at White House **6,** 2531
 assignments at CIA **8,** 3254
 and attempt to blame CIA for Watergate **1,** 195,
 206-208
 and attempted break-in at McGovern headquarters **FR** 27
 attempts to get out of country **4,** 1672
 attitude of other Watergate burglars toward **FR**
 28
 Baldwin identification of **1,** 399
 Barker on **1,** 357-358, 372, 379-81, 382, 383-84,
 385-86
 and Barker's guilty plea **1,** 363-64, 373-74, 380
 and Barker's infiltration of demonstration on
 Capitol steps **1,** 366
 and Bay of Pigs invasion **1,** 360, 363, 370-71 **6,**
 2359

and Bennett **FR** 1124
Benz denies contact with **11**, 4416
blackmail attempt by **8**, 3055, 3117
Buckley's contacts with **11**, 4453
call to Colson demanding more hush money **3**, 969-70
calls to embassies **10**, 3836E
on career **9**, 3661
and Chapin **FR** 184
and charts for Mitchell meeting **2**, 527
CIA aid to **FR** 16-17, 1135-41, 1152-53
CIA background **8**, 3247, 3249
CIA material on, attempts to retrieve from Department of Justice **3**, 977-79
and CIA psychological profile of Ellsberg **8**, 3236 **25**, 12422-24E **FR** 121
Colson and **3**, 932-33, 955, 1206E **4**, 1632
Colson wants Dean to take contents of safe of **3**, 934-35
Colson's taped conversation with **4**, 1419
contact with Barker for Watergate break-in **1**, 374-78, 383-84
contact with Winte **24**, 11562-63
contents of safe
    Dean on **3**, 1256E
    Dean on disposition of **4**, 1362-66
conversation with Hall **3**, 1157E, 1159E
and Cuban community in Miami **6**, 2362
and Cuban liberation movement **1**, 358, 365-67
Cushman on reasons for use of CIA equipment **8**, 3301-3302
Cushman states he has poor judgment **8**, 3307-3308
Dean learns of involvement in Watergate break-in **3**, 932, 1040
Dean on **3**, 921
Dean says Ehrlichman told him to get him out of country **7**, 2829-30
Dean tells Moore about demand for money by **5**, 2053-54
decision to plead guilty **1**, 301-302, 316-117, 329, 330-331 **3**, 973-74, 1053
delivery of equipment to **8**, 3303-3304
demands for money **3**, 967-70, 997 **4**, 1546, 1673 **5**, 1959-60, 1968, 1981-82, 1983, 1986-87, 2063-64, 2071-72 **6**, 2567 **7**, 2734 **8**, 3265
demands on White House **4**, 1381-82, 1403
and Diem cable incident **FR** 125-27
dispute over Ehrlichman's name in Cushman's memos on CIA contacts with **8**, 3295-3300, 3308-10
and Dita Beard matter **6**, 2415 **FR** 128-29
documents from safe **3**, 1036-37
and Ehrlichman **3**, 1267E
Ehrlichman believes he would not talk about Ellsberg matter **6**, 2542
Ehrlichman contacts Cushman on help for **8**, 3281, 3290-91
Ehrlichman learns about involvement in Watergate **6**, 2540-41
Ehrlichman on meeting with Colson about **7**, 2770-71
and electronic surveillance plan for Democratic National Convention **1**, 188
and Ellsberg matter **FR** 14-15

employed by Liddy **2**, 792-93, 856
employment at White House **3**, 858,1157-59E **6**, 2532 **8**, 3257
equipment borrowed from CIA **8**, 3233, 3234, 3255, 3258-59, 3263-64, 3292, 3302
Executive clemency offers to **1**, 163-64, 208-10, 212, 213 **3**, 973-74, 995-96, 1047, 1080 **4**, 1403, 1435, 1484, 1555 **5**, 1862, 1910-11, 2003 **7**, 2847-50 **8**, 3076, 3116 **FR** 64, 66-70
and Executive clemency offers to McCord **FR** 63
false documentation used by **9**, 3853E
FBI check on employment by White House **9**, 3526
FBI instructs Butterfield on probable involvement in Watergate break-in of **FR** 33
and FBI interview of Sloan **2**, 564
and FBI interview with Colson **3**, 1160E
file cabinet **1**, 88
file material
    Ehrlichman's instructions on **3**, 1008
film delivered to CIA by **8**, 3264-65
financial problems **8**, 3261
and first Watergate break-in **1**, 157 **FR** 28
Gray claims Dean lied about office in White House for **3**, 939-40
and Greenspun break-in **24**, 11601-11603
and Gregory **11**, 4636, 4638 **FR** 196-97
on guilty plea **9**, 3692-93
Haldeman on **8**, 3215-16
Harmony on **2**, 459
Helms learns of involvement in Watergate **8**, 3237
Helms on **8**, 3250, 3260-61, 3284
Helms on White House knowledge or lack of knowledge of activities of **8**, 3267-68
hush money paid to **23**, 11110-11
and identity cards for Plumbers **1**, 175
impact of Watergate on **9**, 3890-91E
indictment of **FR** 2
on information from Mardian on Ellsberg **FR** 146
instructions to leave country **4**, 1648 **7**, 2718-20
instructs Segretti to organize support for Nixon's Vietnam policies **FR** 152-53
and intelligence operation in Muskie camp **7**, 2733
interview of DeMotte **FR** 118-19
investigation of financing of Democratic National Convention by **3**, 1151-56E
investigation of Kennedy by **4**, 1532-33
involvement in Watergate coverup **2**, 850-51
Kalmbach's code name for **5**, 2102
and LaRue's payments to Bittman **6**, 2313
leaves Colson's telephone number for Cushman **8**, 3306-3307
letter to Colson **6**, 2608-2609 **FR** 66
letters in CIA documentation provided to Senate Appropriations Committee **9**, 3443, 3834-42E
and Liddy **3**, 1087 **4**, 1352 **6**, 2396
Liddy discusses role in Watergate break-in with LaRue and Mardian **FR** 40
Liddy relates message on bail money from **6**, 2358
Liddy suggests to Magruder as substitute for himself **6**, 2279
and Mardian's belief that CIA was involved in Watergate break-in **6**, 2383-84
material from safe transmitted to FBI by Dean **3**, 948-49

on Bennett's awareness of role of Colson and Hunt at White House **20**, 9366-68

on Bennett's knowledge of White House activities of Liddy **20**, 9374-75

on Bennett's motivation for interest in Greenspun material **5**, 1960-62 **20**, 9355-56

budget for **20**, 9388, 9389-90

changes testimony **20**, 9356-58

on chronology of findings on Ellsberg **9**, 3804-3807

on CIA and intelligence background **9**, 3725-26

on CIA involvement in domestic affairs **9**, 3754-56

claims ignorance of type of derogatory information Greenspun had on Muskie **20**, 9402-9403

closing statement **9**, 3814

and collection of derogatory information on Ellsberg **9**, 3666-70

on Colson refusing to look at photos taken in Fielding's office **9**, 3677

on Colson's knowledge about Gemstone plan **9**, 3715-22, 3776-77

on Colson's knowledge of Plumbers' operations **9**, 3724

on Colson's participation in clandestine operations **9**, 3734-35

on Colson's prior knowledge of Watergate break-in **9**, 3679-84

on contact between Mrs. Hunt and O'Brien **9**, 3691

on contacts with CIA during tenure at White House **9**, 3727-30

on contents of his safe **9**, 3757

on contradictions between executive session and public testimony **9**, 3718-22

contribution to Gemstone plan **9**, 3766

on conversation with Colson on Ellsberg **9**, 3812

on Dahlberg and Mexican money **9**, 3730

on dealings with "Fat Jack" **9**, 3760-62

denies Bennett's allegations that Hunt initiated discussion on forced entry into Greenspun's offices **20**, 9352

denies discussion with Bennett on likelihood of electronic surveillance of Maheu or Greenspun **20**, 9371-72

denies discussion with Winte **20**, 9347

denies doing business with Hughes Tool Co. **20**, 9348

denies receiving offers of Executive clemency **9**, 3795

denies silence was in exchange for money **9**, 3803-3804

denies suspecting foul play in death of wife **9**, 3812

derogatory article on Boudin by **9**, 3673

description of missing evidence **9**, 3751

on desire to withdraw guilty plea **9**, 3664

on destroyed material from his file **9**, 3749, 3762

on differentiation between Gemstone plan and general intelligence-gathering plan **9**, 3746-49

discussion with Bennett after meeting with Winte **20**, 9380

on discussion with Winte on Greenspun break-in **20**, 9358, 9377-78

on discussions on Fielding break-in **9**, 3775

on discussions on future employment for himself or others **20**, 9403-9404

on discussions with Colson on Gemstone **9**, 3766-67

on discussions with Liddy on Las Vegas matter **20**, 9405-9406

on Dita Beard memo **9**, 3791

on double-agent theory **9**, 3741-42

on effort to break into McGovern headquarters **9**, 3686

on Ehrlichman's call to CIA **9**, 3729

on elisions from Pentagon Papers in *New York Times* **9**, 3812

on employment at White House **9**, 3666

on equipment obtained from CIA **9**, 3728, 3730

on evidence withheld at his trial **9**, 3738-39

on executive approval of Gemstone plan **9**, 3720-21

on Executive clemency offers to McCord **9**, 3795

on fabricated Diem cable **9**, 3672-73, 3732-34, 3808-11

on feeling let down by White House and CRP **9**, 3776

on Fielding break-in **9**, 3675-76, 3773-75, 3796

on first conversation with Bennett about Hughes Tool Co. **20**, 9349

on first meeting between Colson and Liddy **20**, 9383

on first meeting with Bennett **20**, 9346, 9349-50, 9352, 9356-57, 9365-66, 9368, 9370-71

on first meeting with Winte **20**, 9346-47, 9350, 9352-53, 9355, 9357-58, 9359, 9374-76, 9377-79

on foreign money received by Democratic National Committee **9**, 3708, 3709-10, 3711, 3712

on Gemstone project **9**, 3741, 3751-52, 3765-67

on Gregory's role at Muskie headquarters **20**, 9366-67

on guilty pleas of Barker, Sturgis, Gonzales, and Martinez **9**, 3787

on his activities as national security or political espionage **9**, 3740-41

on Hughes Tool Co. interest in Maheu-Greenspun relationship **20**, 9346, 9354-55, 9361-62, 9371, 9372-73

identifies "Fat Jack" as John Buckley **9**, 3742-43

instructions for Beard interview **9**, 3753

on intensity of interrogations of **9**, 3663-64

on interview with Conein **9**, 3667-70

on introducing Liddy to Colson **9**, 3748-49

on involvement in Liddy plan **9**, 3678-84

on items missing from his safe **9**, 3790-91

on Las Vegas matter **9**, 3686-87 **20**, 9345-9406

on legitimacy of Watergate break-in **9**, 3707-13

on letters to Colson **9**, 3696-97, 3698, 3757-58, 3807, 3892E, 3897E, 3898E

on Liddy consulting with his superiors **20**, 9393

on Liddy informing him of plan for Watergate break-in **9**, 3792

on Liddy informing his superiors of plan **20**, 9390

on Liddy meeting with Colson **9**, 3683-84

on Liddy indicating high-level interest in Greenspun **20**, 9354, 9357

on Liddy plan **20**, 9385-89

Dean's efforts to get back from Justice Department **9,** 3827E, 3833E
Dean's testimony on **6,** 2569
diagram of Greenspun offices in **20,** 9363-64
discussed at meeting with Colson, Ehrlichman, and Dean **FR** 34-35
disposition of contents of **FR** 35-37
Ehrlichman denies he told Dean to get rid of briefcase from **7,** 2824-28
Ehrlichman on **6,** 2612-16
Fielding and **4,** 1438
Gray and **9,** 3467-71, 3503-3506, 3513-14, 3526-27
Gray denies suspiciousness about **9,** 3531
Gray's destruction of **4,** 1461 **5,** 2106 **7,** 2675-76 **9,** 3508, 3533, 3554, 3624
Hunt examines contents after Watergate arrests **9,** 3689
Hunt on **9,** 3663, 3757, 3789-90
Hunt's motion on materials not turned over to authorities **4,** 1687-88
memos to Haldeman on **8,** 3213-14
Nixon's refusal of subpoena for White House materials and **7,** 2660
opening of **7,** 2822, 2824 **9,** 3757 **FR** 35
in taped Ehrlichman-Gray telephone conversation **7,** 2786 **9,** 3538-39
Huntley, Chet
on enemies list **4,** 1408-1409, 1701-1702E
and impasse on Big Sky Project **4,** 1528-29
memo from Higby to Magruder on discrediting of **10,** 3975, 4127E
Hurlong, Sid 24, 11422, 11423, 11430
Hurricane Camille 6, 2323
Hush money 25, 12403E
Bittman and **FR** 55
and Bittman and Parkinson **7,** 2734
CIA and **5,** 1899-1900
and contribution from Rebozo to LaRue **23,** 11155
Danner denies discussing with Rebozo **24,** 11549
and Davis brothers' contribution **FR** 1001
Dean and **3,** 949-51, 1025-26, 1037 **4,** 1390-93, 1416, 1418, 1589-90 **4,** 1413, 1446-47
Dean asks Kalmbach to raise **3,** 1050
Dean on Kalmbach's role in **3,** 950-51
Dean on legality of **4,** 1426
Dean on White House handling of demands for **3,** 967-71
Dean tells Moore about **5,** 2063-64
Dean-Kalmbach meeting on **4,** 1511-14, 1516
Dean-Moore testimony compared on **5,** 1986
Dean-Nixon meeting on **FR** 57-62
Dean's handling of **4,** 1437-39
discussed at La Costa meetings **3,** 985-86 **5,** 1941-42, 1966-67 **FR** 77
discussions between Liddy, LaRue, and Mardian on **FR** 51
efforts to raise **4,** 1402-1403
Ehrlichman and **FR** 51-52
Ehrlichman on **6,** 2566-75, 2570-75 **7,** 2717, 2726, 2840-45
Haldeman and **FR** 51-52
Haldeman denies knowledge of **7,** 2875

Haldeman discusses with Nixon **FR** 56-57
Haldeman on ethics of **8,** 3092-93
Higby on **23,** 11109-11
Hunt on **9,** 3691-92, 3750
Hunt telephone call to Colson complaining about **FR** 55-56
and Hunt's meeting with O'Brien **9,** 3703-3705
and Hunt's status after death of his wife **3,** 972
Kalmbach and **4,** 1569-71 **5,** 2149 **7,** 2947E **FR** 51-55, 81
LaRue on sources of **6,** 2333-34, 2341-44
LaRue's role in raising and distributing **6,** 2289-99, 2306-2309, 2320-21 **FR** 53, 55
and Lehigh Valley Cooperative Farmers contribution **FR** 481
MacGregor denies knowledge of **12,** 4909
Mitchell and **3,** 1629-32 **4,** 1644, 1658-59, 1672-73 **5,** 2041-42 **FR** 57
Mitchell denies involvement in **4,** 1648-49, 1650 **5,** 1862, 1882-83
Mitchell learns about **4,** 1645-47
Mitchell-LaRue discussions on **23,** 11162
Moore asks Mitchell to raise **5,** 1920-21, 1934-36, 1942, 1969, 2026-27, 2039-43, 2049-53
Moore learns about **5,** 1944, 1945
Moore on **5,** 1958-59
Moore's knowledge about **4,** 1424
Moore's reaction to La Costa discussion on **5,** 1193
Moore's reasons for not telling Nixon about mission to Mitchell on **5,** 2028-29
and Mrs. Hunt **FR** 53
and Nixon **4,** 1521-22, 1538-40, 1567, 1576-77 **7,** 2898 **FR** 60-62
Nixon discusses with Dean **3,** 995, 996, 999, 1017, 1020 **4,** 1381-82, 1402-1403, 1538-40, 1544, 1555 **8,** 3125
O'Brien tells Ehrlichman about **7,** 2734
possible interpretation as defense fund **4,** 1570
pressure from Hunt after Watergate trial for **FR** 57
problems with **4,** 1484
and Rebozo contribution to LaRue **23,** 11161-63, 11164-65
Rebozo discussion with Nixon on **21,** 10140
Stans and **FR** 52
Strachan on **6,** 2463-64
taped telephone conversation between Hunt and Colson on **9,** 3694-96
Ulasewicz and **FR** 51-55
Ulasewicz on use of term **6,** 2249
in Watergate coverup **FR** 51-62
and White House fund of $350,000 **6,** 2295-96 **FR** 56-57
White House questions on **4,** 1567-68
See also Kalmbach, Herbert Warren, testimony of; Ulasewicz, Anthony, testimony of; Watergate coverup
Hushen, John W. FR 48
Huston, Tom Charles 3, 1060 **4,** 1489 **5,** 2089 **23,** 11241, 11260-61
attacks Hoover's objections to Huston Plan **FR** 4-5
and Internal Security Division **FR** 146

Huston, Tom Charles *(Continued)*
   and investigation of Potomac Associates **21**, 9727
   and letterwriting campaigns to senators **FR** 291E
   meeting with Nixon **4**, 1453
   memo from Haldeman on domestic intelligence
      review **3**, 1062, 1324E **4**, 1452-59
   memo from Haldeman on Nixon's approval of
      Huston Plan **FR** 4
   memo on tax-exempt organizations **23**, 11263
   memo to Dean on O'Brien **23**, 11077, 11119-22E
   memo to Haldeman on domestic intelligence re-
      view **3**, 1061, 1062-63, 1325E-29E, 1330E **4**,
      1604
   memo to Haldeman on future air hijackings and
      use of increased intelligence information **3**,
      1062, 1333E
   memo to Haldeman on Hoover's opposition to
      domestic intelligence plan **8**, 3029-30
   memo to Haldeman on IRS and ideological or-
      ganizations with attachments **3**, 1062, 1338-45E
   memo to Haldeman on Subversive Activities Con-
      trol Board **3**, 1062, 1331E
   memo to Helms on domestic intelligence **8**, 3394-
      3401E
   plan for intelligence operations against dissenting
      groups **2**, 854-55
   relationship with Haldeman **8**, 3028, *see also* Hus-
      ton Plan
   telephone call to Barth requesting IRS review of
      activist organizations **FR** 139
   See also Huston Plan
Huston Plan
   demonstrations and dissent as motivation for **FR**
      6-7
   Ehrlichman on **6**, 2527-29
   Haldeman on **7**, 2874 **8**, 3027-30
   Hoover and **7**, 2692 **8**, 3029-30
   and illegality of Fielding break-in **7**, 2817-21
   Mitchell on **4**, 1603-1605, 1636-37 **5**, 1822-24
   Nixon approval of **FR** 3-4
   and presidential power **FR** 3-7
   Weicker on **FR** 1197-98
Hutar, Pat 1, 34 **12**, 5051E
Huzum, Charles A. 9, 3522
Hyatt, Arnold 25, 12147-48
Hyde, Eveline 2, 469, 596, 689
Ianni, John 24, 11611-12 **FR** 956-57, 962
IBM
   McGovern campaign debt to **FR** 555
Ichord, Dick 3, 1332E
Ickes, Harold 25, 12277
Illinois
   Armendariz report on Spanish-speaking campaign
      in **19**, 8793-94
Illinois Democratic party primaries
   CRP vote-siphoning scheme in **FR** 203
   false and misleading literature distributed by Se-
      gretti and his agents during **FR** 171
   Segretti's false advertising during **FR** 174
Immunity
   for Bartolme **13**, 5431
   for Benz **11**, 4403

for Clark **13**, 5416
for Dean **3**, 1019 **4**, 1520, 1554-58, 1558
Dean-Ehrlichman disagreement on **7**, 2744
Dean's efforts to obtain **4**, 1399-1400, 1426-29,
   1440-41
discussed between Dean, Haldeman, and Ehrlichman **7**, 2741-43
discussed in Dean-Nixon meeting **8**, 3072-73
for Edidin **25**, 12221, 12257-58 **FR** 474
Gray waives **9**, 3449
for Hunt in testimony on Fielding break-in **9**,
   3732
Kalmbach does not request **5**, 2091
for Kelly **11**, 4375
letter from Bray to Dorsen on Strachan's **16**,
   7455, 4742E
for Magruder **2**, 783
for Mitchell **5**, 1936
and Office of Public Attorney **FR** 97
for Priestes and Fernandez **13**, 5394
for Segretti **10**, 3979
Select Committee given power to grant **FR** 26
Select Committee witnesses and **4**, 1347, 1348
for Strachan **6**, 2436-38
in taped telephone conversation between Ehrlichman and Colson **7**, 2829-30
in taped telephone conversation between Kleindienst and Ehrlichman **7**, 2750
usefulness in Select Committee investigation **FR**
   28-29
in White House staff discussions **4**, 1384-85
Inaugural Committee
   Harmony on duties at **2**, 473-474
Independent Bancorporation 25, 11773, 11774
Inderfurth, Rick 25, 12196
Individuals Against the War 11, 4543
Indochina issue
   and Mott's letter to Humphrey **25**, 12097
   See also Vietnam issue
Indo-China Peace Campaign 11, 4544
Inflation
   and milk price-support decisions **FR** 680
Informants
   and IRS audits **23**, 11272-73 **FR** 135
   use of
      in Colson memo to Dean **FR** 9
Ingold, Gene 12, 5258E
Inouye, Daniel K.
   attitude toward questioning Stans **2**, 733
   Baker on **8**, 3231-32
   on effect of hearings on reputations **4**, 1559
   Ehrlichman's reaction to **3**, 983
   Ervin on **8**, 3231
   on Griffin exhibits **23**, 10737
   on judgement against Haldeman in 1964 **8**, 3169-
      71
   on leaks from Select Committee **23**, 10734
   letter from Buzhardt with questions for Dean **4**,
      1754-82E
   on line of questioning of Rebozo **21**, 10076,
      10078, 10085
   opening statement **1**, 8
   on prior dealings with Dean **4**, 1561-62

requests records of Internal Security Division **1,** 348-349

thanks Ervin and Baker for remarks about him **8,** 3253

on Vanet's request for recording executive session and reading transcript of previous session **16,** 7085-86

Wilson requests time for statement on **8,** 3227, 3228-29

World War II record **8,** 3231

Inouye, Daniel K., questioning by

Alch **1,** 347-349
Atkins **13,** 5459
Barker **1,** 378-82
Bartolme **13,** 5435
Benz **11,** 4427, 4428
Buchanan **10,** 3957-60
Buckley **11,** 4457-59
Butterfield **5,** 2084
Campbell **12,** 4958
Caulfield **1,** 275-277
Clark **13,** 5418, 5419
Cushman **8,** 3304
Danner **20,** 9534, 9538-39, 9540, 9542, 9550
Dean **4,** 1412-29, 1431-51, 1526-35, 1557-62
Ehrlichman **6,** 2616-25, 2727-37, 2800-2805
Gray **9,** 3503-3508, 3530-33, 3547-50
Haldeman **7,** 2896 **8,** 3100-3104, 3122-24, 3146-49, 3169, 3170, 3181-83, 3199-3202
Harmony **1,** 468-70
Helms **8,** 3253, 3254, 3273
Hunt **9,** 3739-41, 3768-71, 3789-91
Kalmbach **5,** 2127-31, 2171-73
Kehrli **1,** 88-90
Kelly **11,** 4389-91
Kleindienst **9,** 3593-96, 3604-3607
LaRue **6,** 2323-28
Leeper **1,** 112-114
Magruder **2,** 817-23
Malek **18,** 8213-14, 8216-17, 8219, 8223-24
Mardian **6,** 2398-2403
Marumoto **13,** 5311-14
McCord **1,** 171-176, 217-21
McMinoway **11,** 4519-22
Mitchell **5,** 1815-29, 1893-95
Moore **5,** 1990-97
Odle **1,** 26-28, 69-70
Petersen **9,** 3650-52
Porter **2,** 652-55
Reisner **2,** 513-15, 527-28
Segretti **10,** 4017-19, 4044, 4045
Sloan **2,** 602-608
Stans **2,** 726-33, 778-79
Strachan **6,** 2486-89, 2491, 2506, 2507
Taugher **11,** 4552, 4553
Ulasewicz **1,** 291 **5,** 2245-59

Inscoe, Garnett 4, 1573, 1574

letter from Shaffer, McKeever, and Fitzpatrick with enclosures **4,** 1801-1807E

Institute for Policy Studies

and *Quicksilver Times* **10,** 3952, 3955-56
Rogovin's affidavit on **10,** 4370-74E **11,** 4433-35

Intelligence Advisory Committee

McCord on **1,** 201

Intelligence Board (Abuse of Security Committee) 8, 3253

Intelligence Evaluation Committee 8, 3399E

creation of **3,** 916, 1055-56 **7,** 2874-75
Dean on **3,** 926-29

Interagency Dairy Estimates Committee 16, 7516-17

and milk price-supports decision **16,** 7135-36

Interagency Domestic Intelligence Unit

and air hijackings **3,** 1333E
creation of **3,** 1063-64, 1335-37E **FR** 5-6
Huston on Hoover's attitude toward **3,** 1325-29E, 1330E
recommendation for formation of **3,** 1323E

Inter-American Cattlemen's Confederation 15, 6508

Interest groups

memo from Magruder to Mitchell on reports of **19,** 8813-18E

Internal Revenue Code

amendment to provide credit for campaign contributions
Select Committee recommendations for **FR** 572

Internal Revenue Service (IRS) FR 715

Accounts Collection and Taxpayer Service **23,** 11263
and Activist Organizations Committee **FR** 139, 140, 263-66E
and anonymous informants **22,** 10368, 10388 **23,** 11272-73
audit of AMPI **14,** 6117 **15,** 6461, 6464
audit of B & C Investment Co. **23,** 10754-55
audit of Edward C. Nixon **22,** 10605-10606
audit of F. Donald Nixon **22,** 10704-10705
audit of Gibbons **4,** 1447, 1686E
audit of Hughes Tool Co. and O'Brien **22,** 10409
audit of MPI **14,** 6076-78 **15,** 6671-74
audit of New Yorker Films, Inc., DeAntonio, and Talbot **22,** 10385-90 **FR** 136-37
audit of *Newsday* reporter **21,** 10122, 10126 **22,** 10248 **FR** 9, 135-36
audit of O'Brien **21,** 10058-59 **22,** 10249 **FR** 1025-30
audit of Ryland **22,** 10248-49
audits **4,** 1486, 1528, 1530, 1685E
and authorization for committees for campaign contributions **25,** 12188
briefing paper for Haldeman before meeting with Walters on **4,** 1682-85E
briefings to Treasury Department on sensitive case reports **23,** 10926-30
and Brookings Institution **22,** 10356-61 **FR** 142-43
Buzhardt's preparation of Woods letter on Hughes contribution to **23,** 10878-88
Caulfield on "capability at" in memos **22,** 10387-88
Caulfield on relationships with **22,** 10391-95
Caulfield on requests for tax information on individuals and organizations **22,** 10361-79
Caulfield requests for taxpayer information from **FR** 138-39
and checkoff system for campaign contributions **FR** 1168

Internal Revenue Service (IRS) *(Continued)*
and Colson memo to Dean on Gibbons **FR** 136
contacted by individuals within White House on Rebozo case **23**, 11197-98
and Danner's deposition **20**, 9510, 9543-44
disclosure agreement with Cox's office **21**, 10104
document concerning *No Retreat from Tomorrow* and audit of MPI by **17**, 8157E
effort to place White House person in **6**, 2486
efforts by Special Prosecutor's office to obtain disclosure on sensitive case report on Rebozo **23**, 10937
and enemies list **3**, 958 **4**, 1461-62, 1480-81, 1499, 1527, 1535 **FR** 8-9, 51
and Federation of Experienced Americans **18**, 8442-43
and foundations, Buchanan on **10**, 3918-20
Gemmill's contacts on Hughes contribution **23**, 11176-81
and Gulf Oil contribution **13**, 5470
Higby on sensitive case reports to White House from **23**, 11112
and Hughes' campaign contribution **20**, 9408-9409
impact of Watergate on **FR** 1206-1207
and information on Cortese **22**, 10395-96
information to White House from **FR** 134-35
interview of Danner **23**, 11255
interview of Rebozo **21**, 9963-64 **FR** 1010
conflicts in testimony on notification of Rebozo of **FR** 1067
interview with Gemmill **FR** 1019-20
interview with O'Brien, Walters' affidavit on **24**, 11640, 11667-71E
investigation of Eaton **25**, 12308, 12311-12
investigation of F. Donald Nixon **23**, 10938, 11034
investigation of Hertz-Muskie campaign matter **25**, 12261, 12265
investigation of Hughes contribution **FR** 956-62
and analysis of delivery dates **FR** 963-68
investigation of Hughes Tool Co. **FR** 1017-18, *see also* Walters, Johnnie M., testimony of
investigation of Meier **22**, 10647-48 **FR** 1017
investigation of MPI **FR** 715-22
investigation of Rebozo **21**, 9679-85, 10067-68, 10089, 10189-90, 10122-23 **22**, 10205-10206, 10429, 10430, 10435, 10439-42, 10464, 10519-21 **23**, 10878-88, 10891-92, 10930-32, 10938, 11107 **FR** 1016-30, 1054-55
Cox investigation and **23**, 11211-14
return of Hughes contribution and **21**, 10090-92
letter from Lilly to Jacobsen on audit of AMPI by **17**, 8155-56E
letter from Woods on Hughes contribution and **21**, 10107-10108
letter from Worthy to Thrower on "Disclosure of Income Tax Returns to the President" **FR** 252-62E
meeting with Griffin and Gemmill **23**, 11205
memo from Huston to Haldeman on ideological organizations and **3**, 1062, 1338-45E
and minority business enterprises
Barth on **23**, 11260

Nixon's attitude toward investigations of Hughes contribution by **23**, 11012-13
and Nixon's estate plan **6**, 2487-88
and Nixon's friends with tax problems **4**, 1529-30, 1558-59
practices of other administrations on examining tax returns **6**, 2798 **7**, 2800, 2978-3004E
pretext interviews **22**, 10396-97 **FR** 138
purpose of sensitive case reports **23**, 11256-57
relations with White House
Select Committee recommendations on **FR** 1071-73
and Segretti **7**, 2736
sensitive case report on Hughes
Barth on **23**, 11221-30, 11235-44, 11277-78E
sensitive case reports
Johnnie Walters on **24**, 11628, 11629-30
sensitive case reports sent to White House by **21**, 9710-11, 10105 **FR** 134-35
"Special Service Group" **3**, 1338E, 1339E, 1340E, 1341-45E
Special Services Staff **FR** 139-41
subpoena for Danner **24**, 11568
and taxes on Jones' payment to Lilly **16**, 7001-7002
and tax-exempt foundations **FR** 141-43
and transactions between Braniff Airways and CAMFAB **13**, 5490-91
used for political purposes **3**, 1071 **6**, 2486-87 **7**, 2684-86 **FR** 108
and violations of Constitution **FR** 1180
Weicker on use for intelligence-gathering purposes **FR** 1199
and White House domestic intelligence **3**, 1072
and White House enemies list **FR** 132-33
White House requests for audits from **8**, 3135-38
and White House requests for taxpayer information **FR** 137-39
Woods' letter on Hughes contribution to **22**, 10201, 10202-10203, 10272, 10273, 12584E **FR** 1020-22
See also Barth, Roger Vincent, testimony of; Foundations; Haig, Alexander, testimony of; Hughes contribution, return of; Walters, Johnnie M., testimony of

International Association of Machinists
loan to McGovern campaign **25**, 12145
"International Jew, The" **12**, 5026E
International Ladies Garment Workers Union
contribution to McGovern campaign **25**, 12171
Intertel Corp. 20, 9346-47, 9348, 9357, 9403, 9404
Caulfield on **21**, 9716, 9734-35
Davis and **24**, 11611
and interview of Wearley **20**, 9489-90
investigation of Maheu's skimming of Hughes' Las Vegas casino **21**, 9722, 9724
in Operation Sandwedge **FR** 241-43E
Iowa
AMPI sponsored rally for Mills in **15**, 6607-6609, 6866-75
Valentine, Sherman activities in **15**, 6844 **16**, 7029-35

Iowa Cooperative Month 17, 7707-7708 **FR** 915-20
 advertisement announcing **17,** 7722, 7730E
 designation of **FR** 916
Iowa Institute of Cooperation, Ames, Iowa 17, 7707-
 7708
"Iowa project" 15, 6842, 6924-29E
Iran, Shah of 6, 2468
Ireland
 seizure of weapons destined for **1,** 249
IRS
 See Internal Revenue Service (IRS)
Irving, Clifford 20, 9346, 9357, 9367, 9404 **21,** 9987,
 9993 **24,** 11604
 electronic surveillance of **FR** 1123
Isham, Robert O. 14, 5863, 5864, 5924, 5926, 5938,
 5954, 5997-98E, 6005E, 6161, 6178, 6269, 6326 **15,**
 6503 **16,** 7111, 7123, 7261-62 **17,** 7644
 and additional billings to AMPI from Masters **16,**
 6944-46, 6948
 and AMPI arrangement with Valentine, Sherman
 14, 6150, 6157 **15,** 6839, 6850
 and AMPI contributions **15,** 6389, 6644-45
 and AMPI employee checkoff system **FR** 922
 and AMPI payments to Russell **16,** 7308-7309,
 7310
 and AMPI reimbursement scheme **15,** 6529, 6530
 bogus lists from Valentine, Sherman **FR** 881
 and Colson's query to Dean on Corrupt Practices
 Act **FR** 789E
 and decision-making at TAPE **15,** 6689
 discusses Valentine, Sherman with Mehren **16,**
 7345
 discussion with Townsend **14,** 6321
 discussions with Parr on AMPI contributions **15,**
 6889-90
 explanation to Butterbrodt of high fees to Russell
 17, 7628-29
 and financial authorization at AMPI **17,** 7671-72
 handwritten notes by **14,** 5921, 5991E
 Jacobsen and **15,** 6384-85
 and Jacobsen's advice on reporting requirements
 for TAPE **15,** 6509-10
 letter from Harrison on use of political committees for contributions **15,** 6645, 6730-41E
 letter from Parr on mailing of contributions **15,**
 6890, 6931E
 letter from Pierson on legality of loan from TAPE
 to ADEPT **15,** 6640, 6716E
 letter to Betke on resignation from AMPI **17,**
 8163E
 letter to Harrison **15,** 6647
 letter to Harrison on contributions **15,** 6647,
 6742-49E
 letter to Mehren resigning from AMPI **17,** 8159-
 62E
 letter to Van Dyk terminating his consultancy
 with AMPI **16,** 7010-11
 meeting with Pierson and Nelson on AMPI
 repayment scheme **FR** 597-98
 on Mehren's knowledge of AMPI commitment
 FR 712
 memo to Mehren on resignation from AMPI **17,**
 8158-63E
 memo to Nelson on TAPE reports **15,** 6893,
 6932-35E

 and payments to Masters **16,** 7312
 and Pierson **FR** 605
 Pierson's legal advice to **15,** 6385, 6509
 and reimbursement of Russell for political contributions **14,** 5960-61
 and repayment of loan to Lilly **14,** 5921-24, 5938,
 5943-45, 5947
 resignation as treasurer of TAPE **16,** 7286-87 **FR**
 712
 responsibilities for disbursement of TAPE funds
 14, 5912-13 **15,** 6505
 role at MPI **14,** 5909
 role in AMPI **FR** 584
 and TAPE contributions **14,** 5914 **15,** 6524, 6624
 and TAPE loan to ADEPT **FR** 688
 telegram to Jennings on resignation from TAPE
 positions **17,** 8162E
 telephone call to Van Dyk on reporting payment
 to Lilly **16,** 6692, 6998 **FR** 606
 as trustee of TAPE **FR** 585
Israel issue
 bogus press releases on Muskie stationery on **11,**
 4380-81, 4392, 4395
 and Kelly flyers **FR** 171
 McGovern position on **10,** 4079-82E, 4098-4101E
Israeli embassy
 McCord's calls to **9,** 3442
ITT matter 5, 2058
 Anderson column on **17,** 7615, 7624E
 Barth on **23,** 11264-65
 in Butterbrodt conversation with Morris **17,** 7673
 Colson memo to Haldeman on **12,** 4899
 Connally on **14,** 6089-90
 and Dean **4,** 1356
 in Dean telephone call to Walters **9,** 3825-26E
 discussed at La Costa **5,** 1964
 Dita Beard memo on **FR** 127-29
 Ehrlichman believes Watergate hearings will be
 similar to **3,** 984
 Haldeman and **8,** 3216-19
 Kalmbach on milk fund and **16,** 7398-99 **17,** 7615
 and Kalmbach's involvement with AMPI **FR** 711
 and Kalmbach's refusal of AMPI contribution **16,**
 7446
 Kleindienst and **9,** 3475
 and Kleindienst's confirmation hearings **5,** 1948-
 49
 Mardian and **6,** 2416
 memo to Haldeman from Colson on **8,** 3221,
 3373-76E **FR** 29
 Moore on **5,** 1948-50, 2007
 O'Brien and **2,** 790 **5,** 1873-74
 in Priestes-Fernandez dealings **13,** 5333, 5351,
 5361, 5374
 Weicker on **FR** 1175
 See also Beard, Dita
Ives, Burl 18, 8445-46
J & J Addressing and Mailing Service 10, 4026,
 4294E
J. A. Reyes Associates 13, 5287, 5288, 5400 **18,** 8248
 FR 384-385
J.L. Stewart Company 10, 4026, 4302E

J. Walter Thompson Advertising Co. 1, 84-85 7, 2872
Jablonski, Lee 2, 538 4, 1669-70
Jackman, J. Richard 3, 1136E
Jackson, Andrew 10, 3941
Jackson, Brooks 17, 7718
Jackson, Henry M. "Scoop" 2, 731 10, 4168E 13,
   5464, 5478 14, 5885, 5889 17, 7659
   and assault strategy on McGovern 10, 4243E
   attack on "environmental extremists" 10, 4198E
   attacks against 10, 3942, 4187-88E
   Benz on 11, 4411, 4419, 4421-22, 4428
   Benz organizes picket against FR 174-75
   Bernhard on 11, 4655
   dirty tricks against 11, 4381, 4408-4409
   Gulf Oil Corp. contribution to FR 469, 472-73
   headquarters broken into 10, 3970
   and indictment of Hearing 11, 4421
   infiltrator in campaign of 11, 4405, 4407
   letter on Muskie stationery about sexual impro-
      prieties of 10, 3982-83, 3997, 4026, 4279E,
      4280E FR 169-70
   Magruder on 10, 4178E
   Mankiewicz on 11, 4609-10
   and McMinoway infiltration of Humphrey cam-
      paign 11, 4488
   not included in Haldeman's apology 8, 3148
   in primaries 10, 4229E, 4230E
   Segretti letter on 10, 4046-47, 4050
   Segretti letter on Muskie stationery 10, 4032-34
   and Tennessee primary 10, 3975, 4205-4208E
Jackson, Jesse FR 408-409
Jackson, Morton B. 9, 3690, 3754 20, 9348
Jackson, Samuel FR 375
Jackson & Co.
   and contributions to Humphrey campaign 25,
      11772 FR 883-84, 887
Jackson State University
   deaths at FR 1175
Jacobs, C. Bernard 25, 11774
Jacobs, I. Richard
   See Priestes, John J., testimony of
Jacobs, Merrill R.
   affidavit of 12, 5009, 5168-69E
Jacobsen, Jake 14, 5863-64, 5919, 5925, 5968, 5980,
   6106 15, 6624, 6782 16, 6940, 6958, 6968, 7128,
   7247 17, 7684
   and AMPI contributions 15, 6766, 6897, 6898 FR
      594
   and AMPI payback scheme FR 602-604
   and AMPI's contacts with Kalmbach FR 587-91
   and arrangements for meeting between Nunn and
      Mehren 17, 7556, 7557
   arranges meeting between Mehren, Nelson, and
      Connally 16, 7263
   at AMPI strategy sessions 16, 7028
   at meeting with Kalmbach, Mehren, Nelson,
      DeMarco, and Olsen 17, 7610-11, 7612-13
   Butterbrodt and 17, 7637
   and cash contribution for Mills 14, 6318-19
   checks drawn on account of Jacobsen and Long
      to 14, 5935, 5936, 6002E, 6003E 15, 6432-33,
      6436, 6495-96E, 6500E
   and commitment for Connally's assistance in milk
      price supports 14, 6106

and Connally 14, 5975, 5989 16, 7239, 7269-70
   17, 7620
Connally denies discussing political contributions
   with 14, 6053-54, 6069-73
Connally denies meeting with 14, 6068-69
and Connally's meeting with dairymen 14, 6081
contacts with Connally 15, 6557-59, 6560-63,
   6567-68, 6619, 6622 FR 637-38
and contribution for Connally 15, 6648-49
and contributions to Democrats for Nixon 14,
   6087
and contributions to Mills' election campaign 14,
   6167-72 FR 908-10
deliveries of money from AMPI to FR 673
delivers money to Parr for Mills campaign 15,
   6791
discussions with Connally on milk price-support
   decision 14, 6054-58, 6058-60
discussions with Mehren on political contributions
   16, 7290-91
FBI inventory list of safety deposit box of 15,
   6426, 6488-94E
financial arrangements with ADEPT 14, 5898-99
and first meeting between MPI representatives
   and Semer and Jacobsen 16, 7188-89
and formation of TAPE 15, 6507, 6758 FR 584
and Hanman-Connally meeting 14, 5896-97
Harrison and 14, 6266, 6272
indictment for perjury FR 686
informed by Semer of Kalmbach's request for
   $100,000 cash contribution FR 589
involvement in price-support decision 14, 6312
and IRS audit of 15, 6672-73
Kalmbach corrects record on 17, 7805
and Kalmbach-Mehren discussion on antitrust suit
   against AMPI 17, 7615-17
letter from Hanman on discussions with Connally
   14, 5890, 5905E
letter from Lilly on IRS audit of AMPI 17, 8155-
   56E
letter from Lilly on IRS audit of MPI 15, 6671
and loan to Lilly for reimbursement of TAPE 15,
   6527
meeting with Connally on formation of TAPE 14,
   6051-53
meeting with Hanman 14, 5889-90
meeting with Kalmbach, Mehren, and Nelson 14,
   6105-6106 16, 7255-61 17, 7614-16
meeting with Lilly in Austin airport 16, 7102-
   7103
meeting with Mehren to set up meeting with
   Kalmbach 16, 7252-53
meeting with Nelson, Mehren, and Strauss 15,
   6678-79
meeting with Parr, Kalmbach, Semer, and Nelson
   15, 6759-65
meeting with Parr at Austin airport 16, 7091-93
meeting with Semer, Nelson, and Parr in Dallas
   in 1969 16, 7195-97
and meetings between Kalmbach and AMPI representatives in 1972 15, 6658-59
meetings with Connally 14, 6108-09, 6113 15,
   6806-6807 17, 7747-48
meetings with Kalmbach 14, 6124 15, 6666, 6667
   16, 7180 17, 7606, 7607-7608, 7609, 7612, 7613

meetings with Kalmbach and Nelson **15,** 6660-61 **FR** 708-10, 723

meetings with Nelson, Mehren, and Connally **14,** 6073-77 **15,** 6508, 6676

meetings with Mehren **16,** 7236

and Mehren-Kalmbach telephone conversation **17,** 7622

on Mehren's denial of knowledge of AMPI commitment **FR** 712

and Mehren's questions about AMPI campaign commitments **16,** 7248-49

and money paid to Connally **14,** 5962-64

Nelson on advice on TAPE reporting requirements given by **15,** 6509-10

Nelson on contacts with **15,** 6681-83

Nelson on role with AMPI of **15,** 6511-12

and Nelson's commitments to Kalmbach **15,** 6665

Nunn and **17,** 7553

political affiliation **16,** 7252-53

relationship with Mehren **16,** 7298

relationship with Nelson **15,** 6899

and repayment of loan to Lilly **14,** 5934-42

role as legal adviser to Mid-Am and ADEPT **14,** 5897-98

role with MPI and AMPI **14,** 5917

and Semer authorized to contact Kalmbach **15,** 6875

and Semer's meetings with Kalmbach and Gleason **16,** 7194

and source of AMPI contributions **15,** 6879-80

and SPACE **16,** 7062

and TAPE contribution to CRP **15,** 6517, 6519

and TAPE contribution to Kalmbach **14,** 5916

and TAPE contributions to Mills campaign **15,** 6778

telephone call to Connally on March 23 **FR** 651-55

telephone call to Mehren to arrange meeting with Nunn **16,** 7288-89

tells Connally about IRS audit of MPI **14,** 6077

transmittal of AMPI money to Connally **FR** 682-87

use immunity not utilized by Select Committee for testimony of **FR** 582

Jacobsen, Jake, testimony of 15, 6379-6478

on alleged AMPI payment for Connally **FR** 684-85

on AMPI and milk price-support legislation **15,** 6457-58

on AMPI and Vinson Elkins law firm **15,** 6469-70

on AMPI contacts with White House **15,** 6390-91

on AMPI contributions in 1971 **15,** 6408-6410

and AMPI efforts to reduce import quotas **15,** 6405

on AMPI payments to Jacobsen and Long **15,** 6398-6404

on AMPI reimbursement of TAPE **15,** 6391-98

on AMPI's dealings with Kalmbach **15,** 6437-46

and AMPI's efforts to have Nixon attend annual meeting **15,** 6405

on antitrust suit against AMPI **15,** 6465-66, 6469-72

on career **15,** 6379-80

on committees set up in 1971 for dairy coop contributions to Republicans **15,** 6418-19

on Connally's role in obtaining reversal of milk price-support decision **FR** 651-53

on contacts with Connally on price supports for dairy industry **15,** 6407-15

on contacts with Kalmbach **15,** 6449-50, 6456-57

contacts with Mid-America Dairymen, Inc., and Dairymen, Inc. **15,** 6382-83

on contacts with Parr **15,** 6430

on contradictions between *Nader* v. *Butz* deposition and present testimony **15,** 6441

on Corrupt Practices Act and AMPI contributions **15,** 6388-89

on dairy industry contacts with White House **15,** 6418

on delivering cash to Parr for Mills campaign **15,** 6430-35

denies discussing dairy industry contributions with Stans **15,** 6477-78

denies knowing Mitchell **15,** 6478

denies knowledge of AMPI contributions in 1970 **15,** 6406

denies knowledge of dairy coops contributing to Republicans in 1972 **15,** 6468-69

denies knowledge of meeting between Lilly and Connally **15,** 6459-60

on financial arrangements with AMPI **15,** 6383-84

on handling of cash for political contributions **15,** 6429-35

on IRS audit of AMPI **15,** 6461, 6464

on letter from Harrison to Mehren on antitrust suit against AMPI **15,** 6465-66

on Lilly delivery of cash contribution to Kalmbach **15,** 6423

on Lilly loan for AMPI contribution **15,** 6389-98

on meeting between Semer, Parr, Nelson, and Dent **15,** 6457

on meeting with Connally and dairy representatives **15,** 6472-75

on meeting with Kalmbach after meeting with Mitchell **15,** 6464-65

on meeting with Kalmbach and Dairymen, Inc., representatives **15,** 6554-57

on meeting with Kalmbach and Nelson **15,** 6439-41

on meeting with Long and Connally **15,** 6426

on meeting with Mehren, Nelson, and Connally **15,** 6460-66

on meeting with Mehren and Strauss **15,** 6467-68

on meeting with Nelson, Kalmbach, and Mehren **15,** 6442-53

on meeting with Nelson, Mehren, Kalmbach, and Connally **15,** 6451-52

on meetings between dairy coops **15,** 6417-18

on meetings with Nelson, Parr, and Semer on political contributions **15,** 6385-86

on meetings with Nunn on contributions from dairy people **15,** 6476-77

on milk trust contributions to congressional campaigns **15,** 6457

on offering AMPI money to Connally for Democrats for Nixon **15,** 6428-29

on political contribution offered from AMPI to Connally **15,** 6421-25

on purpose of meetings with Kalmbach **15,** 6459

and enemies list **8**, 3158

meeting with Mehren **14**, 6178-85 **16**, 7297-99, 7336-38

Mehren consults with **16**, 7289-90 **17**, 7569 **FR** 734-35

and milk price supports **15**, 6801 **16**, 7330-31

and Mills campaign **15**, 6694

and "No Retreat from Tomorrow" **15**, 6671

and O'Brien's leasing of Government building **23**, 11136E

open letter by Middle East specialists to **10**, 4103-4105E

in Segretti propaganda against Humphrey **10**, 4004

and Sierra Club tax exemptions **10**, 3918

Townsend on visit to **16**, 7107, 7121-22

use of Federal resources by **19**, 8597E, 8598-99E **FR** 363-64

Johnson, Marilyn 1, 32, 35

Johnson, Richard 24, 11614-15

Johnson, Roger E. 16, 7161-62, 7378-79

affidavit with attachment of **17**, 7936-37E

memo to Haldeman on Hillings letter to Nixon **FR** 755E

Johnson, Wallace 3, 980, 984, 1034, 1246E **4**, 1487, 1494 **5**, 1941, 1949, 1965 **8**, 3372E **9**, 3769

and amendments to Senate Resolution **3**, 980

and Dita Beard matter **9**, 3753

tells Dean about his conversation with Baker **3**, 986

Johnson, Walt 8, 3218-19

Johnson, Wes 14, 5874, 5890

Johnston, Al Smart 22, 12562-63E

Johnston, Cynthia 11, 4775E

Joint Committee on Atomic Energy

as depository of Select Committee documents **2**, 602 **3**, 1062

Joint Committee on Internal Revenue Taxation

study of enemies list **FR** 133-34

Joint Fall Peace Fund

sponsors on enemies list **4**, 1726E

Joint Intelligence Oversight Committee

Baker on establishment within Congress of **FR** 1106-1107

Jonas, Charles R., Jr. 4, 1536, 1563-64

Jones, Bob 11, 4766E

Jones, Ed 14, 5984 **17**, 7764, 7768

Jones, James R. 14, 5925, 5958, 5966, 5967 **15**, 6525, 6526, 6774, 6782 **16**, 7028

billing to Lilly for services **17**, 8065E

checks to Lilly **17**, 8056E

documents on payment by MPI for services of **17**, 8066-68E

invoice and check from AMPI for expenses of **17**, 8071-72E

involvement in AMPI payback scheme **14**, 5965 **FR** 607-609

letter and billing to Lilly for services from **17**, 8069-70E

letter from Kennelly to Dorsen on billing to AMPI of **17**, 8061-64E

letter to Ervin on involvement with AMPI **17**, 8058-60E

Mehren on severance from AMPI retainer **16**, 7329-31

professional background **FR** 607

Jones, Jerry 3, 990, 991 **18**, 8201 **22**, 10250 **FR** 382

memo for Higby and Dean on "Options for Jeb Magruder" **3**, 990, 1249-50E **4**, 1577-78

Jones, Kirby

affidavit with attachments of **17**, 7938-43E

and AMPI payback scheme **16**, 6998-7000 **FR** 605-607

check from Ted Van Dyk Associates **16**, 6999, 7043E

check to Lilly **16**, 7002, 7045E

tax forms from Ted Van Dyk Associates **16**, 6999, 7044E

Jones, Lloyd 13, 5507, 5511

Jones, Lyle L.

memo to Rashid on statements made by Gray before Nevada Gaming Commission **26**, 12913-14E

proposed case against Hughes Tool Co. **26**, 12902-12E

report to Rashid on conference with representatives of Hughes **26**, 12923-24E

Jones, Paul R. 1, 35, 74 **13**, 5282-83, 5507 **14**, 5966, 5967 **18**, 8207 **FR** 375

and Black voters and Responsiveness Program **18**, 8256-57, 8259, 8261, 8262, 8265-66, 8267-68, 8270-71, 8278, 8279

memo from Malek on OMBE grants **13**, 5323, 5542E

in memo from Malek to Mitchell on Black Vote Campaign Plan **19**, 8859-60E

memo to Magruder **19**, 8869E

memo to Malek on aid to Wallace **FR** 407

memo to Odle on Jackson and PUSH **FR** 408-409

memos to Malek on meeting with Farmer **18**, 8270, 8419E **19**, 8838E **FR** 405

and OMBE grants **FR** 434-35

and rally in support of mining of Haiphong Harbor **1**, 68-69

and solicitation of contributions from Black recipients of Federal moneys **FR** 409

Weekly Activity Reports to Odle **19**, 8862E, 8867-68E, 8870E, 9341E **FR** 407-09

Weekly Activity Reports to Malek **18**, 8267, 8268, 8273, 8417E, 8418E, 8420-22E **19**, 8848-49E, 8863-68E, 8870-71E, 9342-43E

Jones, Reuben FR 626

Jones, Robert F.

letter to Bernhard on contributions to campaign **11**, 4792-94E

Jones, Roxanne 12, 5187E

Jones, Thomas V. 5, 2126, 2133, 2139, 2149, 2151, 2156, 2159

guilty plea of **FR** 486-87

money to Kalmbach **4**, 2124, 2125 **5**, 2108-2109, 2120-21

See also Northrop Corp.

Jordan, Len 3, 1331E

Jordan, Peter

solicitation of contributions for Lindsay campaign **FR** 558-59, 560

Joseph Cafall Associates **23**, 11254
J-Tec Associates **22**, 10601
Juanich, A. E.
memo of summary of meeting called by Halde-
man **23**, 11100, 11140-42E
Judd, Walter 10, 4218E **12**, 4898
Juliano, James 21, 9701, 9714 **26**, 10339E
and Caulfield's investigation of Meany **22**, 10402-
10403
Justice, Bob 14, 5909, 5947, 5969, 5970, 6319 **15**,
6756
and attorneys' fees used for political purposes by
AMPI **15**, 6781-82
and Mills campaign **FR** 915
Kalish, Donald 11, 4557, 4558, 4559, 4562-63
Kalmbach, Barbara (Mrs. Herbert Warren Kalmbach)
5, 2106 **22**, 10717-18
Kalmbach, Herbert Warren 13, 5505-5506, 5518 **14**,
5889, 6277, 6314 **16**, 7255 **20**, 9454, 9602 **22**, 10696
23, 11249 **FR** 563
affidavit with attachments of **17**, 7944-58E
and American Airlines campaign contribution **13**,
5514 **FR** 448-51
and American Ship Building Co. contribution **FR**
451-53
and AMPI contributions **14**, 6135, 6254, 6300 **15**,
6363, 6386, 6387-89, 6406, 6416-17, 6514-21,
6542, 6691 **16**, 7461 **17**, 7747 **FR** 587-611
Nader v. Butz suit and **FR** 710-11
and antitrust investigation of AMPI **FR** 707-708
and appointments to ambassadorships **FR** 495
and arrangements for AMPI officials to meet
White House officials **FR** 595-96
asks Spater for campaign contribution **13**, 5500
asks Ulasewicz to distribute money for Watergate
defendants **4**, 1590 **6**, 2220-21, 2237-38
at meeting with LaRue and Dean **6**, 2290-91
at meeting with Nunn, Dean, and Evans on milk
producers' contributions **17**, 7649-50
attorney-client privilege for Rebozo and **21**,
10185-87
authorization for disbursement of funds by **2**, 560,
571, 627 **8**, 3078, 3103-3104
authorization for Semer's contact with **15**, 6875
Bartolme on contacts with **13**, 5422, 5423, 5436-
37
on belief in legality of defense fund for Watergate
defendants **FR** 62
and cash contributions from TAPE **16**, 7200-7201
cash disbursements from Sloan to **2**, 535-36, 573,
626, 711-13, 721, 751
and cash disbursements to Strachan **2**, 698
and Caulfield's duties on White House staff **1**, 251
chance meeting with Semer in 1973 **16**, 7205-7208
check from Florida Nixon for President Committee **23**, 10862E
check from Thomas H. Wakefield Special Account **23**, 10863E
checks to Caulfield **23**, 10865-67E
checks to Ulasewicz **FR** 215E
and Chotiner's meeting with Nelson **15**, 6575
and Colson's dealings with AMPI **16**, 7467-68
and "Computer Ideas" **11**, 4631 **25**, 12163

contacts with Danner **24**, 11564
contacts with milk producers **15**, 6827
Nunn on **17**, 7554-55
contacts with Segretti **10**, 4030
contacts with Semer **15**, 6390, 6759-60 **16**, 7218
contacts with Sloan after his resignation **2**, 590,
591
and contributions of milk trusts **15**, 6626-27,
6629, 6632-33
and contributors' lists **22**, 10266
conversation with Rebozo on Hughes contribution
affidavit of O'Connor on **22**, 12577-78E
conversations on money-raising with Ehrlichman
6, 2568-69, 2570-75 **7**, 2737-39
conviction for "selling an ambassadorship" **FR**
492-93
correspondence with Rebozo on Trustee for Clients account **23**, 10872-74E
corroboration of breaking off relations with dairy
people **FR** 726-29
as custodian of 1968 funds **23**, 11085-86
and dairy industry contributions **15**, 6643, 6646
16, 7165-66 **17**, 7541
and de Roulet ambassadorship matter **FR** 501-503
Dean involvement with **7**, 2743-44
Dean tells about Haldeman's destruction of files
4, 1369-70
Dean's memo to Ehrlichman on written retainer
arrangement for **7**, 2812-15
delivery of cash from Lilly to **15**, 6423
demands money from Mehren **14**, 6124-25
and destruction of financial records **2**, 572
discussed at Mehren-Johnson meeting **16**, 7298
discussed at Mehren-Nunn meeting **16**, 7293,
7294, 7295
discussed in Dean-Segretti meeting **10**, 4047
in discussion between Dean and Haldeman **3**,
1230E
discussion with Rebozo on return of Hughes
money **21**, 10111-13
discussion with Semer on use of AMPI contribution **FR** 595
discussions with Griffin on Nixon's purchase of
San Clemente property **23**, 10738-39
discussions with Mehren on antitrust suit and
AMPI contributions **FR** 725-26
discussions with Nunn on milk producers' contributions **17**, 7545-46, 7548
Ehrlichman and **7**, 2840-45
Ehrlichman denies discussing dairy industry contributions with **16**, 7390
Ehrlichman denies knowledge of contact between
dairy people and **16**, 7398-99
Ehrlichman's attitude toward money collection by
7, 2726
Ehrlichman's interview with **7**, 2727, 2764-65,
2768-69
Ehrlichman's notes on meeting with **7**, 2773,
2947E
and employment of Segretti **10**, 3980
ends contact with Ulasewicz **6**, 2244-45
expense money received by **6**, 2238
F. Donald Nixon's reaction to testimony of **22**,
10715-20
and F. Donald Nixon's relationship with Meier
22, 10708-10

financial role in Nixon campaign **1**, 20
financial statement to Stans **2**, 706-707
first contact with Ulasewicz **5**, 2249-50
funds to Ulasewicz from **22**, 10570-71
Garment on meeting between Rebozo and **23**, 11068
and Getty solicitation **FR** 999
Greenspun and **23**, 11032
Greenspun inquiries on Hughes contribution and **21**, 10130
Griffin on testimony of **23**, 10788-89
Griffin's discussions with Rebozo on testimony of **23**, 10787, 10789
Haig denies knowing **23**, 11004
Haig denies knowledge of meeting between Rebozo and **23**, 11031
Haldeman denies arranging surveillance of **8**, 3158-59
Haldeman on funds solicited from milk industry by **16**, 7155-58, 7160-61
Harrison and **14**, 6275
Harrison on AMPI contacts with **17**, 7688-89
Harrison on meeting with **14**, 6258
Higby on payments out of 1968 fund by **23**, 11090-94
in Hillings' letter to Nixon **FR** 620
and Hughes contribution **22**, 10221, 10549-50, 10559-60
and hush money **3**, 949-51, 967, 968, 1026, 1038 **4**, 1369-71, 1416, 1569-71, 1589-90, 1658, 1673 **5**, 1862 **6**, 2306-2307 **7**, 2734 **8**, 3048-49 **FR** 51-55, 81
individuals solicited by and actual contributions **FR** 508-10
informs Mehren that he is terminating discussions on AMPI contributions **16**, 7273-79
involvement in coverup **2**, 837-38 **3**, 1054
itinerary-agenda for meetings of **17**, 7807, 7816E **FR** 760E
Jacobsen arranges meetings between AMPI representatives and **15**, 6437-46 **16**, 7252-53
LaRue and **6**, 2289-99
LaRue gives money to **6**, 2291, 2313-14
LaRue on disbursements to **23**, 11155-56
and legality of distributing money **6**, 2250
letter from Caulfield with travel expenses **22**, 12472E
letter from de Roulet on Connally visit to Jamaica **FR** 503
letter from Rebozo on retention of contributions for administration-connected costs **22**, 1244E
letter from the Mayflower Hotel on registration for **5**, 2209E
letter to Ehrlichman on Trustee for Clients Account for payments to Caulfield **22**, 12473
letter to Segretti on payment for services **10**, 4026, 4268E
letter to Stans on Mulcahy contribution **17**, 7807, 7816E
locates job for Segretti **FR** 183
on March 21 Nixon tape **8**, 3211-12
McKiernan attempts to contact on his testimony on Hughes contribution **22**, 10619
McKiernan on **22**, 10635

meeting with AMPI representatives **16**, 7445-46 **FR** 725-26
meeting with Chotiner **17**, 7689-92
meeting with Chotiner and Kalmbach on March 24 **FR** 667-68
meeting with Chotiner and Nelson on March 24 **FR** 659-67
meeting with Dean on hush money **4**, 1511-14, 1515
meeting with Evans, Colson, and Nelson **15**, 6626
meeting with Jacobsen and Mehren **FR** 723
meeting with Jacobsen and Nelson **FR** 708-10
meeting with Mehren, Nelson, and Jacobsen **14**, 6105-6106 **15**, 6442-51 **16**, 7255-61
meeting with Mitchell on hush money **4**, 1631-32
meeting with Parr, Colson, and Gleason **15**, 6784-86
meeting with Rebozo on disbursal of Hughes contribution to Woods, F. Donald Nixon, and Edward Nixon **22**, 12439-40E
meetings with dairy industry representatives **15**, 6451-52, 6454-57, 6535-41, 6657 **FR** 712-15
meetings with Greenspun **20**, 9607
meetings with Jacobsen **15**, 6464-65
meetings with Mehren **14**, 6122-23, 7249 **16**, 7271-76, 7336 **17**, 7641-43
meetings with Morgan **16**, 7081-82
meetings with Nelson in 1972 **15**, 6658-70
meetings with Parr **15**, 6787-89
meetings with Parr, Semer, Jacobsen, and Nelson **15**, 6759-65
meetings with Semer **16**, 7191-7201, 7204-7205
meetings with Spater **13**, 5494, 5499-5500, 5505-5506, 5508, 5518
Mehren denies knowledge of AMPI involvement with **16**, 7231
Mehren informs Butterbrodt of his refusal to accept AMPI funds for Nixon campaign **17**, 7644-45
Mehren questions Nelson and Jacobsen about relationship with **16**, 7248-49
and Mehren's suspicions about AMPI political commitments **16**, 7333
memo from Dean on bill from Gleason's lawyer **3**, 968, 1231-32E
memo from Dean on draft charter **17**, 7596, 7623E, 8130-34E
and memo from Ehrlichman to Dean on written retainer arrangement with **7**, 2813, 3005-3006E
and memo from Strachan to Haldeman on concern with milk producers' situation **16**, 7468, 7503E
and memo from Strachan to Haldeman on handling of milk money by **16**, 7468, 7469, 7502E, 7504E
memo from Strachan to Haldeman on telephone call of **16**, 7459, 7477E
memo to Ehrlichman on arrangements with Ulasewicz **FR** 231E
and milk industry contributions **16**, 7180, 7182-83, 7400
Mitchell on **4**, 1648-49
Mitchell suggests as contact for AMPI **15**, 6511, 6512-13
money from Rebozo going to Ulasewicz from **21**, 9681

Kalmbach, Herbert Warren *(Continued)*
and money from Stans **2,** 722-23
and money from 1968 campaign **2,** 709-10 **4,**
1581-82 **7,** 2875-76 **8,** 3118-19 **16,** 7157-58 **FR**
505
money paid to Segretti by **7,** 2877 **10,** 3980, 3981-
82, 3986, 3990 **FR** 161, 162, 163
and money to Strachan **2,** 716-17
and money to Wallace's opponent in Alabama
gubernatorial race **4,** 1536-37
Nelson on meetings with **15,** 6636-38, 6675, 6684-
85, 6699
and Northrop Corp. contribution **FR** 487-89
note from Caulfield to **23,** 10864E
note on Trustee for Clients Account **23,** 10869E
Nunn replaces **FR** 733-34
Nunn's work relationship with **17,** 7536
and Parr **15,** 6789-90
payment of Ulasewicz by **FR** 107, 109-110
and payments for Haldeman's polls **8,** 3121
purpose of meetings with dairy industry representatives **15,** 6459
Rebozo and **22,** 10240
Rebozo informs on return of Hughes contribution
22, 10450, 10451
Rebozo mentions Hughes money to **21,** 10110
Rebozo's discussions on Hughes contribution with
24, 11469
and Rebozo's expenditures on Nixon **24,** 11336
FR 941-43
and Rebozo's fundraising role **FR** 999
and Rebozo's leftover money from 1968 campaign
21, 9947, 9948, 9950-51, 9952
records burned **6,** 2293
and rehiring of Sloan by CRP after Watergate **2,**
610
reinvolvement in AMPI contributions **FR** 708-15
rejection of AMPI contribution by **14,** 6121-22 **15,**
6543 **16,** 7446-47
relationship with Mitchell **5,** 1824
relationship with Nixon **15,** 6698
relationship with Semer **15,** 6765
relationship with Strachan **16,** 7456, 7470
requests money from Stans **2,** 702-703, 729, 767-
68
requests to Rebozo for solicitation of contributions **21,** 9974-75
role in fundraising for Nixon's re-election **16,**
7457
role in fundraising in 1969 **21,** 9975
role in Nixon campaign **FR** 505-10
safe-deposit box report to **22,** 12448E
and San Clemente property transaction **23,** 10742,
10750
and Segretti **3,** 963, 1081, 1216E, 1223E, 1299-
1300E **4,** 1374 **10,** 4018
and Segretti coverup **FR** 178, 179
in Segretti's grand jury testimony **10,** 4049
and Semer **15,** 6538 **16,** 7206-7207
Semer delivers cash to **16,** 7206-7207 **17,** 7627
Semer on deposition in *Nader* v. *Butz* by **16,**
7192, 7193-94, 7198, 7205-7208
Semer referred to **17,** 7190
severs connection with AMPI **16,** 7469

and Silbert's questioning of Segretti **10,** 4052
in Silbert-Segretti discussion **10,** 4048
and solicitation of contribution **FR** 447-48
and solicitation of Northrop Corp. contribution
FR 487
Stans' attitude toward after Watergate arrests **2,**
731-32
Stans on suspicions about **2,** 775
and Symington case **FR** 497-501
and TAPE committees **14,** 6315
and TAPE contributions to congressional candidates **16,** 7199-7202
TAPE payment of $100,000 to **14,** 5914-21 **15,**
6830
taped telephone conversation with Ehrlichman **5,**
2215-17E **7,** 2842-44
telephone call from Ehrlichman on milk price-
support decision and $2 million pledge of dairy
industry **FR** 650-51
telephone call to Mehren on April 4, 1972 **16,**
7284-85, 7287-88
telephone call to Rebozo to inform him of resignation from law firm and Richard Nixon Foundation **23,** 10857
telephone call to Ulasewicz asking him to come to
Washington **6,** 2220
telephone calls after Watergate to and from
Mitchell **5,** 1883
telephone calls to Spater on American Airlines
contribution **13,** 5503-5504 **FR** 449
telephone conversation with Ehrlichman on April
19, 1973 **5,** 2215-17E
tells LaRue he wants to end assignment **6,** 2292-
93
tells Sloan to destroy records on cash disbursements **FR** 42
termination of contact with dairy people by **16,**
7398-99
Thomas H. Wakefield Special Account check to
23, 10868E
and Ulasewicz **6,** 2224, 2239, 2242-43, 2245, 2248,
2265, 2268-69, 2270, 2272
Ulasewicz appointment in notes of **FR** 214E
Ulasewicz conveys Mrs. Hunt's messages to **6,**
2242
Ulasewicz on source of authority for **6,** 2262
Ulasewicz warns about handling of money for
Watergate defendants **6,** 2237, 2261
and Ulasewicz's contacts with Bittman **6,** 2225-26
and Ulasewicz's contacts with Caddy **6,** 2222-45
and Ulasewicz's contacts with Mrs. Hunt **6,** 2227,
2235
and Ulasewicz's contacts with O'Brien **6,** 2224
and Ulasewicz's delivery of funds to Bittman **6,**
2256-60
and Ulasewicz's delivery of funds to LaRue **6,**
2232-33
and Ulasewicz's delivery of funds to Liddy **6,**
2231-32
and Ulasewicz's efforts to give money to lawyers
of Watergate defendants **6,** 2222-25
and Ulasewicz's qualms about money **6,** 2267-68
urged to raise funds again **6,** 2297
use of AMPI 1969 contribution **FR** 593, 594

use of code names by **4,** 1512, 1570-71
Wakefield reports expenditures on behalf of Nixon to **24,** 11341-42
wants Ulasewicz for hush money delivery **4,** 1370-71
and Watergate coverup **2,** 822
withdraws from dealings with milk producers **FR** 641

Kalmbach, Herbert Warren, testimony of 5, 2091, 2114, 2115-79 **17,** 7577-7622, 7805-15 **21,** 10181-92 **23,** 10855-61
on advance to Stans of $50,000 **5,** 2095
on advice to Rebozo on IRS investigation of Hughes money **21,** 10189-90
on agreement with Semer **17,** 7805-7806, 7811-12
on amount of money disbursed **5,** 2129-30
on AMPI contributions connected with parity **17,** 7583, 7584, 7589
on AMPI contributions through committees **17,** 7591, 7592-96, 7603-7604
on AMPI disappointment with results of $100,000 contribution in 1969 **FR** 596
on AMPI pledge reaffirmation and reversal of price-support decision **FR** 666
on AMPI's reasons for making 1969 contribution **FR** 592-93
on antitrust suit against AMPI and AMPI contributions **17,** 7611-12, 7615-17
on arranging meeting between Semer and Dent **17,** 7583-84, 7585
on attitude toward Dean **5,** 2100, 2119, 2122, 2129, 2131, 2145-46
on attitude toward Ehrlichman **5,** 2125-26, 2128, 2171
on authorization for Watergate break-in **5,** 2150, 2153, 2171-72
on belief that raising money for Watergate defendants was moral obligation **5,** 2122-23
on Bittman's acceptance of funds for Watergate defendants **5,** 2104
on breaking off contact with "milk people" **FR** 726
on Caddy's refusal to accept funds for Watergate defendants **5,** 2103-2104
on California lawsuit in 1962 election campaign **5,** 2127-28
on calling Stans for money **5,** 2116
on career **5,** 2091-92
on checks sent by Rebozo **21,** 10183-85
on Chotiner-Colson relations **17,** 7601-7602
on Colson's relations with dairy people **17,** 7595, 7609
comparisons with Dean's testimony **5,** 2112-14, 2115-17
on condition of Hughes money **FR** 1058
on confidence in Ehrlichman **5,** 2121
on contact with Liddy at Finance Committee **5,** 2094-95
on contacts with milk people after official contacts end **17,** 7619-20
on contacts with Nixon since Watergate break-in **5,** 2142
on contacts with Semer in 1969 **17,** 7584-85
on contribution from Northrop Corp. **5,** 2108-2109

on correction of record **17,** 7805
on Dean's and LaRue's role in distribution of money for Watergate defendants **5,** 2102, 2104, 2105, 2110-12, 2114
on decision to stop raising money for Watergate defendants **5,** 2110, 2133
on delivery of contribution by Semer **17,** 7581
denies conversations with Nixon or Rebozo on campaign contributions **21,** 10182-83
denies discussing Hughes contribution with Nixon **21,** 10183
denies discussion of Watergate at Finance Committee meeting **5,** 2139
denies prior knowledge or participation in Watergate break-in **5,** 2092
denies relationship between AMPI $2 million pledge reaffirmation and milk price-support increases **17,** 7813-15
denies use of AMPI money by Nixon **17,** 7586
on destruction of files transferred to Finance Committee **5,** 2092, 2094, 2129
on destruction of records of money collected for Watergate defendants **5,** 2111, 2158-59
on diary entries of discussions with Erlichman **23,** 10857-58
on disbursal of campaign contributions to Edward Nixon **23,** 10858
on disbursal of cash to Segretti **5,** 2132
on disbursal of funds into State of Alabama in 1970 senatorial elections **5,** 2142-45
on disclosure problem and contributions **17,** 7604-7606
on discussion with Stans on need for money **5,** 2134
on discussions with Ehrlichman and milk people on AMPI contributions through committees **17,** 7600-7603
on discussions with Haldeman on cash handling of 1968 surplus funds **17,** 7579-80
on discussions with Haldeman on his role in 1972 campaign **17,** 7589-90
on discussions with Haldeman on Semer's delivery of AMPI contribution **17,** 7582
on discussions with Rebozo on Hughes money **FR** 970, 1005-1007, 1009
on Ehrlichman and Dean as contacts at White House **5,** 2093-94
on Ehrlichman taping conversation with **5,** 2173-74
on Ehrlichman's instructions for his meeting with Nelson and Chotiner **17,** 7812-13
on Ehrlichman's instructions on his grand jury testimony **5,** 2161-63
on Ehrlichman's testimony on his break with milk people **17,** 7618-19
on ethics of taking money from Jones **5,** 2120-21
on exhibits proving he stayed at Statler-Hilton on June 29, 1973 **5,** 2138
on first meeting with Dean **5,** 2116, 2151-52, 2176
on General Accounting Office statement on money given to Watergate defendants **5,** 2118
on Getty contribution **FR** 941
and grand jury hearing **5,** 2173-74
on Hillings' letter to Nixon **17,** 7594-95

on reasons for stopping fundraising for Watergate defendants **5**, 2147

on Rebozo asking Gleason about contributions from foreign nationals **23**, 10855-56

on Rebozo's custody of 1968 funds **FR** 1060

on Rebozo's knowledge of payments to Caulfield and Ulasewicz **FR** 942-43

on Rebozo's knowledge of trust fund left over from 1968 campaign **21**, 10183-84

on Rebozo's knowledge of use of campaign funds for payments to Ulasewicz and Caulfield **23**, 10861

on Rebozo's role in fundraising activities in 1969 or 1970 **21**, 10181-82, 10183

recommendations for legislation **5**, 2130

on reconciliation of cash records with LaRue **5**, 2111

on relationship with Nixon **5**, 2093, 2121-22

reports to Rebozo on interviews with Select Committee staff **23**, 10856-57

requests Blech to assist F. Donald Nixon with tax problems **23**, 10858

on role as messenger for Dean, Haldeman, and Ehrlichman **5**, 2172-73

on role as trustee of surplus campaign funds **5**, 2092, 2093 **23**, 10858

on secrecy surrounding money to Watergate defendants **5**, 2128-29, 2156-57

and Segretti matter **5**, 2147

on Semer's representation of AMPI **17**, 7581

on source of AMPI contribution **17**, 7587-88

on sources of money for Watergate defendants **5**, 2145, 2151, 2174-75

on "special project" mentioned in Hillings' letter to Nixon **17**, 7597-98

on Stans' testimony that Ehrlichman and Dean had assured him of legality of money-raising assignment **5**, 2133-34

on surplus funds after 1968 elections **5**, 2128 **17**, 7577-78

on talk with Magruder **5**, 2148-49

on TAPE contributions through committees **17**, 7598

on taped conversation with Ehrlichman **5**, 2177-78

on telephone call from Dean **5**, 2097, 2112

on telephone conversation with Ehrlichman before grand jury testimony **5**, 2161-64, 2165-70

tells Knapp he feels used **5**, 2175

on uneasiness about role in raising and distributing money for Watergate defendants **5**, 2105-2106, 2118, 2132-33, 2145

on use of aliases and code words during distribution of money for Watergate defendants **5**, 2102, 2103

on use of AMPI contribution in 1969 **17**, 7583, 7586-87

on use of milk money **17**, 7605

on use of Ulasewicz as distributor of money for Watergate defendants **5**, 2099, 2113, 2116-18

on use of 1968 surplus funds **17**, 7580-81

on voided checks from AMPI **17**, 7617-18

on Watergate burglars' authorization **5**, 2160-61

Kalmbach, DeMarco, Knapp & Cillingworth 5, 2092

Kampelman, Max 25, 11724, 11725

and Duncan loan to Humphrey campaign **25**, 11798

Kane, Billie 23, 11080 **25**, 12147-48

Kapps, William

affidavit of **12**, 5009, 5151-52E

Kaputkin, Renee 12, 5161E

Karalekas, Steve FR 148

memo to Colson on O'Brien's leasing of Government building **23**, 11084, 11136E

Karam, Joseph 12, 5109E

Kastenmeier, Bob 17, 7659

Katz, Jon 12, 5187E

Katz case **6**, 2592

Kaufman, Frank 16, 7339

Kauper, Tom 17, 7683

Kaupinen, Al 18, 8227 **23**, 11260 **FR** 414

memo from White House on Weeks **18**, 8227, 8364E

memo to Malek on labor problem in Pennsylvania **18**, 8238, 8388E

and Responsiveness Program **18**, 8239

Kaye, Beverly 22, 10267

Kaye, Danny 21, 10056

Kayser, Paul 1, 35

Keating, Kenneth 3, 987

Keeler, W. W.

See Phillips Petroleum Co.

Keema, Alexander W. 16, 7418, 7420-21, 7424

affidavit with attachments of **17**, 7959-68E

memo to Hamilton and Sanders **25**, 11852-60E

Keeney, Albert 21, 10068, 10069, 10091 **23**, 11182 **FR** 1010

Kehrli, Bruce Arnold 3, 941, 1157E **16**, 7457

at June 19 meeting **7**, 2822

at opening of Hunt's safe **3**, 935 **6**, 2612 **7**, 2826

and Chenow's interview with FBI **3**, 941

and conflict in Ehrlichman-Dean testimony **7**, 2718

excused from grand jury testimony **9**, 3619

and Hunt's safe **FR** 35

and material from Hunt's file **3**, 949 **4**, 1363

memo on Hunt **3**, 1158E

memo to Haldeman on expenses for CRP **8**, 3024-26, 3313-15E

role of **6**, 2466, 2467

Kehrli, Bruce Arnold, testimony of 1, 75-95

on Dean's role **1**, 80-81, 82

on Fielding **1**, 93

on financial transactions between CRP and White House **1**, 83-84

on offices of Liddy, McCord, and Hunt **1**, 88

on opening of Hunt's safe **1**, 83

on role on White House staff **1**, 87-88, 93, 94-95

on Shepherd **1**, 89-90

on telephone conversation with Ehrlichman on his files **1**, 90, 91

on telephone conversation with Haldeman after resignation **1**, 90-91

on White House attitude toward his testimony **1**, 82

relationship with McGovern **6**, 2476
in sensitive case report on Hughes **23**, 11237
summary of Gallup poll to **16**, 7006-7007
Van Dyk's poll on **15**, 6882-83
Kennedy, Jackie 22, 10643
Kennedy, John F. 12, 4927 **21**, 9974
and Bay of Pigs **9**, 3877E, 3879-80E
comparisons with Edward Kennedy **10**, 4171E
and Diem cable incident **FR** 125, 127, *see also*
Diem cables
and fall of Diem regime **9**, 3809-11
falsified material in Hunt's safe on **3**, 938
Maheu contribution for deficit in campaign of **24**,
11574-75
plan for National Park honoring **3**, 1117E
political monitoring of Goldwater by **10**, 3946
Stearns on McMinoway's implications about **11**,
4566
See also Kennedy assassination
Kennedy, Robert 1, 250 **9**, 3884E **11**, 4604 **25**, 12098,
12270
campaign activities while attorney general **10**,
3939, 3940
Kennedy assassination
Gray on Diem cables and **9**, 3527
and Hunt's interview with Conein **9**, 3669
Kennedy Center, Washington, D.C. 10, 3954
Kennedy Foundation
Caulfield on financing of *Newsday* article on
Rebozo by **22**, 10374-75
in memos from Caulfield to Dean on *Newsday* article **23**, 11101, 11143-44E
and *Newsday* investigation of Rebozo **21**, 10126,
10127 **23**, 11101
"Kennedy Watch"
memo from Strachan to Magruder on establishment of **10**, 3975, 4164-66E
Kennelly, Thomas A. 4, 1652 **9**, 3635, 3650
letter to Dorsen on Jones's billing to AMPI **17**,
8061-64E
Kensington, Pete 23, 11260
Kent, Jack
See Buckley, John R. (alias of)
Kent State University FR 319E
deaths at **FR** 1174
Keogh 10, 4130E
memo from Haldeman on use of Victor Lasky **10**,
3975, 4129E
Kerner Commission
use of psychiatric profiles **7**, 2674, 2690-91
Kerr, John 12, 4987 **23**, 11167
discusses financial needs of Nunn campaign with
LaRue **23**, 11152-53
Kessler, Don 24, 11436
Key Biscayne, Florida
deliveries of Hughes contribution in **FR** 963-68
Griffin on Nixon's purchase and sale of property
at **23**, 10768-75
Magruder reports to Strachan on meeting in **6**,
2489
Key Biscayne Bank & Trust Co.
Diebold bills for safe-deposit box drilling and keys
to **23**, 10972-74

Rebozo's safety deposit box records from **23**,
10970-71
safety deposit box visitation and rental forms from
23, 10968-69
See also Brown, Jack Warren, testimony of
Key Biscayne Hotel 6, 2301
LaRue on **6**, 2280-82, 2301-2302, 2305-2306,
2312, 2325-26, 2331, 2332-33, 2338-39
LaRue's absences from room at **6**, 2344-45
Mitchell on meeting in **4**, 1613-16
Keys, Martha
letter from Pearlman requesting loan forgiveness
25, 12203E
Khachigian, Kenneth 8, 3124 **9**, 3606 **10**, 3907, 3944,
4182E **11**, 4611
assault book on strategy for undermining McGovern election bid **10**, 3975, 4240-46E
Buchanan and **10**, 3914
and Citizens for a Liberal Alternative **10**, 3933,
3966 **FR** 157-58
and dirty tricks operation **FR** 160
letters to editor drafted by **10**, 4136-44E
memo for Buchanan on McCloskey and Florida
primary **10**, 4193E
memo for Mitchell and Haldeman on Democratic
contenders **10**, 4226-34E
memo to Mitchell, "Attack Organization and
Strategy" **10**, 3975, 4209-20E
memo to Mitchell and Haldeman on Muskie campaign **11**, 4668
plan for activities at Democratic National Convention **10**, 4221-24E
and Sedan Chair I **FR** 191
Kickbacks, to Democratic party 2, 790, 840-41
Kidnappings
Cash case **24**, 11510E, 11511E
in Gemstone plan **FR** 21
in Liddy plan **2**, 788, 839 **3**, 929 **5**, 1815-16
Kilpatrick, Jack 9, 3879E **10**, 4130E
letter from Buchanan on Nixon's press conferences **10**, 4145E
Kilroy, William 12, 5109E
Kimmelman, Henry 11, 4502, 4717E **12**, 5183E **25**,
12116, 12117-18, 12122, 12186
Caulfield's investigation of **22**, 10400-10402
and Cohen **25**, 12189
role in McGovern campaign **25**, 12182
working relationship with Pearlman **25**, 12174-75
King, Stephen B. 12, 5192E, 5193E
King, Thomas 12, 5133E
King Air
and AMPI **14**, 6181-82
Kings Inn Hotel, Miami, Florida 22, 10564
Kingsley, Daniel T. 4, 1409 **13**, 5282, 5293 **18**, 8201,
8203 **19**, 8614E **FR** 416, 417
memo from Freeman on staffing strategy for part-
time boards and commissions **19**, 8882-87E
memo from Herringer on appointment for Wenk
FR 415
memo from Herringer on recommendation and
referral for departmental board or commission
19, 8890E
memo from Horton on patronage **19**, 8891-96E

Kingsley, Daniel T. *(Continued)*
  memo from MacGregor on Bennett **18,** 8226,
    8363E
  and Responsiveness Program **18,** 8183-84, 8226,
    8284-86 **FR** 436-47
  and White House Personnel Office **FR** 414
Kinnard, John 25, 12030-31
Kinsey, Pete FR 148
Kipling, Rudyard FR 1102
Kirby, Jerome 23, 11272
Kirk, Norma 14, 6167, 6319 **15,** 6612, 6776, 6777,
  6830, 6831, 6858-59 **16,** 6990, 7099 **17,** 7669 **FR**
  909, 921
Kirkland, D. 15, 6501
Kirschbaum, Dr. J. 12, 5027E, 5028E
Kirschner Report 19, 9225-26E, 9227E, 9228E
Kislak, Jay I. 22, 12545E **FR** 999, 1000, 1059
  letter from Rebozo with contribution **22,** 12531E
Kissam, Leo T.
  on future legislation **13,** 5476-77
  on incomes of Gulf Oil executives **13,** 5468
  on speculative questions **13,** 5480
  See also Wild, Claude C., Jr., testimony of
Kissel, Dan 13, 5412, 5414, 5429 **FR** 453
Kissinger, Henry 3, 992, 1055 **4,** 1662 **6,** 2409, 2518
  7, 2870 **8,** 3234 **10,** 3913 **11,** 4665, 4884E **23,** 11017
  briefing on ABM issue offered to Hughes by **21,**
    10045, 10047-48, 10231
  and CIA profile of Ellsberg **8,** 3235
  as contact from White House to CIA **8,** 3281
  and domestic intelligence **3,** 1072
  and leaks **3,** 1112E
  plan to kidnap **5,** 1816
  reports on antiwar groups **3,** 917
  role at White House **1,** 91, 92 **7,** 2872 **8,** 2018
  wiretapping of staff of **4,** 1623, 1626-27 **11,** 4885E
  Young tells Malloy he requested CIA psychologi-
    cal profile of Ellsberg **25,** 12422E
Kissinger tapes 3, 1069, 1070 **6,** 2410
  Ehrlichman on **6,** 2533-34
  Mardian on **6,** 2404-2408, 2420
  turned over to Nixon as Presidential papers **6,**
    2534
Kittridge, Marie FR 784E
Kleiboomer, Axel 7, 2751
Klein, Herbert G. 1, 80 **2,** 632 **6,** 2445 **7,** 2801 **8,**
  3193 **10,** 4112E **12,** 4937-38 **13,** 5277 **18,** 8203
  and direct mailings **FR** 153
  memo from Haldeman on use of Lasky **10,** 3975,
    4129E
  memo from Higby on White House polls **FR**
    322E
  memo to Haldeman on ITT matter **8,** 3218,
    3375E
Kleindienst, Richard G. 3, 1014-15, 1317E **9,** 3482
  20, 9551, 9576 **21,** 9712
  advice to Ehrlichman and Haldeman from **4,** 1552
  after Watergate break-in **6,** 2330-31 **8,** 3131
  allows Select Committee to make notes from FBI
    reports **7,** 2664-65
  and antitrust suit against AMPI **17,** 7687 **FR** 724
  appointment of Gray by **9,** 3450

and appointment of special prosecutor for Watergate **9,** 3645
at meeting with Dean and Petersen **7,** 2822 **9,**
  3613-14
attitude toward Select Committee **4,** 1494
and bail for McCord **4,** 1662
calls Petersen after Watergate break-in **9,** 3612-13
and Caulfield **22,** 11039
as contact between Nixon and Select Committee
  3, 991
conversation with Ehrlichman of March 28, 1973
  7, 2714-15
Dean asked to speak with on Watergate **3,** 932
Dean to Haldeman on talking points for meeting
  between Nixon and **3,** 1247-48E
in Dean-Nixon meetings **FR** 84
and Dean's assignment as negotiator with demonstrators **5,** 1841
Dean's meeting after Watergate with **4,** 1419-20
Dean's notes for Nixon on meeting with **4,** 1491-
  94
and Dean's request for FBI interview files **4,** 1358
denies he conducted Watergate investigation **12,**
  4936
discusses destruction of Hunt's files with Gray **9,**
  3495
Ehrlichman discusses immunity with **7,** 2831
Ehrlichman's report on his Watergate investigation to **FR** 90
and Ellsberg matter **9,** 3644
and FBI investigation of wiretapping in Nixon's
  1968 campaign **8,** 3204
and FBI leaks **7,** 2674-75
on FBI reports on Watergate to Dean **3,** 1038-39
and FBI Watergate investigation **9,** 3529
gives CIA documents to Petersen **9,** 3622-23
and Gray confirmation hearings **9,** 3553
Gray on reasons for not reporting suspicions to **9,**
  3536-37
and Gray turning over FBI materials to Senate
  Judiciary Committee **3,** 995
and Gray's recommendation for special prosecutor
  for Watergate case **9,** 3553
and Gray's resignation **7,** 2712
Haldeman wants him to order FBI project on
  1968 bugging **3,** 1240E
Harrison contacts on antitrust suit against AMPI
  17, 7682-83
on Huston memo **4,** 1446-47
instructs Dean to contact DeLoach for information on foreign travels of Kopechne **FR** 118,
  144
interview with Walters **24,** 11622
involvement in coverup **2,** 835
and ITT-Dita Beard matter **FR** 128
letter from Brown on Patman Committee hearings
  5, 2194-95E, 2197-98E
letter from Brown re Banking and Currency Committee investigation into Watergate activities **3,**
  959, 1181-82E
letter to O'Brien on request for Nixon to appoint
  special prosecutor **3,** 1163E
letter to Petersen recusing himself from further involvement in Watergate case **9,** 3573, 3860E
Liddy says Mitchell told him to release Watergate
  burglars **6,** 2353-54

meeting with Ehrlichman and Dean on sentencing of Watergate defendants **9**, 3609

meeting with Ehrlichman taped **4**, 1651

meeting with Ervin and Baker **4**, 1493

meeting with Gray and Petersen **9**, 3491-92

meeting with Moore and Liddy after Watergate arrests **2**, 820

meeting with Nixon **7**, 2758, 2904 **9**, 3627-29 **21**, 10136 **FR** 79

meeting with Nixon and Petersen **7**, 2758 **FR** 91-92

meeting with Petersen on Ellsberg case **9**, 3631

memo from Dean on "Talking Points" for meeting between Haldeman and **3**, 989, 1247-48E

memo from Magruder on million-dollar fund **7**, 2968E

Mitchell wants call made to after Watergate break-in **6**, 2319

and Mitchell's instructions after Watergate break-in **6**, 2314-15

Moore on **5**, 2007-2008

Nixon gives information to **5**, 2072

orders no special treatment of Watergate burglars **FR** 32

and Parkinson's draft of response to Brown **5**, 2205-2207E

Petersen informs about Watergate break-in **9**, 3611-12

and political intelligence **3**, 922

and press statements on Nixon's attitude toward Watergate **7**, 2749

proposed meetings with Baker **4**, 1396

reasons for Dean not telling about meetings with Liddy, Magruder, and Mitchell **3**, 1049-50

recuses himself from Watergate investigation **9**, 3653

report to Nixon on grand jury investigation **7**, 2857

reports to cabinet meeting **8**, 3089

rescinds Gray's order for FBI Watergate files for U.S. Senate **9**, 3553

resignation of **4**, 1492, 1495 **9**, 3653-54

scheduled meeting with Stans **2**, 737

seeks meeting with Ervin and Baker **3**, 992

and Select Committee **4**, 1548-49

speaks to Petersen on Ehrlichman call re Stans' questioning **9**, 3619

and Stans' appearance before grand jury **FR** 47

taped phone conversations with Dean after Watergate break-in **4**, 1356

taped telephone conversation with Ehrlichman **4**, 1500-1501 **7**, 2747-50, 2944-46E

telephone conversation with Nixon on Gray resignation **9**, 3654

tells Dean about meeting with Liddy **3**, 934, 936

tells Ehrlichman Magruder may take Fifth Amendment **7**, 2846

tells Nixon Mitchell and others might be involved in Watergate **5**, 1916

tells Petersen Dean has asked for FBI reports **9**, 3615

and Watergate coverup **2**, 822

and Watergate investigation **7**, 2698

Kleindienst, Richard G., testimony of 9, 3559-3610

on appointment of special prosecutor for Watergate **9**, 3570-72

on appointment with Nixon on April 15, 1973 **9**, 3572-73

on attitude toward Select Committee hearings **9**, 3590-91

on career **9**, 3560

claims lack of knowledge of White House involvement in Watergate **9**, 3602

on contacts with Magruder **9**, 3609

on contacts with Nixon between Watergate break-in and resignation **9**, 3599-3600

on conversation with Ehrlichman on Byrne becoming FBI director **9**, 3570-72

on Dean's efforts to influence FBI investigations of Mexican checks **9**, 3606

on Dean's testimony on relationship between White House and **9**, 3565-66

on Dean's Watergate investigation **9**, 3675-76

on Democratic party and violent demonstrations **9**, 3606-3607

denies knowledge about efforts to blame CIA for Watergate break-in **9**, 3563-64

denies knowledge of Gray giving Dean raw FBI files **9**, 3564

on Department of Justice Watergate investigation **9**, 3600

on Ehrlichman meeting with Byrne **9**, 3604-3605

on Ehrlichman taping conversation with him **9**, 3579, 3588-89, 3593, 3594

on Ehrlichman's call on Stans' testimony **9**, 3594

on Ehrlichman's call to Petersen protesting questioning of Stans **9**, 3580-81

on Ehrlichman's Watergate investigation at White House **9**, 3602

on FBI Watergate investigation **9**, 3582, 3591-92

gets report on Magruder's and Dean's discussions with U.S. Attorneys **9**, 3578-79

on Gray giving Dean FBI files **9**, 3576-77

on Gray nomination hearings **9**, 3598-99

on Gray resignation **9**, 3598-99

on Gray's destruction of Hunt file **9**, 3605-3606, 3609

has no recollection of meeting with Dean and Ehrlichman on July 31, 1972 **9**, 3566-67

on his behavior during Watergate coverup **9**, 3583-84

informs Nixon of White House connection to Ellsberg break-in **9**, 3574-75

on learning about Watergate break-in **9**, 3560, 3561-62, 3595

on learning about White House connection to Ellsberg break-in **9**, 3574-75

on Liddy telling him about Watergate **9**, 3595

on log of telephone calls after Watergate break-in **9**, 3592

on Magruder believed over Sloan **9**, 3582-83

on meeting with Dean and Petersen on Watergate break-in **9**, 3562-63

on meeting with Dean on scope of Watergate investigation **3**, 936-37

on meeting with Helms **9**, 3608-3609

on meeting with Petersen **3**, 1032-33

letter to Ehrlichman reported in *New York Times* **7**, 2661-63

Liddy and **2**, 471 **4**, 1418-19, 1609

and Liddy and Hunt **3**, 1267E

and Liddy plan **7**, 2732

Liddy's calls to after Watergate **3**, 976-77

and Liddy's employment at CRP **4**, 1351, 1352

meeting with Dean and Liddy **4**, 1442-43

memo from Dean on Brookings Institution **22**, 10356-57 **FR** 142-43

memo to Colson on Hunt memo on neutralization of Ellsberg **9**, 3730, 3893E

message to Liddy **3**, 1238E

Mitchell's knowledge about involvement in Ellsberg matter **5**, 1904-1905

and money for Fielding break-in **9**, 3753, 3774

Nixon's instructions to **6**, 2603-2604

note from Ehrlichman on Pentagon Papers Status Report **6**, 2554, 2643-45E

and Pentagon Papers case **6**, 2410

and Plumbers operation **3**, 921 **FR** 120

preliminary report on Fielding break-in submitted to **9**, 3774

recommends Liddy for job at CRP **3**, 927-28

relationship to Erlichman **1**, 78-79

removed from White House staff **5**, 1895

reporting relationship to Ehrlichman **6**, 2531-32

says instructions came from Oval Office **3**, 1080

talks to Magruder about Liddy **2**, 793

telephone conversations with Kleindienst **9**, 3592

and Watergate coverup **2**, 822

See also Fielding break-in; Plumbers

Kromer, Jack **20**, 9419, 9420, 9423

Krulewitch v. *United States* **4**, 1523, 1789-90E

Ku Klux Klan **6**, 2424 **11**, 4475

Kunkel, A.C. **9**, 3466-57, 3501, 3521, 3522, 3535

Kunstler, William **9**, 3712 **12**, 5201E

La Campo, Fredo de **4**, 1687E

La Costa meetings **3**, 982-86 **4**, 1401, 1402, 1404, 1405, 1420, 1500, 1521, 1538 **7**, 2760

Dean on **4**, 1533-35

Dean-Moore testimony compared on **5**, 1941-42, 1986

decision to have Moore ask Mitchell for money at **5**, 2026-27

decisions on dealing with Select Committee hearings at **FR** 76-78

documentary evidence on decisions made at **FR** 78-80

Ehrlichman on **7**, 2849-51

follow-up on decisions of **3**, 986-91

Haldeman denies discussion of defense fund at **8**, 3098

Haldeman on **7**, 2889-92 **8**, 3055-56, 3109

and memos on publicity for campaign disruptions **8**, 3177-79

and Moore asking Mitchell to raise money for Watergate defendants **5**, 2048

Moore on **5**, 1940-42, 1956-57, 1963-67

Moore's attitude toward discussions of Select Committee at **5**, 1992-93

and White House policy on Select Committee **4**, 1460, 1499 **5**, 2006

La Luz magazine **13**, 5325-26

Laaman, Jaan K. **12**, 5135-36E

Labor for America Committee **FR** 157

Labor leaders

on enemies list **4**, 1719E

Labor movement

in Magruder memo on interest groups **19**, 8815-16E

McGovern record on **10**, 4062-65E

in memo from CRP on interest groups **13**, 5534E

Labor unions

campaign activities **FR** 511-14

contributions to McGovern from **25**, 12144-46

and Select Committee questionnaires **FR** 529, 530-33, 540-43

Select Committee recommendation for congressional committee to review political activities of **FR** 513-14

and separate funds for political purposes **FR** 550-51

United Farm Workers, AFL-CIO **FR** 511-12

Lackritz, Marc **1**, 1 **5**, 1947, 1949, 1950, 2062 **11**, 4635-44

on activities oF Chapman's Friends **11**, 4638

on agreement with Edmisten's testimony on Xeroxing money from Davis' exhibits **20**, 9416

agreements with Ambrose and Griffin on line of questioning **22**, 10472

on Brill's activities **11**, 4641

on Burdick's activities **11**, 4639-40

on chart of Democratic primary elections and sabotage activities **11**, 4635-36, 4642-43

on Davis' objections to line of questioning of Danner **24**, 11440, 11442-43, 11452

on Davis' objections to subpoena for Danner **24**, 11388, 11389

on Davis' request for transcript of Danner testimony **24**, 11387-88

on efforts to locate Muse for response to Davis' allegations **24**, 11567

on Freedman's claim of attorney-client privilege for Danner-Davis discussions **24**, 11562

on Freedman's objections to line of questioning of Danner **24**, 11539, 11540-41

on Friedman's activities **11**, 4641

on Gemstone operations **11**, 4636, 4637E, 4638

on Greaves' activities **11**, 4638-39

on Johnson's activities **11**, 4640

on McMinoway's activities **11**, 4639

memo from Beck to Ervin on **11**, 4402-4403

on Muse acting pursuant to Select Committee authorization **24**, 11615

on Norton's activities **11**, 4640

on O'Brien's activities **11**, 4640

on reasons for calling Danner back for further testimony **24**, 11438-39

returns flight log to Wearley **20**, 9465-66

and submission of Danner exhibits by Davis **24**, 11391, 11394, 11395-97, 11398-11400

on subpoena for Winte **24**, 11615-18

on subpoena of Griffin's parents' telephone records **22**, 10417

on United Democrats for Kennedy **11**, 4641-42

informed about Watergate break-in **FR** 32
Kalmbach gives $30,000 to **5,** 2113-14
learns about Watergate arrests **2,** 815
learns Dean plans to tell truth **3,** 1012
letter from Cox to Vinson on guilty plea of **6,** 2634E
letter from Stans requesting payments to Finance Committee **6,** 2636E
letters between Barker, Vinson, Stans and re Finance Committee **6,** 2344, 2635-41E
and Liddy debriefing **4,** 1643 **5,** 1918-20 **FR** 40-41
Magruder on involvement in Watergate **2,** 792, 822
and Magruder urging Porter to commit perjury **2,** 666
and Magruder's coverup story **FR** 44-45
and Magruder's perjury **5,** 1896
in March 21 tape **8,** 3211-12
Mardian and **6,** 2379-80
Mardian contradicts testimony on destruction of Gemstone file **6,** 2356
Mardian on presence at Liddy debriefing **6,** 2358
meeting with Mitchell and Sloan **2,** 544, 592-93
meeting with Sloan on options **2,** 551
meetings after Watergate arrests **2,** 799-800 **5,** 1952, 1953
meetings with Mitchell after Watergate **5,** 1878, 1879, 1880, 1881, 1883, 1885, 1887, 1931
meets Stans about Dahlberg check **2,** 738
Mitchell briefed on Watergate by **4,** 1622
and Mitchell instructing Magruder to destroy Gemstone files **5,** 1877
and Mitchell's attitude toward Liddy plan **5,** 1874-75
money from Sloan and Stans to **2,** 710, 720, 721-22
and money from White House to Watergate defendants **3,** 950-951
on Patman Committee subpoena list **3,** 961
and Porter's efforts to get Government job after Watergate trial **2,** 653, 673-74
present during Colson's telephone call to Magruder urging approval of Liddy plan **2,** 794
and problems between Liddy and Magruder **2,** 791-92, 826
reports to Mitchell on Liddy debriefing **4,** 1644
role at CRP **2,** 791
role at White House **5,** 2172
role in Kalmbach's assignment to raise and distribute cash for Watergate defendants **2,** 849 **5,** 2102, 2104, 2110-11, 2113-14, 2140-42, 2145, 2289-99
role in Watergate coverup **2,** 872
as security agent for Mrs. Mitchell **1,** 393
Sloan returns money from safe to **2,** 548
and Sloan's resignation **FR** 43
Stans' attitude toward after Watergate arrests **2,** 731-32
Stans on money given to **2,** 701-702
Stans on suspicions about **2,** 774-75
Strachan delivers money from White House fund to **6,** 2442-43 **FR** 56
subpoenaed by Patman Committee **3,** 1192E
talks with Eastland on heading up Senate hearings **3,** 980

tells Porter to destroy receipts for cash disbursements **2,** 675
in transcription of taped telephone conversation between Ehrlichman and Kalmbach **5,** 2215E
transfer from White House staff **1,** 80
and transfer of funds from CRP to White House **7,** 2879
urges Sloan to go to California **2,** 550, 581-82, 589 **FR** 43
wants money for White House project after Watergate arrests **2,** 725
and Watergate coverup **2,** 801-803, 805, 822, 849, 855, 857
Watergate information to MacGregor from **12,** 4913
work relationship with Mitchell **4,** 1668
LaRue, Frederick C., testimony of 6, 2277-2345 **23,** 11149-72
admits prior knowledge of break-in to Mardian **6,** 2391
agreement with Watergate prosecutors and **6,** 2278, 2328, 2333
on airline taken to Key Biscayne meeting with Rebozo **23,** 11168-69
on amount given to Nunn campaign from Rebozo contribution **23,** 11165, 11167
on amount of money involved in Kalmbach-Ulasewicz transactions **6,** 2311-14
on argument between Liddy and Magruder **6,** 2279-80
on authorization for Watergate break-in **6,** 2294
on briefing Mitchell on Liddy debriefing **6,** 2288-89, 2318, 2321-22, 2337-38
on budget meetings at CRP **6,** 2316
cannot recollect meeting with Mitchell, Dean, and Kalmbach on January 19, 1973 **6,** 2297
on career **6,** 2279
on cash left over at time of going to U.S. Attorneys **6,** 2299
on code names used by **6,** 2333
on commitments to Watergate defendants **6,** 2307-2309
on conflicts between prior and present testimony on amount of money given by Rebozo **23,** 11154-55
on conflicts with prior testimony on disbursement of money to Nunn **23,** 11156
on contact with Rebozo since campaign contribution pickup **23,** 11169-70, 11170-71
on contacts with Strachan **6,** 2315-16
on conversation with Magruder on Liddy budget **6,** 2303
on decision to send Sloan to California **6,** 2300-2301
denied knowledge of source of commitments to Watergate defendants **6,** 2307-2308
denies business transactions with Rebozo **23,** 11170
denies knowledge of Hughes contribution **23,** 11163
denies knowledge of Mitchell meeting with Nunn **23,** 11167-68
denies meeting with Rebozo in March or August 1972 **23,** 11150-51
denies presence during telephone call between

LaRue, Mrs. Frederick C. 2, 653
Las Vegas matter 7, 2801 8, 3214-15 9, 3735
    Hunt on 9, 3686-87 20, 9345-9406
    McCord on 1, 202
    See also Greenspun, Hank
Las Vegas Sun
    See Greenspun, Hank; Las Vegas matter
Lasky, Victor 2, 823 10, 4130E
    memo from Haldeman to Buchanan, Keogh,
        Klein, and Nofziger on use of 10, 3875, 4129E
Laubenheimer, Merritt R., Jr.
    affidavit of 12, 5009, 5082-83E
Laughter, Si 24, 11416-17
Lavarkas, Paul 23, 11260
Lavasseur, Ray 12, 5092E
"Law and order" issue 10, 4213-14E
Law enforcement agencies
    impact of Watergate on FR 1204-1207
Law Enforcement Assistance Agency 12, 5001
Lawless, Judge 13, 5414, 5429, 5430
Lawrence, Harding L. 10, 4130E 13, 5483
    See also Braniff Airways, Inc.
Lawrence O'Brien v. James McCord 5, 1880-81, 1869
Lawyers' fees
    See Attorneys' fees scheme
Laxalt, Paul (governor of Nevada) 20, 9464, 9484,
    9504, 9575 24, 11448
    affidavit on meeting with Maheu and Dunes Ho-
        tel matter 26, 12921-22E
    and Dunes acquisition matter FR 991, 993
    and Hughes attempted contribution in 1968 FR
        938-40
    letter from Zimmerman on Hughes operations in
        Nevada 26, 12919-20E
    letter to Clark on Hughes operations in Nevada
        26, 12915-18E
Layne, William H. 12, 4987
Lazo, Dr. Mario 1, 369
League of Women Voters
    copy of "Muskie Accountability Project" sent to
        Muskie headquarters by 11, 4695, 4859-83E
Leahy, Charles F. 3, 1137E
Leaks 3, 992, 1068-71
    at FBI 6, 2562, 2613
    Brown's request for FBI check on Leanse ap-
        pointment and 3, 1103-1109E
    of Buzhardt's memo to press 5, 2066
    Davis on Select Committee role in 24, 11601
    Dean, Malek, and Strachan meeting on 3, 1111-
        12E
    on Dean's background while he testifies 3, 1085-
        86
    Ervin talks about "leak in the tapes" 8, 3066
    from Executive Sessions 22, 10563
    from Muskie campaign 11, 4650, 4672-73
    from Select Committee 10, 3903-3904 18, 8235 21,
        9998, 10125 22, 10198-99, 10218, 10559, 10596
        Ambrose on Griffin's testimony and 23,
            10733-34
        Buchanan on 10, 3900-3901
        McKiernan on 22, 10631-32
    Griffin denies being source of 23, 10790

Griffin on effects of 23, 10791
Gurney on FR 1172
Haig on 23, 11026
and Haig's appearance before Select Committee
    staff 23, 10890
Haldeman on 7, 2874-75
Helms on investigation of 8, 3253, 3257-58
and Hunt's material 4, 1365
Krogh's special unit and 6, 2529
McKiernan on 22, 10654
memo from Butterfield to Caulfield on 3, 1107E,
    1109E
memo from Caulfield to Dean on 3, 1108E
memo from Haldeman to Malek on 3, 1113E
memo from Malek to Haldeman on 3, 1114-16E
memo from Strachan to Haldeman on 3, 1111-
    12E
memo to Haldeman from Caulfield on 3, 1101-
    1102E
memos on 3, 919, 1110E
Mitchell on wiretapping after 4, 1623
Nixon assigns Haldeman to handle 8, 3032
note on White House stationery on 3, 1110E
and Pentagon Papers FR 119-20
Rebozo on 21, 10089
and Responsiveness Program 18, 8229-30
Select Committee discussion on prevention of 23,
    10793-94
and Sirica's silence order 22, 10255
White House attitudes toward 3, 919-22
See also SALT talk leaks
Leanse, Jay I.
    leaks on Ehrlichman and 3, 919, 1103-1108E
Leber, Sharon 21, 10015
Leding, Sandy 11, 4773E
Lee, Ruta 12, 5115E
Leeper, Paul W. 1, 75, 118, 119, 122, 123, 412
Leeper, Paul W., testimony of FR 31
    on apprehension of Watergate burglars FR 2
    on Watergate break-in 1, 95-98, 103-114
Lehigh Valley Cooperative Farmers, Inc.
    campaign contribution of 2, 710 FR 481-84
Leighton, F. Beech 22, 10604
Lemay, Jack FR 417
Lennen and Newell 17, 7666
Lenzner, Terry F. 22, 10635, 10683-91
    on Ambrose's objections to line of questioning of
        Griffin 22, 10444-45
    on Blatt's objections to line of questioning of F.
        Donald Nixon 22, 10690-91
    on Buzhardt's claim of attorney-client privilege
        covering discussions with Garment 22, 10541-44
    on Buzhardt's request for copy of transcript 22,
        10539
    on characterizations by Select Committee mem-
        bers of witnesses' testimony 22, 10472
    on Cole's objections to line of questioning of Dav-
        is 22, 10570-71
    on Cole's request for transcript of Davis' inter-
        view 22, 10562
    on Cole's request for transcript of Davis' testimo-
        ny 22, 10589
    on Danner's appearance before grand jury 24,
        11389-90

Lenzner, Terry F. *(Continued)*
and documents sought from Moncourt **22,** 10533-35, 10535-37
on errors in transcript of interview with Moore **5,** 2058-59, 2062
on Executive privilege for source of Buzhardt memo on Dean-Nixon conversations **23,** 10899
on financial records of Edward C. Nixon **22,** 10615, 10616, 10617
on Frates' objections to line of questioning of Rebozo **21,** 9939
on funds held over from 1968 and used in 1972 **22,** 10570-71
on Greer's agreements with Dash **22,** 10533
Greer's criticisms of dealings with **22,** 15033
on Greer's objections to line of questioning of Moncourt **22,** 10514
on Greer's objections to Select Committee's investigation **22,** 10532
on Griffin exhibits **23,** 10738
on Griffin's claims of attorney-client privilege **23,** 10756-60, 10767
on Griffin's records **22,** 10473-74
on Hauser's objections to questions on wiretapping **23,** 11096
interview with Moore **5,** 1994
letter to Davis on arrangements for questioning Hughes **22,** 12451E
in McKiernan protest letter to Ervin and Baker **23,** 10975-76
on McKiernan's request for copies of transcript **22,** 10661, 10662, 10663
memo from Beck to Ervin on **11,** 4404
on method of questioning Moncourt **22,** 10528
on methods of controlling leaks **23,** 10793-94
on need for further questioning of Danner **20,** 9554
on partial waiver by Rebozo on Gemmill's testimony **23,** 11184
on partial waiver of attorney-client privilege by Gemmill **23,** 11189, 11190, 11194-95, 11206, 11207
on pertinency of line of questioning of Griffin **22,** 10470-71
promises to Moore on Segretti matter **5,** 2035
on reasons for questioning McKiernan on electronic surveillance of F. Donald Nixon **22,** 10625
on reasons for wanting to question Davis on 1968 contributions **22,** 10574-75
on Rebozo documents **21,** 10021-24, 10026-38
on Rebozo exhibits **21,** 10010-11
on records on Rebozo's access to safe-deposit boxes **21,** 10017
on relevancy of line of questioning of Griffin **22,** 10472-73
on request to Cox's office for Hunt's memo on Beard **9,** 3791
requests worksheets of Cooper and Lybrand review **23,** 11220
on scheduling of further Griffin testimony **22,** 10475
on sealed transcript of interview with Caulfield **21,** 9720
on sealing of Davis transcript **22,** 10563

on sealing of transcript of Kalmbach testimony on Rebozo and Hughes contribution **21,** 10191-92
on Senate Select Committee resolution on Haig's refusal to testify **23,** 10995
on Senate vote on Griffin testimony transcript **23,** 10734
as source of leaks **22,** 10559
and submission of Danner exhibits by Davis **24,** 11397, 11400-11401
on subpoena for Rebozo **21,** 9937
on Wearley exhibits **20,** 9465-66
Weicker defends his questioning Moore on FBI files **6,** 2486

Lenzner, Terry F., questioning by
Barth **23,** 11228-29, 11233, 11234, 11235-36, 11246, 11247, 11248, 11250
Benz **11,** 4403-15, 4428, 4429
Bernhard **11,** 4644, 4645, 4668-79
Buzhardt **22,** 10539-43, 10544-51, 10553-60 **23,** 10877-78, 10879-82, 10883-84, 10885-90, 10891-98, 10900-10902, 10904-10907, 10908-10909, 10912-13, 10914, 10915-16, 10917, 10918-19
Caulfield **21,** 9704-9706, 9714-23, 9728-31, 9732-33, 9734, 9735-37 **22,** 10349-51, 10354-55, 10356, 10357-59, 10363-64, 10370-78, 10381-82, 10387-90, 10391-95, 10396-97, 10399-10404, 10406, 10407-10
Danner **20,** 9395-97, 9500-13, 9514-22, 9526-27, 9528-29, 9530-34, 9535-38, 9541-48, 9549-51, 9552-54, 9555-60, 9563-64, 9566-75, 9582, 9584-88, 9593, 9598-99, 9603-9604, 9607-12 **24,** 11407, 11410-11, 11426, 11429-32, 11453-54, 11458-60, 11463, 11465, 11473, 11476-78
Davis **20,** 9407-10 **22,** 10571-74, 10580-81, 10582-83, 10588, 10589
Gemmill **23,** 11178, 11180-82, 11184, 11186, 11188, 11192, 11209, 11211, 11217, 11220, 21219
Glaeser **20,** 9410-14, 9417-21, 9424-25
Griffin **22,** 10421, 10429-38, 10444-45, 10451, 10455, 10456, 10458, 10459-60, 10461-65, 10472-74, 10525-27 **23,** 10460-61, 10746-47, 10762-63, 10771-72, 10781-83, 10784-85
Haig **23,** 10849, 10998-11000, 11004-11006, 11011-15, 11018-25, 11026-30
Higby **23,** 11075-76, 11077, 11080-82, 11083-84, 11085, 11087, 11089, 11090-93, 11096, 11097, 11099-11100, 11108-11109
Hunt **20,** 9345-47, 9356-58
Kalmbach **21,** 10181-87 **23,** 10856-61
Kelly **11,** 4376-85, 4402
Lackritz **11,** 4635-44
LaRue **23,** 11156, 11158, 11165, 11168, 11169-71
McKiernan **22,** 10617-19, 10621-27, 10631-33, 10640-41, 10642, 10644, 10645-48, 10649-50, 10653-55, 10658-59
Moncourt **22,** 10487, 10491-92, 10519-20, 10523-26, 10532
Moore **5,** 1946-62, 1991, 2058-73
Nixon, Edward C **22,** 10591-98, 10599, 10600-10603, 10605-10606, 10608, 10610-11
Nixon, F. Donald **22,** 10665, 10678-79, 10680, 10693-95, 10696-10704, 10706-10707, 10709-11, 10712-14, 10715-22, 10722-24, 10726
Rebozo **21,** 9939-41, 9942-43, 9945-57, 9960-64,

9966-67, 9968, 9974-85, 9989-92, 9993, 9994-95,
9998-10000, 10004, 10005, 10006, 10012, 10019,
10041-56, 10057-60, 10062, 10064-65, 10066,
10102-10105, 10110-14, 10116-22, 10126, 10127,
10128-30, 10136-37, 10138-39, 10140, 10143,
10185-86
Reisner 2, 489-97, 530
Simon 23, 10928-29, 10933, 10940, 10943
St. Clair 23, 10850
Stearns 11, 4568-76, 4595-97
Sullivan 12, 5000-02
Ulasewicz 6, 2219-38
Wakefield 24, 11283-85, 11291, 11294-95, 11301,
11303-11304, 11307, 11308, 11312-13, 11314-15,
11317-22, 11323-28, 11333-41, 11342-45, 12286-
88
Wearley 20, 9444-45, 9446-47, 9448-50, 9452-55,
9457, 9458-60, 9464-65, 9466-71, 9472, 9473-76,
9477-79
Woods 22, 10199-10207, 10211-17, 10218-21,
10230-39, 10250-51, 10252, 10255, 10263-74,
10275-79
Leon, Diaz de FR 515, 516, 518
Leonard, George F.
See Liddy, G. Gordon (alias of)
Leonard, Jerris 11, 4454
Leonard, William 3, 1152E
Lepkowski, Stanley J. 13, 5411, 5414, 5420, 5424,
5428
memo from Clark, on payroll deduction 13, 5431,
5777E
statement to FBI 13, 5408
See also American Ship Building Co.
"Letter from the Vietnamese" 12, 5199-5200E
Letterwriting campaigns FR 306E
forgeries by Segretti FR 169-70, 173
generated by White House FR 150-53
Haldeman memo to Magruder on FR 310E
mailroom services specifications form for FR
311E
memo from Buchanan to Nolan on 10, 4256-58E
by Nixon administration FR 286-308E
Smathers and FR 311-13E
on Teamsters Executive Board endorsement of
Nixon FR 314-15E
Levy, Jesse P.
memo from Danner with notes covering expenses
22, 12484-89E
Lewis, Dan 11, 4814E
Lewis, Hobart
Rebozo discusses *Newsday* article with 21, 10128-
29
Lewis, John 25, 12198
Lewis, Willard
affidavit of 12, 5009, 5147-50E
Leyba, Charlie 13, 5629E
Liberty Lobby FR 204
Library of Congress, Washington, D.C.
Select Committee use of computer facility of FR
30
transfer of Select Committee records to FR 1094
See also Computer technology

Liddy, G. Gordon 1, 12-13, 27, 36, 39, 49, 70, 155,
174, 181, 197 2, 515, 554, 561, 713, 744, 809 9,
3722 20, 9610
after Watergate arrests 2, 799, 816 6, i315 9, 3688
alias and papers from CIA 8, 3264, 3294
alias of 1, 359
amount of money given to 9, 3617
arrest of 5, 2013
asked to evaluate Segretti's work FR 165-66
asks Kleindienst to release Watergate burglars FR
32
asks Strachan to have him report to Haldeman instead of Magruder 6, 2466
asks to retain White House pass 3, 928-29
assigned to special unit at White House 6, 2531
assignment in Operation Intercept discontinued 9,
3561
assures LaRue and Mardian he will never reveal
his knowledge of Watergate break-in 6, 2288
at lawyers' conference 1, 326, 350
at meeting with Hunt and ˜Winte 20, 9347, 9348,
9350-53
and attempted break-in at McGovern headquarters FR 27
attitude toward Hunt 6, 2362
attitude toward termination of Las Vegas plan 20,
9401
authority to withdraw funds 2, 571
authorization for Watergate break-up 9, 3777
Baldwin identification of 1, 399
and Barker 2, 463
Barker on 1, 388
and Beard 5, 1874 9, 3791
believes he will not be identified 6, 2359
and Bennett FR 1124
bizarre behavior described by Reisner 2, 497-98
and break-in in Las Vegas 1, 202
brought by Krogh to Mitchell's office 4, 1638-40
budget for 3, 1310E 6, 2429-30, 2496
call to Magruder in California after Watergate arrests 2, 660 6, 2284-85, 2350
career background 4, 1609
cash disbursements from Sloan to 2, 538-39, 540,
543, 544-46, 555, 573-74, 593, 728, 745-46, 800-
803
cash received from Porter 2, 498-99, 500, 657, 658
CIA material to 8, 3393E
and CIA psychological profile of Ellsberg 25,
12425-26E
claims Nixon's authorization 6, 2418-19
and Colson 3, 1266E 9, 3748-49
conflict with Magruder 4, 1414
contact with Kalmbach at Finance Committee 5,
2094-95
convicted in Fielding break-in FR 15-16
as counsel for Finance Committee 2, 707-708, 753
and Dahlberg and Mexican checks 2, 701, 717,
759, 760 3, 942-43 FR 37
Dean and 4, 1413, 1670
Dean explains reasons for Krogh refusing to
speak with 3, 977
Dean on hiring of 3, 921
Dean requests disavowal of his prior knowledge of
Watergate 3, 1005
Dean requests statement from 4, 1449-50

Liddy, G. Gordon *(Continued)*

and Dean's and Mitchell's approval of Watergate break-in **1**, 128-129

Dean's dealings with **4**, 1418-19

and Dean's fear of culpability in Watergate break-in **3**, 1040

Dean's memo for file re conversation with Maroulis on **3**, 1005, 1262E

Dean's relationship with **3**, 1086-87, 1255-56E

in Dean's report to Nixon **8**, 3074

debriefed by LaRue and Mardian **FR** 40-41

decision to blame him for Watergate break-in **2**, 802

declines to testify **2**, 488

and deniability for Mitchell **1**, 219

deposits money in Barker's account **2**, 576

destruction of CRP documents by **1**, 44-45, 61-62 **2**, 485-86 **6**, 2309

dictation of telephone logs to Harmony **2**, 459-62, 466

discharged by Stans **2**, 682, 708, 729, 746

discussed at Mitchell-Haldeman meeting **6**, 2492

discusses Cuban money to Democrats with Hunt **9**, 3793

discussions with Hunt on Las Vegas matter **20**, 9405-9406

and discussions with McCord **1**, 216-17

and disruption of Democratic National Convention **2**, 524

during Watergate burglary **FR** 2

duties of Harmony as secretary for *See* Harmony, Sally, testimony of

and easel **2**, 528

efforts to get him to talk **3**, 1016

efforts to place in IRS **7**, 2684

Ehrlichman and wiretapping by **6**, 2535

Ehrlichman learns of involvement in Watergate break-in **6**, 2539-40

Ehrlichman meeting with Sloan on **2**, 545-46

Ehrlichman on possibility of his talking **6**, 2542, 2564

and electronic surveillance of Muskie's office, and McGovern's headquarters **1**, 153-154

employment at CRP **2**, 785-86, 810, 845-46, 863, 871 **3**, 1264E **4**, 1351-52 **8**, 3033-34 **FR** 18

employs Harmony **2**, 470

and Executive clemency offers to McCord **1**, 228

as fall guy for break-in **4**, 1460-61

and FBI interview of Sloan **2**, 564

firing of **6**, 2307

first meeting with Colson **20**, 9383, 9391-92

and first Watergate break-in **1**, 164, 400 **5**, 1880-81

and funds for proposed Greenspun break-in **20**, 9384-85

gives envelope for Mitchell to Porter **2**, 634, 666-67

Gray on identification and photograph with Hunt of **9**, 3522

and Greenspun break-in **7**, 2801

Haldeman tells Strachan to contact re political intelligence **6**, 2455-56

Harmony's knowledge about intelligence activities of **2**, 475-76

Helms disclaims any relationship between CIA and **8**, 3261-62

hired by CRP **3**, 927-28 **5**, 1924-26

and Hoover funeral demonstration **9**, 3711-12

and Hughes **1**, 202

and Hunt **3**, 1091, 1171E **6**, 2396 **9**, 3716

Hunt on awareness of Hughes loan to F. Donald Nixon **20**, 9373-74

Hunt on description of Gemstone given by **20**, 9386-88

Hunt reports on meeting with Winte to **20**, 9379-80, 9382-83, 9384-85

and Hunt's assignments on political espionage against Democratic presidential candidates **9**, 3684-86

and Hunt's beliefs on authorization for Watergate break-in **9**, 3709

and Hunt's contacts with Fat Jack **9**, 3760-61

in Hunt's notes **9**, 3839E

identified by Baldwin **1**, 405

indictment of **FR** 2

informed by Strachan of Haldeman's instructions to transfer intelligence from Muskie to McGovern **FR** 27

informs Hunt of intended Watergate break-in **9**, 3792

informs Kleindienst of Watergate break-in **9**, 3560, 3561-62

informs McCord of political espionage plan **1**, 183-184

informs Sloan of Watergate arrests **2**, 542

and Internal Security Division **1**, 224

investigation stopped at **4**, 1475

job interview at Department of Justice by Mardian **6**, 2380-81

Kleindienst on **9**, 3595

in Kleindienst-Petersen telephone conversation after Watergate break-in **9**, 3612, 3613

LaRue and Mardian report to Mitchell on debriefing of **5**, 1878, 1880, 1881-82, 1884

LaRue on argument between Magruder and **6**, 2279-80

LaRue questioning of Sloan on **2**, 563-64

LaRue's knowledge of cash disbursements to **6**, 2316-17

and Las Vegas matter **9**, 3686-87

as legal advisor to Sloan **2**, 270

legal relationship with Mardian **6**, 2414-15

and logs of wiretaps **1**, 233

MacGregor on disbursement of funds to **12**, 4923

MacGregor's knowledge about role of **12**, 4910

Magruder and **2**, 474-75, 492-93 **4**, 1642 **6**, 2350

Magruder asks Porter to give cash for dirty tricks to **2**, 633-34, 677

Magruder asks Porter to lie about amount and purpose of money to **2**, 635-36, 643-46, 677

Magruder blames for Watergate **3**, 932

Magruder on coverup of **2**, 800-803

Magruder on reasons for silence of **2**, 819

Magruder says Strachan authorized activities of **6**, 2506-2507

on Magruder telling him not to hire McCord **6**, 2396

Magruder wants Strachan to lie to grand jury about **6**, 2465

in Magruder's briefing of Mardian **6**, 2411-12

Magruder's efforts to have Sloan lie about **2**, 745-46

Malloy affidavit on **9**, 3805

Mardian on dealings with **6**, 2389

Mardian-LaRue debriefing of **5**, 1862, 1870, 1878

Mardian's reaction to **2**, 547

Mardian's relationship with **6**, 2402-2403

and Mardian's suspicions of CIA involvement in Watergate break-in **6**, 2384

mastermind theory on Watergate break-in by **FR** 26

and material taken from Democratic National Committee headquarters **1**, 206

materials given by CIA to **8**, 3302

McCord and **1**, 126-28, 199

and McCord's belief in Mitchell's involvement in Watergate **1**, 160

McCord's opinion of **1**, 149

and McCord's wiretapped phone **1**, 245

media publicizes delivery of cash from Sloan to **5**, 2012

meeting between Stans and Mitchell on money from Sloan to **2**, 726-27, 728

meeting with Colson **9**, 3683-84

meeting with Colson and Hunt on Gemstone plan **FR** 23-24

meeting with Dean, Mitchell, and Magruder **2**, 490-91, 502-503, 519 **3**, 935

meeting with Dean after presentation of intelligence-gathering plan **4**, 1353

meeting with Dean after Watergate break-in **FR** 34

meeting with Hunt after Watergate arrests **9**, 3690-91

meeting with Hunt and Winte in California **20**, 9381, 9394-9400

meeting with Kleindienst **3**, 934

meeting with Krogh and Dean **4**, 1442-43

meeting with Magruder, Dean, Shumway, and Strachan after Watergate break-in **2**, 520

meeting with Mitchell before Watergate break-in **5**, 1875-76

meeting with Moore **2**, 823

and meetings between Mitchell, Magruder, and Dean to plan political espionage **1**, 142-149

meetings with Dean after Watergate arrests **3**, 933, 1266E **4**, 1672

meetings with Magruder **2**, 525

meetings with Mardian on Ellsberg matter **9**, 3786-87

meetings with Stans **2**, 735-37

memo from Hunt on information from Bennett on Greenspun **20**, 9346, 9350, 9352, 9356, 9358, 9368-70

memo to Mitchell on reaction to Nixon's Vietnam speech in Miami **FR** 305-308E

message from Greene to **3**, 977, 1238E

and Mexican checks **FR** 519

and Mexican-Dahlberg transaction **2**, 587-88

and Mitchell **1**, 252 **2**, 463, 478, 481

Mitchell denies talking to **5**, 1882

Mitchell on **4**, 1669

Mitchell on activities of **4**, 1622

Mitchell on contacts with **4**, 1619-20

Mitchell on payments to **4**, 1616-18 **5**, 1847-48

Mitchell on role at CRP of **4**, 1608-1609

on Mitchell's involvement **1**, 162, 341

Mitchell's reasons for reaction to **4**, 1610

money from CRP to **2**, 745 **9**, 3581-83

money to McCord for office rented near McGovern headquarters **1**, 154

motivation for second Watergate break-in **FR** 30-31

in Nixon, Haldeman, and Ehrlichman discussion on Executive clemency **FR** 72-73

Nixon and Dean discuss silence of **4**, 1553-54

Nixon's message to **9**, 3635

and Nixon's statement on everyone coming forward **4**, 1652

Nixon's telephone call to Petersen on **9**, 3650

office space at White House **1**, 88

official post of **9**, 3750

orders to Barker from **9**, 3744

payments to McCord **1**, 169, 170, 188

and *Pentagon Papers* case **6**, 2409, 2427

photograph in CIA material on Hunt **3**, 978

photographs in front of Fielding's office **3**, 1007-1008 **9**, 3529-30 **FR** 75-76

picks up money from Ulasewicz **6**, 2260

plan to blame for Watergate **9**, 3446

and political intelligence **6**, 2493

Porter lies to FBI about amount of money to **2**, 636, 672-73, 677

Porter tells about perjury about money to **2**, 638-42

Porter's knowledge about dirty tricks of **2**, 648, 658, 677

presents plans for intelligence-gathering to Mitchell, Dean, and Magruder **2**, 787-88, 789-91, 811, 838-39, 844-45, 863-64

on pressure from Magruder **6**, 2396

pressures on Sloan to conceal amount of money given to **FR** 41-44

problems with Magruder **3**, 1088

reasons for going to San Diego **20**, 9349

refers to his job for Magruder as "dirty work" **6**, 2279-80

refusal to testify **FR** 20

Reisner on activities of **2**, 491-92, 503

and rejection of Operation Sandwedge **FR** 117

relationship with Hunt **9**, 3788

relationship with Magruder **1**, 59 **2**, 498, 791-93 **4**, 1443, 1619-20

relationship with McCord **1**, 54

relationship with Mitchell **9**, 3609-10

remaining at CRP after presentation of Gemstone plan **FR** 21

reports meeting with Mitchell on Watergate **1**, 233-234

reports to Magruder on wiretap and photography at Democratic National Committee **2**, 796-97

request to Hunt for participation in Gemstone plan **9**, 3764-65

requests easel for meeting with Mitchell **2**, 509-510

resignation of **2**, 548

responsibilities to CRP and Finance Committee **1**, 166

role as general counsel to Finance Committee **2**, 476-77, 696-97, 732

Liddy, G. Gordon *(Continued)*
  role in political espionage **1,** 185 **9,** 3747
  role in Watergate **1,** 158, 165-66, 176, 197-198,
    240-41 **2,** 856-58 **9,** 3713
  role on White House Staff **1,** 79, 81-82
  and Ruby I **FR** 189-90
  and Ruby II **FR** 196
  and Sedan Chair I **FR** 192
  and Segretti **9,** 3771 **10,** 4018
  Segretti meets with **10,** 3983
  and simulated McGovern stationery **2,** 472-73
  Sloan's payments to **6,** 2301 **FR** 41-44
  Stans and **2,** 626, 697-98, 715, 722, 744-45, 751,
    769
  Stans discharges **2,** 737, 770
  Stans' suspicions on **2,** 775
  stories told by **6,** 2380
  Strachan learns about political intelligence role of
    6, 2469
  Strachan tells him to switch intelligence capabili-
    ties to McGovern from Muskie **8,** 3038
  talks off the record with prosecutors **7,** 2754-55
  taping of telephone conversation on kickbacks by
    Democratic National Committee **2,** 840-41
  telephone call to Magruder after Watergate arrests
    2, 654, 798 **6,** 2335
  telephone call to Magruder informing him of Wa-
    tergate arrests **FR** 32
  telephone calls to Krogh after Watergate arrests
    3, 976-77
  telephone conversation with Dean after Watergate
    break-in **4,** 1356
  tells Dean Magruder pushed him **3,** 1035-36
  tells Harmony reasons for discharge from CRP **2,**
    487-88
  tells Hunt there is "high-level" interest in Green-
    spun matter **20,** 9354, 9357, 9359, 9372
  tells Kleindienst that Mitchell wants Watergate
    defendants out of jail **3,** 936
  tells LaRue and Mardian about commitments
    made to Watergate burglars **6,** 2289, 2307-2308
  tells Magruder about intelligence-gathering plan **2,**
    787
  tells Mardian and LaRue he will never talk **6,**
    2398
  tells Mardian Nixon and CIA approved Fielding
    burglary and Beard incident **6,** 2361-62
  tells Mardian White House horrors had authoriza-
    tion of Nixon **6,** 2395, 2397, 2398
  tells McCord Mitchell approved plan **6,** 2304
  tells Moore to have Kleindienst release Watergate
    burglars **6,** 2353-54
  told by Mardian to stay away from Kleindienst **6,**
    2381
  told by Riesner that his plan is approved **4,** 1615
  told to get Hunt out of country **3,** 1049 **4,** 1417
  transfer from CRP to Finance Committee **1,** 16-
    17
  Ulasewicz delivers funds to **6,** 2229-30E, 2231-32
  Ulasewicz on **6,** 2241-42
  visit with Hunt in California after Watergate ar-
    rests **9,** 3783
  visitors to **2,** 470-71, 474-75
  visits Dean and Strachan about his problems with
    Magruder **2,** 793

  and Watergate coverup **2,** 850-51 **3,** 1029
  and Winte **24,** 11560, 11561, 11600
  See also Fielding break-in; Las Vegas matter;
    Plumbers
Liddy, Mrs. G. Gordon 6, 2234, 2251
Liddy charts FR 21
  at Key Biscayne meeting **6,** 2325-26
  cost of **2,** 868
  Dean tells Liddy to destroy **4,** 1353
  Hunt on preparation of **20,** 9388
  Mitchell on **4,** 1610
  used by Liddy **2,** 787-78 **3,** 929, 930 **5,** 1843
Liddy debriefing
  and Beard matter **6,** 2415-16
  and Colson-Mitchell telephone calls **5,** 1929
  Dean briefing of Ehrlichman on **7,** 2823
  Haldeman denies Mitchell reported on **8,** 3043-44
  Mardian memo on **6,** 2403
  Mardian on **6,** 2357-62
  Mardian on confidentiality of **6,** 2430-32
  Mardian's reaction to **6,** 2401-2402
Liddy plan 2, 811 **3,** 930 **6,** 2284
  Colson telephone call to Magruder urging approv-
    al of Liddy plan **6,** 2475-76 **FR** 23-24
  cost of **4,** 1610 **11,** 4673-74
  as crime **5,** 1816
  Dean informs Moore of meetings on **5,** 1969-72
  Dean informs Nixon of **8,** 3074-75
  Dean on **3,** 929-31, 1087-88 **4,** 1352-53, 1413
  Dean tells Ehrlichman about **3,** 934
  Dean tells Ehrlichman and Haldeman about **7,**
    2753-54
  Dean tells Haldeman he won't lie about meetings
    on **3,** 1006
  Dean tells Moore about **5,** 1970-71, 1972, 2053-54
  Dean tells Nixon about **4,** 1542-43
  Dean tells prosecutors about **9,** 3633
  Dean's prior knowledge about **3,** 1048-49 **4,** 1442-
    43
  Dean's reaction to **3,** 1023-24 **4,** 1352-53
  Dean's reasons for not telling Nixon about **4,**
    1353-54
  Ehrlichman informs Nixon of **7,** 2758
  Ehrlichman learns about **7,** 2752
  Ehrlichman says Magruder, Mitchell, and LaRue
    approved **7,** 2766
  Ehrlichman's reasons for not telling Nixon about
    7, 2804-2805
  final meeting approving **2,** 794-95, 811-13
  first meeting on **9,** 3767
  Haldeman and **4,** 1553
  Haldeman denies Dean reported on **8,** 3098-99
  Haldeman on Dean telling him about **8,** 3034-36
  Hunt and **9,** 3678-84, 3734, 3765
  Hunt on **20,** 9385-89
  LaRue hears about **6,** 2277-78
  LaRue on discussion at Key Biscayne meeting of
    6, 2280-81, 2326
  Las Vegas plan and **20,** 9385-88
  Liddy's reaction to rejection of first plan **2,** 788-
    89, 862-63 **9,** 3767-68
  Magruder destroys notes on **2,** 843
  Magruder informs Strachan about **6,** 2452

Magruder says Strachan approved **7,** 2766-67
Magruder tells Dean about White House approval
of **3,** 956
Magruder urged to speed approval of **2,** 793-94,
819-20
Magruder's diary with meetings about **3,** 952-53
Magruder's messages to Strachan on **2,** 824-26
meeting in Mitchell's office on **3,** 1264-65E
memo to Haldeman from Strachan on **6,** 2468-70
Mitchell and **5,** 1854, 1871-72, 1874-75
Mitchell denies approval of **4,** 1613-16 **5,** 1856,
1857-58 **6,** 2305-2306
Mitchell learns about Colson urging Magruder to
begin **5,** 1929-30
Mitchell on **4,** 1609-11 **5,** 1843-46, 1928
Mitchell's reasons for not informing Nixon about
5, 1816-19
Moore says he did not ask Mitchell about **5,**
2062, 2063
Moore told about **5,** 2029
Nixon asks Dean about Haldeman's knowledge of
3, 1015-16
O'Brien informs Ehrlichman about **7,** 2731, 2743
participants in formulation of **2,** 811
and prostitutes at Democratic National Conven-
tion **11,** 4528
reasons for Dean attending meeting on **3,** 1083-84
as starting whole Watergate affair **4,** 1351
Strachan on **6,** 2440-41, 2449, 2469-70
Strachan on Haldeman's knowledge of **6,** 2490
uncovered in Select Committee investigation **FR**
28
use of "chase aircraft" in **20,** 9389
See also Gemstone plan; Key Biscayne meeting
Liebengood, Howard S.
affidavit of **12,** 5016, 5261-64E
Liebengood, Howard S., questioning by
Benz **11,** 4415-19
Hunt **20,** 9347
Kelly **11,** 4385-89
MacGregor **12,** 4912-14
Liebergott, Harvey 9, 3898E
Liedtke, William 2, 699 **FR** 514
Life magazine **9,** 3672 **10,** 4127E
and forged Diem cables **FR** 126-27
and Hughes biography controversy **20,** 9367
Lifflander, Matthew L. 25, 12242, 12245, 12246,
12248, 12255E, 12312, 12314, 12351E
affidavit **FR** 478-79
assures Edidin of Muskie committee payment to
Hertz in exchange for contribution **25,** 12232
correspondence with Shapiro on project for Hertz
Corp. **25,** 12377-80E
and immunity granted to Edidin **25,** 12257-58
invoice to Edidin for additional legal services on
franchise program **25,** 12393E
invoice to Hertz for franchise study **25,** 12336-
37E, 12385E, 12389E, 12394E, 12396E
letter to Brown with check from Muskie campaign committee **25,** 12333-35E
letter to Shapiro on franchise study **25,** 12386E
letter with check enclosed for balance on fee for
franchise study **25,** 12387-88E
memo for file on addition to franchise project **25,**
12392E

note to Shapiro with invoice **25,** 12395E
payment stubs for check in payment for franchise
study **25,** 12390-91E
thank-you letters to contributors to Muskie campaign **25,** 12367-70E **25,** 12275
See also Hertz Corp.
Lifflander, Matthew L., testimony of 25, 12259-98
on allowing Muskie advance men to use his Hertz
credit card **25,** 12270, 12283-85
on billing Edidin for research project **25,** 12291-92
on billing Hertz for project **25,** 12265-66, 12267-
68, 12269, 12277-81
on checks given to Edidin for Muskie contributions **25,** 12275-77
denies knowledge of Hertz arrangement with
Muskie campaign **25,** 12261, 12296
on depositing checks from Edidin **25,** 12294-96
on discussion with Edidin on additional work on
franchise study **25,** 12287-88, 12289, 12292-93
on discussion with Edidin on bills owed to Hertz
by Muskie campaign **25,** 12262-66, 12271-72,
12273-74
on Edidin testimony that he submitted phony bill
to Hertz **25,** 12265-66, 12267-68, 12269
on fees received from Hertz after leaving **25,**
12291-92
on first bill for research project for Hertz Corp.
25, 12280-81
Hertz contribution delivered to **25,** 12233-34
on Hertz policy on renting cars to political groups
25, 12270
informed by Edidin on arrangement made to raise
money for Muskie campaign to pay Hertz bill
25, 12264, 12272-74
on initial agreement with Hertz on study project
25, 12290
on interviewing former Hertz attorneys Mewhinney and Murray for research project for Hertz
25, 12278-79
on lunch with Edidin **25,** 12271
on meetings with Hertz people on project **25,**
12297-98
on memo to Goldstein on settling Hertz account
25, 12282-83
on Muskie campaign workers with Hertz credit
cards **25,** 12269-70
on Muskie's announcement that he was not going
to actively campaign **25,** 12261
on person with Muskie campaign incurring bills
with Hertz Corp. **25,** 12277
on personal contribution to Muskie campaign **25,**
12274, 12285-86
on persons responsible to in Muskie campaign **25,**
12286
on persons writing checks to Muskie campaign for
Edidin **25,** 12296
professional background **25,** 12259
on reasons for charging extra fee for Hertz research project **25,** 12293-94
on reasons for consulting with Edidin on expand-
ing project for Hertz **25,** 12290-91, 12292-93
on referring Edidin to Goldstein **25,** 12288-89
on relationship with Edidin **25,** 12262
on relationship with Petrie **25,** 12281-82

Lifflander, Matthew L., testimony of *(Continued)*
   on role as finance coordinator with Muskie campaign **25,** 12259-61, 12284
   sends letter to Goldstein enclosing Hertz Corp. bills to Muskie campaign **25,** 12272
   on signer of Muskie check in payment of Hertz **25,** 12296-97
   on taking checks to Muskie campaign from Edidin **25,** 12265, 12273
Lill (FBI agent) 5, 1926
Lilly, Robert A. 14, 6326 **15,** 6503, 6781 **16,** 6961, 7111, 7216, 7232, 7449 **17,** 7660
   affidavit with attachment of **14,** 6218-21E
   and AMPI contribution to Muskie campaign **16,** 7214
   and AMPI contributions **15,** 6899
   and AMPI contributions to Democratic congressional and senatorial committees **16,** 7302, 7305-7306 **17,** 7670
   and AMPI contributions to Humphrey's 1970 senatorial campaign **15,** 6547, 6548
   and AMPI relations with Nixon administration **15,** 6759
   and AMPI relationship with Valentine, Sherman **15,** 6850
   and AMPI 1969 contribution **FR** 594
   at meeting at Austin airport with Parr and Jacobsen **16,** 7092
   at meeting at Louisville airport on March 23 **16,** 7071-75 **FR** 655-57
   beneficiary of security agreement between TAPE and Citizens National Bank of Austin **14,** 5926, 5997-98E
   billing from Jones for services **17,** 8065E
   and bogus documents from Valentine, Sherman **FR** 880-81
   cash contributions from Masters to **16,** 6969-72
   and cash contributions to Mills **14,** 6318-19
   chance meeting at Austin airport with Parr, Jacobsen, Long, and Townsend **FR** 686-87
   check from Russell **14,** 5966, 6044E
   check from Van Dyk **14,** 5944, 6018E
   checks from Jones **16,** 7002, 7045E **17,** 8056E
   conflicts with Townsend testimony **16,** 7113-14
   Connally and **15,** 6638
   Connally denies conversation with **14,** 6066-68
   and Connally's role in milk-price support reversal **FR** 654-55
   contact with Connally at Page Airway **15,** 6617-24 **FR** 638-40
   contacts with Masters **16,** 6939
   and contribution for Connally **15,** 6647-48
   and contributions to Democratic and Republican National Conventions' books **16,** 7281
   and contributions to Republicans in 1972 **15,** 6680
   conversation with Connally in airport **14,** 6308-12
   on CTAPE contribution to congressional committees and alleged passthrough to Finance Committee **FR** 736-39
   Dean on use of political tricks by **3,** 1295E
   and decision-making on TAPE political contributions **16,** 7300
   delivers money to Semer **16,** 7202-7203
   delivery of cash to Parr **FR** 908

delivery of funds to Chestnut for Humphrey campaign **17,** 7669
on delivery of money to Jacobsen for Connally **FR** 683-84
delivery of money to Kirk for Mills campaign **17,** 7669
and delivery of money to Semer **15,** 6517
and delivery of 1969 AMPI contribution **FR** 593, 594
discussions with Nelson on reimbursement of TAPE **15,** 6525-28
Harrison and **14,** 6271-72
individuals serving as conduits for repayment of loan to **15,** 6528-35
invoice, check, and voucher from Van Dyk **14,** 5946, 6022-23E
invoice from AMPI to **15,** 6397, 6482E
involvement in cash political contributions **15,** 6776-77
and knowledge of AMPI arrangement with Valentine, Sherman **FR** 878-79
letter and billing from Jones for services to **17,** 8069-70E
letter and check to Berentson for National Republican Senatorial Campaign **16,** 7300, 7363E
letter and check to Terrell for National Republican Campaign Committee **16,** 7300, 7366E
letter from Russell with Muskie's thank-you letter **14,** 6039-40E
letter from Van Dyk on payment to **14,** 5946, 6021E
letter from Van Dyk on withholding slip of **14,** 5944, 6019-20E
letter to Jacobsen on IRS audit of AMPI **17,** 8155-56E
letter to Jacobsen on IRS audit of MPI **15,** 6671
loan for AMPI contribution **15,** 6389-98, 6481E **FR** 598-611
loan repayment scheme and **FR** 909-10
loan to reimburse TAPE **15,** 6527-28
on Long delivering money to Jacobsen for Mills campaign **FR** 910
and Louisville airport meeting **17,** 7731, 7744
meeting with Connally **15,** 6459-60, 6807-13
meeting with Jacobsen in Austin airport **16,** 7102-7103
meeting with Mehren **16,** 7255
on Mehren's report of Kalmbach refusing contribution **FR** 726-28
on Mehren's report on meeting with Connally **FR** 720-21
on Mehren's reports on meetings with Connally and Kalmbach **FR** 715
memo from Mehren on proposal by CTAPE **14,** 6119, 6189E
memo from Van Dyk on contribution to "Maine for Muskie" campaign **14,** 5950, 6025E
and Mills rally in Little Rock **16,** 7099
money delivered to Kirk **15,** 6830, 6831
and money for Connally **15,** 6421-25
Nelson's attitude toward veracity of testimony of **15,** 6612-13
Parr and **15,** 6756, 6766
Parr denies knowledge of loan taken by **15,** 6772
personal notes on conversation with Semer on contribution to Muskie campaign **14,** 5948, 6024E

personal notes on transfers of money **14**, 6178, 6217E

personal notes on various campaign contributions **14**, 5972, 6045-49E

promissory note and renewals to Citizens National Bank of Austin **14**, 5923, 5992-94E

and quid pro quo between contributions and milk price-support decision **FR** 672

reimbursement of **15**, 6532

and relationship between AMPI and Valentine, Sherman **15**, 6578, 6586-87, 6591, 6595-97

repayment of loan to **15**, 6691-92 **16**, 7339

report by Mehren on meeting with Nunn **FR** 735-36

role in AMPI **FR** 584

role in efforts to obtain milk price-support increases **15**, 6556

and Russell payback scheme **FR** 599-602

schedule of various note transactions of **14**, 5935, 5999-6001E

security agreement with Citizens National Bank of Austin **14**, 5926, 5995-96E

solicitation of contributions by **16**, 6940-43, 6948, 6952-53, 6954-55, 6966

on SPACE contribution on March 24 **FR** 658

on strategy for increase in milk price supports **FR** 637

and TAPE contributions to CRP **15**, 6624

and use of conduit system for AMPI contributions to Democrats **FR** 611

Van Dyk on IRS statement of earnings form sent to **16**, 6995-98

Van Dyk on relationship with **16**, 6994-95

Van Dyk payments to **16**, 7000-7002

Van Dyk requested to make reimbursed payments to **16**, 6992-98, 6998-7002

voluntary appearance before House Judiciary Committee **4**, 1557, 1562-63

work relationship with Parr **17**, 6756-57

Lilly, Robert A., testimony of 14, 5907-89, 6105-85

on AMPI board meetings discussions of high attorneys' fees **14**, 5973-74

on AMPI campaign contribution commitments **14**, 6106-6107

on AMPI contributions made as officers' personal contributions **14**, 5929-30

on AMPI contributions to Humphrey **14**, 6160-62

on AMPI contributions to Mills' presidential campaign **14**, 6165-66

on AMPI contributions to Muskie campaigns **14**, 5947-56

on AMPI files on lobbying **14**, 5988-89

on AMPI lobbying **14**, 5975, 5984-88

on AMPI repayment plan for political contributions **14**, 5965-73

on arrangement between AMPI and Valentine, Sherman **14**, 6144-65

association with MPI and TAPE **14**, 5907-5908

attitude toward TAPE contributions **14**, 6134-35

on conflict on dates of delivery of $100,000 to Semer **14**, 5928-29

on Connally **14**, 5975-82

on contacts with Nelson **14**, 5909-10

on contribution to Kalmbach in 1969 **14**, 6135-36

on contributions by TAPE after meetings with Connally **14**, 5982-84

on contributions to Democratic congressional and senatorial campaign committees **14**, 6136-37

on contributions to Humphrey **14**, 6160-62

on contributions to Humphrey campaign in 1968 **14**, 5932

on contributions to Muskie Election Committee **14**, 5948-59

on contributions to Republicans **14**, 6121-25

on delivery of contribution to Semer **14**, 5930-33

denies delivery of TAPE funds to Stans **14**, 5913-14

denies knowledge of solicitation of contributions by Republicans **14**, 5929

on fabrication of Valentine files **14**, 6163-64

on formation and purpose of TAPE **14**, 5911-12

on IRS investigation of income tax returns **14**, 5932-33

on Kalmbach's demand for money from Mehren **14**, 6124-25

on list of names of contributors **14**, 5924-25

on loan **14**, 5933

on loan from Citizens' National Bank **14**, 5921-29

on meeting between Nelson, Jacobsen, Mehren, and Kalmbach **14**, 6105-6106

on meeting with Connally at Page Airways **14**, 6139-40

on meeting with Parr and Nelson **14**, 6151-53

on Mehren-Johnson meeting in 1972 **14**, 6178-85

on Mehren's report on Connally's telephone call to Mitchell **14**, 6115-16

on Mehren's trip to Europe **14**, 6113-15

on Mehren's visit from Nunn **14**, 6125-26

on milk price supports **14**, 6133-34

on money for Connally **14**, 5961-64

on motivation for AMPI contribution **14**, 5929

on Nixon's meeting with milk producers **14**, 6141

on personnel with MPI and AMPI **14**, 5908-5909

on Pierson's role in AMPI repayment plan **14**, 5971-73

on reason for contribution to Republicans **14**, 5916

on reimbursement by MPI **14**, 5932

on reimbursement of his loan **14**, 5956-59

on reimbursement of Russell for political contributions **14**, 5933-47, 5960-61

on relationship and contacts with Connally **14**, 5979-80, 6138-44

on reporting of TAPE contribution **14**, 5917-18, 5919-20

on reports on meetings with Connally **14**, 6107-18

on responsibility for TAPE funds **14**, 5912-13

on role in transmittal of contributions **14**, 6168-78

security agreement with TAPE **14**, 5925-27

on TAPE contributions to Republican and Democratic congressional campaign committees **14**, 6125-36

on TAPE decision on contributions to Democrats and Republicans **14**, 6118-22

on TAPE loan to ADEPT **14**, 5983

on TAPE payment of $100,000 to Kalmbach **14**, 5914-21

on Van Dyk's role in repayment of loan **14**, 5942-55

Loyal Americans for Government Reform 13, 5431, 5769E

Lozano, Diana 18, 8255, 8256, 8281-82 **FR** 396

Ludwig, D. K. 23, 10858, 10859, 11268 **24,** 11402

Ludwig, David 21, 9721

Ludwig, E. D. 24, 11441

Ludwig, Miriam 11, 4543, 4545

Lugar 4, 1703E, 1704E

Lujan, Manuel, Jr. FR 400, 401

Lukens, Dave 14, 6084

LULAC 13, 5293, 5294, 5295 **FR** 402-403

Lund, Albert W. 12, 5042-43E

Lund, Mrs. Rhoda 12, 5120E

Lungren, Dr. John C. 12, 5013
   affidavit of **12,** 5009, 5065-69E

Lyeth, Charlotte
   memo to Rebozo with thank-you letters for
      Courtelis and Kislak **22,** 12546E

Lyman, Arthur L.
   See Palmby, Clarence D.

Lyng, Richard 14, 5875 **15,** 6552, 6656 **16,** 7138-40
   17, 7759, 7776-77 **FR** 626
   letter from Mehren to Nelson on discussions with
      15, 6655, 6750-53E
   meeting with Mehren, Butz, and Campbell **16,**
      7279
   meeting with Mehren and Paarlberg **16,** 7241-42
   meeting with Mehren and Palmby **16,** 7241-42
   and reversal of milk price-support decision **17,**
      7778 **FR** 627-28

Lynn, James 13, 5280 **16,** 7286 **FR** 390-91
   memo from Marumoto on NEDA editorial **13,**
      5400-5401
   memo from Marumoto on *El Diario* editorial **13,**
      5323, 5535E

Lyons, Dennis
   See Fabrega, Camilo, testimony of; Robinson,
      Neal, testimony of

M & R Investment Company
   balance sheet on Dunes Hotel and Country Club
      23, 12939-41E

MacArthur Institute 10, 4119E
   Buchanan on **10,** 3917

MacGregor, Barbara (Mrs. Clark MacGregor) 12,
   4898, 4914, 4921, 4932, 4937, 4938, 4941

MacGregor, Clark 1, 14, 24, 35, 136 **2,** 489, 527, 784,
   872 **3,** 1197E **4,** 1676 **5,** 1886, 1929 **6,** 2349, 2519,
   2784 **8,** 3218-19
   asks Dean to tell him true facts about Watergate
      4, 1578-79
   at Cabinet meeting at Camp David **18,** 8194
   at press conferences after Watergate arrests **2,** 850
   believes coverup story **2,** 851
   CRP memo from Todd on Final Report of Older
      Americans Division **19,** 9051-54E
   Dean wants to brief on coverup **3,** 1034
   diary subpoenaed **3,** 952-53
   Ehrlichman wants full statement on Watergate
      from **7,** 2725-26
   and grants **FR** 383
   Gray complains about White House interference
      with FBI Watergate investigation to **FR** 39

and Gray's telephone conversation with Nixon **9,**
   3524

Haldeman and **7,** 2877, 2878

Mardian fails to inform **6,** 2419

Mardian's efforts to give him facts **6,** 2430-31

meeting with Marumoto **13,** 5283

meeting with Mehren, Albert, and Mills **16,** 7318-
   20

memo from Buchanan about points of weakness
   in McGovern campaign **10,** 3975,4250-51E

memo from Buchanan on political suggestions for
   attacks on McGovern **10,** 3975, 4254-55E

in memo from Colson to Haldeman on ITT **8,**
   3372E

memo from Malek on Older Americans pamphlet
   19, 9212-16E

memo from Malek on "Older Americans Progress" **FR** 421

memo from Todd on final report of Older Americans Division **19,** 9051-54E

memo to Colson on request for information on
   new labor committee **FR** 336-50E

memo to Ehrlichman and Shultz on milk price
   supports **FR** 813-14E

memo to Ehrlichman and Shultz on Rice's memo
   on dairy industry problems **FR** 805E

memo to Kingsley on Bennett **18,** 8226, 8363E

Nixon requests report from **7,** 2803-2804

Nunn's reporting relationship with **17,** 7536

progress report on Older Americans Division
   from Malek **19,** 9212-16E

questions CRP staff on involvement in Watergate
   break-in **2,** 528-30

refuses to discuss Watergate with Mardian **6,**
   2375, 2403-2404

and Responsiveness Program **18,** 8226

role in CRP **1,** 14, 16 **2,** 513

role on White House staff **1,** 79-80, 91, 92

says Ehrlichman lied to him **7,** 2803-2804

and Segretti coverup **FR** 185-86

taped telephone conversation with Ehrlichman **7,**
   2814, 2815, 3007-3008E

telephone call from Gray **9,** 3462, 3530-31, 3536,
   3541

Washington Post article about statement and news
   release of **12,** 4905, 5019-21E

MacGregor, Clark, testimony of
   asks Chapin about Segretti **12,** 4905
   on attitude toward Watergate **12,** 4932
   on campaign financing recommendations **12,**
      4927-28
   on Dean investigating Watergate **12,** 4922-25
   on decision to replace Mitchell **12,** 4940-41
   on decision-makers in campaign **12,** 4931
   on Democratic National Committee lawsuit
      against CRP **12,** 4923-24
   denies being figurehead in Nixon campaign **12,**
      4944-45
   denies contacting Nixon at Gray's request **12,**
      4916-20
   denies Ehrlichman made request for complete
      statement on Watergate **12,** 4907-3908
   denies knowledge of hush money **12,** 4909
   denies knowledge of Watergate coverup **12,** 4908-
      4909

cash disbursements from Sloan to **2**, 538, 540, 744-45

and cash disbursements from Sloan to Liddy **2**, 539, 615, 773-74

and cash disbursements to Liddy **5**, 1847

and Chapman's Friends **FR** 199-200

Colson and **4**, 1543

and Colson's demonstration projects **2**, 512

and Colson's involvement in Watergate **3**, 1266E

complaints about Segretti to **FR** 165

and concern over McCord's letter to Sirica **FR** 70-71

and concern over unravelling of coverup **FR** 82-83

concern with intelligence capacity of CRP **4**, 1608

confidential memo from Haldeman on generating support for administration's Vietnam position **10**, 3975, 4120-26E

confidential memo to Mitchell on discretionary fund at Commerce Department **2**, 695-96

confidential memo to Mitchell on use of Federal resources in election campaigns **19**, 8595-96E

conflict with Liddy **4**, 1414

conflicts between his testimony and Dean's **4**, 1442-43

contacts with Kleindienst **9**, 3609

contacts with McCord **1**, 146

contradicts Strachan's testimony **9**, 3648-49

and CRP finances **5**, 1846

and CRP hiring of Liddy **3**, 1255-56E

Dean aids with grand jury testimony **3**, 1038 **4**, 1382

Dean asks Kalmbach to meet with **5**, 2148-49

Dean believes involved in Watergate **7**, 2901

Dean tells Ehrlichman and Haldeman about perjury of **7**, 2754

Dean tells Kleindienst about Watergate involvement of **4**, 1419-20

Dean tells Moore about perjury of **5**, 1970-71

Dean tells Nixon about Watergate involvement of **4**, 1425 **8**, 3117

Dean-Petersen discussion on grand jury testimony of **9**, 3617-18

and Dean's involvement in Watergate **4**, 1420-21

and Dean's name omitted from list of those attending meetings on Liddy plans **4**, 1417

and Dean's prior knowledge of Watergate **4**, 1379-80

and Dean's promise of Executive clemency **4**, 1443-44

delegated authority at CRP by Mitchell **4**, 1607

and Democrats for Nixon **16**, 7471

and destruction of Gemstone bill **2**, 484-85

and dirty tricks **2**, 647-48, 679

discussions with Haldeman after Watergate break-in **8**, 3097-98

discussions with LaRue on money given to Liddy **6**, 2317

discussions with U.S. Attorneys reported to Kleindienst **9**, 3578-79

efforts to get Sloan to perjure himself **2**, 543, 545, 548-49, 550, 566, 581, 583-85, 611, 612-13, 614, 708-9, 770, 772, 776-77 **FR** 42-43

Ehrlichman's knowledge of involvement in Watergate of **7**, 2845-46

and electronic surveillance of O'Brien **9**, 3785

employment problems after Watergate **3**, 990-91, 1243E, 1251E **4**, 1380, 1577-78 **5**, 1895, 1921 **7**, 2886-87

Executive clemency for **4**, 1634 **FR** 70-71

and film strips of memos from Muskie's offices **2**, 669-70

and first Watergate break-in **7**, 2733 **FR** 29

Gemstone material in file for Mitchell **2**, 503-504

and Gemstone plan **FR** 21, 22-23

Haldeman contradicts testimony of **8**, 3056-57

Haldeman on relationship with **7**, 2886-88

Haldeman wants Dean to talk to **3**, 1042

Haldeman's opinion of **8**, 3129

and Haldeman's private polls **6**, 2498-99

and hiring of Greaves **11**, 4639

and hiring of Liddy **5**, 1924-26

Hunt on Liddy plan and **9**, 3679

Hunt on responsibility for Watergate **9**, 3778

in Hunt's notes **9**, 3839E

immunity for

  and litigation on television and radio coverage of Senate Select Committee hearings **FR** 1079-80

and immunity powers of Select Committee **FR** 28

indicates to LaRue that he had prior knowledge of Watergate break-in **6**, 2285, 2340

and infiltration of peace vigil by Brill **FR** 198-99

informed by Dean about newspaper stories that they had prior knowledge about Watergate **3**, 1004

informed by Dean that he won't lie about meetings where Liddy presented intelligence-gathering plans **3**, 1006-07

informs LaRue of Watergate break-in **6**, 2335

informs Mitchell of amount of cash disbursed to Liddy **2**, 547

informs Reisner of approval of Liddy plan **FR** 25

instructions to Liddy on hiring of McCord **6**, 2396

instructions to Reisner on shredding of documents after June **2**, 506-508, 510-11

instructs Odle and Reisner to remove Gemstone files **FR** 32-33

and intelligence plans **4**, 1413

interview with Ehrlichman **7**, 2765-66

on involvement of Mitchell, Dean, LaRue, and Mardian in coverup story **FR** 44-45

Kalmbach's attitude toward **5**, 2175-76

Kleindienst has no recollection of discussion with Ehrlichman and Dean about possible involvement in Watergate of **9**, 3567

LaRue on argument between Liddy and **6**, 2279-80

LaRue on meetings regarding perjury by **6**, 2292

LaRue on prior knowledge of Watergate break-in of **6**, 2328-30

LaRue's discussions on Key Biscayne meeting with **6**, 2283-84

and Lehigh Valley Cooperative Farmers, Inc., contribution **FR** 481

letter to Reitz on ACTION **FR** 150

and Letters to Editor program **FR** 298E

Liddy and **1**, 17 **2**, 475, 492-93, 503 **4**, 1644

and Liddy budget **6**, 2496

Magruder, Jeb Stuart *(Continued)*

and Liddy plan **3**, 929, 930-31 **4**, 1352, 1353, 1413-14, 1611, 1613-16 **5**, 1816 **20**, 9385

on Liddy plan discussion at Key Biscayne meeting **FR** 24-25

Liddy pressured for better surveillance by **6**, 2304

and Liddy's hiring at CRP **3**, 928, 1264E **4**, 1351

lies to Mitchell about amount given Liddy **6**, 2381, 2392

MacGregor on being used by **12**, 4930

MacGregor on revelations of **12**, 4910

MacGregor questions about involvement in Watergate activities **2**, 529

Mardian contradicts testimony on destruction of Gemstone file **6**, 2356-57, 2374-75

Mardian contradicts testimony on Liddy trip to see Kleindienst on release of Watergate burglars **6**, 2353-54

Mardian denies knowing perjury plans of **6**, 2371-74

Mardian denies testimony of **6**, 2371-72, 2373-74

McCord on perjured testimony by **1**, 241-242

and McMinoway's reports **11**, 4479

meeting with Dean and Mitchell **4**, 1634-35 **FR** 89-90

meeting with LaRue, Mardian, Dean, and Mitchell **3**, 1035-36 **6**, 2286, 2355-57

meeting with LaRue, Mitchell, and Flemming in Key Biscayne **23**, 11150

meeting with Liddy, Dean, Shumway, and Strachan after Watergate break-in **2**, 520

meeting with Mitchell and LaRue at Key Biscayne **2**, 490-91, 503, 505 **4**, 1668-69

meeting with Strachan before his grand jury testimony **6**, 2465

meeting with U.S. Attorneys **7**, 2903-2904

meetings after Watergate arrests **2**, 738-39 **3**, 935

meetings with Dean, Liddy, and Mitchell **2**, 490-91, 502-503

meetings with Dean after Watergate **4**, 1672 **12**, 4906

meetings with Liddy **2**, 525

meetings with Mitchell after Watergate **5**, 1878, 1879, 1881, 1883

meetings with White House staff **2**, 505-506

memo from Higby on formation of citizens committees to run ads against opposition senators **FR** 155

memo to Mitchell on "Matters of Potential Embarrassment" **FR** 165

and memos to Mitchell **6**, 2494

Mitchell contradicts his testimony on Liddy plan **4**, 1611

Mitchell denies he showed him Gemstone files **4**, 1619, 1641

Mitchell instructs him to destroy Gemstone files **5**, 1877

and Mitchell on Colson **5**, 1933-34

Mitchell on influences to supersede his orders to **4**, 1640-41, 1670-71

Mitchell on involvement in Watergate of **5**, 1850-51

Mitchell on testimony of **4**, 1662-63

Mitchell refuses to fire **6**, 2430

Mitchell says Nixon would have fired if informed about Watergate **5**, 1828

Mitchell tells him to destroy sensitive files **6**, 2286

and Mitchell's acceptance of Liddy **4**, 1639

and Mitchell's attempts to have Chief Wilson contacted after Watergate break-in **6**, 2331

and Mitchell's authorization of payments to Liddy **4**, 1617-18

Mitchell's hiring of **5**, 1819, 1820

Mitchell's reasons for not telling FBI about Watergate activities of **5**, 1927

and Mitchell's request for accounting on money to Walker **8**, 3190

and money to Liddy **7**, 2698-99

Nixon denies he had prior knowledge of Watergate **9**, 3549

Nixon informed about stories on **8**, 3126

Nixon wants Ehrlichman to interview **7**, 2757

on Nixon's denial of White House connection to Watergate **2**, 861

O'Brien reports to Ehrlichman on talk with **7**, 2731-36

on O'Brien's activities in ITT case **5**, 1873

Odle returns file to **1**, 67

on Patman Committee subpoena list **3**, 961

and payments by Sloan to Porter **2**, 537

payments for "expenses" to **6**, 2324, 2325

and payments to Liddy **2**, 697

perjured testimony of **1**, 244 **4**, 1417, 1426, 1565, 1625-26, 1628-29, 1633-34, 1643-44 **5**, 1859, 1865-66, 1896-98, 1914-15 **7**, 2845 **8**, 3043 **9**, 3582-83, 3650-51 **FR** 44-46

and pickets at Whittier College **FR** 174

plans to run for office in California **3**, 990

and political espionage **11**, 4641

and Porter's admission of perjury on money to Liddy **2**, 638-42, 643-44

and Porter's cash disbursements ordered by **2**, 658-60

and Porter's efforts to get government job after Watergate trial **2**, 653

and Porter's perjury **FR** 45

and pressure on Liddy for break-in **6**, 2359-60, 2396

pressures on Sloan from **FR** 41

problems with Liddy **3**, 1088

questioned by Ehrlichman **7**, 2727

reassures Mitchell on Harmony testimony **2**, 464, 467-68

and reconvening of grand jury after conviction of "Watergate Seven" **25**, 12403E

Reisner on activities to disrupt Democratic party campaign **2**, 523-25

Reisner on emptying files of **2**, 525-26

Reisner's duties as executive assistant of **2**, 489

relationship with Dean after Watergate **3**, 989-90

relationship with Liddy **1**, 59, 149 **2**, 498, 791-93, 826-27, 863 **4**, 1443, 1619-20 **6**, 2465-66

relationship with Mitchell **2**, 522-23

removal of files by **1**, 45-49, 52-53, 62-67, 70-71, 72-74

reports to Strachan on Liddy plan **2**, 791 **3**, 1024 **6**, 2489

requests meeting with Reisner after Watergate break-in **2**, 508-10, 517

and re-registration scheme in California **FR** 204
research on utilization of Federal resources by
other presidential campaigns **FR** 363-64E
role at CRP **1**, 16, 20, 21 **4**, 1657 **FR** 18-19
role in Watergate break-in **5**, 1859
and Ruby I **FR** 187-90
and Sandwedge proposal **1**, 252
and Sedan Chair I **FR** 190-92
and Sedan Chair II **FR** 192-96
in Silbert affidavit **25**, 12407-10E
Sloan denies financial reports to **2**, 616
Sloan reports approaches to U.S. Attorneys to **2**,
552
and Sloan testimony at Watergate trial **7**, 2698-99
and Sloan's payments to Liddy **5**, 2012
Strachan calls after learning about Watergate
break-in **6**, 2456-57
Strachan denies learning about Liddy plan from **6**,
2449
Strachan denies seeing Gemstone file from **6**,
2451-52
Strachan on truth-telling capabilities of **6**, 2503
on Strachan's authorization for Liddy's activities
6, 2506-2507
on Strachan's knowledge of Liddy plan **FR** 26-27
Strachan's relationship with **6**, 2440-42
subpoenaed by Patman Committee **3**, 1193E
talking paper on letterwriting campaigns to
Haldeman **FR** 292-93E
talks to Federal Prosecutors **4**, 1635
taped telephone conversation with Dean with attached Camp David envelope **3**, 1004, 1258-60E
taped telephone conversation with Haldeman **7**,
2888
telephone call from Colson on Liddy plan **6**, 2284
FR 23-24
telephone call from Liddy after Watergate break-
in **2**, 654 **6**, 2284-85
telephone call from Liddy informing him of Watergate arrests **FR** 32
telephone call to Dean blaming Liddy for Watergate break-in **3**, 932 **4**, 1356
telephone call to Reisner after Watergate arrests
2, 515, 522, 528
telephone conversation with Colson **2**, 517-18
telephone conversation with Haldeman after Watergate arrests **8**, 3039
tells Dean that Colson pressured him into using
Liddy's plans **3**, 954
tells Dean that Mitchell approved Liddy's plan **3**,
1088
tells LaRue about his role in Watergate break-in
6, 2284
tells LaRue about Liddy's involvement in Watergate break-in **6**, 2287, 2336
tells LaRue that Mitchell approved Liddy plan **6**,
2305, 2339
tells Mardian about Watergate break-in **6**, 2349-50
tells O'Brien Strachan told him to rehire Liddy **7**,
2733
tells Porter names of people he expects to be indicted **2**, 646, 660, 664
tells Porter Nixon wants everyone to tell the truth
2, 640
tells Reisner to inform Liddy his plan was approved **5**, 1846

tells Sloan to comply with Liddy's requests for
money **FR** 26
tells Stans that Liddy will handle security at
Republican National Convention **2**, 728
tells Strachan about Liddy plan **6**, 2452
testimony at trial **1**, 343-344 **2**, 584-85
testimony before grand jury **3**, 952-53
testimony before U.S. Attorney discussed between
Kleindienst and Nixon **9**, 3585-88
threats to Haldeman **4**, 1577-78
transfer to CRP **1**, 80
urged by Colson to start Liddy plan **5**, 1929-30
verification of cash disbursements by **2**, 555
and Watergate break-in **5**, 1858 **FR** 27-28, 30-31
and Watergate coverup **3**, 1310E
and write-in campaign for Kennedy in New
Hampshire **FR** 202
and Young Voters for the President **FR** 200-201
Magruder, Jeb Stuart, testimony of
on activities since Watergate break-in **2**, 853-54
on agreement with prosecution **2**, 810
and approval of Liddy's project **2**, 826
on attitude toward effect of Watergate on his life
2, 853-54
on behavior after Watergate arrests **2**, 798-800,
820
believes meetings with Haldeman, Ehrlichman,
and Dean were taped **2**, 832
on campaign decision making **2**, 817-18
career background **2**, 784
on cash disbursement to Lasky **2**, 823
on CIA defense **2**, 867
on Colson's telephone call urging approval of Liddy's intelligence-gathering plan **2**, 793-94, 819-
20, 857-58
on contents of Gemstone file **2**, 848
cooperates with U.S. Attorneys **2**, 808
on Dean discussion on deniability for Mitchell **2**,
872-73
on Dean preparing him for grand jury testimony
2, 869-70
on Dean reporting coverup to Ehrlichman and
Haldeman **2**, 803-804
Dean tells him he won't be indicted **2**, 823-24
on Dean's denial of involvement in Watergate
planning meetings **2**, 806, 842-43, 864-65
on Dean's involvement in Watergate affair **2**, 862-
63
on Dean's role in coverup **2**, 848-49
on decision to destroy Gemstone file **2**, 800
denies knowledge about Gemstone file to Reisner
2, 504-505
on discrepancies between Sloan's testimony and
his own **2**, 867-68
discussion with Harmony on her testimony **2**, 871
discussions with Sloan on amount of money given
to Liddy **2**, 800-801, 820, 867-68
on early concept of intelligence-gathering operations **2**, 810-11
on employment at CRP **2**, 784-85
on Executive clemency **2**, 804-805, 807-808, 809-
10, 819, 850
expresses reservations about Liddy's intelligence-
gathering plan **2**, 813
on failures of Watergate coverup **2**, 805-806

4130-45E

to Haldeman on use of Antitrust Division to curb media unfairness **FR** 145

to Horton on memo from Timmons to Magruder on campaign plan **19,** 8604-05E

to Horton referring Timmons' memo on Martin's plan for use of Federal resources in campaign **19,** 8604-8605E

to Kleindienst on million-dollar fund **7,** 2968E

to Malek on coordinating functions for campaign organization **1,** 451-53E

to Mitchell, "Democratic and Republican Contenders" **10,** 3975, 4174-84E

to Mitchell about plans for activities at the Democratic National Convention **10,** 3975, 4221-24E

to Mitchell on Cabinet Committee **FR** 395

to Mitchell on CRP assuming White House support activities **4,** 1655-56

to Mitchell on Democratic '72 Sponsors Club **10,** 3975, 4196E

to Mitchell on discretionary fund at Commerce Department **2,** 696, 874, 899E

to Mitchell on funding of telephone plan for Florida primary **4,** 1810-13E

to Mitchell on grantsmanship **1,** 40, 41, 449E

to Mitchell on interest group reports **19,** 8813-18E

to Mitchell on interest in federal resources **19,** 8595-96E

to Mitchell on La Raza Unida **FR** 397-98

to Mitchell on Muskie candidacy **11,** 4654

to Mitchell on "Resource Development" **FR** 362-63

to Mitchell on tracking presidential contenders **10,** 3075, 3975, 4185-91E, 4225-34E

to Mitchell on utilization of Federal resources for campaign purposes by Eisenhower, Johnson, and Humphrey **19,** 8598-99E

to Mitchell regarding Muskie campaign organization **11,** 4695, 4889-91E

to Nixon on Cambodia bombing reaction and response **FR** 317-19

to Strachan on use of White House computer for 1972 campaign **19,** 8600-8603E **FR** 364

from Buchanan about Florida primary **10,** 3975, 4192-95E

from Dean for files on call from Dent **3,** 991, 1251E

from Failor **12,** 5016, 5017

from Failor on McGovern-Shriver confrontation **12,** 5017, 5265-66E

from Haldeman about press coverage for administration **10,** 3975, 4112E

from Haldeman on advertisement suggestions on Cambodia policy **10,** 3975, 4128E

from Haldeman on Harris poll on students' attitudes **10,** 4126E

from Haldeman on letterwriting campaign to Senators opposing Nixon's positions **FR** 150-51

from Haldeman on telegrams to Humphrey **FR** 286E

from Higby on discrediting Huntley **10,** 3975, 4127E

from Jones on 8th Annual Convention of Opportunities Industrialization Centers of America, Inc. **19,** 8869E

from Jones to Higby and Dean entitled "Options for Jeb Magruder" **3,** 990, 1249-50E **4,** 1577-78

from Malek **1,** 54-55, 56-59, 451-53E

from Odle on payments to McCord **1,** 52

from Porter on infiltrators of Democratic party campaign **FR** 352E

from Rietz on ACTION **FR** 285E

from Strachan **10,** 4132E

from Strachan on establishment of "Humphrey Watch" and "Kennedy Watch" **10,** 3975, 4164-66E

from Timmons on campaign plan discussed in memo from Magruder to Horton **19,** 8604-05E

with copies of citizen letters to Severeid **FR** 296-97E

Maguire, Richard 14, 5925, 5968-70 **15,** 6510, 6526, 6781

and AMPI payback scheme **FR** 610-11

and formation of TAPE **15,** 6504-6505, 6757

Mahan, Dennis 9, 3486

Mahan, John 3, 1331E

Maheu, Peter R., interview with 20, 9432, 9433, 9501 **FR** 951, 960

shows Danner copies of checks to local state committees for Nixon-Agnew in 1968 **20,** 9512-15 **FR** 949

summary of **FR** 952-53

Maheu, Robert A. 21, 9962 **22,** 10221, 10269 **23,** 10963

and ABM issue **20,** 9596

and atomic testing in Nevada **20,** 2592 **21,** 10041-44 **24,** 11578-79

authorization of Hughes' contribution **20,** 9531-32, 9533, 9564

and Bell's delivery of contribution to Danner **FR** 953-54

Buzhardt and **23,** 10905

and Castro assassination attempt **21,** 9719

Caulfield investigation of relationship with O'Brien **21,** 9715-19 **22,** 10404-10

checks payable to **24,** 11396, 11526-35E

conflict with Hughes **21,** 9722, 9724, 9987-88

and contact with FBI on Dunes acquisition matter **FR** 992

correspondence with Hughes on Dunes Hotel acquisition **26,** 12775-89E

Danner changes testimony on presence during delivery of Hughes contribution **24,** 11464-66, 11467, 11476-78

Danner informs about Rebozo's concern over partisanship of Hughes Tool Co. **20,** 9530

and Danner's delivery of contribution to Key Biscayne **20,** 9536-37, 9543

and Danner's expense vouchers **22,** 12480E, 12481E

Davis investigation of **24,** 11568-69

and delivery of Hughes contribution **FR** 962

discussions with Davis on campaign contributions **24,** 11574-79

discussions with Davis on TWA litigation **24,** 11579-82

discussions with Rebozo on TWA lawsuit **21,** 10048-50

and Dunes Hotel acquisition **20,** 9576, 9580 **FR** 997

Maheu, Robert A. *(Continued)*
effort to deliver Hughes contribution to Nixon **FR** 959
efforts to make Hughes contribution through Laxalt **FR** 938-40
efforts to obtain moneys from Henley **24,** 11573
employs Humphrey's son **20,** 9529
first meeting with Danner **20,** 9498
on flights on Hughes' plane **20,** 9479, 9480
in Florida at time of Danner's visit with Rebozo **21,** 10043-44
Gemmill on role in Hughes contribution **23,** 11200
and Greenspun **20,** 9376, 9380
and Hayes-Metzner letter **FR** 995
and Hughes contribution **20,** 9511, 9516-17 **22,** 1612 **24,** 11418
and Hughes' interest in Greenspun break-in **20,** 9384
informs Rebozo of reasons for Hughes hiring O'Brien **21,** 10056, 10057-58
interview on "Sixty Minutes" **23,** 11079, 11132-33E
and IRS investigation of Hughes Tool Co. and Meier **24,** 11631
Laxalt affidavit on meeting with **26,** 12921-22E
meeting with Danner in Las Vegas in 1968 **24,** 11446-48, 11449
and Meier **24,** 11594
memo from Colson to Dean on conflict between Hughes and **23,** 11079, 11134-35E
money sent by Henley to **FR** 958-59
Rebozo and **20,** 9524
receives money from Sands Casino in 1968 **FR** 939
relationships with Mafia figures **21,** 9721-22, 9723
representatives paying expenses for presidential advance party **21,** 9722-23
retains O'Brien **24,** 11589-94
on sources of money for Hughes contributions **FR** 960
suggests Mitchell be consulted on TWA litigation **20,** 9605-9606
trip to Washington with Rebozo and Maheu **21,** 10055-56
trip with Danner and Rebozo **21,** 10053-55 **24,** 11548
trip with Danner to see Rebozo **20,** 9535-36
and TWA litigation **1,** 299 **20,** 9565, 9567
Wearley denies flying him to Texas for visit with President Johnson **20,** 9458
Maheu, Robert A., interview with 9, 3686 **20,** 9477 **22,** 10272 **23,** 11255
and analysis of delivery dates of Hughes contribution **FR** 962-68
authority with Hughes organization **20,** 9451
conflicts with Rebozo testimony **FR** 1054-55
Danner informs of Rebozo's awareness of O'Brien retainer with Hughes Tool Co. **20,** 9529
on Dunes Hotel acquisition **FR** 983-84
on flight with Danner and Rebozo **20,** 9448, 9458-60
on flights on Hughes' plane **20,** 9469, 9473, 9476-77, 9480-81
Greenspun and **20,** 9346, 9349, 9354-55, 9361-62, 9372-73

hotel bill from Sonesta Beach Hotel **26,** 12842-46E
hotel registration and bill from Madison Hotel, Washington, D.C. **26,** 12836-38E
on Hughes decision to contribute to Nixon campaign through Rebozo **FR** 935
on Hughes knowledge of campaign contributions **FR** 933
instructions to Danner on Hughes contribution **24,** 11540-44
Jones report to Rashid on conference with **26,** 12923-24E
and Nevada Airport Operations Co. **20,** 9443-44
O'Brien and **22,** 12051
and Rebozo's efforts to get contribution from Hughes in 1968 **20,** 9495-97, 9498-99, 9500-9501, 9505
on reimbursement to himself for campaign contribution to Humphrey in 1968 **FR** 959
on Sands withdrawal **FR** 956-58
suit against Hughes Tool Co. in 1970 **20,** 9541
summary of **FR** 951-52
Wearley forbidden to fly aircraft for **20,** 9430
Wearley on knowledge of his position in Hughes organization **20,** 9452
Wearley on role at Summa Corp. **20,** 9432-33
See also Hughes-Rebozo investigation; Maheu-Hughes litigation
Maheu, Mrs. Robert A. 20, 9473
Maheu & Associates 20, 9433
Maheu-Hughes litigation
and Davis **24,** 11568
Davis on Select Committee interference with **24,** 11611-12
Muse statement on role in providing information to court **24,** 11615-16
Mai, Nguyen 12, 5199-5201E
Maine
anti-Nixon demonstrations in **12,** 5084-94E
"Maine for Muskie" campaign 14, 5950, 6025E
Maine State Federated Labor Council 12, 5085E
Maine sugar industry
investigation of Muskie and **21,** 9726-27
Maisey 25, 12145-46
Malek, Frederick V. 1, 13, 17, 40, 59, 71, 449E **2,** 602 **13,** 5282, 5304 **22,** 10250 **23,** 11260
activity report from Jones **18,** 8267, 8268, 8417E, 8418E
at Cabinet meeting **18,** 8193-94
briefings of department and agency chiefs on Responsiveness Program **FR** 379
and budget committee **5,** 1846
and cancellation of Responsiveness Program **18,** 8184
and Crawford Plan **FR** 277
and Department of Labor **FR** 431-32
dispute with Ehrlichman **12,** 4944
and EEOC-University of Texas matter **FR** 410
Evans' projects and **18,** 8439
and Farmer grant **FR** 406
and Flemming **18,** 8483
and funding for Federation of Experienced Americans **18,** 8442, 8447-48 **FR** 428
general plan for Responsiveness Program **FR** 367-

73

and Government brochures published in 1972 **18,** 8473-75

Haig on contacts with **23,** 11035-36

and Horton's draft on Federal resources **FR** 365, 367

and initiation of Responsiveness Program **18,** 8175-79

and IRS **4,** 1684E

letter to Dorsen on Responsiveness Program **19,** 8748E

and Marumoto **13,** 5275, 5276

and OMBE grants **FR** 434-36

and Pentagon Papers matter **6,** 2504

and Porter's efforts to get Government job after Watergate trial **2,** 653, 673-74

progress report to Haldeman on Responsiveness Program **18,** 8181-83 **FR** 410-12

progress report to MacGregor on Older Americans Division **19,** 9212-16E

and project to curtail leaks **3,** 921, 922

and recruitment of White House staff **1,** 86

request from Kaupinen on Labor Department return of Local 454,
    Dock and Wharf Builders, subpoenaed records **FR** 411

and Responsiveness Program **18,** 8181

role in CRP **1,** 14, 16, 31-32

role on White House staff **1,** 78

takes blame for Haldeman **4,** 1490 **6,** 2489

on Target Dates for State Selection of Spanish-speaking Chairmen **19,** 8650-51E

unsigned note on telephone call from Todd **18,** 8475, 8577E

and Walters **4,** 1682E

Weekly Reports from Jones **19,** 8863-68E, 8870E

and White House leaks **FR** 120

and White House Personnel Office **FR** 414

Malek, Frederick V., testimony of 18, 8199-8290

on attitude toward Black support **18,** 8267

on Civil Service Commission investigation of GSA and HUD **18,** 8228

on Clarke's affidavit on GSA contract awards **18,** 8244-45

on competitive service positions and White House **FR** 418-19

on concern about leaks in Responsiveness Program **18,** 8229-30

on contact with Mitchell on Responsiveness Program for Black groups **18,** 8258-59, 8261-63, 8265-66, 8272

on Davison's role with Responsiveness Program **18,** 8252-53

on Dent's role in campaign **18,** 8289

on difficulties of election campaigns **18,** 8279

disagrees with Marumoto's interpretation of Responsiveness Program **18,** 8278-80

on function Of White House Personnel office **18,** 8225-30

on goals of Responsiveness Program **18,** 8210-11

on government career **18,** 8199-8200

on grant requested by Farmer **18,** 8270-73

on grants and contracts awards **18,** 8280-81

on grants for La Raza Unida and Southwest Council of La Raza **18,** 8253-54

on grantsmanship **18,** 8231-32, 8276-77

on grantsmanship and Spanish-speaking enterprises **FR** 393-94

on grantsmanship by Democrats **18,** 8251-52

on Haldeman's initiation of Responsiveness Program **18,** 8208, 8209-10

on Haldeman's response to progress reports on Responsiveness Program **18,** 8243

on Hatch Act and Government employees participating in election campaign activities **18,** 8282-84

on HUD and Responsiveness Program **18,** 8245-46

on importance of Responsiveness Program **18,** 8241-43

on Kingsley's reports to Haldeman on Responsiveness Program **18,** 8284-86

on Labor Department and Responsiveness Program **18,** 8339-40

on legality of Responsiveness Program **18,** 8286-88

on Marumoto and Armendariz "signing off" on grants **18,** 8249-50

on meeting with Mitchell, Ehrlichman, Shultz, and Nixon **18,** 8205-8206

on meetings with group directors to explain Responsiveness Program **18,** 8232-33

on memos describing his roles in campaign **18,** 8210-8206

on Nixon's attitude toward his campaign role **18,** 8204-8207

on OMBE grants and Jenkins **18,** 8268-69

on organization of his staff **18,** 8230-31

on patronage **18,** 8223-25

on people in CRP reporting to him **18,** 8207-8208

on political activities of White House employees **18,** 8275-76

on programs similar to Responsiveness Program in other administrations **18,** 8288-89

on progress reports to Haldeman on Responsiveness Program **18,** 8231-39

on "puffing" of reports to Haldeman on Responsiveness Program **18,** 8241

on purposes of Responsiveness Program **18,** 8212-20

on report to Haldeman on Camp David meeting **18,** 8232-33

on responsibilities as Special Assistant to the President **18,** 8200-8201

on responsibilities of members of Congress compared with members of CRP **18,** 8222

on Responsiveness Program and Black groups **18,** 8256-80

on Responsiveness Program and legal and regulatory actions **18,** 8220-21

on role of Marumoto and Armendariz in Responsiveness Program **18,** 8246-55

on role of Responsiveness Program **18,** 8280

on Spanish-speaking Americans appointed to administration posts **18,** 8224

on special recruiting project **18,** 8203

on staff at White House **18,** 8201

on termination of Responsiveness Program **18,** 8285-86

Malek memos
  on DOL responsiveness **19,** 9338-40E
  on Marumoto's "Brown Mafia" title for memos
    13, 5278
  on OMBE grants **13,** 5282-83 **FR** 434-35
  on organization and implementation of new re-
    sponsibilities **18,** 8202, 8305-10E
  to Armendariz on La Raza Unida **FR** 398
  to Brown, Marumoto, Jones, and Armendariz on
    OMBE grants **13,** 5323, 5542E
  to Cole on Social Security increase **19,** 9223E
  to Cole on White House staff support for Nixon
    re-election **18,** 8208, 8325-41E
  to Conde on Spanish-speaking task force media
    team **13,** 5323, 5593-98E
  to Finch on Farmer **19,** 8837E **FR** 406
  to Haldeman on alternative roles in re-election ef-
    fort **18,** 8201, 8291-96E
  to Haldeman on Department of Labor migrant
    worker program grant **FR** 433
  to Haldeman on increasing Executive Branch re-
    sponsiveness **18,** 8208, 8311-19E
  to Haldeman on Responsiveness Program **18,**
    8234, 8380-86E **FR** 441
  to Haldeman on results of Camp David meeting
    18, 8233, 8367-69E
  to Haldeman on White House staff support for
    Nixon re-election **18,** 8208, 8320-24E
  to MacGregor on Older Americans pamphlets **19,**
    9212-16E **FR** 421
  to Magruder **1,** 54-55, 56-59, 451-53E
  to Marumoto **13,** 5281
  to Mitchell and Haldeman on meeting to discuss
    role in re-election effort **18,** 8201, 8297-8304E
  to Mitchell on Black Vote Campaign Plan **18,**
    8258, 8414-16E **19,** 8859-61E **FR** 377-78
  to Novelli on HEW film **18,** 8479, 8582E
  from Anderson and Davidson on Responsiveness
    Program **18,** 8232, 8366E
  from Armendariz on La Raza Unida **13,** 5321
  from Armendariz on Spanish-speaking organiza-
    tional chart **13,** 5322-23, 5648-49E
  from Armendariz on the Raza Unida Party na-
    tional convention **13,** 5323, 5677-78E
  from Armendariz on Zavala County grant **18,**
    8253, 8405E
  from Clarke on Black vote field plan **18,** 8258,
    8406-13E
  from Evans on brochures **18,** 8473, 8574E
  from Evans on Flemming's advance scheduling
    18, 8483, 8584E
  from Flemming on Stack **18,** 8237, 8387E
  from Grinalds on military voters **19,** 9332-37E
  from Haldeman on leaks **3,** 922, 1113E, 1114-16E
  from Heringer on Responsiveness briefing of
    Mitchell **18,** 8208, 8342-47E
  from Horton on patronage **19,** 8891-96E
  from Jones on activity report **18,** 8268, 8273,
    8418E, 8420-22E
  from Jones on meeting with Farmer **18,** 8270,
    8419E **19,** 8838E **FR** 405
  from Jones on Weekly Reports **18,** 8273, 8420-
    22E **19,** 8848-49E, 8863E, 8864E, 8865E,
    8871E, 9342-43E
  from Kaupinen on labor problem in Pennsylvania
    18, 8238, 8388E

  from Magruder on coordinating functions for
    campaign organization **1,** 451-53E
  from Mardian re Crawford's proposed Black Vot-
    er Program **19,** 8742E-47E
  from Marumoto on activity report for Spanish-
    speaking people **13,** 5323, 5556-60E, 5561-65E,
    5566-70E, 5571-75E, 5576-78E, 5579-82E, 5583-
    87E, 5599-5606E, 5607-10E, 5613-16E, 5617-
    21E, 5624-26E, 5629-34E, 5637-42E, 5643-47E,
    5658-62E, 5666-68E, 5670-76E, 5681-84E,5686-
    91E, 5692-96E
  from Marumoto on Nixon's participation in Span-
    ish-speaking activities **19,** 8641-49E
  from Marumoto to **13,** 5278-96
  from Todd on Federation of Experienced Ameri-
    cans **19,** 9235-41E **FR** 427
  from Todd on HEW film **18,** 8479, 8583E
  from Todd to Mitchell on Older Americans Divi-
    sion through **19,** 9055-9134E
  from Todd to Mitchell with proposed campaign
    plan for Older Americans Division **19,** 9055-
    9134E
  from Yeutter on agricultural campaign materials
    17, 8167E
Malkin, Edgar W. 25, 12244, 12249, 12251, 12298,
  12350E **FR** 475, 479-80
  invoices to Hertz Corp. **25,** 12344-46E
Malloy, Barnard Mathis 9, 3727 **22,** 10729-30
  affidavit on psychological profile of Ellsberg pre-
    pared by CIA **9,** 3085, 3812 **25,** 12421-26E
  and Ellsberg psychological profile **FR** 13
  Hunt's dealings with **9,** 3805-3806
Malone, Walter 2, 875
Maloney, Mike 25, 11722, 11731, 11749
Maloy, Paula E.
  affidavit of **12,** 5009, 5143-46E
Manatt, Chuck 25, 12167
Manchester, New Hampshire
  demonstration at Nixon Headquarters in **12,** 5127-
    34E
Manchester, New Hampshire, Police Department 12,
  5009, 5135-42E
  bombed **12,** 5127E, 5133-34E
Manchester Union Leader **12,** 5009, 5127-34E
  and bogus contribution to McCloskey **FR** 198
  and Canuck Letter **10,** 3975, 4264-65E **FR** 207
  See also "Canuck" letter
Mandel, Bus 12, 5171E
Mankiewicz, Frank 10, 4168E **11,** 4502, 4497, 4520,
  4582, 4661, 4668, 4681, 4717E **12,** 5183E **13,** 5290
  18, 8251 **25,** 12101, 12109, 12123, 12124, 12126
  Barash on testimony of **12,** 5267-72E
  Bernhard complains to **11,** 4671
  counteractions against **3,** 1177E
  efforts by McCord to bug telephone of **FR** 197
  Pearlman on working relationship with **25,** 12174
  and Tuck's employment by McGovern campaign
    25, 12192
  and U-13 incident **25,** 12160, 12162
Mankiewicz, Frank, testimony of 11, 4601-34
  on academic and professional background **11,**
    4604
  on Buchanan memos **11,** 4605-4608

on Connally heading Democrats for Nixon **11,**
4625-26
on contents of his book **11,** 4621-22
on Democratic candidates disrupting one another
11, 4620-21
on Democrats for Nixon **11,** 4625-26
denies that McGovern campaign got materials
from Internal Security Division of Justice Department **11,** 4631
on dirty tricks against McGovern campaign **11,**
4611-12, 4627-31
on effects of dirty tricks on Democratic party
campaigns **11,** 4603-4604, 4612-13
on evidence that Chapin's memorandum to Segretti on dividing Democrats was carried out
11, 4607-4609
on Haldeman's testimony on dirty tricks by
Democrats **11,** 4602-4603
on impact of dirty tricks **FR** 205-206
on impact of dirty tricks against Humphrey campaign **11,** 4613-14
on impact of Segretti activities **FR** 173
on Jackson-Humphrey letter **11,** 4609-10
on McGovern campaign methods for information
gathering **11,** 4626-27
on McMinoway's activities **11,** 4616-18
on McMinoway's testimony on anti-Muskie activities at Milwaukee McGovern headquarters **11,**
4617-18
on memo from Hart on Muskie campaign **11,**
4620-21
on Mott's role in McGovern campaign **11,** 4623-.
24
opening statement **11,** 4601-4604
political background **11,** 4604
on political spying **11,** 4632
on previous political campaigns **11,** 4609
on proposal to plant infiltrator in Nixon campaign
11, 4624-25
recommendations on legislation or code of ethics
in political campaigns **11,** 4618-20, 4633-34
role in McGovern campaign **11,** 4604-4605
on security at Doral **11,** 4617
on Segretti **11,** 4606-4607
on Segretti's activities against Muskie **11,** 4609-12
on telephone tapping at McGovern headquarters
11, 4632
on Tuck's activities **11,** 4615-16, 4626
on use of dirty tricks in campaigns **11,** 4622-23,
4627
on 5 o'clock club in 1964 campaign **11,** 4622-23
Mannino, Edward F.
See Stearns, Richard G., testimony of
Mansfield, Mike 2, 875 **3,** 1331E **14,** 6257
and efforts to retrieve CIA material on Hunt from
Justice Department **3,** 978
Manual for the Republican Convention, The **12,** 5198-
5218E
Manuel, Eleanor
affidavit with attachment of **17,** 7985-87E
Marchetti, Victor 1, 194, 215-16
in Hunt's notes **9,** 3838E
and plan to blame CIA for Watergate break-in **1,**
313-314

Marciszewski, Stephen 25, 12127
Marcuse, Hans 3, 1152E
from Armendariz on Spanish-speaking organizational chart **13,** 5322-23, 5648-49E
Mardian, Robert C. 23, 11264
after Watergate arrests **2,** 661-62, 798 **5,** 1849,
1852
asks Dean to obtain CIA assistance in Watergate
investigation **3,** 945-46
at meeting on June 19 **FR** 33-34
at meeting on Kleindienst Nomination hearings **5,**
1947-48
at meeting with Dean, Mitchell, LaRue, and Magruder **6,** 2286, 2354, 2355-57
at meeting with LaRue and Liddy **6,** 2286-89
at meetings to plan Magruder's grand jury testimony **4,** 1624 **6,** 2292
at Slovak World congress **12,** 5027E
ballot security and **26,** 10339E
and Black supporters **18,** 8260
and CIA **4,** 1415
and conflict between Liddy and Magruder **4,** 1443
contacts with Helms since Inauguration Day **8,**
3251
contacts with Mitchell after Watergate **5,** 1877
and Crawford Plan **FR** 377
and CRP internal investigation of Watergate affair
2, 563, 564
Dean shows FBI files to **4,** 1361
debriefing of Liddy and **5,** 1905 **FR** 40-41
debriefing report to Mitchell on Beard episode **5,**
1919-20
on Democratic party and violence to security **8,**
3124
discussions with Bittman **FR** 51
efforts to warn MacGregor on CRP involvement
in Watergate **12,** 4906-4907
and *Ellsberg* case **6,** 2309-10, 2348
and FBI reports on Watergate investigation **3,** 945
gives Ehrlichman Kissinger tapes **6,** 2533-34
and hush money **3,** 969
and information from Internal Security Division
1, 217 **3,** 1056-57
information to Plumbers on Ellsberg **FR** 146
instructed by Mitchell to have Liddy speak to
Kleindienst on possibility of releasing McCord
FR 32
and Intelligence Advisory Committee **1,** 201
involvement in coverup **3,** 943, 1026, 1054
and ITT case **5,** 1949 **8,** 3372E
and ITT-Dita Beard matter **FR** 129
and leaks **3,** 1056
letter from Crawford with proposal for Black Voter Program **19,** 8743-47E
and Liddy debriefing **4,** 1643 **5,** 1918-20 **6,** 2309-
10, 2318
on Liddy taking Beard away from Washington
FR 128
Liddy tells Hunt he is action officer **9,** 3783
and logs of wiretaps between newsmen and White
House staffers **3,** 1069
MacGregor on warnings from **12,** 4932
and Magruder's perjury **5,** 1896

Mardian, Robert C. *(Continued)*
McCord and **1**, 177-178, 224
meeting with Ehrlichman, Buzhardt, Krogh, Young, and Macomber **7**, 2670
meeting with LaRue and Mitchell on Liddy debriefing report **6**, 2321-22
meeting with Mitchell, Magruder, and Dean afer Watergate **3**, 1035-36
meeting with Mitchell and LaRue **4**, 1671-72
meeting with Sloan after Watergate arrests **2**, 547, 548, 569, 580, 619
meetings after Watergate arrests **2**, 799-800 **5**, 1952, 1953
meetings with Liddy on Ellsberg matter **9**, 3786-87
in meetings with Mitchell, O'Brien, and McPhee **5**, 1906, 1907-1908
meetings with Mitchell after Watergate **5**, 1878, 1879, 1880, 1881, 1883, 1885, 1887, 1931
meetings with Stans and LaRue on Dahlberg check **2**, 738
memo to Malek re Crawford's proposed Black Voter Program **19**, 8742-47E
Mitchell briefed on Watergate by **4**, 1622
and Mitchell's attempts to have Chief Wilson contacted after Watergate break-in **6**, 2331
money given to LaRue **6**, 2291
participation in Watergate coverup **2**, 801-803, 857
on Patman Committee subpoena list **3**, 961
and Plumbers unit **9**, 3772-73
and problems between Magruder and Liddy **3**, 1088
and reports to McCord from Internal Security Division **1**, 237
reports to Mitchell on Liddy's debriefing **4**, 1644
Sloan reports on cash disbursements to **FR** 42
subpoenaed by Patman Committee **3**, 1193E
telephone call to Stans on California trip with Sloan **2**, 776
tells Dean about talk with Nixon on wiretap logs of suspects in leaking **3**, 920
tells Stans to give cash on hand to LaRue after Watergate arrests **2**, 702
and transmission of Justice Department information to Plumbers **9**, 3780
and use of CIA **5**, 1899
wants Dean to get FBI reports on Watergate investigation **3**, 944 **4**, 1358
wants Gray to slow down Watergate investigation **3**, 945
and Watergate coverup **2**, 803, 805, 822
Mardian, Robert C., testimony of 1, 13, 16, 22, 34, 55, 195 **2**, 557, 558, 592, 653, 658, 769, 774, 866 **3**, 949 **4**, 1621 **5**, 1950 **6**, 2345-85, 2387-2436 **9**, 3691
on ABA Code of Professional Responsibility and failure to voice suspicions **6**, 2432-34
on actions after learning truth from Liddy **6**, 2375-76
agrees to review Dean and Magruder testimony **6**, 2388
on approval for Liddy budget **6**, 2429-30
asks LaRue about prior knowledge of break-in **6**, 2391
assigned by Mitchell to handle Watergate legal matters **6**, 2352, 2414

and attorney-client privilege **6**, 2345-46, 2378-79, 2402-2403
on authorization for Watergate break-in **6**, 2394-98
on Bittman's fee **6**, 2394
on briefing from Magruder after Watergate break-in **6**, 2410-12
on calls to Liddy after Watergate arrests **6**, 2352-53
on career after Watergate **6**, 2346, 2347-48
on CIA involvement in Watergate break-in **6**, 2383-84
on confidentiality of Liddy debriefing **6**, 2430-32
on dealings with Liddy while at Justice Department **6**, 2389
on Dean saying he thought Colson was clean **6**, 2381
on Dean's claim that he reviewed FBI reports **6**, 2389-90
on Dean's testimony that he suggested use of CIA **6**, 2368
denies asking for or reading FBI 302 reports **6**, 2370-71
denies involvement in coverup **6**, 2377
denies knowledge about Magruder's perjury **6**, 2371-74
denies knowledge of dirty tricks or Liddy plan **6**, 2347
denies knowledge of discussion of destruction of Gemstone file **6**, 2356-57
denies knowledge of Kalmbach money raising and distributing efforts **6**, 2368-69
denies knowledge of money passed to LaRue **6**, 2364-65
denies meetings with Liddy, Magruder, and LaRue **6**, 2401
denies prior knowledge of Watergate break-in **6**, 2349
denies telling Magruder to erase diary entries **6**, 2374-75
denies wiretap requests by Internal Security Division **6**, 2428-29
on discussion about destruction of documents **6**, 2378
on discussions after news of Watergate break-in **6**, 2412-14
on discussions of Watergate with Mitchell **6**, 2399-2400
on discussions with Mitchell on Liddy's budget **6**, 2416
on duties at CRP **6**, 2348-49
on duties in 1968 campaign **6**, 2348
on efforts to inform MacGregor **6**, 2375, 2403-2404, 2419, 2430-31
on efforts to resign from CRP **6**, 2394
on information to McCord from Internal Security Division **6**, 2398-99, 2427-28
on involvement of White House staff members in Watergate **6**, 2415
joins CRP staff **6**, 2346-47
on Kissinger tapes **6**, 2404-2408
and Kleindienst hearings **6**, 2348
on learning about money disbursed to Liddy **6**, 2363-64
on learning about Watergate break-in **6**, 2349-51

learns about dirty tricks and Black advance from Magruder **6**, 2351-52
legal relationship with Liddy **6**, 2414-15
on Liddy destroying documents **6**, 2362
on Liddy's application for attorney's job at Department of Justice **6**, 2380-81
on Liddy's budget **6**, 2361
on Liddy's claim of authorization for activities from Nixon **6**, 2418-19
on Liddy's opinion of Hunt **6**, 2396
on Liddy's request for bail money **6**, 2362-63
on Magruder lying to Mitchell about amount of money given to Liddy **6**, 2381, 2392
on McCord's allegations that national security was reason for Watergate break-in **6**, 2400
on McCord's testimony on information from Internal Security Division **6**, 2398-99
meetings with Mitchell, Magruder, and LaRue after Watergate break-in **6**, 2350, 2351
on meetings with Parkinson and O'Brien **6**, 2369-70
on memo prepared for Mitchell **6**, 2430, 2432
mistaken for LaRue and vice versa **6**, 2380
on Mitchell's logs **6**, 2379
on Mitchell's order to forget memo on Liddy debriefing **6**, 2403
on Mitchell's press statement after Watergate arrests **6**, 2413-14
on Mitchell's refusal to fire Magruder and Porter **6**, 2430
on money given to Liddy **6**, 2381
on Mrs. Hunt's visit to O'Brien **6**, 2367-68
on Nixon's knowledge about Watergate **6**, 2398
note after telephone conversation with Stans **6**, 2367, 2642E
on objections to Mitchell's press statement **6**, 2375
objections to questions on role in Internal Security Division **6**, 2425-27
opening statement **6**, 2346-47
on passing money from Sloan to LaRue **6**, 2366, 2367
on payments to Watergate defendants **6**, 2367-69
on Pentagon Papers case **6**, 2408-10
on political dissent **6**, 2423
on professional ethics and conscience over Watergate **6**, 2401-2402
on purported comment to Brennan on demonstration leaders **6**, 2435
reaction to Mitchell's press statement after Watergate arrests **6**, 2417-18
on reasons for his involvement in Watergate coverup **6**, 2392
on reasons for not telling Department of Justice about Liddy's revelations **6**, 2416
on reasons why no one discussed coverup with Nixon **6**, 2384
on reelection of Nixon outweighing other considerations **6**, 2377
on relationship with Hoover **6**, 2434
on relationship with Sullivan **6**, 2422
reports to Mitchell on Liddy debriefing **6**, 2362, 2363
on role as head of Internal Security Division of Justice Department **6**, 2420-29
and Sloan **6**, 2365

on Sloan's trip to California **6**, 2300, 2365-66
on talks with Hoover **6**, 2390
on trip to San Clemente in July 1972 to see Nixon **6**, 2392-93
on use of attorney-client privilege **6**, 2382-83
on use of attorneys in Internal Security Division in investigative function **6**, 2434-35
on wanting to resign from CRP **6**, 2377
on Watergate break-in theory **6**, 2415
on White House horror stories **6**, 2401
on White House lack of confidence in FBI and Justice Department **6**, 2390-91
Mardian, Mrs. Robert C. 2, 653
Mardian, Sam 12, 5046E
Mardian Construction Co., Phoenix, Arizona 6, 2348
Marfino, Daniel 20, 9415
Margoulis, Peter 1, 326 **5**, 2130
Marijuana
and assault strategy on McGovern **10**, 4242E
arrests for possession of at Century Plaza demonstration **11**, 4559
legalization of **11**, 4670
McGovern record on **10**, 4067-68E
Marijuana and Dangerous Drugs Task Force 1, 270
Marik, Dr. Robert 1, 10, 35, 57 **19**, 8663E **FR** 302E
memo from Armendariz with final report on Spanish-speaking campaign effort **19**, 8820-34E, 8754-96E
Marine Midland Bank, New York City
and return of Hughes contribution **20**, 9411, 9412 **FR** 1016
Maritime Administration
and American Ship Building Co. claim cost account **FR** 453
Maritime Advisory Committee 10, 4088E
Marks, J. David 25, 11761, 11790, 11809
Marks, Leonard 16, 7471
Marony, Kevin 9, 3574, 3630, 3631
memo from Martin **9**, 3575
Maroulis, Peter 3, 1005 **4**, 1451 **9**, 3635, 3650
and Dean **4**, 1452
Dean requests statement from Liddy from **4**, 1449-50
Dean's memo for file re conversation concerning Liddy with **3**, 1005, 1262E
Mitchell and **4**, 1673
money from LaRue to **6**, 2296
Marriott, John 22, 10708-10709, 10730
F. Donald Nixon and **22**, 10646, 10647
Marriott Corp. 22, 10679
F. Donald Nixon as consultant for **22**, 10674
and F. Donald Nixon's relationship with Meier **22**, 10708-10709
Marschalko, Lajos 12, 5026E
Martin, Dr. Edwin H. 9, 3575, 3898E
Martin, Edward J.
See McCord, James (alias of)
Martin, John 1, 217, 230 **3**, 1056, 1058 **5**, 1949 **9**, 3574 **19**, 9098E **FR** 129
information to CRP from **FR** 146-47, 178-81
and McCord **FR** 146

Martin, Lloyd 3, 1117E
Martin, Mrs. Lloyd 3, 1117E
Martin, Michael, Jr. FR 166, 168
  political espionage activities 11, 4640
Martin, Paul 10, 4130E
Martin, Preston 19, 8604-8605E
  plan for use of Federal resources FR 364
Martin, William FR 492
Martina, Edward 22, 10513
Martinez, Eugenio 1, 51, 108, 234 2, 856 9, 3486, 3755
  arrest of 1, 106
  Barker recruits 1, 375
  CIA comments on Select Committee report on
    FR 1164
  convicted in Fielding break-in FR 15-16
  and Executive clemency 1, 212-213
  expenses of 1, 385
  and Fielding break-in 9, 3676
  and first Watergate break-in FR 28
  Helms on 8, 3263
  information from CIA to FBI on employment of
    9, 3426-37
  involvement in Watergate 1, 375
  and lawyers' meeting 1, 326
  meets with Segretti in Miami 10, 4011-12
  money for 6, 2235, 2252
  relationship with CIA 8,3247-48, 3249 FR 1145-
    49, 1150-51
  role in Watergate break-in 1, 367 FR 1
  See also Cuban Watergate burglars; Plumbers;
    Watergate defendants
Marumoto, William 13, 5350-51, 5532E, 5535E 18,
  8201, 8268, 8269 19, 8633E, 8640E
  and Cabinet Committee FR 396
  Ehrlichman on campaign role of 18, 8197
  Fernandez denies discussions on grants with 13,
    5399-5401
  and grants 18, 8219
  and La Raza Unida FR 399
  letter to Hernandez on support for Nixon's re-
    election FR 401
  Malek disagrees with interpretation of Responsive-
    ness Program by 18, 8278-80
  Malek on role in Responsiveness Program 18,
    8246-55
  and OMBE grants FR 434-35
  preparation of plan on Spanish-speaking campaign
    FR 374
  role in Spanish-speaking efforts FR 381
  Weicker on line of questioning of 13, 5308-10
  "Weekly Report for Brown Mafia" to Colson FR
    383
  and White House Spanish-Speaking Constituent
    Group Task Force 19, 8675-77E
  work relationship with Malek 18, 8204
Marumoto, William, testimony of 13, 5274-5326
  on accomplishments of Nixon Administration 13,
    5302
  on activities after election day 13, 5304
  on AP report of resignation statement 13, 5312-13
  on appointment offer to Hernandez 13, 5294-96
  on Arenas contribution 13, 5324-25

  on attitude of Nixon administration toward Span-
    ish-speaking Americans 13, 5314-15
  on campaign contribution from Arenas 13, 5298-
    5300
  on campaign contributions from Hispanic Ameri-
    can minority enterprises 13, 5298-5300
  on cancellation of SER grant 13, 5312
  on "Capitalizing on the Incumbency" memo 13,
    5278-79
  on career after election 13, 5312
  career background 13, 5274
  on conflicts in testimony during executive session
    of Select Committee 13, 5307
  on contracts for minority enterprises related to
    campaign contributions 13, 5296-5300
  on CRP and Finance Committee and grants to
    Hispanic Americans 13, 5276-77
  on deletion of material in Census Report for 1972
    on status of Spanish-speaking population 13,
    5324
  denies grants were tied in with campaign contri-
    butions 13, 5316-23
  denies violations of Hatch Act 13, 5313-14
  on Development Association grant 13, 5318-20
  on development of Spanish-speaking Federal em-
    ployees list 13, 5286
  on duties at White House 13, 5275-76
  on editorial by NEDA employee opposing Guerra
    appointment as director of OMBE 13, 5279-80
  on efforts to terminate Pena FR 403
  on ending of Sanchez' grant 13, 5302-5303
  on Executive pardon for Tijerina 13, 5315, 5316
  on firing of Pena 13, 5293-94, 5303-5304
  on government appointments for Hispanic Ameri-
    cans 13, 5281-82
  on Government contracts to minority businesses
    13, 5317
  on Government contracts to Spanish-speaking
    firms 13, 5284-85
  on grant for Development Associates 13, 5290-93
  on grant to Mexican American Unity Council FR
    390
  on grant to Service Employment Redevelopment
    13, 5288-89
  on grant to Southwest Council of La Raza FR
    392-93
  on grants for Hispanic Americans 13, 5301-5308
    FR 382
  on grants to persons opposing administration FR
    386-87
  on Hernandez matter 13, 5317-18 FR 402
  on identification of list of grants and contracts for
    Hispanic Americans 13, 5296
  on La Raza Unida grant 13, 5320-22
  on loss of grant by Development Associates FR
    388-89, 390
  on meeting with Ramero of La Luz magazine 13,
    5325-26
  on Nixon Administration achievements 13, 5312-
    13
  opening statement 13, 5274-75
  on organization of Spanish-speaking task force FR
    381-82
  political background 13, 5275-76

on preferential grant-giving **13,** 5280-93

on public announcements of awards and grants by Congressmen and Senators **13,** 5300-5301

on reasons for interest in programs for Hispanic Americans **13,** 5275

on recruiting of Hispanic Americans to Government jobs **13,** 5301

on Responsiveness group **FR** 373

on SER grant **13,** 5312

on soliciting of campaign contributions from Hispanic Americans for Nixon campaign **13,** 5277

on sources and uses of contributions made to National Hispanic Finance Committee **13,** 5304-5305

on Spanish-speaking organizational chart **13,** 5323

on Spanish-speaking voters Responsiveness Program **FR** 380-81

on "Weekly Report for the Brown Mafia" memo **13,** 5278

on weekly reports to Colson and Malek **13,** 5278-96

on White House Responsiveness group and political contributions from grantees or contract receivers **13,** 3505-3506

on work load **13,** 5315-16

on Zazueta attending Democratic Convention as McGovern delegate **13,** 5289-90

Marumoto memos

on appointments of Spanish-speaking persons by Nixon Administration **19,** 8698-8703E

on attempts to fire Pena **FR** 402-403

on grants **FR** 383, 384

to Clarke on appointment of Hernandez to Federal bench in Texas **FR** 401-402

to Clarke on Hernandez **13,** 5323, 5663-65E

to Colson and Malek on activity report for Spanish-speaking (people) **13,** 5323, 5556-87E, 5599-5610E, 5613-16E, 5617-21E, 5624-26E, 5629-34E, 5637-42E, 5643-47E, 5658-62E, 5666-68E, 5670-76E, 5681-84E, 5686-91E, 5692-96E

to Colson and Malek on efforts to hold back Census Bureau report on Spanish-speaking Americans **FR** 404-405

to Colson and Malek on Hernandez **FR** 401

to Colson and Malek on OEO grant to Mexican American Unity Council **FR** 390

to Colson on report for Brown Mafia **13,** 5323, 5536-50E

to Colson on Weekly Activity Report for the Spanish Speaking **13,** 5323, 5551-55E, 5599-5606E, 5607-10E

to Davison on Development Associates **13,** 5323, 5635-36E

to Davison on Sanchez and grant to Development Associates **FR** 387

to Lynn on NEDA editorial **13,** 5400-5401

to Lynn on NEDA grant **FR** 390-91

to Malek and Colson on President's participation in Spanish-Speaking Activities **19,** 8641-49E

to Rodriguez and Armendariz on Romero **13,** 5323, 5611-12E

from Armendariz on characteristics of persons and families of Mexican, Puerto Rican, and other Spanish origin **13,** 5323, 5627-28E

from Armendariz on La Raza Unida **13,** 5678E

from Malek on OMBE grants **13,** 5323, 5542E

Marx, Gene 16, 7068

Marx, Louis

FBI interview of **7,** 2661-63, 2664-65

and Hoover **7,** 2671-72

and Hoover's reluctance to investigate Ellsberg case **7,** 2663-64

Maryland Committee for the Re-Election of the President 2, 714

Massad, L. A.

memo to authorized signers in Hertz Corp. **25,** 12325E

Massiah v. *U.S.*. **9,** 3486

Masters, Frank D. 14, 5925, 5968 **15,** 6525,6526, 6773 **16,** 7312

and AMPI reimbursement scheme **FR** 922

billings to AMPI for legal fees and expenses **16,** 6968, 6981E

billings to MPI for legal fees and expenses **16,** 6944, 6974-80E

check and invoice from AMPI **16,** 6943, 6973E

check from AMPI **16,** 6950, 6982E

check from MPI to **16,** 6947, 6982E

involvement in AMPI payback scheme **15,** 6529 **FR** 609-10

and repayment to Lilly **14,** 5967

Masters, Frank D., testimony of 16, 6937-72

on annual income in 1969 and 1970 **16,** 6953

on billings to AMPI **16,** 6943-52, 6953, 6957-58

on budget discussions at AMPI board meetings **16,** 6955-57

career **16,** 6937-38

on cash contributions to Lilly **16,** 6969-72

on contacts with Lilly **16,** 6939

on contacts with Nelson **16,** 6938-39

on contribution to Humphrey campaign **16,** 6966-67

on contribution to Mills for presidential campaign **16,** 6953-54, 6964-65

on contributions to Muskie's presidential campaign **16,** 6967

denies contribution to Nixon campaign **16,** 6967

denies knowledge of AMPI destruction of documents **16,** 6959

denies knowledge of AMPI or TAPE political contributions to presidential campaigns **16,** 6959-60

denies knowledge of political contributions by AMPI or TAPE **16,** 6941-42

denies knowledge of Valentine, Sherman relationship with AMPI **16,** 6960-61

denies knowledge of Wagner & Baroody **16,** 6961

denies reimbursement for contributions **16,** 6943, 6966-67

denies solicitations for political contributions from AMPI employees **16,** 6965-68

on duties for AMPI **16,** 6938-39

on exhibits requested by Select Committee **16,** 6972

on formation of TAPE **16,** 6939

on import quotas issue **16,** 6967-68

on law firms associated with **16,** 6937-38

on lawyers involved in antitrust suit against AMPI **16,** 6958

Masters, Frank D., testimony of *(Continued)*
on lawyers representing AMPI **16**, 6939-40, 6961-64
on Lilly soliciting contributions for State Democratic Party in Austin, Texas **16**, 6940-43, 6948, 6952-53, 6954-55
on motivations for political contributions to Lilly **16**, 6954-55
on relations with other dairy coops **16**, 6938, 6968
on role in antitrust suit against AMPI **16**, 6957-59
on source of funds for political contributions to Lilly **16**, 6943
Masters and McManus
See Masters, Frank D., testimony of
Mastrangelo 19, 8607E
Mastrovito, Michael FR 1157
Mathis, Anthony 16, 7235 **FR** 670
Matukonis, J. A. 11, 4857E
May Day demonstrations 4, 1447-48 **6**, 2425
McGovern on **10**, 4244E
Maye, Mike 19, 8815E
Mayflower Hotel, Washington, D.C.
Dean-Kalmbach meeting in **4**, 1511-14, 1515
letter stating Kalmbach was not registered between June 1 and July 1, 1972 **5**, 2209E
Segretti at **10**, 4024
Mays, John 16, 7075
McCandless, Robert C.
See also Dean, John W., III, testimony of
McCann, Dr. Kevin FR 781E
McCarthy, Eugene 4, 1557 **10**, 3969-70, 4198E **25**, 12111, 12157, 12158
bogus letter to delegates for **10**, 4026, 4296-97E
bogus letters on attempt to sabotage McGovern candidacy **10**, 4026, 4301E
Mott and **25**, 12098
Mott campaign contribution to **25**, 12116
older voters in Gallup polls and **19**, 9079E
in primaries **10**, 4229E
Segretti actions against **10**, 4002-4003
McCarthy, Joe 2, 855
McCarthy hearings 3, 985
McCarthyism 1, 8 **17**, 7697
McCaughan, J. W. 22, 12536E
McClellan, George B. 3, 1331E **4**, 1557
McClintock, Lynn Rae 22, 10267
McCloskey, Paul N. 1, 23, 396 **3**, 1134E
McCloskey, Pete 25, 12118 **FR** 153
attack strategy for **10**, 4188E
business community supporters **3**, 1136-37E
Caulfield directs Ulasewicz to investigate New Hampshire campaign of **FR** 116-17
and Florida primary **10**, 4193-95E
intelligence information on New Hampshire campaign of **3**, 926, 1134-48E
literature against **25**, 12194
Magruder on **10**, 4178-79E
memo from Khachigian to Buchanan on **10**, 4193E

McCloskey campaign 10, 4173E
and Caulfield **3**, 925 **4**, 1605
Colson and bogus contributions to **FR** 197-98
funding of **3**, 1137-38E
McCone
cablegrams from Richardson to **9**, 3809
McCord, James W., Jr. 1, 12, 35, 45, 51, 108, 112, 116 **2**, 514 **3**, 1173E **4**, 1621, 1661 **6**, 2220
Alch on **1**, 313-314, 316-319, 321, 323-325, 329-330, 330-333, 346, 350-352
Alch on motivation for Watergate break-in **1**, 336-37
Alch on reasons for silence **1**, 299
Alch on relationship with **1**, 294-310, 312-56
allegations about Dean and Magruder **9**, 3532
allegations that Democratic party was threat to national security **6**, 2400
anonymous letter to Caulfield **FR** 63-64
and approval of Liddy plan **5**, 1846
arrest of **1**, 46, 106, 113, 128, 187 **2**, 727, 729, 798-99, 815, 828, 859 **3**, 932
article in *Armed Forces Journal* **9**, 3485-87, 3521-22, 3542, 3543, 3848-49E
assigns Baldwin to monitor visitors to Kennedy's senatorial office **FR** 119
bail for **1**, 305-307, 321, 323 **4**, 1662
and Bailey **4**, 1574-75
and Baldwin **1**, 409
Baldwin takes van to home of **9**, 3737
and Baldwin's involvement in Watergate break-in **1**, 398-406, 411-13
and Baldwin's surveillance activities **1**, 395-96, 397
Barker and **1**, 361
Barker on role of **1**, 376
belief of legality of Watergate **1**, 341-342, 353-354
believed double agent **2**, 798-99
on Bittenbender perjury **9**, 3445
and Caldwell **1**, 302-303
calls to foreign embassies **1**, 276, 298, 320, 338-40 **3**, 975-76, 1236-37E **9**, 3442
Caulfield on relationship with **1**, 253-60, 264-67
Caulfield's meetings with **1**, 257-58
Caulfield's offer of Executive clemency to **1**, 271-73 **3**, 974-76 **7**, 2771
Caulfield's reasons for messages to **1**, 275-276
CIA background **8**, 3237, 3247, 3249
Colson tells Ehrlichman about stories he is telling **7**, 2801
CRP payments to **1**, 52
Cushman states he doesn't know **8**, 3302
Danner on discussions of testimony of **24**, 11561-62
Dean on **4**, 1378-79
Dean tells Nixon he doubts silence of **4**, 1545
Dean's messages to **1**, 318, 326
discussion on having Bailey meet with **4**, 1580
discussion with Barker on Executive clemency **1**, 362-63
document on relevancy of intercepted communications **3**, 976, 1236-37E
during Magruder's testimony at trial **1**, 343-44

and efforts to bug McGovern headquarters **FR** 27-28

in Ehrlichman-Kleindienst taped conversation **7,** 2749, 2945E

electronic bugging devices placed in O'Brien's and Oliver's telephones by **FR** 28-29

and electronic surveillance portion of Gemstone plan **9,** 3747

Executive clemency offers to **3,** 1079-80 **9,** 3795

and FBI interview of Sloan **2,** 565

FBI requests for W-4 forms of **1,** 26

fee paid to Alch by **1,** 312

and Fensterwald **1,** 322-23, 346

Fensterwald on **7,** 3012-15E

files of **1,** 53

finances of **1,** 333

and Gemstone plan **9,** 3765

Gray on FBI efforts to interview **9,** 3485-86

and Greenspun break-in **7,** 2801

and Gregory **FR** 197

and guilty plea **1,** 336-37

and hearsay evidence **4,** 1523

Helms on responsibilities at CIA **8,** 3250, 3259-60

hiring by CRP **1,** 253, 270-271

hiring of Baldwin by **9,** 3736

and Hughes Tool Co. **20,** 9403-9404

Hunt discusses Baldwin with **9,** 3714-15

Hunt on role in Watergate break-in **9,** 3710-11

in Hunt's notes **9,** 3838E

and Hunt's theory that Baldwin was double agent **9,** 3738

impact on Watergate principals **2,** 806-807

information from Internal Security Division to **2,** 824 **3,** 1056-57, 1073 **6,** 2427-28

informs Caulfield he will testify on Watergate break-in **FR** 65-66

and involvement of CRP in Watergate break-in **6,** 2319

and knowledge of plan for Greenspun break-in **20,** 9402

and Las Vegas plan **20,** 9393

legal fees **1,** 359

and legality of Watergate **1,** 356

letter to Alch on plan to prove wiretap on his telephone **1,** 339-340

letter to Caulfield **1,** 280-83

letter to Sirica **1,** 186-87, 303, 306-307, 321-322, 342-346 **2,** 640, 641, 643 **3,** 1002-1003 **4,** 1385, 1422, 1550-51 **5,** 1913-14, 1930, 2005 **FR** 27-28

impact on Stans **2,** 731-32

and unravelling of Watergate coverup **FR** 82-83

letters to Helms and others at CIA **9,** 3440-47

Liddy on **6,** 2359, 2396

Liddy speaks to Kleindienst about release of Watergate burglars **FR** 32

Liddy tells Dean about role in Watergate break-in of **3,** 933

logs of intercepted telephone conversations at Democratic National Committee given to Liddy **FR** 29

and logs of wiretapped conversations from Baldwin **1,** 401, 410-11

Magruder denies knowledge of his participation in Liddy's plan **2,** 793

and Magruder's worries over Watergate coverup **2,** 805

and Martin **FR** 146

meets with Caulfield **FR** 64-65, 65-66

memo to Alch on "Shift of Focus of Publicity" **1,** 297-98

memos of wiretaps to Harmony **2,** 466-67

memos taken by Baldwin from bag of **1,** 406-407

messages from Dean through Caulfield to **3,** 1089

Mitchell on **4,** 1613, 1632

in Mitchell's press statement after Watergate arrests **6,** 2413

Mitchell's relationship with **4,** 1649-50 **5,** 1824-25

on Mitchell's role in Watergate break-in **4,** 1620

moves Baldwin to Howard Johnson Motel **1,** 395

Mrs. Hunt and **6,** 2243

Nixon's knowledge about **4,** 1382

note to Caulfield **1,** 315-16

note to Caulfield on CIA taking blame for Watergate **3,** 974, 1235E

O'Brien on behavior of **7,** 2736

O'Brien memo to Nixon on **3,** 1162E

Odle and **1,** 27, 29

Odle on arrest of **1,** 42-43

office space at White House **1,** 88

official post of **9,** 3750

Pennington break-in at home of **FR** 1127-30

plan on wiretapping **1,** 281-83

and plan to blame CIA for Watergate **1,** 300, 313-16, 321-22, 328-29, 334-35, 350-51

polygraph test suggested by Alch for **1,** 335, 336

possible indictment of **1,** 295-96

proposed book by **1,** 297, 320-21, 333

reaction to pleading guilty to one charge and being Government witness **1,** 349

recapitulation of testimony by Baker **1,** 154-155

receives revolver from LaRue **1,** 253

recipient of data obtained by **5,** 2011

recollection of Hunt's comments **1,** 297

recruitment of Baldwin by **1,** 391-93

refuses hush money **FR** 59

relationship with Alch during trial **1,** 304-305, 343-44, 349-53

relationship with Liddy **1,** 54

request by Baker for further information from **1,** 191-192

requests to testify again **1,** 311-12

on responsibilities of Plumbers during Watergate break-in **1,** 158

retained as consultant to Security Consulting Groups **3,** 1126E

role at CRP **1,** 38

role in Watergate break-in **1,** 367-69 **9,** 3713, 3714 **FR** 1

says fair trial is impossible **9,** 3446

says Liddy told him Mitchell approved Watergate break-in plan **6,** 2304

selection of Alch as his attorney **1,** 341

signature on record of time of arrival and departure from 315 9th St., N.W., Washington, D.C. **FR** 273-76E

silence doubted **5,** 1862

skill as wireman **1,** 292

talks with other Watergate defendants **1,** 342-43

telephone call to Odle **1,** 42-43

telephone message to Porter from **2,** 662

McCord, James W., Jr. *(Continued)*
   tells Alch of Mitchell's approval of Watergate operation **1**, 341-42
   testimony on intelligence reports to Sloan and Stans **7**, 2976-77E
   threatens to implicate Parkinson **7**, 2734
   Ulasewicz and **1**, 279-80, 285-92 **6**, 2270-71
   and wiretap plan **1**, 338-340
McCord, James W., Jr. testimony of 20, 9401-9402 **24**, 11603
   on attempt to blame CIA **1**, 206-208
   attempts to enter McGovern headquarters **1**, 164
   on attitude toward Watergate break-in **1**, 125
   attorneys for **1**, 187
   on automobile used by Caulfield **1**, 237
   on Baldwin's monitoring of wiretap **1**, 232-233
   on bugging of CRP **1**, 203-205
   on CIA involvement in Watergate **1**, 129-130
   contacts with Dean **1**, 176
   on contingency plan in event of arrest **1**, 175
   on cost of political espionage **1**, 184-85
   demonstration of wiretapping by **1**, 235-237
   on deniability for Mitchell in Watergate **1**, 218-19
   on electronic surveillance of Muskie and McGovern **1**, 153-54
   on Ellsberg case **1**, 171
   on employment at Republican National Committee **1**, 205-206
   on employment in CRP **1**, 151, 183
   on Executive clemency offers **1**, 208-210, 231-32 **FR** 63-66
   first knowledge of political espionage plan **1**, 183-84
   on first Watergate break-in **1**, 156-58, 164 **FR** 28
   on Government denial of tap on his telephone **1**, 139
   on hiring and arming of Baldwin **1**, 158-159
   on identity cards **1**, 175
   on illegality of his activities **1**, 159, 165
   on illegality of Watergate operation **1**, 171-75
   on income **1**, 216, 220-21
   on information from Internal Security Department **1**, 178-81, 217-18, 221-24, 229-32, 237, 246-47
   on involvement of Mitchell, Magruder, and Dean in political espionage **1**, 142-49
   on involvement of Nixon and Mitchell in Watergate **1**, 163-64
   on involvement with Liddy **1**, 126-28
   on Las Vegas matter **1**, 202
   on letter to Caulfield on effort to blame CIA for Watergate **1**, 196-97
   on Liddy's character **1**, 149
   on Magruder's perjury at trial **1**, 241-42, 244
   on meeting with Mitchell and Magruder **1**, 146-48
   on Mitchell's reported involvement in Watergate **1**, 233-34
   on money found on Plumbers **1**, 149, 210, 241
   on money received after arrest **1**, 130
   on motivation for activities **1**, 128-29, 159-160, 166-68, 199-203
   on offers of Executive clemency **1**, 161-62, 228-29
   opening statement **1**, 125
   on payments from Liddy **1**, 188
   on pressures applied to Watergate defendants to blame Watergate on CIA **1**, 192-99

on pressures to plead guilty and remain silent **1**, 131-41, 149-53
on professional background **1**, 125-26
on reasons for not telling Alch about alleged involvement of Dean and Mitchell in Watergate break-in **1**, 242-243
on reasons for prior silence about political pressure on **1**, 141
on reasons for silence at trial **1**, 242-43, 247-48
on reasons for taking Fifth Amendment in regard to contact with Mardian **1**, 177-78
on reasons for turning down Executive clemency offers **1**, 232
on relationship between Liddy and Magruder **1**, 149
on relationship with Barker **1**, 210-12
on relationship with Caulfield **1**, 182-83
on relationship with Mitchell **1**, 162-63
on reports of violence in Miami **1**, 234
on role in CRP **1**, 126
on rumor of Baldwin being double agent **1**, 226-227
on Russell **1**, 218
on salary and expenses for Watergate operations **1**, 168-70
on "Sanction of the Watergate Operation" **1**, 199-202
on sources of Executive clemency offer **1**, 167-68
on suspected wiretapping of his telephone **1**, 198-99, 227-28, 243-46
on telephone calls to local embassies **1**, 219-20
on telephone conversations with Baldwin **1**, 225-27
on trip to Florida **1**, 187-88
on typing of wiretap logs by Harmony **1**, 233
on use of tapes on door during Watergate break-in **1**, 238-41
on violence threatened against CRP **1**, 174-75
on Watergate break-in participants **1**, 234-35
on Watergate trial **1**, 241-242
on White House control of CIA **1**, 195-96
McCord and Associates 9, 3487
McCormack, John W. 7, 2797
McCracken, Dr. 14, 6061, 6062, 6063
McCrea, Sloan 22, 12530E **24**, 11281, 11310
McCroskey, Sam 14, 6296
McDonald, Merle 11, 4705E
McDonald, Robert 20, 9432, 9433
McDonald, Steve FR 561-62
McDowell, James 12, 5126E
McDowell, Joseph E. 3, 1141E
McEvoy, John 11, 4774E, 4817E
McGahan, Pat 25, 12023
McGinn, John 12, 5113E
McGinnis, Joe 10, 3970
McGovern, George 1, 26, 172, 174, 396 **10**, 4198E **12**, 4927, 5046E
   affidavit denying knowing McMinoway **11**, 4743E
   after Watergate **11**, 4625
   agents from Muskie campaign transferred to **9**, 3761-62
   and anti-Humphrey activities of **11**, 4525-27, 4608-4609

anti-Muskie activities of workers of **11**, 4485-86, 4501-4502, 4515-16, 4522-24, 4524-25
attitude of ADEPT toward **14**, 5888
attitude toward demonstrations **11**, 4573
Barker's attitude toward **1**, 382
bogus pamphlet about Humphrey and **11**, 4492-93
book by Buchanan and Khachigian on **10**, 3975, 4240-46E
Buchanan and ads against **10**, 3928-30
Buchanan memo on **11**, 4606
Buchanan on **10**, 3921, 3925-26
Buchanan on name calling by **10**, 3936
Buchanan on political memos on **10**, 3961-63
Buchanan on reasons for Democratic party nomination of **10**, 3901-3902
Caulfield on investigation of fundraising by **21**, 9727-28
circular entitled "George McGovern's Real Record on the War" **10**, 4026, 4298E **11**, 4387
Davis' attitude toward **22**, 10564
and demonstrations against Nixon **8**, 3081
dirty tricks against **11**, 4611-12, 4627-31 **12**, 5017
efforts to connect with communists **8**, 3205-3206
and Ellsberg **12**, 5019E
financing of United Farmworkers demonstration against Nixon **12**, 4950-51, 4954, 4959, 4960
FTS telephone lines **25**, 12196
fundraising by **3**, 1180E
Haldeman requests political intelligence on **6**, 2455
hiring of Tuck by **7**, 2876 **11**, 4616
impact of dirty tricks against Humphrey on **11**, 4613-14
impact of dirty tricks against Muskie on **11**, 4612-13, 4614
impact of dirty tricks on **11**, 4603-4604, 4684
information from Secret Service to Colson on **FR** 148
and Jews for McGovern-Shriver **12**, 4968, 4973
La Raza Unida promises to condemn **FR** 398, 399
and leaflets linking Nixon with Nazis **12**, 4970, 4973
letter to Ervin on campaign debt settlements and transfer of funds to senatorial campaign **FR** 556-58
letter to Ervin re his campaign financing **25**, 12214-18E, 12219-20E
letter to Hall on wheat sales to Soviets **10**, 4090-94E
letter to Montoya concerning recognition of McMinoway **11**, 4588-89, 4617, 4743E
letters campaign on abortion stand of **10**, 4256-58E
in Los Angeles see Taigher, Frederick Joseph, testimony of
and Los Angeles demonstration against Nixon **9**, 3606-3607
MacGregor statement on **12**, 5019-20E
Mankiewicz's role in campaign of **11**, 4604-4605
and material from Internal Security Division of Justice Department **11**, 4631
material published about **10**, 3934, 4059-4106E
McMinoway and **11**, 4717E
and Meany **10**, 4060E

meeting with AMPI representatives **16**, 7009-10
meeting with Mehren **16**, 7313
memo from Buchanan on campaign of **10**, 4259-63E
memo from Buchanan to Haldeman on "McGovern Assault Book" **10**, 3975, 4252-53E
memo from Buchanan to Macgregor, Haldeman, and Colson on political suggestions for attacks on **10**, 3975, 4254-55E
memo from Buchanan to Mitchell and Haldeman about manner of responses of **10**, 3975, 4248-49E
memo from Buchanan to Mitchell and Haldeman about strategy on **10**, 3975, 4235E, 4237-39E
memo from Colson to Dean about checks on key staff members of **10**, 3975, 4247E
and memo on communist money behind demonstrations **8**, 3171-74
and Middle East issue **11**, 4582-86
Mott's decision to support **25**, 12095-96
Mott's role in **11**, 4600
Muskie supporters blame for dirty tricks **11**, 4669-70, 4671
newspaper advertisements against **10**, 4026, 4275-78E
Nixon believes responsible for student demonstrations **3**, 1100E
and "Nixon Is Treyf" leaflet **12**, 4967, 4970, 4973
Ohio headquarters broken into **10**, 3970
older voters in Gallup polls and **19**, 9079E
and peace movement **3**, 1242E
and Pentagon Papers **10**, 3914
in Philadelphia **11**, 4712E
plan for unsigned booklet on **FR** 205
and plan to spy on Agnew's plane **12**, 5010
political intelligence on **3**, 923, 924, 934 **6**, 2470, 2476 **9**, 3685-86, 3689 **11**, 4626-27
in primaries **10**, 4168E, 4229E, 4232E
report to CRP from Secret Service agent on **23**, 10942
response to assault strategy against **10**, 4248-49E
Secret Service report to Dean on **3**, 1071-72
Segretti activities against **10**, 3983, 4005-4006, 4011
and Segretti's activities against Muskie **10**, 4031-32
and Segretti's activities in Florida primary **10**, 4020-21
and Spanish-speaking voters **19**, 8771-73E
staff members added to enemies list **4**, 1707-11E
Stearns on **11**, 4567, 4568, 4569, 4574, 4581
stories linking him to communist money **10**, 3972-74
suggested speakers against **10**, 4245E
as target of Gemstone plan **9**, 3747
transcript of interview on *Today Show* **10**, 4095-97E
unsigned article from *Time* magazine against **10**, 3933, 3934
Van Dyk gives summary of Gallup polls to **16**, 7006-7007
vetoes spy plan **12**, 5184E
victory in California **11**, 4714E
and violence against Nixon campaign **8**, 3149-53

McGovern, George *(Continued)*
See also McGovern campaign
"McGovern Assault Book"
  memo from Buchanan to Haldeman on **10**, 3975,
    4252-53E
McGovern campaign
  and anti-Nixon leaflets **12**, 5056-58E
  and anti-war demonstration in Boston **12**, 5114E
  attempted break-in at headquarters of **9**, 3792 **FR**
    27-28, 197
  Citizens for Liberal Alternative pamphlet planted
    in **FR** 158
  debt settlements by **FR** 554-57
  and Gregory **FR** 197
  impact of Segretti's dirty tricks on **FR** 173
  and labor unions **FR** 551
  letter for Taugher to Dash on **25**, 12419-20E
  Liddy instructions on **FR** 27
  Masters denies contribution to **16**, 6967
  McCord's attempts to enter **1**, 164, 399-400
  and McMinoway **FR** 195-96
  McMinoway aid to anti-Muskie activities of **11**,
    4485
  McMinoway as member of security staff at Miami
    convention headquarters of **11**, 4497-4500, 4519-
    20
  McMinoway infiltration of **11**, 4492-94, 4715E
  McMinoway on infiltration of **11**, 4556, 4715-16E
  McMinoway's testimony on anti-Muskie activity
    by **11**, 4617-18
  memo from Buchanan to MacGregor about points
    of weakness in **10**, 3975, 4250-51E
  memo from Failor to Magruder on confrontations
    with **12**, 5017, 5265-66E
  memo from Howard to Failor on McGovern Plat-
    form booklet **FR** 360E
  memo on disruptions of **FR** 354-57E
  Mott financial commitment to **25**, 12116-18
  and Mott's negative advertising **25**, 12106
  and Muniz campaign **18**, 8254
  plan for electronic surveillance of **1**, 153-54, 184
  preparation of pass by Harmony for **2**, 463
  surveillance of **4**, 1622
  transfer of funds from Presidential to senatorial
    committees **FR** 553-54, 557-58
  and Tuck **25**, 12115
  union support for **FR** 511
  use of telephones in Los Angeles headquarters for
    demonstration organizers **FR** 208-209
  workers on list given by Dean to Walters **FR** 133
  and Young Voters for the President demonstra-
    tions **FR** 200-201
  See also Brindze, Paul, testimony of; Mott, Ste-
    wart, statement of; Pearlman, Marian, testimony
    of; Rubin, Miles L., statement of; Stearns, Rich-
    ard G., testimony of
McGovern Campaign Committee
  campaign irregularities **12**, 5120-24E
  transfer of funds from McGovern for President,
    Inc., to **25**, 12177

McGovern Central Control Fund
  gift to Farm Workers Political Education Fund
    FR 512
"McGovern Record--A Critical Appraisal, The" 10,
  3934, 4061-87E
McGovern workers
  and anti-Nixon leaflets **12**, 5059-60E
  McMinoway document on infiltration in Miami of
    11, 4556, 4717E
  McMinoway on types of **11**, 4532
McGowan, Joe 24, 11638
McGrath, Eugene 24, 11403
  correspondence with Danner **24**, 11393, 11460-62,
    11512-18E
McGrath, James 3, 1058, 1066
McGrory, Mary 8, 3155
  on enemies list **4**, 1696E, 1698E
McGuire, Dick 15, 6525
McGuire, Joseph 12, 5115E
McHale, James A. 12, 5174E
McKean, John 25, 12195-96
McKenna, Terry 14, 5966
McKenna (FBI agent) 1, 390
McKenzie, Barbara 11, 4543, 4571, 4572, 4573-74,
  4575
McKenzie, Donald 12, 5109E
McKiernan, Stanley W.
  Buzhardt informs of newspaper story on Rebozo
    giving Hughes money to Nixon's brothers and
    Woods **22**, 10546-49
  Buzhardt on contacts with **23**, 10904
  on contacts with F. Donald Nixon after learning
    of Kalmbach's testimony **22**, 10716, 10717
  discussions with Buzhardt on Nixon brothers tes-
    tifying before Select Committee **23**, 10906
  efforts to contact Rebozo and Woods after Kalm-
    bach testimony **22**, 10728-29
  on F. Donald Nixon's Separation & Recovery
    Systems investment **22**, 10702
  on Hallamore Homes stock transaction in booklet
    on Nixon brothers **22**, 10697-98
  on IRS meeting with F. Donald Nixon **22**, 10705
  letter to Ervin and Baker on treatment of F. Do-
    nald and Edward Nixon **23**, 10975-77, 10984-
    87E
  mailgram to Ervin on Nixon brothers' inability to
    comply with new subpoena **23**, 10988E
  mailgram to Muse on documents requested from
    Nixon brothers--**23**, 10990E
  meeting with Nixon brothers **22**, 10719-22, 10723-
    24 **23**, 11024-25
  memo for Nixon on F. Donald and Edward Nix-
    on **23**, 10906
  on memo to Nixon on meeting **22**, 10723
  pamphlet on Nixon brothers **23**, 11071
  telegram from Muse on compliance with subpoena
    for Nixon brothers **23**, 10898E
  transcript of executive session testimony of Ed-
    ward C. and F. Donald Nixon given to **23**,
    10977
  See also Nixon, Edward C., deposition of; Nixon,
    F. Donald, deposition of

McKiernan, Stanley W., deposition of 22, 10615-35, 10637-63

appointment of Mitchell as liaison with Nixon brothers 22, 10641
attempts to contact Frates 22, 10620
attempts to contact Kalmbach on his testimony on Hughes contribution 22, 10619
attitude toward Mitchell 22, 10644-45
attitude toward Watergate break-in 22, 10639
Buzhardt as liaison in White House for Nixon brothers 22, 10621-22
claims no correspondence exists for Edward C. Nixon 22, 10617
on contact with White House representative on Nixon brothers 22, 10637-38
on contacts with Miller on booklet on Nixon brothers 22, 10638-40
denies knowledge of Nixon brothers' meetings with Ehrlichman, Haldeman, and Mitchell 22, 10640-42
denies White House investigation of Watergate Committee 22, 10659
on destruction of memo sent to Nixon 22, 10658-59
on discussion of electronic surveillance of F. Donald Nixon at meeting with Nixon brothers 22, 10626
on discussion with Buzhardt on *Vesco* case 22, 10621
on discussion with Nixon on effect of adverse publicity on F. Donald Nixon's relationship with Marriott 22, 10630
on discussion with Nixon on F. Donald Nixon's activities 22, 10633
on discussion with Nixon on Hughes contribution 22, 10632-33
on discussions on Meier and Hatsis paying F. Donald Nixon's travel expenses 22, 10645-48
on discussions with Buzhardt 22, 10617-22, 10633-34
on efforts to contact Frates 22, 10653
on F. Donald Nixon's business transactions 22, 10643-44
on first knowledge of Hughes contribution and Rebozo 22, 10651-52
on meeting with Nixon 22, 10634, 10635, 10656-58
on meeting with Richard M., F. Donald, and Edward C. Nixon on *Vesco* case and Watergate investigation 22, 10622-30
on meeting with Wilson 22, 10653-55
on meetings with Buzhardt 22, 10648-53
on memo on meeting with Nixon brothers on *Vesco* case and Watergate investigation 22, 10624-25, 10627-28
on murder of Cleveland's associates 22, 10642-43
on Nixon's attitude toward full disclosure to Watergate Committee 22, 10632
on preparation of booklet on Nixon brothers 22, 10645-46
on reaction of Buzhardt and F. Donald Nixon to full disclosure concept 22, 10631-32
on receiving copies of transcript 22, 10661-63
on relationship with Nixon brothers 22, 10637
on report to Mitchell on Nixon brothers 22, 10638, 10640
on report to Nixon on Watergate Committee interviews of Nixon brothers 22, 10658
on search for booklet on Nixon brothers 22, 10652
on subpoena for Edward Nixon 22, 10615-17
on White House reaction to giving booklet on Nixon brothers to Senate Watergate Committee 22, 10630-31
on wiretapping of F. Donald Nixon 22, 10659-61

McKiernan, Stanley W., testimony of 23, 10977-83
on agreement with Select Committee counsel on oral modification of list of materials called for in subpoena for F. Donald and Edward C. Nixon 23, 10979-83
on reading letter to Ervin and Baker into record 23, 10977

McLaren, Richard W. 16, 7442-43 20, 9455
affidavit of 17, 7977-84E
affidavit on Dunes Hotel acquisition and Justice Department Antitrust Division 26, 12851-56E
and "anticrime" factor in Dunes decision FR 992-94
and antitrust suit against AMPI 17, 7682, 7688
Danner and 20, 9576-77
on discussions with Mitchell on Dunes Hotel acquisition matter FR 990-91
and Dunes acquisition matter FR 989-91, 993-98
on filing suit against AMPI FR 708
forwarding of memo on antitrust suit against AMPI to Mitchell FR 700-701
Harrison on confirmation of 17, 7687
and Hoover memo on Dunes Hotel acquisition 26, 12878E, 12879E, 12899-12901E FR 991-92, 997-98
letter to Dorsen on *U.S.* v. *AMPI* 17, 8151-54E
memo for attorney general on Dunes Hotel acquisition by Hughes 26, 12876-77E, 12897-98E
memo from Mitchell on antitrust suit against AMPI FR 768-69
on Mitchell and Hayes letter to Metzner FR 996
on Mitchell's rejection of request for grand jury investigation of AMPI FR 701-702

McLaughlin, Delbert J.
See Benz, Robert M.

McLaughlin, Joe 11, 4711E

McLauglin, John 22, 10367, 10368

McLean, Joe 12, 5114-15E

McMahan, Ron 13, 5414, 5429

McMinoway, Michael W. 2, 659 11, 4531, 4705-4706E
affidavit from McGovern denying knowing 11, 4743E
Barash on testimony of 12, 5267-72E
communication with Stone during political spying operations 11, 4402
Democratic candidates' headquarters infiltrated by 11, 4480, 4482-83
diary of activities of 11, 4402-4403, 4531, 4556, 4705-06E, 4709-11
document of on infiltration of McGovern staff in Miami 11, 4556, 4717E
letter from McGovern to Montoya concerning recognition of 11, 4588, 4743E
Mankiewicz on activities of 11, 4616-18

McMinoway, Michael W. *(Continued)*
McGovern's letter to Montoya denying he has ever met **11**, 4588-89
money received by **11**, 4639
notes on Wisconsin Muskie primary **11**, 4707-4708E
political analysis of California **11**, 4556, 4714E
political analysis of Philadelphia **11**, 4556, 4712-13E
predictions on Wisconsin primaries **11**, 4708E
record of financial transactions with Rainer **11**, 4556, 4718E
resume of activities of **11**, 4556, 4703-04E
and Sedan Chair II **FR** 192-96
Southwick affidavit denying knowing **11**, 4892-95E

McMinoway, Michael W., testimony of
on activities at Democratic National Convention **11**, 4496-4500
on activities in California primary campaigns **11**, 4492-94
on aliases used by **11**, 4492
on attitude of Humphrey campaigners toward **11**, 4489-90
attitudes toward political intelligence gathering **11**, 4505-13, 4530-36
on belief that he was working for Republican party **11**, 4480
on contact for political spying assignment **11**, 4478-79
on contacts with Stone after Watergate break-in **11**, 4494-95
denies contact with Republican National Committee or White House **11**, 4501
denies fraud **11**, 4510-11
denies knowing Segretti **11**, 4491-92
denies knowing Zimmer **11**, 4491
denies use of code names **11**, 4501
denies violation of Florida Criminal Code **11**, 4521
on difference between his activities and Watergate break-in **11**, 4495-496
on disruption of Humphrey fundraising dinner in California **11**, 4525-26
on effects of infiltration on Humphrey campaign **11**, 4493-94
on effects of infiltration on Muskie campaign **11**, 4483-85
on FBI investigation **11**, 4478
on first contact with Stone **11**, 4478, 4479-80
on future actions **11**, 4536
on giving Muskie schedule to Humphrey supporters **11**, 4523-24
on hiring as security guard for McGovern headquarters **11**, 4503, 4519-20, 4532
on identity of employer **11**, 4519, 4520-21
on income from intelligence gathering reported in income tax return **11**, 4519
on infiltration of Humphrey campaign in Philadelphia **11**, 4486-91
on infiltration of McGovern headquarters in Washington, D.C. **11**, 4556, 4715-16E
on instructions from Stone **11**, 4529
on intelligence gathering between Democratic

party primary candidates **11**, 4502, 4514-16
on intelligence gathering vs. demonstrating and radical disruption as more injurious to political system **11**, 4528-29
on learning about Watergate break-in **11**, 4494-95
on learning of Strachan's testimony about use of his reports **11**, 4479-80
on materials obtained for Stone by **11**, 4480-81
on McGovern campaign workers heckling Muskie **11**, 4501-4502
on McGovern supporters demonstrating against Muskie **11**, 4515-16, 4522-24
on McGovern victory **11**, 4715-16E
on meeting with Barash **11**, 4519-20
on method of infiltrating Muskie headquarters in Milwaukee **11**, 4481-82
on newspaper reporters infiltrating political campaigns **11**, 4530
on payments received from Stone **11**, 4479
on Philadelphia diary **11**, 4487-91
on political background **11**, 4478, 4511-12, 4521, 4529
recommendations for laws on political ethics **11**, 4518-19
on role as security guard at Democratic National Convention **11**, 4502-4505, 4510, 4529
on transmission of materials to Stone **11**, 4500
on use of prostitutes at Democratic National Convention **11**, 4503-4505, 4516-17, 4527-28, 4499-4500

McMurry, Paula **22**, 10513
McMurtrie, Sandra A. **FR** 888
affidavit on contribution to Humphrey campaign **25**, 11920 **FR** 888-90
McNally, John **1**, 308, 336
McNamara, Morton **10**, 3964 **25**, 11730
McNelis, Charles A.
See Jacobsen, Jake, testimony of
McPhee, Rhoemer **2**, 753 **3**, 957 **19**, 8607E
at meetings **5**, 1953
discussions with Richie on Democratic party civil suits **7**, 2889
involvement with Mitchell **5**, 1906, 1907-1908
and Richie **5**, 1908-1910, 1953
McPherson, Harry
See Bernhard, Berl, testimony of
McPhillips, Alice **22**, 10267
McWilliams, A.L. **14**, 5909, 6178
Meany, George **10**, 3958
bogus call from Hart impersonator to **11**, 4604, 4628-29
Caulfield's investigation of **22**, 10402-10404
and McGovern **10**, 4059E
and unsigned anti-McGovern article **10**, 3933, 3934
"white paper" **10**, 4060E
Media
at Dean's house after Gray's statement **3**, 1002-1003
Buchanan accuses Select Committee of leaks on his appearance to **10**, 3900-3901
campaign memo on **10**, 4215E

Mehren, Dr. George L. *(Continued)*

meetings with Nunn **14,** 6125-26, 6179 **15,** 6683-84 **17,** 7553, 7554, 7555-62, 7566-67 **FR** 733-34

memo from Isham enclosing correspondence on resignation from AMPI **17,** 8158-63E

memo to Lilly on proposal for RNC by CTAPE **14,** 6119, 6189E

memo to Nelson **15,** 6655-56

and motivations for contributions to Nixon campaign **15,** 6698

Nelson on denial of knowledge of meeting between Nelson, Jacobsen, and Kalmbach **15,** 6661-62

and Nelson's commitments to Kalmbach **15,** 6670

and Nelson's meetings with Kalmbach **15,** 6440, 6664-65, 6667

and Nunn **14,** 6130

rejects contributing for Nixon **17,** 7559

replacement of Nelson by **16,** 7011

reports on fulfilled commitment to Russell **17,** 7631, 7632

reports to Lilly on Connally's telephone call to Mitchell **14,** 6115-16

reports to Lilly on meeting with Johnson **FR** 735-36

reports to Lilly on meeting with Nunn **FR** 735-36

reports to Lilly on meetings with Connally **14,** 6107-18

role in AMPI **FR** 584

and Russell **FR** 601-602

and Russell payback scheme **FR** 600

and Russell's refusal to explain high fees **17,** 7629-30

on support from Mills on milk price-support issue **FR** 906

and TAPE contribution to Mills **17,** 7659

telephone conversation with Kalmbach on antitrust suit **17,** 7621-22

tells Butterbrodt that Kalmbach refused funds from AMPI **17,** 7644-45

tells Pepper to talk with Beauford **17,** 7718

timing of trip to Europe **14,** 6113-15

and Townsend's preparations of papers on milk price supports **14,** 6304

and voided CTAPE checks **17,** 7648

Mehren, Dr. George L., testimony of 16, 7229-7348

on advice from L. B. Johnson **16,** 7296

on AMPI arrangements with Russell **16,** 7306-12

on AMPI bonus scheme **16,** 7314, 7347-48

on AMPI checkoff system for Mills **16,** 7340-41

on AMPI contributions to congressional campaigns **16,** 7337-38

on AMPI contributions to Mills campaign **16,** 7313-16, 7324-25, 7341-43

on AMPI decision making on political contributions **16,** 7299-7300

on AMPI employees working in Mills campaign **16,** 7341

on AMPI paying for Mills rally **16,** 7343-44

on AMPI payments to Russell **16,** 7348

on AMPI political contributions and second milk price-support decision **16,** 7241

on AMPI relationship with Valentine, Sherman **16,** 7344-47

on AMPI severance of Jones from retainer **16,** 7329-31

on career background **16,** 7229-30

on checks drawn on CTAPE account **16,** 7281-86

on conflicts between Nelson's testimony and **16,** 7250-51

on Connally's telephone call to Mitchell **16,** 7267-69

on consulting with J. B. Johnson after meeting with Nunn **16,** 7289-90

on CTAPE decision to contribute to congressional campaign committees **16,** 7290-91

on decision making on TAPE political contributions **16,** 7321-22, 7325-26

on decision to consult L. B. Johnson **16,** 7291-92

on denials of AMPI commitment **16,** 7298-99

denies Jacobsen informed him of AMPI commitments **16,** 7269-70

denies knowing Chotiner **16,** 7237

denies knowledge of AMPI campaign commitments **16,** 7248-49, 7332-34

denies knowledge of AMPI contributions **16,** 7232

denies knowledge of contacts between MPI and AMPI representatives and Kalmbach in 1969 **16,** 7231

denies knowledge of meeting between Nelson, Jacobsen, and Kalmbach **16,** 7249-50

denies link between AMPI commitments to Nixon campaign and antitrust suit against AMPI **16,** 7261-63

denies remembering call from Kalmbach on April 4, 1972 **16,** 7284-85, 7287-88

on discussions about past contributions of TAPE with legislators **16,** 7320-21

on discussions with Butterbrodt on AMPI commitments **16,** 7247-48

on discussions with Nunn on TAPE contributions to congressional campaigns **16,** 7300-7306, 7348

on discussions with Talmadge and Eastland on antitrust suit against AMPI **16,** 7335-36

on efforts to ascertain commitments and responsibilities of AMPI **16,** 7245-49

on Isham's resignation as treasurer of TAPE **16,** 7286-87

on Jacobsen-Connally relationship **16,** 7239

on Kalmbach terminating discussions on AMPI contributions **16,** 7273-79

on lawyers representing AMPI in efforts to obtain milk price-support increase **16,** 7236

on meeting with Butz, Campbell, and Lyng **16,** 7279

on meeting with Connally **16,** 7263-71

on meeting with Hardin on reaction to reversal of milk price-support decision **16,** 7242-44

on meeting with Harrison **16,** 7253-55

on meeting with J. B. Johnson **16,** 7297-99, 7336-38

on meeting with Jacobsen to discuss meeting with Kalmbach **16,** 7252-53

on meeting with Kalmbach after meeting with Connally **16,** 7271-76

on meeting with Lyng and Paarlberg **16,** 7241-42

on meeting with Lyng and Palmby **16,** 7241-42

on meeting with MacGregor, Albert, and Mills **16,** 7318-20

on meeting with McGovern **16,** 7313

on meeting with Nelson, Jacobsen, and Kalmbach **16,** 7255-61

on meeting with Nunn **16,** 7292-97

on meeting with Strauss **16,** 7279-81

on meetings with Harrison and Jacobsen **16,** 7236-37

on meetings with Kalmbach **16,** 7249, 7336

on meetings with Mills, Poage, and Albert **16,** 7334

on milk price supports **16,** 7327-29, 7331-32

on Mills role in milk price-support issue **16,** 7326-27

on motivation for meeting with Connally **16,** 7266-67

on *Nader* v. *Butz* **16,** 7244-45

on Nelson and Jacobsen meeting with Kalmbach **16,** 7251

on Nelson's comments on Chotiner and Colson **16,** 7237-7239

on Parr's denial of AMPI commitment **16,** 7316-17

on Parr's requests for reorganization of AMPI **16,** 7251

on pressures to contribute to Nixon campaign **16,** 7287-88

on reasons for agreeing to meet with Nunn **16,** 7090-91

on responsibilities at AMPI **16,** 7230

on retaining Wright to investigate Russell payments **16,** 7339-40

on role in contributions from TAPE to presidential primary candidates **16,** 7321-22

on role in milk price-support decision **16,** 7317-18, 7233-45

on TAPE contribution to Eastland **16,** 7334

on TAPE contributions to legislators **16,** 7323-26

on TAPE contributions to presidential primary candidates **16,** 6313-16

on telephone call from Connally to Dole **16,** 7268, 7269

on telephone call from Jacobsen to arrange meeting with Nunn **16,** 7288-89

on Van Dyk's and Connell's role in milk price-support issue **16,** 7326

Meier, John H. 19, 9324-25 **20,** 9454, 9506, 9508, 9510, 9588, 9595-96, 9675E **21,** 9701, 9703 **22,** 10279, 10609, 10625 **23,** 10927, 11103, 11174

and atomic tests in Nevada **24,** 11579

Barth on IRS sensitive case report on Hughes **23,** 11221, 11230-32, 11235-37

Davis denies knowledge of relationship between F. Donald Nixon and **24,** 11594-95

Edward Nixon denies financial dealings with **22,** 10611-12

Ehrlichman and **22,** 10611

Ehrlichman and F. Donald Nixon's relationship with **22,** 10707-10708

and F. Donald Nixon **20,** 9598-9604 **22,** 10633, 10645-48

F. Donald Nixon discusses with Buzhardt **22,** 10556

and F. Donald Nixon's travel expenses **22,** 10731

hotel registration receipts **22,** 12461E

and Hughes contribution to Rebozo **FR** 937-38

IRS investigation of **22,** 10647-48 **FR** 1017

Kalmbach and F. Donald Nixon's relationship with **22,** 10708-10

McKiernan on **22,** 10651

Rebozo and **24,** 11444

Rebozo on relationship between F. Donald Nixon and **21,** 10118-21

relationship with Danner **20,** 9604

trips with F. Donald Nixon and Hatsis **22,** 10709, 10714-15, 10729-30

Walters on

See Walters, Johnnie M., testimony of

Melcher, Robert 13, 5412, 5413, 5414, 5429 **16,** 7216

guilty plea by **FR** 459

See also American Ship Building Co.

Mellilli, Conrad 12, 4978, 4981-82

Mellott, Lloyd R.

letter from Barrick on return of illegal Gulf Oil campaign contribution **13,** 5466, 5806E

letter to Parkinson on Gulf Oil contribution **13,** 5466, 5804-05E

Members of Congress for Peace Through Law 25, 12095

Memorandum of Law, Admissibility of Hearsay Statements of a Conspirator 4, 1783-90E

Meritorious Police Award

to Caulfield **1,** 249, 250

Merman, Ethel 12, 5115E

Merrill, Frederick 11, 4461, 4890E

Metcalf, Senator 4, 1702E **8,** 3113

Metzner, Charles M. 20, 9586-87 **24,** 11580 **26,** 12855-56E **FR** 996

letter from Hayes on Dunes acquisition matter **FR** 995-96

letter from Hayes on Hughes Tool Co. transactions **26,** 12937-38E

Mewhinney, Larsh B. 25, 12251, 12275, 12278-79, 12280, 12297-98, 12314, 12321 **FR** 475

affidavit **FR** 481

Mexican Americans

memo from Armendariz to Marumoto on characteristics of persons and families whose origin is **13,** 5323, 5627-28E

in memo on Spanish-speaking voters **19,** 8621-23E

opinion polls and analysis of results in California **19,** 8678-82E

Mexican checks 2, 748-50, 574, 892E-895E **3,** 944 **4,** 1415 **7,** 2694-95 **8,** 3042

and Allen contribution **FR** 514-22

CIA and FBI and **2,** 774 **6,** 2564

in civil suits against CRP **5,** 1906

Dean's calls to Gray on not investigating **9,** 3534, 3535

Ehrlichman and **5,** 1860

Ehrlichman and Haldeman discussion with Walters **3,** 946

and FBI investigation of Watergate **3,** 942-43 **7,** 2782 **9,** 3509-12

Gray on **9,** 3515-16, 3522-23

Gray tells Walters about **8,** 3239-40, 3270

Gray testimony on CIA-FBI relations on Watergate and **9,** 3451, 3452, 3453-54, 3455, 3456, 3457, 3458, 3463-64, 3466

and reasons for Nixon's decision on milk-price
supports **FR** 579-81
selected documents **FR** 755-828
on total contributions to Nixon campaign **FR** 743
and Vesco case **FR** 582
and White House refusal of information **FR** 617-
18, 618N
Milk import quotas
AMPI news release on speech given by Butterbrodt on **15,** 6545, 6703E
and meeting between Kalmbach and Dairymen,
Inc., representatives **15,** 6455
memo from Harrison to Special Counsel to the
President on **14,** 6296, 6328-30E
Milk price-support issue 15, 6560-75 **16,** 7119-21
ADEPT and **14,** 5869-80
Alagia on SPACE contributions to Republicans
and **16,** 7062-84
and AMPI contribution to Belcher **15,** 6879
and AMPI contributions **14,** 6137 **15,** 6881 **17,**
7603, 7607
and AMPI representatives meeting with Kalmbach **15,** 6445-46
and AMPI's reaffirmation of $2 million pledge **17,**
7813-15
announcement by USDA of reversal of decision
on March 25 **FR** 668-70
announcement of March 12 decision on **FR** 627
Associated Dairymen, Inc., paper on **14,** 6304,
6332-62E
Associated Milk Producers, Inc., press release on
15, 6703E
at meeting between Mehren, Nelson, and Connally **16,** 7265
bill introduced by Humphrey on **25,** 11880E
Butterbrodt on AMPI and **17,** 7635-39
and campaign contributions **15,** 6694-95
Campbell on **17,** 7750-90
congressional pressure on administration on **16,**
7401
and Connally **14,** 5975-82
Connally-Jacobsen discussions on **14,** 6054-58,
6058-60
and Dairy Week in Washington memo from Stevens **FR** 798-99E
and decision on dairy industry contributions to
Republican fundraising dinner **FR** 642
decision to increase **15,** 6568-70
Department of Agriculture decision-making proc-
ess prior to March 23, 1971 **FR** 623-28
and destruction of AMPI files **15,** 6895-96
Ehrlichman on **16,** 7381-90, 7399-7400
Gifford memo to White House on **FR** 815E
Haldeman on **16,** 7167-68, 7183-84
and Hanman on attitudes of ADEPT toward
Republican fundraising dinner **17,** 7732-34
Hanman on dairy industry contributions and **17,**
7735, 7744
Hardin discusses reaction to second decision with
Mehren **16,** 7242-44
Harrison on **14,** 6279-80
Hillings' letter to Nixon on **15,** 6701-6702E **FR**
757-58E
historic and legal background **FR** 623-24

Humphrey speech in Senate on **25,** 11879E
Humphrey's support for legislation to raise **FR**
881-83
Jacobsen on AMPI's efforts in Congress on **15,**
6457-58
Jacobsen on contacts with Connally on **15,** 6407-
15
Kalmbach on **17,** 7596-97
letter from Hanman to Baumann on role of
TAPE, ADEPT, and SPACE in decision on **17,**
8139-40E
letter from Hanman to Beezley on **17,** 8127E
letter from Hanman to Connally on **14,** 6080,
6099-6101E
letter from Healy to Hardin on announcement of
16, 7134, 7153-54E
letter from Powell to Mr. and Mrs. Spidle on **17,**
8141-42E
letter-writing campaign and **16,** 7326
Masters denies representation of AMPI in **16,**
6957
and meeting between Mehren, MacGregor, Albert,
and Mills **16,** 7318-20
and meeting between Nixon, Parr, and Nelson **15,**
6794
meeting between Nixon and dairy farmers on **14,**
6060-65
and meetings with Connally **14,** 6107-18
Mehren on **16,** 7327-29, 7331-32
Mehren's role in **16,** 7233-45, 7317-18
memo from Campbell to Rice with proposed press
release on **FR** 855-56E
memo from Farrington to USDA Administrator
of Commodity Operations on **17,** 8117-26E
memo from MacGregor to Ehrlichman and Shultz
on **FR** 813-14E
memo from Rice to Shultz on **FR** 806-807E
memo from Shultz to Ehrlichman on telephone
call from Mills on **17,** 8128E
and milk producer contacts with Connally **FR**
637-40
milk producers' reaction to **FR** 671-73
Morris on **16,** 7440-41
Mott on campaign contributions tied to **25,**
12107-12108
and *Nader* v. *Butz* **FR** 710-11
Nelson on **15,** 6655-58, 6688-89
Nelson on AMPI efforts to obtain increases in **15,**
6552-59
Nelson on connection between campaign contributions and **15,** 6633-35
Nelson on contacts with Connally and **15,** 6617-
24, 6676
Nixon's decision related to dairy industry contributions **FR** 621-23
Nunn on **17,** 7551
organization chart of decision making on **FR**
759E
Paarlberg on **16,** 7514-31
Parr on **15,** 6800-29
reaction at Department of Agriculture **FR** 668-70
in Rice memo **FR** 800-803E
rumors at Kick-Off 1972 Republican Dinner
about reversal in decision on **FR** 659
Select Committee chart of bills for 1971 on **17,**
8143-46E

contribution from Masters to **15,** 6971 **16,** 6964-65

contributions from dairy industry to **16,** 7400

failure to appear for Select Committee interview **FR** 908, 925

and Gallup poll on presidential candidates in 1972 **16,** 7007

Gulf Oil Corp. contribution to **FR** 469

informed by Arnold of Wild contribution **25,** 12023-24

invitation to Ames, Iowa, rally **17,** 7722

Jacobsen delivers money to Parr for **15,** 6430-35, 6791

Johnson activity for **17,** 7667-69

letter from Oswald to Peterson on support of **17,** 7719, 7727-28E

Little Rock rally in 1971 for **14,** 6320 **16,** 7090-91, 7098

Masters on contributing to presidential efforts of **16,** 6953-54

meeting with Albert **16,** 7118-20

meeting with Mehren, MacGregor, and Albert **16,** 7318-20

Mehren and **16,** 7334, 7336

memo from Shultz to Ehrlichman on telephone call from **17,** 8128E

and milk price-support issue **16,** 7317, 7326-27, 7383, 7399, 7401-7402 **FR** 630, 805E

money delivered by Townsend for **16,** 7088-90

Parr soliciting contributions for **16,** 7096-97

Pepper on telephone call from **17,** 7709-10

press release with excerpt from appearance on "Washington Straight Talk" **25,** 12070-71E

and review of CTAPE contributions **17,** 7572-73

speech to Texas Legislature **16,** 7091, 7107-7108

statement on unsolicited invitation to Ames, Iowa, rally **FR** 917

and support of legislation favorable to dairy producers **FR** 905-908

support of milk price-support legislation and AMPI contributions **FR** 905-908

TAPE contributions to **15,** 6776-79 **16,** 7313-16, 7322-26 **17,** 7659-62

telephone call to Pepper **FR** 916

Townsend denies delivering AMPI money to Little Rock office for rally for **16,** 7100

Townsend on AMPI contributions for **16,** 7100-7103

and Valentine, Sherman **16,** 7112, 7113

See also Draft Mills for President Committee; Mills campaign; Mills campaign finances report

Mills campaign

AMPI file on **25,** 12077-87E

assignment of AMPI employees to **FR** 911-15

Johnson refuses to answer questions on **17,** 7695-98

Kinnard contribution to **25,** 12030-31

Mid-Am contributions to **17,** 7746-47

Robeson memo to Sanders re campaign committees **25,** 12033-67E

services rendered by AMPI employees to **FR** 911-15

solicitation of donations from AMPI employees for **FR** 920-23

3M contribution to **FR** 484

See also Arnold, Carl, testimony of

Mills campaign finances report

on contributions from AMPI **FR** 904-23

and Gulf Oil Corp. contribution **FR** 923-25

limitations on investigation **FR** 903-904

3M Corp. contribution **FR** 925-27

Millspaugh, Peter 1, 40, 449E **18,** 8224

memo to Flemming on resources of incumbency **18,** 8223, 8358-62E **19,** 8606-12E

memos to Flemming on patronage **FR** 364-65

note with attachments from Horton on White House papers **18,** 8209, 8348-57E

Milwaukee, Wisconsin

Benz sets up dirty tricks operation in **11,** 4413

McGovern campaigners activities against Muskie in **11,** 4486

Segretti's activities against Humphrey's primary campaign in **10,** 3984

Milwaukee McGovern headquarters

and Liddy plan **2,** 463, 481 **3,** 1683-84 **4,** 1413, 1542, 1543 **6,** 2304 **9,** 3765

McMinoway diary on **11,** 4705-4708E

Minneapolis Star **17,** 7605

Minnesota Committee to Re-elect the President 12, 5120-24E

Minnesota Mining & Manufacturing Co.

campaign contribution of **FR** 484-86

Minnesota Republican Party 12, 5120-24E

break-in at Republican Campaign Headquarters in **12,** 5125-26E

Minnick, Walter 3, 969

Minnick, William 12, 5174E

Minority Business Enterprise (OMBE)

See Office of Minority Business Enterprise

Mioler, Senator 15, 6867

Miranda v. *Arizona* **9,** 3486

Mirelez, Peter FR 385, 389

Mirto, Robert

"Memo to the File of Alfred C. Baldwin III" **1,** 389-90

See also Baldwin, Alfred C., III

Mississippi

campaign laws in **11,** 4675

Mitchell, George 11, 4768-77E, 4780E, 4781E, 4814E **FR** 473

Mitchell, John N. 1, 12, 13, 34, 35, 172, 225 **2,** 555, 602, 653, 702 **3,** 1205E, 1240E **5,** 1950

advice to Nixon on Watergate problems **4,** 1548-49

advises LaRue to make $75,000 delivery to Bittman **6,** 2298

after Watergate arrests **2,** 661-62 **6,** 2412

alleged involvement in Watergate **1,** 242-43

and AMPI contributions **15,** 6452 **17,** 7611-12

AMPI lawyers and **16,** 6959

and AMPI referral to Kalmbach **FR** 588

and Antitrust Division decision on Dunes Hotel matter **FR** 989-98

and antitrust suit against AMPI **15,** 6467 **17,** 7682 **FR** 705, 706-708, 724

apology to Nixon on Watergate **5,** 2020

appointment sheets **26,** 12824E, 12832E, 12833E

Mitchell, John N. *(Continued)*

appointments and telephone call memos **26,** 12929-36E

appoints Mardian counsel for CRP on Watergate issue **6,** 2352, 2414

approval of cash disbursements by Sloan **2,** 537-38, 539, 627

approval of Liddy for assignment at CRP **FR** 18

and approval of Liddy's budget **6,** 2361, 2430

approves LaRue's disbursement of $75,000 **6,** 2320-21, 2324

approves Liddy's intelligence-gathering plan **2,** 794-95, 811-13, 826, 855-56 **3,** 1088

asked by Moore to raise hush money **5,** 1969, 2048-53

asks Dean to get FBI interview files **4,** 1358

asks Dean to have Caulfield speak to McCord **3,** 974-75

asks Dean to obtain CIA assistance in Watergate investigation **3,** 945-46

asks Dean to prevent disclosure of Dahlberg check **FR** 37

assurances to Magruder **2,** 804-805, 836-37

assures Dean he is not being set up **3,** 956

at CRP budget meetings **6,** 2316

at Key Biscayne meeting **6,** 2302, 2331, 2332-33, 2339

at Liddy's first presentation of intelligence-gathering plan **2,** 787-88, 838, 844-45, 863-64 **3,** 929-31

at Liddy's second presentation of intelligence-gathering plan **2,** 789-91

at meeting with Malek, Ehrlichman, Shultz, and Nixon **18,** 8205-8206

at meetings to plan Magruder's testimony before grand jury **6,** 2292

at Nixon-Dean meeting **4,** 1549-50

at San Clemente meetings **4,** 1510-11

and attempts to involve CIA in Watergate investigation **4,** 1368

attitude toward protection of Nixon from Watergate information **8,** 3184

attitude toward White House horrors **6,** 2543

and attorney general's right to order wiretaps **1,** 356

as authority for Watergate break-in **7,** 2801 **9,** 3708-3709

authority on disbursement of funds **2,** 555, 560, 573

and authorization of money to Liddy **FR** 26

authorization to Magruder for cash disbursements **5,** 2012-13

and Bailey asked to see or talk to McCord **4,** 1575

and booklet on Nixon brothers **22,** 10652

briefed on Liddy debriefing **6,** 2342

briefed on Responsiveness Program **FR** 379

and Buchanan's political strategy **10,** 3926

campaign activities while still attorney general **10,** 3938-39

and campaign press releases **10,** 3938-39

campaign role after resignation **12,** 4945

and cash disbursement to Liddy **2,** 744, 795-96

and Caulfield **3,** 925-26

Caulfield as aide to **1,** 252-253

and Chapman's Friends **FR** 199-200

and CIA aid **4,** 1415

and commitments to Watergate defendants **6,** 2310

communication with Haldeman **6,** 2501

confidential memo from Magruder to **2,** 695-96

conflicting testimony on Key Biscayne meeting and hush money **6,** 1928

Connally's meeting with AMPI representatives and **15,** 6462, 6464

contacts with Davis **24,** 11613

contacts with Helms since Inauguration Day **8,** 3251

contacts with Semer on AMPI contributions **15,** 6386-87

and contributions from dairy groups in 1969 **16,** 7156

conversation with Chotiner on antitrust suit against AMPI **17,** 7683-84, 7686-87

and coverup of White House horrors **FR** 41

and creation of Intelligence Advisory Committee **3,** 1066

and CRP **1,** 14, 16

and CRP activities while attorney general **7,** 2752

CRP memo from Todd on Older Americans Division **19,** 9055-9134E

and Dahlberg checks **2,** 701 **3,** 942

daily schedule **26,** 12847-50E, 12893-96E

Danner and **21,** 10044-45

and Danner's investigation of Dunes Hotel acquisition **20,** 9572-75, 9577-85

Dean and **4,** 1413

Dean believes Ehrlichman and Haldeman are setting him up as scapegoat **3,** 1011-13

Dean discusses involvement with Nixon **8,** 3117

Dean informs Moore about meetings on Liddy plan with **5,** 1969-72

Dean informs of Hunt's threats against Ehrlichman **3,** 999

Dean informs of O'Brien's visit to Haldeman **3,** 1010

Dean on approval of Liddy plan **3,** 1088

Dean protests on Nixon announcement of "Dean report" **4,** 1368

Dean reports on Gray's theories on Watergate to **3,** 944

Dean tells Haldeman and Ehrlichman about role in Liddy plan meetings of **7,** 2753-54

Dean tells Kleindienst about Watergate involvement of **4,** 1419-20

Dean tells that he will tell everything **4,** 1395

in Dean-Nixon discussion on hush money **FR** 59

on Dean's "indictable" list **5,** 1988

Dean's memo on meeting with **3,** 1011, 1308-10E

death threats against **2,** 861

and Democratic civil suits **3,** 957 **4,** 1575-76

and deniability for Watergate break-in **1,** 218-219 **2,** 872-73

denial of knowledge about surplus funds from 1968 campaign **5,** 2126-27

denies offering Magruder Executive clemency **FR** 70-71

denies receiving Gemstone material **FR** 30

discusses payments to Liddy with Stans **2**, 697

discussion with Kalmbach on antitrust suit against AMPI **17**, 7616

discussion with LaRue on hush money **23**, 11162

discussion with LaRue on Nunn campaign **23**, 11161

discussions with Haldeman after Watergate break-in **8**, 3097

discussions with LaRue on money given to Liddy **6**, 2316-17

discussions with Mardian on Liddy budget **6**, 2416

discussions with Rebozo **21**, 10045

and Dunes Hotel acquisition efforts by Hughes **23**, 11055, 11056-57

efforts by White House to blame for Watergate **FR** 91

efforts to block Patman Committee hearings **3**, 960, 961, 962

Ehrlichman denies discussions on dairy industry issues with **16**, 7399

Ehrlichman interview with **7**, 2729

Ehrlichman on **1**, 279

Ehrlichman on reaction to Plumbers operation **7**, 2780-82

in Ehrlichman-Kleindienst taped conversation **7**, 2945E

and employment of Caulfield **1**, 250-251

and Executive clemency offers **3**, 1080 **FR** 64, 72

expects to be witness at grand jury **5**, 2043

F. Donald Nixon and **22**, 10639

and F. Donald Nixon's Hallamore Homes stock transaction **22**, 10643, 10644

FBI interview of **9**, 3456

and Gemstone documents **FR** 29-30

grand jury appearance of in Silbert affidavit **25**, 12416-17E

grand jury testimony discussed at Nixon-Dean meeting **5**, 2065

and Gray's nomination as FBI Director **9**, 3487-88

and Greenspun break-in plans **20**, 9379

Haldeman and **7**, 2877, 2878

Haldeman on conversation about "taking rap" for Watergate **8**, 3168-69

Haldeman on reasons why Nixon didn't question **8**, 3127

Haldeman wants Dean to talk to **3**, 1042

and Haldeman's memo to Dean on DeLoach firing by Kendall **8**, 3204-3205

Harmony and **2**, 470

and Hayes letter to Metzner **FR** 996

hears taped conversation between Hunt and Colson **3**, 970

and hiring of Liddy by CRP for intelligence gathering **2**, 786, 810, 845

Hoover memos on Dunes Hotel acquisition to **FR** 997-98

Hoover objects to Huston Plan to **FR** 4-5

Hughes instructs Danner to meet with on Dunes acquisition **FR** 983-84

Hunt assumes Liddy informed about Greenspun matter **20**, 9354

Hunt on Liddy plan and **9**, 3679

Hunt on responsibility for Watergate **9**, 3776, 3778

in Hunt-Colson taped conversation **9**, 3888E

and Hunt's belief in legality of Watergate **9**, 3764

and Hunt's demands for money **7**, 2853

in Hunt's notes **9**, 3836E, 3839E

and Hunt's status after death of his wife **3**, 972

and hush money **3**, 950, 969, 970, 985-86, 987 **4**, 1371, 1402, 1484 **5**, 1967, 2149 **5**, 1966-67

on importance of Nixon victory **10**, 3922, 3923

information to Stans after Watergate arrests **2**, 865-66

informed about Watergate break-in **FR** 32

informed by Dean that CIA will not assist in Watergate investigation **3**, 949-50

informed by Dean that he won't lie about meeting where Liddy presented intelligence-gathering plans **3**, 1006-07

informed by LaRue and Mardian of Liddy debriefing **FR** 41

instructions to LaRue after hearing about Watergate break-in **6**, 2314-15

instructs LaRue to contact Rebozo for campaign contribution for Nunn campaign **23**, 11152-53, 11163, 11164, 11166

and Intelligence Advisory Committee **1**, 201 **4**, 1457

and intelligence-gathering plan against antiwar leaders and supporters **3**, 916, 1059 **4**, 1413

interview with Johnnie Walters **24**, 11622

and investigation of mob infiltration of Hughes hotels **20**, 9572-75

invites Mardian to join campaign **6**, 2346-47

involvement in Watergate **1**, 127, 128, 129, 130, 139, 142-49, 157-60, 163, 165, 166-67, 173, 341-42, 409 **2**, 569, 803, 804, 805, 818, 822 **3**, 11053-54 **4**, 1425, 1497 **7**, 2749-50, 2901-2902, 2903

and IRS sensitive case reports **24**, 11635, 11636

and ITT matter **8**, 3372-76E

and ITT-Dita Beard memo **FR** 128

Jacobsen denies knowing **15**, 6478

and Jacobsen-Kalmbach meeting **17**, 7608, 7609

and Johnnie Walters' appointment as IRS Commissioner **24**, 11623-24

Kalmbach and **16**, 7158

Kalmbach feels used by **5**, 2175

Kleindienst on his reaction to involvement in Watergate of **9**, 3587, 3588

and Kleindienst recusing himself from Watergate investigation **9**, 3860E

LaRue and **2**, 577, 578 **3**, 1311E **6**, 2291

LaRue and Mardian report on Liddy debriefing to **6**, 2288-89, 2337-38, 2402, 2416, 2417, 3318

LaRue on information given to **6**, 2336-38

LaRue on involvement in coverup **6**, 2324

LaRue on Key Biscayne meeting **6**, 2280-82

LaRue on motivations for participation in coverup **6**, 2340-41

LaRue on reaction when learning about Watergate arrests **6**, 2330-31

LaRue on relationship with **6**, 2278

learns of Watergate arrests **2**, 815 **6**, 2285

and Lehigh Valley Cooperative Farmers contribution **FR** 481, 482

Mitchell, John N. *(Continued)*
 letter from Sloan on money to Walker **8**, 3190-92, 3324E
 and Liddy's employment at CRP **3**, 927-28 **4**, 1351
 Liddy sent to inform Kleindienst of Watergate break-in by **9**, 3562
 as Liddy's authorization for Watergate break-in **9**, 3792
 and Liddy's claim about his attempts to get McCord out of jail **6**, 2381
 Liddy's intelligence plan and **2**, 787-88 **3**, 930, 1264-65E **20**, 9385-87
 Liddy's visit to office of **2**, 527
 logs of meetings of **6**, 2379
 MacGregor on secrecy of **12**, 4930-31
 MacGregor replaces as directer of CRP **12**, 4899-4900, 4940-41
 Magruder and **2**, 547
 Magruder as liaison to **6**, 2494
 Magruder lies about money to Liddy to **6**, 2392
 Magruder on Malek's memo to **1**, 451-53E
 Magruder shows material from first break-in to **2**, 797, 827
 Magruder tells Mardian he approved budget for dirty tricks and Black advance **6**, 2351-52
 and Magruder's authority to tell Sloan to make payments **2**, 715, 773-74
 and Magruder's discussion with Harmony **2**, 871
 and Magruder's employment at CRP **2**, 784
 and Magruder's employment problems after Watergate **3**, 990
 Magruder's meetings with **2**, 490-91, 492, 503, 505, 665-66
 and Magruder's talks with Prosecutors **2**, 864
 and Magruder's urging Porter to commit perjury **2**, 666
 Mardian contradicts testimony of **6**, 2371, 2372-73
 Mardian on discussions about Watergate with **6**, 2399-2400
 Mardian tells Liddy he will report to **6**, 2358
 Mardian works at CRP with **6**, 2348-49
 Mardian's changes in press statement of **6**, 2375
 on Mardian's knowledge of Magruder's perjury **6**, 2372-73
 McCord and **1**, 126, 186 **3**, 976
 and McCord remaining silent **4**, 1545
 McCord's meetings with **1**, 162-63, 176
 McKiernan's opinion of **22**, 10644-45
 and McKiernan's report on Nixon brothers **22**, 10638, 10640
 McLaren affidavit on Dunes Hotel acquisition matter and **26**, 12851-52E, 12855E
 and McMinoway **FR** 193
 and media reports on Watergate **5**, 2018
 meeting with Danner and Rebozo **FR** 937-38
 meeting with Danner on acquisition of Dunes Hotel by Hughes Tool Co. **22**, 12429E
 meeting with Dean, LaRue, and Kalmbach on hush money **5**, 2110-11
 meeting with Dean, Liddy, and Magruder **2**, 490-91, 502-503, 519 **3**, 935, 952-53
 meeting with Dean and Magruder on coverup story **2**, 808, 841 **4**, 1398
 meeting with Haldeman **7**, 2881

 meeting with Haldeman, Ehrlichman, and Dean on immunity issue **7**, 2745
 meeting with Haldeman, MacGregor, and Nixon **12**, 4943
 meeting with Haldeman after Key Biscayne meeting **6**, 2476-77 **8**, 3180-81
 meeting with Haldeman on Sandwedge proposal **6**, 2492
 meeting with Kalmbach, Dean, and LaRue **5**, 2176
 meeting with LaRue, Dean, Mardian, and Magruder **6**, 2286, 2355-57
 meeting with LaRue, Magruder, and Flemming in Key Biscayne **23**, 11150
 meeting with Liddy and Dean **3**, 928, 1150E **7**, 2753
 meeting with Magruder, LaRue, Mardian, and Dean after Watergate break-in **FR** 33-34
 meeting with Magruder after McCord's letter is made public **2**, 806-807, 833
 meeting with Mardian, Magruder, and Dean after Watergate **3**, 1035-36
 meeting with Moore after La Costa **5**, 1952, 1968-69
 meeting with Moore on raising of hush money **4**, 1511
 meeting with Nixon, Dean, Ehrlichman, and Haldeman **3**, 1000-1002
 meeting with Nunn **23**, 11167-68
 meeting with O'Brien and Alch **4**, 1580-81
 meeting with Rebozo and Danner in 1968 **20**, 9506-10
 meeting with Semer in 1970 **16**, 7209-10
 meeting with Sloan after Watergate arrests **2**, 544, 561-62, 578, 592-93, 618-19, 628, 627
 meeting with Stans after Watergate arrests **2**, 703-704, 725, 734-35, 737-38
 meeting with Stans and Magruder after Watergate arrests **2**, 809, 868-69, 870
 meeting with Stans on money to Liddy **2**, 726-27, 728, 769
 meetings after Watergate arrests **2**, 739, 799-800, 816-17, 841-42 **5**, 1953
 and meetings between Haldeman and Kalmbach on dairy industry contributions **16**, 7161
 meetings with Danner on Dunes acquisition **22**, 10231 **FR** 984-89
 meetings with Haldeman, Ehrlichman, and Nixon brothers **22**, 10640-42
 meetings with Kalmbach **FR** 707
 meetings with LaRue prior to April 7 deadline **23**, 11156
 meetings with Moore, Mardian, and Kleindienst on confirmation hearings for Kleindienst **5**, 1946-48
 meetings with Nixon **3**, 1084-85
 meetings with Wild **13**, 5467, 5470-71, 5481
 memo from Buchanan and Khachigian on Muskie campaign **11**, 4668
 memo from Dean on domestic intelligence **3**, 1063-64
 memo from Dean on Operation Sandwedge **3**, 926, 1149E
 memo from Magruder on funding of telephone plan for Florida primary **4**, 1810-13E

memo from Magruder on grantsmanship **1**, 40, 41, 449E

memo from Magruder on Muskie candidacy **11**, 4654

memo from Stans on budget matters **2**, 696, 900-905

memo on discretionary fund at Commerce Department from Magruder **2**, 696, 874, 899E

memos from Magruder to **2**, 503, 504

message from Liddy to Kleindienst on freeing Watergate defendants **3**, 936

Moore and **5**, 1939, 1940, 1942, 2000-2001

Moore assigned to discuss raising money for Watergate defendants with **FR** 77

Moore denies meeting with Haldeman and **5**, 2062-63

Moore on meetings listed in log of **5**, 1953

Moore on request for money raising to **5**,1986, 2026-27, 2039-43, 2048-49

Moore states he never asked about meetings on Liddy plan with **5**, 2062, 2063

Moore's and Dean's testimony on request to raise hush money **5**, 1958-59

Nixon wants accounting of his pre-June 17 activities **3**, 1000

Nixon wants Ehrlichman to interview **7**, 2757

Nixon wants meeting between Dean, Ehrlichman, Haldeman, and **4**, 1548

in Nixon-Ehrlichman discussions on Executive clemency **FR** 73

on Nixon's advisory group **6**, 2519

Nixon's handling after Watergate **8**, 3162-63

and Nunn's assignment to Finance Committee **17**, 7541

Nunn's work relationship with **17**, 7536, 7549, 7554

and Operation Sandwedge **3**, 924-25 **4**, 1444-45

opposition to Huston plan **8**, 3030

orders Mardian not to prepare memorandum on Liddy debriefing **6**, 2403

participation in Watergate coverup **2**, 801-803, 857

on Patman Committee subpoena list **3**, 961

and Phillips Petroleum Co. contribution **FR** 491

and political espionage plan **1**, 183

Porter takes Liddy's envelope for **2**, 634, 666-67

and Porter's efforts to get Government job after Watergate trial **2**, 653

and preparation of booklet on Nixon brothers **22**, 10646, 10648

press statement after Watergate break-in **6**, 2285, 2319, 2413-14, 2417-18

and pre-Watergate intelligence gathering **3**, 1055, 1065

prior knowledge about Watergate break-in **3**, 1048, 1049 **6**, 2309, 2391

protection by Caulfield **1**, 252-253

questioned by Ehrlichman **7**, 2727

questioned by MacGregor about Watergate **2**, 529-30

reaction to Dean's intelligence-gathering plan **4**, 1352, 1353

reaction to first Watergate break-in **2**, 815

reaction to Gemstone file **2**, 871

reaction to Gemstone plan **FR** 21, 22

reaction to Liddy plan at Key Biscayne meeting **6**, 2281

reaction to Liddy's request for bail money **6**, 2363

reaction to Liddy's second plan **2**, 790-91

reaction to news of Watergate break-in **6**, 2311-12

reads FBI reports on Watergate investigation **3**, 945

on reasons for coverup **6**, 2311

reasons for McCord's silence on **1**, 247-248

reasons for resignation **7**, 2724-25

reassured by Magruder on Harmony testimony **2**, 464, 467-68

Rebozo denies discussing Hughes money with **21**, 10110

Reisner on material in Magruder's file for **2**, 494-95, 503-504

rejection of McLaren's request for grand jury investigation of AMPI **FR** 701-703, 707-708

rejects Caulfield for position of chief U.S. marshal **FR** 109

rejects Sandwedge Plan **FR** 17-18

relationship with Colson **16**, 7464-65, 7467 **17**, 7609

relationship with Dean **3**, 1036

relationship with Ehrlichman **3**, 1050

relationship with Haldeman **2**, 818

relationship with Liddy **9**, 3609-10

relationship with Magruder **2**, 522-23

relationship with Nixon **3**, 1051, 1052

relationship with Stans on budget committee **2**, 704, 763-66

report to Haldeman and Ehrlichman on Liddy debriefing **8**, 3043-44

and reports on violence **1**, 179, 181

requests copy of Muskie's speech taken from his office **2**, 670

and re-registration scheme in California **FR** 204

resignation **FR** 44

resignation from CRP after Watergate arrests **2**, 548 **3**, 951 **5**, 1951-52, 2008 **6**, 2338 **8**, 3165-67

and Responsiveness Program **18**, 8188, 8212

and Responsiveness Program for Black groups **18**, 8258-59, 8261-63, 8265-66, 8272

role at CRP **1**, 18, 21, 24, 40-41, 54-55, 57-58, 59 **2**, 784-85, 846-47 **12**, 4931

role at CRP after MacGregor becomes director **12**, 4905-4906

role in Kalmbach ending negotiations for AMPI contributions **16**, 7276-77

role in Watergate affair **2**, 855-57

role on budget committee **2**, 773-74

and Ruby I material **FR** 189

as scapegoat **3**, 1047, 1092-93 **4**, 1383

scheduling of appearance by **4**, 1430

and Segretti **FR** 186

Semer and **15**, 6386 **16**, 7189, 7190, 7192

and Semer-Kalmbach meeting **17**, 7585

and Semer's call to Kalmbach **17**, 7578

Shapiro's references to in Ehrlichman's notes **7**, 2802

Sloan denies financial reports to **2**, 616

Sloan expresses concern over Liddy money to **FR** 41

and Sloan's money to Liddy **2**, 616 **9**, 3581

Mitchell, John N. *(Continued)*

and solicitation of Gulf Oil Corp. contribution **FR** 469

as source of assurances to Watergate defendants **2,** 810, 849, 850

as source of money to Bittman **6,** 2312

Stans' attitude toward after Watergate arrests **2,** 731-32

Stans' letter to on budget reductions **2,** 742

statement on Watergate break-in **FR** 33

Strachan at same law firm as **6,** 2445-46

subpoenaed by Patman Committee **3,** 1193E

suggested as fundraiser for hush money **5,** 1941-42

suggests break-in at Greenspun's office in Las Vegas **2,** 790

suggests TAPE contact with Kalmbach **15,** 6511, 6512-13

summary of testimony by Baker **5,** 2020-2021

tape of meeting with Ehrlichman **7,** 2736-37

telephone call from Connally on antitrust suit against milk coops **14,** 6075-76

telephone call from Connally to **14,** 6078-80, 6115-16

telephone call from Johnnie Walters on Ryland **24,** 11635

telephone call to Nixon after Mardian report on Liddy debriefing **6,** 2417

telephone call to Nixon after report on Liddy debriefing **6,** 2318, 2321-22

telephone conversation with Connally **16,** 7267-69

tells Dean he plans to "stonewall" charges **3,** 1310E

tells Magruder he will deny complicity in Watergate **2,** 646

tells Magruder to brief Mardian on Watergate break-in **6,** 2359

tells Magruder to destroy documents **6,** 2286, 2317

tells Mardian to forget writing memo about Watergate **6,** 2375

tells Moore Dean should not testify **7,** 2752-53

in transcription of taped conversation between Kalmbach and Ehrlichman **5,** 2215E

and use of White House fund for Watergate defendants **FR** 56

wants Dean to get FBI reports on Watergate investigation **3,** 944

and Watergate coverup **3,** 943, 1026

and White House horrors **7,** 2831-33

and White House intelligence operations **4,** 1456

and White House money **6,** 2343

and White House staff **1,** 83

and White House staff transfers to CRP **1,** 83

and Whitney **FR** 504

Whitney memo to **2,** 873-74

Wild and Mills visit to confirm Nunn's credentials with CRP **13,** 5461-62

and wiretapping of White House staffers' conversations with newsmen **3,** 921

working relationship with Haldeman **8,** 3026

and write-in campaign for Kennedy in New Hampshire **FR** 202

See also Mitchell memos

Mitchell, John N., testimony of 4, 1601-81 **5,** 1816-92, 1893-1936

on actions after Watergate arrests **4,** 1621-22

on actions Nixon would have taken if he had known about Watergate break-in and coverup **5,** 1828-29, 1834

on Anderson column on ITT case **5,** 1873-74

on attitude toward grand jury hearings **4,** 1628-29

on attitude toward Magruder perjury **5,** 1865-66

on attitude toward Watergate break-in **5,** 1869

on attitude toward Watergate coverup **4,** 1632-33

on awareness of Magruder's involvement in Watergate **4,** 1623-24

on behavior after Watergate arrests **5,** 1849-50

career background **4,** 1602

on Caulfield-McCord talks **4,** 1649-50

on Caulfield's contacts with McCord **4,** 1632

on civil deposition given in Democratic party suit against CRP **4,** 1643

on Colson pushing Magruder **5,** 1933-34

on Colson reassuring Hunt of Executive clemency **5,** 1910-11

on Colson's campaign duties **5,** 1928-29, 1930-31

on conflicting testimony during Democratic party civil suit and Select Committee hearing **5,** 1880-81

on conflicting testimony on knowledge of Liddy debriefing **5,** 1922-24

on conflicting testimony with Magruder, Dean, and Stans testimony **5,** 1830

on contact with mutual friends of Nixon or White House staff members **5,** 1911

on contacts with Liddy **4,** 1669

on contradictory testimony on his role with CRP and Republican party **4,** 1653-59

on conversations with Colson after Watergate **5,** 1931-32

on conversations with Liddy **4,** 1619-20

on conversations with Nixon about Watergate **5,** 1861

on Dean stopping plan for firebombing of Brookings Institution **4,** 1647

on Dean's reaction to Liddy plan **4,** 1611-12

on Dean's role as liaison between CRP and White House **4,** 1624

on Dean's role at White House **5,** 1904

on Dean's testimony **4,** 1646, 1647-51, 1663, 1664, 1665, 1670, 1671-72, 1673-74, 1678-79, 1680 **5,** 1851

on Dean's testimony about McPhee approaching Judge Richey **5,** 1908-1910

on Dean's testimony about White House involvement in coverup **5,** 1890

on Dean's verification of White House horror stories **4,** 1647

on Dean's worries about being fall guy for Watergate **4,** 1649

on deciding not to meet further with Nixon **5,** 1916

on delegation of authority to Magruder **4,** 1607

on Democrats for Nixon **5,** 1931-32

denies approval of Liddy plan **5,** 1845-46, 1856, 1857-58 **FR** 25

denies Democratic National Committee was target for electronic surveillance in revised Liddy plan **4,** 1611 denies discussions of CIA support **5**, 1899-1900

denies discussions with Nixon on Watergate **4**, 1645

denies involvement in hush money payments **4**, 1649

denies involvement in Watergate **5**, 1870, 1915-16

denies knowledge of Hunt working with Liddy **5**, 1848

denies knowledge of Hunt's requests for money **4**, 1663

denies meeting with Ehrlichman on Magruder's testimony before grand jury **5**, 1898

denies meeting with Mardian, LaRue, and Dean **4**, 1645-46

denies Nixon ever asked about his knowledge of Watergate break-in or White House horror stories **5**, 1912

denies Nixon involvement in Watergate break-in and/or coverup **5**, 1829

denies reporting on meetings with Liddy **4**, 1613

denies role in Watergate break-in **4**, 1620

denies seeing Gray since Watergate **5**, 1934

denies talking with Liddy or Hunt **5**, 1882

denies telling Magruder to destroy Gemstone files **5**, 1877

on destruction of documents **4**, 1622

on dirty tricks **4**, 1670

discusses Fifth Amendment with Dean **4**, 1679-80

discusses Sandwedge proposal with Dean **FR** 115-16

on discussions after Watergate arrests **5**, 1852-53

on discussions with Haldeman about Watergate **5**, 1859-60

on discussions with Nixon on political intelligence during other campaigns **4**, 1667-68

on discussions with Nixon on Select Committee hearings **4**, 1663-64

on Ehrlichman's interview with Magruder **5**, 1915

on Executive clemency for Hunt **5**, 1862

on Executive privilege **5**, 1821-22, 1863-64

on FBI investigation of Watergate **5**, 1829, 1926-27

on FBI reports **4**, 1678-79

on financial responsibilities at CRP **5**, 1846-47

on Gemstone file **4**, 1618-20, 1641-42

on Haldeman and Ehrlichman resignations **5**, 1894-95

on Haldeman-Magruder meeting **4**, 1634

on hearing that McCord might not remain silent **5**, 1862

on hiring of Watergate principals **5**, 1819-20

on hush money **4**, 1629-32, 1645-47, 1672, 73 **5**, 1862, 1882-83 **FR** 57

on Huston plan **4**, 1603-1605 **5**, 1822-24

on influences on Magruder to supersede his orders **4**, 1640-41, 1670-71

informs Dean of Liddy debriefing **5**, 1883

on intelligence reports to CRP **5**, 1842-43

on Interagency Evaluation Committee **4**, 1637

on investigation of Watergate break-in and coverup **5**, 1827-28

on involvement in civil cases **5**, 1905-1908

on involvement in White House horror stories **4**, 1624-25

on involvement of staff in Watergate break-in **5**, 1858

on ITT and Beard matter **5**, 1873-74

on Key Biscayne meeting **4**, 1613-16 **5**, 1918, 1928, 1930

on knowledge of Ehrlichman's role in coverup **5**, 1860

on knowledge of Liddy's background **4**, 1609

on knowledge of Liddy's role at CRP **4**, 1608-1609

on knowledge of planned bombing of Brookings Institution **5**, 1861

on knowledge of Segretti matter **5**, 1861-62

on knowledge of Watergate details **5**, 1858-59

on Krogh bringing Liddy to his office **4**, 1638-40

on Krogh's activities **4**, 1639

on Krogh's and Ehrlichman's involvement in Ellsberg matter **5**, 1904-1905

on LaRue withholding information from him **5**, 1933

on LaRue's presence at Key Biscayne meetings **4**, 1615-16

on LaRue's testimony on Liddy plan **5**, 1875

on last meeting with Nixon **5**, 1911

on learning about Ellsberg matter **5**, 1890-92

on learning about Watergate break-in **5**, 1848-49

on legislation to prevent irregularities in election campaigns **5**, 1821

on Liddy debriefing **4**, 1644-45 **5**, 1878, 1880, 1881-82, 1884, 1918-20

on Liddy hiring by CRP **5**, 1924-26

on Liddy plan **4**, 1609-13 **5**, 1843-45

on Liddy's intelligence work **5**, 1848

on logs **4**, 1619, 1669-70 **5**, 1885-86, 1887-88

on Magruder and Dean talking to Federal Prosecutors **4**, 1635

on Magruder's allegations about his involvement in Watergate **5**, 1915-16

on Magruder's appointment at CRP **4**, 1606

on Magruder's involvement in Watergate break-in **4**, 1623 **5**, 1850-51

on Magruder's perjury **4**, 1624, 1625-26, 1628-29 **5**, 1859, 1914-15

on Magruder's testimony before Select Committee **4**, 1662-63

on Magruder's testimony that he approved Liddy plan **4**, 1614-15

on Mardian debriefing report on Beard matter **5**, 1919-20

on Mardian debriefing report on Diem cables **5**, 1920

on meaning of "White House horrors" **4**, 1653

on meeting between Hoover and Nixon on 1968 wiretappings **4**, 1667

on meeting with Dean, Haldeman, and Ehrlichman **5**, 1888

on meeting with Dean, Magruder, and Liddy **4**, 1609-11

on meeting with Dean and Nixon **4**, 1635

on meeting with LaRue and Magruder at Key Biscayne **4**, 1668-69

on meeting with Liddy and Dean **4**, 1637-38

on meeting with Liddy before Watergate break-in **5**, 1875-76

on meeting with Liddy on June 15 **5**, 1875-76

on meeting with Magruder **4**, 1633-34

Mitchell, John N., testimony of *(Continued)*
on meeting with Magruder and Dean **4**, 1634-35
on meeting with Magruder before grand jury testimony **5**, 1896-98
on meeting with Mardian, Magruder, and Sloan **4**, 1659-60
on meeting with Nixon, Dean, Haldeman, and Ehrlichman **5**, 1863
on meeting with Sloan **5**, 1884
on meeting with Stans on Dahlberg and Mexican checks **4**, 1659-60
on meetings after Watergate break-in **4**, 1622 **5**, 1851-53, 1881-82, 1931-32
on meetings and telephone conversations with Nixon **4**, 1674-79
on meetings in log book **5**, 1878-81, 1883, 1884
on meetings prior to Watergate **5**, 1815-16
on meetings with Dean after Watergate **5**, 1876-77
on meetings with Ehrlichman being taped **4**, 1651-52
on meetings with Liddy **5**, 1875-76
on meetings with Mardian and LaRue **4**, 1671-72 **5**, 1878
on meetings with McPhee, Mardian, and O'Brien **5**, 1907-1908
on meetings with Nixon after Watergate break-in **4**, 1633, 1665
on meetings with White House staff members on Patman Committee **5**, 1898-99
on money given to Liddy **5**, 1847-48
on money remaining after 1968 campaign **4**, 1658-59
on Moore asking him to help raise money for defendants **5**, 1920-21, 1934-36
on Nixon learning about Watergate and coverup **4**, 1680-81
on Nixon removing people from White House staff after learning about coverup **5**, 1894-95
on Nixon's behavior after Dean tells him about Watergate **5**, 1894-95
on Nixon's chances for reelection at time of Watergate break-in **4**, 1642-43
on Nixon's fidelity to truth-telling **5**, 1865
on Nixon's involvement in Watergate break-in or coverup **4**, 1627-28, 1636
on Nixon's reaction after learning of White House staff members involved in Watergate **5**, 1921
on Nixon's reaction if he had known about White House horrors **5**, 1895
on Nixon's refusal to testify before Select Committee or to give access to presidential papers **5**, 1867
on Nixon's refusal to turn material over to Select Committee **5**, 1838
on Nixon's statement of April 17, 1973, about "beginning new intensive inquiries" into Watergate **5**, 1888-90
opening statement relinquished by **4**, 1602
opinion of Dean **5**, 1841-42
on payments to Liddy **4**, 1616-18
on people consulted relative to Watergate **5**, 1877
on persons involved in responding to Democrats' civil litigation **5**, 1877
on Plumbers operation **4**, 1605

on political activities while serving as attorney general **5**, 1856-57
on political intelligence **4**, 1602
on possibility of becoming scapegoat for Watergate **4**, 1665-66
on power to authorize electronic surveillance **4**, 1603
on presidency **5**, 1830-33
on protection of good name of President **5**, 1829
on protection of presidency **5**, 1908-1909
on reaction to McCord's revelations **5**, 1913-14
on reaction to Nixon's announcement of "Dean Report" **5**, 1900-1901
on reasons for denying knowledge of Liddy debriefing during **5**, 1870
on reasons for not asking Colson about White House horrors **5**, 1932-33
on reasons for not informing Nixon about White House horrors **4**, 1628 **5**, 1825-28, 1830-37, 1853-55, 1865, 1866-68, 1872-73, 1882, 1884-85
on reasons for not informing Nixon of Liddy plan **4**, 1632-33 **5**, 1816-19
on reasons for not informing Nixon on Watergate **4**, 1666-67 **5**, 1827-28, 1830-37, 1853-55, 1865, 1866-68, 1872-73, 1882
on reasons for permitting Magruder's perjury **4**, 1643-44
on reasons for resigning as head of CRP **5**, 1886
on reasons why telephone conversations with Nixon appear on White House logs and not on his logs **5**, 1887-88
on relationship between civil suits and Watergate coverup **5**, 1899
on relationship with Haldeman in operation of CRP **4**, 1607-1608
on relationship with Kalmbach **5**, 1824
on relationship with McCord **5**, 1824-25
on relationship with Nixon **4**, 1602 **5**, 1839-41
on reports from Dean **5**, 1904
on resignation as campaign director **4**, 1664-65 **5**, 1885
on response to Liddy plan **5**, 1871-72
on responsibility for cash disbursements at CRP **4**, 1656-69
on role at CRP **4**, 1606-1607
on role in meetings with Magruder, Mardian, LaRue, and Dean after Watergate **5**, 1902-1903
on running of political campaigns **5**, 1820
on security measures at CRP **4**, 1668
on sources of information after Watergate break-in **5**, 1849
on Strachan's responsibilities **4**, 1608
on Strachan's role as liaison between White House and CRP **5**, 1860-61
on supposed isolation from Nixon **4**, 1665-66
on suppression of White House horror stories **5**, 1905 **5**, 1903-1904
on talks with Nixon after Kleindienst and Petersen name him as possibly involved in Watergate **5**, 1916
on talks with White House people on Watergate **4**, 1661-62
on telephone call to Maroulis **4**, 1652
on telephone calls between his home and White House **5**, 1912-14

on telephone conversation between reporter and Mrs. Mitchell **5**, 1936

on telephone conversation with Nixon after Watergate arrests **5**, 1879, 1886-87

on telephone conversations with Dean after Watergate **5**, 1879-80

on telephone conversations with Kalmbach after Watergate **5**, 1883

on testimony in new grand jury investigation compared with previous grand jury hearing **5**, 1916-18

on timing of learning about Watergate break-in **4**, 1660-61

on Ulasewicz **4**, 1606 **FR** 117

on Watergate break-in **4**, 1621-22, 1642 **FR** 27-28

on Watergate coverup **4**, 1624-26, 1671-72 **5**, 1853

on Watergate incident as "ridiculous caper" **5**, 1850

on White House horror stories **4**, 1622, 1653 **5**, 1826

on White House horror stories distinguished from Watergate break-in **5**, 1901-1902, 1903

on willingness to protect Nixon **5**, 1869, 1921-22

on wiretapping after SALT leaks **4**, 1626-27

Mitchell, Martha (Mrs. John N. Mitchell) 1, 126, 186 **3**, 1310E **4**, 1646, 1665, 1675 **5**, 1824 **6**, 2280, 2301 **12**, 4940 **22**, 10639-40

Baldwin hired as security officer for **1**, 158-159, 186, 225, 392-93, 394-95

calls to White House **5**, 1913

campaigns for Nixon **8**, 3165-66

death threats against **2**, 861

FBI interview with **5**, 1927 **9**, 3545

on her husband being fall guy **5**, 1936

Kalmbach's calls to Mitchell and **5**, 1883

McCord traveling with **5**, 1825

and meetings between Mitchell and Nixon **3**, 1084-85

and Mitchell's resignation as head of CRP **5**, 1885

threats against **1**, 174, 201, 203

Mitchell memos

for McLaren on antitrust suit against AMPI **FR** 768-69

from Buchanan about McGovern responses **10**, 3975, 4248-49E

from Buchanan and Khachigian, "Attack Organization and Strategy" **10**, 3975, 4209-20E

from Buchanan and Khachigian on Democratic contenders **10**, 4226-34E

from Buchanan on basic attack strategy **10**, 3975, 4236E

from Buchanan on McGovern strategy **10**, 3975, 4235E, 4237-39E

from Buchanan on Tennessee primary **10**, 4205E

from Buchanan on *New York Times* article about Jackson's strategists seeking earlier Tennessee primary **10**, 3975, 4205-08E

from Cole on support for Nixon's Vietnam speech **FR** 301-304E

from CRP on interest groups **13**, 5323, 5533-34E

from Dent on meeting with southern Black leaders **19**, 8613-14E **FR** 365

from Heringer to Malek on Responsiveness briefing of **18**, 8208, 8342-47E

from Magruder, "Democratic and Republican Contenders" **10**, 3975, 4174-84E

from Magruder about plans for activities at the Democratic National Convention **10**, 3975, 4221-24E

from Magruder on Cabinet Committee **FR** 395

from Magruder on CRP assuming White House support activities **4**, 1655-56

from Magruder on Democratic '72 Sponsors Club **10**, 3975, 4196E

from Magruder on interest group reports **19**, 8813-18E

from Magruder on interest in Federal resources **19**, 8595-8596E

from Magruder on Muskie campaign organization **11**, 4695, 4889-91E

from Magruder on previous memo about contender tracking and strategy **10**, 3975, 4225-34E

from Magruder on "Resource Development" **FR** 362-63

from Magruder on tracking presidential contenders **10**, 3975, 4185-91E

from Magruder on use of Federal resources by Eisenhower, Johnson, and Humphrey **19**, 8598-99E **FR** 363-64

from Malek on Black Vote Campaign Plan **18**, 8258, 8414-16E **19**, 8859-61E **FR** 377-78

from Malek on meeting to discuss role in re-election effort **18**, 8201, 8297-8304E

from Odle and Evans on "Citizens Campaign for 1972" **FR** 325-35E

from Strachan to Haldeman on agenda for **16**, 7466, 7500-0E

from Todd on Flemming **19**, 9093-94E

from Todd through Malek on Older Americans Division **19**, 9055-9134E

from White House on exploitation of "fissures" within Democratic party **10**, 3975, 4197-4204E

to Hoover on Dunes Hotel acquisition **23**, 11057-58

on La Raza Unida to **FR** 397-98

Mittler, Austin 1, 134 **9**, 3794

Mobile Crime Unit 1, 114

search of Watergate complex by **1**, 106-107

Moczygemba, Arthur 15, 6703E

Model Cities grant in Los Angeles

Malek on **18**, 8219-20

Mollenhoff, Clark 3, 992 **4**, 1489, 1559, 1560 **5**, 2056-57 **23**, 11227, 11228, 11260 **FR** 252E

asks IRS for tax returns **FR** 137-38

and investigation of Muskie's association with Maine sugar industry **21**, 9726-27

Moncourt, Nicole 21, 9949, 10052 **23**, 10956 **24**, 11310

Greer on documents of **22**, 10533-37

Greer's objections to line of questioning of **22**, 10514-15

Griffin's dealings with on transfer of Rebozo's account to B & C account **23**, 10753-54

letter to Stans with receipted slip for contributions **22**, 12570-71E

Moncourt, Nicole, testimony of 22, 10485-10537
  on bookkeeping assignments 22, 10486, 10488-89, 10500, 10511-14
  on business or financial dealings with Rebozo 22, 10500
  checks missing from Rebozo's personal account 22, 10506-10509
  on contents of Rebozo's safe-deposit box 22, 10502-10503, 10523-26
  contributions for CRP received by Rebozo 22, 10518-19
  correspondence file for Smathers 22, 10519
  denies contact between Rebozo and Colson, Haldeman, or Ehrlichman 22, 10521
  denies knowledge of Abplanalp or Griffin borrowing money from Rebozo 22, 10498
  denies knowledge of business transactions between William and Charles Rebozo 22, 10529-30
  denies knowledge of Hughes contribution 22, 10518
  denies knowledge of instructions to Wakefield in Rebozo's safe-deposit boxes 22, 10522
  denies typing or filing material related to Hughes contribution 22, 10487
  denies unusual increases in compensation 22, 10530-31
  on duties performed for Nixon 22, 10489
  on employment history 22, 10485-86
  on first knowledge of Hughes contribution 22, 10516
  on Fishers Island transaction 22, 10529-30
  Greer's objections to line of questioning of 22, 10533-37
  on IRS investigation of Rebozo 22, 10519-21
  on lock changes on Rebozo's safe-deposit boxes 22, 10528-29
  on materials furnished to IRS 22, 10520-21
  on Nixon's business dealings with Abplanalp 22, 10510-11
  on payment of legal fees by Rebozo 22, 10531-32
  on predecessor as Rebozo's bookkeeper 22, 10511
  on Rebozo's bank accounts 22, 10505-10506, 10516-10
  on Rebozo's business and financial dealings 22, 10510, 10521-22
    with Abplanalp or Griffin 22, 10398-99, 10497
    with Danner 22, 10495-97
    with Edward Nixon 22, 10499
    with F. Donald Nixon 22, 10493-94
    with Nixon 22, 10490-93
    with Smathers 22, 10513-14, 10521
    with Woods 22, 10494-95
  on Rebozo's correspondence files 22, 10487-88
  on Rebozo's correspondence with Golden 22, 10486-87
  on Rebozo's finances 22, 10515-18, 10526
  on Rebozo's loan from Hudson Valley Bank 22, 10497-98, 10504-10505
  on Rebozo's loan from Palmetto Bank & Trust Co. 22, 10498, 10503-10505
  on Rebozo's personal expenses 22, 10509-10
  on Rebozo's safety deposit boxes 22, 10501-10503
  on Rebozo's use of other names 22, 10489-90
  on Rebozo's will 22, 10522-23

on records kept on Rebozo's loans 22, 10512-14
on retention of Rebozo's financial records 22, 10527-28
on Wakefield's Special Account for Rebozo 22, 10506, 10508

Mondale, Fred 16, 7338
Monday 10, 4189E, 4198E
Money
  Alch's contribution to committee to investigate the assassination of the President 1, 323
  amount received by Porter from Sloan 2, 634-35
  AMPI payments to Jacobsen and Long 15, 6398-6404
  approved budget for Liddy's intelligence-gathering plan 2, 794
  at CRP, O'Brien tells Ehrlichman about 7, 2752
  bail for McCord 1, 305-307, 321, 323
  bill from Gleason's lawyer for Common Cause lawsuit defense 3, 1231E-32E
  budget for Liddy plan at Key Biscayne meeting 6, 2281
  budget for Subversive Activities Control Board 3, 1331E
  to "Chapman's Friends" FR 199-200
  check to Baldwin from Finance Committee 1, 455E
  checks sent from Rebozo to Kalmbach 21, 10183-85
  for citizens committee ads FR 156
  cost of Las Vegas plan 20, 9388, 9389-90
  cost of Liddy's first plan 4, 1610
  cost of manpower at anti-Nixon demonstration at Century Plaza Hotel, Los Angeles 11, 4722E
  cost of polls 8, 3121
  cost of Watergate operation 1, 220-21
  cost of wiretapping equipment 1, 236
  CRP expenses in memo from Kehrli to Haldeman 8, 3026, 3313-15E
  CRP transfers of $350,000 to White House 5, 2095-96
  Dean's financial records 4, 1515
  Dean's personal use 4, 1572-73, 1582-87, 1590-95
  Dean's reference to in discussion with Walters on Cubans' responsibility for Watergate 9, 3412-13
  disbursements made by Porter 2, 657-60
  disbursements to Liddy 5, 1847-48
  discretionary fund at Commerce Department 2, 873-74
  distributed by Kalmbach for Alabama senatorial elections 5, 2142-45
  Ehrlichman's receipt of campaign funds 7, 2858-59
  fee paid to Alch by McCord 1, 312
  fee paid to Kelly 11, 4377
  for Fielding break-in 9, 3774
  to finance re-registration of American Independent party voters 11, 4643-44
  financing of Democratic National Convention 3, 1151-56E
  found on Mrs. Hunt's body 9, 3507, 3515
  found on Watergate defendants 1, 108, 109, 149, 355-356 2, 621-22, 815, 828, 830 5, 2011-12 9, 3515-16, 3714 FR 31
  from communists to demonstrators in Haldeman memo to Dean 8, 3171-74

from foreign source to Democratic National Committee as rationale for Watergate break-in **9**, 3708, 3709-10, 3711, 3712

from Mrs. Hunt to Barker **1**, 359

from Mrs. Hunt to McCord **1**, 210, 241

from Kalmbach to Segretti **10**, 3990

from Reitz to Buckley **11**, 4443

from White House back to CRP **8**, 3195-98

given to Dean by Strachan **3**, 935-36

given to Hunt by Bittman prior to his sentencing **9**, 3707

given to Kalmbach **2**, 702-703

given to LaRue **2**, 701-702 **6**, 2293

given to Liddy by Porter **2**, 633-34, 643-46

given to Liddy by Sloan **9**, 3581-83

given to McCord **1**, 150

given to Wallace's opponent by Kalmbach **4**, 1536-37

Haldeman on reasons for not using campaign funds for Watergate defendants **8**, 3148-49

Harmony's salary at Inaugural Committee **2**, 474

honorarium paid to Muskie for speaking at AMPI convention **16**, 7018-19

in Hunt's conversation with Colson **9**, 3779

Hunt's payments at White House **20**, 9347

Kalmbach on surplus funds from 1968 campaign **5**, 2093

Kalmbach's payments to Segretti **3**, 1299E-1300E **FR** 162, 163

lack of financial support for Republican senatorial candidates in South **6**, 2483-85

left over from 1968 campaign **4**, 1581-82, 1658-59 **5**, 2143 **8**, 3118-19

letter from Sloan to Mitchell on accounting of $2,000 made available for Walker **8**, 3190, 3324E

to Liddy, Porter's reasons for perjury on **2**, 638-42

to Liddy, Sloan testimony on **7**, 2698-99

Liddy's budgets for intelligence-gathering **2**, 788

Lilly loan for AMPI contribution **15**, 6389-98

to McCord from Republican National Committee **1**, 216

McCord's salary with CRP **1**, 168-70, 230

for McGovern supporters to promote activity against Muskie **11**, 4516

meeting notes on campaign spending **3**, 968, 1226-30E

memo from Kehrli to Haldeman on CRP general budget items **8**, 3024-26

not mentioned in FBI interview of Sloan **2**, 565

offered to Connally by Jacobsen **15**, 6421-25

offered to McCord **1**, 141

one million dollars discussed at Nixon-Dean March 21 meeting **8**, 3068-69, 3211

paid by Benz to Griffin **11**, 4431

paid by Benz to Hearing for placing stink bombs at Muskie picnic **11**, 4413

paid by Buckley to Wyatt **11**, 4450, 4451, 4453

paid by CRP to Baldwin **1**, 393, 394

paid by Hunt to Fat Jack **9**, 3761

paid by Mrs. Hunt to Bittman **9**, 3692, 3693-94

paid by Kalmbach to Segretti **10**, 4030

paid by Reitz to Buckley **11**, 4445-46

paid by Segretti to Kelly and Benz **10**, 3983

paid for surveillance, infiltration, dirty tricks, etc. **11**, 4638, 4639, 4640,4644

paid to Barker for Ellsberg and Watergate break-ins **1**, 357-358, 360, 384-85

paid to Benz by Segretti **11**, 4404-4405

paid to Mrs. Caulfield **22**, 10247

paid to Greaves **FR** 191

paid to Gregory **FR** 197

paid to Hunt and Mrs. Hunt **9**, 3798, 3799E, 3800-3802

paid to Kelly **11**, 4386

paid to McMinoway **11**, 4505-4506 **FR** 192

paid to O'Brien by Hughes Tool Co. **21**, 9956

paid to political infiltrators by Benz **11**, 4405

paid to Watergate defendants **3**, 936 **9**, 3711

paid to Wyatt **11**, 4440

passed from Sloan to LaRue **6**, 2366, 2367

payments for expenses at CRP **6**, 2324-25

payments to Liddy **4**, 1616-18

payments to McCord **1**, 188

payments to Ulascewicz **1**, 290

planned budget for Watergate operation **1**, 145

for police protection at political functions **12**, 5001-5002

provided by Liddy as contingency money for Hunt **9**, 3689

Ragan's checks made out to Caulfield **21**, 9700

received by McCord **1**, 243

received by McMinoway **11**, 4519

received by Segretti from Kalmbach **10**, 3986

Reisner's salary at CRP **2**, 518, 527-28

rent for McCord's room near McGovern's headquarters **1**, 154

reported discretionary fund of $1 million at Commerce Department **2**, 695-96

for re-registration scheme in California **FR** 204

returned by LaRue to Finance Committee **6**, 2334-35

salary increases for White House staff members moved to CRP **8**, 3023

Segretti's salary **10**, 3980, 3981-82

sent to Hunt through Bittman **9**, 3724-25

source of payment to Caulfield **1**, 270

spent for ad in or support of Hanoi-Haiphong bombing **6**, 2461-62

spent on Federal elections **11**, 4686, 4687

spent on Muskie campaign compared with money for Liddy plan **11**, 4673-74

spent on Segretti's operation **10**, 4021

Stans one-million-dollar fund **7**, 2791

Strachan on transfer of $350,000 from CRP to White House **6**, 2461-64, 2494-96, 2497-2500

transferred from CRP to White House **8**, 3047-50, 3115-16, 3119-20 **12**, 4909

turned over to Sloan by Kalmbach **5**, 2094

Ulasewicz's salary **1**, 291 **6**, 2268-69, 2270, 2272

for Watergate break-in **9**, 3723

in White House **6**, 2295-96, 2297

See also Campaign contributions; Financial matters; Hush money

Monocle Restaurant, Washington, D.C. 1, 213, 214, 300, 313, 314, 322, 335

Monro, Sterling **13**, 5464 **14**, 5478
Monroe, Charles M. **1**, 113
Montgomery County, Ohio, CRP **12**, 5009, 5163-64E
Montoya, Joseph M. **1**, 141
    on Ambrose's objections to line of questioning of
        Griffin **23**, 10786, 10787
    asks to be excused from hearing of Harrison **14**,
        6262
    on conflicts in testimony of Ehrlichman and oth-
        ers **7**, 2772
    on effects of Watergate **9**, 3550
    on Frates' objections to line of questioning of
        Rebozo **21**, 9959
    on Frates' statement that Bellino and Armstrong
        were out to "get" Rebozo **21**, 10123-24
    on Harrison's request for open hearing **14**, 6246
    on impact of leaks on Griffin **23**, 10791
    on leaks **23**, 10793
    letter from McGovern denying he has ever seen
        McMinoway **11**, 4588-89, 4617, 4743E
    on Marumoto's testimony on Spanish-speaking
        voters FR 380-81
    on memo from Failor to Magruder **12**, 5016, 5017
    on Nixon attempts to "buy" Spanish-speaking
        voters **13**, 5308
    opening statement **1**, 9
    political contributions to opponents of **14**, 6255,
        6257
    requests Select Committee subpoena Buzhardt **4**,
        1430
    and rulings on Griffin's attorney-client privilege
        claims on testimony re Rebozo and Abplanalp
        23, 10757, 10758-59, 10760, 10761, 10765-68,
        10774, 10775, 10776, 10777, 10778, 10779
Montoya, Joseph M., questioning by
    Alch **1**, 349-353
    Atkins **13**, 5457, 5458
    Barrett **1**, 115-116
    Barth **23**, 11224, 11226, 11252-35
    Bartlome **13**, 5435, 5436
    Benz **11**, 4427, 4428
    Bernhard **11**, 4684, 4685
    Buchanan **10**, 3965-71
    Buckley **11**, 4457-59
    Butterfield **5**, 2084-86
    Campbell **12**, 4958-61
    Caulfield **1**, 269-273
    Dean **3**, 1074-95 **4**, 1508-11
    Fernandez **13**, 5386-99
    Gray **9**, 3508-12, 3534-37, 3550, 3551
    Haldeman **8**, 3109-13, 3125-27, 3153-57, 3174-77,
        3178, 3189
    Hanman **14**, 5868, 5873-79, 5880-81
    Harmony **2**, 478-81
    Harrison **14**, 6278-79
    Heller **12**, 4972-74
    Helms **8**, 3250
    Hunt **9**, 3746-49, 3775-79, 3793-96
    Kalmbach **5**, 2115-21, 2176, 2177
    Kehrli **1**, 93-95
    Kelly **11**, 4398-4400
    Kleindienst **9**, 3599-3603
    LaRue **6**, 2315-22

MacGregor **12**, 4921-26
Malek **18**, 8204, 8206-8207
Mankiewicz **11**, 4627-34
Mardian **6**, 2410-18
Marumoto **13**, 5301-08, 5325, 5326
McCord **1**, 182-188, 227-132
McMinoway **11**, 4519-22⁻
Mitchell **5**, 1839-56
Moore **5**, 2048-58
Odle **1**, 36-41, 72-74
Petersen **9**, 3656-58
Porter **2**, 672-76
Preistes **13**, 5353-55
Rebozo **21**, 9960, 9965-66, 9968-69, 9971-72,
    10103
Reisner **2**, 522-27
Robinson **13**, 5492
Segretti **10**, 4012-15
Sloan **2**, 614-25
Spater **13**, 5518, 5519
Stans **2**, 709-17
Stearns **11**, 4589, 4590
Strachan **6**, 2473-78
Sullivan **12**, 5005, 5006
Ulasewicz **6**, 2267-70
Walters **9**, 3423-26
Wild **13**, 5478, 5479
Montoya, Joseph M., statement of FR 1167-69
Monuments
    plot to destroy **1**, 250
Moody, Richard **16**, 7135
Moore, Charles **15**, 6503
Moore, Diane V.
    and Muskie campaign **11**, 4658, 4695, 4815-16E
Moore, George C. **8**, 3401E
Moore, Jack
    affidavit of **12**, 5009, 5174-75E
Moore, James, questioning by
    Danner **24**, 11464-69, 11537-40
Moore, Jan D. **20**, 9428
Moore, Jonathan **18**, 8461
Moore, Paul **1**, 43
Moore, Powell **1**, 34, 55 **2**, 799 **5**, 1877, 1953, 2063
    accompanies Liddy during request to Kleindienst
        to release Watergate burglars FR 32
    at meetings after Watergate arrests **5**, 1952
    call to Mardian after Watergate arrests **6**, 2353
    Kleindienst on work relationship with **9**, 3561
    Liddy and **6**, 2381
    with Liddy when Kleindienst is informed about
        Watergate break-in **9**, 3560, 3561-62
Moore, Richard Anthony **2**, 850 **3**, 956, 967, 979,
    980, 982, 1010, 1210E **4**, 1402 **5**, 1877 **7**, 2743 **11**,
    4568 **12**, 4943
    advice to Dean **4**, 1397, 1434-35
    asks Mitchell to raise hush money **5**, 1920-21,
        1934-36
    assigned to discuss fundraising for Watergate de-
        fendants with Mitchell FR 77
    at La Costa meetings with Haldeman, Ehrlich-
        man, Dean **3**, 982-86
    at meetings with Nixon and Dean **4**, 1381, 1402,
        1404-1405, 1406

confidential memo from Buchanan on topics for discussion at meeting of June 24, 1971 **10,** 3975, 4173E

conversation with Dean after McCord's letter to Sirica is read in open court **3,** 1003-04

conversations with Dean on Watergate **FR** 89

Dean and **4,** 1397, 1541

Dean discusses hush money with **3,** 997

Dean protests about Nixon's announcement of "Dean report" to **4,** 1368

Dean shows FBI files to **4,** 1362

discussions with Dean on coverup **3,** 997 **4,** 1579

discussions with Dean on his concern about becoming fall guy **4,** 1579

has FBI reports during talk with Strachan and Chapin **6,** 2485-86

in hypothetical question and answer session to prepare Ziegler for press conference **3,** 965, 1200-1208E

interviews Mitchell on Liddy plan meetings **7,** 2752-53

Kleindienst and **9,** 3595

meeting with Liddy **2,** 823

meeting with Liddy and Kleindienst after Watergate arrests **2,** 820

meeting with Mitchell on raising money for Watergate defendants **4,** 1511

meeting with Nixon **3,** 996

meeting with Strachan and Chapin on Segretti matter **6,** 2485-86

and Mitchell's responsibility for raising hush money **3,** 987

and Nixon's handling of Segretti matter **FR** 183

and presidential press conferences **3,** 1075

reads FBI reports on Watergate investigation **3,** 945

relationship with Dean **4,** 1421-22

says Dean was assigned to write report at La Costa **4,** 1421-22

and Segretti coverup **FR** 187

and Segretti matter **FR** 184-85

skeptical of newspaper reports during political campaign **5,** 2121

summation of Segretti involvement in Watergate by **3,** 1010, 1294-1307E

talks with Dean **4,** 1518

telephone conversation with Dean on Watergate problems **3,** 1004-05

and Watergate coverup **2,** 823

on White House response to Segretti matter **10,** 4043

Moore, Richard Anthony, testimony of 5, 1938-62, 1963-2048, 2049-73

advises Nixon to speak to nation about coverup **5,** 1984

asked to talk to Mitchell on hush money **5,** 1966-67

at meeting with Nixon, Ziegler, and Dean **5,** 1943

attitude toward La Costa meeting discussion of Select Committee members **5,** 1992-93

biographical sketch **5,** 1946

on briefing for his testimony before Select Committee **5,** 1991-92

on Buzhardt memo inaccuracies **5,** 2065, 2068

on career **5,** 1938, 1998-2002

claims he told U.S. Attorneys about Hunt's demands for money **5,** 2064

on community activities in Los Angeles **5,** 2001

on comparisons of his testimony with Dean's **5,** 1985-88

on conflicts on testimony on remembered conversations **5,** 2040

on connecting Watergate to Segretti matter **5,** 2035

on contradictory testimony on his request that Mitchell raise money for Watergate defendants **5,** 2049-53

credibility of **5,** 1998

on Dahlberg and Mexican checks **5,** 1993-94

on Dean talking about meeting on Liddy's plans **5,** 1970-71, 1972

on Dean telling him about Ehrlichman's involvement in Ellsberg matter **5,** 1989

on Dean telling him about Hunt's demands for money **5,** 1981-82, 2053-54, 2063-64

on Dean telling him about Magruder perjury **5,** 1970-71

on Dean telling Nixon about Watergate coverup **5,** 1939, 1945, 1959-60, 1977-78 1979, 1980-81, 1982, 1986-87

on Dean testimony **5,** 2004-2006, 2043-44

on Dean's call from Camp David **5,** 1971-72

on Dean's hints about activities of Plumbers **5,** 1972

on Dean's indictable list **5,** 1988-90

on Dean's suggestion that FBI investigate Select Committee members **5,** 1975-76, 1995

on Dean's testimony about discussion of money at La Costa **5,** 1941-42

on Dean's testimony on hush money **5,** 1958-59

on decision to ask Mitchell to raise hush money **5,** 1941-42

denies discussions of Watergate in meetings with Nixon and Dean **5,** 1953-54, 1959

differentiated from other witnesses **5,** 1997-98

on difficulty in remembering dates **5,** 2059

discusses Dean's charges with Nixon **5,** 1982-83

on discussion of Mitchell's problems with grand jury and Vesco at meeting with Nixon and Dean **5,** 2067

on discussion with Mitchell **5,** 1942-43

on discussions with Nixon on Watergate **5,** 1955-56

on duties at White House **5,** 2002

on errors in transcript of interview with Lenzner **5,** 2058-59

on factors preventing knowledge of White House staff involvement in Watergate **5,** 2020-2021

on Fielding break-in **5,** 1960-62

on Garment's request for his testimony after Mitchell's **5,** 1990

on Gray hearings and Dean **5,** 1943

on Haldeman, Ehrlichman, and Dean's involvement in Watergate coverup **5,** 2007

on Hunt remaining on White House payroll after Fielding break-in **5,** 2016-17

on Hunt's demands for money **5,** 1944

on hush money **5,** 2027, 2042-43

Morgan, Edward L. **14,** 6082 **15,** 6905 **16,** 7374 **20,**
9477, 9478, 9479, 10190 **21,** 9969-70 **22,** 10227,
10279, 10622 **23,** 11057, 11261 **24,** 11402, 11403,
11408, 11415, 11418-20, 11430, 11437, 11438,
11442 **26,** 1294E **FR** 986
  advice from Alagia on loan from SPACE to
    ADEPT **16,** 7084
  and Alagia's purchase of Republican fundraising
    dinner tickets **16,** 7070
  at meeting with Maheu, O'Brien, and Davis **24,**
    11590-91
  on attorney-client relationship and Kalmbach-
    Rebozo discussions **21,** 10187
  brief on school busing by **24,** 11458
  business dealings with Danner **20,** 9497-98
  conversations with Danner on Hughes contribu-
    tion **24,** 11549-50
  Danner and **FR** 935
  Danner denies he was present at meetings in New
    York in 1968 **20,** 9506
  Danner denies telling Rebozo about personal con-
    tribution from **20,** 9500
  and Danner's meeting with Maheu **24,** 11447
  and Dunes Hotel acquisition **20,** 9580 **FR** 996
  Ehrlichman asks advice on Getty contribution for
    White House social events **FR** 941
  flights with Wearley **20,** 9454
  and Hughes contribution **24,** 11418, 11440, 11441
  letter to Maheu with data on Nevada hotel opera-
    tions **26,** 12825-31E
  meeting with Danner and Rebozo **20,** 9498-99
  meeting with Danner and Rebozo on Hughes con-
    tribution in 1968 **21,** 9939-44
  meeting with Mitchell, Danner and Rebozo **21,**
    9976-77
  meeting with Rebozo and Danner **20,** 9505-9506
    FR 936-37
  and Rebozo's efforts to get contribution from
    Hughes in 1968 **20,** 9495-97, 9498-99, 9500-
    9501, 9503, 9505
  See also Kalmbach, Herbert W., testimony of
Morgan, Reuben T. **19,** 8872-81E
Morics, Smitty **23,** 11273
Moroney, Kevin **3,** 1057
Morris, Benjamin W. **22,** 12540E
Morris, Dwight **17,** 7664
  Butterbrodt contradicts testimony of **17,** 7650-51,
    7672-73
  cover letter from Hamilton and Sanders on ques-
    tionnaire of **16,** 7447, 7454E
  meeting with Butterbrodt **17,** 7648-51
Morris, Dwight, testimony of **16,** 7439-50
  on AMPI contributions and milk price-support is-
    sue **16,** 7440-41
  on AMPI's political perspective **16,** 7441-42
  on antitrust suit against AMPI **16,** 7442-47
  denies knowledge of AMPI contributions in 1969
    and 1970 **16,** 7440
  on discussions with Butterbrodt on antitrust suit
    against AMPI **16,** 7444-45, 7447-50
  on formation of TAPE **16,** 7440-41
  on Kalmbach's refusal of AMPI contribution **16,**
    7446-47
  on meeting between Mehren, Butterbrodt, and
    Kalmbach **16,** 7445-46

official positions with AMPI and other dairy organizations until 1972 **16,** 7439
questionnaire of Select Committee completed by
  16, 7447, 7451-53E
on telephone call threatening Parr **16,** 7447-48 **FR**
  636-37
on trip to and from Washington, D.C **16,** 7447-50
Morrison, John, statement of **25,** 11747-64, 11809
  on Chestnut taking proceeds of Duncan loan to
    California **25,** 11758-59
  on claim against him for Duncan loan **25,** 11752-
    53
  claims no knowledge of Humphrey campaign fi-
    nances **25,** 11763-64
  on contributions to Humphrey campaign **25,**
    11763
  denies keeping petty cash in his desk **25,** 11760
  denies knowledge about campaign contributions
    25, 11760-61
  denies knowledge of Loeb contribution **25,** 11759
  denies political services for Humphrey before
    January 1972 **25,** 11750-51
  discussions with Humphrey **25,** 11763
  and Duncan loan to Humphrey campaign **25,**
    11751-53, 11800
  on expenses paid by Humphrey campaign **25,**
    11764
  on financial dealings of Humphrey campaign **25,**
    11753-54
  on fundraising activities for Humphrey campaign
    25, 11749-50
  on other deputy campaign managers in Humphrey
    campaign **25,** 11749
  on participation in handling of proceeds of Dun-
    can loan **25,** 11754-59
  on proceeds from Duncan loan left in his desk **25,**
    11756-58
  on records of Humphrey campaign **25,** 11762
  on relationship with Thatcher before 1972 **25,**
    11751
  on removal of cash from his desk **25,** 11761
  on role in Humphrey campaign **25,** 11721-22,
    11748-49
  on taking proceeds of Duncan loan to West Vir-
    ginia **25,** 11755-56
  on travel for Humphrey campaign **25,** 11764
Morrison, Paul **10,** 3975, 4265E **11,** 4810E
Morse, Wayne **3,** 1141E
Mortan, Ben, Jr. **14,** 6080
Morton, Bruce **12,** 5017 **FR** 200
Morton, Robert **2,** 541
Morton, Rogers **12,** 5027E
Morton, Thurston **13,** 5461
Moser, John **14,** 5875
  at meeting between Nixon and dairy coop re-
    presentatives **16,** 7063
  deposition in Nader v. Butz **16,** 7067-68
  meeting with Alagia on SPACE contributions to
    Nixon's reelection campaign **16,** 7069
  role in Dairymen, Inc. **FR** 585
  and SPACE **16,** 7065

Moskow, Michael H.
  memo for under secretary on Responsiveness program committee within ASPER **19,** 8809-10E
Moskowitz, Larry 12, 5085E, 5093E
Mote, Thomas 9, 3491
Mott, Stewart Rawlings 3, 1138E **10,** 4245E, 4284E **11,** 4599-4600, 4612, 4623, 4629-30, 4668, 4678-79 **12,** 5183E **25,** 12182
  Accountability Project **11,** 4681
  campaign flier entitled: "Disgusting--the Secret Money in Presidential Politics" **25,** 12133E
  on enemies list **4,** 1696E
  and Lewis contribution to McGovern campaign **25,** 12198
  memo from Hodgkin to Sanders on presidential contributions by **25,** 12136E
  and Muskie's Florida campaign **11,** 4664-65
  negative advertising paid for by **25,** 12132-33E
  role in McGovern camapaign **11,** 4623-24
  in Segretti material against Muskie **10,** 4004-4005
  Segretti use doctored reprint of ad by **FR** 172
Mott, Stewart Rawlings, statement of 25, 12091-12130
  on ads taken in newspapers on campaign **25,** 12105-12106
  on assets **25,** 12094
  on attitude toward Muskie Accountability Project **25,** 12129-30
  on background of Newton **25,** 12109-10
  on campaign contributions **25,** 12116-23
  on campaign contributions through donative sales of stock **25,** 12118-19, 12121-22
  on candidate-contributor relations **25,** 12098
  on compliance with Campaign Finance Act **25,** 12121
  on consultation with McGovern campaign staff on Muskie Accountability Project **25,** 12109-10, 12111
  on contacts with Muskie campaign staff on Muskie Accountability Project material **25,** 12104-12105
  on contributors to Muskie campaign **25,** 12106-12107
  on decision to support McGovern for **25,** 12095-96
  on disclosure of campaign contributions **25,** 12118
  on discussions on Muskie Accountability Project **25,** 12100-12101, 12123-25
  on Dobrovir's inquiry into Stone's disclosure **25,** 12121
  on GAO reports **25,** 12110
  on Gwirtzman letter **25,** 12106
  on influence of Muskie Accountability Project **25,** 12128-29
  on involvement with Tuck **25,** 12113-14
  on legal opinions on donative sales of stocks **25,** 12122
  on letter to Humphrey in 1968 **25,** 12096-97
  on material distributed on Picker's involvement in pornography **25,** 12106
  on meeting with Muskie in 1971 **25,** 12098-99
  on meetings with political candidates **25,** 12098
  on Muskie Accountability Project **25,** 12099-12107, 12110-12, 12127-28

on Muskie's failure to disclose names of contributors **25,** 12128-29, 12130
  on negative ads on Muskie **25,** 12129
  on occupation **25,** 12091-92
  on offices maintained by **25,** 12092-94
  on opinions of Hart and Mankiewicz on Muskie Accountability Project material **25,** 12125
  on payment for Muskie Accountability Project **25,** 12123
  on political activities **25,** 12094, 12095
  on principles behind campaign contributions **25,** 12107-12108
  on publications other than Muskie pamphlet **25,** 12112-13
  on reaction of McGovern staff to negative ads on Muskie **25,** 12126
  on signing name to Muskie Accountability Project **25,** 12110
  on Sixtus Corporation **25,** 12110, 12122-23
  on solicitation by McGovern of campaign contribution **25,** 12117
  on source of material on Muskie **25,** 12127
  on sources for Muskie Accountability Project material **25,** 12101-12102, 12123
  on Spectemur Agendo foundation **25,** 12092-93
  on staff **25,** 12092-93
  on *The Reliable Source* **25,** 12112, 12113-14
  on truthfulness of negative research **25,** 12115-16
  on unfair advantage of wealthy contributors over average wage earners **25,** 12120
  on use of offices for political activities **25,** 12095
  on use of term "draft dodger" in Muskie material **25,** 12103-12104
Moulds, Darlene 23, 11260
Moulton, Sandy 11, 4774E
Mountain, Barry 1, 205, 231, 271
  and Caulfield's employment by CRP **1,** 253
  memo on security measures to Republican National Committee employees **3,** 1130-32E
Mounts, Robert T. 12, 5196E
Mucher, Gus 14, 6060
Mudge, John 3, 1135E
Mudge, Rose, Guthrie, and Alexander 6, 2445-46 **25,** 12122 **FR** 451
  and TWA litigation **24,** 11580-82
Mudgett, Fred A. 25, 12265
  letter from Lifflander on franchises for Hertz project **25,** 12382-84E
Mueller, Jim 16, 7076, 7077, 7078, 7081
Mulcahy, Jack
  and Tell It To Hanoi Committee **FR** 154
Mulcahy, John A. 16, 7396 **17,** 7592, 7600 **FR** 506, 507
  campaign contributions **17,** 7807
  letter from Kalmbach to Stans on contribution of **17,** 7807, 7816E
Mullen, William G. 11, 4461, 4890E
Mullen & Co. 9, 3698, 3690 **20,** 9347, 9365, 9366 **24,** 11593-94
  Hunt fired by **9,** 3898E
  relationship with CIA **FR** 1121-26, 1151-52

Muskie, Edmund S. *(Continued)*

letter from Morrison to Loeb at *Manchester Guardian* **10,** 3975, 4265E

letter to Jackson campaign manager from "A Former Muskie Staff Worker" **10,** 4026, 4279E

letter to Nelson acknowledging campaign contributions **16,** 7016, 7058E

letter to Russell expressing appreciation for help **16,** 7217, 7227E

letter to senators receiving fraudulent mailing on Kennedy attributed to him **11,** 4852E

Magruder on **10,** 4175E, 4176-77E

Mankiewicz on activities at Milwaukee McGovern headquarters against **11,** 4617-18

Mankiewicz on Segretti's materials against **11,** 4611-14

mass mailing fraudulently attributed to **11,** 4695, 4847-49E

Masters denies contribution to **16,** 6967

McGovern activities against **11,** 4485-86, 4501-4502

McMinoway gives schedule to Humphrey supporters **11,** 4523-24

McMinoway infiltration of Milwaukee headquarters of **11,** 4481-82

memo from Buchanan to Nixon about **10,** 3975, 4146-53E

memo from Chapin to Segretti on activities against **10,** 3989-90

memo from Magruder to Mitchell on **11,** 4654

memo on strategy for campaign of **11,** 4817-46E

and Mott **11,** 4623-24

Mott document on **11,** 4599-4600

Mott meeting with **25,** 12098-99

newspaper advertisements against **10,** 4026, 4275-78E

and Nixon's chances for re-election at time of Watergate break-in **4,** 1642

older voters in Gallup polls and **19,** 9878E

pamphlet issued by Citizens for a Liberal Alternative against **10,** 3933-34, 3944, 4055-58E

partial list of recipients of fraudulent mailing attributed to **11,** 4695, 4850-51E

political intelligence against **2,** 472, 501 **3,** 923, 924, 934 **9,** 3685-86 **10,** 3924-25

political pranks against **6,** 2502

position on Black Americans **10,** 3969, 3983

poster "Help Muskie Support Bussing More Children Now" **10,** 3996, 4267E

in presidential polls **FR** 666

press conference on meeting with Black leaders in Watts **10,** 3966

in primaries **10,** 4155-56E, 4169E, 4231E

proposed amendment to Freedom of Information Act **11,** 4676-77

purpose of dirty tricks against **11,** 4393-98

and race issue **10,** 4269E, 4270E

reaction to attack on Mrs. Muskie **11,** 4401-4402

results of Harris polls vs. Nixon and Wallace **11,** 4695, 4764-65E

results of Harris polls vs. Nixon **11,** 4695, 4764-65E

and Ruby I **FR** 187-90

Segretti activities against **10,** 3982-83, 3987-88, 3991-92, 3995-4000, 4004-4005 **FR** 162, 163, 169, 176-78

Spanish newspaper advertisement about **10,** 4026, 4281E

speaks at AMPI convention **16,** 7017-19, 7023

staged demonstrations against **11,** 4485

stinkbombs at picnic for and at headquarters of **10,** 3982 **11,** 4382, 4412-13, 4414

stolen documents from **11,** 4814E

Stoubaugh article on **10,** 4289E

summary of voting record of **11,** 4600, 4744-63E

surveillance of **FR** 168

TAPE or AMPI contributions to **15,** 6548

as target of Gemstone plan **9,** 3747

thank-you note to Nelson **14,** 6033E

transfer of intelligence gathering to McGovern **6,** 2470

Ulasewicz activities and **FR** 110, 111

and unsigned memo about signs at demonstrations and rallies **10,** 4026, 4269E

wiretapping of campaign **11,** 4884-85E

withdrawal from presidential race

Las Vegas matter and **20,** 9348, 9353

Wyatt as political infiltrator in campaign of **11,** 4439-46

See also Bernhard, Berl, testimony of; "Canuck" letter; Democratic party primaries; Greenspun, Hank; Las Vegas matter; Muskie Accountability Project; Muskie campaign

Muskie, Jane 10, 3967-68 **11,** 4775E

"Newsmakers" column about **10,** 4026, 4282-83E

Muskie, Steve 11, 4774E

Muskie Accountability Project

influence of **25,** 12128-29

letter from Gwirtzman to **25,** 12106-12107, 12131-32E

mailing list for **25,** 12103

Mott on **25,** 12099-12107, 12109-10, 12122-30

sent to Muskie headquarters by League of Women Voters **11,** 4695, 4859-83E

sources for **25,** 12101-12102

sources used for **25,** 12104

Muskie campaign 14, 5947-56, 6024E

AMPI contributions to **14,** 5947-59, 6024E **15,** 6615-16, 6831 **16,** 7012-23, 7055-56E, 7213-16

and AMPI payments to Russell **16,** 7340

and Canuck letter **FR** 207

and Citizens for a Liberal Alternative **FR** 158

contributions to **14,** 5950, 6025E

copy of "Muskie Accountability Project" from League of Women Voters to **11,** 4695, 4859-83E

Edidin contacts Lifflander on bills owed to Hertz Corp. by **25,** 12262-66, 12271-72, 12273-74

Evans-Novak column reprinting excerpts from memo of staff of **11,** 4695, 4814E

financial reports of **11,** 4767-85E

fundraising guidelines of counsel for **11,** 4695, 4805E

fundraising reports of **11,** 4695, 4792-99E

general guidelines for fundraising **11,** 4800-4803E

and Gregory **FR** 196-97

and Hertz Corp.

See Edidin, Sol M., testimony of

impact of dirty tricks on **FR** 206

infiltration of **11,** 4695, 4815-16E **FR** 167

and investigation of Wilkes **22,** 10398-99

letter from Barry to Robinson on campaign contributions and tax matters **11,** 4806-4808E

letter from Russell on campaign contribution to **16,** 7015, 7057E

letter from Semer to Parr on **14,** 5951, 6028E

letter from Van Dyk to Nicoll on contributions to **14,** 5951, 6026-27E

letter on appreciated properties and gift tax committees as contributions for **11,** 4695, 4806-08E

letter returning corporate contributions to **4695,** 4809E

Lilly on contributions to **14,** 5950-56

material sent from Mott to **25,** 12104-12105

McMinoway infiltration of **FR** 193-94

memo from Magruder to Mitchell regarding organization of **11,** 4695, 4889-91E

memo from Nelson on campaign contributions **11,** 4804E

memos dealing with fundraising practices and policies for **11,** 4695, 4800-04E

miscellaneous notes and correspondence on contributions to **14,** 5951, 6029-40E

report of receipts and expenditures **25,** 12352-66E

Rubin contribution to **25,** 12156

and Sedan Chair I **FR** 190-92

and Semer **16,** 1789 **FR** 709-10

Semer on AMPI contribution to **16,** 7213-14

Semer on fundraising efforts for **16,** 7210-11, 7213-14

TAPE contributions to **15,** 6615-16

Whitaker affidavit on indebtedness of **11,** 4786-89E

and write-in campaign for Kennedy in New Hampshire **FR** 202

Wyatt infiltration of **FR** 188-90

Muskie Election Committee 14, 5866

thank-you notes to Russell from **14,** 6030E, 6031E

"Muskie Watch, The" 10, 3915-17, 3921, 3922, 3935, 3975, 4146-53E

Buchanan on **10,** 3936, 3965-67

Mankiewicz on **11,** 4605-4606

Musser, Dr. Marc J. 19, 9242-44E

My Lai incident

Caulfield on investigation of source of **22,** 10377-78

and Fund for Investigative Journalism **FR** 143

Myer, Benny 20, 9506

Myer, Johnny 21, 10121

Myers, Fred S.

letter from Barrick on return of contribution of Goodyear Tire & Rubber Co. to FCRP **13,** 5526, 5856E

letter to Parkinson on return of contribution of Goodyear Tire & Rubber Co. to FCRP **13,** 5526, 5855E

"Myth of Six Million" 12, 5026E

Nader, Ralph 5, 1899 **13,** 5465

Nader v. *Butz* **15,** 6441, 6445, 6523-24 **16,** 7181 **17,** 7690

Buzhardt's affidavit in **23,** 10918-19

Campbell on preparation of affidavits for **17,** 7780-82

documents identified in search of White House re-

cords pursuant to subpoena duces tecum in **17,** 8094-8017E

Haldeman on **16,** 7182-83

Hardin affidavit in **FR** 669

and impact on Kalmbach relations with milk producers **FR** 710-11

impact on White House **FR** 732-33

Kalmbach and **17,** 7610

and Kalmbach's attitudes toward milk industry contributions **17,** 7611

Kalmbach's deposition in **17,** 7807

Mehren on **16,** 7244-45, 7258

memo from Dean to Colson on **FR** 867E

memo from Dean to Ehrlichman on **16,** 7397 **FR** 863-66E

memo from Dean to Haldeman and Ehrlichman on **16,** 7470, 7510-12E

memo from Dean to Haldeman on **16,** 7470, 7505-09E

Moser's deposition in **16,** 7067-68

Nelson's deposition in **15,** 6562-67, 6645

Parr on **15,** 6893-95

Semer on Kalmbach deposition in **16,** 7192, 7193-94, 7198, 7205-7208

Strachan memo to Haldeman on Kalmbach and **17,** 7610

White House refusal of documents and **FR** 618N

Napolitan, Joseph 21, 9701

Nardone, Benito 9, 3726

Natalie, Ronald 11, 4644

Nathan, Herb

See Pearlman, Marian, testimony of

National Association of Advertisers 20, 9403-9404

National Association of Cable Television 5, 1999

National Association of Small Business Investment Companies 9, 3474-75

National Citizens for Fairness to the Presidency, Inc. et al. v. *Senate Select Committee, et al.* **FR** 1080

National City Bank of Minneapolis

Fellows on leave of absence from **25,** 11766

Fellows' position with **25,** 11773-74

National Committee for the Impeachment of the President

supporters on enemies list **4,** 1727E

National Council of Agricultural Employers 25, 12183

National Council on Senior Citizens, Inc. 18, 8448 **19,** 9225-26E

Evans on funding of **18,** 8441-8442

National Council on the Aging 18, 8457-58 **19,** 9228E **FR** 425

contract at OEO **18,** 8443-45

Evans on funding for **18,** 8441-8442, 8448

National Dairy Council 17, 7657

National defense

and assault strategy on McGovern **10,** 4243E, 4261E

McGovern on **10,** 4083-85E

National Economic Development Association (NEDA) 13, 5279-80

Fernandez on **13,** 5388-93, 5394-99

letter from Villalobos to Peterson and Kleppe on **13,** 5743-46E

National Economic Development Association (NEDA)
(Continued)
    memo from Marumoto to Lynn on grant for **FR**
    391
    report from Villalobos to Fernandez on **13**, 5749-
    67E
National Guard
    and violence at Republican National Convention
    12, 4995
National Hispanic Finance Committee 13, 5537E
    activities of **FR** 522-26
    Armendariz report on **19**, 8776E
    and contributions from minority enterprises **13**,
    5277, 5288, 5298-99, 5304-5305, 5360-66
    contributions received by **13**, 5304-5305
    fact sheet on **19**, 8686E
    and grantsmanship **FR** 386
    Reyes and **18**, 8274
    See also Fernandez, Benjamin, testimony of
National Iranian Oil Co.
    agreement with Ashland Petroleum **13**, 5454
National Jewish Youth for Humphrey 12, 4964, 4965
National Labor for Peace Organization
    on enemies list and **4**, 1705-1706E
National Lawyers Guild 11, 4543
National Maritime Committee to Re-Elect the President FR 512-13
National Milk Producers Federation 15, 6553 **16**,
    7134
National Peace Action Coalition 11, 4543
National Press Club, Washington, D.C.
    speech by Edward Kennedy on Pakistan at **3**,
    1118E
National Republican Campaign Committee
    check from National Republican Senatorial Campaign **16**, 7408, 7415E
    check to National Republican Senatorial Campaign **16**, 7408, 7414E
    checks from National Republican Congressional
    Committee **16**, 7418, 7432-33E
    checks to FCRP **16**, 7422, 7434E
    expenditure voucher of TAPE for contribution to
    16, 7300, 7365E
    letter and check from Lilly to Terrell for **16**,
    7300, 7366E
    receipt to TAPE for contribution to **16**, 7300,
    7367E
National Republican Congressional Committee
    check from Republican National Associates Committee **17**, 8172E
    checks to Republican Campaign Committee **16**,
    7418, 7432-33E
    expenditure voucher from TAPE for contribution
    to **16**, 7300, 7358E
    receipt for contribution from TAPE **16**, 7300,
    7359E
    transfers of funds to Republican National Finance
    Committee
        See Clancy, Lynda E., testimony of; Odell,
        Robert P., testimony of
National Republican Heritage Groups 12, 5030E

National Republican Senatorial Campaign
    check from Republican Campaign Committee **16**,
    7408, 7414E
    check to Republican Campaign Committee **16**,
    7408, 7415E
    expenditure voucher for TAPE contribution to **16**,
    7300, 7354E, 7362E
    letter and check from Lilly to Berentson for **16**,
    7300, 7363E
    letter and check from Mehren to Dominick for
    16, 7300, 7355-56E
    receipt for TAPE contribution to **16**, 7300, 7357E,
    7364E
National Republican Senatorial Committee
    check from Republican National Associates Committee **17**, 8172E
    checks from Republican Campaign Committee **17**,
    8171E, 8173E
    transfers of funds to Republican National Finance
    Committee
        See Clancy, Lynda E., testimony of; Odell,
        Robert P., testimony of
National Retired Teachers Association 18, 8451 **19**,
    9227-28E
National Review **FR** 1119
National Rifle Association 10, 4057E
National security
    as Barker's motivation for participation in Watergate break-ins **1**, 360, 365-67, 375, 385-86, 387
    and containment of Watergate investigation **7**,
    2884-85
    and documents discussed by Select Committee **3**,
    1062
    Ehrlichman links to Ellsberg matter **6**, 2541-53
    and Ehrlichman's refusal to discuss wiretapping of
    F. Donald Nixon **FR** 113
    and electronic surveillance **FR** 104-106
    and Ellsberg case **5**, 2070-71 **7**, 2815 **8**, 3304-3305
    Executive privilege and **5**, 1864
    as Hunt's motive for Watergate break-in **9**, 3739-
    40
    and Huston Plan **FR** 3
    and information on wiretaps from McGovern
    headquarters **2**, 468-69
    and Nixon's instructions to Petersen on Watergate
    investigation **7**, 2696-97
    and paragraph missing in memo from Krogh to
    Young and Ehrlichman **7**, 2702-10
    Plumbers' activities and **9**, 3740-41
    as reason for Watergate break-in **9**, 3793
    and suspension of Fourth Amendment **8**, 3207
    Wilson on Ellsberg case and **6**, 2589-93
    and wiretap on Kraft **21**, 9687-88
National Security Act of 1947
    Helms on **8**, 3235
National Security Agency 6, 2409
National Security Council 1, 76 **9**, 3846E
    relationship with White House staff **1**, 79
    and SALT talk leaks **4**, 1627
National Socialist White Peoples Party 12, 5223E
National Student Association 10, 3919 **11**, 4585
    Stearns and **11**, 4583

National Veterans Committee for the Re-election of the President **19**, 9283-9305E

National Voter Registration Association FR 912

National Welfare Rights Organization (NWRO) **12**, 5187E

National Women's Political Caucus **10**, 4059E

Naughton, James M. **10**, 4257E **11**, 4815-16E

Naval Academy **9**, 3473-3474

Navarro, Anna **11**, 4659, 4775E, 4814E

Nazis
  Nixon accused of softness on **12**, 5027-30E

Neal, Edward B. **20**, 9428

Near East Report **11**, 4582, 4586
  Stearns letter to **11**, 4584

NEDA
  See National Economic Development Association (NEDA)

Nedzi subcommittee **9**, 3495

Neiburger, Colin **12**, 5159E, 5161E, 5162E

Neideffer, David L. **12**, 5097E, 5098E
  letter to Hopkins on vandalism at Baltimore CRP headquarters **12**, 5100-5101E

Nelsen, Alice **22**, 10267

Nelson, Bob **25**, 12277

Nelson, Harold S. **14**, 5863, 5871, 5874, 5876, 5877, 5912, 5915, 5927, 5931, 5953, 5973, 5975, 5978, 5989, 6106, 6164, 6183, 6216E, 6258, 6314, 6315, 6326 **15**, 6466 **16**, 7111, 7014-15, 7123, 7128, 7247, 7282, 7398 **17**, 7784 FR 583
  on $2 million pledge to Colson in 1970 FR 613-14
  after meeting with Nixon FR 646
  Alagia on opinion of **16**, 7083-84
  and AMPI aid to Mills campaign **14**, 6150, 6151, 6156 **15**, 6855 FR 872
  and AMPI arrangement with Valentine, Sherman **14**, 6150, 6151, 6156 **15**, 6855 FR 872
  and AMPI commitment to Johnson **14**, 6183-84
  and AMPI committees **14**, 6301, 6302
  and AMPI contributions **15**, 6409-10, 6415-19, 6774-75
  and AMPI contributions to Muskie campaign **16**, 7012
  and AMPI payments to Russell **16**, 7309
  on AMPI pledge reaffirmation and reversal of price-support decision FR 666
  and AMPI rally for Mills **17**, 7665
  and AMPI reimbursement to TAPE **15**, 6393
  and AMPI relations with Nixon administration **15**, 6759
  and AMPI repayment plan **14**, 5967
  and assignment of AMPI employees to Mills campaign FR 911
  at Jacobsen-Kalmbach meeting **17**, 7607-7609
  at meeting at Louisville airport **14**, 6309, 6310 **16**, 7071-75 FR 655-57
  at meeting between Chotiner and Kalmbach **17**, 7690
  at meeting with Hillings, Harrison, Evans, and Parr **15**, 6788
  at meeting with Kalmbach **14**, 6124
  at meeting with Mehren and Connally **16**, 7263-71
  at meeting with Semer and Jacobsen **16**, 7188-89
  at meetings with Connally **14**, 6108-6109
  at Mehren-Kalmbach meeting **17**, 7645
  at Nixon's meetings with dairy industry representatives **16**, 7139
  attitude toward Republican fundraising dinner **15**, 6828
  authorizes Lilly loan for payment to Connally FR 684
  and budget discussion at Las Vegas AMPI board meeting in 1970 **16**, 6957
  Campbell and **17**, 7750
  and Campbell's requests for political contributions **16**, 6783
  on Chestnut's awareness of AMPI-Valentine, Sherman arrangements FR 875
  and Chotiner **16**, 7237
  on Chotiner's call on reversal of milk price-support decision FR 649
  and conduit system for political contributions to Democrats FR 611
  conflicts between Mehren's testimony and **16**, 7250-51
  Connally denies meeting in 1972 with **14**, 6059
  Connally on relationship with **14**, 6052-53
  contacts with Kalmbach **15**, 6437-46
  and contributions to Mills campaign FR 909, 910
  and destruction of AMPI files **15**, 6896
  discusses AMPI commitments with Mehren **16**, 7245-47
  discussions with Parr on AMPI contributions through committees **15**, 6886-87
  and dispensation of TAPE funds **14**, 5912
  and efforts to have Nixon attend AMPI 1970 convention **15**, 6792 **17**, 7634 FR 616
  end of employment by AMPI **16**, 7087
  explanation to Butterbrodt of high fees to Russell **17**, 7628-29
  and financial authorization at AMPI **17**, 7671-72
  and formation of Dairymen Inc. **16**, 7061
  and formation of SPACE **16**, 7061 FR 586
  and formation of TAPE FR 584
  and Gallup polls **16**, 7004
  and Gleason's request for AMPI cash contribution **15**, 6768
  Harrison letter on commitment to Republicans to **14**, 6269-71
  and high attorney fees **14**, 5974
  and increased AMPI retainer to Van Dyk **16**, 7022-23
  informed by Semer of Kalmbach's request for $100,000 cash contribution FR 589-591
  instructs Lilly to deliver cash to Parr for Mills FR 909
  Jacobsen and **15**, 6380-81, 6384, 6454
  and Johnson **14**, 6179
  and Johnson's activities for Mills campaign **17**, 7668
  and Jones retainer by AMPI **16**, 7330
  knowledge of AMPI arrangement with Valentine, Sherman FR 879
  letter from Harrison objecting to political contributions for unopposed candidates and candidates on both sides of one race **14**, 6251-52

Nelson, Harold S., testimony of 15, 6501-6700
on amount committed to Kalmbach 15, 6662-63
on AMPI and Johnson's book 15, 6696-97
on AMPI board meetings 15, 6529, 6531-32
on AMPI contacts with Kalmbach 15, 6512-15
on AMPI contribution to CRP 15, 6514-21
on AMPI contribution to Humphrey in 1968 15, 6531
on AMPI contributions in 1972 15, 6658-6700
on AMPI contributions through committees in 1970 15, 6542
on AMPI contributions to Democratic Presidential candidates 15, 6613-17
on AMPI corporate funds contributed to Mills 15, 6612-13
on AMPI efforts to obtain milk price-support increases 15, 6552-59
on AMPI people bragging about price-support decision 15, 6656
on AMPI's relationship with Mills 15, 6603-13
on antitrust suit against AMPI 15, 6673-77
on assistants at MPI and AMPI 15, 6503-6504
on Associated Dairymen, Inc., document on milk price-support increases 15, 6556-57
on association with dairy coops 15, 6502
on attitude toward antitrust suit against AMPI 15, 6688
on attorneys retained by TAPE 15, 6510-11
on checks issued to committees provided by Kalmbach 15, 6641-77
on commitments to Nixon campaign in return for increase in milk price supports 15, 6694-96
on communication with other dairy leaders 15, 6699
on compensation from AMPI 15, 6506
on Connally's involvement in milk price-support decision reversal FR 654
on contacts with Connally for milk price-support increases 15, 6557-58, 6560-63, 6567
on contacts with Jacobsen in April 1972 15, 6681-83
on contacts with Long in 1972 15, 6681-82
on contribution to Connally 15, 6647-49
on contributions by ADEPT and SPACE 15, 6627-32
on contributions of TAPE through committees in 1971 15, 6685-86
on contributions to Nixon's campaigns 15, 6626-6700
on coordination of dairy coop contributions 15, 6535
current employment as general manager of American Grain and Cattle 15, 6506
on decision-making process for use of TAPE funds 15, 6689
denies contributions to Republicans by TAPE in 1972 15, 6679-80
denies discussing political contributions with Connally 15, 6677
denies discussions of TAPE contributions with Harrison 15, 6534-35
denies knowledge of AMPI representatives meeting with Ehrlichman 15, 6555
denies knowledge of cash delivery on behalf of AMPI to Gleason 15, 6535

denies meeting with Mehren on contributions to Republicans before April 7 15, 6680-81
on deposition in *Nader* v. *Butz* 15, 6562-67
on discussion with Hardin on desired meeting between Nixon and dairy leaders 15, 6550
on discussions of antitrust suit against AMPI with White House people 15, 6687-88
on discussions with Lilly on reimbursement of TAPE 15, 6525-28
on efforts to have Nixon attend AMPI convention 15, 6549
on efforts to have Nixon attend dairy meetings 15, 6521
on efforts to obtain milk price-support increases 15, 6560-75
exhibits brought by 15, 6501-6502
on formation of TAPE 15, 6504-6505, 6507-11
on Government people he met with on milk price supports 15, 6555-56
on Harrison's contacts with administration 15, 6523
on Hillings letter to Nixon 15, 6544
on import quotas 15, 6543-46
on Iowa rally for Mills 15, 6609-10
on irregularity of contributing through committees to Nixon campaign 15, 6646-47
on IRS audit of Milk Producers, Inc., tax returns 15, 6671-74
on Jacobsen's advice to Isham on TAPE reporting requirements 15, 6509-10
on Jacobsen's contacts with Connally 15, 6567-68
on Jacobsen's role with AMPI 15, 6511-12
on Kalmbach 15, 6665-66
on learning of milk price-support decision 15, 6639-40
on learning that milk price supports would be increased 15, 6568-70
on legality or illegality of TAPE contribution to CRP 15, 6518-19
on letter from Cashen on photographs taken at White House 15, 6546, 6704E
on letter from Harrison on contributions to opposed candidates only 15, 6533-34
on letter from Hillings to Nixon 15, 6541-42
letter from Mehren on discussions with Lyng and Palmby 15, 6655, 6750-53E
on Lilly contact with Connally at Page Airways 15, 6617-24
on list given to Harrison of people to attend meeting with Nixon 15, 6553-54
on loan from TAPE to ADEPT 15, 6535
on meeting between Colson and dairy industry representatives in 1970 15, 6539-41
on meeting between Kalmbach and dairy industry representatives on 1970 15, 6535-38
on meeting with Alagia 15, 6685
on meeting with Chotiner on milk price supports 15, 6570-75
on meetings with Connally and Mehren 15, 6668-69, 6675-78
on meeting with Gleason 15, 6521
on meeting with Jacobsen, Mehren, and Connally 15, 6508
on meeting with Jacobsen and Kalmbach 15, 6660-61

New York Times **3**, 1082 **5**, 1959 **6**, 2604-2605
on blaming of CIA for Watergate **1**, 199
claims Ehrlichman is in favor of release of Nixon tapes **7**, 2687
CRP letterwriting campaign to **FR** 152
on Griffin returning Hughes contribution **22**, 10427
and Huston plan **7**, 2818
on infiltration of Diane Moore into Muskie campaign **11**, 4695, 4815-16E
and Intelligence Evaluation Committee **1**, 201
investigation of Rebozo **21**, 10085
letter from Krogh to Ehrlichman reported in **7**, 2661-63
McCord memo on CIA in **1**, 309
Op Ed page **10**, 4130E
on political spy in Muskie campaign **11**, 4815-16E
prints questions for Dean prepared by Buzhardt **4**, 1431, 1432
publication of Pentagon Papers by **3**, 919, 921 **7**, 2875 **FR** 119-20
on Rebozo returning Hughes contribution **23**, 10800E
source of "Dean Papers" **2**, 601-602 **4**, 1557
on Tennessee primary **10**, 4206E
New Yorker Films, Inc. FR 145
Caulfield on investigation of **22**, 10385-90
Newman, Elva FR 784E
Newman, Paul
on enemies list **4**, 1696E
Newsday **4**, 1530 **23**, 11266
article on Rebozo **3**, 1072 **FR** 9
Caulfield on investigation of **22**, 10370-74
Higby on White House memos on **23**, 11098-99, 11101-11102
investigation of Rebozo **21**, 9677-79, 9681-82, 10085-86, 10122 **22**, 10247-48 **23**, 10924 **24**, 11546-47 **FR** 135-36
IRS audit of Greene and **21**, 10126, 10368-70 **22**, 10248
memos from Caulfield to Dean on **23**, 11101, 11143-44E
Rebozo denies discussing libel suit against **21**, 10128-29
rumor of financing by Kennedy Foundation for Rebozo articles **21**, 10126
"Newsmakers"
column about Jane Muskie **10**, 4026, 4282-83E
Newspaper advertisements
anti-Muskie-McGovern **10**, 4026, 4275-78E
about Muskie in Spanish **10**, 4026, 4281E
See also Advertising
Newspaper polls
CRP "packing" of **FR** 152
Newspapers
and information about Watergate break-in **4**, 1460
source stories on Dean's allegations about Nixon **4**, 1440-41
See also Media
Newsweek **4**, 1437 **9**, 3884E
article about Dean's prospective testimony **4**, 1441
article on Mrs. Muskie **11**, 4392-93, 4396, 4401-4402
memo from Haldeman to Dean on "The Periscope" from **23**, 11076, 11115-16E

memo from Safire to Haldeman on article on O'Brien in **23**, 11076, 11114E
Newton, Vern 25, 12127
background of **25**, 12109-10
and Muskie Accountability Project research **25**, 12101, 12102
Nicholas, Anthony 14, 5915-20, 5923, 5925, 5927-28 **16**, 6961
See also Lilly, Bob A., testimony of
Nichols, Lou 26, 10339E
Nicolai 9, 3882E, 3883E, 3886E
Nicoll, Don 11, 4773E **14**, 5949 **16**, 7016, 7017, 7214
and AMPI contributions to Muskie campaign **16**, 7012
letter from Van Dyk on contributions to Muskie campaign **14**, 5951, 6026-27E
Nidecker, John 19, 8606E, 8607E
Niebuhr, Reinhold 10, 3937
Niefeld, Joann Rogers
affidavit of **12**, 5009, 5095-96E
Nieley, Bob FR 166
Nigrelle, Joe 14, 5966, 6044E
Nigro, Edward 20, 9428, 9432, 9433, 9446, 9601 **FR** 956-57, 962
Niles, Henry E. 3, 1141E
Nixon, Barbara (Mrs. F. Donald Nixon) 22, 10672, 10680-81, 10717-18, 10728
Nixon, Donald A. 17, 7587 **22**, 10488
Hughes loan to **20**, 9373-74
Rebozo and **20**, 9506, 9507-9509, 9510
Nixon, Edward C. 20, 9454 **22**, 10488 **23**, 10928
at meeting with F. Donald and Richard Nixon and McKiernan **22**, 10655-56
business or financial dealings with Rebozo **21**, 10134 **22**, 10499
Buzhardt and **22**, 10648 **23**, 10904
Buzhardt informs of newspaper story on Hughes contribution money given to him **22**, 10545, 10546, 10550
Buzhardt's relationship with **22**, 10555-56
campaign funds given to **23**, 10896
denies receiving funds or gifts from Rebozo **FR** 1052
discussion between Muse and McKiernan on documents called for in subpoena of **23**, 10982-83
discussion between Wilson and McKiernan on **22**, 10654-55
Ehrlichman approves payment of campaign funds to **23**, 10859-60
employed by Richard Nixon Foundation **23**, 10857, 11103-11104
Haig and **22**, 10655
Haig on allegations about Hughes money and **23**, 11013
Kalmbach disburses campaign funds to **23**, 10858, 10859
in Kalmbach's testimony **FR** 1006, 1064
McKiernan letter to Ervin and Baker on treatment of **23**, 10975-77, 10984-87E
and McKiernan's discussion with Buzhardt on newspaper story on Hughes contribution **22**, 10618-19

IRS interview of **23,** 10943
IRS investigation of **23,** 10938
in IRS sensitive case report on Hughes Tool Co.
23, 10928, 11221, 11222, 11225-26, 11228,
11230-32, 11236-37, 11277-78E
and IRS sensitive case reports **23,** 11251
in Johnnie Walters briefings to Shultz on Hughes-
Meier investigation **24,** 11629, 11633
Kalmbach and **23,** 10857-58
Kalmbach testimony on Rebozo disbursal **FR**
1006
and Kalmbach's discussions with Greenspun **23,**
11032
in Kalmbach's testimony **FR** 1064
loans to **21,** 9969-70, 9988
McKiernan denies discussion of his business activities with President **22,** 10633
McKiernan letter to Ervin and Baker on treatment of **23,** 10975-77, 10984-87E
McKiernan on booklet on **22,** 10638-40
McKiernan on wiretapping of **22,** 10659-61
and McKiernan's discussion with Buzhardt on
newspaper story on Hughes contribution **22,**
10617-22
meeting with McKiernan and Richard and Edward Nixon **22,** 10622-30 **23,** 11024-25
meetings with Ehrlichman, Haldeman, and Mitchell **22,** 10640-42
and Meier **20,** 9598-9604 **23,** 11103
Mitchell and **22,** 10639
Moncourt denies Rebozo has file on **22,** 10486
money from 1968 campaign fund given to **23,**
10860-61
monitoring by Caulfield of wiretap of **FR** 112-13
Onassis and **22,** 10643
Pearson's publicity on loan taken in 1958 by **21,**
9942-43
photographed at Orange County Airport **21,**
9702-9703
press statement on newspaper stories about money
from Hughes **22,** 10549, 10556-58
Rebozo and **24,** 11444-45
Rebozo tells Kalmbach he disbursed part of
Hughes money to **21,** 10189
Rebozo's uneasiness over Hughes contribution and
FR 936
relationship with McKiernan **22,** 10637
relationship with Meier **21,** 10118-21
relationship with Meier and Hatsis **22,** 10625
and search for booklet on Nixon brothers **22,**
10652
and Simon's report on IRS investigation of Nixon
23, 11061
subpoena for **23,** 10991-92E
telephone conversation with Buzhardt on newspaper story on Hughes contribution **22,** 10551-52,
10554-55
trip to Dominican Republic **21,** 9701, 9702, 9719-
20
trips to Switzerland and Hawaii **22,** 10646
Walters informed of impending IRS interview of
24, 11643
wiretapping of **23,** 10942
Woods denies discussing Hughes contribution
with **22,** 10234

Woods denies knowledge of file on **22,** 10268-69
Woods denies knowledge of surveillance of **22,**
10269-70
Nixon, F. Donald, deposition of 22, 10665-10732
on accountants employed by **22,** 10669-70
on bank accounts held by **22,** 10670, 10671
on business dealings with Cleveland **22,** 10675-77
on conversation with Malloy **22,** 10729-30
denies anyone attempting to extort money from
him **22,** 10732
denies borrowing money at usurious rates **22,**
10732
denies business or financial transactions with
Rebozo **22,** 10666-68
denies business or financial transactions with
Richard Nixon, Woods, or Kalmbach **22,** 10696
denies compensation to Meier for his travel expenses **22,** 10731
denies discussing money owed Hallamore with
anyone other than Mitchell **22,** 10698
denies discussing possible appearance before Senate Watergate Committee with Nixon, Haig,
Garment, or Buzhardt **22,** 10724-26
denies discussing testimony with anyone other
than counsel **22,** 10725-27
denies discussion with White House on Kalmbach's testimony **22,** 10719
denies knowledge of San-Bar CDs as support for
his loan at United California Bank **22,** 10712-14
denies Rebozo, Richard Nixon, or anyone at
White House attempted or paid bill on his behalf **22,** 10732
denies statements of personal expense for inauguration **22,** 10698-10700, 10713-14
discussions with Ehrlichman on association with
Meier **22,** 10707-10708
discussions with Kalmbach on relationship with
Meier **22,** 10708-10
Ehrlichman's and Rebozo's visit to Hallamore
Homes project **11,** 10684-89
on employers and fee arrangements with corporations since 1969 **22,** 10673-77
financial dealings with San-Bar Electric Corp. **22,**
10695-96
on first knowledge of Hughes contribution
through Rebozo **22,** 10710
on health status **22,** 10665
on Hughes acquisition of Air West **22,** 10730
on IRS audit **22,** 10704-10705
and Kalmbach's testimony **22,** 10715-20
last visit with Rebozo **22,** 10726-27
loan from Hallamore to **22,** 10678, 10679, 10680-
83
McKiernan's memo to President on meeting **22,**
10722-23
on meeting with Richard and Edward Nixon and
McKiernan **22,** 10719-22, 10723-24
on personal finances **22,** 10671-73
on possible reasons for Rebozo stating that he
gave money to him **22,** 10728
on President asking Ehrlichman and Rebozo to
visit Hallamore Homes project **22,** 10687, 10688
on property owned by **22,** 10675-77
on purchase of additional Hallamore Homes stock
22, 10691-95

attitude toward full disclosure to Watergate Committee **22,** 10632

attitude toward immunity for Dean **FR** 93-95

attitude toward immunity for White House staff **7,** 2831

attitude toward Malek's role in campaign **18,** 8206-8207

attitude toward Select Committee hearings **4,** 1459-61 **5,** 1941, 1943, 1957-58, 1973-74, 1975, 2021-22

attitude toward White House staff members involved in Watergate **5,** 1921

and audit of B & C Investment Co. **23,** 10755

authorization for creation of Plumbers unit **7,** 2780-81

authorization for investigation of Ellsberg matter **7,** 2771

and awarding of grants and contracts **18,** 8190-91

awareness of illegality of Fielding break-in **7,** 2820-21

bill for diamond earrings addressed to Rose Mary Woods **26,** 12767-69E

boat trip with Rebozo during Watergate investigation **21,** 10136-39

and booklet on Edward and F. Donald Nixon to Watergate Committee **22,** 10630

and break-in at Fielding's office **12,** 5065-69E

briefed by Colson on milk industry pledge to campaign **16,** 7376-77

briefing book before press conferences **3,** 1074-75

and brochure, "The President Speaks to Older Americans" **18,** 8484, 8585-87E

Brown declares there are no safety deposits for at Key Biscayne Bank & Trust Co. **23,** 10961

Brown on invoices or work orders signed on behalf of **23,** 10961-63, 10965

Buchanan memos to **11,** 4605-4606

Buchanan on reasons for election of **10,** 3901, 3961

and Buchanan's investigation of foundations **10,** 3916-17

Buchanan's political relationship with **10,** 3904-3905

business dealings with Rebozo **22,** 10130-33, 10490-93

business dealings with Abplanalp **22,** 10510-11

Butterfield proclaims belief in innocence of **5,** 2090

Buzhardt states he made no effort to inform on newspaper story on Hughes contribution **22,** 10547-48, 10553-54

Buzhardt's discussions on his brothers with **22,** 10556-57

Byrne and **6,** 2617-18, 2619

and California lawsuit in 1962 election campaign **5,** 2128

calls Petersen about Gray resigning **9,** 3625-26

Camp David meeting with Danner and Rebozo **24,** 11472-76 **FR** 1011-12

campaign of 1962 **8,** 3169-70

and campaign plan for older voters **19,** 9115-16E

Caulfield on Executive clemency and **1,** 277-278

Caulfield's belief he was serving **1,** 274-75

certificates of deposit issued to **21,** 10078-79, 10088

chances for re-election at time of Watergate break-in **4,** 1642-43

Chapin on protection of **2,** 545

check from Griffin **23,** 10796E

and claim of Executive privilege for Haig testimony **23,** 10995-96

on Colson discussing hush money **4,** 1522

Colson memo on Open Hour Event **FR** 779-84E

communications from Petersen **FR** 80-82

communications with Dean in Buzhardt memo sent to Thompson **23,** 10897-10900

compared to Hitler **10,** 3967, 3973-74

concern about leaks **6,** 2603-2604

concern for F. Donald Nixon's health **22,** 10649, 10656-57

concern over CIA and FBI investigation **7,** 2694-95, 2823-24, 2833

confidential memo to Shultz in preparation for conference with **24,** 11648-50

congratulates Dean on handling of Watergate **FR** 48, 49-50

Connally informs of milk producers contributions **FR** 654

and Connally's impact on reversal of milk price-support decision **FR** 640

contacts with Kleindienst between Watergate break-in and resignation **9,** 3599-3600

contacts with Petersen **9,** 3648-49

contacts with Walters **9,** 3404

on content of tapes **8,** 3092

convenes independent panel on Watergate **3,** 1261E

conversation with Rebozo and Danner **21,** 9965-6, 10094-96, 10097-99

in conversations between Mitchell and Mardian **6,** 2400

conversations with Haig on Hughes-Rebozo matter **23,** 11027-30

conversations with Mitchell about Watergate **5,** 1861

correspondence from Beck to Sporrer on "After-action Report" following visit to Los Angeles of **11,** 4561, 4719-26E

correspondence with Ervin and Baker on materials relating to domestic intelligence operations **3,** 1060-61

cost of visit to Century City **11,** 4725-26E

counterbalances to media reports on Watergate **5,** 2019-21

and Cox's investigation of Rebozo and Hughes contribution **22,** 12442E **23,** 10888

credibility of vs. credibility of Dean **3,** 1044

daily schedule **1,** 85-86

and dairy industry conventions **16,** 7208-7209

Danner denies discussing ABM or nerve gas issue with **20,** 9497

Danner denies discussing requests for direct contributions to **20,** 9500-9501

Danner denies discussion of campaign contributions to pay expenses of **24,** 11453-54

Danner introduces Rebozo to **FR** 934

Danner-Rebozo discussions on business dealings of **20,** 9525

Danner's visit to Walker Cay with **24,** 11450-52

Nixon, Richard M. *(Continued)*

Davis and Crosby and **20,** 9521

and Dean and Mitchell's offers of Executive clemency to Magruder **2,** 804-805, 836-37

Dean expresses concern about impact of Watergate break-in on **FR** 35

Dean informs fully on Watergate coverup **3,** 992-93, 998-1000

Dean informs of Liddy plan **FR** 23

Dean informs that he is testifying to government prosecutors **3,** 1015-17 **4,** 1553-56

Dean informs that Strachan had prior knowledge of Watergate break-in **FR** 26

Dean on **4,** 1467-83

Dean on access to **4,** 1488-90

Dean prepares agenda for meeting with Haldeman on La Costa decisions **3,** 987-88

Dean proposes he create independent panel to investigate Watergate **3,** 1004-05

on Dean Report **3,** 955-56, 1211-13E **4,** 1510 **5,** 2003

Dean tells Moore about discussion on coverup with **5,** 1981

and Dean's appearance before grand jury **4,** 1428-29

and Dean's effort to write report at Camp David **5,** 1971

and Dean's implication of Haldeman in Watergate coverup **8,** 3095-96

on Dean's investigation of Watergate **7,** 2720, 2882-83 **9,** 3576

and Dean's meeting agendas **4,** 1482-83

Dean's message before going to Federal Prosecutors **3,** 1015, 1313E

and Dean's negotiations with Federal Prosecutors **4,** 1554-55

Dean's notes on Kleindienst for **4,** 1491-94

Dean's reasons for not telling about Liddy's intelligence-gathering plan **4,** 1353-54

Dean's reporting relationship with **6,** 2525-26

and Dean's requests for tax information **22,** 10362

and Dean's resignation **FR** 92-93

and Dean's suggestion that FBI investigate campaign practices of Select Committee members **5,** 1975-76, 1995

and decision to blame CIA for Watergate **1,** 195

decision to bomb North Vietnam **7,** 2870

decision to reverse milk price-support decision **FR** 648

delegation of political role to others **6,** 2518-19

and DeMarco **23,** 11250

and Democrats civil suit **3,** 1028

Democrats for Nixon dinner for **14,** 6083-84

demonstration at Century Plaza Hotel against **11,** 4719-24E

and demonstrator at his inauguration **4,** 1440

denial of discussing Hughes contribution with Danner and Rebozo **FR** 936

denies any White House connection to Watergate **2,** 861

denies Dean and Magruder had prior knowledge about Watergate **9,** 3549

denies Rebozo raised and maintained funds for his personal behalf **22,** 12449-50E **FR** 1051

designation of Rebozo as agent for **24,** 11302-11305

and difference of opinion between Ehrlichman and Dean on immunity for White House staff **7,** 2745

directives on Chappaquiddick incident **10,** 3936

discusses Executive clemency for Hunt with Dean **4,** 1555

discusses leaks at Cabinet meeting **3,** 921

discussion of Hallamore Homes project with F. Donald Nixon **22,** 10687, 10688

discussion of Hughes contribution **FR** 1024-25

discussion of hush money with Dean **FR** 58-60

discussion with Danner on role in 1968 campaign **24,** 11409-11

discussion with Dean on Select Committee hearings **FR** 79-80

discussion with Haig on testifying before Select Committee **23,** 11025

discussion with Moore on Segretti matter during press conference briefings **5,** 2006-2007

discussion with Petersen on immunity for witnesses **9,** 3629-30

discussion with Petersen on payments to Watergate defendants **FR** 62

discussion with Rebozo on ABM **21,** 10050

discussion with Rebozo on O'Brien's involvement with Hughes **21,** 10058

discussions with Danner in 1968 **20,** 9502, 9503

discussions with Dean on Watergate coverup **4,** 1400-1408

discussions with Gemmill on IRS investigation of Rebozo **23,** 11193-94

discussions with Haig on Hughes contribution **23,** 11011-12 **FR** 1024-25

discussions with Mitchell **4,** 1644

discussions with Mitchell on Executive privilege **4,** 1663-64

discussions with Moore on Watergate **5,** 1955-56

discussions with Rebozo and Danner on contributions **20,** 9540

discussions with Rebozo on Hughes contribution **21,** 10101-10103

discussions with Rebozo on money for Watergate defendants **21,** 10140

disruption of "People to People" rally in California **12,** 4948-51, 4953, 4955-63

and domestic intelligence **6,** 2527

draft statement from Dean re grand jury's investigation into Watergate and leave-of-absence requests from Haldeman, Ehrlichman, and Dean **3,** 1018, 1317-18E

draft statement on Watergate investigation **3,** 1317-18E

and efforts to block Patman Committee hearings **3,** 960

efforts to have Mitchell take blame for Watergate **FR** 91

efforts to obtain information on Watergate break-in **7,** 2802-2803

efforts to obtain milk price-support increases **15,** 6564-65

Ehrlichman characterizes **6,** 2513

Ehrlichman denies discussing grantsmanship plan with **18,** 8195-96

Ehrlichman denies he offered Executive clemency for Hunt **6,** 2610-12

Ehrlichman denies telling about hush money **7,** 2726

Ehrlichman on his loyalty to **7,** 2864

Ehrlichman on opponents of **6,** 2518

Ehrlichman on powers under Constitution of **6,** 2569

Ehrlichman on prior knowledge of Watergate break-in by **6,** 2587

Ehrlichman on problems of his administration **6,** 2512-13

Ehrlichman on staff of **6,** 2523, 2524

Ehrlichman refuses to testify on discussions with **16,** 7393

Ehrlichman reports findings of inquiry to **7,** 2724, 2757-58, 2857

and Ehrlichman-Byrne meeting **9,** 3605

Ehrlichman's discussions on Watergate with **6,** 2554-55

and Ehrlichman's interest in IRS sensitive report on Hughes **23,** 11229-30

Ehrlichman's reasons for keeping information away from **7,** 2804-2805

Ehrlichman's suggestion that everyone should go before grand jury **8,** 3071-73

on Ellsberg and Pentagon Papers **FR** 119-20

and Ellsberg case **9,** 3607-3608, 3631-32, 3644

and enemies list **3,** 958-59 **4,** 1481, 1527-28 **FR** 9

Ervin on necessity of obtaining White House tapes from **7,** 2658

Ervin's reasons for not discussing impeachment of **FR** 1097

and establishment of Cabinet Committee on Opportunities for Spanish-Speaking People **FR** 394

and Executive clemency offers **1,**167-68,228-229, 257, 273, 326, 328 **2,** 807 **3,** 973-74, 995-96, 1017, 1020, 1029, 1042 **4,** 1379, 1674 **5,** 1522, 1910-11 **FR** 63

Executive Order 11478: Equal Employment Opportunity in the Federal Government **19,** 8706-8707E

on Executive privilege **1,** 81 **5,** 1821-22

expresses confidence in Dean after Dean's revelations **5,** 2054-58

factors involved in milk price-support decision of **FR** 580-81

and FBI **3,** 1071

and FBI Ellsberg investigation **5,** 2016 **7,** 2672-73, 2695-98, 2783-84

and FBI leaks **6,** 2557-58

and FBI reports on Watergate investigation **3,** 944

fees paid to Wakefield **24,** 11342-43

Fensterwald threats about **1,** 308, 322-323, 328, 335-336

and Fielding break-in **4,** 1491 **6,** 2501, 2551, 2604 **7,** 2692-93

film on Checkers speech of **22,** 10383-84, 10388-89

financial arrangements for San Clemente purchase **23,** 11086-87

financial dealings between Woods and **22,** 10225-26

financial dealings with Rebozo **22,** 10230 **23,** 10781-83, 10784-85 **24,** 11344

firing of Cox by **FR** 32

and first milk price-support decision **16,** 7381

and Fitzgerald fired from Air Force **4,** 1560

friends with tax problems **4,** 1529-30

fundraising dinner for **15,** 6816-17 **16,** 7069-71

Garment's positions with since 1969 **23,** 11053

and Gemmill **23,** 11183

Gemmill and Buzhardt discuss testimony on conversations with **23,** 11215-16

Gemmill on legal relationship with **23,** 11218

gifts from Rebozo and Abplanalp **23,** 10781-82, 10784-85

glad investigation stopped at Liddy **4,** 1475

and grantsmanship memo from Magruder to Mitchell **1,** 449E

Gray believes Dean is speaking for **9,** 3482

and Gray confirmation hearings **7,** 2789 **9,** 3598-99

Gray informs that CIA had no involvement in Watergate **9,** 3429

and Gray resignation **7,** 2790

on Gray turning over FBI information to Senate Judiciary Committee **3,** 993

Gray's and Walters' concern about **9,** 3535-36

and Gray's destruction of Hunt's papers **7,** 2675-76, 2677-78 **9,** 3505-3506

Gray's letter to **9,** 3495-96

Gray's warning to **9,** 3531

and Gray's withdrawal of nomination **9,** 3545-46

and Greenspun information **20,** 9353

Griffin on purchase and sale of Key Biscayne property by **23,** 10768-66

Haig informs of IRS investigation **23,** 11064, 11065-66

Haig on belief he had no knowledge of Hughes contribution **23,** 11027

and Haig's discussions with Richardson on Cox investigation **23,** 11015

Haldeman declares he had no knowledge of Watergate or coverup **7,** 2867 **8,** 3088-89

Haldeman denies discussing Responsiveness Program with **18,** 8179-80, 8182

Haldeman on **8,** 3227

Haldeman on accomplishments of **7,** 2867-71

Haldeman on awareness of milk fund of **16,** 7184

Haldeman on demonstrations against **8,** 3079-81

Haldeman on handling of Watergate situation by **8,** 3160-61, 1362

Haldeman on personal use of campaign contributions by **16,** 7158

Haldeman on reporting methods **8,** 3216

and Haldeman's access to tapes **7,** 2893 **8,** 3050

Haldeman's association with **6,** 2521-22 **7,** 2873 **8,** 3017

Haldeman's schedule and schedule of **6,** 2467-68

Haldeman's travels with **6,** 2467

handling of Watergate situation **8,** 3162-63

Helms on **8,** 3256

Helms' reasons for not going to **8,** 3256

and Helms' resignation as CIA Director **8,** 3257

and Helms-Walters meetings **8,** 3062, 3064

Herge willing to lie to **2,** 645

Hillings' letter to **14,** 6253-54, 6260-64 **15,** 6541-42, 6544, 6701-02E, 6789-90, 6814, 6884 **16,** 7161-63 **17,** 7546, 7594-95 **FR** 619-21, 695, 757-58E

Ehrlichman on **16,** 7377-81

Nixon, Richard M. *(Continued)*

and Hoover's attitudes toward domestic intelligence **3**, 1325-29E

on Hoover's information that his 1968 campaign was bugged **4**, 1477-78

and Horton's "Discussion Draft" on grants **FR** 365-67

and Hughes contribution **FR** 936-37, 1069-70

Hunt on authorization for Watergate and **9**, 3764

Hunt on re-election of **9**, 3898E

on Hunt's demands for money **5**, 1983 **8**, 3142

Hunt's threats on impeachment of **1**, 196

and hush money **4**, 1402-1403, 1521-22, 1538-40, 1567, 1571

and Huston plan **4**, 1604

ignorance of Watergate involvement of White House staff **5**, 2017-19

impact of Mitchell's apology on **5**, 2020

impact of Watergate coverup on **4**, 1420

impeachment investigation of **FR** 23

information on Watergate given to **7**, 2722, 2810-11 **8**, 3057-58

informed by Dean of Colson call to Magruder on Gemstone plan **FR** 24

informed by Haig of Simon's report on IRS investigation of Hughes contribution **23**, 10999, 11001

informed by Haldeman of delivery of White House fund to LaRue **FR** 56-57

informed by Rebozo of return of Hughes contribution **21**, 10007-10008, 10062-64

informed of Fielding break-in **9**, 3630-31

informs Dean about meeting with Baker **3**, 991-92

informs Government that Dean is seeking immunity in exchange for testimony **3**, 1019-20

instructions on Eagleton **10**, 3940

instructions to Ehrlichman on Watergate investigation **6**, 2557-66

instructions to Gray on Watergate investigation **7**, 2711

instructions to Haldeman on testimony on White House tapes in letter from Buzhardt to Wilson **8**, 3132, 3320E

instructions to Rebozo to maintain fund for control by White House staff rather than Republican National Committee **22**, 12427-28

instructs Dean to report directly to him on Watergate **3**, 991

interest in purchasing San Clemente property **23**, 10738-39

interest in White House public relations activities **FR** 153

interest in 1969 contributions for congressional campaigns **20**, 9526-28

on investigations of Watergate **4**, 1509-10 **5**, 2016 **7**, 2798-99 **8**, 3073-74, 3112-13

invited to attend AMPI convention **17**, 7581 **FR** 596

involvement in Watergate **1**, 163-64, 166-67 **3**, 914, 1009, 1027-31, 1351 **4**, 1371-73, 1380-84 **5**, 1838

involvement in Watergate coverup **4**, 1462-64, 1537-56

on involvement of Haldeman, Ehrlichman, and Dean **4**, 1432, 1435-36

involvement or noninvolvement in Watergate as central theme of Watergate investigation **8**, 3181

and IRS and friends of **4**, 1558-59

IRS audit of **23**, 11059-60

and IRS audits of enemies **4**, 1535

and IRS investigation of Rebozo **21**, 9680 **22**, 12441-42E

and IRS sensitive case reports **23**, 10928 **24**, 11635, 11636

Kalmbach assumes he knew about money for Watergate defendants **5**, 2147

Kalmbach denies contact since Watergate break-in with **5**, 2142

Kalmbach denies discussing Hughes contribution with **21**, 10183

Kalmbach denies use of AMPI money for personal use of **17**, 7586

Kalmbach's activities for **5**, 2092

and Kalmbach's commitment to Symington **FR** 499

Kalmbach's reasons for not going to **5**, 2146, 2147-48, 2154-56

and Kissinger tapes incident **6**, 2405-2406, 2407-2408

Kleindienst, Petersen, and Dean decide to contact on Watergate matter **9**, 3563

Kleindienst reports on Dean's and Magruder's testimony to U.S. Attorneys **9**, 3579-80, 3583-84

Kleindienst informs of White House connection to Fielding break-in **9**, 3574-75

and Kleindienst's resignation **9**, 3593, 3597-98, 3653-54

knowledge about Watergate coverup **4**, 1460-61

knowledge of campaign practices **FR** 107

knowledge of dairy industry contributions **16**, 7386

knowledge of Haldeman's private polling **6**, 2498

knowledge of Hunt's blackmail threats **7**, 2853

knowledge of IRS interviews of Rebozo and F. Donald Nixon **24**, 11651, 11652

knowledge of McKiernan's discussions with Buzhardt **22**, 10634

knowledge of money from CRP to White House **8**, 3120

knowledge of Special Investigations Unit **6**, 2564-65

Krogh claims he authorized Fielding break-in **3**, 1007

and Krogh's report on FBI Ellsberg investigation **7**, 2667

lack of knowledge about Watergate related to White House staff system **8**, 3184-88

LaRue as voluntary special consultant to **23**, 11149

LaRue on willingness to lie to protect **6**, 2327

LaRue's reasons for not reporting to **6**, 2310-11

leaflets distributed in Berkeley against **12**, 5056-58E

leaflets on **12**, 5081E

and leaks to newsmen **3**, 1056

learns about laundering of hush money from Dean **3**, 996

learns of involvement of Mitchell, Magruder, and Dean **4**, 1429

letter from Chapin to Hardin on milk producers' meeting with **17**, 8135E letter from Dean requesting indefinite leave of absence **3**, 1018, 1316E

letter from Dean requesting right to Xerox his files **4**, 1531-32

letter from Ervin requesting tapes **5**, 2137, 2178-79

letter from Harrison to Hardin on arranging meeting with **15**, 6553, 6705-08E

letter from Hillings on implementation of section 22, Tariff Commission recommendations **14**, 6253, 6285-86E

letter from Hoover to Krogh on top-secret material **6**, 2626, 2655E

letter from Select Committee requesting information on Rebozo's alleged use of campaign contributions for Nixon's personal expenses **26**, 12527-42E

letter to Charles Wallace **19**, 8852E

letter to Ervin refusing to submit tapes **6**, 2478-79 **7**, 2657-58, 2907E **8**, 3100, 3105

letter to Haig invoking Executive privilege and directing him not to testify **23**, 10849-50

letter to Shultz prohibiting Secret Service personnel from testifying before Select Committee **5**, 2136-37

letters given to Dean on his resignation **3**, 1017, 1314-15E

letterwriting campaign on Vietnam policy of **FR** 311-13E

liability ledger from First National Bank of Miami **26**, 12771-72E

Liddy claims authorization by **6**, 2359, 2395, 2397, 2398, 2418-19

and Liddy's legal work **4**, 1352

linked with Nazis by Anderson columns **12**, 4970

list of participants for meetings with dairy leaders on March 23, 1971 **FR** 843E

listening devices in offices of *See* Nixon tapes; Nixon's listening devices

loan for purchases of Key Biscayne properties **22**, 12436-38E

loan from First National Bank of Miami **24**, 11336-40

loans to Rebozo **21**, 10132

MacGregor denies Gray asked him to call **12**, 4015-22

MacGregor expresses trust in **12**, 4911

MacGregor's political association with **12**, 4898-99

Magruder implicates in Watergate plans **3**, 990

Magruder on **2**, 816, 818, 837-38

Magruder on Dean's meetings with **2**, 843-44

Magruder on role in campaign decision making **2**, 817-18

and Magruder staying at CRP after Watergate **3**, 1050

and Maheu contribution in 1968 **24**, 11575

and Maheu's retainer for Mudge, Rose, Guthrie and Alexander **24**, 11580-82

and Malek's plan for Responsiveness Program **FR** 370

and Malek's role in campaign **18**, 8204-8205

Mardian denies knowledge of involvement in Watergate of **6**, 2398

Mardian's visit to **6**, 2392-93

Marumoto on attitude toward needs of Hispanic Americans of **13**, 5274-75, 5312-13

McCord and **1**, 182

and McCord's implications on involvement in Watergate **1**, 160

and McCord's letter to Sirica **4**, 1550-51

and McGrath's letter to Danner on Panama Canal treaty **24**, 11461-62

McKiernan on reaction to Donald F. Nixon's problems **22**, 10630

meeting on world development **17**, 7635-36

meeting with advisers on March 23 on milk price supports **FR** 647-48

meeting with AMPI representatives **14**, 5874-77

meeting with Baker **3**, 983-89

meeting with Campbell, Hardin, and other agricultural officials before meeting with dairy leaders **17**, 7782-83

meetings with dairy industry leaders **14**, 6060-64, 6141, 6265, 6279 **15**, 6414, 6802 **16**, 7063-66, 7137-43, 7159-60, 7164-65, 7168-69, 7376-77, 7382, 7522-23 **17**, 7731, 7759-64 **FR** 636-37, 643-46, 844-54E, 857-58E

Ehrlichman on **16**, 7387-90

meeting with Ehrlichman and Hardin **14**, 6280

meeting with Ehrlichman and Schultz **FR** 646-47

meeting with Gray **7**, 2712

meeting with Haig on IRS investigation of Rebozo **FR** 1013

meeting with Haldeman, Ehrlichman, Malek, Mitchell, and Shultz **18**, 8205-8206

meeting with Haldeman, MacGregor, and Mitchell **12**, 4943

meeting with Hardin, Schultz, Connally, and Campbell before meeting with dairy leaders **17**, 7763-65, 7767-70

meeting with heads of security agencies **8**, 3027-28

meeting with Huston on domestic intelligence **4**, 1453

meeting with Kleindienst and Petersen **7**, 2904 **9**, 2628-29 **FR** 91-92

meeting with MacGregor **12**, 4941-42

meeting with McKiernan **22**, 10632-33, 10655-58

meeting with McKiernan and Nixon brothers **22**, 10622-30, 10634, 10635, 10719-24

meetings on hush money **FR** 60-62

meetings on March 23 on milk price supports **FR** 642-57

meetings with Danner and Rebozo **20**, 9503-9505, 9538-39 **23**, 10894-95, 11005-11006, 11019-20 **24**, 11439-42 **FR** 1066-67

meetings with Dean
Executive privilege for Dean and **3**, 994
White House statement on reasons for **4**, 1422
See also Nixon-Dean meetings

meetings with Dean and Haldeman **4**, 1371-73 **5**, 1838

meetings with Ehrlichman **6**, 2584-87 **7**, 2807-2809, 2822, 2823, 2848-49

meetings with Haldeman **7**, 2888-89

meetings with Kleindienst **9**, 3567-69, 3572-73, 3584-88, 3592 **FR** 79

meetings with Mitchell **3**, 1084-85 **5**, 1911

meetings with Moore **5**, 1950-52, 1982-85, 1998

Nixon, Richard M. *(Continued)*
meetings with Moore and Dean **5,** 1973-77
meetings with Nelson and Parr **15,** 6550-51, 6793-94, 6796-98 **17,** 7634-35 **FR** 617
meetings with Parr **15,** 6814-15, 6817-18, 6821
meetings with Stans after Watergate arrests **2,** 726, 772
memo from Campbell to Whitaker on materials for meeting with milk producers **17,** 8136-38E
memo from Cole to Mitchell on support of Vietnam speech of **FR** 301-304E
memo from Dean re congressional hearings regarding Watergate **3,** 980, 1239E
memo from Dean to DeMarco, Evans, and Kalmbach on charter for committees working for renomination of **17,** 8130-34E
memo from Harrison on milk import quotas **14,** 6296, 6328-30E
memo from Magruder to Haldeman on public relations after press conference of **10,** 3975, 4130-45E
memo from Marumoto to Malek and Colson on participation in Spanish-speaking activities **19,** 8641-49E
memo from Nelson to Dent on invitation to address Associated Dairymen Inc. to **15,** 6769, 6909E
memo on response to reaction on Cambodian bombing **FR** 317-19E
memo to Dean on student demonstrations **3,** 918, 1100E
memo to Haldeman on public relations aspects of Lindsay victory in New York **10,** 3975, 4111E
memos for file from Whitaker on meeting with Connally, Hardin, Shultz, Rice, Ehrlichman, and Whitaker **FR** 860-61E
memos from Buchanan
"EMK--Political Memorandum" **10,** 3975, 4167-72E
on Kennedy candidacy **11,** 4659-60
on left influence in Democratic party **10,** 3975, 4114-19E
on Muskie campaign **11,** 4656, 4667-68
on "Muskie Watch" **10,** 3915-17, 3975, 4146-53E
on tax-exempt foundations **FR** 141-42
"The Resurrection of Hubert Humphrey" **10,** 3975, 4154-63E
message to Liddy on cooperating with prosecutors **9,** 3635
message to Magruder to tell truth **2,** 851, 852
messages to Magruder through Haldeman **2,** 872
and milk import quotas **16,** 7380
and milk price supports **14,** 6065 **FR** 621-23
and million-dollar discussion **4,** 1576-77
and Mitchell **8,** 3127
Mitchell denies he requested information on break-in or White House horror stories **5,** 1912
Mitchell discusses Watergate with **4,** 1661
Mitchell on **4,** 1627-28, 1636 **5,** 1829
Mitchell on actions he would have taken if informed on Watergate **5,** 1828-29, 1834
Mitchell on attitude toward protection of good name of **5,** 1829
Mitchell on concern over political intelligence **4,** 1667-68

Mitchell on meetings and telephone conversations with **4,** 1674-79
Mitchell on Presidency as institution **5,** 1830-33
Mitchell on probable reaction to White House horrors **5,** 1895
Mitchell's call to after Liddy debriefing report **6,** 2321-22
Mitchell's efforts to keep information from **5,** 1905
Mitchell's reasons for not informing about Liddy's plans **5,** 1816-19
Mitchell's reasons for not informing about White House horrors **4,** 1628 **5,** 1825-28, 1830-37, 1853-55, 1865-68, 1872-73, 1882, 1884-85
Mitchell's reasons for not informing on Watergate **4,** 1632-33, 1666-67 **5,** 1827-28, 1830-37, 1853-55, 1865, 1866-68, 1872-73, 1882
Mitchell's relationship with **5,** 1839-41
and Mitchell's resignation as head of CRP **4,** 1665 **5,** 1885, 1886
Mitchell's supposed isolation from **4,** 1665-66
Moncourt's bookkeeping duties for **22,** 10489
Moore denies discussions on Segretti matter with **5,** 2026
Moore discusses Ellsberg case with **5,** 2061
Moore encourages Dean to inform **5,** 2044, 2054
Moore hired by **5,** 1999-2000
Moore on **5,** 2009, 2067-69
Moore on lack of awareness of Hunt-Liddy activities **5,** 1944-45
Moore tells about Ehrlichman's involvement in Ellsberg case **5,** 1961-62
Moore urges him to tell nation about coverup **5,** 1984
Moore's meetings with **5,** 1950-52, 1982-85, 1998
Moore's political association with **5,** 1939
Moore's reasons for not discussing Dean's stories with **5,** 1972
Moore's reasons for not informing of suspicions **5,** 2027-29, 2044-45
Moore's role in Dean's decision to tell about Watergate coverup **5,** 1939, 1945, 1977-78, 1979, 1980-81, 1982, 1986-87
and national security issue **7,** 2706-2708
Nelson on awareness of TAPE contributions of **15,** 6625-26
Nelson on milk price-support decision and meetings with **15,** 6656-57
news of subpoena to obtain logs of meetings with Dean **2,** 231-32
news summaries to after Watergate **10,** 3948
newspaper stories with Dean's allegations against **4,** 1440-41
not mentioned in Sloan's meetings after Watergate **2,** 593, 594
notes from Petersen re Erlichman, Haldeman, Strachan, and Watergate investigation **9,** 3634, 3875-76E
obsessions over demonstrators and leaks **3,** 1022
Odle on **1,** 9-10
opening statement for meeting with dairy leaders **FR** 827E
and opportunities for Spanish-speaking people **13,** 5302
orders Petersen to avoid investigation of Ellsberg case **5,** 2070-71

Parker memos on proposed meeting between dairy leaders and **FR** 794-97E

partnership document for San Clemente property **23,** 10804-18E

and Patman committee **4,** 1479, 1566, 1575

payment of expenses by Rebozo for **22,** 12438E **26,** 12953-55E

payments for improvements on Key Biscayne property **FR** 1036

and Pentagon Papers case **6,** 2409-10, 2530

and Petersen's advice on Watergate investigation **9,** 3613-14

Petersen's reports on Dean's information to **9,** 3634

petition project for a million signatures from Spanish-speaking endorsers **19,** 8659-60E

photograph with Nelson and Parr **17,** 8093E

and plan to blame Mitchell for Watergate **3,** 1013-14

and Plumbers **7,** 2693

policies on older Americans **19,** 9085-92E

Porter's loyalty to **2,** 649, 678

precedents for testimony before Select Committee **4,** 1557, 1562-63

press conference on Muskie appearance at Whittier College **10,** 3992

press conferences **5,** 1973 **7,** 2707, 2709, 2762-63 **8,** 3026-27 **12,** 4924-25, 4935-47

press statement denying practice of brokering ambassadorships **FR** 492

press statement on appointment of Flemming as Special Consultant on Aging **19,** 9095E

press statement on Dean Report **FR** 47

and pre-Watergate Intelligence gathering **3,** 1055-74

prior knowledge of Watergate **2,** 663-64

proclamation on dairy import quotas **15,** 6798-99 **FR** 621

prohibits use of Fort Wayne story in publicity on campaign disruptions **8,** 3179-80

proposed meeting with Baker **3,** 988

and proposed merger between American Airlines and Western Airlines **13,** 5509-10

and purchase of earrings from Winston **FR** 1047-48

and purchase of house for David and Julie Eisenhower **21,** 10132-33

and purchase of Smathers' home **24,** 11452-53 **FR** 939-40

on purpose served by House Un-American Activities Committee **5,** 2047-48

qualities wanted for White House staff **8,** 3128, 3130

raises possibility of complete disclosure to Dean **FR** 88-89

on raising $1 million **8,** 3117

reaction to Dean telling him about coverup **3,** 1047 **5,** 1894-95, 1996-97

reaction to Dean's statement that Haldeman, Ehrlichman, and Dean are indictable **4,** 1548

reaction to demonstrator near White House **FR** 7

reaction to Kleindienst and Petersen telling him Mitchell and others might be involved in Watergate **5,** 1916

reaction to media on White House involvement in Watergate **8,** 3125-27

reaction to Safeguard ad **FR** 320-31E

reaction to Woods' report on missing portions of tapes **21,** 10139

on realization about coverup **4,** 1522-23

reasons for Dean not telling about coverup **3,** 1049 **4,** 1357

reasons for formation of Plumbers unit **9,** 3783

reasons for milk price-support decision **FR** 673-77

reasons for not contacting Department of Justice, FBI, etc., on new information **5,** 2071-72

reasons for reversal of milk price-support decision by **FR** 666-67

reasons for Stans not telling about payments to Liddy **2,** 770-72

reasons for using Ehrlichman instead of Dean for investigation **7,** 2750

reasons why Walters did not go to **9,** 3438, 3440 and Rebozo **20,** 9453, 9481

Rebozo as agent for **24,** 11333-36 **FR** 943-44

Rebozo denies discussing Hughes contribution with **21,** 9940-41, 9977

Rebozo denies discussing TWA lawsuit with **21,** 10049

Rebozo denies discussion of contributions with **21,** 9975

Rebozo discusses return of Hughes contribution with **21,** 10090 **FR** 1004

Rebozo expenditures on behalf of **23,** 10781-83, 12445-47E **24,** 11311-24, 11454

Rebozo on ABM issue discussion with **21,** 10048

Rebozo tells Davis he will be informed of contribution **22,** 10565, 10580

Rebozo tells Kalmbach he requested meeting on Hughes contribution **21,** 10189

Rebozo's material on ABM to **22,** 10230-31

Rebozo's payment of expenses for **FR** 1031-32

receipt prepared for signature on Hughes contribution **FR** 953

recommendation that he discuss leaks at Cabinet Meeting **3,** 1116E

record on Spanish-speaking Americans **19,** 8627E, 8634-37E

and reduction of dairy import quotas **15,** 6544-45

and refinancing of San Clemente property **23,** 10751

refusal to appear before Select Committee **5,** 1866, 1867

reimbursements to Rebozo **FR** 1032, 1035, 1036, 1044-45, 1051

relationship with Cushman **8,** 3305-3306

relationship with Gray **9,** 3474-75

relationship with Griffin **22,** 10412-13

relationship with Hillings **15,** 6625-26

relationship with Kalmbach **5,** 2093 **15,** 6761

relationship with Kleindienst **9,** 3594

relationship with Moore **5,** 1990

relationship with Rebozo **20,** 9499 **21,** 10063

relationship with Walters **9,** 3431-32

relationship with White House staff **1,** 80-81, 91-92 **3,** 1024-25, 1051-52

and release of Ehrlichman's interview notes **7,** 2737

remodeling of home in Key Biscayne **24,** 11544

report by Moore on Segretti matter to **5,** 2023

Nixon, Richard M. *(Continued)*
  and reports from Ehrlichman **7,** 2716-17
  reports from Haig on IRS investigation of Rebozo
    23, 11003
  reports on Watergate to **8,** 3078-79
  and request for equipment from Hunt **8,** 3258-59
  requests Ehrlichman talk to Rebozo about libel
    suit against *Newsday* **21,** 9677-78
  requests for action on anti-administration media
    FR 269-72E
  requests private transcriber for McKiernan's tes-
    timony **22,** 10661, 10662
  requests Stans not be compelled to testify before
    grand jury **7,** 2790, 2791, 2806
  and re-registration of American Independent
    Party voters **11,** 4643-44
  and resignations of Dean, Kleindienst, Haldeman,
    and Ehrlichman **4,** 1495
  response to Democratic party civil suits **3,** 956-57
    FR 74
  response to McGovern **10,** 4249E
  and Responsiveness Program **18,** 8243
    Ehrlichman on **18,** 8189-92
  results of Harris polls vs. Muskie **11,** 4695, 4764-
    65E
  results of Harris polls vs. Muskie and Wallace **11,**
    4695, 4764-65E
  and return of Hughes contribution **23,** 11007
  reversal of milk price-support decision
    statutory restrictions on **FR** 667
  and Russell **22,** 12050
  and Ryland **24,** 11635
  sale of Key Biscayne property to Griffin **24,**
    11332-33
  sale of San Clemente property **23,** 10739-40
  and sanction of Watergate operation by Mitchell
    and Dean **1,** 199
  schedule for appearances at veterans groups **19,**
    9276-79E
  and school milk program **17,** 7639
  and security problems **7,** 2874-75
  and Segretti matter **3,** 966, 1221E **4,** 1374 **5,** 2037
    10, 4018 **FR** 182-83
  and Select Committee **4,** 1493-94
  Select Committee chart of vetoes of **17,** 8149E
  Select Committee letters on Presidential papers to
    5, 1937-38
  and Select Committee request for meeting and
    materials **13,** 5530-31 *see also* Nixon tapes
  selection of Kalmbach as personal counsel **5,**
    2121-22
  sends Dean to Camp David **4,** 1394, 1395, 1550
    FR 89
  in sensitive case report on Hughes **23,** 11237
  and "separation of powers" instead of "Executive
    privilege" **4,** 1508
  share in Fishers Island **21,** 9679
  Shultz report on meeting with economic advisors
    FR 819-20E
  Sixteen-Point Program to assist Spanish-speaking
    Americans in joining Civil Service **19,** 8704-
    8705E, 8708-8709E
  Sloan on loyalty to **2,** 608-609
  Spanish-speaking appointees **13,** 5539-41E

  Special Message on Aging **19,** 9102E
  and Special Unit **7,** 2832
  speech on truth-telling in **5,** 1864-65
  speech on Watergate of May 22, 1973 **FR** 1118
  staff member present at meetings of **5,** 2087-88
  and Stans confirmation hearings **4,** 1483
  Stans on **2,** 726
  statement of April 17, 1973 **7,** 2857-58 **8,** 3079
  statement of April 30, 1973 **9,** 3489-90, 3545,
    3596-97, 3601-02, 3652-53 **FR** 95-96
  statement of May 22, 1973 **4,** 1627 **6,** 2555 **7,**
    2696-97, 2858
  statement of October 5, 1972 **5,** 1855
  statement on campaign contributions **FR** 618-19
  statement on "Dean Report" **3,** 1075-76
  statement on Ellsberg break-in **6,** 2552-53
  statement on everyone involved in Watergate
    coming forward **4,** 1652
  statement on Executive privilege **23,** 10853
  statement on lack of involvement of White House
    staff **5,** 1967-68
  statement on March 21 **5,** 2057-58 **7,** 2769-70
  statement on new Watergate developments **7,** 2758
  statement on White House Watergate investiga-
    tion **5,** 1888-90
  statements on FBI Watergate investigation and
    White House **FR** 40
  Strachan and Mitchell at same law firm as **6,**
    2446
  Strachan on communication between Haldeman
    and **6,** 2501
  Strachan on estate plan for **6,** 2487-88
  and Strachan's memos to Haldeman **6,** 2488
  suggests "White Paper" for Senate **5,** 1944
  summit conference with Brezhnev **2,** 875
  Supreme Court nominations **10,** 4199E
  suspicions about his involvement in Watergate **5,**
    1836
  swimming pool for, in summary of meeting called
    by Haldeman
    23, 11140-42E
  talks to Colson about Executive clemency for
    Hunt **3,** 1047
  talks with lawyer in Key Biscayne **5,** 1984
  in taped telephone conversation between Ehrlich-
    man and Kalmbach **5,** 2216E
  tasks after Watergate break-in **6,** 2519-20
  Taugher on Haldeman's testimony on violence
    and dirty tricks by Democrats against **11,** 4537-
    55
  telephone call from Hunt to Barker prior to
    speech on mining of Haiphong Harbor **9,** 3745,
    3746
  telephone call from Mitchell after Mardian report
    on Liddy debriefing **6,** 2417
  telephone call to Mitchell **5,** 1879
  telephone call to Nelson **15,** 6549-50, 6793 **17,**
    7634 **FR** 616
  telephone calls to Danner **21,** 10066-68
  telephone calls to Dean after Sirica reads
    McCord's letter **3,** 1003 **FR** 89
  telephone calls to Petersen **9,** 3632, 3636, 3650
  telephone conversation with Connally on milk
    price supports on March 23 **FR** 643

telephone conversation with MacGregor **12,** 4940-41

telephone conversations with Gray **9,** 3415, 3432, 3440, 3462, 3464-65, 3489-90, 3497-98, 3506-3507, 3523-25, 3527, 3531, 3536, 3541 **12,** 4939 **FR** 39-40

telephone conversations with Mitchell after Watergate arrests **5,** 1886-88

tells Dean to deal directly through him **3,** 1078-79 **4,** 1400-1401, 1495

tells Ehrlichman Petersen said he tried to get Hunt out of country **7,** 2718

tells Haig about Rebozo's role as recipient of campaign contributions **23,** 11017, 11018

tells Haig Rebozo did not use Hughes money **23,** 11024

tells Haig that none of Hughes money was given to Woods or Nixon brothers **FR** 1025

tells Haldeman Rebozo has funds for legal defense **23,** 11074-75, 11082-84

tells MacGregor he does not recollect telephone call from him on July 6 **12,** 4917-20

tells Mardian to deliver Sullivan reports to Ehrlichman **6,** 2393

tells Moore about Dean's charges **5,** 1982-83, 2010, 2069-70

tells Moore Dean told him about Hunt's demands for money **5,** 2054

tells Petersen he heard Dean has been immunized **9,** 3630

tells Petersen to forget about investigating Fielding break-in **9,** 3631

time spent on Watergate by **7,** 2871

tour in Latin America **9,** 3431-32

Townsend on **14,** 6313

trip to Bahamas in 1968 **FR** 962

trip to China **3,** 1301E

on trip with Rebozo, Danner, and Abplanalp **24,** 11407-11408

and use of FBI **5,** 1976

and use of IRS against political enemies **FR** 133

veto power in White Paper on milk price-support decision **FR** 676-77

victory dinner in 1969 for **15,** 6521-23

and violent demonstrations in San Francisco **3,** 1307E

visit with Rebozo and Danner in May 1973 **20,** 9548-50

and waiver of attorney-client privilege for Gemmill testimony **23,** 11208

Wakefield claims attorney-client privilege on testimony on **24,** 11279, 11280, 11284, 11286-88, 11290-94, 11297, 11300-11302, 11303-11305, 11306, 11307, 11308, 11313, 11329, 11343-45

Wakefield reports to Kalmbach and DeMarco on expenditures on behalf of **24,** 11341-42

Wakefield's checks for expenses of **24,** 11312, 11316-17, 11320-22, 11372-84E

in Walters' memo on conversation with Gray **9,** 3822E

Walters on reasons for not going to **9,** 3434-35

wants Dean to brief cabinet **4,** 1517-18

wants Dean to go before grand jury **7,** 2754

wants Kleindienst to meet with Baker **4,** 1396

and Watergate break-in **4,** 1407, 1467, 1521

and Watergate coverup **4,** 1465-66 **7,** 2883-84 **9,** 3586

Watergate coverup and re-election of **2,** 856 **3,** 936, 937

and Watergate investigations **8,** 3126-27

and Weicker's protest about Sixth Amendment violation by Haldeman's testimony on tapes **8,** 3065-66

whereabouts during Key Biscayne meeting **6,** 2325

Whitaker memo in preparation for meeting with dairy industry leaders **FR** 821-28E

on White House and Watergate **5,** 1860

White House log of phone calls and visits to **1,** 92-93

on wiretapping in 1968 **3,** 993 **8,** 3189

and wiretapping of plane in 1968 **3,** 981, 982 **4,** 1667

withdraws approval of Huston plan **FR** 4

Woods denies Rebozo met with since last testimony **22,** 10215-16

Woods on diary of **22,** 10257

Woods on habit of saving everything **22,** 10267-68

Woods on personal finances of **22,** 10253

Woods on work relationship with **22,** 10218

and Young **10,** 4009

See also Committee to Re-Elect the President (CRP); Nixon tapes; Nixon-Dean meetings; Nixon's listening devices; Nixon's press conferences; Richard Nixon Foundation

Nixon, Tricia

See Cox, Tricia Nixon

Nixon Cabinet

and Responsiveness Program **18,** 8179, 8189, 8193-94 **FR** 379

wants Dean to brief on Watergate **4,** 1517-18, 1544-45

Nixon Campaign Headquarters, Roosevelt Hotel, New York

demonstrations at **12,** 5151-52E

Nixon Campaign Headquarters, Fall River, Massachusetts

vandalism at **12,** 5107-09E

"Nixon Is Treyf" leaflet 12, 4908, 4965-69, 4971-72, 4973, 4976-79, 5022E, 5059-60E

Nixon Library 5, 2074, 2077

Nixon re-election campaign

budget for **FR** 507

confidential memo on plans to capture the Spanish-speaking vote for **19,** 8617-8712E

improper activities directed against **FR** 207-10

political strategy of **FR** 158-60

and use of incumbency

See Responsiveness Program

violence against CRP and Republican campaign offices **12,** 5107-09E, 5151-52E **FR** 210

Nixon tapes 5, 2076-77

argument over subpoena on Haldeman requiring him to turn over to Select Committee **8,** 3053-54

Baker on **FR** 1114

Baker proposal of special panel for review of **7,** 3659-60

Butterfield on requests for **5,** 2089-90

Ervin on Select Committee's handling of **2,** 601-602

February 27 **3,** 991-92 **4,** 1400, 1483-84
February 28 **3,** 992-93 **4,** 1401-1402
March 1 **3,** 993-94
March 6 **3,** 994
March 7 **3,** 994-95
March 8 **3,** 995
March 13 **3,** 995-96 **4,** 1401-1404, 1521-22, 1538-40, 1567-68 **5,** 2003 **7,** 2892 **8,** 3115, 3142-46
March 14 **3,** 996 **5,** 1943
March 15 **3,** 996 **4,** 1404-1405
March 16 **3,** 996 **4,** 1405
March 17 **3,** 996-97 **4,** 1405
March 19 **3,** 997 **4,** 1405-1406 **5,** 1944
March 20 **3,** 997 **4,** 1406-1407, 1540-41
 Moore on **5,** 2065-68, 2068-69
March 21 **3,** 998-1000 **4,** 1380-84, 1396-97, 1426, 1516-18, 1541-46 **7,** 2714-16, 2856-57 **8,** 3604, 3067-68, 3115-18, 3167-68 **FR** 57-61
 Haldeman on **7,** 2896-98
March 22 **4,** 1548-50, 1635
September 15 **4,** 1474-82 **8,** 3124-25, 3138-42 **FR** 48-51
on Stans' libel action against O'Brien **FR** 75
in 1972 **4,** 1521, 1569-68 **7,** 2888-89
Nixon's listening devices
activation of **5,** 2075-76, 2086
in Cabinet room **5,** 2076, 2086-87
installation of **5,** 2074-75, 2077
in locations other than White House **5,** 2083-84
mechanics of **5,** 2084-85
and meetings with foreign dignitaries or heads of state **5,** 2080
operation of **5,** 2079-80
persons knowing about **5,** 2077-78
reasons for **5,** 2077, 2083, 2087-88
reasons for lack of at Key Biscayne, San Clemente, etc. **5,** 2085-86
and rumors of previous devices in former administrations **5,** 2079
secrecy surrounding **5,** 2088
and telephones **5,** 2076-77
test of system **5,** 2080-81
Nixon's press conferences
after Watergate arrests **2,** 850
of August 29 **7,** 2882-83
Buchanan and **10,** 3905, 3947
Buchanan letter to Kilpatrick on **10,** 4145E
called by Mitchell after Watergate break-in **5,** 1848-49
discussed in Dean-Nixon meetings **4,** 1402-1404
and MacGregor **4,** 1578-79
of March 15, 1973 **5,** 1943
and Mollenhoff raising Fitzgerald case **4,** 1560
on opening of liaison office in Peking **3,** 996
preparations for **3,** 965, 1074-75, 1200-1208E **4,** 1403-1404 **5,** 1973
on Select Committee **4,** 1463
No Retreat from Tomorrow (Johnson) **14,** 6181 **15,** 6671, 6696-97, 6906 **17,** 8157E
Nofziger, Lyn 2, 541, 542, 573, 751 **4,** 1688E **10,** 4112E, 4130E **12,** 4950 **23,** 11101
and Caulfield's investigation of Kennedy Foundation financing of *Newsday* article on Rebozo **22,**

10375
and Colson's plan to firebomb Brookings Institution **FR** 125
and DeAntonio film **22,** 10380-81, 10384-85
and derogatory information to press **FR** 143-44
and enemies list **4,** 1408-1409, 1690E **FR** 8, 131
instructions to Ulasewicz **FR** 110
memo from Buchanan on topics for discussion **10,** 3975, 4173E
memo from Haldeman on use of Lasky **10,** 3975, 4129E
memo to Haldeman on Huntley **4,** 1701-1702E **8,** 3213-14
use of money disbursed to **2,** 621
No-Knock laws 7, 2692
Nolan, Betty FR 303E
and CRP letterwriting campaign **FR** 151-52
on memo from Buchanan on bogus "Letter to the Editor" **10,** 3975, 4256-58E
Nollen, Jack 24, 11624
North Carolina
Buckley's political activities in **11,** 4455-56, 4460
North Texas Milk Producers 15, 6502
Northrop Corp.
campaign contributions of **FR** 486-89
scheme to conceal corporate contribution **FR** 447
See also Jones, Thomas
Norton, Bob FR 168
Norton, James Robert 7, 2735 **10,** 4026, 4273-74E **11,** 4640 **FR** 166
Novak
See Evans and Novak
Novelli, William D. 18, 8467, 8468, 8469
memo from Malek on HEW film **18,** 8479, 8582E
memo from Todd on HEW film **18,** 8479, 8580E
memo to Todd and Evans on Older Americans brochures **18,** 8471, 8566-68E **FR** 420-21
November Group 1, 32 **17,** 7555-56, 7561 **18,** 8469
Liddy and **2,** 476
and Spanish-speaking voters **19,** 8654E
suspected wiretapping of **1,** 204-205
Nuberg, Esther 25, 12284
Nunez, Carlos 13, 5340
affidavit on campaign contributions to Hispanic Finance Committee **13,** 5371, 5736E
affidavit on role in Fernandez contact with Priestes **13,** 5371
and contact between Fernandez and Priestes **13,** 5366-67, 5367-68
and Priestes contribution **FR** 522
Nunn, Lee 2, 558, 602, 695, 704, 734 **3,** 1228E **13,** 5478, 5481, 5506 **14,** 5889 **16,** 7424 **17,** 7600
and alleged passthrough of CTAPE contribution from congressional committees to Finance Committee **FR** 741, 742-43
and American Airlines contribution **13,** 5502 **FR** 448
and AMPI contributions through committees **14,** 6259, 6264, 6270 **16,** 7261, 7420-21, 7423, 7459-60 **FR** 689, 733-34
and budget committee **5,** 1846
Clancy testimony on TAPE contribution and **16,** 7404-7405, 7406-7407, 7408-11

on enemies list **FR** 9

FBI removal of tap on telephone **9**, 3595

and Gemstone plan approval **FR** 25

Hughes' retainer of **23**, 10943 **FR** 949, 954-55

Hunt on plan to have electronic surveillance of **9**, 3785

income from Hughes Tool Co. **21**, 9956

information from IRS to White House on **21**, 9711

information wanted on **2**, 858

involvement in Hughes operation **21**, 10056-58

IRS audits of **FR** 137, 1025-30

and IRS Hughes report **23**, 11251

IRS investigation of relationship with Hughes Tool Co. **21**, 9683-84

in IRS sensitive case report on Hughes Tool Co. **23**, 10928

and ITT case **2**, 790 **5**, 1873-74

Johnnie Walters on IRS investigation of **24**, 11638-42, 11644-46

leasing of Department of Transportation building in Washington, D.C. **23**, 11084, 11136E, 11137E

letter from Dean on request to Nixon for appointment of Special Prosecutor **3**, 1163E

letter from Kleindienst on request to Nixon for appointment of Special Prosecutor **3**, 1163E

letter of complaint to IRS on second audit **23**, 11225

letter to Nixon requesting appointment of Special Prosecutor

  memos from Dean to Haldeman and Ehrlichman on **3**, 943, 1161-68E

and Mafia figures **21**, 9733-36

Mardian's meetings with **6**, 2369-70, 2430, 2431-32

McCord's motivations for wiretapping **1**, 174-75

memo from Haldeman to Dean on Hughes' retainer of **8**, 3214-15, 3221, 3369-71E

memo from Huston to Dean on **23**, 11077, 11119-22E

memos to and from Dean and Haldeman on **23**, 11114-18E

in Miami during Watergate break-in **1**, 401-402

on Nixon administration and IRS **7**, 2978-79E

in Operation Sandwedge **FR** 240E

political espionage activities against **1**, 128 **3**, 923-24 **10**, 3946-47 **11**, 4640

postponement of IRS interviews until after elections **24**, 11642

relationship to Hughes organization **20**, 9528-29, 9530

reopening of IRS audit on **24**, 11653

retained by Maheu **24**, 11589-94

retainer with Hughes Tool Co. **20**, 9604 **22**, 10249

and settlement of civil suit **7**, 2735

Stans' libel suit against **4**, 1471-72, 1478 **FR** 75

as target of Liddy plan, Mitchell on **4**, 1611

telephone tapped by McCord **1**, 157 **FR** 28-29

three-way telephone call from Shultz, Walters, and Barth to Ehrlichman on tax report on **23**, 11223-24, 11243

in wiretaps **2**, 465-66, 468

O'Brien, Obie 19, 8888-90E

O'Brien, Pat FR 167-68

O'Brien, Paul 1, 195 **2**, 517, 563, 709 **3**, 957 **4**, 1649 **5**, 1935

Alch and **1**, 348

at FBI interviews of CRP staff persons **FR** 46

calls Dean on problems with Hunt **3**, 973

contact with Mrs. Hunt **9**, 3691

Dean believes he was set up **3**, 1010

on dirty tricks **7**, 2735-36

discusses status of civil suits with Ehrlichman **7**, 2735

discussions with Bittman **6**, 2313

Ehrlichman interviews **7**, 2751-52

Ehrlichman reports to Nixon on interview with **7**, 2757

and Executive clemency offers to Watergate defendants **1**, 210 **3**, 1080 **FR** 64

Haldeman and **4**, 1577-78

on Haldeman ordering Watergate **7**, 2902

and Hunt's demands for money **4**, 1382, 1546

in Hunt's notes **9**, 3842E

and hush money **3**, 971 **4**, 1402 **6**, 2224, 2320

informs Dean about Hunt's status after death of Hunt's wife **3**, 971

informs Dean that Hunt wants to plead guilty **FR** 66

interviewed by Ehrlichman **7**, 2727, 2731-36

involvement in coverup

  Dean on **3**, 1054

MacGregor on role at CRP of **12**, 4909-10

Magruder implicates Nixon in Watergate plans to **3**, 990

and Magruder's proposed meeting with Reisner **2**, 508-509

and McCord **FR** 64

McCord letter on misinformation on CIA given to **9**, 3446

meeting with Dean for report on La Costa meeting **3**, 986-87

meeting with Hunt **9**, 3703-3705, 3707

meeting with Mitchell, McPhee, and Mardian **5**, 1907-1908

meeting with Mitchell and Alch **4**, 1580-81

meeting with Sloan **2**, 549-50, 777-78

and meetings after Watergate arrests **5**, 1952

meetings with LaRue **6**, 2291-92

meetings with Mitchell **4**, 1549-50 **5**, 1905-1906

messages from Bittman on demands for hush money **3**, 969

messages on hush money from Hunt to Dean **3**, 997

and Mitchell as scapegoat **3**, 1093

and Porter's decision to admit perjury to grand jury **2**, 638-39, 640-42, 643-44

reads FBI reports on Watergate investigation **3**, 945

recommends Hampton as counsel for Segretti **FR** 183

refuses funds for Watergate defendants **5**, 2104 **6**, 2267

reports to MacGregor **12**, 4923-24

O'Brien, Paul *(Continued)*
Sloan tells about cash disbursal to Liddy **FR** 43
and Sloan's disclosure of Magruder's effort to
have him perjure himself **2,** 557-558
on Stans' indictability **7,** 2735
tells Dean about Hunt-Colson relationship **3,** 933
tells Dean about McCord's letter to Sirica **4,** 1385
tells Ehrlichman about Liddy plan meetings **5,**
2085 **7,** 2731-32
tells Ehrlichman about plant in Muskie camp **7,**
2732-33
tells Ehrlichman Dean is key Watergate problem
in White House **7,** 2733-34
tells Mardian about Mrs. Hunt's visit **6,** 2367-68
in transcription of taped telephone conversation
between Ehrlichman and Kalmbach **5,** 2215E,
2216E
Ulasewicz and **FR** 110
and Watergate coverup **2,** 857
and White House strategy for Select Committee
hearings **FR** 76
**Occupational Safety and Health Administration
(OSHA)**
and Responsiveness Program **19,** 8801-8803E **FR**
432-33
Oceanographic Fund
Edward C. Nixon and **22,** 10600
O'Connell, Jack 21, 9736-37 **FR** 241-42E
O'Conner, Ed 12, 5113E
O'Connor, James H. 5, 2174 **21,** 10188 **23,** 10856 **25,**
11775 **FR** 1064
affidavit on Kalmbach's report on discussion of
Hughes contribution with Rebozo **22,** 12577-
78E **FR** 1007-1008
pre-April 7 records of Humphrey campaign in office of **25,** 11770, 11771
on taped conversation between Ehrlichman and
Kalmbach **5,** 2162, 2167
O'Connor, Patrick J.
Schaller letter on Humphrey fundraiser to **25,**
11973E
O'Connor, Paul 7, 2947E
October 14, Coalition 11, 4543
Odell, Robert P. 13, 5362 **16,** 7405
conflicts between Nunn's testimony on senatorial
campaign contributions and **17,** 7561-62
memo from Stans on thank-you letters to contributors **2,** 747, 908E
and TAPE contributions **16,** 7407, 7408, 7411-12
and transfer of funds from Senatorial and Congressional Campaign committees to Finance
Committee **17,** 7569
Odell, Robert P., testimony of 16, 7417-31
on CTAPE contributions to national Republican
committees **16,** 7418-26
on dairy industry contributions in 1971 **16,** 7425-
26
denies knowledge of AMPI $2 million pledge pri-
or to White House White Paper **16,** 7424-25
on financial positions of congressional and
senatorial committees relative to Finance Committee to Re-Elect the President **16,** 7426-31
on persons in position to authorize transfers of
funds to Finance Committee **16,** 7423
on present and prior chairmen of Finance Com-

on press contacts **16,** 7425
on Strachan memo to Haldeman on "Milk
Money" **16,** 7426
Odle, Mrs. 1, 70
Odle, Robert C., Jr. 1, 166 **2,** 549, 602, 659 **6,** 2350
affidavit of **12,** 5009, 5013-14, 5188-93E
and Chapman's Friends **FR** 199-200
differences between Reisner's testimony and testimony of **2,** 516
FBI interviews **9,** 3526
and Gemstone bill **2,** 483
and Gemstone file **2,** 515, 525-26, 530
instructed by Magruder to remove Gemstone files
FR 32-33
on Liddy's behavior after Watergate arrests **FR** 32
list of employees of CRP and Finance Committee
1, 28, 437-447E
memo for Timmons on dividing the Democrats
10, 4204E
memo from Jones on Weekly Activity Report **19,**
8862E, 8867-68E, 8870E, 9341E
memo from McCord on security at Republican
Convention **1,** 406
memo on citizens committees in 1972 campaign
FR 156
memo to Bungato on envelopes for delivery to
Haldeman **FR** 353E
memo to Mardian from **6,** 2428
memo to Mitchell on "Citizens Campaign for
1972" **FR** 325-35E
money from Porter to **2,** 659
on Patman Committee subpoena list **3,** 961,
1193E
and removal of Magruder's file **2,** 495, 496, 505,
510-11, 798
and reports on violence **1,** 179, 181
role in CRP budget meetings **6,** 2316
on Stans' role **2,** 741-42
and Watergate break-in plans **1,** 183
and Watergate coverup **2,** 823
Weekly Report from Jones **19,** 8862E, 8870E
on White House campaign in response to Nixon's
resumption of bombing of North Vietnam **FR**
152
Odle, Robert C., Jr., testimony of 1, 9-75
on access to files in CRP **1,** 37-38
on activities of CRP **1,** 27
on April 17th **1,** 70-71
on clearances for CRP personnel **1,** 71-72
contacts with Sloan **2,** 597
on CRP electronic equipment **1,** 31
on CRP liaison with White House **FR** 19
on demonstrations against Nixon **FR** 209
on destruction of CRP records **1,** 26-27, 50-51,
59-61
on "Gemstone" file **1,** 49-50
hiring by CRP **1,** 39
on Hunt **1,** 69-70
on June 17th **1,** 41-50
on knowledge of dirty tricks **1,** 39
on knowledge of Watergate break-in **1,** 27-28
on Liddy's destruction of CRP documents **1,** 44-
45, 61-62
and McCord **1,** 126, 146, 176

on McCord's travel funds **1**, 38
on memo from Malek to Magruder **1**, 56-59, 451-453
on Mitchell's role at CRP **1**, 40-41
opening statement **1**, 9-10
on organization of CRP **1**, 10-36
on payment for rally in support of Nixon's mining of Haiphong **1**, 68-69
on payments to McCord **1**, 52
on relationship between Liddy and Magruder **1**, 59
on relationship between McCord and Liddy **1**, 54
on removal of Magruder's files **1**, 28-30, 45-49, 52-53, 62-67, 70-71, 72-74
on return of file to Magruder **1**, 67
on role at CRP **1**, 36
on role at CRP after Watergate **1**, 67-68
transfer to CRP from White House staff **1**, 80
on *Washington Post* stories **1**, 51
on Watergate defendants **1**, 39
on White House relationship to CRP **1**, 54-55
O'Donnell, Andrew J. 6, 2466, 2467 **23**, 11179
Office of Economic Opportunity (OEO) 19, 8613E, 8615E
Buckley's employment at **11**, 4436-37, 4445, 4457
documents related to Grant No. 30064 of **18**, 8458, 8530-32E
and Federation of Experienced Americans grant **18**, 8439, 8443-45, 8481 **FR** 426-28
and grants **18**, 8234-36
grants to Spanish-speaking Americans **FR** 382, 383, 384-85
memo from Marumoto to Colson on grants by **13**, 5543-46E, 5699E
and Older Americans **19**, 9229-30E
and Responsiveness Program **18**, 8252
speaking schedule for Spanish-speaking appointees from **13**, 5539-41E
Office of Emergency Preparedness 13, 5454-55
Office of Management and Budget (OMB) 16, 7132
list from Malek to Doresen with departmental contacts for "Responsiveness Program" **19**, 8748E
Malek as Deputy Director of **18**, 8199
in memo from Millspaugh to Flemming **19**, 8607E
and milk price-support decision **16**, 7518 **17**, 7751, 7752, 7753 **FR** 631-32
Office of Minority Business Enterprise (OMBE) 13, 5314, 5535E, 5542E
appointments to **13**, 5279-80
Ehrlichman on criticisms of **18**, 8194-95
grant to Ultra-Systems, Inc. **FR** 385-86
and grantsmanship **18**, 8249, 8268-70 **FR** 407-408
Malek memo on grants **13**, 5282-83
memo from Amendariz to Bayer on proposals for **13**, 5653-57E
memo from Bayer to Armendariz and Rodriguez on status of proposals for **13**, 5323, 5652-57E
resistance to Responsiveness Program **FR** 434-36
Office of Public Prosecutor FR 442
Baker on establishment of **FR** 1105-1106
Gurney on opposition to appointment of **FR** 1172-74
Select Committee recommendation of establishment of **FR** 96-100

Ogarrio, Manuel 8, 3239 **9**, 3421
and Mexican checks **FR** 514-21
See also Mexican checks
Ogden Foods
F. Donald Nixon's employment at **22**, 10673-74
O'Grady, J. Terrance
meeting with assistant U.S. attorneys on Baldwin as Government witness **1**, 389-90
O'Hanlon, Richard, questioning by
Chestnut **25**, 11743-44
Cole **25**, 11813-14
Eaton **25**, 12323
Fellows **25**, 11783-84
Lifflander **25**, 12292-93, 12297
Morrison **25**, 11764
Pearlman **25**, 12199-12201
Rubin **25**, 12167-70
Ohio State University 10, 4070E
Ohrenstein, Manfred
and attorney-client privilege in relationship between Hertz and Lifflander **25**, 12266-67
opening statement on immunity granted to Edidin **25**, 12257-58
See also Lifflander, Matthew L., testimony of
Oil Import Appeals Board 13, 5455
Oil import quotas
and Gulf Oil contribution to CRP **13**, 5471
Okin, Robert 11, 4461, 4891E
Older Americans Act 19, 9098E
Older Americans Brochures FR 419-23
confidential memo from Evans on **19**, 9217-23E
copies of **19**, 9157-9204E
General Accounting Office report on **19**, 9135-56E
memo from Evans to Todd on **19**, 9207-11E
memo from Todd to Flemming, Rensselaer, Keller, and Evans on **18**, 8485, 8593E
memos on publication of **19**, 9217-9223E
published in 1972 **18**, 8463-78, 8484-86
Older Americans Division, CRP
appointment of Flemming as Special Consultant on Aging to Nixon **19**, 9093-95E
and Domestic Council Cabinet on Aging **19**, 9096-9103E
Field Operation through April 1, 1972 **19**, 9121-23E
Final Report of **19**, 9051-54E
financing of **19**, 9125E
form letter to state Nixon chairmen on **19**, 9133-34E
memo for Public Information Offices on Aging Program Information **19**, 9205-9206E
memo from Todd through Malek for Mitchell with Campaign Plan **19**, 9055-9134E
memo from Todd to MacGregor on Final Report of **19**, 9051-54E
progress report from Malek to MacGregor **19**, 9212-16E
proposed campaign plan for **19**, 9055-9134E
proposed organization chart for **19**, 9125E
and Responsiveness Program **FR** 419-28
state field organization plan **19**, 9126-32E

on attitude toward second milk price-support
decision **16,** 7144-46
on behavior of dairymen at convention in Chicago
16, 7149, 7151
on contacts with Nelson and Parr **16,** 7139
on duties in Department of Agriculture **16,** 7130
on education and training in agricultural area **16,**
7129-30
on first decision on milk price supports **16,** 7131-
37
on Government posts held by **16,** 7129, 7130
on involvement in milk price-support decisions **16,**
7130-51
on lack of knowledge of reversal of price-support
decision **FR** 627-28
on learning about change in milk price-supports
decision **16,** 7142
on meetings at White House on milk price-support decisions **16,** 7137-43
on milk price-support decision related to political
contributions **16,** 7148-51
on phasing out price supports **16,** 7146-47
on reasons for not attending Chicago convention
of dairymen **16,** 7151
on role as president of Commodity Credit Board
16, 7143-44
on role of Interagency Dairy Supply Estimates
Committee **16,** 7135-36
Pan American Airlines
and acquisition efforts of Resorts International **23,**
10792
Panama Canal issue
in letter from McGrath to Danner **24,** 11460-62
Panarites, Sylvia 1, 32, 34, 35
Panzarino, Frank
letter to Silverstein on transmittal of after-action
report for Operation Dade **12,** 5015, 5196-
5218E
Paradise Island
Rebozo on trip to **21,** 10054
Parelman, Sam 11, 4490, 4712E
Parker, Dan FR 490
Parker, David 10, 3906 **12,** 5133E **16,** 7164 **23,** 11064
attends Moore interview with Select Committee
staff **5,** 1991-92
memos on proposed meeting between Nixon and
dairy industry leaders **FR** 794-97E
Parker, Doug 5, 1948-49 **23,** 11060
Parker, Glenn FR 204, 205
Parker, John
affidavit of **17,** 7990-91E
Parker, William W. 19, 9246-47E
Parkinson, Kenneth Wells 1, 196 **2,** 508, 558, 563,
698, 709, 808 **4,** 1470, 1576, 1598, 1623 **5,** 1935 **17,**
7663
at FBI interviews of CRP staff persons **FR** 46
at meetings after Watergate arrest **5,** 1953
and civil suit **6,** 2356
Dean shows FBI files to **4,** 1361
on Dean's "indictable" list **5,** 1989
and Dean's testimony on McPhee's approaches to
Judge Richey **5,** 1910
and Democratic civil suits **3,** 957 **4,** 1575-76

discussed in taped telephone conversation between
Colson and Hunt **9,** 3784
discussions with Bittman **6,** 2313
draft of Kleindienst's response to Brown **5,** 2205-
2207E
and efforts to block Patman Committee hearings
3, 959, 960, 961 **FR** 74
and Executive clemency offers **1,** 210
and hush money **4,** 1391 **6,** 2320
involvement in coverup
Dean on **3,** 1054
and LaRue's payment to Bittman **6,** 2294
letter from Firestone on contributions to CRP **13,**
5526, 5854E
letter from Heininger on contribution to CRP **17,**
7653, 7674-77E
letter from Herbert J. Miller, Jr., on return of
American Airlines' illegal contribution to CRP
13, 5504, 5839E
letter from Mellott on origin of $100,000 contri-
bution to CRP being Gulf Oil **13,** 5466, 5804-
05E
letter from Myers on return of contribution of
Goodyear Tire & Rubber Co. to CRP **13,** 5526,
5855E
letter to Atkins on source of contribution to CRP
13, 5445 **FR** 460
letter to Barrick on return of contribution of
Goodyear Tire & Rubber Co. to CRP **13,** 5526,
5857E
letter to DeYoung and Firestone on listing of individual contributions **13,** 5525-26
letter to Firestone on contribution to CRP **13,**
5526, 5852-53E
letter to Garry Brown **5,** 2208E
letter to Goodyear Tire & Rubber Co. **FR** 467
letter to Lawrence **FR** 463
letter to Mr. and Mrs. Orin E. Atkins on their
contribution to CRP **13,** 5448, 5796E
letter to Wild on $100,000 contribution to CRP
13, 5466, 5803E
letter to Wild on listing of contributors from Gulf
Oil **13,** 5466 **FR** 472
MacGregor on role at CRP of **12,** 4909-10
and Magruder and Porter's testimony before
grand jury **5,** 1897
Magruder tells about coverup to **2,** 802
Mardian's meetings with **6,** 2369-70
McCord threatens to implicate in Watergate **7,**
2734
and McPhee's talks with Richey **5,** 1910
meeting with Porter **2,** 667-68, 673
meeting with Sloan **2,** 549-50, 581, 777-78
meetings with LaRue on money for Watergate defendants **6,** 2292
meetings with Mitchell **5,** 1905-1906
meetings with Mitchell, Stans, and McPhee **5,**
1907
memo from Dean on 1972 political filings **3,** 961,
1183-89E
memo re counteractions on Democratic party civil
suit **3,** 957, 1173-80E
Mitchell contacts after Watergate **5,** 1887
and Porter's decision to admit perjury to grand
jury **2,** 638-39, 640-42, 643-44, 667-68

Parkinson, Kenneth Wells *(Continued)*
 reads FBI reports on Watergate investigation **3,** 945
 relays conversations with Bittman on cash needs of Watergate defendants **6,** 2295
 reports to MacGregor **12,** 4923-24
 Sloan tells about cash disbursal to Liddy **FR** 43
 in taped telephone conversation between Colson and Hunt **9,** 3797
 tells Mardian about Bittman's fee demands **6,** 2368
 and Watergate coverup **2,** 857
 and White House strategy for Select Committee hearings **FR** 76
Parks, Robert 17, 7718
Parnham, Arnold L. 9, 3426
 memos re "Cleo" **9,** 3465
Parochial schools issue
 and assault strategy on McGovern **10,** 4242E
Parole Board
 Nixon administration use of **FR** 277-80E
Parr, David L. 4, 1791E **14,** 5863, 5871, 5874, 5877-78, 5881, 5885-86, 5892, 5909, 5912, 5922, 5953, 5958, 5969, 5973, 5975, 5978, 5985, 6082, 6106, 6154, 6161, 6168, 6258-59, 6271, 6326 **15,** 6525, 6637 **16,** 6965, 7108, 7111, 7123, 7128, 7324, 7449
 and ADEPT campaign commitment **17,** 7741
 after meeting with Nixon **FR** 646
 and Albert-Mills meetings **16,** 7119
 on AMPI $2 million pledge to Colson in 1970 **FR** 613
 and AMPI arrangement with Valentine, Sherman **14,** 6150, 6151 **FR** 875-76
 and AMPI checkoff system for Mills **16,** 7040-41
 and AMPI committees **14,** 6301, 6302
 and AMPI contributions **14,** 5966 **15,** 6409-10, 6415-19
 and AMPI contributions to Humphrey's 1970 senatorial campaign **15,** 6547
 and AMPI contributions to Muskie campaign **16,** 7012
 and AMPI efforts to obtain milk price-support increases **15,** 6552
 and AMPI employee checkoff system for Mills **FR** 922
 and AMPI rally for Mills in Ames, Iowa **17,** 7664, 7666
 and AMPI reimbursement scheme **15,** 6530-31
 and AMPI relationship with Mills **15,** 6603, 6605, 6607-6609, 6611, 6612, 6613
 and AMPI relationship with Valentine, Sherman **15,** 6579, 6581, 6582, 6584-86, 6587, 6595
 at airport during Lilly-Connally conversation **14,** 6309, 6310 **15,** 6618, 6620, 6621
 at LBJ ranch with Townsend, Arnold, and Mills **16,** 7121-22
 at meeting at Louisville Airport **6,** 7071-75 **17,** 7731-40
 at meeting between Kalmbach and dairy industry representatives **15,** 6535-38
 at meeting with Semer and Jacobsen **16,** 7188-89
 at milk producers' meeting with Kalmbach in 1970 **17,** 7590-91, 7593-94
 at Nelson's meetings on milk price supports **15,** 6555

at Nixon's meetings with dairy industry representatives **16,** 7139
 on attending kick-off 1972 Republican Dinner on March 24 **FR** 658-59
 Campbell and **17,** 7750
 and cash contributions for Mills **14,** 6318-19
 and checkoff system for contributions to Mills **14,** 6321
 commitments to Republicans **14,** 6276
 contacts with Masters **16,** 6939
 and contributions through committees to Nixon campaign **15,** 6628, 6631, 6645-46
 and contributions to Mills' election campaign **14,** 6168-72
 delivery of money by Townsend to Goss from **16,** 7097-98
 delivery of money for Mills by Townsend for **16,** 7090-91
 denies AMPI commitment to Nixon campaign to Mehren **FR** 712
 denies AMPI made $2.6 million commitment to Nixon campaign **16,** 7316-17
 and destruction of documents in AMPI Little Rock, Arkansas, office **14,** 6322-25
 discussions with Campbell on milk price supports **17,** 7766
 discussions with Hanman on Louisville Airport meeting **17,** 7743-44
 efforts to have Nixon attend first AMPI convention **17,** 7634
 and formation of Dairymen, Inc., and SPACE **16,** 7061
 and Gallup polls **16,** 7004
 informs Mehren of AMPI checkoff system for Mills **16,** 7314
 informs Mehren of reasons for Dallas meeting **16,** 7251
 Jacobsen and **15,** 6380-81, 6384
 Jacobsen delivers cash for Mills campaign to **15,** 6430-35
 Jacobsen on contacts with **15,** 6430
 learns of Nixon plans to raise milk price supports **FR** 637
 letter from Chotiner on use of political committees for contributions **15,** 6888, 6930E
 letter from Connell on meeting in Louisville **15,** 6835, 6911E
 letter from Hanman on cover letter to Chotiner **14,** 6315, 6372E
 letter from Hanman on TAPE committees **14,** 6315-16
 letter from Semer on Muskie campaign **14,** 5951, 6028E
 letter from Valentine enclosing invoices for Iowa project **15,** 6842, 6924-29E
 letter from Valentine on AMPI's payment to Valentine, Sherman **15,** 6840, 6923E
 letter of recommendation of Chestnut from Connell to **25,** 11839E
 letter to Hanman **14,** 6280-81
 letter to Hanman on contributions to political committees **14,** 6315, 6373-77E
 letter to Isham on mailing of contributions **15,** 6890, 6931E
 letter to Nelson on objectives and progress reporting within MPI **15,** 6756, 6907-08E

Malek on **18**, 8223-30, 8232-34, 8289, 8290
memo from Freeman to Kingsley on Staffing
Strategy for Part-time Boards and Commissions
19, 8882-87E
memo from Horton to Malek and Kingsley on
targets of **19**, 8891-96E
in memos from Millspaugh to Flemming **19**,
8606-12E **FR** 264-65
recommendation and referral for departmental
board or commission **19**, 8888-89E
and White House Personnel Operation **19**, 8892-
96E, 8897-98E
Patterson, John 3, 1331E
Pauco, Dr. Joseph 12, 5027-28E, 5029E
Payne, Nancy 3, 1135E
Payroll deductions
and Tennessee Eastman Co. Volunteers for Better
Government contributions **FR** 553
Peace Action Council 11, 4543
Peace Corps 11, 4604 **13**, 5290
Pearlman, Marian Rachel 25, 12122, 12151 **FR** 555
letter to Keys requesting loan forgiveness **25**,
12203E
letters to McGovern creditors **FR** 554-55
Pearlman, Marian Rachel, testimony of 25, 12173-
12202
on amount received by McGovern campaign **25**,
12175-76
on becoming involved with McGovern campaign
25, 12174
on Branner's role in McGovern campaign **25**,
12175
business association of **25**, 12173
on cash contributions to McGovern campaign **25**,
12180-81
on cash kept in McGovern headquarters **25**,
12197-98
on Citizens for McGovern **25**, 12178-79
on committees used by McGovern campaign for
contributions **25**, 12198-99
on decentralization of fundraising **25**, 12202
denies knowledge of anonymous contributions to
McGovern campaign **25**, 12185-86
denies knowledge of dirty tricks **25**, 12194-95
denies knowledge of McGovern Campaign Committee transfer of funds to United Farm Workers **25**, 12183
on direct mail receipts by McGovern campaign
25, 12201
on financial condition of McGovern campaign **25**,
12176
on identity of Rich Cohen **25**, 12188-91
on largest contributors to McGovern campaign
25, 12182
on meeting with McGovern staff on cash contributions **25**, 12181-82
on method for placing short-term employees on
payroll of McGovern campaign **25**, 12190
on payment of telephone canvassers for McGovern campaign **25**, 12196
on personal contributions to McGovern campaign
25, 12188
persons responsible to in McGovern campaign **25**,
12174-75

on principal fundraisers of large gifts to McGovern campaign **25**, 12182
on reasons for McGovern campaign setting up
committees for contributions **25**, 12186-88
on recommendations for reform or improvement
of future presidential campaigns **25**, 12200-
12201
on records of McGovern campaign **25**, 12184-85,
12186
role as national finance director of McGovern
campaign **25**, 12173-74
on Rubin's cash expenditures for McGovern campaign **25**, 12181
on salaries paid by McGovern campaign **25**,
12174
on stock contributions to McGovern campaign **25**,
12201
on telephone canvassing of Democratic party
Convention delegates by McGovern campaign
workers **25**, 12194-96
on third-party contribution from Lewis **25**, 12198
on total receipts of McGovern campaign **25**,
12199-12200
on transfers made from McGovern's Presidential
Committee to Senate Committee **25**, 12176-80
on Tuck's relationship to McGovern campaign **25**,
12191-94
on Tuck's request for money **25**, 12192-94
on working relationship with Kimmelman **25**,
12174-75
on Zafferoni contribution **25**, 12202
Pearson, Drew 4, 1687E **21**, 9955, 9969-70, 10116
and F. Donald Nixon's loan in 1958 **21**, 9942-43
Morgan and
Rebozo's uneasiness over Hughes contribution
and **FR** 936
Pell, Claiborne 12, 5027E
on campaign contributions and appointments of
ambassadors **FR** 494
Peloquin, Bob 20, 9375, 9519 **23**, 10792
Pelski, William 13, 5330-31, 5347, 5352-53, 5355
Pemberton, Haywood 4, 1525-26
Pena, Ed 13, 5293-94, 5303-5304 **18**, 8240
attempts to discharge from Equal Employment
Opportunity Commission **FR** 402-403
memo from Florence to Armendariz on **13**, 5323,
5669E
Pendergast, Tom 10, 3068
Penn Camera Exchange, Inc. 11, 4442, 4698E
Pennington, Lee R., Jr. FR 1156
CIA comments on report on **FR** 1161-62
destruction of documents in McCord residence by
FR 1127-30
Pennsylvania
vandalism against Nixon campaign in **12**, 5173E
Pennsylvania Democratic primaries
Segretti picketing activities during **FR** 176
Pennsylvania State College 17, 7757, 7801-03E
Pennsylvania Voice **10**, 4026, 4289E
article on Muskie in **10**, 3998-99
"Penny-a-plate" rally 12, 5114E

Pennzoil FR 514
and Mexican checks FR 518-19
Pentagon Papers case 6, 2565 11, 4544 20, 9347
Buchanan on 10, 3912
Cushman on transmittal of material to official in Soviet Union 8, 3304-3305
and establishment of Special Investigations Unit in White House 7, 2875
Haldeman's knowledge about 6, 2504
and Hunt 3, 1267E
Hunt and Liddy and 1, 81-82
Mardian and 6, 2408-10, 2420, 2425
and Mardian's role at Internal Security Division 6, 2427-28
memos on 6, 2643-45E, 2646-51E
and motivation for false Diem cables 9, 3808-11
and Plumbers unit 8, 3032
publication of 3, 919, 921 FR 119-20
as reason for establishment of Plumbers 8, 3103 FR 12
and setting up of Krogh's special unit 6, 2530-31
See also Ellsberg case; Fielding break-in
Pentland, Robert, Jr. 22, 12534E
"People Are Coming to San Diego, The" 10, 3956, 4107-08E
"People to People" Nixon caravan
violence at rally of 12, 4948-51, 4953, 4955-63
Pepper, Gerald R. 17, 7707-25 22, 10582
letter to Ray on Mills rally 17, 7719, 7726E
letter to REC managers on "Cooperative month" 17, 7720, 7729E
and rally for Mills 17, 7665
Pepper, Gerald R., testimony of
on agreement with Ray that cooperatives had been used for Mills campaign 17, 7717, 7718-19
on Ames, Iowa, rally 17, 7708-7709, 7714-17 FR 916-18
on bank account set up for Mills rally in Ames, Iowa 17, 7715-16
on bipartisan nature of Mills rally 17, 7721, 7723-25
on Iowa Cooperative Month 17, 7707-7708
on Mills spokesperson stating invitation to Ames, Iowa, rally was unsolicited 17, 7714
on nature of Mills appearance at Ames, Iowa, rally FR 919
on report of Wright, Lindsay, and Jennings to AMPI 17, 7721-22
on role as executive director of Iowa Institute of Cooperation 17, 7707-7708
on telephone call from Mills 17, 7709-10, 7722-23
on telephone interview by Beauford 17, 7718
on thank-you letter to Mills 17, 7717
on trip to Washington of executive board of Iowa Institute of Cooperation 17, 7711-13
on use of Mills rally to further Mills presidential campaign 17, 7719-25
Peretz, Marty and Anne 25, 12147
Perfectly Clear; Nixon from Whittier to Watergate (Mankiewicz) 11, 4621-22
Perkins, Ed 24, 11626

Perman, Ronald 25, 12222, 12223, 12227, 12255E FR 474-75
advised by Edidin of resolution of Muskie campaign rental bill problem 25, 12234
discussion with Edidin on paying Hertz for Muskie campaign car rentals through attorney fee system 25, 12230-31
Edidin believes he had no knowledge of Hertz arrangement with Muskie campaign 25, 12239
Permanent Committee on Investigations of the Committee on Government Operations of U.S. Senate 13, 5454 FR 139
Petersen, Henry E. 3, 936, 937, 944, 1008, 1015, 1016, 1083, 1313E 4, 1552, 1553, 1652 5, 1889 8, 3284 9, 3482, 3602-3603, 3609 20, 9575
advice to Nixon on Ehrlichman's resignation 7, 2809
advice to Nixon on Haldeman 8, 3096
affidavit 6, 2607, 2652-54E
asked by Ehrlichman not to require Stans to testify before grand jury 7, 2699-2701
at meeting with Nixon 9, 3592
and Caulfield's investigation of Virgin Islands Corp. 22, 10400, 10401-10402
communications with Nixon and coverup FR 80-82
and Criminal Division investigation of MPI FR 722
and Dean resignation 7, 2678
Dean tells about Gray having Hunt's files 9, 3469, 3470
Dean tells about materials from Hunt's safe 3, 949 4, 1365, 1588
and Dean's efforts to retrieve Hunt photos from CIA FR 75-76
and Dean's involvement with Segretti 3, 963-64
on Dean's reaction to Watergate break-in FR 35
denies he conducted Watergate investigation 12, 4936
discusses Magruder testimony with Dean FR 46
discussion with Nixon on payments to Watergate defendants FR 62
and efforts to get Liddy to talk 3, 1016
Ehrlichman says he refused to obey order to leave Stans alone 9, 3564-65
and Ellsberg case 7, 2676
and Fielding break-in 6, 2552, 2606-2607 7, 2681
Gray denies having Hunt's files 9, 3470-71
Gray denies receiving documents from Dean to 3, 1033
Gray lies to 9, 3498
Gray tells him about Hunt files 9, 3538
and Gray's destruction of Hunt files 7, 2678
Haldeman denies knowing 8, 3127
informs Kleindienst of Watergate break-in FR 32
informs Kleindienst of White House connection to Fielding break-in 9, 3574
Kleindienst on 9, 3566
letter to Patman re public hearings into financial aspects of Watergate "bugging" incident 3, 961, 1194-99E 5, 2199-2204E
meeting with Dean on White House and Watergate 3, 1032-34
meeting with Kleindienst 7, 2758

meeting with Kleindienst, Titus, and Silbert **9**, 3578-79

meeting with Kleindienst and Dean after Watergate break-in **9**, 3562-63

meeting with Kleindienst and Gray on **9**, 3491-92

meeting with Kleindienst and Nixon **FR** 91-92

meeting with Nixon **4**, 1558 **7**, 2904 **8**, 3058 **21**, 10136

memo from Kleindienst recusing himself from further involvement in Watergate investigation **9**, 3573, 3860E

memo to Ehrlichman on Ellsberg break-in **6**, 2553-54

Nixon gives new information to **5**, 2072

Nixon's call on Liddy's remaining silent **4**, 1554

and Nixon's decision on Dean's resignation **7**, 2807-2808

and Nixon's decisions after April 15 **7**, 2807-2808

Nixon's instructions on Watergate investigation and national security to **7**, 2696-97

opposed to appointment of special prosecutor for Watergate **9**, 3570-71

ordered by Nixon to avoid investigation of Ellsberg case **5**, 2070-71

reaction to Watergate break-in **9**, 3528

report to Nixon on grand jury investigation **7**, 2857

reports to Nixon **8**, 3079

requests delay in Patman hearings **FR** 74

responsibility for Watergate **9**, 3551-52

and Segretti coverup **FR** 179

shows Dean CIA material on Hunt **3**, 978

and Stans appearance before grand jury **FR** 47

and Stans excused from grand jury testimony **7**, 2790, 2791 **9**, 3580-81

telephone call from Kleindienst after Liddy informs him of Watergate break-in **9**, 3562

tells Nixon, Mitchell and others might be involved in Watergate **5**, 1916

tells Dean to ask Gray for FBI interview files **4**, 1358

tells Gray they are expendable and Haldeman and Ehrlichman are not **9**, 3525, 3547

tells Gray to get lawyer **9**, 3492

and Watergate investigation **3**, 1317E

and White House staff members appearing before grand jury **3**, 954

Petersen, Henry E., testimony of 9, 3611-59

on appointment of special prosecutor **9**, 3639-40, 3645-46, 3647

on attitude toward Senate Watergate hearings **9**, 3655-56

career **9**, 3611, 3643

on CIA involvement in Watergate investigation **9**, 3616-17

on Colson, Kehrli, and Young questioned in conference room by prosecutors **9**, 3619

on contacts with Nixon **9**, 3648-49

on conversation with Dean on response to Brown's letter on Patman investigation **9**, 3621-22

on Dean testimony **9**, 3652

and decision to exclude dirty tricks of Segretti from Watergate investigation **9**, 3620-21

denies knowledge of Stans receiving transcript of

his testimony **9**, 3620

denies receiving summary from Silbert on possible implication of others higher than Liddy **9**, 3655

on Department of Justice Watergate investigation **9**, 3612, 3620, 3637-40, 3658-59

on discussion with Dean on Magruder's grand jury appearance **9**, 3617-18

on discussion with Nixon on immunity for witnesses **9**, 3629-30

on discussions with Gray on giving Dean FBI reports **9**, 3614-16

on documents from CIA to Kleindienst **9**, 3622-23

and Ellsberg matter **9**, 3644

on Executive privilege and White House tapes **9**, 3656-58

on FBI Watergate investigation **9**, 3612

on grand jury subpoenas **9**, 3646

on Gray resignation **9**, 3625-26, 3654

on Gray's destruction of documents from Hunt's safe **9**, 3624-36

on Haldeman and Dean's attempting to get CIA to stop FBI investigation on Mexican money **9**, 3648

on immunity for Dean **9**, 3643

on information from Dean on Haldeman and Ehrlichman's involvement in Watergate matter **9**, 3632-36

on information given to Nixon **9**, 3649

on information received from Dean **9**, 3632-36

informs Nixon of Fielding break-in **9**, 3630-31

on involvement of Nixon **9**, 3635-36

on Kleindienst resignation **9**, 3653-54

on learning about Fielding break-in **9**, 3630

on learning about Watergate break-in **9**, 3611-12

on loyalty **9**, 3644

and Magruder's testimony before grand jury **9**, 3650-51

meeting on June 20, 1972, with Dean and Kleindienst **9**, 3613-14

on meeting to brief Kleindienst on Dean's testimony **9**, 3627

on meeting with Kleindienst, Dean, and Ehrlichman on leniency for Watergate defendants **9**, 3626-27

on meeting with Nixon **9**, 3627-29

meets with Kleindienst on Nixon's orders on Ellsberg case **9**, 3631-32

on negotiations of agreement for Dean's testimony **9**, 3627

Nixon discusses immunity for Dean with **9**, 3630

on Nixon's message to Liddy **9**, 3635

on Nixon's statement of April 30, 1973, on intensive new inquiries into Watergate **9**, 3652-53

on Nixon's telephone call on Liddy cooperating **9**, 3650

notes given to Nixon re Ehrlichman, Haldeman, and Strachan and Watergate investigation **9**, 3634, 3875-76E

on Office of Attorney General as serving President or American people **9**, 3644-45

on Patman and Watergate hearings **9**, 3647

political affiliation of **9**, 3643

on questioning of White House staff members in private **9**, 3619-20

Pico, Reinaldo
  and second Watergate break-in 1, 235
Pierce, Morgan E. 15, 6392
Pierson, W. DeVier 14, 5863, 5922, 5924, 5925, 6296, 6298-99 15, 6504, 6525, 7346
  advice on reporting requirements of TAPE 15, 6509, 6510
  Alagia informs of SPACE decision on loan to ADEPT 16, 7084
  and AMPI reimbursement scheme 14, 5965-66, 5971-73 15, 6529 FR 604-605
  at AMPI strategy sessions 16, 7028
  check signed by 17, 8056E
  and formation of ADEPT FR 586
  and formation of TAPE 15, 6757
  informs AMPI leaders of TAPE reporting requirements FR 596-97
  letter to Isham on TAPE loan to ADEPT 15, 6640, 6716E FR 688
  meeting with Nelson and Isham FR 597-98
  meeting with Nelson on reporting requirements for TAPE 15, 6524-26
  Mehren on role in milk price-support increase efforts 16, 7236
  Nelson on transactions with 15, 6528, 6529
  and SPACE 16, 7060
  and TAPE contributions 15, 6385, 6524
Pike, Thomas 2, 604
Pillot, Madeline 14, 5910, 5911
Piltero, Dan 1, 35
Pinkertons 3, 1132E
  and security at Republican national headquarters 3, 1125E
Pinkney, Arnold 25, 11749
Pinkstaff, Marsha 11, 4773E
Pioneer Systems 25, 12137, 12142-43
Pipefitters Local 562 v. *United States* FR 550-51
Pitt, William, the Elder 6, 2630-31
Pittsburgh, Pennsylvania
  Benz sets up dirty tricks operation in 11, 4413
Plamdon case 6, 2590, 2591, 2592, 2593
Playboy
  interview with McGovern 10, 4077-78E
Pleasant, William D. 15, 6618, 6808
  affidavit of 17, 7992-93E
Plotkin, Benjamin, questioning by
  Alagia
    16, 7066, 7082-84
  Arnold 25, 12027-28, 12031-32
  Clancy 16, 7412-13
  Ehrlichman 16, 7401-7402 18, 8196-97
  Mehren 16, 7276-78
  Palmby 16, 7146-47, 7150-51
  Semer 16, 7211-18
  Townsend 16, 7103-7104
Plumbers unit 3, 1022
  arrest of 1, 106, 111, 112-13
  attorneys for 1, 109, 111-12
  Barker on 1, 358
  Buchanan on 10, 3912-13
  Buzhardt on 23, 10918
  Chenow testimony and 3, 941

CIA connections of 1, 326
Colson's knowledge of activities of 9, 3724
and concept of presidential power FR 12-17
Dean on creation of 3, 921, 1091
and dissatisfaction with performance level of FBI 7, 2680-81
Ehrlichman on 6, 2529-33 7, 2693
Ehrlichman on justification for use of 6, 2625-29 7, 2780-82
and Ellsberg matter FR 119-24
and Fielding break-in 5, 1919, 1961-62 FR 12, 13, 696
Haldeman on 8, 3030-32, 3103
Haldeman's knowledge about 6, 2504
Helms denies knowledge about 8, 3282
Hunt on 9, 3722
identity papers 1, 112-113, 175
Kleindienst on 9, 3592
list of 1, 116
MacGregor claims lack of knowledge about 7, 2803
Mardian claims lack of knowledge about 6, 2389, 2415
McCord on association with 1, 128
memos in Hunt's safe on FR 35
memos in Hunt's safe to Colson on 3, 937-38
Mitchell denies knowledge of 4, 1638-39
Mitchell learns about 5, 1904-1905
Mitchell on 4, 1605
Mitchell on origins of 4, 1636-37
and national security 7, 2696
Nixon and 6, 2603-2604
origin of name 9, 3735
Petersen denies knowledge of 9, 3623
prior roles in White House 1, 79
reasons for creation of FR 12
reasons for Fielding break-in by 9, 3781-83
Weicker on FR 1201-1202
wiretapped information on Ellsberg from FBI to 9, 3786
See also Watergate break-in; Watergate burglars
Poage, W. Robert 14, 5984, 5986-87, 6252 15, 6555, 7120, 7216, 7317, 7318, 7320, 7321 FR 907
  Mehren and 16, 7334
  and milk price-support issue 16, 7399
  TAPE contributions to 16, 7323-24
Podesta, Robert 1, 32, 35
Podesta, Tony 25, 12277
Pokorney, Gene 11, 4617-18
Police Department, Miami, Florida
  "Chronological Log of Events" on 1972 convention week 12, 5219-57E
Polin, Mike 11, 4490
Polin, Mim 11, 4710E
Political enemies
  See Enemies list
Political espionage 1, 26
  against McGovern campaign 11, 4628-31
  Buchanan on 10, 3924-25, 3958-59, 3961-63
  Buckley's attitude toward 11, 4457-59
  chart illustrating a variety of individuals engaged in 11, 4635, 4637E
  cost of 1, 184-185

and Greaves **11**, 4639

and Magruder **2**, 501, 515

Magruder's efforts to help with employment problems **2**, 821, 831-32

on Magruder's perjury **2**, 852

memo to Magruder on infiltrators of Democratic party campaigns **FR** 352E

Mitchell refuses to fire **6**, 2430

on Patman Committee subpoena list **3**, 961

perjury by **FR** 44-46

petty cash disbursed by **2**, 498-99, 500

plea to perjury for false statements **25**, 12404E

and political spying **2**, 501

and review of Ruby I material **FR** 188-89

role on budget committee **2**, 704

and Sloan's questions on use of cash disbursement **2**, 553

Sloan on activities of **2**, 614-15

Stans on cash disbursements to **2**, 698, 744-45

subpoenaed by Patman Committee **3**, 1193E

testimony before grand jury **5**, 1897

transfer to CRP from White House staff **1**, 80

and Watergate coverup **2**, 823, 851

Porter, Herbert Lloyd, testimony of 2, 631-55, 657-80

on amount of money received from Sloan prior to April 7 **2**, 634-35

asked by Magruder to lie about amount of money to Liddy **2**, 635-36, 643-46, 665-66, 677

asked not to mention Reisner **2**, 672

on attempt to get Government job after Watergate trial **2**, 653, 673-74, 676

on career background **2**, 632

cash disbursements made by **2**, 657-60

on changes in campaigning **2**, 651

consults Herge on Magruder's request that he lie **2**, 645-46

denies knowledge about Watergate **2**, 679

denies knowledge of use of money given to Liddy **2**, 677

destroys records of disbursements **2**, 652-53, 674-75

on destruction of records at CRP **2**, 663

on disbursal of $69,000 **2**, 657-60

disbursements by Sloan to **2**, 625-26, 751

on discrepancies between Sloan's testimony and his own on amount of cash disbursed **2**, 659

on documents from Muskie's office as legal or illegally obtained **2**, 670-71

on duties at CRP **2**, 675-76

on effects of Watergate on his life **2**, 651

on Haldeman's role as White House liaison with CRP **2**, 674

on lack of knowledge about illegal activities **2**, 664

on learning about Watergate break-in **2**, 635, 653-54

on Liddy's envelope for Mitchell **2**, 634, 666-67

on lies to FBI about amount of money to Liddy **2**, 636, 672-73, 677

on lies to grand jury about amount of money to Liddy **2**, 636, 637, 643, 672, 673

on loyalty to Nixon as reason for perjury **2**, 649, 678

on Magruder's asking him to give cash to Liddy **2**, 633-34

on Magruder's comments on investigation after Watergate arrests **2**, 664-65

on Magruder's prior knowledge of Watergate break-in **2**, 646

on Magruder's reaction after learning about Watergate break-in **2**, 660-61

on Magruder's statement that he had perjured himself 12 times **2**, 654

on material sent to Strachan at White House **2**, 671

on meeting with Mitchell and Magruder **2**, 663

on meetings in California after Watergate arrests **2**, 661-62

on Mitchell telling Magruder he would deny complicity in Watergate **2**, 646

on motivations for his perjury **2**, 654-55

on Nixon involvement in Watergate **2**, 663-64

opening statement **2**, 631

on persons responsible for cash disbursements **2**, 652

on purchase of microfilm viewing equipment **2**, 668-69

on reasons for cash disbursements to Liddy **2**, 659-60

on reasons for perjury on money to Liddy **2**, 646-52, 676

on reasons for seeking immunity **2**, 678

on reasons for telling about his perjury **2**, 638-42

on reports from people in prank or sabotage department **2**, 678-79

role in Finance Committee **2**, 657

on shredding Liddy's envelopes for Mitchell **2**, 667

on surrogate candidate program **2**, 632-33

on telephone message from McCord after Watergate arrests **2**, 662

tells about his perjury for first time **2**, 637, 643-44

on typing of stolen documents **2**, 650

Portland, Oregon

Segretti's activities in **10**, 4017-18, 4019

"Possible Violations of Criminal Laws and Hatch Act by Veterans Administration Employees in Connection with the 1972 Presidential Campaign" 19, 9242-48E

Post, Dr. Jerrold 25, 12421E

Post (printer of Gemstone stationery) 2, 461-62

Postal officials

exchange of correspondence with Muskie regarding fraudulent mailing **11**, 4695, 4853-57E

Potomac Associates FR 143

Caulfield on investigation into **21**, 9727

Powell, Joy 14, 5897

Powell, William A.

14, 5874, 5897

letter on reason for reversal of milk price-support decision **FR** 671

letter to Mr. and Mrs. Spidle on milk price-support decision **17**, 8141-42E

role in Mid-Am **FR** 586

Powers, Ken 12, 5113E

of U.S. Dept. of Agriculture excerpting speech of
  Campbell **17**, 7757, 7801-03E
Weicker and Haig plan **23**, 11036
of White House on milk price-supports decision
  17, 8073-92E
White House statement on Camp David meeting
  of Nixon, Rebozo, and Danner **23**, 10894-95
Preston, Donald C. 12, 5102E
Prete, Inspector (D.C. Police Department) 1, 114
Price, Jack 20, 9441, 9486, 9487
Price, Mel 3, 1062
Price, Ray 4, 1489 **22**, 10621
confidential memo from Buchanan on topics for
  discussion at meeting **10**, 3975, 4173E
function on White House staff **1**, 76, 78, 82
Priestes, John J. 13, 5361-62, 5366-5401
bill from Manger-Hay-Adams Hotel **13**, 5332,
  5705E
conflicts with Hunt's testimony **9**, 3799E, 3800-
  3802
immunity status of **13**, 5394-95
letter from Barker to Ervin on testimony on Stans
  of **13**, 5706-5707E
note from Dunnells to Stans on **13**, 5348, 5713E
reasons for contribution to National Hispanic Finance Committee instead of CRP **13**, 5387-88
Sloan's statement on meeting with Stans and Fernandez **13**, 5380
Stans instructs Fernandez to return check from
  13, 5380-81
Stans statement on **13**, 5345-47, 5708-13E
See also John Priestes Homes, Inc.; National Hispanic Finance Committee
Priestes, John J., testimony of 13, 5327-57
businesses working under **13**, 5327
on call to Pelski **13**, 5330-31
on contacts with Fernandez **13**, 5328-39, 5339-45,
  5348-51, 5353-55, 5356
and FHA suspension **13**, 5327-39, 5340-45
on meeting Sloan **13**, 5334-35
on meeting with Stans and Fernandez **13**, 5335-
  37, 5341-45, 5348-50
on motivation for attempted contribution **13**, 5350
on motivation for testifying **13**, 5356
plea bargaining agreement made by **13**, 5339
returns check to Woolin **13**, 5339
says Fernandez expected appointment as secretary
  of commerce **13**, 5355-56
telephone call to Pelski **13**, 5352
Priestes Development Corp. 13, 5327
Privacy rights
and public disclosure **FR** 892-93
and Select Committee recommendation for private
  sessions of senatorial committees **FR** 1085-86
Procochino, Mario 10, 4111E
Progressive Labor Party 11, 4543
"Project Find" 18, 8463 **19**, 9135-36E
Evans on **18**, 8477-78
**"Proposed Communications Support Program for the
  Older Americans Division, CRP" 18**, 8465, 8536-
  62E

Proposition 22 12, 4959-60
at protest rally against Nixon **12**, 4949
Prostitutes 2, 788, 839, 863-64 **3**, 929 **4**, 1610 **9**, 3741
at Democratic National Convention **11**, 4449-
  4500, 4516-17, 4527-28
in Gemstone plan **FR** 21
"Protocols of the Elders of Zion" 12, 5026E
Providence Journal **23**, 11027
Proxmire, William 1, 396 **3**, 1331E
Psychological profiles 7, 2673-74
Cushman on **8**, 3310-11
and Ellsberg case **25**, 12421-26E **FR** 121, 1140-44,
  1153-54
Helms on **8**, 3258
use of **7**, 2690-91, 2692-93
Public Affairs Analysts
Caulfield investigation of **21**, 9712, 9713
Public Attorney
See Office of Public Prosecutor
Public Citizen, Inc.
See Nader v. *Butz*
Public Opinion Survey, Inc.
check from Ted Van Dyk Associates, Inc. **16**,
  7003, 7045E
Public opinion surveys
See Gallup polls; Polls
Puerto Ricans
memo from Armendariz to Marumoto on charac-
  teristics of **13**, 5323, 5627-28E
in memo on Spanish-speaking voters **19**, 8623-24E
and Nixon campaign in New York City **19**, 8789-
  92E
Purcell, Graham 14, 5984
**Pure Milk Products Cooperatives, Fond du Lac, Wis-
  consin 14**, 5875
PUSH FR 408-409
Quakers
infiltration of **11**, 4641
Quicksilver Times **10**, 3952, 3955-56
and demonstrators against Muskie **11**, 4383-84
in Rogovin affidavit **10**, 4370-74E **11**, 4434
Quigley, Clarence 25, 11772
Quinn, Sally FR 742
Quinn, Thomas E., Jr.
See Harmony, Sally, testimony of
Race issue
and assault strategy on McGovern **10**, 4244E,
  4245-46E
Humphrey on **10**, 4162-63E
Kennedy and **10**, 4171E
and McGovern **10**, 4250E
See also Black Americans; Black voters
Radel, Robert 16, 7110
Radio programs
letter from Brenneman to Brody on **18**, 8461,
  8533-35E
Radunz, Diane 20, 9583
Rafferty, James 1, 109, 187
Ragan, John 3, 1125E
activities in Chile **21**, 9699-9700
Caulfield obtains telephone company installer cre-
  dentials for **21**, 9692-93

business or financial dealings with Davis brothers
or Winn-Dixie or subsidiaries **22,** 10569-70
business or financial dealings with Edward Nixon
22, 10499
business or financial dealings with Wakefield **24,**
11281-84
Buzhardt denies discussion of Hughes contribution with **23,** 10877
Buzhardt denies knowledge of contributions received by other than Hughes contribution **23,**
10919
Buzhardt learns of Hughes contribution to **22,**
10540, 10544-45
Buzhardt on newspaper story about use of
Hughes contribution by **22,** 10544-60
and Buzhardt's preparation of Woods' letter to
IRS **23,** 10878-88
calls Griffin to discuss problem **22,** 10413-14
campaign contribution given to LaRue **23,** 11152-
71
and campaign funds used for payments to Ulasewicz and Caulfield **23,** 10861
cash funds on hand of **FR** 1050-51
Caulfield denies discussing Hughes contribution
with **22,** 10407
changes lock on safety deposit box **22,** 10528-29
FR 971-72
check from Precision Valve Corp. to **26,** 10538E
check to Wakefield **22,** 12471E
checks missing from personal account of **22,**
10506-10509
confidential memo prepared by Johnnie Walters
on Hughes investigation and **24,** 11648-50
conflicts in testimony with Danner **24,** 11445-46
connections with fundraising organizations or
committees **22,** 10605
contact with LaRue after campaign contribution
pickup **23,** 11169-71
contacts with Danner in 1968 **24,** 11401-32
contacts with Danner in 1973 **24,** 11432-38
contributions received for CRP **22,** 10518-19
and contributions through Danner from Hughes
in 1968 **20,** 9495-97, 9498-99, 9500-9501, 9503-
9505
conversations with Haig on Hughes contribution
23, 11023-24
conversations with Nixon **23,** 11072
correspondence files of **22,** 10487-88
correspondence with campaign contributors **22,**
12529-74E
correspondence with Danner **24,** 11392-93, 11455-
60, 11462, 11503-11E, 11519-24E
correspondence with Kalmbach on Trustee for
Clients Account **23,** 10872-74E
counsels consulted with on Hughes contribution
23, 11184-85
Cox investigation of **22,** 10462 **23,** 10888-89
and Crosby and Davis **20,** 9519-21
Danner delivers contribution to **3,** 955-56 **20,**
9531-39, 9563
Danner denies discussion on special fund with **24,**
11454
Danner informs of IRS deposition **20,** 9543-44

Danner introduces Nixon to **FR** 934
Danner on reasons for his belief that Hughes
should contribute to 1970 congressional campaigns **20,** 9528-30
and Danner's arrangements for, returning contribution to Hughes **20,** 9552-54, 9557-60
Danner's deliveries of Hughes contribution to **20,**
9538-40 **24,** 11539-40
and Davis brothers contribution **22,** 10562-63,
12429-30E **FR** 1000-1001
and Davis' decision to make campaign contribution **22,** 10568-69
Davis denies having business or financial transactions with **22,** 10584-87
Davis on meeting to make contribution with **22,**
10564-67
Davis on trust in **22,** 10572-73
delivery of Hughes contribution to **24,** 11464-68
denies contacts with Danner since last session of
Senate Committee **24,** 11551-52
designated as acting agent for Nixon in Key Biscayne **24,** 11302-11305 **FR** 943-44
discusses F. Donald Nixon's role in 1968 campaign with Danner **20,** 9509, 9510
discusses Hughes Tool Co. job offer with Danner
20, 9511-12
discusses *Newsday* investigation with Danner **24,**
11546-47
discussion with Haig **22,** 10212-13
discussion with Kalmbach on financial matters **21,**
10188-89
discussion with Smathers on Hughes contributions
20, 9545
discussion with Wearley **20,** 9453-54
discussion with Woods on Hughes contribution
22, 10271-73
discussions with Bartlett on cashier checks **23,**
11210
discussions with Danner on Hughes' contributions
in 1968 **20,** 9512-17
discussions with Danner on Hughes' retainer of
O'Brien and employment of Humphrey's son
FR 949
discussions with Danner on IRS investigation **24,**
11558-59
discussions with Danner on Meier-F. Donald Nixon problem **20,** 9598-9604
discussions with Danner on return of Hughes contribution **24,** 11475-76
discussions with Davis on Hughes contribution
24, 11587-88
discussions with Griffin on Hughes contribution
22, 10461-62, 10469-70
discussions with Griffin on need for loan **23,**
10755
discussions with Haig on IRS investigation **23,**
11003-11004
discussions with Woods **22,** 10212
discussions with Woods on problems in Hughes
organization **22,** 10221
documents of **22,** 10536
documents related to safety deposit boxes of **23,**
10955-59
and Dunes Hotel acquisition **20,** 9578-79, 9581

Rebozo, Charles Gregory "Bebe" *(Continued)*

Edward C. Nixon denies financial or business transactions with **22,** 10592, 10606-10608

efforts to return Hughes contribution **22,** 10446-48 **24,** 11585-86

Ehrlichman asked by Nixon to discuss proposed lawsuit against *Newsday* with **21,** 9677-78

Ehrlichman on IRS investigation of **21,** 9679-85

F. Donald Nixon and **22,** 10617

F. Donald Nixon denies having business or financial transactions with **22,** 10666-68

financial status of **FR** 1044-46

first meeting with Danner **FR** 934

first meeting with Gemmill **23,** 11186

first meeting with Griffin on Hughes contribution **22,** 10427-38

and Fishers Island transaction **22,** 10529

flight with Danner and Maheu **20,** 9458-60

flights on Hughes' plane **20,** 9474

flights with Wearley **20,** 9461

and fund for administration-connected costs in Florida **FR** 941-43

fundraising activities in 1969 **FR** 940-41

fundraising role in 1972 campaign **FR** 998-1001

funds provided to B & C Investment Co. by **23,** 10742-44

Garment on meeting between Kalmbach and **23,** 11068

Garment recommends lawyer for **23,** 10999-11000

Gemmill and **FR** 1014-16

Gemmill instructs him to copy serial numbers of Hughes money **23,** 11176, 11202-11203

Gemmill on contact re Hughes contribution with **23,** 11176-80, 11185-88

Gemmill on reasons for keeping Hughes contribution **23,** 11186-88, 11195-96

and Gemmill's efforts to ascertain if Hughes money had remained in place **23,** 11203-11204

goes to Europe **FR** 1071

and Golden **24,** 11460

and Greer **24,** 11287-88

Griffin denies discussing testimony with **22,** 10462-63

Griffin discusses interview with Select Committee staff with **23,** 10787-88, 10790-91

Griffin informs on IRS audit of B & C Co. **23,** 10755

Griffin on first meeting with **22,** 10411-12

Griffin on loan of $225,000 to **23,** 10760-65

Griffin on reasons for selling Abplanalp his share of San Clemente partnership **23,** 10747

Griffin's attorney-client relationship with **23,** 10756-60, 10765-68, 10774-79

Griffin's billings to **23,** 10765

Griffin's interoffice memo on loan for **23,** 10847E

and Griffin's loan from Precision Valve Corp. **23,** 10773-74

Griffin's trips to Florida and **22,** 10417-24, 10425

Haig denies discussion of meeting with Kalmbach **23,** 11031

Haig discusses IRS investigation with Gemmill **23,** 11190, 11191-93, 11195

Haig on discussions with Richardson on Cox investigations of **23,** 11013-15, 11020

Haig on return of Hughes contribution by **23,** 11006-11009

Haig recommends Gemmill to **23,** 11023, 11065-68

and Haldeman's and Ehrlichman's legal expenses **22,** 12428E, 12439E

in Haldeman's memo to Dean on Hughes-O'Brien connection **23,** 11080

Haldeman's memo to Ehrlichman on contact of Getty planned by **22,** 12469E

and Hallamore's loan to F. Donald Nixon **22,** 10689-90

Higby denies knowledge of funds to Haldeman and Ehrlichman from **23,** 11108-11109

Higby denies knowledge of payment of Nixon's expenses by **23,** 11100

Hughes contribution to Garment on **23,** 11059-71, *see also* Hughes contribution

Hughes' decision to contribute to Nixon campaign through **FR** 935

informed of forthcoming IRS interview **24,** 11651-52

informs Griffin of agreement with Gemmill **22,** 10449

informs Kalmbach of disbursal of Hughes contribution **22,** 12439-40E

informs Woods that he spoke with Griffin **22,** 10213-14, 10216

instructions to Wakefield on safety deposit box **22,** 10522 **24,** 11296

interest payments on loans **FR** 1044

and investigation of O'Brien-Hughes relationship **21,** 9718

and IRS audit of Greene **22,** 10368-70

IRS investigation of **21,** 9684-85 **22,** 10519-21, 12441-42E **23,** 10891-92, 10938, 11107 **FR,** 135, 1016-30

and IRS investigation of Hughes Tool Co. and Meier **24,** 11633-34

in IRS sensitive case report on Hughes Tool Co. **23,** 10928, 11221, 11222, 11225-26, 11228, 11230-32, 11235-37, 11277-78E

Kalmbach and attorney-client privileges for **21,** 10185-86

Kalmbach informs of resignation from law firm and Richard Nixon Foundation **23,** 10857

Kalmbach memo on discussions on Hughes contribution with **21,** 10187-91

Kalmbach on checks sent by **21,** 10183-85

Kalmbach on knowledge of disbursal to Caulfield **21,** 10185

Kalmbach on questions on contributions from foreign nationals to Gleason from **23,** 10855-56

Kalmbach reports on interviews with Select Committee staff to **23,** 10856-57

and Kalmbach's testimony **22,** 10560

Kalmbach's testimony on disbursal of Hughes contribution by **FR** 1006

and Kovens **FR** 278E

letter from Danner on atomic testing **20,** 9587-88, 9591-98, 9674E

letter from Danner on news releases about Meier **20,** 9588, 9675E

letter from McGrath to **24,** 11461

letter from Select Committee to St. Clair requesting information and documents from Nixon on use of campaign funds by **22,** 12527-42E letter from Stearns to Schulte of First National Bank of Miami with payment of note of **26,** 12773E

letter from Tuccillo to Muse on money returned by **22,** 12515-17

letter from Woods to Bartlett re campaign contribution delivered by Danner to **26,** 10283E

letter to Kalmbach on retention of contributions for administration-connected costs **22,** 12444E

letter to Stans with campaign contributions **22,** 12530E

letter to Stans with check from Gerity **22,** 12429E

and loan for Nixon's purchase of Key Biscayne properties **22,** 12436-38E

loan from Hudson Valley National Bank to **22,** 10470-71, 10497-98, 10504 **23,** 10756-57, 10801E

loan from Palmetto Bank & Trust Co. to **22,** 10498, 10503-10505

loan from Precision Valve Corp. to **23,** 10802-10803E

maintains fund for "administration-connected costs" **22,** 12428E

McKiernan and **22,** 10653, 10655

McKiernan on **22,** 10634

McKiernan on first knowledge of Hughes contribution through **22,** 10651-52

McKiernan's efforts to contact **22,** 10728-29

meeting with Abplanalp and Danner **20,** 9563-64

meeting with Danner and Garcia **24,** 11445

meeting with Danner and Morgan **20,** 9498-99, 9505-9506 **FR** 936-37

meeting with Danner in 1969 on campaign contributions from Hughes for 1970 congressional elections **20,** 9515-17

meeting with Danner on nerve gas dumping issue **20,** 9596

meeting with Danner on TWA litigation **20,** 9566-68

meeting with Gemmill in Philadelphia **22,** 10452

meeting with Nixon and Danner at Camp David **22,** 10218-19 **23,** 10894-95, 11005-11006, 11019-20 **24,** 11472-76 **FR** 1011-12, 1066-67

meeting with Nixon and Danner in 1968 **20,** 9503-9505 **24,** 11439-42

meeting with Woods and Nixon **22,** 10273-74

meetings with Danner and Mitchell **20,** 9506-10 **24,** 11444-45 **FR** 937-38

meetings with Danner on 1969 contributions **20,** 9526-27

and Meier-F. Donald Nixon relationship **21,** 9705

memo from Danner on ABM **20,** 9597-98

memos from Caulfield to Dean on *Newsday* and **23,** 11101, 11143-44E

Moncourt denies contact between Colson, Haldeman, or Ehrlichman and **22,** 10521

Moncourt denies knowledge of existence of will for **22,** 10522

Moncourt on content of safe-deposit box of **22,** 10523

Moncourt on duties as bookkeeper for **22,** 10486

Moncourt on files kept by **22,** 10486-87

Moncourt on finances of **22,** 10409-10, 10515-18, 10526-27

Moncourt on safety deposit boxes maintained by **22,** 10501-10503

and Moncourt's legal fees **22,** 10531-32

money to Kalmbach for Caulfield and Ulasewicz payments **21,** 9681 **23,** 10860-61 **FR** 942-43

New York Times article on return of Hughes contribution **23,** 10800E

Newsday article on **3,** 1072 **23,** 10924, 11101-11102 **FR** 9, 135-36, 144

Nixon and Gemmill discuss IRS investigation of **23,** 11193-94

Nixon asks Haig to find lawyer for **23,** 10999, 11000

Nixon denies payment of expenses by **22,** 12449-50E **FR** 1051, 1069-70

Nixon tells Haldeman funds for legal defense are available from **23,** 11074-75, 11082-84

and Nixon's purchase and resale of Key Biscayne property **23,** 10769-75

and Nixon's purchase of Smathers' house **24,** 11425-26

and Nixon's request to contact Getty for contribution **22,** 12443E

and Nixon's sale of San Clemente property **23,** 10739-41

notification of IRS interview
conflicts in testimony on **FR** 1067

partial waiver of attorney-client privilege for Gemmill testimony **23,** 11173, 11174, 11182, 11184, 11186, 11194-95, 11206-11207, 11210, 11211, 11218

partnership agreement with Abplanalp in B & C Investment Co. **23,** 10823-44E

partnership document for San Clemente property **23,** 10804-18E

payment from Florida Nixon for President committee **21,** 9681

payment of Nixon's expenses by **22,** 12438E **23,** 10781-83, 10784-85 **24,** 11311-29 **FR** 1031-32

payment of Nixon's fees to Wakefield by **24,** 11343

and payments for alterations and furnishings for Nixon's Key Biscayne properties **22,** 12430-36E, 12445-47E, 12641-12726E, 12739-45E

personal financial statements **22,** 12729-38E

purchase of Key Biscayne property **24,** 11332

and real estate in Florida **24,** 11428-29

reasons for returning Hughes contribution **20,** 9569

records kept on loans by **22,** 10512-14

refusal of bank records to Select Committee **FR** 1071

relationship with Abplanalp **22,** 10452

relationship with Davis **22,** 10569

relationship with F. Donald Nixon **22,** 10705-10707, 10709

relationship with Griffin **23,** 11204-11205

relationship with Haig **23,** 11016-17

relationship with LaRue **23,** 11171

relationship with Nixon **20,** 9499

relationship with Wakefield **24,** 11281

remodeling of home in Key Biscayne **24,** 11545

removal of Hughes contribution from safety deposit box by **FR** 1015

retention and destruction of financial records of **22,** 10527-28

on campaign funds left over after 1968 election **21,** 9945-52

on certificate of deposit issued to Nixons **3,** 1078-79

on committee investigators **21,** 10086

on concern about O'Brien's involvement in Hughes operation **21,** 10056-58

on conflict on dates of delivery of money from Danner **21,** 9963-64

on consulting with Griffin and Gemmill on return of Hughes contribution **21,** 9994, 9995

on consulting with Nixon on return of Hughes contribution **21,** 9994, 9995

on contacts with Danner on return of Hughes contribution **FR** 1010-11

on contacts with Dean **21,** 10065-66

on contribution from A. D. Davis **21,** 10116-18

on Danner's delivery of contribution **21,** 9962-66, 9977, 9983-85

on Danner's efforts to give him contribution from Hughes in 1968 **21,** 9939-44

on Danner's relationship with Mitchell **21,** 10044-45

on Danner's telephone records **21,** 9976

on decision to hold on to Hughes contribution **21,** 9986-89

on decision to return money to Hughes **21,** 10089-10100

on decision to take Hughes contribution in 1970 **21,** 9961-62

denies anyone else had access to Hughes money **21,** 10143

denies connection between Hughes contribution and Dunes Hotel acquisition **FR** 984-85

denies consulting with Danner on whether to keep Hughes contribution **21,** 9992

denies counting Hughes contribution money **21,** 9989

denies CRP paid his legal expenses **21,** 10140

denies discussing Hughes contribution with Danner, Maheu, and Davis **21,** 10055-56

denies discussing Hughes contribution with Nixon **21,** 9940-41, 9977, 10104

denies discussing Hughes money with Mitchell **21,** 10045, 10110

denies discussing libel suit against *Newsday* with Fielding **21,** 10128-29

denies discussing TWA lawsuit with Danner **21,** 10054

denies discussion with Dean or Ehrlichman on O'Brien-Hughes-Maheu relationships **21,** 10129

denies discussions with Nixon on contributions **21,** 9975

denies ever making statement that Hughes money had been used **21,** 9999

denies fundraising role **FR** 998-99

denies knowing that Cox's office had disclosure agreement with IRS **21,** 10103-10104

denies knowledge of Greenspun memos in Hughes' handwriting **21,** 10130

denies knowledge of Morgan inquiring about Hughes contribution **21,** 10059

denies knowledge that Ehrlichman received IRS sensitive case reports **21,** 10105

denies obtaining IRS audit of *Newsday* reporter **21,** 10122

denies official fundraising responsibilities in 1969 **21,** 9974-75

denies press reports on his connection with Cuban Watergate burglars **21,** 10105-10106

denies use of Hughes contribution **21,** 10116 **FR** 1066

on deposit of cashier's check for $50,000 **21,** 10079-80

on discussing Hughes contribution with Danner **21,** 9952-73, 10041-44

on discussing Hughes contribution with Danner and Morgan **21,** 9939-40

on discussing Hughes contribution with Haig **21,** 10108-10109

on discussing Hughes contribution with Kalmbach **21,** 1011-13 **FR** 1004-1005, 1009

on discussing Hughes contribution with Nixon **21,** 10101-10103

on discussing Hughes money with Smathers **21,** 10106-10107

on discussing IRS investigation with Ehrlichman **21,** 10068-69

on discussing missing portions of Nixon tapes with Woods **21,** 10139

on discussing money for Watergate defendants with Nixon **21,** 10140

on discussing TWA lawsuit with Danner and Maheu **21,** 10048-50

on discussion of *Newsday* article with Lewis **21,** 10128-29

on disposition of money from Danner **21,** 9966-72, 9978-83, 9985-86

on Dunes Hotel acquisition efforts **21,** 10044-45

on entries into safety deposit boxes **21,** 10014-16

on finances **21,** 10070-89

on financial dealings with Nixon **21,** 10130-33

on financial dealings with Smathers **21,** 10083-84

on Fishers Island negotiations **21,** 10082

on flights on Hughes plane **21,** 10050-51, 10053

on Gemmill obtaining Woods' letter to IRS **21,** 10107-10108

on handling of Hughes contribution before returning it **21,** 9990-92

on Hughes contribution **FR** 935-36

    conflicts with other testimony **FR** 1053-67

    summary of **FR** 1068-69

on impact of investigation on his business **21,** 10085

on information given to Woods **21,** 10006-10007

on informing Nixon about Hughes contribution **21,** 10007-10008

on informing Nixon about retaining Gemmill **21,** 10102

on informing Nixon of return of Hughes contribution **21,** 10062, 10063-64

on informing Woods of Hughes contribution **21,** 10000, 10001-10003

on initiator of Hughes contribution **FR** 1053

on intensity of IRS investigation of his finances **21,** 10122-23

on intentions of informing Nixon of Hughes contribution after elections **21,** 9978

on intentions of turning Hughes contribution over to appropriate finance committee **21,** 9982

on IRS audit of *Newsday* reporter **21,** 10126

Rebozo, Charles Gregory "Bebe", testimony of
(Continued)
on IRS audit of O'Brien **21,** 10058-59
on IRS investigation of Hughes contribution **21,** 10067-68
on Kalmbach's requests for solicitation of contributions **21,** 9974-75
on keys to safety deposit boxes **FR** 971
on leaks **21,** 10089
on letter from Danner **21,** 10059
on loan from Hughes to F. Donald Nixon **21,** 9969-70
on loans from Nixon **21,** 10131-32
on locations of discussions with Nixon **21,** 10139
on meeting with Danner at San Clemente **21,** 9975-76
on meeting with Danner in Washington **21,** 10094
on meeting with Kalmbach on Hughes contribution **FR** 1061-62, 1065-66
on meeting with Morgan, Danner, and Mitchell **21,** 9976-77
on meeting with Nixon and Danner at Camp David **21,** 10094-96, 10097-99
on meeting with Whitaker in 1973 **21,** 9961
on meetings with Gemmill and Rose **21,** 10073-74
on Meier and F. Donald Nixon **21,** 10118-21
on *Newsday* investigation **21,** 10122
on Nixon tapes **21,** 10137-39
on notifying Wakefield of disposition of Hughes contribution in event of his death **21,** 10008-10009
on O'Brien's income from Hughes Tool Co. **21,** 9956
on payment of Nixon's expenses **FR** 1051-52
on persons informed about Hughes contribution **21,** 9988-89, 10006-10009, 10109-13
on purchase of house for David and Julie Eisenhower **21,** 10132-33
on purpose of Hughes contribution **21,** 9960
on reasons for calling Whitaker to be present at counting of Hughes contribution **21,** 9995-98
on reasons for cash contributions **21,** 10117-18
on reasons for not discussing Hughes contribution with Abplanalp **21,** 10101
on reasons for precautions taken with Hughes contribution **21,** 9969-70
on reasons for refusing Hughes contribution **21,** 9955-56, 10120
on reasons for removing wrappers from Hughes contribution **21,** 9983
on reasons for return of Hughes contribution **FR** 1003-1005
reasons for uneasiness over Hughes contribution **FR** 936
on referral to Gemmill **21,** 10061-62
on refusal of money from Danner **21,** 9957-58
on return of Hughes contribution **21,** 9970, 9993-98, 10060-65, 10113-16
on rumor of Kennedy Foundation financing *Newsday* articles **21,** 10126, 10127
on safety deposit boxes held by, in Key Biscayne Bank and Trust Co. **21,** 10009-15
scheduling of **21,** 10018-19, 10037-38
on secrecy of Hughes contribution **21,** 10003-10006

states Woods did not discuss Hughes contribution with Nixon **21,** 10105
on stock purchases **21,** 10081-82
on storage of Hughes contributions **FR** 968-72
on subpoenaed records **21,** 10029-30
summary of **FR** 954-56
on taking Hughes contribution out of bank for return **21,** 9995-98
on transaction with Danner for $1,000 **21,** 10087-88
on trip to Abplanalp's place with Danner **21,** 10100-10101
on trip with Maheu and Danner **21,** 10053-56
on trips to Las Vegas **21,** 10051, 10053, 10056
on use of Hughes contribution in 1969 **21,** 9960-61
on use of name "Charles Gregory" **21,** 10051-52, 10065, 10079
on use of Nixon's telephone in Executive office **21,** 10066-68
on wrappers on Hughes money **FR** 970
Rebozo, Donald 22, 10486, 10487
Rebozo, William 24, 11305
"Recommendations, Top Secret, Handle VIA COMINT Channels Only Operational Restraints on Intelligence Collection" document 4, 1452-59
"Recommended Action Plan for Career Military Voter Group" 19, 9335-37E
Reed, Dan 22, 10604
Reed, Tom 1, 34
Reese, Al FR 174
Reese, Mary Virginia 10, 4280E
Reeves, Jim 16, 7102
Reeves, Richard 25, 12102, 12111-12
Reeves and Harrison 15, 6542 **16,** 7168
and Chotiner **FR** 633
Chotiner joins firm **15,** 6806
Regency Hotel, New York 5, 2105
Regina v. *O'Connell* **4,** 1785E
Regional Electric Cooperatives
letter from Pepper on "Cooperative Month" to managers of **17,** 7720, 7729E
Register (IRS) **23,** 11181, 11182, 11219
Regulatory agencies
government interference with **FR** 410-12
impact of Watergate on **FR** 1207-1208
Rehnquist, William 2, 670 **11,** 4447, 4452
Reichardt, Field 3, 1134E
Reid, Fergus, III FR 560-61
Reimbursement schemes
for campaign contributions
and Carnation Co. **FR** 464
See also Attorneys' fees scheme
Reisner, Robert A. 1, 12, 32, 34
call from Magruder on Liddy plan **5,** 1846
and clearance for CRP personnel **1,** 71-72
excerpts from log kept by **2,** 490, 878E-888E
failure to interview **FR** 47
and "Gemstone" file **1,** 50
informed by Magruder of approval of Liddy plan **FR** 25
instructed by Magruder to remove Gemstone files **FR** 32-33

MacGregor denies learning about Gemstone project from **12**, 4907
and Magruder's worries over Watergate coverup **2**, 805-806
Porter and **2**, 674
Porter asked by Magruder not to mention **2**, 672
removal of Magruder's files by **1**, 28, 29, 30, 45-47, 52-53, 62-67, 72-74 **2**, 798, 800-801
reviews Porter's financial records **2**, 652, 653
Strachan and **6**, 2440
telephone call from Magruder to **4**, 1615
and Watergate coverup **2**, 822
Reisner, Robert A., testimony of 2, 489-530, 794
asks Magruder about Gemstone file **2**, 504-505
on attack file **2**, 530
career background **2**, 518, 527-28
on cash paid to "Sedan Chair 2" **2**, 499-500
on comparison of Odle's testimony with his **2**, 516
on contacts prior to testimony **2**, 521
on conversation between Magruder and Porter **2**, 501
on demonstration at Hoover's funeral **2**, 500, 515
on destruction of documents after Watergate arrests **2**, 506-508, 526-27
on diaries of meetings **2**, 490-91, 502-503
on duties as Magruder's executive assistant **2**, 489
on easel **2**, 527
on FBI interviews at CRP after Watergate arrests **2**, 521-22
on Gemstone files **2**, 513-15
on Gemstone stationery **2**, 493-94
on giving Mitchell Gemstone material **FR** 30
on Liddy and Magruder **2**, 492-93
on Liddy's role **2**, 497
on MacGregor's role as head of CRP **2**, 513
on Magruder and Colson **2**, 512
on Magruder memos to Mitchell **2**, 503
on Magruder-Mitchell relationship **2**, 522-23
on Magruder's attempts to meet with him before his testimony **2**, 508-10
on Magruder's meetings with White House staff members **2**, 505-506, 519
on Magruder's references to Liddy's activities **2**, 490
on Magruder's role in disruption of Democratic party campaign **2**, 523-25
on Magruder's trip to Florida to meet with Mitchell **2**, 492, 503
on meeting between Magruder, Liddy, Dean, Shumway, and Strachan on June 19 **2**, 520
on meetings between Magruder and Mitchell **2**, 522-23
on personal opinion of Liddy **2**, 497-98
on photographs in Mitchell's files **2**, 494-95
on possible plants in CRP **2**, 502
on reasons for not informing MacGregor about Magruder's involvement **2**, 528-30
on refusal of meeting with Magruder and O'Brien **2**, 517
on removal of material from Magruder's desk **2**, 495-97, 511-12
on shredding files after Watergate break-in **2**, 501-502
on telephone call from Magruder after Watergate arrests **2**, 522, 528

on telephone calls from other witnesses **2**, 515
on telephone conversation between Magruder and Colson **2**, 517-18
transmits message from Magruder to Liddy **2**, 493
Reliable Source, The **25**, 12112, 12113-15
Reno, Robert H. 3, 1137E
Rensselaer, Bernard van
memo from Todd on second Older Americans brochure **18**, 8485, 8593E
"Report to Older Americans, A" 19, 9165-74E
Republic of New Africa 3, 1341E
Republican Campaign Committee
check to Republican Congressional Campaign Committee **17**, 8170E
checks to Republican Senatorial Campaign Committee **17**, 8170E, 8171E, 8173E
Clancy testimony on financial dealings of **16**, 7403-13
Republican Congressional Campaign Committee
check from Republican Campaign Committee **17**, 8170E
check from Republican National Finance Committee **17**, 8169E
letter from Harrison to Hanman on names and addresses of **14**, 5883, 5901-02E
Republican fundraising dinners
for Black supporters **18**, 8259-60
dairy industry contributions to **FR** 641-42
and meeting at Louisville airport **17**, 7732-40
in telephone call between Campbell and Nelson **17**, 7775-76
Republican National Associates Committee
check to National Republican Congressional Committee **17**, 8172E
check to National Republican Senatorial Committee **17**, 8172E
Republican National Committee
and attempts to infiltrate Muskie campaign **11**, 4658
distinguished from CRP **12**, 4951-52
and hush money **6**, 2335
letter-writing campaign of **FR** 151
McCord employed by **1**, 205-206, 230-31, 271
memo from Mehren to Lilly on proposal by CTAPE for **14**, 6119, 6189E
payments to McCord **1**, 216
and proposal by CTAPE **14**, 6119, 6190E
relationship with CRP **1**, 20, 22-23, 24-25, 39-40
role in election campaign **9**, 3922
security measures at **3**, 1124E, 1125-27E, 1130-32E
Strachan and **1**, 79
thank-you letter to Davis **22**, 10572, 10576
Republican National Convention of 1972
article about demonstrations at **10**, 3956, 4107-08E
attack strategy for **10**, 4218E
"Chronological Log of Events" of week of **12**, 5015, 5219-57E
demonstration of pregnant Black woman at **10**, 3923
experiences of Graser during week of **12**, 5016, 5258-60E

Malek on **FR** 393-94

and Marumoto's request to Villalobos for demonstrators in front of *Los Angeles Times* office **FR** 403-404

and neutralization of potential opponents **FR** 391-93

organization of **FR** 381-82

and Pena matter **FR** 402-403

and Raza Unida matter **FR** 397-400

and Tijerina matter **FR** 400-401

and staffing of Federal positions **FR** 414-19

telephone report from Davison to Hamilton on **19**, 8752E

U.S. Department of Labor memos on **19**, 8797-8812E

and Veterans' Administration **FR** 429-30

See also Black voters; Federal resources; Malek, Frederick V., testimony of; Older Americans; Spanish-speaking voters

Reston, James 10, 4113E

Retail Clerks' Union

loan to McGovern campaign **25**, 12145

Retired Armed Services Men for Nixon 9, 3474

Revenue sharing

Muskie on **10**, 4149E

Reyes, Joseph A. 13, 5287, 5373, 5400 **18**, 8275

Reynaldo, Ectore

subpoenaed by Patman Committee **3**, 1193E

Reynolds, Anita 21, 10081-82 **22**, 10503

Rhatican, Bill FR 356E

Rhodesian Chrome Bill

Byrd amendment to **20**, 9514

Rhylick, Lawrence T. 24, 11611-12 **FR** 956-57, 962

Rhyne, Charles 20, 9502

identifies Paul Rhyne **22**, 10234

on leaks from Senate Watergate Committee **22**, 10263

on length of time for Woods' interview **22**, 10276-77, 10280

objections to line of questioning of Woods **22**, 10254-56

on procedures for interview of Woods **22**, 10193-94, 10195

on relevancy of questioning of Woods **22**, 10224-25, 10227

on Sirica's Court Silence Order **22**, 10263

See also Woods, Rose Mary, testimony of

Rhyne, Paul 22, 10234

Ribicoff, Abraham 10, 4162E

Rice, Dr. Donald B. 16, 7132, 7133, 7385, 7388 **17**, 7756, 7763, 7789 **FR** 678

Campbell on **17**, 7751

on meeting with Nixon on March 23 **FR** 647-48

memo for Shultz on dairy problems **FR** 806-807E

memo from Campbell with proposed press release on reversal of milk price-supports decision **FR** 855-56E

memo on March 12 milk price-supports decision **FR** 632

memo to Shultz and Ehrlichman on price supports, school lunch program, and dairy import quotas **FR** 800-803E, 804E

and milk price supports **17**, 7753

Rice University 9, 3473-74

Richard Danner, et al. v. *Senate Select Committee, et al.*. **FR** 1080, 1083-84

Richard Green Building Corp. 13, 5344

Richard Nixon Foundation

employment of Edward C. Nixon at **22**, 10601-10602, 10603-10605 **23**, 11103-11104

Kalmbach resigns from **23**, 10857

Richards, Dick 1, 34

Richards, Mary Jane 23, 10967

Richardson, Elliot L. 9, 3646 **12**, 5115E **18**, 8461, 8478 **19**, 9053E

Buzhardt denies discussing investigation of electronic surveillance with **23**, 10915

cablegrams to McCone **9**, 3808

conversations with Haig **23**, 11032-33

discussions with Buzhardt on investigations by Cox **23**, 10915-17

Haig on discussions of Cox investigation with **23**, 11013-15, 11020

Haig's discussions with and Executive privilege **23**, 11031-32

Haig's telephone call on Cox investigation of Rebozo **23**, 10888-89, 10891, 11214-15, 11216-17 **FR** 1022-23

memo for Domestic Council Committee on Aging **19**, 9102-9103E

on Nixon's knowledge of Fielding break-in **5**, 1962

nomination as attorney general **1**, 293, 310

resignation of **FR** 1081

role on White House staff **1**, 82

Richey, Charles R. 3, 1176E **4**, 1472 **7**, 2889

Dean discussion with Nixon on **8**, 3210

and Democratic party civil suit **3**, 957 **4**, 1575, 1576

McPhee and **5**, 1953

Mitchell on McPhee's discussions with **5**, 1908-1910

order prohibiting public statements on Watergate **12**, 4909

and Stans' libel action against O'Brien **FR** 75

Richman, David 12, 5151E

Richman, Jerome S.

See Priestes, John J., testimony of

Rickless contribution to Humphrey campaign 25, 11810, 11811-12

Rietz, Kenneth 1, 32, 35 **2**, 627, 658, 668, 671 **7**, 2732, 2733 **12**, 5017, 5265E **FR** 302E

and Brill's infiltration of peace vigil **FR** 198

Buckley discusses Hunt with **11**, 4453

and Buckley's political espionage **11**, 4458

complaints about Segretti to **FR** 165

ends contacts with Buckley **11**, 4443

and infiltration of Quaker group **11**, 4641

memo to Magruder on ACTION **FR** 285E

memo to Magruder on disruptions of McGovern campaign **FR** 356-57E

and political spying in Muskie campaign **11**, 4438-43

relationship with Buckley **11**, 4437-40, 4451-52

and Ruby I **FR** 187-90

Rietz, Kenneth *(Continued)*
and Young Voters for the President **FR** 200-201
Riggs, Ronald
letter from Stock to **12,** 5009, 5120-24E
Rise and Fall of the Third Reich, The **11,** 4426
Rivers
See Ulasewicz, Anthony T.
Rizzo, Frank 10, 4057E, 4171E **11,** 4709E
Robert R. Mullen & Co. 9, 3726
Roberts, Charles 12, 5046E
Roberts, Gene 1, 32, 34, 454E
Roberts, Walter Donald 15, 6392
Robertson, B. M. 13, 5522
Robeson, Brenda
memo to Sanders on Hart and Stauffer contributions to Mills Presidential campaign committees **25,** 12068-69E
memo to Sanders re AMPI flights into Minneapolis **25,** 11847-51E
memo to Sanders re campaign committees for Mills contributions **25,** 12033-67E
Robinson, Bill 11, 4642 **12,** 5133E
Robinson, Eliot
letter from Barry on campaign contributions and taxes **11,** 4806-4808E
Robinson, Neal, testimony of 13, 5489-93
denies knowledge of CRP connection to Braniff-CAMFAB transaction **13,** 5490
on reimbursement of Braniff by executive officers **13,** 5493
on transactions between CAMFAB and Braniff-Airways **13,** 5489-93
Rocha, Father 18, 8482
Roche, Delia 23, 10966
Roche, John P. 11, 4586
Rockefeller, Nelson 3, 992 **4,** 1675 **5,** 1929, 1931 **10,** 4213E **12,** 4926-27, 5061E, 5063E, 5064E
Rockefeller, Winthrop 16, 7450
Rockefeller Foundation
Buchanan on **10,** 3951-52
Rodrigues, Enrique 23, 10967
Rodrigues, Maria 23, 10966
Rodriguez, Antonio F. 13, 5281, 5283, 5284, 5286-87, 5289, 5293, 5294, 5322, 5536E, 5537E **19,** 8675E **FR** 381, 383
campaign contribution from Arenas and **13,** 5299-5300
Fernandez denies discussion on grants with **13,** 5399-5401
and grants to persons opposing administration **FR** 387
and Hatch Act **13,** 5313
letter to Trevino on SBA meeting **13,** 5323, 5699E
memo from Bayer on status of OMBE proposals **13,** 5323, 5652-57E
memo from Herringer on Surrogate Plan **13,** 5651E
memo from Marumoto on Romero to **13,** 5323, 5611-12E
memo to Herringer on surrogate plan **13,** 5323, 5650-51E

and OMBE grant to Ultra-Systems, Inc. **FR** 385-386
Rodriguez, Jim 12, 5010
affidavit of **12,** 5009, 5170-72E
Rogers, James 6, 2518 **FR** 958
and immunity for Dean **FR** 95
Rogovin, Mitchell 7, 2979E **10,** 3955
affidavit of **10,** 3977, 4360-74E **11,** 4433-35
Rohatyn, Felix 5, 1949, 2058
Rolbin, Herbert 3, 1152E
Rollins, John 23, 11268 **FR** 506, 507
Romero, Ed 13, 5325-26
Romero, Fred E.
memo from Marumoto to Rodriguez and Armendariz on **13,** 5323, 5611-12E
memo to Hans on Older Worker Project **19,** 9232-33E
Romney, George 12, 5134E **22,** 10687
Priestes says Fernandez promised Stans would contact **13,** 5330, 5333, 5335-36, 5341, 5344, 5349
Roosevelt, James 11, 4585 **12,** 5059E
Root, Elihu 5, 1939
Rose, H. Chapman 21, 10073-74, 10110 **22,** 10451 **23,** 10999, 11000-11001, 11022-23, 11060-61, 11064-65, 11183, 11193, 11220, 11269
Barth and **23,** 11208
recommends Gemmill to Garment **23,** 11066-67
telephone call to Gemmill on Haig's testimony **23,** 11215-16
"Rosemary Woods' list" 17, 8168E
Rosenzweig, Harry 12, 5046E
Rosselli, John 21, 9719
Rossides, Gene 3, 923, 1086 **6,** 2389 **9,** 3561
Rossiter, Clinton 10, 3939
Roth, Clifford 13, 5414
Rothblatt, Henry 1, 169, 324, 326, 329, 363
and Barker's guilty plea **1,** 373
source of fees for **1,** 359
Rotunda, Ron 1, 1
Roulet, Vincent de FR 493, 494, 496, 499, 500
campaign contributions and ambassadorships and **FR** 501-503
Rouse, Charles 20, 9428
Rouse, Frank 4, 1533 **8,** 3202
Roush, Larry F. 18, 8244 **FR** 412
affidavit of **18,** 8244, 8397-98E
Rove, Carl 11, 4641 **FR** 165
Roycroft, Howard F.
affidavit of **12,** 5009, 5181E
Rubin, Jerry 11, 4715E
See also Jerry Rubin Fund
Rubin, Miles L. 11, 4630 **25,** 12182
cash expenditures for McGovern campaign **25,** 12181
and literature against McCloskey **25,** 12194
Rubin, Miles L., statement of 25, 12137-71
on activity in McGovern's Presidential campaign **25,** 12137-38
on banking practices of McGovern campaign **25,** 12153-54

on contributions and loans from unions **25,**
12144-46
on contributions to McGovern **25,** 12139-43,
12146-50
on contributors desiring anonymity **25,** 12154-55
denies he alleged Republican campaign sabotaged
McGovern campaign through Computer Ideas
25, 12165
denies knowledge of transfers of funds from
McGovern campaign to senate campaign committee **25,** 12159
denies reimbursement of donors to McGovern
campaign by corporations **25,** 12148
on files from McGovern campaign **25,** 12150-51
on first meeting with McGovern **25,** 12138
on forgiveness of loans to McGovern campaign
25, 12151-53
on Hefner contribution **25,** 12170
on ILGWU contribution **25,** 12171
on loans to McGovern campaign **25,** 12141-42,
12167-68
on McGovern campaign use of Computer Ideas
25, 12163-66
on New Hampshire primary and McGovern staff
25, 12138-41
on personal contributions to McGovern campaign
25, 12155-56
on pre-April 7 contributions to McGovern campaign **25,** 12154-55
on principal business connections **25,** 12137
on recommendations for financing of election
campaigns **25,** 12169-70
on record-keeping for contributions to McGovern
campaign **25,** 12149-51
on reference in Hunter book to U-13 incident on
Humphrey trip to Las Vegas **25,** 12160-63
on results of fundraising efforts for McGovern **25,**
12168-69
on role as fundraiser in McGovern campaign **25,**
12143-51
on role of Samuels in McGovern campaign **25,**
12170-71
on Sheridan's role in McGovern campaign **25,**
12159-60
on statement sent to contributors to McGovern
campaign on gift tax laws **25,** 12153
on structure of McGovern campaign **25,** 12144
on taxes paid for personal contributions **25,** 12169
on third-party contributions to McGovern campaign **25,** 12156
on United Farm Workers and McGovern campaign **25,** 12166-67
on Zafferoni contribution **25,** 12156-58
Rubin, Nancy 25, 12155, 12156, 12166, 12169
Rubin, Sam 3, 1138E
Ruby I FR 187-90
Magruder on **2,** 848
See also Buckley, John
Ruby II
See Gregory, Thomas
Ruckelshaus, William 4, 1627
and Caulfield **22,** 10395
resignation of **FR** 1081

Rueff, Bill 12, 4987
Rumsfeld, Donald 1, 81 **10,** 4212E
role at White House **1,** 91, 92
Runyon, Harley 12, 5117E
Runyon, Mrs. Harley 12, 5117E
**Rural & Urban Community Development Services,
Inc. 19,** 9229E
**Rural Pennsylvania Committee for McGovern-Shriv-
er 12,** 5174E
Russell, Dick 21, 10127
Russell, Louis
cleared by McCord **1,** 218
Woods on **22,** 10250-52
Russell, Steve 25, 12280
Russell, Stuart H. 14, 5923, 5925, 5953, 5958, 5966,
5974, 6175, 6251 **15,** 6465, 6466 **16,** 6939, 6963,
7011-12, 7013, 7055-56E, 7282 **17,** 7667
and AMPI contributions **14,** 6172-73, 6176 **15,**
6773-74
and AMPI contributions to Muskie campaign **15,**
6616 **16,** 7015, 7016, 7019
and AMPI loan repayment scheme **15,** 6528-30
FR 599-602, 910, 921-22
AMPI payments to **16,** 7306-12, 7348
and AMPI relationship with Valentine, Sherman
15, 6853
and antitrust suit against AMPI **15,** 6674 **16,**
6958, 7444 **17,** 7685-86 **FR** 703-705
Butterbrodt on billings to AMPI as conduit for
campaign contributions **17,** 7628-33
check and check authorization from AMPI for legal fees and expenses **16,** 7307, 7368-71E
check made out to cash by **14,** 5964, 6042E
check to Lilly from **14,** 5966, 6044E
checks to Van Dyk from **16,** 7012-13
as conduit for AMPI funds for Muskie **15,** 6831
contribution to Muskie campaign **16,** 7213-14,
7216-17
delivery of AMPI cash by **15,** 6779-80
and destruction of AMPI files in Little Rock **15,**
6895-96
letter from Harrison on antitrust suit against
AMPI **16,** 7262, 7351E **17,** 7687-88 **FR** 771
letter from Muskie expressing appreciation for
help **16,** 7217, 7227E
letter to Heininger on Department of Justice complaint **16,** 7262, 7349-50E
letter to Lilly with Muskie's thank-you letter **14,**
6039-40E
letter to Muskie Election Committee on campaign
contribution to **14,** 6034E **16,** 7015, 7057E
letter to Weitz on delivery of cash to Townsend
15, 6779-80
letter to Weitz on money delivered to employees
of AMPI **15,** 6779, 6910E
Lilly attempt to obtain money for Connally from
FR 683-84
and Lilly payments to Kalmbach **15,** 6853
and loan from AMPI **17,** 7631-32
and money for Connally **14,** 5961-65
and money to Lilly **FR** 686-87
note on Belcher campaign funds **14,** 5958, 6041E
reimbursement for political contributions **14,**
5960-61

Russell, Stuart H. *(Continued)*
and repayment of Lilly's bank loans **14**, 5956-57, 6166-67
as source of contribution for Belcher **15**, 6878-79
and TAPE cash political contributions **15**, 6777-78
telephone conversation with Harrison on antitrust suit against AMPI **17**, 7680-81
termination of employment by AMPI **17**, 7633
thank-you notes from Semer for contributions to Muskie Election Committee **14**, 6030E, 6031E
Townsend on cash from **16**, 7093, 7095-96
Wright retained by AMPI to investigate payments to **16**, 7339-40

Russian Embassy
See Pentagon Papers matter

Rybicki, R. A.
memo to Cooper on Hertz charge privileges to political parties **25**, 12327E, 12328E

Ryland, Dr. Kenneth 23, 11227, 11230, 11268 **FR** 137
IRS case against **24**, 11655
telephone call from Johnnie Walters to Mitchell on **24**, 11635
Woods on advice to **22**, 10248-49

Ryne, William
See Woods, Rose Mary, testimony of

Sabatino, Louis 23, 10771

Sachs, Sidney S.
on Dash's list of Hunt's duties at White House **9**, 3808
on FBI interviews with indicted persons **9**, 3486
on Hunt's attorney-client privilege **9**, 3698-3703
informs Lenzner that Hunt wants to change his testimony on conversations with Winte, Liddy, and Bennett **20**, 9356
and IRS interviews of Ryland **24**, 11655
on length of interviewing sessions with Hunt **20**, 9377
requests break and/or early completion of session **9**, 3784, 3785
on Select Committee request that Gray turn over names of all FBI agents involved in Watergate investigation **9**, 3543
on sentencing of Hunt **9**, 3731
See also Hunt, E. Howard, testimony of

Sachs, Sidney S., questioning by
Walters
24, 11641, 11643

Sachs, Stephen H.
See Gray, Louis Patrick; Walters, Johnnie M., interview of

Sacks, Ervin 23, 11203

Safe Streets Act of 1968 4, 1603 **6**, 2592

Safer, John FR 494-95

Safire, Bill 6, 2445 **10**, 4111E
memo to Haldeman re *Newsweek* article on O'Brien **23**, 11076, 11114E

Sale, Jon 14, 6263, 6274 **15**, 6524, 6525, 6527

Salinger, Pierre 10, 4168E **11**, 4502, 4717E

Salk, Erwin Abner 3, 1141E

SALT talks 6, 2565
and leaks on **3**, 1111-12E **4**, 1623 **6**, 2565, 2604
Plumbers and **FR** 12
wiretapping after **4**, 1626-27
and Nixon's reaction to Pentagon Papers case **6**, 2410
Watergate and **1**, 7

Saltonstall, Leverett 12, 5115E

Salute to the President Dinner
in investigation of Veterans' Administration employees **19**, 9242-47E
and violation by General Services Administration employees by solicitation of ticket sales to **19**, 8872-81E **FR** 413-14

"Salute to Victor Reuther, A"
sponsors on enemies list **4**, 1728-29E

Salvodelli, Steve 24, 11437

Samuels, Howard 25, 12109, 12171
contribution to McGovern campaign **25**, 12170-71

San Clemente meeting
See La Costa meeting

San Clemente property
document on **23**, 10804-18E

San Diego, California
demonstrations at **4**, 1612

San Francisco, California
anti-Nixon demonstrations in **3**, 1100E **8**, 3205 **12**, 5012, 5070-72E

San Francisco Examiner
on demonstration in San Francisco against Nixon **12**, 5063-64E

San Geanero Festival, Greenwich Village, New York
disruption of **FR** 201

San-Bar Electric Corp.
certificates of deposit given as support for F. Donald Nixon's loan at United California Bank **22**, 10712-14
F. Donald Nixon as consultant at **22**, 10675
financial dealings with F. Donald Nixon **22**, 10695-96

Sanchez, Leveo 4, 1553 **13**, 5290-93, 5301, 5302-5303, 5318-20, 5625-36E **18**, 8251, 8252 **21**, 10116
letter from Russell Hamilton, Jr., on changed status of his business **13**, 5323, 5685E
See also Development Associates

Sanchez, Manuel 20, 9549

Sanchez, Phillip 13, 5539E, 5678E **FR** 365

Sandburg, Carl 4, 1562-63

Sanders, Donald G. 14, 5940, 6087-88
on amounts paid by AMPI to Valentine, Sherman **15**, 6860
on Cochrane's request for transcript of Morrison interview **25**, 11747
cover letter to Morris on questionnaire for Select Committee **16**, 7447, 7454E
in dispute over Johnson's appearance **17**, 7694
on Dorsen's comments on limitations of questions to Van Dyk **16**, 7014
letter from Deloss Walker re AMPI-related files **25**, 12076-87E
letter from Higgins re total receipts of Mills for President Committee **25**, 12075E
letter from Joe Walters with Andreas check **25**, 11953-55E

on list of loans made by Cole to Humphrey campaign **25,** 11792, 11793E

memo from Costa and Keema **25,** 11852-60E, 11969-72E

memo from Costa on Humphrey campaign bank accounts **25,** 11960-68E

memo from Hodgkin re presidential contributions by Mott **25,** 12136E

memo from Robeson on campaign committees for Mills contributions **25,** 12033-67E

memo to Robeson re AMPI flights into Minneapolis **25,** 11847-51E

on questions being asked Townsend **16,** 7109-10

on subpoena for Cole **25,** 11792, 11815

on Williams' objection to line of questioning of Arnold **25,** 12025

Sanders, Donald G., questioning by 16, 7316-48 **17,** 7597-98

Arnold **16,** 7125-28 **25,** 12019-24, 12028, 12030-31

Butterbrodt **17,** 7632-33, 7657-72

Campbell **17,** 7782-86, 7787-88

Chestnut **17,** 7700-7702 **25,** 11719-32, 11733-39, 11740, 11745-46

Cole **25,** 11804-11806, 11808-13

Edidin **25,** 12236-42, 12248-49, 12250

Ehrlichman **16,** 7399-7401

Fellows **25,** 11773-83, 22884-85

Haldeman **16,** 7183-85

Hanman **17,** 7745-47

Harrison **14,** 6280

Jacobsen **15,** 6457-59

Kalmbach **17,** 7607, 7621-22, 7811-14

Lifflander **25,** 12285-92, 12294-96

Lilly **14,** 5984-89, 6124-25, 6130-38, 6139-59, 6164, 6167-68, 6176-83

Marumoto **13,** 5296-5301

Masters **16,** 6948-49, 6961-67, 6969-71, 6972

Mehren **16,** 7274-76

Morrison **25,** 11747-59, 11761-64

Mott **25,** 12108-12114, 12116-21, 12127-29

Nelson **15,** 6582-88, 6591, 6595, 6597-98, 6599-6601, 6604-6609, 6612-17, 6623, 6689-97

Nunn **17,** 7569-73, 7574

Parr **15,** 6829-33, 6847-51, 6851-60, 6864-72, 6875-83

Pearlman **25,** 12173-97, 12202

Pepper **17,** 7707-22

Rubin **25,** 12137-51, 12153-67, 12170-71

Stans **2,** 704-709

Townsend **16,** 7096-7103, 7109-21

Van Dyk **16,** 7011-28, 7033-35, 7036-37, 7041-42

Williams **17,** 7695-98

Sands Hotel, Las Vegas

as source of Hughes contribution **FR** 956-58

Wearley transports money to **20,** 9450-51

Sandwedge Plan 2, 786, 862 **3,** 1087, 1124E **4,** 1608

Acree on **FR** 139

Barth denies familiarity with **23,** 11273

Caulfield and **FR** 113-17

Caulfield on **1,** 252 **21,** 9728-37 **22,** 10341-56

Caulfield on destruction of documents on **22,** 10354-55

and concept of presidential powers **FR** 17-18

and Dean **4,** 1413 **FR** 114-15

Dean on **3,** 924-26

Dean's knowledge about **4,** 1442

Dean's reaction to **3,** 1023

discussed at Haldeman-Mitchell meeting **6,** 2492

Ehrlichman on **6,** 2536-37

Haldeman on **8,** 3032-33

and IRS audits **22,** 10391

memo from Dean to Mitchell **3,** 926, 1149E

Mitchell on **4,** 1605

and O'Brien's intelligence efforts **21,** 9736

and penetration of McCloskey's volunteer headquarters in Washington, D.C. **3,** 1145E

as precursor to Gemstone **FR** 117

proposed budget and other memos relating to **3,** 925, 1121E-32E

Woods denies knowledge of **22,** 10242-46, 10278

written report on **FR** 240-51E

Sanford, Terry 10, 4227E

Santa Fe International Drilling Co. 22, 10701

Santanello, Floyd 23, 10966

Santarelli (of Department of Justice) 22, 10399

Sarbaugh, John FR 700

and antitrust suit against AMPI **FR** 703-705

and Heininger's reference to political contributions **FR** 704

Sarber, Margaret 12, 5159E

Sargent, Francis W. 12, 5115E

Sargent, Mrs. Francis W. 12, 5115E

Sarno, J. 23, 11269

Saunders, Mr. and Mrs. Charles 2, 710 **6,** 2636E

Savy, William

and Northrop campaign contribution scheme **FR** 487-89

Scaife, Richard 17, 7594 **FR** 506, 507

Schaeffer, Jack 20, 9571, 9572

Schaller, Jerome D. FR 893, 894

memo on declining to contribute to Humphrey fundraising affair **25,** 11973E

memo to Opstad re request by Mills for President Committee for 3M contribution **25,** 12088-90E

memos to Opstad and Bennett on Humphrey dinner in Minnesota **25,** 11974-75E

and 3M contribution to Mills campaign **FR** 926-27

Scheckarski, Frank 16, 7314, 7340

Scheuer, Sandy FR 1175

Schlesinger, Arthur 1, 300, 313, 329, 334 **8,** 3296 **10,** 4241E

asks for memo from Walters on his February 21, 1973, meeting with Dean **9,** 3419

call from Dean on materials at FBI **9,** 3438-39

and Dean's request for Hunt's material **3,** 978-79 **9,** 3833E

Helms and **8,** 3273

McCord letter on **9,** 3444

and plan to blame CIA **1,** 215

requests affidavit from Walters on his contacts on Watergate case **9,** 3419

takes over as CIA Director **1,** 194

telephone call from Dean **9,** 3417-18

Schmults, Edward C. **23,** 10926
    on Simon's telephone logs **23,** 10933-34
    See also Simon, William E., testimony of
Schnapper, Eric 3, 1135E
Schneiderman, Rebecca FR 700
Schochet, Barry, questioning by
    Harrison **14,** 6264, 6278-80
    Paarlberg **16,** 7513-24, 7525-26, 7527, 7529-31
    Palmby **16,** 7135-36, 7149
School milk program 17, 7634, 7639
    and AMPI contributions to Muskie **16,** 7017
    and dairy industry contributions **FR** 580
    Parr on **15,** 6792-93, 6794-95, 6881
    renewal of **FR** 616
    in Rice memorandum **FR** 800-803
Schorr, Daniel 4, 1490, 1528 **8,** 3155, 3175
    on enemies list **4,** 1696E, 1698E
    FBI investigation of **3,** 1071 **6,** 2489
    Haldeman and FBI investigation of **8,** 3156-57 **FR**
        144
Schreck, Albert R. 3, 1138E
Schroeder, Kenneth
    See Barth, Roger Vincent, testimony of
Schroeder, William FR 1175
Schubert, Richard F.
    memo for under secretary on Responsiveness Pro-
        gram **19,** 8807-8808E
Schulman, Howard FR 512-13
Schulte, James E. 26, 12773E
Schultz, Daniel 1, 362
Schultz, George
    pressure from Congress for milk price-support in-
        creases **FR** 630
Schultz, Richard L.
    affidavit of **12,** 5009, 5048-50E
    on agreement with Eaton on appearance preceding
        formal execution of immunity order **25,** 12299
    on attorney-client privilege **23,** 11207
    on Cole's objections to line of questioning of Dav-
        is **22,** 10574-75
    on Edidin appearing prior to formal order entered
        for immunity **25,** 11221
    and IRS audit of O'Brien **FR** 1026-29
    on Ohrenstein's protest on immunity granted to
        Edidin **25,** 12258
    on Rebozo documents **21,** 10088
    telephone calls to Ehrlichman and Haig to report
        on IRS sensitive cases **23,** 10928-29
Schultz, Richard L., questioning by
    Barth **23,** 11255-59
    Bartolme **13,** 5432-35, 5438
    Buzhardt **23,** 10923
    Clark **13,** 5417, 5418
    Danner **20,** 9562-63, 9581-83 **24,** 11559, 11564,
        11565
    Eaton **25,** 12299-12315, 12323-24
    Edidin **25,** 12242-48, 12249, 12250-51
    Glaeser **20,** 9421-24
    Griffin **22,** 10472
    Haig **23,** 11034
    Lifflander **25,** 12259-85, 12296-98
    Malek **18,** 8280-81

Wakefield **24,** 11288
Walters **24,** 11625-27
Wearley **20,** 9437, 9438, 9439, 9440, 9442-43,
    9446, 9450-52, 9457, 9458, 9485-87, 9491
Wild **13,** 5467-69
Schumacher, Charles 20, 9444
Schwartzberg, Sid 10, 4125E
Scott, Harold B.
    and corporate group solicitation program **FR** 544-
        48
Scott, Hugh 2, 875 **14,** 6257
    letter from Carroll **FR** 481-82
    suspected as source of leaks **3,** 1101E
Scott, Mike 1, 35
Scott, Rita Sue 23, 10966
Scott, Robert M.
    See also Hunt, E. Howard, testimony of
Scott, Sandra 20, 9583
Scott, Stan FR 275
**Seafarers Political Action Donation Committee
    (SPAD) FR** 512-14
Seale, Bobby 12, 5201E
Search warrants
    issued after Watergate break-in **1,** 111, 113
Sears, John P.
    See Caulfield, Jack, testimony of
Seaton, William R. 13, 5442, 5444
    bank record of $100,000 payment to **13,** 5448,
        5795E
    and transmittal of campaign contribution from
        Ashland Petroleum to CRP **13,** 5443
Secret Service
    at Milwaukee Muskie headquarters **11,** 4707E
    Butterfield as White House liaison with **5,** 2074
    and demonstrator at Nixon's inauguration **4,** 1440
    and expected demonstrations **8,** 3151
    and installation of Nixon's recording devices **5,**
        2077
    and intelligence-gathering for White House **3,**
        1071-72
    and knowledge of Nixon's listening devices **5,**
        2077
    and McCord's employment by CRP **1,** 229
    in McGovern headquarters at Democratic Nation-
        al Convention **11,** 4497-99
    present at opening of Hunt's safe **7,** 2826
    reports to CRP on Democratic presidential candi-
        dates from agents of **23,** 10942
    and rumors of use of tapings by other administra-
        tions **5,** 2084
    and Strachan's examination of files in Executive
        Office Building **6,** 2505-2506
    surveillance of F. Donald Nixon **21,** 9702-9703
    White House misuse and attempted misuse of **3,**
        1071 **FR** 147-48
    and Wilkes investigation **22,** 10399
    and wiretapping **23,** 10911
    wiretapping of F. Donald Nixon by **21,** 9700-9707
        23, 10942
    work liaison with Treasury Department **23,**
        10925-26

Secretaries (unnamed)
and AMPI's relationship with Mills' **15,** 6604, 6605-6606
at CRP
1, 32
Butterfield's **5,** 2077-78, 2080
Gray's (Marjorie) **9,** 3402
Haldeman's **8,** 3035-36
Young's **6,** 2565

Securities and Exchange Commission (SEC)
Danner denies approaching on Dunes Hotel acquisition matter **20,** 9584-85
Danner's deposition to **20,** 9587 **24,** 11565-66
and investigation of Hallamore Homes stock transactions **22,** 10643, 10644
ITT investigation **FR** 128

Security
at White House **5,** 2074
and computer technology use **FR** 1088, 1091
memos from Dalbey on **9,** 3480, 3843-45E, 3446-47E
and report on CIA activity in Watergate incident **FR** 1115

Security Consulting Group 3, 1124E-29E

Sedam, Glenn J., Jr. 1, 32, 35 **2,** 519 **5,** 1878, 1879 **6,** 2321, 2322
memo to Flemming on Tennessee primary **10,** 4207-08E

Sedan Chair I 2, 523 **6,** 2472 **FR** 190-92
Strachan and **6,** 2441, 2442, 2468-70

Sedan Chair II FR 192-96
Magruder on **2,** 848
Reisner on **2,** 499-500, 514
See also McMinoway, Michael W.

Sedlak, Polly 19, 9124E

Segal, Marvin
See Mitchell, John N., testimony of

Segretti, Donald H. 2, 524, 708, 732 **3,** 1010, 1081 **11,** 4604, 4666
activities during primaries **FR** 166-78
aliases used by **FR** 162, 164
appearance before grand jury **3,** 964, 965
attempted coverup of activities of **FR** 178-83
and attorney-client relationship and Dean **9,** 4022-23, 4035-42
attorneys representing **FR** 183
bank deposit slip, telephone statement of, and cashier's check to **10,** 4026, 4311-13E
bank forms and receipt to **10,** 4026, 4286-88E
Benz and **11,** 4409
Benz employed by **11,** 4403-4405, 4415
Benz's activities and **11,** 4417
Buchanan on decision to hire **10,** 3923-24
Buchanan on lack of impact of **10,** 3901-3902
Chapin and **7,** 2736
and Citizens for a Liberal Alternative pamphlet **FR** 158
communication with Kelly **11,** 4378-79
complaints to CRP about activities of **FR** 165
conversation with Benz on Democratic National Convention **11,** 4414
Dean on allegations that he showed FBI interviews to **3,** 1254E
Dean on coverup of activities of **3,** 962-66

Dean's meeting with, after Watergate arrests **4,** 1373-74
discusses Florida primary with Kelly **11,** 4378
distribution of false and misleading campaign literature by **FR** 168-73
draft of Chapin's sworn deposition on **3,** 1214-21E
draft of Strachan's sworn deposition on **3,** 1222-25E
forges signatures on telegrams supporting Nixon's Vietnam policies **FR** 153
false advertisements placed by **11,** 4379 **FR** 173-74
false ordering of food, flowers, and beverages by **FR** 176-77
FBI interview of **FR** 178
and Florida campaign **11,** 4663
grand jury appearance of **FR** 179-80
Haldeman on **2,** 598, 608, 627
hiring of **FR** 160-63, 186
and Humphrey-Jackson letter **11,** 4411
identification of exhibits by **9,** 4025-26
immunity for **10,** 3979
indictment of **11,** 4421 **FR** 170
instructions from Chapin to **FR** 162-63
Kalmbach job offer to **FR** 183
Kalmbach's disbursal of cash to **5,** 2132
and Kelly, *see* Kelly, Martin Douglas, testimony of
Kelly on hiring by **11,** 4376-77
letter from Chapin entitled "Politics" **10,** 4271-72E
letter from Kalmbach concerning payment for services **10,** 4026, 4268E
and Liddy **6,** 2470
MacGregor asks Chapin about role of **12,** 4905
Mankiewicz denies knowing **11,** 4606-4607
on March 21 tape **8,** 3077
McMinoway denies knowing **11,** 4491-92
meetings with Dean **3,** 962-63
memo from Chapin on Muskie's Whittier College appearance **11,** 4656-57
memo from Dean to Haldeman on **3,** 967, 1210-25E
Mitchell on knowledge about **5,** 1861-62
money from Kalmbach to **7,** 2814
newspaper story that Dean showed him FBI interview files **4,** 1360-61
note entitled "Politics" addressed to **10,** 4026, 4271-72E
notes in "Personal Directory" notebook **10,** 4026, 4350-68E
organizing of pickets by **FR** 174-76
payment to **8,** 3119
poster suggestions for **10,** 4290-91E
prison sentence of **FR** 170
proposed press statement of **FR** 181-82
receipts from Towne Motel, Florida, of **10,** 4303-09E
recruitment by **FR** 166-68
relationship with Chapin **FR** 163-165
relationship with Hunt and Liddy **FR** 165-66
and stinkbombs at Muskie picnic **11,** 4413, 4414
summary of activities of **1,** 163-65
and surveillance of Muskie **FR** 168

in Dean-Nixon March 21 meeting **8,** 3116
Dean's written report for Nixon on **3,** 967
in draft of Dean report **3,** 1212-13E
Ehrlichman on learning about Chapin's role in **7,** 2846-47
Ehrlichman-Dean meeting on **7,** 2760
in Ehrlichman-Kleindienst taped conversation **7,** 2944E
Haldeman on **7,** 2876-77
Kalmbach and **5,** 2147
Kalmbach's testimony before grand jury on **5,** 2130
MacGregor's press statement on **12,** 4943
meeting between Chapin, Strachan, and Moore on **6,** 2485-86
and meeting to prepare Ziegler for press conference on Watergate **3,** 1202E, 1203E, 1205-06E, 1208E
Moore and **5,** 1954-55, 2006-2007
Moore on **3,** 1010, 1294E-1307E **5,** 2022-26, 2030-39, 2043-45
Petersen on decision to exclude from Watergate investigation **9,** 3620-21
in Silbert affidavit **25,** 12411-14E
Strachan on **6,** 2501-2502
Strachan takes blame for Haldeman on **6,** 2488-89
White House press response to **FR** 184-87
Ziegler's response to **3,** 1082-83
Seidita, Jo 11, 4538, 4542, 4543, 4545, 4570-71, 4572
Select Committee
See Senate Select Committee on Presidential Campaign Activities
Semer, Bob 14, 6150
Semer, Milton P. 14, 5928-29, 5951, 5954-55, 6072 **15,** 6511, 6767 **21,** 10183 **25,** 12104
agreement reached with Kalmbach at time of delivering AMPI contribution **17,** 7805-7806, 7811-12
and AMPI contacts with Kalmbach **15,** 6512-15 **FR** 587-91
and AMPI's contribution to CRP **15,** 6515 **17,** 7811-12
and AMPI's contributions to Muskie campaign **16,** 7012
and arrangements for AMPI officials to meet White House officials **FR** 595-96
at AMPI strategy sessions **16,** 7028
authorization for contact with Kalmbach **15,** 6875
Colson and **17,** 7609
contacts in administration for AMPI **15,** 6512-15
contacts with Kalmbach **15,** 6390, 6759-60 **16,** 7218
contacts with Kalmbach in 1969 **17,** 7584-85
contacts with Kalmbach on AMPI contributions **15,** 6386, 6387-89
contacts with Mitchell on AMPI contributions **15,** 6386-87
and contributions to Muskie Election Committee **14,** 5948
and conversation with Lilly on contribution to Muskie campaign **14,** 5948, 6024E
delivery of AMPI contribution to Kalmbach **17,** 7581, 7627
and delivery of 1969 AMPI contribution **FR** 593, 594

first meeting with Kalmbach **17,** 7578-79
Harrison as successor to **17,** 7593
and Jacobsen **FR** 709-10
Kalmbach and **15,** 6537-38 **16,** 7155-56, 7373, 7374, 7375, 7377, 7378
Kalmbach's notes on meetings with **17,** 7588-89
Kalmbach's reasons for telling Flanigan about contacts with **17,** 7588
letter from Gleason on Department of Agriculture advisory board positions **16,** 7208, 7225E
letter from Gleason on Nixon fundraising dinner **15,** 6521-23
letter to Parr on Muskie campaign **14,** 5951, 6028E
Lilly and **14,** 5930-33
Lilly delivery of cash for Kalmbach to **14,** 5914-21
meeting with Dent **17,** 7583-84, 7585
meeting with Nelson, Parr, and Dent **15,** 6391, 6457, 6520-21
meetings with Gleason **15,** 6386
meetings with Kalmbach **17,** 7581-85 **FR** 589-91
meetings with Kalmbach, Parr, Jacobsen, and Nelson **15,** 6759-65
meetings with Nelson, Parr, and Jacobsen on political contributions **15,** 6385-86
Mitchell and **15,** 6386
and Muskie campaign **17,** 7609
opening statement to Select Committee **16,** 7187, 7219-20E
relationship with Kalmbach **15,** 6765
relationship with Parr **15,** 6764-65
replaced by Harrison as AMPI lawyer for White House matters **FR** 613
thank-you notes to Russell for contributions to Muskie Election Committee **14,** 6030E, 6031E
Semer, Milton P., testimony of 16, 7187-7218
on AMPI contribution to Muskie campaign **16,** 7213-14, 7215-16
on blacklisting by White House **16,** 7210, 7212-13
on chance meeting with Kalmbach in 1973 **16,** 7205-7208
on contacts with Gleason **16,** 7196
on decision on amount of TAPE contribution **16,** 7198-99
on delivering money to Kalmbach **16,** 7204-7205, 7211-12
denies discussing contributions with Kalmbach **16,** 7192-93
on first meeting with MPI representatives **16,** 7188-89
on formation of TAPE **16,** 7189
on involvement in fundraising for Muskie campaign **16,** 7210-11, 7213
on Kalmbach's deposition in *Nader* v. *Butz* **16,** 7192, 7193-94, 7198, 7205-7208
on Kalmbach's use of milk money **16,** 7206
on meeting with Dent **16,** 7206-7208
on meeting with Gleason **16,** 7189-91
on meeting with Mitchell in 1970 **16,** 7209-10
on meeting with Nelson, Parr, and Jacobsen in Dallas in 1969 **16,** 7195-97
on meetings with Kalmbach **16,** 7190, 7191-94, 7195-7201, 7404-7405
on motivation for TAPE contributions **16,** 7194,

Semer, Milton P., testimony of *(Continued)*
7197
on Nixon and dairy industry conventions **16,**
7208-7209
on organization of White House under Nixon **16,**
7195-96
on professional background **16,** 7187-88
on reasons for cash contribution **16,** 7197-98,
7200-7201
on receiving delivery of money from Liddy **16,**
7202-7203
on relationship with Mitchell **16,** 7189
on role as fundraiser for Muskie **16,** 7189, 7218
on Russell's contribution to Muskie campaign **16,**
7216-17
on TAPE contributions to congressional candidates **16,** 7199-7202
Semer, White & Jacobsen 15, 6511
See also Jacobsen, Jake, testimony of; Semer, Milton P., testimony of
Senate
discussion on Subversive Activities Control Board
budget in **3,** 1331E
Senate Appropriations Committee
Hunt letters in CIA documentation provided to **9,**
3443, 3834-42E
Senate Armed Services Committee
hearings on St. George matter **FR** 1119-20
Senate Committee on Government Operations
open hearings on controversial organizations **3,**
1341E
Senate Finance Committee
Talmadge on nonpartisanship of **8,** 3138
Senate Foreign Relations Committee
Helms' classified testimony to **8,** 3262-63
Senate Resolutions pertaining to Select Committee
Senate Resolution 60 **3,** 981-82 **6,** 2425-27 **FR**
1231-44
Baker on limitations of **11,** 4466-67, 4471
text of **1,** 427-35 **2,** 751
Senate Resolution 132 **FR** 1248
Senate Resolution 194 **FR** 1245-47
Senate Resolution 278 **1,** 435-36
Senate Resolution 327 **FR** 1249-50
Senate Select Committee Final Report
campaign financing recommendations **FR** 563-77
on campaign practices
Introduction **FR** 107-109
Introduction to
on characterization of Watergate **FR** 23, 24-25
and determination of legal guilt or innocence
FR 23
on function of report **FR** 24-25
on investigative procedures **FR** 27-31
on organization of Committee and selection of
staff **FR** 25-27
on public hearings **FR** 31-32
recommendations of Committee **FR** 23, 25
on relationship of report to impeachment issue
FR 23
legislative recommendations
on bar association's study of attorney-client
privilege **FR** 1074
on disclosure by president and vice president
to GAO on all income and expenditures by

themselves and their spouses **FR** 1073-74
on IRS-White House relations **FR** 1071-73
letter of transmittal from Ervin to Eastland of **FR**
5
recommendations for legislation
on awarding of Federal grants and loans **FR**
442-43
on campaign contributions **FR** 443-44
for Congress overseeing executive branch operations **FR** 444
on congressional subpoenas **FR** 1084-85
on establishment of Congressional Legal Service **FR** 1085
on fraudulently interfering with Government
function **FR** 442
on Hatch Act **FR** 444
on Public Attorney **FR** 442
on senatorial committees or staffs taking testimony and evidence in private sessions **FR**
1085-86
Silbert letter to Dash on unfavorable inferences
about U.S. Attorney's Office for D.C. investigation in **25,** 12401-12404E
See also CIA Watergate investigation; Computer
technology; Domestic intelligence; Hughes-
Rebozo investigation; Humphrey campaign;
Milk Fund Report; Mills campaign finances report; Senate Select Committee litigation; *statement entries for* Baker, Howard H., Jr., Ervin,
Sam J., Jr., Gurney, Edward J., Montoya, Joseph M., Weicker, Lowell P., Jr.
Senate Select Committee litigation
*Application of United States Senate Select Commit-
tee on Presidential Campaign Activities* **FR** 1079-
80
*National Citizens for Fairness to the Presidency,
Inc., et al.* v. *Senate Select Committee, et al.* **FR**
1080
Richard Danner, et al. v. *Senate Select Committee,
et al.* **FR** 1080, 1083-84
Senate Select Committee v. *Nixon* **FR** 1079, 1080-
83
on taking of testimony in executive sessions **FR**
1083-84
**Senate Select Committee on Presidential Campaign
Activities**
appointment of staff by **FR** 26-27
areas of investigation of campaign practices **FR**
107-108
"Authority to Investigate" memo of **23,** 10995-96
Baker on role of **5,** 1837
Dean, Mitchell, Nixon meet on March 22 on **4,**
1635
Dean suggests FBI investigation of campaigns of
members of **5,** 1975-76, 1995
and Dean's request for privilege against testifying
3, 912-13
denial of request by special prosecutor of Watergate case **2,** 457-458
discussed at La Costa meetings **4,** 1533-35
discussed at White House **4,** 1396-97
document entitled "Authority to Investigate" **23,**
10996, 11038-41E
efforts to discredit **3,** 1090

Short, Bob 11, 4697E
Showalter, David 12, 5162E
Shredding machines
    at Republican National Headquarters **3,** 1132E
    in CRP offices **1,** 27
Shriver, Sargent 11, 4628 **13,** 5290 **18,** 8251
    dirty tricks against **12,** 5017
    Sanchez and **FR** 387
    and Young Voters for the President demonstra-
      tions **FR** 200
    See also McGovern campaign
Shultz, George P. 3, 1001, 1102E **7,** 2745, 2747 **14,**
    5872, 5875 **16,** 7326-27 **23,** 10999
    at meeting with Nixon and dairy leaders **14,** 6061-
      64 **16,** 7388 **17,** 7761
    attitude toward dairy price supports **16,** 7450
    bogus call to Ervin on Nixon decision to make
      tapes available to Select Committee **6,** 2354-55,
      2360-61
    briefings on IRS sensitive case reports **24,** 11628
    confidential memo from Johnnie Walters on
      Rebozo and F. Donald Nixon's involvement in
      IRS Hughes investigation **24,** 11648-50
    conversation with Campbell **17,** 7751, 7752
    Haig informs about IRS investigation of Rebozo
      23, 11003
    handwritten notes by Walters for briefing with **24,**
      11628, 11657-64E
    and IRS investigation of Hughes Tool Co. **23,**
      11253
    and IRS sensitive case reports **23,** 11222 **24,**
      11635-36
    and Johnnie Walters leaving IRS **24,** 11656
    letter to Ervin containing Nixon's orders against
      Secret Service personnel testifying before Select
      Committee **5,** 2136-37
    meeting with Ehrlichman, Walters, and Barth on
      IRS investigation of Hughes Tool Co. and
      O'Brien **21,** 9683-84
    meeting with Hardin and Ehrlichman **16,** 7383-84
    meeting with Nixon and Ehrlichman on March 23
      FR 646-47
    meetings with Walters on Hughes-Meier investiga-
      tion **24,** 11628-37
    meets with Walters and Barth on O'Brien tax re-
      port **23,** 11223-24, 11241
    memo for Staff Secretary on President's Meeting
      with Connally, Burns, Shultz, and McCracken
      FR 819-20E
    memo from Clark on Rice memo on dairy indus-
      try problems **FR** 805E
    memo from MacGregor on milk price supports
      FR 813-14E
    memo from Rice on dairy industry issues **FR** 800-
      803E, 806-807E
    memo from Walters on IRS interview with Rebo-
      zo **FR** 1001-1003
    memo from Walters on "IRS Investigation Involv-
      ing Howard Hughes Interests and Associates"
      24, 11675-78E
    memo to Ehrlichman on telephone call from Mills
      on milk price supports **17,** 8128E
    memo to Walters to proceed with interviews of
      Rebozo and F. Donald Nixon **24,** 11651

    and milk price-support issue **16,** 7327, 7401
    in Nelson's deposition in *Nader* v. *Butz* **15,** 6562-
      63, 6565-66
    and political enemies list **FR** 133
    and Responsiveness Program **18,** 8177-88, 8188-89
      FR 378
    and sensitive case report on Hughes **23,** 11236
    Simon's duties and **23,** 10925
    telephone conversation with Ehrlichman, Walters,
      and Barth re O'Brien tax case **24,** 11638, 11640-
      41, 11644-46
Shumway, DeVan A. 1, 17, 34 **2,** 861 **4,** 1409 **5,** 1877
    12, 5046E
    denies slandering Stearns **11,** 4592-93
    and enemies list **4,** 1693E
    and Liddy's letter to *Washington Post* **5,** 1875
    and MacGregor's news releases **12,** 4904
    meeting with Magruder, Dean, Liddy, and Stra-
      chan after Watergate break-in **2,** 520
    and slander campaign against Stearns **11,** 4567
    statements after Watergate arrests **2,** 859, 860
Shure, H. William, questioning by
    Hunt **20,** 9352
    Ulasewicz **6,** 2238-45
Sibley, Marion
    on Wakefield's claim of attorney-client privilege
      24, 11291, 11293, 11294
    See also Wakefield, Thomas H., testimony of
Siciliano, Rocco 2, 734
Sickles, General 4, 1557
Siegel, Morris 11, 4439, 4450, 4697E
Sierra Club 10, 3919
Silberman, Laurence 18, 8445
    resistance to Responsiveness Program **FR** 431-33
Silbert, Earl J. 1, 111, 113, 295, 389-90 **2,** 552, 583-
    85 **3,** 1169E **4,** 1440 **6,** 2462 **9,** 3574
    affidavit on questioning of Segretti **FR** 180
    affidavit on Watergate investigation by United
      States Attorney's Office for District of Co-
      lumbia **25,** 12505-18E
    announces another grand jury hearing **9,** 3804
    at meeting with Kleindienst, Petersen, and Titus
      on April 14 **9,** 3578-79
    and CIA blame for Watergate **9,** 3446
    conflict on date of knowledge about Fielding
      break-in **7,** 2681
    discussion with Segretti **10,** 4048
    Ehrlichman's call on harassment of Stans by **9,**
      3618-19
    and exclusion of Segretti's dirty tricks from Wa-
      tergate investigation **9,** 3620-21
    and Fielding break-in **6,** 2552
    in Hunt's notes **9,** 3842E
    and hush money **6,** 2463-64
    informs Petersen on negotiations with Dean **9,**
      3630
    Kleindienst on **9,** 3567
    knowledge of Segretti's activities **10,** 4049-50
    letter to Dash accompanying affidavit **25,** 12401-
      12404E
    memo to Ehrlichman on Fielding break-in **6,**
      2553-54
    Porter and **2,** 673

and release of grand jury testimony to Senate Select Committee **25,** 12402-12403E
ruling on attorney-client privilege **6,** 2382
sentencing of McCord by **7,** 3014
silence order, Woods' testimony and **22,** 10254-56
and theory of Liddy as mastermind of Watergate **FR 26**

Six Crises (Nixon) **5,** 2047-48

Sixth Amendment
and Haldeman's testimony on Nixon tapes **8,** 3065-66

Sixtus Corporation
Mott on **25,** 12110

"60 Minutes" 7, 2815-16
on Hughes controversy **21,** 9724
on Hughes-Maheu, Dean-Caulfield memos **23,** 11079, 11132-33E

Sizemore, Larry 14, 5966

Skelton, Donald 21, 10068, 10069, 10091 **24,** 11435 **FR** 961, 1010

Slater, Ronald H. 13, 5414
affidavit of **13,** 5431, 5792-93E
affidavit on delivering envelope from American Ship Building Co. to CRP **13,** 5422-23
on American Airlines "good government fund" **13,** 5508
on contribution to CRP **13,** 5510-12
on motivation for contribution to CRP **12,** 5512-15, 5518 **13,** 5507
on proposed merger between American Airlines and Western Airlines **13,** 5508-10, 5512-14

Sloan, Debbie (Mrs. Hugh W. Sloan, Jr.) 6, 2365 **7,** 2699

Sloan, Hugh W., Jr. 1, 10, 13, 20, 22, 80, 181 **2,** 459, 689, 695, 704, 734 **4,** 1485 **6,** 2636E **12,** 4922 **13,** 5381, 5506 **17,** 7548
access to cash **2,** 721, 762
advised by LaRue to take Fifth Amendment **2,** 778
amount offered by Priestes in statement of **13,** 5380
and AMPI committees **14,** 6275
asks Porter about use of money **2,** 650
and budget committee **5,** 1846
call from Dean on Fifth Amendment privileges **3,** 1039
cash disbursement to Kalmbach **2,** 711
cash disbursements by, Stans and **2,** 714-19, 721, 751
and cash disbursements to Liddy **2,** 659-60, 697-98 **5,** 1847
cash disbursements to Porter **2,** 698
on cash receipts of Finance Committee until April 7 **2,** 750-51
chart entitled "transactions of April 7, 1972, Cash Deposits and Disbursements, including 'committed' items" **2,** 891E
and committees for milk producers' contributions **FR** 689
and coverup **2,** 873
and Dahlberg and Mexican checks **2,** 748, 759-60 **3,** 942
and dairy co-op contributions through committees **17,** 7541

and Dean and Haldeman's campaign spending discussion **3,** 1228E
and delivery of American Airlines campaign contribution **13,** 5502
discusses resignation with Stans **2,** 770
discussions with LaRue on amounts given to Liddy **6,** 2316-17
and discussions with prosecuting attorneys **9,** 3582-83
on efforts to involve him in Watergate coverup **FR 41-44**
efforts to talk to Ehrlichman **7,** 2699
on extent of cash contributions **FR** 567-68
FBI interrogation of **9,** 3582
Fernandez on reputation of **13,** 5376-77
and Fifth Amendment **4,** 1418
and formation of National Hispanic Finance Committee **13,** 5362
gives full statement to Federal prosecutors **FR** 43-44
and hush money **3,** 968 **4,** 1658
Kalmbach on amount of cash transferred to in 1972 **17,** 7580
Kalmbach turns over campaign funds to **5,** 2094
LaRue informs him of his options with grand jury **6,** 2300
on LaRue's role in Watergate investigation **6,** 2310
letter to Mitchell on payment to Walker **8,** 3190-92, 3324E
Magruder gives authorization for Liddy to draw money for intelligence-gathering operation **2,** 795-96
Magruder's efforts to have him perjure himself **2,** 708-709, 745-46, 770, 776-78, 800-801, 820, 867-68 **9,** 3617 **FR** 42-43
Mardian calls Stans on California trip of **2,** 776
media publicizes delivery of cash to Liddy by **5,** 2012
on meeting between Stans and Mitchell on money to Liddy **2,** 726-27
meeting with Ehrlichman after Watergate arrests **2,** 738, 772-73
meeting with Ehrlichman on cash disbursements to Liddy **FR** 42
meeting with Kalmbach in Washington **5,** 2096
meeting with Magruder, Dean, Strachan, and Liddy after Watergate arrests **2,** 799, 816
meeting with Mitchell, Magruder, and Mardian **5,** 1884
memo from Stans on bumper strips, banners, pins, etc. **2,** 746, 906E-907E
memo from Stans on depositing checks promptly **2,** 747-48, 763
memo from Stans on thank-you letters to contributors **2,** 747, 908
and Mexican checks **2,** 699, 757 **FR** 519
Mitchell and **4,** 1659-60
money given to Liddy by **6,** 2381 **9,** 3581-83, 3638 **FR 26**
money to LaRue **6,** 2291, 2320, 2366, 2367 **23,** 11155
O'Brien says he took cash home the night of Watergate break-in **7,** 2735
on Patman Committee subpoena list **3,** 961

Sloan, Hugh W., Jr. *(Continued)*
and payments to Liddy **4,** 1617
phone call to Dean after Watergate arrests **4,** 1356
Porter and **2,** 676
and Porter's financial records **2,** 653
and Priestes contribution **13,** 5334-35, 5341, 5349, 5353, 5376
reports to Stans on cash disbursements **2,** 714
requests meeting with Dean after Watergate arrests **3,** 933
resignation of **FR** 43
on results of public disclosure of Milk Fund **FR** 693-94
role at Finance Committee **17,** 7550
role in campaign **5,** 2010
role in fundraising **16,** 7461
role on budget committee **2,** 742, 763
and Select Committee investigation **FR** 28
sent on vacation **5,** 1884
in Silbert affidavit **25,** 12407-10E
and solicitation of funds by Colson **17,** 7552
with Stans in California **2,** 776-78
Stans is requested to seek his cooperation in cove-rup **2,** 809, 836, 869
Stans on character of **2,** 743-44
Stans on differences in recollections of **2,** 780
statement of **13,** 5379, 5741-42E
statement on meeting with Priestes, Fernandez, and Stans **13,** 5379-80
statement on Stans' contact with Fernandez **13,** 5741-42E
subpoena by Patman Committee **3,** 1193E
tells Mardian about money disbursed to Liddy **6,** 2363-64
tells Mardian he is being pressured to lie by Magruder **6,** 2364
tells Parkinson and O'Brien about cash disbursals to Liddy **FR** 43
testimony at Watergate trial on money to Liddy **7,** 2698-99
told by O'Brien and Parkinson to join Stans in California **FR** 43
told that Mitchell authorized money for Liddy **4,** 1615
trip to California **6,** 2300-2301
vacation trip of **6,** 2365-66
and Watergate coverup **2,** 822
on Woods' list of contributors **FR** 692
Sloan, Hugh W., Jr., testimony of 2, 532-99, 602-31
on activities in California **2,** 591-92, 619-20
advised by LaRue to take Fifth Amendment **2,** 582
on amount of money handled by **2,** 535, 594-96
on anonymous contributions to CRP **2,** 606-607
on assumption money was spent legally **2,** 603-604, 607-608, 617
on boat ride on Potomac **2,** 622-23
on budget committee members and functions **2,** 602-604
on cash disbursements
  authorization by Stans **2,** 625-26
  to Hitt **2,** 541
  to Kalmbach **2,** 535-36, 607-608
  to Kalmbach for Haldeman **2,** 607-608
  to Lankler **2,** 540-41, 554, 573, 605

to Liddy **2,** 538-39, 540, 548-49, 587, 613, 614, 615, 621
to Magruder **2,** 540
Mitchell and **2,** 537-38, 616, 617
to Porter **2,** 536-37, 538-39, 615
to Stone **2,** 541-42
to Strachan **2,** 536, 612, 613
on compliance with Campaign Disclosure Act **2,** 559-61
on contacts with Ehrlichman and Dean after Watergate break-in **2,** 556
on contacts with Kalmbach and Stans after resignation **2,** 590, 591
on contributions of stocks and securities **2,** 604-605
on conversation with LaRue after Watergate arrests **2,** 544, 577-78
on conversations with Dean **2,** 589-91
on Dahlberg and Mexican checks **2,** 574-76, 587, 617, 620
on destruction of records of contributions and dispersals **2,** 571-72, 594, 605-606, 626
on disbursements and records **2,** 570-72, 606-607, 615-16, 627-28
on discussion with Cole **2,** 545
on duties at Finance Committee **2,** 534, 559, 570, 595-96
on effects of Campaign Spending Act **2,** 553-55
on effects of Corrupt Practices Act **2,** 539-40
on employment by CRP **2,** 532-35
on employment problems after Watergate **2,** 598, 608-609
on extent of concern expressed after Watergate **2,** 628-29
on FBI interview **2,** 544, 564-65, 566
on final report to Stans on cash disbursements **2,** 546-47
on finances in 1968 campaign compared with 1972 **2,** 555
on his participation in Watergate interviews **2,** 563-65
on knowledge about Liddy's use of funds **2,** 620-21
on "laundering checks" **2,** 627
on loan to Hitt **2,** 558-59
on Magruder's efforts to change his testimony on amount given to Liddy **2,** 543, 556-58, 581, 613-14, 624-25
on meeting with Chapin after Watergate arrest **2,** 545, 579, 593-94, 599, 611-12, 623
on meeting with Ehrlichman after Watergate arrests **2,** 579-80, 593-94, 599, 621, 622, 623-24
on meeting with Haldeman **2,** 597-98, 608-10, 611, 612-13, 613-14, 626-27
on meeting with LaRue on cash disbursement to Liddy **2,** 549, 630
on meeting with LaRue on resigning **2,** 551
on meeting with Mardian after Watergate arrests **2,** 580
on meeting with Mardian on cash disbursements **2,** 547
on meeting with Mitchell after Watergate arrests **2,** 544, 561-62, 579, 592-93, 618-19
on meeting with Parkinson and O'Brien **2,** 549-50, 581

on meeting with Silbert on Magruder pressure **2,** 583-84

on meeting with Stoner, Glanzer, and Campbell **2,** 552, 565-66

on Mexican-Dahlberg transaction **2,** 587-88, 617, 620

on missing financial records **2,** 573

on Mitchell's probable knowledge of disbursements to Liddy and Porter **2,** 616

on money deposited to Barker's account **2,** 576-77

on money found on Watergate burglars **2,** 621-22

on money taken to White House **2,** 577-78

and officials with authority to make cash disbursements **2,** 560, 617

on personal ethics and handling funds **2,** 570

on persons with access to safes **2,** 596

on pick-up arrangements for contributions to Finance Committee **2,** 617-18

on Porter's activities **2,** 614-15

on procedures for cash disbursements **2,** 596-97

rehired by CRP after Watergate **2,** 609-10

resignation from Finance Committee **2,** 534, 551-52, 565

retains counsel **2,** 552

returns money from safe to LaRue **2,** 548

on revisions in Campaign Expenditures Act **2,** 566-69

on Stans' financial instructions after Campaign Spending Act **2,** 554-56

takes Bermuda vacation **2,** 547-48

takes money from safe home **2,** 547

testifies before grand jury **2,** 552

on those authorized to disburse funds **2,** 571

urged to go to California after Watergate break-in **2,** 550, 581-83

on use of cash disbursements **2,** 552-53

on Watergate trial **2,** 556-557

Slovak World Congress 12, 5027E

Small Business Administration 13, 5323, 5699E

extracts of policy regulations of **13,** 5324, 5700-04E

and grants to Hispanic Americans **13,** 5289-92

and National Economic Development Association **13,** 5743-46E

regulations pertaining to award of contracts and grants **13,** 5323-24

and Responsiveness Program **18,** 8262

Smalley, Robert A. 25, 12222-23, 12255E

and arrangement with Muskie campaign for free Hertz cars **25,** 12230, 12236-37, 12252-53E

Edidin denies informing him of outstanding bills to Muskie campaign **25,** 12243

leaves Hertz Corp. **25,** 12227

telephone call to Edidin on provision of vehicles for Muskie campaign **25,** 12224-25

See also Hertz Corp.

Smathers, George 20, 9478 **21,** 9679, 10122 **22,** 10270, 10513-14, 10519, 10582 **24,** 10408, 10414, 10416, 11427, 11434

business dealings with Rebozo **22,** 10513-14, 10521

contacts with Danner **24,** 11551

conversation with Colson on Kovens parole **FR** 147, 277-80E

Danner and **FR** 934

Davis denies discussing campaign contributions with **22,** 10582

discussions with Danner on Hughes contributions **20,** 9544-45

discussions with Rebozo on Hughes money **21,** 10106-10107

financial dealings with Rebozo **21,** 10083-84

introduces Nixon to Danner **FR** 934

and letterwriting campaign on Nixon's Vietnam policy **FR** 311-13E

Nixon's purchase of Key Biscayne home of **24,** 11425-26, 11452-53 **FR** 939-40, 1048

Wakefield and **24,** 11330

Smith, C. Arnholt 24, 11444

Smith, Carroll 20, 9428, 9447

Smith, H. Allen 11, 4463

Smith, Helen 22, 10215

Smith, J. T.

report to Garment on Hughes Tool Co. Air West and Dunes Hotel matters **23,** 11053-59

Smith, Jeff 11, 4715E

Smith, John N.

memorandum for Haldeman on form for memoranda **1,** 89, 454E

Smith, Ken 1, 32, 35 **12,** 5265E

Smith, Kent FR 506, 507

Smith, Neal 16, 7338

Smith, Preston 15, 6430

Smith, Rodney 11, 4624

Smith, Ron 25, 12115

Smith, Stephen FR 241E

Snow, Michael

See McMinoway, Michael

Social Security

memo from Evans to Cole on increase in **19,** 9222E

Society of Ex-FBI Agents, New York City

McCord obtains Baldwin's resume from **1,** 391

Solomon, Dick 25, 12147

Solomonsen, Bruce 25, 11724, 11725

and Loeb contribution **25,** 11726, 11727, 11805

Sonesta Beach Hotel

bill to Maheu **26,** 12842-46E

Sorensen, Ted

and *Newsday* article on Rebozo **21,** 10127

South, Charles FR 462

contacts with Fabrega **13,** 5484-88

South Dakota

Valentine, Sherman work for AMPI in **16,** 7029, 4035-41

Southern Christian Leadership Conference 10, 3952

Southern Elections Fund 16, 6983

Southern Milk Producers Association 17, 7649

plans to separate from AMPI **16,** 7445

Southwick, Thomas P. 11, 4485, 4515-16, 4532, 4717E

and disruption of Muskie's television appearance **11,** 4523

letter and affidavit to Select Committee from **11,** 4892-95E

and McGovern activities against Muskie campaign **11,** 4485, 4486

on return of contribution to American Airlines
13, 5504

Special Committee on Aging
GAO Report to **18,** 8450, 8489-8529E
Subcommittee on Aging, Committee on Labor
and Public Welfare, U.S. Senate report on Federation of Experienced Americans **18,** 8449,
8450-57

Special Investigations Unit
authorizations from Ehrlichman on wiretaps by **6,**
2534-35
Ehrlichman on termination of **6,** 2556
Haldeman on **7,** 2875
Nixon's knowledge of **6,** 2564-65

Special Political Agricultural Community Education
See SPACE

Special prosecutors
accounting by Segretti to **10,** 3982
agreement with LaRue **6,** 2333
appointment of **FR** 1106
and IRS investigation of Rebozo **23,** 11003, 11020
Petersen on appointment of **9,** 3645-46, 3647

Special Subcommittee on Human Resources 19, 9242-
48E

Spector, Arlen 18, 8238

Sperling, Godfrey 10, 4182E, 4245E

Spidle, Floyd S.
letter from Powell on milk price-support decision
17, 8141-42E

Spiegel, Albert A. 12, 4966, 4969, 4977, 5059-60E
letter from Essrig **12,** 4969, 5025E

Spivack, Leo J. 25, 12275

Spock, Dr. Benjamin 3, 1141E **25,** 12098

Sporrer, Louis L.
report on Century Plaza Hotel anti-Nixon demonstration from Beck to **11,** 4561, 4719-26E

Springfield, Massachusetts
violence at Nixon Campaign Headquarters in **12,**
5116-19E

Spurgeon, D. Lonnie 14, 5872, 6296

Squier, Robert 11, 4780E, 4781E, 4814E, 4817E

SST issue
and assault strategy on McGovern **10,** 4243E
Muskie on **10,** 4151E

St. Clair, James D. 22, 10548, 10554 **23,** 11081
at discussion between Garment and Buzhardt on
newspaper story on Hughes contribution **22,**
10553
and Haig testimony **23,** 10850-53, 10997
and letter from Nixon directing Haig not to testify **23,** 10849-50
letter to Ervin on behalf of Nixon on Nixon-
Rebozo financial relationship **22,** 12449-50E **FR**
1051, 1069-70
and Select Committee inquiry on Rebozo payments for Nixon's expenses **FR** 1049
See also Haig, Alexander M., Jr., testimony of

St. George, Andrew FR 1119-20

St. Louis Post-Dispatch **4,** 1448 **11,** 4520 **18,** 8235

St. Peter, George 16, 6940, 6961, 6963

Staats, Elmer 3, 962

Stable Society Council 13, 5431, 5769E

Stack, Michael 18, 8234, 8236-39, 8387E
and Fannie Mae inquiry **FR** 411-12

Stafford, Gordon 13, 5414 **20,** 9448 **FR** 453

Stahlbaum, Lyn 14, 5985, 5988-89

Stanley, Earl
letter to Taptich on Dean's employment record at
law firm of Welch and Morgan **3,** 1045-46

Stanley, Edward T. FR 110

Stans, Maurice H. 1, 13, 14, 17, 181 **2,** 475, 481,
550, 583, 596, 602, 605, 627 **5,** 2010 **12,** 4922 **16,**
7417, 7423 **20,** 9455 **24,** 11444
and American Ship Building Co. claim **FR** 452
and AMPI contributions to Republicans **15,** 6447
on anonymity of contributions **2,** 729-31 **13,** 5448
asks Kalmbach to meet with Sloan after Watergate arrests **5,** 2096-97
asks Kalmbach to take trusteeship of funds from
1968 campaign **23,** 10858
asks Moore to help with public relations after
Watergate arrests **5,** 1952-53
asks Webb for list of contributors from Ashland
Petroleum **13,** 5444-45
asks Wild for list of contributors from Gulf Oil
13, 5466
at meetings after Watergate arrests **5,** 1952, 1953
Atkins on relations with **13,** 5459
Atkins on telephone call soliciting contribution
from **13,** 5440-41, 5450-51, 5457-58
authorization of cash disbursements by Sloan **2,**
625-26
and awareness of Semer-Kalmbach meeting and
agreement **17,** 7806-7807
and Better Government Association of Gould,
Inc. **FR** 552
and Braniff Airways, Inc., contribution **FR** 462,
463
and budget committee **5,** 1846
called to testify before grand jury **3,** 954
and cash disbursement to Liddy **5,** 1847, 1848
cash kept in offices by **5,** 2012
Casson affidavit on **7,** 2969-70E
confirmation hearings **3,** 1243E **4,** 1483, 1485
contacts with Sloan after his resignation **2,** 590
contacts with Spater **13,** 5502-5503, 5509-10
and contribution from 3M **FR** 485-86
and contributors' lists **22,** 10238, 10265
conversations with Sloan in California after Watergate arrests **2,** 620
and corporate group solicitation program **FR** 546-
47
correspondence with Rebozo on campaign contributions **22,** 12530E, 12548E, 12551E, 12556E,
12558E, 12571E, 12573E, 12574E
Dahlberg and **9,** 3463
and Dahlberg check **2,** 588 **2,** 701, 749 **3,** 942 **5,**
2011 **FR** 37
and de Roulet ambassadorship **FR** 501
on Dean's "indictable" list **5,** 1989
declines to appear at scheduled Patman hearings
FR 74
and Democrats for Nixon **16,** 7471

Stans, Maurice H. *(Continued)*

and destruction of financial records **2**, 572, 606
and destruction of Kalmbach's records **5**, 2129
discussion with Danner **20**, 9506
divides money in safe with Sloane **2**, 547, 548,
   580, 581
Ehrlichman and grand jury testimony of **7**, 2699-
   2701, 2797-98 **9**, 3594
Ehrlichman's telephone call to Kleindienst on
   questioning of **9**, 356, 465
Ervin's characterization of **13**, 5348, 5716-32E
excused from grand jury testimony **7**, 2790-93,
   2806 **9**, 3618-20, 3636-38, 3640-42
   Kleindienst on **9**, 3580-83, 3584
Fernandez' opinion of **13**, 5373
and Finance Committee **2**, 533
and finances at CRP **5**, 1847
and formation of National Hispanic Finance
   Committee **13**, 5360, 5362
and GAO investigation **3**, 962
and Goodyear Tire & Rubber Co. contribution
   13, 5521-22, 5523, 5525, 5527, 5529 **FR** 465-67
and grand jury testimony **3**, 1033 **9**, 3647
   in Silbert affidavit **24**, 12414-16E
Griffin and **11**, 4430
and Gulf Oil Corp. contribution **FR** 470, 471
Harrison and **14**, 6265-66
and hush money **3**, 950, 968-69, 970, 1025 **4**,
   1391, 1392, 1438, 1673 **5**, 2100, 2156 **FR** 52
information from Mitchell about Watergate affair
   2, 865-66
informed by Kalmbach of AMPI payment
   schedule **17**, 7612
instructions to Sloan on Campaign Spending Act
   2, 554-56
instructs Fernandez to return Priestes' check **13**,
   5380-81
interrogation by prosecutors **FR** 47
involvement in Watergate **2**, 569
involvement in Watergate coverup **2**, 835-36
   Dean on **3**, 1054
and Lehigh Valley Cooperative Farmers contribution **FR** 483, 484
Jacobsen denies discussing dairy industry contributions with **15**, 6477-78
and Kalmbach **7**, 2940 **16**, 7158
Kalmbach asks for money **5**, 2095, 2134
Kalmbach informs of payment to F. Donald Nixon from surplus 1968 funds **23**, 10860-61
Kalmbach turns over campaign records to **5**, 2094
and Kalmbach's contacts with Semer **17**, 7583
Kalmbach's destruction of originals of records
   given to **5**, 2158-59
Kalmbach's trust funds and **21**, 10184
and LaRue **23**, 11155
and Leanse appointment **3**, 1105E
letter from Barker to Ervin on **13**, 5348, 5706-
   5707E, 5714-15E
letter from Garry Brown to **5**, 2196E
letter from Kalmbach on Mulcahy contribution
   17, 7807, 7816E
letter from Moncourt with receipted slip for contributions **22**, 12570-71E
letter from Rebozo with campaign contributions
   22, 12530E

letter from Rebozo with check from Gerity **22**,
   12429E
letter from Thurmond to Select Committee on **4**,
   1563, 1793E
letter from Vinson on contribution of Mr. and
   Mrs. Atkins **13**, 5448, 5797E
letter from Vinson requesting refund to Ashland
   Petroleum **13**, 5445-46
letter to A. D. Davis **22**, 12576E **FR** 1000-1001
letter to Ervin from Wilkinson, Cragun and Barker law offices on cancellation of grand jury testimony **2**, 685, 897-98E
letter to executive committee of Finance Committee **16**, 7428-29
letter to Hamilton on memo to Mitchell and
   Haldeman from **19**, 8615-16E
letter to LaRue requesting payment to Finance
   Committee **6**, 2636E
letter to Mrs. Swanke on distribution of campaign
   funds **16**, 7429, 7436E
libel suit against O'Brien **3**, 1174-75E, 1178-79E
   4, 1472 **FR** 75
and loan to Hitt **2**, 558
MacGregor on meeting with Dean and **12**, 4908
on Magruder's authority from Mitchell **2**, 555,
   795-96
Mardian's notes on telephone conversations with
   6, 2367, 2642E
and Mardian's role in money going to LaRue **6**,
   2365
and McPhee's participation in discussions of
   Democratic National Committee suit **5**, 1906-
   1908
meeting with Fernandez and Priestes **13**, 5335-37,
   5361, 5376-79
meeting with Magruder and Mitchell after Watergate arrests **2**, 868-69, 870
meeting with Mitchell and Magruder **2**, 809
meeting with Sloan on cash disbursements **2**, 546-
   47, 615
meetings with Mitchell **4**, 1660
meetings with Mitchell, McPhee, and Parkinson
   5, 1907
meetings with Wild **13**, 5463-64, 5467, 5473,
   5478-79
memo from Byers on industry-by-industry campaign solicitations **FR** 548-50
memo from Jobe **7**, 2967E
memo from Sloan on deposit of Abel check **2**,
   910E
memo to Sloan on deposit of checks **2**, 909E
on Mitchell's responsibilities for expenditures at
   CRP **4**, 1656-69
money from Ashland Petroleum delivered to **13**,
   5444
and money passed from Sloan to LaRue **6**, 2366,
   2367
money to LaRue from **6**, 2320, 2497
and National Hispanic Finance Committee **FR**
   522
note from Dunnells on Priestes **13**, 5348, 5713E
Nunn and **17**, 7536
and Nunn-Mehren meeting **17**, 7556-57
O'Brien says he took cash home the night of Watergate break-in **7**, 2735

and Patman Committee hearings **3**, 959-60, 1181-82E

on Patman Committee subpoena list **3**, 961, 1193E

and payments by Sloan to Porter **2**, 537

and payments to Liddy **4**, 1617-18

and Phillips Petroleum Co. contribution **FR** 489-92

and Priestes contribution **13**, 5330, 5333, 5338, 5341-45, 5348-50 **FR** 522-26

reaction after Watergate **2**, 569

Rebozo and **22**, 10240

and Rebozo's retention of Hughes contribution **22**, 10236

refers Semer to Gleason **16**, 7189

and reports from Sloan on finances **2**, 616

and Republican fundraising efforts **17**, 7547

request to defer testimony before Select Committee **2**, 680-87

role at Finance Committee **17**, 7550, 7551, 7552

role in campaign **12**, 4931

role in CRP **1**, 21

safe-deposit box report received from Kalmbach **22**, 12448E

says Dean and Ehrlichman had assured Kalmbach of legality of money-raising assignment **5**, 2133-34

seeks Sloan's return to campaign after Watergate **2**, 609-10

Sloan and **2**, 536, 539, 541

Sloan joins in California **FR** 43

and Sloan's disbursal of funds **2**, 571, 573

Sloan's final report to **2**, 873 **FR** 42

and Sloan's resignation **2**, 551-52 **FR** 43

Sloan's statement on meeting with Priestes and Fernandez **13**, 5380

and solicitation of campaign contributions **13**, 5465

solicitation of contribution from Ashland Oil Co. **FR** 459-61

and solicitation of contribution from Northrop Corp. **FR** 487

as source of Woods' contributors' list **22**, 10233-34

and Spater **FR** 449

statement by Sloan on Fernandez contact with **13**, 5741-42E

statement on Priestes contribution **13**, 5708-12E

statement on Priestes testimony **13**, 5345-47

and surplus 1968 campaign funds **5**, 2092

and TAPE funds **14**, 5913-14

telephone call from Kalmbach for money **5**, 2116, 2131

tells Fernandez to return Priestes' check **13**, 5386

tells Sloan he should pay funds to Liddy **FR** 26

thank-you letter to Courtelis **22**, 12547E

in transcription of taped telephone conversation between Ehrlichman and Kalmbach **5**, 2215

and transfer of funds from presidential to congressional campaign committees **FR** 739-41

and transfer of funds from senatorial and congressional campaign committees to Finance Committee **17**, 7566, 7571, 7574

Vinson's correspondence with **6**, 2299

and Watergate coverup **2**, 822 **3**, 943 **4**, 1571-72

Stans, Maurice H., testimony of 2, 687-782

on amount of cash kept in CRP offices **2**, 761-62

attitude on use of money **2**, 741-42

on attitude toward LaRue, Mitchell, and Kalmbach after Watergate arrests **2**, 731-32

on his behavior after learning about Watergate break-in **2**, 681-82

on campaign contributors **2**, 781-82

on campaign spending **2**, 772

on career **2**, 694-95, 743

on cash contributions **2**, 713, 750-56

on cash disbursements **2**, 711-17, 719-21

to Liddy **2**, 722, 744-45

to Porter and Liddy **2**, 693

by Sloan **2**, 721

to White House **2**, 716-17

cash received after April 7 **2**, 710-11

on cash received prior to new law **2**, 709-10

on CIA and FBI involvement in Mexican checks issue **2**, 774

claims no intentional violation of laws on campaign financing **2**, 689-93

closing statement **2**, 779-82

on connection between Finance Committee and Watergate **2**, 740

contacts with Nixon after Watergate arrests **2**, 726, 766

on cooperation with inquiring bodies **2**, 688-89

on Dahlberg check **2**, 699-701, 717, 748-50, 759-61

and Dean **2**, 722

denies conferences on Watergate coverup **2**, 725-26

denies knowledge of intelligence-gathering operations **2**, 705

denies knowledge of Watergate break-in or sabotage program **2**, 689, 693-94

on destruction of campaign records **FR** 891-92

on destruction of Finance Committee records **2**, 692, 751-56

on differences between Sloan's recollections and his own **2**, 780

on discharging Liddy **2**, 729, 737, 746, 770

on disclosure of contributors' names **2**, 731

on elimination of cash transactions from political system **2**, 742-43

on employment by Finance Committee **2**, 696

on FBI questioning him **2**, 772

on financial transaction with Lankler **2**, 714

on financial transactions with Agnew dinner **2**, 756-57

on financial transactions with LaRue **2**, 721-22

on fund at Commerce Department to be used for Nixon's re-election **2**, 695-96

on fundraising trip to California and Iowa **2**, 775-76

on his behavior after Watergate arrests **2**, 724-26

indictment in Vesco case **2**, 680-87

informs FBI that Sloan has resigned **2**, 770

on Kalmbach's money carried over from 1968 **2**, 706-707

on Kalmbach's request for money for White House project **2**, 702-703, 729, 767-68

on lack of awareness of cash disbursements **2**, 706

on ethics of campaign aiding demonstrations **11,** 4579-80, 4597-99

on his testimony in executive session **11,** 4572

on information on Shumway as source of slanders against him **11,** 4592-93

on insufficient notice of appearance from Select Committee **11,** 4565-66, 4569

on interview by majority staff **11,** 4568

on learning about use of McGovern headquarters telephones for demonstration against Nixon **11,** 4575-76

on McGovern campaign policy toward demonstrations **11,** 4572-73

on McGovern campaign practices **11,** 4567

on McMinoway's implications about Robert Kennedy **11,** 4566

on Mott **11,** 4599-4600

on Mott document on Muskie **11,** 4599-4600

on Muskie's voting record **11,** 4600

opening statement **11,** 4565-68

on organization of McGovern campaign **11,** 4574, 4581

on organizational meeting at McGovern headquarters in Los Angeles on anti-Nixon demonstration **11,** 4570-77

on petition from McGovern campaign workers in California **11,** 4569-70

on recommendations for resources of political campaigns aiding demonstrations **11,** 4596-97

relevance of **11,** 4594-95

on relevance of hypothetical questions **11,** 4595-96

on role in McGovern campaign **11,** 4569

on Select Committee investigating Democrats **11,** 4576-78

on slanders against him **11,** 4567, 4576-77, 4582-86

on views on Middle East **11,** 4583-84

Steel Seizure case **6,** 2590, 2594

Stein, Herb 10, 4248E

on enemies list **4,** 1698E

Stein, Howard 3, 1138E **8,** 3155

on enemies list **4,** 1695E

Steinberg, Jonathan R. 19, 9247E

Steinbrenner, George M., III 13, 5431, 5777E

Bartolme on meetings with **13,** 5427-30

Bartolme on motivations for campaign contributions **13,** 5435

and bonus plan for illegal campaign contributions to CRP **13,** 5420-38

Clark on dealings with **13,** 5407, 5417

destruction of records on bonuses **13,** 5424

gives employees expense money for weekend **13,** 5413-14

indictment of **FR** 458-59

and instructions on record keeping on bonuses and campaign contributions **13,** 5425

meetings with Bartolme, Lepkowski, and Clark on false statements to FBI re American Ship Building Co. political contributions **13,** 5411, 5412-13

meetings with Clark **13,** 5415-16

meetings with employees prior to grand jury hearing on campaign contributions **13,** 5414

personal contributions to CRP **13,** 5423-24

reasons for not going to special prosecutor **13,** 5418

See also American Ship Building Co.

Steinem, Gloria 10, 4059E **12,** 5183E

Stennis, John 7, 2809

and Nixon tapes

See Stennis Compromise

Stennis, Mrs. John 22, 10423

Stennis Compromise 23, 11014, 11020 **FR** 1081

Stephans, Alan J. 12, 5181E

Stephens, Tom 19, 8597E

Sterile telephones 9, 3752, 3760, 3789

Stetler, Marvin FR 594

affidavit with attachments of **17,** 7994-8000E

and AMPI contribution **15,** 6389-90

Lilly loan application and **15,** 6392

and TAPE contribution to Kalmbach **14,** 5918-19

Stevens, Gary

memo on political pressure from Dairy Week in Washington **FR** 798-99E

Stevenson, Adlai 10, 3972

Stewart, Dick 11, 4774E

Stinkbombs

Benz on legality of use of **11,** 4427-28

used by Segretti **FR** 177

Stobaugh, Blair 10, 4026, 4289E

Stock, Arthur J.

affidavit and letter of **12,** 5009, 5120-24E

Stock contributions

to McGovern campaign **25,** 12149-50, 12201

to Muskie campaign **11,** 4651

Stone, Roger 2, 658, 659, 662 **FR** 158

and bogus contribution to McCloskey **FR** 198

contacts with McMinoway **11,** 4402, 4478-80, 4494-95, 4530, 4705-06E, 4711E

materials from McMinoway to **11,** 4480-81, 4500

recruitment of McMinoway by **11,** 4703E, 4704E

and Sedan Chair II **FR** 192-96

Stone, W. Clement 2, 541-42, 573, 627, 721, 751, 756, 780 **11,** 4505-4506 **17,** 7592 **23,** 11268 **24,** 11444 **FR** 506, 507

Mott on GAO and Justice Department treatment of **25,** 12121

Stoner, James R. 2, 286, 552, 557, 565-66, 572 **3,** 1039

letter to Select Committee with Sloan's statement **13,** 5379-80, 5740E

See also Sloan, Hugh W., Jr., testimony of

Stoner, Treese & Ruffner 13, 5379-80

Storer Broadcasting Co. 5, 1999

Stover, Bill 1, 35

Strachan, Gordon C. 1, 18, 24-25, 54, 71 **2,** 572, 720, 824 **3,** 941, 954, 1229E **4,** 1409 **5,** 2071

advice on government service **8,** 3175-76

and AMPI contributions through committees **17,** 7602-7603

and AMPI political commitments **16,** 7333

asks Dean for name of lawyer to head up demonstration intelligence operation at CRP **3,** 927

behavior after Watergate arrests **2,** 842

in Buzhardt memo **5,** 1817

Strachan, Gordon C. *(Continued)*

cash disbursements from Sloan to **2**, 536, 612

and clearance for CRP personnel **1**, 72

and conflict between Magruder and Liddy **4**, 1414

contradictions between Magruder's testimony and **9**, 3648-49

Dean tells Nixon he gave fruits of bugging to Haldeman **8**, 3115

on Dean's "indictable" list **5**, 1989

delivery of money from White House fund to La-Rue **FR** 56

denies Magruder's allegations **7**, 2768

destruction of files by **3**, 1035, 1088 **4**, 1357, 1415 **5**, 1900, 1901 **7**, 2745, 2880-81

and destruction of Haldeman's files **3**, 1091 **3**, 934 **4**, 1372

draft of sworn deposition on Segretti matter **3**, 1222-25E

Ehrlichman and **7**, 2717

Ehrlichman on his advice to young Americans on Government service **7**, 2864-66

Ehrlichman's interview with **7**, 2767-68, 2864

employment after Watergate **5**, 1921

employment of Segretti by **10**, 3980, 3985, 4050

ends contact with Segretti **10**, 3988

and enemies list **4**, 1409 **6**, 2487

and enemies project **4**, 1529

and FBI files held by Dean **4**, 1362

gives money for Dean to hold **3**, 935, 1025

Haldeman denies telling him to transfer intelligence capabilities from Muskie to McGovern **8**, 3038

Haldeman denies testimony on cleaning file **8**, 3037-38, 3097

Haldeman's opinion of **8**, 3129-30

and Haldeman's polling instructions **8**, 3121

and hiring of Segretti **FR** 160-61, 162

and hush money **3**, 968, 969, 971 **4**, 1390, 1391, 1438

informed about approved Liddy plan **2**, 794-95, 826

informed by Magruder of first break-in **2**, 826

informs Dean of scheduled FBI interview of Segretti **3**, 962-63

informs Liddy of Haldeman instructions to transfer intelligence from Muskie to McGovern **FR** 27

interrogation by prosecutors **9**, 3633

interviewed by Moore on Segretti matter **5**, 1954, 1955

involvement in Watergate **3**, 1053-54

Kalmbach and **16**, 7158

knowledge of Dean taking money for personal use **4**, 1587, 1588

knowledge of first Watergate break-in **FR** 29

and knowledge of Gemstone plan **FR** 26-27

LaRue's relationship with **6**, 2315-16

and leaks at White House **3**, 921

letter from Bray to Dorsen on immunity for **16**, 7455, 7472E

and letterwriting campaign **FR** 151

liaison role between CRP and Haldeman **2**, 504, 785, 824-26, 826-27, 828, 830-31, 834-35, 846-47, 858-59 **3**, 1024, 1088-89

liaison role between CRP and White House **5**, 1860-61, 2013

Liddy and **2**, 471

and list of Muskie's campaign contributors **4**, 1495

Magruder says he approved Liddy plan **7**, 2766-67

Magruder's messages to Haldeman **2**, 819

and McMinoway's reports **11**, 4479

meeting with Dean, Liddy, Sloan and Magruder after Watergate arrests **2**, 816

meeting with Dean after Watergate arrests **3**, 933-34

meeting with Magruder, Dean, Liddy, and Shumway after Watergate break-in **2**, 520

Mitchell on responsibilities of **4**, 1608

money from Kalmbach **2**, 716-17

money to Dean **4**, 1374-77

money to Haldeman **5**, 1989

money to Kalmbach **2**, 724

money to LaRue **6**, 2296, 2320, 2334, 2343

and money to White House from CRP **2**, 872 **7**, 2878-80

note from Colson to **16**, 7456, 7473E

in notes from Petersen to Nixon on Watergate investigation **9**, 3634, 3875-76E

Nunn's reporting relationship with **17**, 7547

Porter on documents sent to **2**, 671

questioned by Ehrlichman **7**, 2727

reaction to Liddy's intelligence-gathering plan **2**, 813

receives copies of material filmed in Muskie's offices **2**, 670

receives money from Kalmbach for White House **5**, 2095-96

as recipient of enemies list **4**, 1409

recommends to Haldeman that Colson not be informed of continued solicitations of dairymen **FR** 710

Reisner shows Gemstone material to **FR** 30

relationship with Segretti **10**, 3980

reports from Magruder on meetings with Dean, Mitchell, and Liddy **2**, 789, 791, 839

requests meeting with Dean after Watergate arrests **3**, 932

and requests to Magruder for intelligence information **FR** 24

responsibilities at CRP **8**, 3023-24

role in campaign **7**, 2877-78

role in CRP **1**, 30-31 **7**, 2766-67 **FR** 19

role in Watergate coverup **2**, 857

role on White House staff **1**, 79, 89 **2**, 793 **8**, 2019-20

Segretti and **3**, 965-66, 1212-13E **4**, 1374 **10**, 3982, 4029, 4030

and Segretti coverup **FR** 178, 180, 181

and Segretti matter **3**, 1295E-1307E **7**, 2877

Segretti told by Dean not to mention him to FBI **3**, 963

and Segretti's activities **10**, 4013

shown Gemstone material by Magruder **2**, 797-98

shreds Haldeman's file **FR** 165

and solicitation of funds by Colson **17**, 7552

source of money to LaRue **6**, 2343

and surveillance of Kennedy **3**, 922-23

sworn statement planned by Dean for **3**, 1210E

on talking paper for Haldeman on intelligence capability **6**, 2470-71 talks to Magruder on problems with Liddy **2**, 793, 825-26

telephone call from Magruder after Watergate arrests **2**, 799, 827-28

telephone call to Dean after Watergate arrests **4**, 1356

tells Dean about orders to destroy materials in Haldeman's files **3**, 1048

tells Dean about problems between Magruder and Liddy **3**, 1088

tells Dean he destroyed material from Haldeman's files after break-in **4**, 1672 **FR 34**

tells Liddy to transfer his "capability" from Muskie to McGovern **FR 197**

tells Magruder that Liddy should not be involved directly in intelligence-gathering activities **2**, 843

tells Magruder to rehire Liddy **7**, 2733

transcript of application for and order conferring immunity upon **6**, 2436-38

and Watergate coverup **2**, 822

working relationship to Haldeman **6**, 2526-27 **8**, 3154

Strachan, Gordon C., testimony of 6, 2436-2507 **16**, 7455-71

on ad paid for out of $350,000 **6**, 2499

on aides to President recording telephone conversations **6**, 2506

on AMPI $2 million commitment **16**, 7458-59

on AMPI commitment to Nixon re-election **16**, 7468-69

on AMPI contribution through committees **16**, 7459-60

on attack ads **6**, 2474-75

attitude toward working for Government **6**, 2477-78

on career **6**, 2445-46

with Chapin and Moore on Segretti matter **6**, 2485-86

cleans out files after Watergate break-in news **6**, 2457-59, 2505

on Colson and milk money **16**, 7467-68

on Colson's memo to Haldeman on antitrust suit against AMPI **16**, 7464, 7466-67

on Colson's role on White House staff **6**, 2487

on Dean's ability to recollect **6**, 2450-51

on Dean's advice before FBI interview **6**, 2464

on Dean's relationship with Haldeman **6**, 2449-50, 2460-61

on Dean's testimony on Magruder's statement that he had authorized Liddy's activities **6**, 2506-2507

on Dean's truthfulness **6**, 2477

denies attending coverup meetings **6**, 2491

denies discussing price supports with Ehrlichman or Whitaker **16**, 7457-58

denies knowledge of Colson's "special project" funded by AMPI money **16**, 7462-63

denies knowledge of funnelling of money from Republican senatorial and congressional campaign committees to Finance Committee **16**, 7471

denies Magruder showed him Gemstone file **6**, 2451-52

on destruction of documents after Watergate arrests **6**, 2473-74, 2490-91

on destruction of political matters memos to Haldeman **6**, 2442

on dirty tricks **6**, 2474-76

on discussion of milk money between Haldeman and Dean **16**, 7458-59

on duties after 1970 re contributions **16**, 7455-56

on duties as staff assistant to Haldeman **6**, 2446-47

on Ehrlichman's and Haldeman's roles at White House **6**, 2501

on electronic surveillance in Liddy plan **6**, 2455-56

on FBI interview on Segretti matter **6**, 2502

on fundraising by Democrats for Nixon **16**, 7471

gives Dean list of documents he destroyed **6**, 2459

on grand jury testimony **6**, 2499-2500

on Haldeman as superior at White House **6**, 2503-2504

on Haldeman's assignment to contact Liddy **6**, 2455-56

Haldeman's calls monitored by **6**, 2493

on Haldeman's duties **6**, 2466-68

on Haldeman's instructions on fund solicitation **16**, 7462-63

on Haldeman's instructions to clean files **6**, 2471-72 **8**, 3061-62

on Haldeman's interest in political intelligence **6**, 2450

on Haldeman's private polls **6**, 2487-99

on Haldeman's role in campaign **6**, 2447-48

on Haldeman's staff **6**, 2466-67

on Haldeman's telephone monitoring system **6**, 2453-54

on Haldeman's testimony in conflict with his own **6**, 2504-2505

on Haldeman's work habits **6**, 2447, 2456

and hush money **6**, 2463-64

on identification of exhibits **16**, 7456-57

informs Haldeman he cleaned files **6**, 2459-60, 2472

on intent to tell truth **6**, 2438-39

on Kalmbach's rejection of AMPI contribution **16**, 7469

on learning of Liddy plan from Magruder **6**, 2452

on Liddy budget **6**, 2496

and Liddy-Magruder relationship **6**, 2466

on Liddy's role at CRP **6**, 2469

on likelihood of Dean disclosing facts to Haldeman **6**, 2451

on Magruder informing him of Gemstone plan **FR** 21, 23

on Magruder testimony that he knew about Liddy plan **6**, 2449

on Magruder's perjuries **6**, 2503

on Magruder's report after Key Biscayne meeting **6**, 2489

on material sent to Haldeman **6**, 2466

meeting with Haldeman after Watergate break-in **6**, 2458

on meeting with Magruder before grand jury testimony **6**, 2465

on meetings Haldeman attended on intelligence-gathering proposals **6**, 2492-94

meets with Haldeman before testifying before grand jury **6**, 2464-65

and CIA **8**, 3262

CIA credentials of **1**, 326

in Dean-Walters telephone call **9**, 3825-26E

identified by Baldwin **1**, 405

and lawyer's meeting **1**, 326

money for **6**, 2235, 2252

role in Watergate break-in **1**, 367 **FR** 1

See also Watergate defendants

Subversive Activities Control Board 6, 2425 **7**, 2692

Huston memo to Haldeman on **3**, 1062, 1331-32E

Sullivan, Jeremiah P., testimony of 12, 4996-5007

on arrests at demonstration against Nixon in Boston **12**, 5003, 5004

on connection between Vietnam war and violent demonstrations **12**, 5003

on demonstration at Nixon fundraising dinner in Boston **12**, 4996-5000

on intellience gathering prior to anti-Nixon demonstration in Boston **12**, 5000

on police ability to control demonstrations **12**, 5004, 5005-5006

recommendations to prevent violence at campaign functions **12**, 5000-5001

Sullivan, Maggie 20, 9583

Sullivan, William 3, 992, 993, 1056, 1069 **6**, 2389, 2421

and Ellsberg matter **6**, 2531

and FBI involvement with other Presidents **3**, 1071

and Kissinger tapes incident **6**, 2404-2408

and logs of wiretapped conversations between newsmen and White House staffers **3**, 920-21, 1069-71

memo **4**, 1387-88

relationship with Mardian **6**, 2422

and tapes **6**, 2392-93

Summa Corporation

and return of money to Davis **20**, 9422

See also Davis, Chester C., testimony of; Golden, James; Whearley, Robert Franklin, testimony of

Summary of investigation of "Possible Violations of Criminal Laws and Hatch Act by Veterans Administration Employees in Connection with the 1972 Presidential Campaign" 19, 9242-47E

Summers, W. Dennis, questioning by

Harrison **17**, 7679-81, 7685-88

Summit, Paul 11, 4892E

Sunday News **19**, 8836E

Supersonic transport

See SST issue

Supreme Court

Buchanan's recommendations on appointments to **10**, 3927

and electronic surveillance decision **FR** 105

and *Ex parte Millikin* case **6**, 2631

and *Hammerschmidt* v. *United States* **FR** 438-39

and *Linde* v. *United States* **8**, 3207, 3329-68E

on problem of publicity and fair trial **2**, 682-83

on separate corporate or union funds for political purposes **FR** 550-51

and *United States Civil Service Commission, et al.* v. *National Association of Letter Carriers, AFL-CIO, et al.* **FR** 438

See also Plamdon case; *Steel Seizure* case

Surrogate candidate program 2, 680

Porter on **2**, 632-33

Surveillance operations 1, 3, 26

See also Political intelligence

Suskind, Irving 20, 9404

Sutter, John Joseph

prestatement of **6**, 2219-20

See also Ulasewicz, Anthony T.

Suttle, Leo 14, 5922 **15**, 5959-60, 6503, 6525

and AMPI reimbursement scheme **15**, 6530-31

Svihlik, Charles FR 166

Swanke, Mrs. Albert Homer

letter from Republican National Finance Committee to **16**, 7428-29

letter from Stans on distribution of campaign funds **16**, 7429, 7436E

Swimming pool

at Nixon's Key Biscayne property **FR** 1038-41

Swinford, Irma 22, 10604

Swiss banks

and campaign contributions by corporations **FR** 459, 465-66

Sydnor, Norris FR 409

Sylvester, Ray 5, 2209E

Symington, J. Fife FR 494, 496

campaign contributions and ambassadorship and **FR** 497-501

interview with Select Committee staff **FR** 501

Symington, Stuart 8, 3244 **21**, 10127

Szebedinsky, Geno 12, 5026E, 5029E

Tabourian, Andre 13, 5501, 5502 **FR** 448

TAC unit

and Watergate break-in **1**, 96, 109, 110

Taft, Robert 12, 5027E

Tagawa, Walter 3, 1118E

Talbot, Daniel FR 145

Caulfield investigation of **22**, 10385-90

Talmadge, Herman E. 16, 7320, 7321-22 **20**, 9569

on breaking and entry **6**, 2601

on claim of attorney-client privilege for Segretti-Dean relationship **10**, 4022-23

on Cole's objections to line of questioning of Davis **22**, 10570, 10571, 10574-75, 10578, 10579, 10580

on Cole's request for transcript of Davis' testimony **22**, 10589

discussions with Mehren on antitrust suit against AMPI **16**, 7335

in dispute over Johnson's appearance **17**, 7693, 7694, 7695

and milk price-support issue **16**, 7317, 7318, 7399, 7401

on Nixon tapes **8**, 3091

on political secrecy **2**, 833-34

ruling on sealing Davis' testimony **22**, 10563-64

ruling on Wearley exhibits **20**, 9465

on Stans' career **2**, 743

TAPE contributions to **16**, 7323-24

on tax-exempt foundations **10**, 3949-50

votes in favor of motion for litigation against Nixon to procure tapes **7**, 2663

Teapot Dome scandal **2**, 778 **FR** 65, 96
  compared with Watergate **FR** 1101
  Select Committee to investigate **FR** 25
Ted Van Dyk Associates **FR** 606
  check to Jones **16**, 6999, 7043E
  check to Public Opinion Survey, Inc. **16**, 7003,
    7045E
  checks and statements to AMPI **16**, 7003, 7008,
    7047-48E, 7050-54E
  letter from AMPI with checks for Muskie cam-
    paign **16**, 7013, 7055-56E
  statement from Gallup Organization for services
    16, 7003, 7046E
  statement from Nickel for services **16**, 7007,
    7049E
  tax forms for Jones **16**, 6999, 7044E
Teeter, Bob **1**, 34
Telephone conversations
  Adler-Comegys **FR** 995
  alleged between Magruder and Colson **2**, 517-18
  anonymous to Rubin
    on Humphrey trip to Las Vegas **25**, 12160-63
  Barth-Rebozo on forthcoming IRS interview **23**,
    11232, 11233-34, 11245-48
  Beauford-Pepper **17**, 7718
  between Mitchell's home and White House **5**,
    1912-14
  Boggs-Caulfield after second Watergate break-in
    1, 279
  bogus, from McGovern committee **11**, 4628-29
  bogus, in New Hampshire primary **11**, 4660-61
  Buzhardt-Edward Nixon on press story about
    Hughes contribution **22**, 10550, 10594-95
  Buzhardt-McKiernan on newspaper stories on
    Hughes money **22**, 10546-49
  Campbell-Nelson after reversal of milk price-sup-
    port decision **17**, 7770-72, 7773-75
  Campbell-Parr **17**, 7734-35, 7737, 7738
  canvassing of Democratic party Convention dele-
    gates by McGovern campaign workers **25**,
    12194-96
  Caulfield-Ehrlichman after second Watergate
    break-in **1**, 279
  Caulfield-McCord **1**, 152-153, 161-62
  Chotiner-Nelson on Nixon's reversal of milk
    price-support decision **FR** 649
  Colson-Hunt on Ellsberg matter **FR** 120-21
  Colson-Magruder on Liddy plan **2**, 793-94 **6**,
    2284, 2302-2303 **FR** 23-24
  Connally-Dole **16**, 7268, 7269
  Connally-Mitchell **14**, 6115-16 **15**, 6462, 6464 **16**,
    7267-69
  Connally-Mitchell on antitrust suit against milk
    cooperatives **14**, 6075-76
  Connally-Mitchell on milk price supports **14**,
    6078-79
  Connally's records of **14**, 6056, 6080, 6092-94E
  Cushman-Ehrlichman on Hunt **8**, 3283, 3294
  to Dahlberg on checks **2**, 701
  Danner-Gemmill **23**, 11175
  Danner-Rebozo **20**, 9521-22
  Davis-Gemmill on return of Hughes contribution
    23, 11177-78, 11199
  to Dean after McCord's letter to Sirica is read in
    open court **3**, 1102-1003

  to Dean after Watergate arrests **3**, 932
  by Dean after Watergate break-in **4**, 1356
  Dean-Colson after Watergate arrests **3**, 932-33
  Dean-Gray on not interviewing Ogarrio or Dahl-
    berg **9**, 3534, 3535
  Dean-Gray on Walters' visit **9**, 3499
  Dean-Haldeman at Camp David **7**, 2901-2902
  Dean-Kalmbach **5**, 2097, 2112
  Dean-Maroules **4**, 1449, 1450
  Dean-Moore from Camp David **5**, 1971-72, 1987-
    88
  Dean-Moore on Watergate problems **3**, 1004-05
  Dean-Nixon on Watergate **3**, 998
  Dean-Petersen on Magruder grand jury testimony
    9, 3651
  Dean-Schlesinger **9**, 3417-18
  Dean-Treese urging Sloan to take Fifth Amend-
    ment at Barker trial **2**, 585-86
  Dent-Walters **24**, 11622
  and distribution of hush money **5**, 2100-2101,
    2102, 2116, 2117-18
  during Kalmbach's and Ulasewicz's distribution of
    hush money **6**, 2221
  by Eaton after IRS call **25**, 12312-14
  Ehrlichman requests Barth to inform Rebozo of
    IRS interview **23**, 11231, 11245-46
  Ehrlichman-Barth on tax report on O'Brien **23**,
    11224, 11243-44
  Ehrlichman-Gray on Dean handling Watergate
    investigation **9**, 3508-3509
  Ehrlichman-Kalmbach **5**, 2161-70, 2173-74 **7**,
    2737-39
  Ehrlichman-Kehrli after resignation **1**, 90, 91
  Ehrlichman-Kleindienst **9**, 3564-65, 3577-78
  Ehrlichman-Kleindienst on Select Committee **4**,
    1500-1501
  Ehrlichman-Petersen on Stans' testimony before
    grand jury **9**, 3580, 3618-19
  Ehrlichman-Walters on Barth's status at IRS **24**,
    11624
  English-Edidin on Hertz rentals **25**, 12240-41
  Fensterwald-Alch **1**, 308-309
  Fernandez-Priestes **13**, 5331, 5332
  Gemmill-Davis **24**, 11586-87
  Gemmill-Garment **23**, 11175, 11199
  Gemmill-IRS **23**, 11178-79
  Gray-Dean **9**, 3453-54, 3455-56, 3457
  Gray-Dean on CIA involvement in Watergate
    investigation **3**, 947
  Gray-Helms for meeting between representatives
    of FBI and CIA **8**, 3241
  Gray-MacGregor **9**, 3530-31, 3536 **12**, 4914-22,
    4937-39
  Gray-Walters **9**, 3438
  Greaves **FR** 192
  Griffin-Rebozo **22**, 10425-29
  Griffin-White House after interview with Select
    Committee staff **23**, 10788
  Haig-Richardson **FR** 1022-23
  Haig-Richardson on Cox investigation **23**, 10888-
    89, 10891, 11214-15, 11216-17
  Haldeman-Kehrli after resignation **1**, 90-91
  Haldeman-Magruder after Watergate arrests **2**,
    799, 828-29, 858-59
  Hunt-Barker on Nixon's forthcoming speech on
    mining of Haiphong Harbor **9**, 3745, 3746

Stans-LaRue and Mardian after Watergate arrests
2, 569
Stans-Mardian 6, 2366-67
Stans-Webb on list of contributors from Ashland
Petroleum 13, 5444-45
Stans-Wild 13, 5473
Stans-Wild for list of contributors 13, 5465
Strachan-Dean on Segretti 3, 962-63
Strachan-Magruder after Watergate break-in 6,
2456-57
threatening, against Baltimore CRP 12, 5098-99E
threatening, to Nixon supporters 12, 5117E
threatening, to Parr 16, 7447-48
Todd-author of unsigned note to Malek 18, 8475,
8577E
Ulasewicz-Mrs. Hunt 6, 2234-36
Ulasewicz-McCord 1, 253-254, 279-80, 285-92 FR
64
White House-Parr FR 636-37
Wild-Arnold before guilty plea on contribution
25, 12024, 12026
See also Taped conversations
Telephones
of Subcommittee on Air and Water Pollution Office, memo from Billings on 11, 4695, 4886-87E
See also Sterile telephones; Telephone conversations
Television
Colson meeting with network chief executives FR
281-84E
fundraising for McGovern on 25, 12168-69
litigation involving coverage of Senate Select
Committee hearings on FR 1079-80
public hearings of Select Committee on FR 31-32
See also Media
Tell It To Hanoi Committee 6, 2461-62 8, 3121 FR
154-55, 156
bogus ads by FR 318E, 324E
statement of account for FR 316E
Temple, Glenda 16, 6997, 7003
Temple, Larry 15, 6411, 6412, 6426
Tennessee Eastman Co.
payroll deductions by Volunteers for Better Government of FR 553
TerHorst, Jerald F. 9, 3807 FR 123
affidavit denying use of Hunt's material on Bou-
din 9, 3759, 3895-96E
Hunt testimony on article prepared for 9, 3673
Terker, Harry 4, 1787-88E
Terker, Richard 4, 1787-88E
Terrar, Edward 16, 7419, 7424 FR 739, 740
Terrell, Ed
letter and check from Lilly for National Republi-
can Campaign Committee 16, 7300, 7366E
Terrorism
and Caulfield's job with New York City Police
Department 1, 249
as Davis' reason for reluctance to discuss amount
of 1972 campaign contribution 22, 10562-63
Ehrlichman on 6, 2512-13
Mardian and 6, 2424

Texas
Armendariz report on Spanish-speaking campaign
in 19, 8785-88
Texas ad hoc Fund Raising Committee FR 514
Texas Democratic primaries
Segretti activities in FR 168
Texas Legislature
Mills speech to 16, 7107-7108
Texas Republican party 12, 5009, 5176-80E
Thatcher, Paul 25, 11722, 11741, 11755, 11790,
11809 FR 887
and Backers for Humphrey bank forms 25, 11889-
92E
Brooks check to 25, 11888E
business association with Fellows 25, 11766,
11774
check to Chestnut, Burkard, and Brooks trust account 25, 11887E, 11889E
and computer program for Humphrey campaign
25, 11737
discusses Loeb case with Humphrey FR 897
discusses Loeb contribution with Chestnut 25,
11727
and Duncan loan to Humphrey campaign 25,
11796-97, 11799, 11800
Fellows' information on pre-April 7 records to 25,
11777-78
and Humphrey campaign records 25, 11734
and loan to Humphrey campaign 25, 11741-43
and Loeb contribution 25, 11805-11806
and money left in Morrison's desk 25, 11757-58
Morrison's relationship with before 1972 25,
11751
and removal of cash from Morrison's desk 25,
11761
requests Fellows to review Humphrey campaign
books 25, 11774
responsibility for recordkeeping 25, 11771
Theberge, Roger 12, 5093E
Thieu, Nguyen Van 3, 1009
Thigpen, Dr. Neal D. 12, 5015-16, 5261E
letter to Select Committee 12, 5016, 5261-64E
Thigpen, Mrs. Neal D. 12, 5016
"13 Mistakes of Kennedy, The" 3, 993
Thomas, E. Perry 20, 9563
Thomas, Jane 4, 1592-94
Thomas, Pat 16, 6938
Thompson, Fletcher 12, 5076E
Thompson, Fred D. 3, 1246E 4, 1488
affidavit and detailed notes of telephone conversation with Buzhardt 4, 1794-1800E
on audience demonstrations during Ehrlichman
testimony 7, 2863, 2904, 2905
on Baker's request that counsels annotate with
page references to previous testimony 8, 3044
and Buzhardt memo, *see* Buzhardt memo
and discrepancy on date of Nixon-Dean meeting
4, 1567-68
on FBI reports shown to Segretti 10, 4009-10
on Frates' objections to line of questioning of
Rebozo 21, 9951
on hearsay evidence 9, 3813

Ulasewicz, Anthony T., testimony of
on activities for Caulfield in 1968-71 **FR** 109-111
on admission that serving as contact with
McCord was illegal **6,** 2270-71
on advising Kalmbach to stop handling money for
Watergate defendants **6,** 2237, 2243-44
after last contact with Kalmbach **6,** 2244-45
on airline travel with money **6,** 2226
on amount given to Mrs. Hunt **6,** 2245 **9,** 3750
on amounts asked for by Mrs. Hunt **6,** 2235-36,
2252-56
asked by Kalmbach to distribute money for Watergate defendants **6,** 2220-21
on assignments from Caulfield **6,** 2263-64
on assignments from Ehrlichman **6,** 2265, 2266
assumes Mrs. Hunt is in contact with someone
else **6,** 2242-43
attitude toward distributing funds for Watergate
defendants **6,** 2239-40
attitude toward investigative activities **6,** 2275-76
on authorization for deliveries of money to Watergate defendants **6,** 2262
on belief that distributing funds for Watergate defendants was legal **6,** 2248-49
on Caulfield's investigative assignments to him **6,**
2265-66
on consequences if cash were not delivered to Liddy **6,** 2241-42
contacted by Caulfield and interviewed by Ehrlichman for investigative job **6,** 2220
on contacts with Bittman **6,** 2225-27, 2228E
on contacts with Caddy **6,** 2249
on contacts with Mrs. Hunt **6,** 2227, 2228-30E,
2231, 2246, 2250-56 **9,** 3691-92
on current status of Watergate principals **6,** 2276
on delivery of funds to LaRue **6,** 2232-33
on delivery of money to Bittman **6,** 2256-60
on delivery of money to Hunt **6,** 2260
on delivery to Liddy **6,** 2229-32, 2260
denies contact with members of law-enforcing
agencies **6,** 2245-46, 2247
denies Mrs. Hunt discussed pardons or light sentences **6,** 2246, 2247
denies receiving instructions from anyone other
than Caulfield **6,** 2263
on determination of amounts for Watergate defendants **6,** 2262
duties on White House staff **1,** 291
on efforts to give money to lawyers of Watergate
defendants **6,** 2222-25
on end of assignment with Kalmbach **6,** 2246
on feelings of being used **6,** 2262
on feelings of suspicion **6,** 2261
on first contact with Kalmbach **6,** 2249-50
on first delivery of money to Mrs. Hunt **6,** 2236
on hiring by Caulfield and Ehrlichman **6,** 2238-39
on increased demands for money **6,** 2307
on investigative assignments for Caulfield **6,** 2268-
76
investigative work while on Kalmbach's payroll **6,**
2245-47, 2268-69, 2270
on last delivery of money for Watergate defendants **6,** 2237-38
on legality of distribution of money for Watergate
defendants **6,** 2244

lists deliveries and amounts of money for Watergate defendants **6,** 2221-22
on method of delivery **6,** 2268
on money delivered to Hunts **6,** 2228
on money found on Mrs. Hunt's body **6,** 2262-63
on Mrs. Hunt's attitude toward increasing demands for money **6,** 2241-42
on nontraceability of money for Watergate defendants **6,** 2241
photographs used during interrogation of **6,** 2228-
30E, 2276
on phrase "under the table" used by Mrs. Hunt **6,**
2248-49
on possibility of losing money for Watergate defendants **6,** 2240-41
on present-day residence and employment **6,** 2261
on previous experience with cash deliveries **6,**
2240
on reasons for calling McCord **6,** 2271
on reasons for not telling Caulfield about assignment with Kalmbach **6,** 2244, 2260
on salary and expense money received by himself
and Kalmbach **6,** 2238
on secrecy of assignment to distribute money to
Watergate defendants **6,** 2239-40
telephone contacts with Mrs. Hunt **6,** 2234-36
telephone conversations with Hunt **6,** 2233-34
on telling Mrs. Hunt he could not negotiate over
money **6,** 2242
tells Kalmbach methods for maintaining confidentiality of transactions **6,** 2221
on timing of questioning legality of money assignment **6,** 2267-68
on uneven distribution of money to Watergate defendants **6,** 2242

Ultra Systems, Inc., Newport Beach, California 13,
5400
OMBE grant to **FR** 385-86
Umberger, Mary 12, 5162E
Underwood, Cecil 3, 1130E **11,** 4437
Union Oil Co., California 13, 5456
United Auto Workers (UAW)
loan and contribution to McGovern campaign **25,**
12145-46
United California Bank
F. Donald Nixon's account at **22,** 10695-96,
10703-10704
San-Bar certificate of deposit given as support for
F. Donald Nixon's loan at **22,** 10712-14
United Dairy Association 17, 7657
United Democrats for Kennedy 11, 4641-42, 4671
letter from Robin Ficker, chairman, to New
Hampshire voter **10,** 3968, 3975, 4266E
United Farm Workers
anti-Nixon demonstration in Fresno, California
12, 4949-51, 4953, 4955-63, 5051-54E
and lettuce boycott **19,** 8772-73E
and McGovern campaign **25,** 12166-67, 12183 **FR**
511-12
and proposition 22 **12,** 4959-60
violence and **12,** 4959, 4960

Veterans Administration
investigation of Hatch Act violations by employees of **19**, 9242-48E
and Responsiveness Program **FR** 429-30
"Veterans Administration and Older Americans, The" **19**, 9201-9204E
Veterans Committee To Re-Elect the President
Campaign Plans for Veterans' Leaders **19**, 9248-82E
document on Veterans' Administration **FR** 429-30
Vice-Presidential elections
MacGregor on **11**, 4688-89 **12**, 4928
Vicky Holding Corp.
purchase of Nixon's San Clemente property by **23**, 10771, 10772
Viega, Frank 13, 5280, 5400, 5535E **FR** 391
Vietnam issue
and assault strategy on McGovern **10**, 4245E
as basis for campaign contribution decisions Mott on **25**, 12108
confidential memo from Haldeman to Colson, Buchanan, Cole, and Magruder on generating administration's position on **10**, 3975, 4120-26E
Humphrey on **10**, 4162E
leaflet on referendum on **10**, 4121E
McGovern on **10**, 4077-79E
McGovern record on **10**, 4072E
Muskie on **10**, 4148E
Nixon's speech on mining of Haiphong Harbor **9**, 3745, 3746
Vietnam Veterans Against the War (VVAW) 1, 201, 202, 234 **12**, 5085E, 5092-93E, 5223E, 5224E
at demonstration at Century Plaza, Los Angeles **11**, 4559
at meeting for planning demonstration against Nixon in Los Angeles **11**, 4543
demonstration in May 1971 **3**, 917
and McGovern campaign **FR** 146
office at Democratic National Committee or McGovern headquarters **1**, 223-224
Vietnam War
and anti-Nixon leaflets **12**, 4972, 5022-23E
circular on McGovern's record on **10**, 4026, 4298E
classified material in Hunt's safe on **3**, 937, 938
demonstration in Los Angeles against **11**, 4538-55
infiltration of antiwar demonstrations **FR** 198-99
leaflet for rally in Columbus, Ohio **12**, 5160E
Nixon and **7**, 2869-71
opponents of policies on enemies list **8**, 3155
in telephone conversation between Nixon and MacGregor **12**, 4941
and violent demonstrations **12**, 5003
See also Vietnam issue
Vietnamese Committee for Solidarity with the American People 12, 5199-5201E
Vietnamese Student Union for Peace 11, 4543
Vietnamization
and strategy for career military voters **FR** 430-41
Viglia, William 13, 5462-63. 5464
and Gulf Oil Corp. contribution **FR** 469

Villa, Pete 13, 5293-94, 5669E **FR** 403
Villalobos, Alfred R. 13, 5391, 5396-99 **FR** 391, 403-404
letter to Fernandez with report on NEDA **13**, 5749-67E
letter to Peterson and Kleppe on charges made against Fernandez **13**, 5394, 5743-46E
Villareal, Carlos 18, 8248
Vinas, Julian 13, 5371
Vine, John
See Edidin, Sol M., testimony of
Vinson, Elkins 15, 6469-70
Vinson, Fred M., Jr.
on correspondence with Stans re return of LaRue's leftover money to Finance Committee **6**, 2299
on LaRue's absences from room at Key Biscayne **6**, 2344-45
on LaRue's agreement with Federal prosecutors **6**, 2327-28
on LaRue's return of money to Finance Committee **6**, 2334-35
letter from Barker enclosing letter from Stans to LaRue **6**, 2635E
letter from Barrick on return of Ashland Petroleum contribution **13**, 5448, 5798-99E
letter from Cox to **6**, 2328, 2634E
letter to Stans on contribution of Mr. and Mrs. Atkins **13**, 5448, 5797E
letter to Stans requesting refund to Ashland Petroleum **13**, 5445-46
letters to Barker on LaRue's payments to Finance Committee **6**, 2637E, 2638E, 2639E, 2641E
memo to Lindenbaum on Dunes Hotel acquisition proposal **26**, 12925-26E
requests copy of transcript of LaRue testimony **23**, 11171-72
See also Atkins, Orin E., testimony of; LaRue, Fred C., testimony of
Violence
affidavits in lieu of testimony on **12**, 5007-17
against Baltimore CRP **12**, 5097-5101E
against Republican campaign in 1973 **8**, 3149-53
against Washington CRP **12**, 5188-93E
at Boston anti-Nixon demonstration **12**, 5033E
at Democratic National Convention in 1968 **12**, 4990, 4992
at demonstration against Nixon at Century Plaza, Los Angeles **11**, 4558-59
at Fall River, Massachusetts, Nixon Campaign Headquarters **12**, 5107-09E
at Fresno, California **12**, 5051-54E
at GOP Minnesota headquarters **12**, 5125-26E
at Lungren's office **12**, 5065-69E
at Nixon campaign dinner in Boston, *see* Sullivan, Jeremiah P., testimony of
at Nixon rally in California **12**, 4948-51, 4953, 4955-63
at Republican National Convention, *see* Carter, Tim Lee, testimony of
bombing at Madison **3**, 1332E
bombing of Manchester, New Hampshire, police station **12**, 5135-42E
Democratic party and **9**, 3606-2607

Violence *(Continued)*
during Nixon campaign, Haldeman on **8,** 3079-81
during Nixon's trip around South America **9,**
3404
expected by McCord **1,** 186-187, 234
fire at Austin, Texas, Republican Headquarters
12, 5176-80E
fire at Phoenix, Arizona, Nixon headquarters **12,**
5034-47E
Haldeman's claim of firebombed Nixon headquarters **11,** 4560-61
Higby asks Dean for list of Democrats' activities
relating to **3,** 1241E
and Huston Plan **7,** 2874
and intelligence reports to CRP **5,** 1842
and McCord's motivation for participation in Watergate **1,** 186-87, 199-202, 203, 242, 295, 297,
337
McGovern record on **10,** 4069-70E
and Nixon campaign in Manchester, New Hampshire **12,** 5127-34E
in plans for use of advance people **FR** 201-202
in Portland, Oregon **3,** 1330E
reports from Internal Security Division of Justice
Department to CRP on **1,** 178-181, 217-18, 246-
47, 348-49, 353
Strachan communicates with Haldeman on **8,**
3033
threatened against CRP, McCord on **1,** 174-175
vandalism against Albuquerque, New Mexico,
Nixon Campaign Headquarters **12,** 5143-46E
Virdin, D. O.
memo for file on establishment of Activist Organizations Committee **FR** 263-66E
Virgin Islands Corp.
Caulfield's investigation of **22,** 10400-10402
**Virginia Hispanic Finance Committee to Re-Elect the
President 13,** 5288
Visney, Tom FR 166, 174
political espionage activities **11,** 4640-41
Voice alteration device
requested from CIA by Hunt **8,** 3264, 3268
Volpe, John A. 12, 5115E **18,** 8475-77
Von Tobel
transcript of discussion with Gray and Dickerson
on Dunes Hotel acquisition **26,** 12790-91E
Vote siphoning schemes
and CRP **FR** 202-205
Voter registration
Baker recommendations on reform of **FR** 1111
Wachtel, Harry FR 297E
Wagner, Carl 9, 3502, 3678, 3729, 3756
Wagner & Baroody
AMPI and **15,** 6651-55
Colson and **15,** 6469
Kalmbach denies knowledge of **17,** 7598-99
Masters denies knowledge of **16,** 6961
Parr denies knowledge of **15,** 6892-93
payments from AMPI **FR** 694-98
"Wake Up Liberals" 10, 3934, 4055-58E
Wakefield, Thomas H. 20, 9610 **21,** 9946, 9948, 9949,
9951-52, 9961, 9971, 9981, 9990-91, 10002, 10064,
10075-77, 10143 **22,** 10237, 10272, 10453, 10489,
10502 **23,** 11178, 11185 **24,** 11279-11345 **FR** 942

accounts of **FR** 1037
check from Rebozo **22,** 12471E
check to Florida Finance Committee **24,** 11281,
11346E
checks in payment for Nixon's expenses **24,**
11312, 11316-17, 11320-22, 11372-84E
checks to Catalina Pools, Inc. **24,** 11312, 11372-
74E
checks to Finance Committee **24,** 11281, 11346E
correspondence on campaign fundraising and contributions **24,** 11352-69E
interviewed by Armstrong **24,** 11286-87, 11291-94
and invoices for Nixon **23,** 10962-63
and keys to Rebozo's safety boxes **21,** 10013
letter from Rebozo to
conflicts in testimony on **FR** 1057-58
Moncourt denies knowledge of Rebozo's instructions in safe-deposit box to **22,** 10522
and Nixon's purchase and sale of Key Biscayne
property **23,** 10770, 10772, 10773
Rebozo's instructions to **21,** 10008-1009 **FR** 969
and Rebozo's safe deposit box **21,** 10016
receipts for contributions made by **24,** 11281,
11347-51E
and return of Hughes contribution **FR** 1014
safe-deposit box records, lease, and visitation card
24, 11370E
Select Committee subpoena for records on Special
Account of **22,** 12585-86E
special account for Rebozo **22,** 10506, 10508
subpoena duces tecum for **24,** 11279-80
Wakefield, Thomas H., Special Account FR 942
check to Kalmbach from **23,** 10863E, 10868E
and payment of Ulasewicz **23,** 10860
signature card for **24,** 11297, 11371E
Wakefield on **24,** 11282-83, 11307-11309
Wakefield, Thomas H., testimony of 24, 11279-11345
on appearance of money in Rebozo's safety deposit box **24,** 11294-95
on attorney-client privilege with Nixon and Rebozo **24,** 11308, 11313, 11329, 11339, 11343-45
on attorney-client relationship with Nixon and
Rebozo **24,** 11279, 11280, 11284, 11286-88,
11290-94, 11297, 11298, 11300-11302, 11303-
11305, 11306-11307, 11308 **FR** 969
on bank accounts held by **24,** 11306-10
on Buchanan's stock in Fishers Island Corp. **24,**
11284, 11285
on business or financial relationships with Rebozo
24, 11281-84
denies instructions from Nixon or his designate
24, 11345
on difference between attorney account and trustee account **24,** 11307-10
on discussing waiver of attorney-client privilege
with Buzhardt **24,** 11341
on discussions with Greer and Frates on waiver of
attorney-client privilege **24,** 11288
on fees received from Nixon **24,** 11342-43
on financial transactions re Conden Corp. **24,**
11305-11306
on joint account with Rebozo **24,** 11282-83
on Key Biscayne land transaction **24,** 11338-40

on keys to Rebozo's safety deposit boxes **24,** 11289 **FR** 971-72, 1058

on knowledge of Hughes contribution **24,** 11295

on meeting with Ehrlichman and Rebozo **FR** 943-44

on meeting with Nixon and Rebozo **FR** 943

on money in Rebozo's safety deposit box **24,** 11295-96

on Nixon's loan from First National Bank of Miami **24,** 11336-40

on Nixon's sale of Key Biscayne property to Griffin **24,** 11332-33

on offices held in corporations **24,** 11281-82

on partnership between Rebozo, Abplanalp, and Nixon **24,** 11331-33

on Rebozo as agent for Nixon **24,** 11333-36

on Rebozo paying bills for Nixon **24,** 11311-29

on Rebozo purchasing Key Biscayne property **24,** 11332

on Rebozo's instructions re safety deposit box **24,** 11296

on Rebozo's trust account **FR** 1034

on records brought to hearing **24,** 11281

on relationship with Rebozo **24,** 11281

on reporting expenditures on behalf of Nixon to Kalmbach and DeMarco **24,** 11341-42

on return of Hughes contribution **24,** 11289-90

on safety deposit box held with Rebozo **24,** 11283, 11286, 11295-96

on Thomas H. Wakefield Special Account with Rebozo **24,** 11297-98

on Wakefield, Hewitt & Webster trust account **24,** 11298-11301

Wakefield, Thomas H., Trust Account
and payment for Nixon's Key Biscayne property improvements **FR** 1034-47

and transfers from Florida Nixon for President Account **FR** 1047

Wakefield, Hewitt & Webster trust account
deposit slip for **24,** 11323, 11385E

and Rebozo's payment of Nixon's expenses **24,** 11311-29

Wakefield on **24,** 11298-11301

Walker, Charlie
Barth's briefings on IRS sensitive case reports to **24,** 11631

Walker, Deloss 14, 6161 **17,** 7667
letter to Sanders re AMPI-related files **25,** 12076-87E

Walker, Ronald H. 10, 4190E **11,** 4639 **13,** 5414
on activities of advancemen **FR** 201-202

and Charlotte, North Carolina, demonstrations **8,** 3191

confidential memo from Buchanan **10,** 3975, 4173E

and dirty tricks operation **FR** 160

Haldeman on duties of **8,** 3190-92

letter to Mitchell from Sloan on accounting of $2,000 Haldeman requested for **8,** 3190, 3324E

memo from Dean on Wilkes to **22,** 10399

memo to Haldeman on Charlotte, North Carolina, demonstrations **8,** 3151-53, 3190, 3322-23E

and Sedan Chair I **FR** 190

Walker, Roy FR 453

Walker, Sonny 19, 8616E

Walker and Associates, Inc. 17, 7666
and order from AMPI for bumper stickers for Mills **FR** 922-23

Wall Street Journal **16,** 7464, 7492-93E
and dairy industry contributions in 1971 **16,** 7425

Wallace, Charles 18, 8273-74 **FR** 409
affidavit on allegations concerning SBA contacts **19,** 8854-56E

documents relating to **19,** 8848-58E

form letter on support for Nixon **19,** 8850-51E

letter from Hershman to Dash on allegations about **19,** 8857-58E

Small Business Administration contract to **FR** 406-407

Wallace, Don
affidavit of **17,** 8001E

Wallace, G. C. "Gus" 19, 9243E

Wallace, George C. 1, 396 **2,** 477 **10,** 4060E, 4226E
AMPI contributions to **15,** 6548, 6613-15, 6830-31 **16,** 7114

and attack strategy **10,** 4227-29E

attempted assassination of **1,** 201 **9,** 3735

bogus Muskie literature against **11,** 4410

campaign in California **11,** 4714E

campaign in Philadelphia **11,** 4712E

campaign money used for opponents of **8,** 3093-94

campaign of **11,** 4652

campaign of 1970 against Brewer **16,** 7206

Colson asks Hunt about **3,** 1170E

CRP and **2,** 541

and dirty tricks in Florida campaign **11,** 4663-64

on enemies list **4,** 1556-57

and fissures in Democratic party **10,** 4200E

in Florida primaries **11,** 4662

and funds going into Alabama campaigns in 1970 **5,** 2144-45

Haldeman on support for candidate opposing **7,** 2875-76

Kalmbach gives money to opponent of **4,** 1536-37

in memo from Magruder on interest groups **19,** 8817-18E

money given to opponent **4,** 1581-82

and Muskie's defeat in Florida primary **10,** 3902

and plan to investigate Bremer **FR** 129

in primaries **10,** 4232E

Republican support of Brewer candidacy against **FR** 594, 595

and re-registration of American Independent party voters **11,** 4643-44

results of Harris polls vs. Nixon and Muskie **11,** 4695, 4764-65E

Segretti literature on **FR** 169

and Segretti's activities in Florida primary **10,** 4020

Wallace, Glenn C. FR 429

Wallace, Henry 10, 4074E

Wallace, Mike 7, 2815-16 **10,** 3962

Wallace, Tom 10, 4026, 4302E

Wallace & Wallace Fuel Oil Co., Inc. 18, 8273-74 **FR** 406-407
form letter on minority enterprise advancements in "8-A Program" **18,** 8273, 8423-26E

Wallace & Wallace Fuel Oil Co., Inc. *(Continued)*
  questionnaire on Nixon's re-election **19**, 8853E
Wallenstein, Elaine FR 562-63
Wally Cruttenden & Co. 22, 10678
Walters, Dave 2, 979 **3**, 1072, 1080, 1154E
Walters, Joe A.
  letter from Dash on confidentiality of affidavits
    25, 11926-28E
  letter to Costa with confirmation statements of
    sale of Archer-Daniels-Midland stock **25**,
    11929E
  letter to Dash with affidavits of McMurtrie, Hast-
    ings, and Andreas **25**, 11918-22E
  letter to Sanders with Andreas check **25**, 11953-
    55E
  letters to Costa re deposits to Jackson and Com-
    pany by Backers for Humphrey **25**, 11897-
    11906E
  loan to Humphrey campaign **25**, 11773
  memo from Costa and Keema to Sanders on
    meeting on Humphrey campaign finances with
    25, 11969-72E
  objections to taking of Fellows' testimony **25**,
    11765
  objects to Sanders' statement on GAO report of
    Humphrey campaign finances **25**, 11782
  requests transcript of Fellows testimony **25**, 11785
  See also Chestnut, Jack L., statement of; Fellows,
    Ben E., testimony of; Morrison, John, statement
    of
Walters, Johnnie M. 22, 10358 **23**, 10927
  affidavit re O'Brien meetings with IRS **24**, 11640,
    11667-71E
  Barth and **22**, 10358-59
  Barth on relationship with **23**, 11248
  and Barth showing sensitive case reports to Ehr-
    lichman **FR** 134
  and Barth's call to Rebozo **23**, 11232
  correspondence referring to White House oppo-
    nents list **24**, 11656, 11684-11716E
  handwritten notes **24**, 11672-74, 11679
  handwritten notes for briefing with Connally **24**,
    11632, 11665E
  handwritten notes for briefing with Shultz **24**,
    11628, 11657-64E
  and IRS audit of O'Brien **FR** 1026, 1027, 1028-29
  and IRS investigation of MPI **FR** 716-17
  in IRS Talking Paper **4**, 1683-84E
  meeting with Ehrlichman, Shultz, and Barth on
    IRS investigation of Hughes Tool Co. and
    O'Brien **21**, 9683-84
  meetings with Dean on enemies list **23**, 11244
  meets with Shultz and Barth on O'Brien tax re-
    port **23**, 11223-24, 11241
  memo from Haldeman on IRS responsiveness **8**,
    3136-37
  memo in IRS interview of Rebozo and F. Donald
    Nixon **23**, 11244-45
  in memo on IRS and enemies list **FR** 8-9
  memo to Shultz on IRS interview with Rebozo
    24, 11675-78E **FR** 1001-1003
  and political enemies project **FR** 132-33
  and sensitive case reports by IRS to Treasury De-
    partment **23**, 10926, 10927

and tax-exempt foundations **FR** 142
Walters, Johnnie M., interview with 24, 11621-56
  on appointment as Commissioner of Internal
    Revenue Service **24**, 11623-25
  on awareness of problems with Barth's role in
    IRS **24**, 11627
  on Barth's relationship to Administration **24**,
    11625-26
  on briefing in Las Vegas on Hughes-Meier investi-
    gation **24**, 11633-34
  on briefings to Shultz on Hughes-Meier investiga-
    tion **24**, 11628-37
  career at IRS and with Federal Government **24**,
    11621-22
  on cases handled while Assistant Attorney Gener-
    al of Tax Division **24**, 11623
  changes Barth's assignments at IRS **24**, 11625-26
  on confidential memo on Rebozo and F. Donald
    Nixon involvement in IRS Hughes investigation
    24, 11648-50
  on Connally's role in Hughes-Meier investigation
    24, 11630-31
  on conversation with Simon on Rebozo and F.
    Donald Nixon involvement in Hughes investiga-
    tion **24**, 11647-48
  on decision to proceed with IRS interview of
    Rebozo and F. Donald Nixon **24**, 11650-51
  on delays in IRS interviews of prominent in-
    dividuals **24**, 11654-55
  denies discussing IRS cases with Nixon **24**, 11653
  denies discussion of Hughes or Rebozo cases with
    Ehrlichman, Mitchell, or Kleindienst **24**, 11646-
    47, 11653
  on first knowledge of tax cases involving Hughes
    Tool Co. and Meier **24**, 11627-28
  on handling of sensitive case reports **24**, 11628
  on information on requests for interviews of
    prominent individuals **24**, 11642-43
  on IRS case against Ryland **24**, 11655
  on IRS investigation of O'Brien **24**, 11644-46
  on IRS material to Dean **24**, 11634
  on IRS staff opinions of Barth **24**, 11625
  on meeting with Malek on Barth's status **24**,
    11625
  on meetings with Shultz and Connally **24**, 11636-
    37
  on notification of IRS intent to interview Rebozo
    and F. Donald Nixon **24**, 11643
  on notification to Rebozo and F. Donald Nixon
    of forthcoming IRS interviews **24**, 11651-52
  on postponement of O'Brien interviews by IRS
    until after elections **24**, 11642
  on purpose of IRS sensitive case reports **24**,
    11629-30
  on reasons for leaving IRS **24**, 11656
  on recruitment for position as Assistant Attorney
    General of Tax Division **24**, 11621-23
  on relationship with Gemmill **24**, 11621
  on reopening of IRS audit of O'Brien **24**, 11653
  reports to Shultz on sensitive case reports **24**,
    11635-36
  on status of Barth at IRS related to appointment
    of commissioner **24**, 11624-27
  on status reports on Hughes investigation **24**,
    11638

uncovering of Watergate facts by **7,** 2762-63
on wiretaps on Halperin and Lake **11,** 4695, 4884E
Ziegler on reports in **3,** 1082
See also Anderson, Jack; Segretti matter

Washington Star **11,** 4439, 4697E
on Humphrey's free taxi rides in **11,** 4438-39, 4450
on responsibility for Watergate **1,** 197

"Washington Straight Talk"
excerpt from Mills appearance on **25,** 12070-71E

Water Pollution Control, Inc. **21,** 10087

Watergate
CIA destruction of tapes on **FR** 1131-34
as country's greatest tragedy **6,** 2480
Dean learns of **3,** 931-38, 1265-66E
Dean's list of indictable persons **3,** 1013, 1312E
Dean's reactions to **3,** 1039-40
Ervin on antidote for **FR** 1103
Ervin on reasons for **FR** 1101-1103
Ervin review of **FR** 1098-1101
Haldeman on perspective on **7,** 2868
Heller on youth reaction to **12,** 4974-75
Hunt's actions after **9,** 3688-90
impact on political system **FR** 1212-22
impact on reputations of White House people **8,** 3130-33
Kleindienst on **9,** 3591
MacGregor on impact on Nixon campaign **12,** 4912-14, 4932
Magruder's behavior after learning about **2,** 798-800
Mankiewicz on impact of **11,** 4601-4604
McGovern campaign and **11,** 4625
meeting in California after **2,** 661-62
Nixon on investigation of **12,** 4924-25
Nixon's fact-finding efforts on **8,** 3073-74
preparations for Ziegler press conference on **3,** 1200-1208E
and Rebozo's decision to return Hughes contribution **21,** 9993-94
and return of Hughes money **21,** 10115
Select Committee attitude toward **FR** 23, 24-25
Sheridan investigation of **25,** 12159-60
Stans on role in **2,** 785-86
status among other issues at White House **6,** 2519-20
and termination of Responsiveness Program **18,** 8285-86

Watergate break-in
American Presidency and **1,** 7-8
attempt to blame on CIA **1,** 206-208
attempted **1,** 377
Baldwin's role in **1,** 398-406, 411-13
Barker on **1,** 358, 367-69, 371, 383-84
Barker's motivation for participation in **1,** 358, 360, 365-67, 372, 383
Barker's role in **1,** 382-83
Barrett on **1,** 115-116
believed legal action by Hunt **9,** 3738, 3739
Buchanan on **10,** 3971-72
Buchanan on impact on election of Nixon **10,** 3902-3903
Buchanan on news summaries to Nixon on **10,** 3947-48

Buckley's reaction to **11,** 4453
budget approval for **4,** 1644
Caulfield's telephone call to Ehrlichman after **1,** 279
CIA and **1,** 129-130 **2,** 774
Barker on **1,** 360, 379-81
Colby denies CIA knowledge of **FR** 1159
Colson tells Ehrlichman about plans for **7,** 2801
conflict in Helms testimony on discussion at Helms-Walters-Ehrlichman-Haldeman meeting **8,** 3244-47, 3249
considered legal action by Hunt **9,** 3739-40
contingency plan in event of arrest **1,** 175
cost of **1,** 220-221
and CRP relations to White House **FR** 18-20
Cubans and **9,** 3820E
Danner-Rebozo discussions on **24,** 11548-49
Davis-Bennett discussions on **24,** 11602
Dean learns about **4,** 1356
Dean on Nixon's involvement in **4,** 1407
Dean on reasons for concern of White House over **3,** 1022
Dean proposes independent commission on **7,** 2742
Dean reports to Nixon on **7,** 2896-97
Dean suggests Cuban conspiratorial plot to Walters **9,** 3412-13
Dean's list of those involved in **3,** 1053-54
Dean's presumed involvement in **4,** 1379-80
Dean's prior knowledge about **3,** 1022-24
democratic system and **1,** 2-3
deniability for Mitchell **1,** 218-219
destruction of CRP records after **1,** 26-27
dirty tricks after **11,** 4376
discussion between Abplanalp, Danner, and Rebozo **24,** 11472
in discussions between Danner and Rebozo **24,** 11463
distinguished from White House horror stories by Mitchell **5,** 1900-1902, 1903
double-agent theory of **9,** 3528
Ehrlichman denies prior knowledge of **6,** 2579-80
Ehrlichman learns about **6,** 2539-41, 2554, 2580-87
Ehrlichman on problem to White House created by **6,** 2556-57
Ehrlichman tells Gray that Dean will handle White House investigation of **9,** 3508-3509
Ehrlichman's actions after **7,** 2759
Ehrlichman's handwritten notes of interviews on **7,** 2730, 2915-43E
Ehrlichman's inquiry on **7,** 2750-57
enemies list as concept leading to **FR** 7-12
Ervin reviews **2,** 855-57 **7,** 2790-91
expenses and salaries for **1,** 168-170
facts uncovered immediately after **4,** 1460
first **FR** 28-29
Magruder reports to Strachan on **2,** 843
McCord on **1,** 164
Mitchell on **4,** 1618
Mitchell's conflict of testimony on knowledge of **5,** 1880-81
and Gemstone plan **1,** 206 **9,** 3746-47, 3792 **FR** 20-27
Gray learns about **9,** 3450

White House accusation that Dean was involved in **4,** 1412-14
See also Watergate burglars; Watergate defendants

Watergate burglars
aliases of **1,** 112-113, 116
apprehension of **FR** 31
arrests of **FR** 2
cash found on **2,** 621-22, 761
CIA backgrounds and connections of **9,** 3427-28
CRP financing of **5,** 2013-14
indictment of **FR** 48
and Mexican checks
See Mexican checks
money found in possession of **2,** 576-77
motivations of **FR** 28

Watergate Committee
See Senate Select Committee on Presidential Campaign Activities

Watergate complex 1, 99E, 1006
aerial photographs **1,** 99E, 100E
Watergate building in relation to Howard Johnson's Motor Lodge **1,** 101E

Watergate coverup
civil suits and **5,** 1899
and conflicts in testimony on September 15 meeting **8,** 3124-25
and Dahlberg and Mexican checks **FR** 37
Dean attempts to end **3,** 1000
Dean blamed by White House for **4,** 1415-29
Dean exposes to prosecutors **3,** 1008-09
Dean on Nixon's knowledge about **4,** 1567
Dean tells Moore about **5,** 2043-44
Dean tells Nixon about **3,** 998-1000, 1046-47 **4,** 1381, 1541-46 **4,** 1400-1408
Dean tells Nixon about his involvement in **3,** 992-93
and Dean-Nixon meetings **FR** 48-51, 83-89
Dean's Camp David report on **3,** 1006, 1263-93E
Dean's claim that he informed Nixon on September 15, 1972 of **7,** 2889
Dean's decision to end **4,** 1518
Dean's decision to inform Nixon about **5,** 1939, 1945, 1977-78, 1979, 1980-81, 1982, 1986-87
and Dean's efforts to retrieve Hunt photos of Fielding break-in from CIA **FR** 75-76
Dean's involvement in **4,** 1414-15
Dean's list of those involved in **3,** 1053-54 **4,** 1571-72
as Dean's main campaign duty **4,** 1591
Dean's reasons for exposing **3,** 1094
Dean's reasons for participation in **3,** 1040-41
Dean's role in **3,** 1026-27 **4,** 1357-58
and Democratic National Committee suits against CRP **FR** 74-75
and disposition of contents of Hunt's safe **FR** 35-37
during first three days after break-in **FR** 32-35
and efforts to blame Mitchell **FR** 91
and efforts to block Patman Committee hearings **3,** 959-62
Ehrlichman on Dean's involvement in **7,** 2743-44
and Ehrlichman's Watergate investigation **FR** 90
Ervin on extent of **FR** 1100-1101

extent of **FR** 31-32
Gray on **9,** 3503
Gray on Dean's efforts to stop FBI investigation and **9,** 3511-12
Gray's suspicions of **9,** 3523
guilty pleas of Watergate defendants as confirmation of **FR** 31-32
Haldeman on **7,** 2883-84
Haldeman's description of **8,** 3199-3200
Haldeman's discussions with Dean on his own vulnerability on **8,** 3077-78
Helms on efforts to use CIA in **8,** 3273
help sought from CIA on **3,** 1037
and hush money **FR** 51-62
initial success of **FR** 48
and Kalmbach **4,** 1369-71
Kleindienst and **9,** 3583-84
knowledge on White House staff of **4,** 1438-39
La Costa meetings on **3,** 982-86
LaRue on Dean's and Mitchell's awareness of **6,** 2324
LaRue on involvement in **6,** 2277-78, 2323-24
LaRue on motivation for **6,** 2311
LaRue on reasons for involvement in **6,** 2306, 2326-27, 2340-41
MacGregor denies knowledge of **12,** 4908-4909
MacGregor on need for **12,** 4914
Magruder names participants in **2,** 822-23, 834-36
Magruder on **2,** 800-804, 816-17, 818, 837-38, 848-49, 850-51, 852-53, 869-73
Magruder on failure of **2,** 805-806
Magruder on his participation in **2,** 801-803
and Magruder perjury **FR** 44-46
and Mardian-LaRue-Liddy meeting **FR** 40-41
Mardian's reasons for involvement in **6,** 2392
Mardian's testimony conflicting with others on his role in **6,** 2377
and meeting at San Clemente **4,** 1510-11
Mitchell and **5,** 1817-18
Mitchell denies discussion at White House on **5,** 1889-90
Mitchell denies knowledge of **4,** 1671-72
Mitchell on Dean's role in **5,** 1900-1901
Mitchell on Dean's testimony on **4,** 1648
and Mitchell's meeting with Dean **3,** 1309E
Mitchell's role in **4,** 1624-26
Moore denies discussions with Nixon and Dean on **5,** 1959
Moore denies knowledge of **5,** 1968
Moore encourages Dean to tell Nixon about **5,** 2044
Moore on involvement of Haldeman, Ehrlichman, or Dean in **5,** 2007
Moore on Nixon's possible knowledge of **5,** 2005-2006
Moore urges Nixon to tell nation about **5,** 1984
motivations for **2,** 856-57
and Nixon **4,** 1462-64
Nixon and Dean on **3,** 1027-31
Nixon's denial of involvement in **3,** 1077
Nixon's involvement in **3,** 1372-73 **9,** 3433
Nixon's knowledge of **4,** 1400-1407 **5,** 2021
Nixon's reaction after Dean tells him about **5,** 1893-95
Nixon's speech condemning Dean on **3,** 1076-79

Weicker, Lowell P., Jr. *(Continued)*
  on political spying **11**, 4631-32
  on possibility of conflict between Ehrlichman's
    and Haldeman's testimony **7**, 2863
  on presence of Senator at closed sessions **18**, 8256
  on qualities of White House staff reflected on by
    Watergate **8**, 3130, 3132
  on Rebozo documents **21**, 10020-21, 10023-24,
    10025, 10026, 10027, 10028, 10029, 10031,
    10032, 10033-34, 10035, 10036, 10037, 10136,
    10142
  relationship with Gray **9**, 3489
  on relevance of questions on anti-Nixon demon-
    stration at Century Plaza, Los Angeles **11**,
    4594-95
  on Republicans **4**, 1504
  rulings during Buzhardt testimony **23**, 10918,
    10919, 10920
  on scheduling Rebozo's testimony **21**, 9973,
    10018-19, 10037-38, 10139
  on Slater's voluntary testimony **13**, 5517-18
  on St. Clair's interpretation of Nixon's instruc-
    tions to Haig on executive privilege **23**, 10850-
    51, 10853
  on tactics used by Republicans in 1972 campaign
    8, 3174
  in taped telephone conversation between Klein-
    dienst and Ehrlichman **4**, 1500-1501 **7**, 2944E
  on tapes as repository of truth **8**, 3108-3109
  told by Gray that he had destroyed Hunt files **7**,
    2676-77
  on use of word Communist **8**, 3205-3206
  wants Sullivan as witness **3**, 1070-71
  on Watergate investigation ordered by Nixon **9**,
    3652-53
  on White House attitude toward Select Committee
    hearings **4**, 1497
  White House efforts to embarrass **4**, 1502-1503
Weicker, Lowell P., Jr., questioning by
  Atkins **13**, 5458
  Baldwin **1**, 391-409
  Barker **1**, 382-83
  Barrett **1**, 115
  Benz **11**, 4421-25, 4431, 4432
  Buchanan **10**, 3960-65, 3971-75
  Buckley **11**, 4459-63, 4474-76
  Butterfield **5**, 2086-88
  Buzhardt **22**, 10551, 10552 **23**, 10878-80, 10882,
    10884-86, 10889, 10900, 10902-03, 10907-09,
    10915-16
  Caulfield **1**, 273-275
  Connally **14**, 6071-73, 6078, 6079, 6088-89
  Cushman **8**, 3308, 3309
  Danner **19**, 9302
  Dean **3**, 1055-59, 1063-74 **4**, 1495-1504
  DeYoung **13**, 5529, 5530
  Ehrlichman **6**, 2625-30 **7**, 2663-79, 2773-90, 2811-
    14, 2861-63
  Gray **9**, 3489-94, 3522-25, 3545-47
  Haig **23**, 11000-11001, 11004, 11006-11, 11015-18,
    11022, 11025, 11032-33
  Haldeman **8**, 3104-3109, 3127-32, 3149-53, 3171-
    74, 3189-95, 3203-3207
  Harmony **2**, 476-78

  Helms **8**, 3273-76, 3280
  Hunt **9**, 3698, 3701-3703, 3741-46, 3771-75, 3786-
    89, 3797-3802
  Kalmbach **5**, 2121-27, 2173-76
  Kehrli **1**, 90-93
  Kleindienst **9**, 3596-99, 3607, 3608
  LaRue **6**, 2333-38
  Leeper **1**, 114
  MacGregor **12**, 4914-21, 4935-45
  Magruder **2**, 823-33
  Mankiewicz **11**, 4631, 4632
  Mardian **6**, 2403-10, 2419-29, 2434-35
  Marumoto **13**, 5308-10
  McCord **1**, 176-181, 221-27
  McMinoway **11**, 4533-36
  Mitchell **5**, 1869-92
  Moore **5**, 2029-45
  Odle **1**, 28-32, 34, 35, 70-72
  Petersen **9**, 3652-56
  Porter **2**, 668-71
  Priestes **13**, 5350-5353
  Rebozo **21**, 9958, 9966, 9969-71, 9986-89, 9993-
    97, 9999-10001, 10017-19, 10056-57, 10060-64,
    10069-70, 10105-06
  Reisner **2**, 510-13, 528-30
  Segretti **10**, 4015-17, 4034-37, 4041-44, 4051
  Shoffler **1**, 124
  Sloan **2**, 608-14
  Spater **13**, 5516-18
  Strachan **6**, 2481-85, 2504-06
  Sullivan **12**, 5003, 5004
  Taugher **11**, 4555
  Ulasewicz **6**, 2266, 2270-76
  Walters **9**, 3427-31, 3447, 3448
Weicker, Lowell P., Jr., statement of FR 1175-1229
  on Bill of Rights and Watergate FR 1189-95
  on due process of law and Watergate FR 1195-96
  on future "Watergates" FR 1228
  on impact of Watergate on electoral process FR
    1219-22
  on impact of Watergate on Government depart-
    ments FR 1208-12
  on impact of Watergate on intelligence communi-
    ty FR 1197-1204
  on impact of Watergate on law enforcement agen-
    cies FR 1204-1207
  on impact of Watergate on political system FR
    1212-22
  on impact of Watergate on regulatory agencies
    FR 1207-1208
  on impact of Watergate on Republicans FR 1227-
    28
  on Kent State and Jackson State FR 1174
  on legislative recommendations FR 1228-29
  on politics FR 1226-27
  on prelude to Watergate FR 1175-76
  on Presidential powers in Constitution and Water-
    gate FR 1178-87
  on seriousness of Watergate FR 1222-26
  on U.S. Constitution related to Watergate FR
    1176-96
  on writing of Watergate Final Report FR 1222-23

Weiglin, Fred **25**, 12233
Weil, Gordon **10**, 4247E
Weinberger, Cap **3**, 1115E
Weisgerber, Joseph A. **19**, 8872-81E
Weiss, Brownston, Rosenthal, Heller and Schwartz-
man **25**, 12245
Weiss, Jesse **3**, 1152E
Weitz, Alan S. **14**, 6148
affidavit with attachments of **14**, 6222-44E **17**,
8002-11E
on documents produced by Townsend **14**, 6294-95
on Harrison's request for open hearing **14**, 6245-
46
on justification for questioning Haldeman on con-
tributions in 1969 **16**, 7156-57
letter from Russell on money delivered to employees of AMPI **15**, 6779, 6910E
letters from Mehren **16**, 7187, 7220-23E
on request for public hearing for Townsend **14**,
6293-94
Weitz, Alan S., questioning by **17**, 7686-87
Alagia **16**, 7059-82, 7084
Butterbrodt **17**, 7625-32, 7633-57, 7673
Campbell **17**, 7749-82, 7786
Connally **14**, 6051-87
Ehrlichman **16**, 7373-99
Haldeman **16**, 7155-83
Hanman **14**, 5859-73, 5881-95 **17**, 7731-40, 7747-
48
Harrison **14**, 6246-55, 6660-78, 6280-81 **17**, 7681,
7688-92
Jacobsen **15**, 6379-6419, 6421-57, 6459-78
Kalmbach **17**, 7577-97, 7598-7621, 7805-11
Lilly **14**, 4919-20, 5907-14, 5921-24, 5933-47,
5956-84, 6105-23, 6125-30, 6136-39, 6158-60,
6164-71, 6173-76
Masters **16**, 6937-45, 6945-48, 6949-61, 6968-69,
6972
Mehren **16**, 7229-74, 7278-7316
Nelson **15**, 6501-75, 6617-88, 6697-6700
Nunn **17**, 7535-69, 7573-75
Paarlberg **16**, 7524-25, 7526, 7527, 7528-29, 7531
Parr **15**, 6791-6829, 6885-6906
Semer **16**, 7187-7211, 7218
Townsend **14**, 6293-6327
Van Dyk **16**, 6983-7011
Welch and Stanley
Dean's former employment at **3**, 1045-46
Welfare
and assault strategy on McGovern **10**, 4243-44E
and McGovern **10**, 4260-61E
Welfare rights protesters **12**, 5187E
Welling, Elaine **20**, 9583
Wells, Bernard **3**, 1058, 1066
Wells, Dr. Benjamin B. **19**, 9244-45E
Welsey, Burke **23**, 11233
Wenk, William **19**, 8888-90E **FR** 415
documents on recommendation and referral for
departmental commission of **19**, 8888-90E
Werner, Dave **13**, 5537E **25**, 12227
Edidin denies he had knowledge of Hertz arrange-
ment with Muskie campaign **25**, 12236, 12240

Werner, Robert **25**, 12224
Wertheim, Ronald B. **4**, 1564
West, Jack **12**, 5046-47E
West, Mickey **24**, 11573 **26**, 12788E
West Side Peace Committee (Los Angeles) **11**, 4544
West Virginia
Buckley's political activities in **11**, 4455, 4460
gubernatorial campaign of 1964 in **11**, 4471
Western Airlines
proposed merger with American Airlines **13**,
5503, 5508-10, 5512-14 **FR** 449
Western Union
money order receipt to Doug Kelley **10**, 4026,
4310E
Westwater, Joseph J. **14**, 5871, 5890, 5892, 5895,
6080, 6082, 6143 **15**, 6417, 6900, 6904-05
at meeting with Connally **15**, 6472-75
and contribution to Finance Committee **FR** 732
letter to Connally on federal programs relating to
dairy industry **14**, 6080, 6095-98E
meeting with Kalmbach and Morgan **15**, 6454-57
role in Dairymen, Inc. **FR** 585
and SPACE participation in efforts to obtain increased milk price supports **16**, 7062-63
and SPACE purchase of tickets for Republican
fundraising dinner **16**, 7076
Westwater, Lou (Mrs. Joseph Westwater) **16**, 7075
Westwater, Paul **15**, 6556
Wexler, Ann **11**, 4774E
"What the FBI Almost Found" (McCord) **9**, 2848-
49E, 3521-22
Whitaker, John C. **4**, 1702E **15**, 6806 **17**, 7756 **20**,
9455-58
and briefing paper for Nixon for meeting with
dairy industry leaders **FR** 644-45
letter from Harrison on dairy industry parity **15**,
6634, 6714-15E
memo for record on Nixon's meeting with dairy
industry leaders **FR** 857-58E
memo from Campbell on materials for Nixon
meeting with milk producers **17**, 8136-38E
memo on Rice's recommendation on milk price
supports **FR** 810-12E
memo to Ehrlichman on suggested meeting with
Hardin **FR** 818E
memo to Nixon on meeting with dairy industry
leaders with attachments **FR** 821-28E
memos for Nixon's file on meetings with Connally, Hardin, Shultz, Rice, Ehrlichman, and Whitaker on March 23, 1971 **FR** 860-61E
Whitaker, Kenneth **15**, 6634 **16**, 7382, 7385, 7387 **17**,
7759 **21**, 9961, 9964, 9970, 10006 **22**, 10453 **23**,
11203, 11204 **24**, 11289, 11290
at Nixon's meeting with dairy industry representatives **16**, 7388
briefing papers for Nixon on dairy industry contributions **16**, 7386
letter from Harrison on milk price-support increases to **FR** 634
and milk price supports **16**, 7399 **FR** 635
on opening of safety deposit box with Hughes
contribution **FR** 970
Rebozo on **21**, 9995-96, 9997-98

Ehrlichman tells Kleindienst he is interrogating on Watergate **9**, 3577-78

former employees of J. Walter Thompson Advertising Co. **1**, 84-85

and FBI Watergate investigation **9**, 3526, 3556-57

Gray's attitude toward **9**, 3496

Haldeman on functions of **7**, 2971-72

Haldeman on Nixon's selection of **7**, 2869 **8**, 3128-32

investigation of **9**, 3613

involvement in Watergate, countervailing forces preventing Nixon's knowledge about **5**, 2020-2021

Kehrli on payroll **1**, 87, 94-95

Liddy's telephone conversations with **2**, 471-72

linked by media to Watergate **8**, 3113

Magruder's meetings with **2**, 505-506

memo from Dean on dealing with political enemies **4**, 1689-90E

memo from Malek to Cole on support for Nixon re-election by **18**, 8208, 8325-41E

memo from Malek to Haldeman on support for Nixon re-election by **18**, 8208, 8320-24E

Moore's reactions to articles implicating in Watergate **5**, 1993-95

Nixon on grand jury testimony of **3**, 1318E

Nixon's attitude toward testifying before Select Committee **4**, 1463-64

organization, and access to Nixon **4**, 1488-90

organization chart **1**, 75-76, 77, 78-80, 84-85

personnel referrals for career and non-career placements **19**, 8899-8902E

questioning by prosecutor's office **9**, 3619-20

questions for Dean **4**, 1412-29

recruitment of **1**, 86-87

secretarial system **16**, 7378

size of **1**, 86, 94

Stans on organizational structure of **2**, 766

subordinates taking blame for superiors on **4**, 1490 **6**, 2489

transfers to CRP **1**, 80, 93-95

and Watergate articles in newspapers **5**, 2009-19

White House tapes
See Nixon tapes

White House White Paper on "The Milk Price-Support Decision" 17, 8073-92E **FR** 673-82

and congressional pressure **FR** 906

and dairy industry $2 million pledge **FR** 680-82

and Humphrey's support for legislation to raise supports **FR** 881-83

on Nixon's meeting with advisers on March 23 on milk price supports **FR** 647

on Nixon's meetings with Nelson and Parr **FR** 617

on Nixon's milk price-support decision **FR** 622

on Nixon's proclamation on dairy import quotas **FR** 621

White Papers
on Hillings' letter to Nixon **FR** 620-21

See also White House White Paper on "The Milk Price-Support Decision"

White v. *United States* **9**, 3657

Whiteaker, Patricia
affidavit on debts of Muskie campaign **11**, 4786-89E

Whitehorn, Stanley 25, 12122

Whitmer, K. 21, 9998

Whitmore
Van Dyk on role in AMPI contributions to Muskie campaign **16**, 7013-14

Whitney, Cornelius Vanderbilt 17, 7550 **FR** 496
campaign contributions and ambassadorships and **FR** 504-505

Whitney, Richard P. 2, 695 **7**, 2959E, 2967E, 2968E
memo to Mitchell **2**, 873-74

Whittaker, Ken 16, 7168-69 **20**, 9605

Whitted, Dr. Steve 14, 6296

Whitten, Les 12, 5028E, 5029E

Whittier College 11, 4669 **FR** 174
Muskie's appearance at **10**, 3991-92 **11**, 4656-57 **FR** 191

Nixon family vault at **22**, 10611

"Who Is Our Candidate for President" leaflet 12, 4969, 4979-81, 5023-24E

"Why Doesn't Muskie Tell the Truth?"
See Muskie Accountability Project

"Why Labor Can't Support George McGovern" leaflet FR 157

Wicker, Tom 8, 3155 **10**, 4227E
on enemies list **4**, 1698E

Wikof, Chevalier 4, 1557

Wild, Claude C., Jr. 17, 7550
Arnold informs Mills of planned guilty plea of **25**, 12026-27

Arnold's reaction to contribution of **25**, 12025-26

guilty plea of **FR** 925

and Gulf Oil Corp. contribution to Mills campaign **25**, 12021-30 **FR** 923-25

and Gulf Oil Corp. contributions **FR** 469-73

letter from Parkinson on $100,000 contribution to FCRP **13**, 5466, 5803E

motivations for cash contribution to Mills campaign **25**, 12028

telephone call to Arnold on planned guilty plea on Gulf Oil contribution **25**, 12024, 12026

See also Gulf Oil Corp.

Wild, Claude C., Jr., testimony of 13, 5460-81
on amounts of contributions to CRP **13**, 5472-73

on authorization for campaign contributions by Gulf Oil Corp. **13**, 5465

on campaign contributions as "customary" **13**, 5478-79

on campaign contributions to Jackson's and Mills' campaigns **13**, 5464-65

on delivery of campaign contributions **13**, 5478

denies discussions of possibility of disclosure with Nunn or Stans **13**, 5467-68

denies requests for cash contributions **13**, 5468

duties at Gulf Oil Corp. **13**, 5460

on first contribution to CRP **13**, 5462-63

on Gulf Oil Corp. press release on reasons for campaign contribution **13**, 5479

on impact of public disclosure on contributions **13**, 5479-80

on incomes of Gulf Oil Corp. executives **13**, 5468

on questions to Ehrlichman relating to indictment against him **16,** 7396

on relevancy of Butterfield memo to Haldeman **8,** 3146-47

on relevancy of Haldeman memo to Walters on IRS **8,** 3136-37

requests time for statement to Select Committee re Senator Inouye **8** 3227, 3228-29

requests transcript of taped Hunt-Colson telephone conversation **7,** 2853

on scheduling of hearings for Haldeman's opening statement **7,** 2854-55

on Stans' deposition before grand jury **7,** 2793

on tape of Ehrlichman interview with Mitchell **7,** 2737

and Zweig opinion **7,** 2805-2807

See also Ehrlichman, John D., testimony of; Haldeman, Harry Robins, testimony of

Wilson, Richard O. 22, 12530E, 12554-55E

Wilson, T. 11, 4613

on bogus Segretti pamphlet against Humphrey **10,** 4002

Wilson, Will 20, 9575

Wilson, Woodrow 2, 833-34

meets with Foreign Relations Committee **4,** 1557

Wimer, David J. FR 387-88

letter to Wise on grant to National Conference of Southwest Council of La Raza **FR** 392

memo to Wise on OASA involvement and efforts in key states **19,** 8797-98E

Winchester, Lucy 4, 1409

Winchester, Roy 2, 574

and Mexican checks **FR** 518-19

Winn-Dixie Stores, Inc. 22, 10518 **24,** 11330

Anderson column on contribution of **26,** 10590E

effort to purchase Tropicana **22,** 10583 **24,** 11408-09

and IRS case involving Corrupt Practices Act **23,** 11268-69

Rebozo and **22,** 10585-87

See also Davis, A. Darius, testimony of

Winston, Harry FR 1047-48

See also Harry Winston, Inc.

Winte, Ralph 9, 3686-87 **22,** 10606

contact with Hunt **24,** 11562-63

Danner on discussions of rumor about Rebozo denying receipt of Hughes contribution **24,** 11554-55

Danner on contacts with Hunt of **24,** 11560-61, 11562

Davis claims attorney-client privilege on interview with **24,** 11605-11609

Davis-Lackritz argument on appearance for testimony **24,** 11615-18

and diagram of Greenspun offices **20,** 9363-64

discussion with Davis **24,** 11596-11601

flights on Hughes' plane **20,** 9482

Hunt's report to Liddy on meeting with **20,** 9384-85

letter from Ervin denying request for open hearing for **24,** 11615-16, 11619E

meetings with Hunt **20,** 9375-79 **24,** 11598-99

Davis discusses with Bennett **24,** 11603-11604

on rumor about documents in Greenspun's posses-

sion **20,** 9346-47, 9350-53, 9355, 9357-58, 9359, 9374-75

meetings with Hunt and Liddy **20,** 9347, 9348, 9350-53, 9358, 9359, 9381, 9394-9400

on reporting to Gay about discussion with Hunt **24,** 11608

scheduled appearance of **20,** 9611, 9612

Wearley and **20,** 9489

Wiretap logs

related to newsmen and White House staffers **3,** 920-21, 1068-71

See also Nixon tapes

Wiretapping

by Anderson **4,** 1687E

at McGovern headquarters **11,** 4632

attorney general's power to **1,** 356

Baldwin's monitoring of **1,** 232-233

countermeasures at Republican National headquarters **3,** 1126E

of Democratic National Committee **2,** 796-97 **9,** 3548

demonstration by McCord **1,** 235-237

of F. Donald Nixon **21,** 9700-9707

Haldeman admits knowledge of **8,** 3046

of Halperin and Lake **11,** 4695, 4884-85E

Harmony's attitude toward **2,** 487-88

Hauser objects to questions to Higby on **23,** 11096, 11097

of Institute for Policy Studies **11,** 4435

of journalists and Kissinger's staff members **4,** 1623

Kalmbach worried about **5,** 2118

of Kraft **3,** 919 **21,** 9687-99 **23,** 10911-13

in Liddy's presentation of intelligence-gathering plan to Mitchell, Dean, and Magruder **2,** 789-90, 791

Mardian denies Internal Security Division asked for **6,** 2428-29

by McCord of Democratic National Committee headquarters **1,** 128, 157-58

on McCord's telephone **1,** 139, 153, 198-99, 219-20, 227-28, 243-46, 256-57, 258, 259, 338-40

Caulfield on **1,** 275-276

McCord's efforts to prove **9,** 3442, 3443

Nixon authorizing **6,** 2591-92

of Nixon during 1968 campaign **3,** 981, 982 **4,** 1667

in Nixon's 1968 campaign **8,** 3204

Odle on **1,** 27

on Oliver's telephone **9,** 3651-52

and Plumbers **6,** 2533

Porter on transcriptions of **2,** 650

and Special Investigations Unit **6,** 2534-35

on telephones at Democratic party headquarters **9,** 3595-96

See also Huston Plan; Nixon tapes

Wisconsin Democratic primaries

literature distributed by Segretti and his agents during **FR** 171

Wisdom, Forest 14, 6324 **15,** 6756 **17,** 7715

Wise, Flora 12, 4949, 5052E

Wise, Richard J. FR 432

memo from Tupper on Responsiveness Program **19,** 8811-12E

Wright report 16, 7231-32 17, 7663, 7665, 7666-67, 7669, 7672
  as Butterbrodt's source of information 17, 7627, 7630, 7647, 7649-50
  Pepper disputes content of 17, 7722
Wrights, Ken
  money from Porter to 2, 659
"Writer, The"
  See Hunt, Howard E. (alias of)
"Writer's wife, The"
  See Hunt, Mrs. Howard E. (alias of)
Wurf, Jerry 10, 4060E
Wyatt, Donald 22, 10367, 10368
Wyatt, Elmer 11, 4472, 4657, 4658, 4672 FR 552
  first meeting with Buckley 11, 4450
  as infiltrator 11, 4449
  interview with Select Committee staff 11, 4445
  money received from Buckley 11, 4445
  as political spy in Muskie campaign 11, 4439-46
  and Ruby I FR 188-90
Wyman, Gene 25, 11750, 11789
  role in Humphrey campaign 25, 11722
Wyman, Sidney FR 996-97
Wymore, James F. 12, 5046E
  affidavit of 12, 5009, 5034-47E
Xerox
  and McGovern presidential campaign debt FR 555
Yacht
  in Liddy's intelligence-gathering plans 2, 788
Yancey, Gary 11, 4406, 4409 13, 5442, 5451-52, 5454
Yeutter, Clayton 1, 35 2, 736 15, 6902, 6904
  and contributions from milk producers FR 729
  memo to Herringer on appointment to presidential board or commission for Wenk FR 415
  memo to Malek on agricultural campaign materials 17, 8167E
  and recommendation and referral for departmental board or commission 19, 8888-89E
Yippies 12, 5214E, 5216E, 5217E
  news release 12, 5218E
Ylvisaker, William FR 552-53
Yorty campaign 11, 4714E
  document attempts to sabotage McGovern candidacy by 10, 4926, 4301E
  and forged letters from Barron FR 173
  Segretti blames for bogus McCarthy letters 10, 4003-4004
Young, David 1, 79, 81 3, 927, 941, 954, 1267E 4, 1438 6, 2409 7, 2670 9, 3456, 3722
  authorization to Hunt and Liddy for Ellsberg break-in 6, 2547
  Buchanan's relationship with 10, 3913
  and Chenow briefing FR 46-47
  and Chenow's testimony to FBI 3, 941
  and CIA psychiatric profile of Ellsberg 8, 3235-36
  and contents of Hunt's safe FR 35
  and Diem cables 9, 3732 FR 125-26
  excised paragraph from memo from Krogh to 7, 2702-10
  excused from grand jury testimony 9, 3619, 3636-37
  and Fielding break-in FR 122

and Hunt 3, 1172E
informs Helms of his assignment to Ehrlichman's staff 8, 3234
and leaks 3, 1114E
in Malloy's affidavit on CIA psychological profile of Ellsberg 25, 12422-23E, 12425E
and material in Hunt's safe 3, 938, 948
memo to Colson on Hunt memo on neutralization of Ellsberg 9, 3730, 3893E
memo to Ehrlichman on Ellsberg 10, 3911-12
memo to Ehrlichman on Pentagon Papers matter 6, 2554, 2646-51E
memo to Ehrlichman on press image for Ellsberg 7, 2670-71
note from Ehrlichman with Pentagon Papers Status Report 6, 2554, 2643-45E
and Plumbers' unit 3, 921
and reasons for creation of Plumbers FR 120
reporting relationship to Ehrlichman 6, 2531-32
request to Macomber for Hunt's access to State Department files 9, 3772
See also Ellsberg break-in; Plumbers
Young, Lawrence 10, 4007-4009
Young, Whitney 10, 4152E
Young Americans for Freedom 10, 4120-26E
Young Republicans 11, 4403
  contributions after Watergate 13, 5478
  and letterwriting campaign FR 151
Young Socialist Alliance 11, 4544
  bogus contribution to McCloskey campaign from FR 198
Young Voters for the President 11, 4641 FR 200-201
  of Oklahoma 12, 5009, 5168-69E
Youth International Party
  See Yippies
Zaffaroni, Alex 25, 12147, 12202
  contribution to McGovern campaign 25, 12156-58
Zarb, Frank G. 18, 8203
  memo for undersecretary on Department of Labor responsiveness to special needs 19, 8799-8800E
Zavala County grant 18, 8253-54 FR 398-400
  memo from Armendariz to Malek on 18, 8253, 8405E
Zazueta, Richard 13, 5289-90
Zeibert, Duke 24, 11420
Ziegler, Ron 2, 850, 861 3, 921, 980, 995, 996, 997, 1001, 1046-47 4, 1383, 1405, 1485, 1508, 1549 5, 1972, 1983, 1991 7, 2720 10, 4029, 4112E 21, 10110 22, 10240, 10622
  announcement that White House was not conducting inquiry on Watergate break-in FR 33
  at meetings with Nixon, Dean, and Moore 5, 1943
  briefings 3, 1074-75, 1081, 1082-83 7, 2761-62
  and Camp David meeting of Nixon, Rebozo, and Danner FR 1012
  and Dean investigation of Watergate 7, 2721
  Dean's meetings after Watergate with 4, 1420
  and Dean's response to Gray 3, 1002
  and Dean's written report on Watergate 3, 967 4, 1378
  denies Segretti revelations 10, 4043-44
  discussion with Haig on Camp David meeting of Nixon, Danner, and Rebozo 23, 11005-11006